Routledge Handbook of Religion and Politics

D0217800

From the United States to the Middle East, Asia and Africa, religion has become an increasingly important factor in political activity and organisation. This Handbook provides a definitive global survey of the interaction of religion and politics.

Featuring contributions from an international team of experts, it examines the political aspects of all the world's major religions, including such crucial contemporary issues as religious fundamentalism, terrorism, the war on terror, the 'clash of civilisations' and science and religion.

Four main themes addressed include:

- The World Religions and Politics
- Religion and Governance
- Religion and International Relations
- Religion, Security and Development

Bibliographies at the end of each chapter guide the reader towards the most up-to-date references on various topics. In addition, large amounts of information make this book an indispensable text for students, academics and the wider public interested in the dynamic relationship between politics and religion.

Jeffrey Haynes is Professor of Politics at London Metropolitan University, UK. He is the author of 17 previous books and over 100 journal articles and chapters in edited volumes.

Contributors: John Anderson, Michael D. Barr, Steve Bruce, James Chiriyankandath, Gerard Clarke, Adam Dolnik, Jonathan Fox, Paul Freston, Peter Friedlander, Rohan Gunaratna, Jeffrey Haynes, David Herbert, Allen D. Hertzke, Atsuhiro Katano, John Madeley, Payam Mohseni, Andrea Mura, Mohammad Nafissi, Brenda O'Neill, Thorleif Pettersson, Shmuel Sandler, Giorgio Shani, Andrea Teti, Noah J. Toly, David Wessels and Clyde Wilcox.

Routledge Handbook of Religion and Politics

Edited by
Jeffrey Haynes

LONDON AND NEW YORK

First published 2009
by Routledge
2 Park Square, Milton Park, Abingdon, Oxon, OX14 4RN

Simultaneously published in the USA and Canada
by Routledge
711 Third Avenue, New York, NY 10017

Routledge is an imprint of the Taylor & Francis Group, an informa business

© 2009 Editorial selection and matter, Jeff Haynes; individual chapters, the contributors

Typeset in Bembo by Keyword Group Ltd.

British Library Cataloguing in Publication Data
A catalogue record for this book is available from the British Library

Library of Congress Cataloging in Publication Data
Routledge handbook of religion and politics / edited by Jeff Haynes.
    p. cm.
 1. Religion and politics. I. Haynes, Jeffrey.
 BL65.P7R78 2008
 322′.109—dc22   2008012961

ISBN 10: 0-415-41455-5 (hbk)
ISBN 10: 0-203-89054-x (ebk)
ISBN 13: 978-0-415-60029-3 (pbk)
ISBN 13: 978-0-415-41455-5 (hbk)
ISBN 13: 978-0-203-89054-7 (ebk)

Contents

Figures

Tables

Contributors

John Anderson, University of St Andrews, UK

Michael D. Barr, Flinders University, Australia

Steve Bruce, University of Aberdeen, UK

James Chiriyankandath, London Metropolitan University, UK

Gerard Clarke, Swansea University, UK

Adam Dolnik, Institute of Defence and Strategic Studies, Singapore

Jonathan Fox, Bar-Ilan University, Israel

Paul Freston, Calvin College, USA

Peter Friedlander, La Trobe University, Australia

Rohan Gunaratna, Institute of Defence and Strategic Studies, Singapore

Jeffrey Haynes, London Metropolitan University, UK

David Herbert, Open University, UK

Allen D. Hertzke, University of Oklahoma, USA

Atsuhiro Katano, Rakuno Gakuen University, Japan

John Madeley, London School of Economics, UK

Payam Mohseni, Georgetown University, USA

Andrea Mura, Loughborough University, UK

Mohammad Nafissi, London Metropolitan University, UK

Brenda O'Neill, University of Calgary, Canada

Thorleif Pettersson, Uppsala University, Sweden

Shmuel Sandler, Bar-Ilan University, Israel

Giorgio Shani, Ritsumeikan University, Japan

Andrea Teti, University of Aberdeen, UK

Noah J. Toly, Wheaton College, USA

David Wessels, Sophia University, Japan

Clyde Wilcox, Georgetown University, USA

Introduction

Jeffrey Haynes

Prior to the eighteenth century and the subsequent formation and development of the modern (secular) international state system, religion was a key ideology that often stimulated political conflict between societal groups. However, following the Peace of Westphalia in 1648 and the subsequent development of centralised states first in Western Europe and then via European colonisation to most of the rest of the world, both domestically and internationally, the political importance of religion significantly declined.

In the early twenty-first century, however, there is a resurgence of – often politicised forms of – religion. This trend has been especially noticeable in the post-cold war era (that is, since the late 1980s), notably among the so-called 'world religions' (Buddhism, Christianity, Confucianism, Hinduism, Islam and Judaism). Regarding important events in this context, many observers point to the Iranian revolution of 1978-9 – as it marked the 'reappearance' of religion (in this case, Shii Islam) as a significant political actor in Iran, a country that like Turkey, with its Sunni Muslim majority, decades before had adopted a Western-derived, secular development model.

Since the late 1970s, numerous other examples of the growing political influence of religion have been noted – with the partial exception of Europe, especially its western segment. Europe is widely seen as an exception, because most regional countries are now very secular, with religion squeezed from public life. Among 'developed' countries and regions, however, Europe's position contrasts with that of the USA. More than half of all Americans claim regularly to attend religious services, three or four times the European norm. In addition, eight words – 'In God We Trust' and the 'United States of America' – appear on all US currency, both coins and notes. The continuing popular significance of religion in the USA is to some degree a cultural issue, deriving in part from the worldview of the original European settlers in the seventeenth and eighteenth centuries, many of whom shared an Anglo-Protestant culture. This has stayed an important cultural factor until the present time.

Elsewhere in the world, since the late 1970s we have seen increased political involvement of religious actors within many countries, as well as internationally. Much attention is often focused upon so-called 'Islamic fundamentalism', particularly in the Middle East, to the extent that a casual observer might assume that the entire region is polarised religiously and politically between Jews and Muslims. This is partly because both groups claim 'ownership' of various holy places, including Jerusalem, while conflict between them is also a result of the plight of the continu-ing conflict between Israel and the (mostly Muslim) Palestinians. There are also other political issues in the region – notably the large number of non-democratic gov-ernments – that have also encouraged widespread political involvement of vari-ous Islamist actors.[1] In addition, Islamists are also active in, *inter alia*, Africa, Central Asia, and South East and East Asia.

However, it is not only Islamists who pursue political goals related to religion. In officially secular India, there have been significant recent examples of militant Hinduism; many stemmed from, but were not confined to, the Babri Masjid mosque incident at Ayodhya in 1992. This event was instrumental in transforming the country's political landscape, to the extent that a 'Hindu fundamentalist' political party, the Bharatiya Janata Party (BJP), swiftly grew to political prominence. From the mid-1990s, the BJP served in several coali-tion governments and until May 2004 – when the BJP lost power to a resurgent Congress Party - it was the leading party in government.[2] In addition, Jewish religious parties currently serve in the Olmert government in Israel, while the Roman Catholic Church was a leading player in the recent turn to democracy in, among others, Poland, South Africa and several Latin American countries. In sum, there are numerous examples of recent religious involvement in politics in various parts of the world, in both domestic and international contexts.

Debates about the current political importance of religion also include a focus upon various issues that can be grouped together under the rubric: 'Religion, Security and Development'. What unites them is a common concern with the impact of religion on conflict and devel-opment issues and outcomes. Among them can be noted Samuel Huntington's controversial thesis about 'clashing civilisa-tions', with religion and culture key

factors, while others stress the potential of religion to help resolve political conflicts and be a major component of peacebuild-ing. Scholars also focus upon the influence of religion on various manifestations of ter-rorism and, more generally, the post-9/11 'War on Terror' (now known as 'The Long War'), as well as the significance of religion in relation to the develop-mental position of females. Finally, a new religion-linked controversy has emerged: a debate between 'religion and science' on the relative scientific merits of Darwin's Theory of Evolution and 'Intelligent Design'.

In sum, a variety of religious actors and factors are now involved in various politi-cal issues and controversies. For many observers, this 'return' of religion is both novel and unexpected: until recently, it appeared that religious actors could safely be ignored in both politics and interna-tional relations because they appeared to be collectively insignificant. Now, how-ever, governments, analysts and observers would all agree that things have changed in various ways. This book examines the recent 'return' of religion to politics and international relations.

The book approaches this issue as fol-lows. The first part of the book comprises eight essays under the collective heading: 'The World Religions and Politics'. The fol-lowing religions are examined: Buddhism, Christianity: Protestantism, Christianity: Catholicism and the Catholic Church, Confucianism, Hinduism, Sunni Islam, Shia Islam, and Judaism. The overall aim is to illustrate the contention that in recent years, around the world, each of these reli-gious traditions has engaged for a variety of reasons with a variety of political issues and controversies.

In the second part of the book, the focus turns to the relationship between 'religion and governance'. The seven essays that comprise this section are on the fol-lowing topics: secularisation and politics, religious fundamentalisms, religion and the state, religion and democracy, religion and political parties, religion and civil society, and religious commitment and socio-political orientations.

The third part is concerned with 'religion and international relations', and comprises four essays; religion and international relations theory, religion and foreign policy, religious transnational actors and politics, and religion and globalisation.

The final part of the book is made up of five chapters on the overall theme of 'religion, security and development' and includes the following topics: terrorism, conflict prevention and peacebuilding, religion and gender, faith-based development aid, and religion, climate change and human suffering.

In short, the overall rationale for the project is to provide a definitive survey of what is currently happening in relation to the interaction of religion and politics, both domestically and internationally, with regard to a variety of issues.

Examining a more general and complex relationship between religion and politics in the contemporary world, the book discovers that, apparently irrespective of which religious tradition we are concerned with, many religious ideas, experiences and practices are all significantly affected by the impact of globalisation on both politics and international relations. The impact of globalisation is encouraging many religions to adopt new or renewed agendas in relation to a variety of religious, social, political and economic concerns. It is also stimulating many religious individuals, organisations and movements to look not only at local and national issues and contexts but also to focus on regional and international environments. We will see that in many cases such concerns are focused in two generic areas: *social development and human rights*; and *conflict and conflict resolution*.

Social development and human rights

Most analyses of religion and politics focus on economic, social and/or cultural issues, including the economic range and social and cultural significance of the activities of transnational corporations (TNCs). This often leads to the perception that TNCs are taking economic power both from governments and citizens. This comes in the context of what is often understood as significant downsides to economic globalisation: the apparent mass impoverishment of already poor people, especially in the developing world. These circumstances have led to a new focus for numerous religious organisations, concerned with trying to redress these imbalances, reflecting more generally a concern with multiple – social, economic and human rights – concerns. This focus is manifested in various ways, including: new religious fundamentalisms, support for anti-globalisation activities, such as anti-World Trade Organisation protests, and North/South economic justice efforts. In sum, recent religious responses to globalisation have often included a stress on social interests, manifested in various ways, which together go way beyond the confines of what might be called 'church' or more generally 'religious' life.

These concerns are now increasingly pursued within inter-faith contexts. In recent years, various inter-faith religious forums have sought to bring sustained concern to social development issues – and by extension – human rights issues through an inter-faith focus. For example, there is the well known World Faiths Development Dialogue (WFDD), an initiative that, encouraged by the World Bank, sought to map areas of convergence among various separate religious faiths' development agendas. Many shared a focus on relationships of service and solidarity, harmony with the earth, and the vital but – necessarily limited – contribution of

3

material progress to human development and satisfaction.

A senior World Bank figure, Katherine Marshall, delivered a speech in April 2005 that seemed to be especially significant in emphasising that the World Bank no longer believed 'that religion and socio-economic development belong to different spheres and are best cast in separate roles – even separate dramas'. This observation was based on a recognition that around the world both religious organisations and (secular) development agencies often share similar concerns: how to improve (1) the lot of materially poor people, (2) the societal position of those suffering from social exclusion, and (3) unfulfilled human potential in the context of glaring developmental polarisation within and between countries, which the World Bank now accepts, has arisen in part because of the polarising impact of globalisation (Marshall 2005). Marshall's speech also emphasised that while in the past religion was understood by the World Bank to be primarily concerned with 'otherworldly' and 'world-denying' issues, it now accepted that religion can play a significant role in seeking to achieve developmental goals for millions of people, especially in the developing world. The Bank also now recognises that issues of 'right' and 'wrong', as well as those linked to social and economic justice, are central to the teachings of *all* the world religions (that is, Buddhism, Christianity, Hinduism, Islam and Judaism). This realisation is influential in highlighting: (1) how relatively marginal most current manifestations of religious fundamentalism are, yet (2) at the same time, potentially increasingly the likelihood that disadvantaged people might turn to various religious fundamentalisms compared to people who are happy and confident in their developmental positions.

Reflecting such concerns, recent years have seen regular 'Leaders' Meetings', convened to enable religious leaders to try to address these issues. One such meeting was held in Canterbury, England, in October 2002, hosted by James Wolfensohn, then president of the World Bank, and Dr George Carey, at the time head of the worldwide Anglican communion of around 70 million people. The main purpose of the meeting was to bring together an important group of leaders 'from the world's faith communities, key development organisations, and from the worlds of entertainment, philanthropy and the private sector'. Linked to the Millennium Development Goals announced in 2000, with the aim of achieving them by 2015, key themes addressed at the meeting included: poverty, HIV/AIDS, gender, conflict and social justice. Participants accepted that poverty, HIV/AIDS, conflict, gender concerns, international trade and global politics explicitly link all the world's countries and peoples – rich and poor – into a global community. Another main theme was the dualistic impact of globalisation, with its differential impact on rich and poor countries. The meeting revealed a growing sense of religious solidarity that highlights the urgency of developing shared responsibility and partnership to deal with collective problems facing humanity. Yet it is crucial to move from talk to action: as much more needs to be done to progress from expressions of shared religious solidarity in response to shared development problems to a realisation of practical plans involving collaboration between the worlds of faith and development in confronting major development issues (Marshall and March 2003).

Conflict and conflict resolution

The second issue that informs many of the chapters of this book is also linked to the impact of globalisation: religion's involvement in both conflict and conflict resolution in various parts of the world. A starting point for our analysis in this regard was to note that globalisation both highlights and encourages religious pluralism. But religious responses may well be different. This is because some religions, including Judaism, Christianity and Islam (sometimes known as the 'religions of the book', because in each case their authority emanates principally from sacred texts, actually, similar texts) claim what Kurtz calls 'exclusive accounts of the nature of reality', that is, only *their* religious beliefs are judged to be *true* by adherents (Kurtz 1995: 238).

As globalisation results in increased interaction between people and communities, the implication is that not only are encounters between different religious traditions likely to be increasingly common but also that there will be various outcomes as a result: some will be harmonious, others will not. Sometimes, the result is what Kurtz has called 'culture wars' (Kurtz 1995: 168). These can occur because various religious worldviews encourage different allegiances and standards in relation to various areas, including the family, law, education and politics. As a result, conflicts between people, ethnic groups, classes and nations can be framed in religious terms. Such religious conflicts seem often to 'take on "larger-than-life" proportions as the struggle of good against evil' (Kurtz 1995: 170). This may be noted in relation to certain religious minorities who may regard their own existential position – for example, Muslim minority communities in Thailand, the United Kingdom, France, the Philippines and India – to be unacceptably weakened because of actual or perceived pressure from majority religious communities – Buddhists in Thailand, Christians in Britain, France and the Philippines, and Hindus in India – to conform to the norms and values of the religious and cultural majority.

There are many examples of religious involvement in recent and current national and international conflicts. For example,

stability and prosperity in the Middle East is a pivotal goal, central to achieving general peace and the elimination of poverty in the region. Yet the Middle East is particularly emblematic in relation to religion – in part because the region was the birthplace of the world's three great monotheistic religions (Christianity, Islam and Judaism). This brings with it a legacy not only of shared wisdom but also of conflict – a complex relationship that has impacted in recent years on countries as far away as Thailand, the Philippines, Indonesia, the United States and Britain. A key to peace in the region may well be achievement of significant collaborative efforts among different religious bodies, which along with external religious and secular organisations, for example from Europe and the United States, may through collaborative efforts work towards developing a new model of peace and cooperation to enable the Middle East to escape from what many see as an endless cycle of religious-based conflict. Overall, this emphasises that religion may be intimately connected, and not only in the Middle East, *both* to international conflicts and their prolongation *and* to attempts at reconciliation of such conflicts. In other words, in relation to many international conflicts, religion can play a significant, even a fundamental role, contributing to conflicts in various ways, including how they are intensified, channelled or reconciled. In addition, we also saw that religion has a key part to play in resolution of conflicts in other parts of the world, including South Asia (notably India/Pakistan) and Africa (for example, in relation to the recently ended civil war in Sudan). We also noted its involvement in the still simmering civil war in Sri Lanka, between the minority (Hindu) Tamils and the majority (Buddhist) Sinhalese.

In sum, religion is becoming a more important factor in relation to both politics and international relations in many parts of the world; yet, it would be incorrect only to focus on the links with conflict. To do so, would mean that we would be likely to overlook the many recent and current examples of religious involvement in attempts at conflict resolution. On the other hand, the fact remains that many current international conflicts have religious aspects that can exacerbate both hatred and violence and make the conflicts themselves exceptionally difficult to resolve. Hans Kung, an eminent Roman Catholic theologian, claims that

> the most fanatical, the cruelest political struggles are those that have been colored, inspired, and legitimized by religion. To say this is not to reduce all political conflicts to religious ones, but to take seriously the fact that religions share in the responsibility for bringing peace to our torn and warring world.
>
> (Hans Kung, quoted in Smock 2004)

Such concerns are echoed in Samuel Huntington's (1993, 1996) controversial thesis of a 'clash of civilisations', a topic that has filled international debates, especially since 9/11. This thesis was erected upon Huntington's belief that there is a serious 'civilisational' threat to global order that has become especially apparent after the cold war. It is rooted in the idea that there are competing 'civilisations' that engage in conflict that affects outcomes in international relations in various ways. On the one hand, there is the 'West' (especially North America and Western Europe) with values and political cultures deemed to be rooted in liberal democratic and Judaeo-Christian concepts, understood to lead to an emphasis on tolerance, moderation and societal consensus. On the other hand, there is supposedly a bloc of allegedly 'anti-democratic', primarily Muslim, countries, believed to be on a collision course with the West.

A key problem with Huntington's thesis, however, is that there are actually no 'civilisations' that act politically or in international relations in uniform and single-minded ways. Instead, wherever we look – for example, the United States, Europe, Israel, the Muslim countries of the Middle East – what is most notable is the *plurality* of beliefs and norms of behaviour that are apparent even in allegedly cohesive and uniform civilisations. It is useful to bear these concerns in mind when thinking about the role of religion in relation to conflict in both domestic and international contexts. It is important not to overestimate religion's potential for and involvement in large-scale violence and conflict – especially if that implies ignoring or underestimating its involvement and potential as a significant source of conflict resolution and peacebuilding. It is also important to recognise that, especially in recent years, numerous religious individuals, movements and organisations have been actively involved in attempts to end conflicts and to foster post-conflict reconciliation between formerly warring parties (Bouta *et al.* 2005). This emphasises that various religions collectively play a key role in international relations and diplomacy by helping to resolve conflicts and build peace. The 'clash of civilisations' thesis oversimplifies causal interconnections between religion and conflict, in particular by disregarding important alternate variables, including the numerous attempts from a variety of religious traditions to help resolve conflicts and build peace. When successful, religion's role in helping resolve conflicts is a crucial component in wider issues of human development because, as Ellis and ter Haar note: 'Peace is a precondition for human development. Religious ideas of various provenance – indigenous religions as well as world religions – play an important role in *legitimising or discouraging violence*' (my emphasis; Ellis and ter Haar 2004).

Overall, the book's chapters make it clear that religion has now reappeared as an important domestic and international political actor in part because of the impact of deepening globalisation, which has led to an expansion of channels, pressures and agents via which norms are diffused and interact through both transnational and international networks and interactions. As a result, religious actors now pursue a variety of political goals both nationally and internationally that in many cases links their concerns to the economic, social and political consequences of globalisation.

Notes

1 An Islamist is a believer in or follower of Islam, someone who may be willing to use various political means to achieve religiously derived objectives.
2 The secular Congress Party emerged as the largest party following the elections of April/May 2004. The breakdown of seats in the 542-seat Lok Sabha was: Congress and allies: 220; BJP and allies: 185; Others: 137.

Bibliography

Bouta, T., Ayse Kadayifci-Orellana, S. and Abu-Nimer, M. (2005) *Faith-based Peace-building: Mapping and Analysis of Christian, Muslim and Multi-faith Actors*, The Hague: Netherlands Institute of International Relations

Ellis, S. and ter Haar, G. (2004) *Religion and Development in Africa*, background paper prepared for the Commission for Africa.

Huntington, S. (1993) 'The clash of civilisations?', *Foreign Affairs*, 72, 3, pp. 22–49.

Huntington, S. (1996) *The Clash of Civilizations*, New York: Simon and Schuster.

Kurtz, L. (1995) *Gods in the Global Village*, Thousand Oaks, CA: Pine Forge Press.

Marshall, K. (2005) 'Faith and development: Rethinking development debates', June. Based on a presentation at the Conference on Religious NGOs and Development Institutions in Oslo, Norway, on 7 April.

Marshall, K. and March, R. (2003) *Millennium Challenges for Development and Faith Institutions*, Washington, DC: The World Bank.

Smock, D. (2004) 'Divine intervention: Regional reconciliation through faith', *Religion*, 25, 4. Available at http://hir.harvard.edu/articles/1190/3/, accessed 1 September 2005.

Part I

The world religions and politics

Buddhism and politics

Peter Friedlander

The past

Buddhists sometimes describe the relationship between Buddhism and politics by saying that when the Buddha was born it was prophesied that he could either become a ruler of the world, a 'Wheel-turning Monarch' (*cakravartin*), or become a Buddha (Khosla 1989: 32; Walshe 1987: 205). This idea – that the roles of secular ruler and spiritual leader are two distinct paths – stands at the heart of Buddhist tradition. Both are leaders: the secular ruler establishes security and prosperity in this world and the Buddha leads the people towards spiritual liberation. This notion of the two separate, but complementary, roles has contributed greatly towards the compatibility of Buddhist ideas on governance and modern Western conceptions of the separation between the church and state.

It needs to be borne in mind that the modern idea that religion and politics are two separate aspects of human life was not known in ancient India. Both were seen as manifestations of one underlying principle: *dharma*. The word *dharma* (Pali *dhamma*) has meanings that relate to the notions of the true nature of things in themselves, or duty, virtue or morality (Rahula 1974: 181). It often occurs in compounds as in *Buddha-dharma*, which is normally translated as the 'The Buddhist

religion' but could equally well be thought of as 'Buddhist morality' or 'the nature of things as taught by the Buddha'. Alongside this, the term *Raja-dharma* is also found. In this case, *dharma* would not be translated as 'religion' but rather as 'the duties/morality of a king'. In each case, whether for the *raja*, the king, or for the Buddha, what matters is that each upholds an aspect of the *dharma*. *Rajniti* is another word that relates to the notion of 'politics' in classical Indian languages. It is formed from *raja*, 'king', and *niti* which has a range of meanings which centre around the notion of appropriate conduct and according to context range in translation from morality to policy. So *Rajniti* can be understood as meaning 'the policies/morality/code of conduct of a king'. What is important to notice here is that neither *Rajadharma* nor *Rajaniti* relates to a system of representation of the people but, rather, to the notion of how a king should conduct himself.

In 1999 Ian Harris edited a work on Buddhism and politics in Asia in which he argued that the Western notion that religion and politics are exclusive categories should be set aside when discussing Buddhism as it has always had a political dimension (Harris 1999: vii). A traditional Buddhist description of this relationship as complementary, rather than exclusive, was to speak of there being two wheels of the *dhamma*, one wheel being the wheel of *dhamma* turned by the Buddhist monastic community and the other being the wheel of secular rule turned by the king or *Cakkavatti* ('Wheel-turning Monarch') (Reynolds 1972).

It is also important to bear in mind that to simply define religion as a system of belief would not be in accord with traditional Buddhist views. The traditional Buddhist formula that describes Buddhism contains three elements: the Buddha, the *dharma* and the *sangha*. The Buddha is the founder of the tradition. The term *dharma* covers the range of meanings discussed above and the *sangha* is the community of followers of the Buddha and the *dharma* which includes both monks and nuns and laymen and -women. Richard Gombrich (1971) argued that the distinction between seeing religion simply in terms of precept, the modern Western model, and seeing it as related to its practice, the dominant pre-modern Asian model, was fundamental to understanding how the Buddhist tradition relates to society, and hence to politics.

There is also a large body of ancient Indian literature on the duties of the king, which include: the protection of the people, the maintenance of social order and administration of justice (Flood 1998: 71). Buddhist notions of kingship share in this heritage and include as prime duties of the king that he should conquer without violence but through maintaining justice and that he maintains law and order within the boundary of the kingdom so that people can be prosperous and free from danger (Walshe 1987: 443).

Indications of the relationship between Buddhism and the state are found in the texts of the Pali canon which constitute the earliest Buddhist texts to survive to the present day. Two points need to be considered here. First, they contain descriptions of what constitutes a desirable relationship between a king and the Buddhist community. Second, they contain two distinct models for governance itself.

Theravada Buddhist tradition identifies ten duties of a king, the *dasarajadhamma*, which include: liberality, morality, self-sacrifice, honesty and non-violence (Rahula 1985: 84–85). The role of the *sangha* is to advise the king, and to influence him so that his policies uphold values that further the *dhamma*.

There are also Buddhist texts which explicitly state that the Buddhist community must follow the laws of the land as laid down by the king. In the *vinaya* texts (codes of monastic conduct) it is stipulated that a criminal cannot be accepted as a monk into the *sangha* and that monks and nuns cannot make use of the king's property without making payment for it. In other words, it is explicit that Buddhists must follow the laws of the land. In fact even the severity of the punishment for a theft by a monk was decided on the basis of the equivalent civil offence. A monk was to be expelled from the *sangha* if the amount he stole was the same as that in a civil case which would cause the king, or his official, to banish a layperson from a country (Horner 1970: 73–74).

On how the *sangha* is to influence the king, the texts depict an ideal in which the king is a willing patron of Buddhism and upholds its teachings. In the section of the Pali Canon called the *Mahavagga* there is an idealised account of this relationship. It starts by showing how the Buddha convinces the former royal priests, the *Jatilas* of Gaya, to become his followers and then takes their place as the king's chief spiritual advisor (Horner 1982: 47). Archaeological evidence suggests that this picture is only partly true and rather than simply supplanting earlier traditions what happened was that Buddhism became one of the spiritual traditions, along with those of the Brahmins, Jains and Ajivakas which received state patronage (Thapar 2000).

There are two models of how the state should be governed in the Pali Canon. In one model, found in the *Agganna sutta*

(Walshe 1987: 407–415) there is a description of how men came to be ruled by elected leaders, called the *Maha-samata*, the 'People's Choice'. In the other model, such as found in the *Cakkavati-Sihanada Sutta* (Walshe 1987: 395–405), the rulership of the state is decided on the basis of a person being born with certain marks on their body, such as wheel patterns on the soles of their feet, which show that they will be a universal monarch. In the second model there is no suggestion that the universal monarch needs the general consensus of the people to rule. Rather, his rule is dependent on his upholding the *dharma* and ensuring the wealth and prosperity of the state. As long as the king rules according to *dharma* the heavens revolve according to their proper pattern, but when he deviates from the *dharma* and rules for his personal benefit then the heavens no longer follow their proper pattern and he falls from power. A possible reason for the existence of these two models is that during the time of the Buddha there were two types of state in existence. The Buddha himself was born in what is sometimes called a 'village republic' (*ganatantra*) in which the leaders were elected from amongst the people on a temporary basis. However, during the Buddha's lifetime most of the 'village republics' were absorbed into developing kingdoms ruled by hereditary monarchs.

The next significant evolution in these early ideas on the relationship between the Buddhist *sangha* and the state happened during the rule of the Emperor Asoka (269–243 BCE). Buddhist legend has it that he converted to Buddhism and then ruled according to Buddhist teachings. Contemporary scholarship has questioned the degree to which Asoka was actually a Buddhist in the modern sense as he seems to have also continued to patronise all religions (Norman 1997: 113–130) and it might be safer to say that the historical Asoka took it upon himself as part of his

rule to propagate a version of the *dharma* of a king which seems heavily influenced by Buddhism.

It is Buddhist legend, rather than history, which has had the most influence in South and South East Asia and in these legends Asoka became the archetypal example of how a ruler should patronise Buddhism. According to the legends he started out as a cruel ruler who constructs a prison which is a hell on earth but he is converted by miracles performed by a Buddhist monk who accidentally gets imprisoned in it. After his conversion he becomes a patron of the Buddhist monastic *sangha* and having broken up the ten existing funerary monuments, *stupas*, associated with the Buddha, ordered the construction of 84,000 Buddhist monuments throughout his realm. This linkage of the ruler, royal patronage and monumental architecture is what makes him an archetype for royal patronage of Buddhism. It is the Asoka of legend who became the model for later Buddhist kings in South East Asia who sought to emulate his role as state patron of Buddhism (Strong 1983).

The historical Emperor Asoka, as opposed to the Asoka of legend, erected a number of edicts throughout his kingdom. Most of these were written in a script called *Brahmi*, but within a few centuries people forgot how to read this script and it was not until the early nineteenth century that it was deciphered again (Keay 1988: 39–63). When they were deciphered and translated they were a revelation as they contained a depiction of Asoka quite different from the legends. In these edicts he describes how he took to the practice of *dharma* after the slaughter involved in his conquest of Kalinga, an area of eastern India, and how he then abandoned violence and took to the practice of *dharma* as a means of spreading his influence. The linkage between Asoka and patronage of Buddhism and monumental architecture is, however, attested in the edicts, as in

13

them he describes how he went on pilgrimage to the Buddhist sacred sites and had monuments built at them. That he also was concerned with how the *sangha* was run is evident from the edicts in which he warned against splits in the *sangha* and indicates that the state would intervene in such matters and expel from the monastic community those who caused splits in the *sangha*. Some of the edicts also describe how he appointed *dharma* officers to superintend the lay people. Whether this actually refers to spreading the Buddha *dharma*, as Buddhists mostly understand it nowadays, or whether it means more upholding the law, in a secular sense, is a matter for debate. The Asoka of the edicts is not really the same as the Asoka of the legends, yet it came to be rapidly synthesised with them and a picture was drawn of Asoka by popular historians, such as H.G. Wells, in which he was a modern liberal ruler who patronised Buddhism (Wells 1936: 111–112). Buddhists also conflated the Asoka of legend and history when it was convenient. Norman points out that in the edicts Asoka sends *dharma* emissaries to spread word of his rule, like ambassadors to neighbouring countries, but in Buddhist traditions this becomes conflated with the sending of messengers to spread the Buddha *dharma* to nearby countries, which was a separate matter all together (Norman 1997: 128). In the eyes of most Asian Buddhists Asoka has become the critical figure in defining the relationship between Buddhism and politics as he is now seen as having been not only the first legendary Buddhist emperor, but also the first historical ruler of a Buddhist state.

As Buddhism spread through Asia it also encountered cultures in which different notions of kingship were current. In each case Buddhist tradition seems to have adapted by absorbing elements of local traditions into Buddhism. In the case of central Asia, Buddhist traditions absorbed elements of the Iranian figure of the divine monarch and in the case of East Asia elements of the Chinese concept of the king as the ruler of heaven were fused with Buddhist ideas. This can be seen in the way that there is a proliferation of celestial Buddhas in Himalayan and central Asian Buddhist traditions whose iconography often shows features such as crowns and solar imagery, while Amitabha Buddha as the sovereign ruler of the land of bliss (*sukhavati*) in Chinese Pure Land Buddhism also reflects a shift towards emphasising the status of the Buddha himself as ruler, rather than as spiritual teacher as he is seen in South Asian traditions.

A vital element in how Buddhism developed as an Asian religion was the tradition of monastic missions to spread the *dharma*. This started from the time of the Buddha himself when individual monks were sent to distant areas to teach Buddhism and it continued as long as Buddhism flourished in India.

There is also a complex history of the inter-relationship of Buddhist traditions in Asia. After Buddhism was established in China monks at various times from there went back to India in order to gain further insight into the teachings and the codes of monastic conduct. Likewise, Sri Lankan and Burmese traditions were often involved with contacts with each other. These monastic contacts were the precursors of colonial period contacts between Buddhist traditions in Asia, and show Buddhism had a pan-Asian dimension to it in pre-colonial times.

During the colonial era profound changes in Buddhism and its relationship to politics took place. Many of these changes can be understood by studying some of the leading reformers and considering the political dimensions of their activities. The most significant figure for Sri Lanka was Anagarika Dharmapala (David Hewaviratne 1864–1893) who was a lay Buddhist reformer who donned robes in 1881 and gave himself the title *Anagarika Dharmapala* ('Homeless Protector of the Dharma'). He was very involved with Madame Blavatsky and Colonel Olcott, the founders of the western nineteenth-century spiritualist and mystical movement called the Theosophical Society, during their visits to Sri Lanka in which they became Buddhists in 1873. He also visited Japan in 1889, and the USA, for the Parliament of Religions in 1893 and Shanghai in 1893 as well as spending many years in India after he founded the Mahabodhi society in 1891 with the aim of reclaiming the temple at Bodhgaya from the Hindus. His role as a nationalist is now remembered in Sri Lanka as much for his being a Buddhist reformer and this points to the way in which Buddhism became a symbol in Asian states for anti-colonial rhetoric.

In the case of China similar prominent Chinese reformers and activists included Yang Wenhui (1837–1911) who met Dharmapala when he came to Shanghai in 1893, and Tai Hsu (1890–1947). Tai Hsu's ideas on reform of the *sangha* were influential and included the involvement of the *sangha* in community and government affairs (Lopez 2002: 85–90).

In Japan a similar reformer was Shaku Soen (1859–1919) who was a Rinzai tradition Zen monk who studied at Kamakura, then Keio University, and then travelled to Sri Lanka where he lived as a Theravada monk and studied Pali for some years and was a Japanese Representative at the 1893 world parliament of religions in Chicago. Judith Snodgrass has argued that during the Meiji period there was a major re-evaluation of the relationship between the Buddhist *sangha* and the state which sprang from both government efforts to harness Buddhism as a patriotic force and Buddhist efforts to engage in social and political aspects of reform (Snodgrass 2003: 115–136).

Lopez has argued in his book *Modern Buddhism* (2002) that Yang and Dharmapala, amongst others, were prominent figures in the development of what he describes as modern Buddhism. Lopez's argument is that Modern Buddhism shares in many aspects of the 'projects of modernity' and sees itself as rejecting ritual and magical elements, stresses equality over hierarchy, the universal over the local and the individual over the community. It sees itself, he argues, as a return to origins, to the Buddhism of the Buddha himself (Lopez 2002: xi).

Whether or not one accepts that the notion of Modern Buddhism is valid, it points to the ways that Buddhism had changed during the colonial period and contemporary Buddhism in Asia is the heir to not only ancient traditions, but also to modern ideologies from the anti-colonialist nationalist movements.

The present

Estimates of the total number of Buddhists in the world today vary widely, between around two hundred to five hundred million, with quite possibly a rough estimate being around three hundred and fifty million. We also need to distinguish between relative percentages of Buddhists in different countries and numbers of Buddhists in different countries. The internet site 'Adherents.com' estimates the numbers as shown in Table 2.1.

There are, however, major problems with figures like these. For instance, the number of Buddhists in Japan is very open to question. In Japanese census forms it is possible to tick more than one option for religion, and many people mark themselves as being both Shinto and Buddhist at the same time. This points to a problem in how categories of religious adherence are conceived of, why should it not be possible to belong to more than one religion at the same time? Also there are problems due to issues such as what constitutes

Table 2.1 The largest Buddhist communities

Top ten in terms of numbers		Top ten in terms of %	
China	102,000,000	Thailand	95
Japan	89,650,000	Cambodia	90
Thailand	55,480,000	Myanmar	88
Vietnam	49,690,000	Bhutan	75
Myanmar	41,610,000	Sri Lanka	70
Sri Lanka	12,540,000	Tibet	65
South Korea	10,920,000	Laos	60
Taiwan	9,150,000	Vietnam	55
Cambodia	9,130,000	Japan	50
India	7,000,000	Taiwan	43

Source: Adherents.com (Adherents.com is a website which aggregates data from a wide range of sources and is regarded by many scholars as a reasonably accurate guide to the number of adherents of different religions.)

a country. The Tibetan community in exile regards Tibet as being a region which is larger than the Chinese government's view on what constitutes the Tibetan Autonomous Region, so that whilst some figures would suggest that there are around six million Tibetans, who would virtually all describe themselves as Buddhists, other figures might be lower or higher. I will now look at the top ten countries in terms of number of Buddhists and then at Western countries.

China

The two main issues which dominate discussions of Buddhism in China are the degree to which there is religious freedom and the treatment of the Tibetans. During the Cultural Revolution period (1966–76) there was a wholesale attack on Buddhist cultures, peoples and monasteries. However, there has been an enormous resurgence of interest in Buddhism since liberalisation began in the late 1970s. By 2003 there were around 13,000 monasteries and around 180,000 monks and nuns. It is striking that though this figure also includes 120,000 belonging to Tibetan orders in Tibet and adjacent regions of China, the total also includes around 8,000 Theravada monks in Yunnan

and around 50,000 Mahayana monks and nuns from the Han community. In addition to the problem of finding economic support for their activities, Buddhist organisations have also had to deal with being treated as foci of the tourist industry and transformed into money-making enterprises. Partly this is because the number and strength of lay Buddhist organisations is still low and the monasteries cannot look to them for support as they would in the Buddhist countries of South East Asia. Political figures such as Chairman Jiang Zemin have even advocated the use of Buddhist morality (*de*) in the political sphere (Yin 2006). It is notable that the term used here for virtue is 'de'. This is the same word for virtue as appears in the title of the Daoist classic the 'Tao Te Ching' (Pinyin: Dao De Jing) and is not, as such, a particularly Buddhist term but a more general traditional Chinese term for virtue. The idea of promoting traditional virtues, rather than democratic rights, as 'Asian values' is one that shows how Buddhist ideas can be used by many different camps in politics. The emphasis, however, in the regulations issued by the government in 2004 is on the management of religion in such a way as to ensure it does not disrupt society or threaten the government's authority but acts to promote economic development (Miller 2006).

Japan

Talking to young Japanese people one normally gets very little sense of enthusiasm about Buddhism, and few people seem to take seriously the notion that the New Komeito Party is a Buddhist political party. The Komeito or 'Clean Government Party' is often spoken of as a Buddhist party. This is because it was formed in 1964 by the lay Buddhist Soka Gakkai organisation, which is itself an offshoot of the Nichiren Buddhist tradition (Hardacre 2006). In 1999 Komeito reformed and became the 'New Komeito' Party, but its policies do not appear to have any Buddhist aspect to them at all. Indeed, the New Komeito party on its website takes pains to point out that it is not affiliated with any religious groups and there have been no formal links between it and the Soka Gakkai apart from at the time of its foundation in 1964 ('New Komeito's Views on Politics and Religion in Japan'). The issue of how religion relates to politics in Japan was also raised during the period when Junichiro Koizumi was Prime Minister (2001–06), as he made annual visits to the Yasukuni Shrine to fallen soldiers in which the names of a number of war criminals are honoured. This is, however, a Shinto shrine so it does not directly bear on the relationship of Buddhism to politics in Japan beyond pointing to the sensitivity of the relationship between religion and politics in contemporary Japan and suggesting that there are limits on the degree to which any religion can be seen to be a part of Japanese polity.

Thailand

It has to be borne in mind that as around 95% of Thais are Buddhists, all sides of the political spectrum claim Buddhist affiliations at times for their ideologies. During the period when Thaksin Shinawatra was Prime Minister of Thailand (2001-06) the main change that took place was the rise of successful businessmen, such as Thaksin Shinawatra himself, in the political sphere. At times Shinawatra linked his market reform concept of a 'social contract' to Buddhist ideas. In a speech he gave in 1999 on the influence of the Buddhist reformer Buddhadasa (1906–93) he proposed that Buddhadasa had said: 'Politics is *dhamma* and *dhamma* is politics'. He then claimed that what Buddhadasa, and by implication Buddhist reformers, wanted was a government of men of moral integrity, and he was himself such a person (Phongpaichit and Baker 2004: 137).

The Thai scholar Kitiarsa (2006) has also argued that Thaksin's downfall in 2006 was actually due to his failing to convert his power into virtue in the sense of acting like a moral Buddhist leader. As an example of opposition to Thaksin's rule he also quotes the engaged Buddhist campaigner Sulak Sivaraksa who described Thaksin as the embodiment of Mara, a devil-like figure in some Buddhist traditions, and argued that Thai democracy should be based on 'good governance, a righteous ruler, and Buddhist Dhammic kingship'. In the light of his being deposed due to questions about corruption the depth of his commitment to Buddhist ideals seems very open to question.

In regards to ethnic separatism in the south, Thaksin's approach was to blame it on bandits and deny a link to militant Islam and attempt to crack down on violence while trying to increase development funding to the area. The extent to which Thailand's own military and police forces, and their actions, were also involved with the situation is not clear, but what is notable is that disputes over whether it was gangsterism, separatism, Islamic fundamentalism, or even simple opposition to Thaksin Shinawatra's government became endemic during this period. In this context then, although it is impossible not to regard the conflict has having been to some degree a conflict between Buddhists and Muslims, it is also apparent that whilst politicians did not talk up this aspect of the issue during the period when Thaksin Shinawatra was in power, his reforms contributed to exacerbating it (Phongpaichit and Baker 2004: 234-239). It remains to be seen how the new military government which came to power in 2006 will respond to these challenges.

Vietnam

Religious freedom, or the lack of it, is a dominant issue in the discussion of Buddhism in Vietnam. The current regime has a very fluid attitude towards Buddhism and other religions; it publicly supports religious traditions whilst at the same time seeking to stamp out superstitions. This means that whenever it dislikes any particular grouping it labels it a superstition and can ban it (Do 1999; King 1996). The leading Buddhist monk, Thich Nhat Hahn, who left Vietnam in 1966, has only been able to return once to Vietnam for a visit in 2005. Even then his visit was a source of considerable controversy as monks in Vietnam argued that the government was using his visit to show they were liberal in their attitude to Buddhism, whilst at the same time increasing repression of Buddhists and the 'Unified Buddhist Church of Vietnam' which was banned in 1981 ('UBCV Patriarch Thich Huyen Quang Declines to Meet Thich Nhat Hanh in Binh Dinh').

Myanmar

In Myanmar (formerly Burma) there is the apparently paradoxical situation of a military junta taking the role of guardians of the Buddhist tradition. The central conundrum

at the forefront of many international observers' minds is how members of the Buddhist *sangha* can support and relate to such a governing system. Up until 1990 large parts of the *sangha* supported pro-democracy elements and the National League for Democracy (NLD) led by Aung San Suu Kyi. Following the 1990 election, which was won by the NLD, but the results of which were ignored by the government, the military set out to suppress opposition to it in the *sangha*. This culminated in the police attacking a meeting of 7,000 monks in Mandalay to which 20,000 monks responded by boycotting the regime (Mathews 1999). The government then set out to drive elements hostile to it from the *sangha* and adopt for itself a Buddhist dimension to its policies and to appropriate Buddhist rhetoric to legitimate its rule. The *mangala sutta* has been heavily promoted as a basis for government policy and the generals began to appear from time to time on television in white robes, like lay Buddhists observing the eight precepts on special days (Houtman 1999). The notion of virtue is also contested in Burmese politics. Both Aung San Suu Kyi and the regime put forward that what they are doing is acting on Buddhist principles and promoting Buddhist virtues. Yet, clearly, their aims and ideals are diametrically opposite in relation to whether a democratic system of government is favourable. Despite the occasional incidents of protest by the *sangha* it now appears that the situation is one in which the regime maintains a tight control of the *sangha* and many in the *sangha* support its promotion of Buddhist values.

Sri Lanka

The continuing conflict between the (mainly Hindu) Tamils and the (mostly Buddhist) Singhalese has dominated the relationship of Buddhism to politics in Sri Lanka since 1980. The background to this goes back not only to Angarika Dhammapala's reforms of the nineteenth century which sought to 'purify' singhalese Buddhist traditions and remove elements from it which were seen as Hindu in origin, but also to the movement towards the politicisation of the Sangha in which Walpole Rahula was influential, but which was opposed by the early post-independence leaders such as D.S. Senanayake. Rahula in his seminal pre-independence work of 1946, *Bhikshuvage Urumaya* ('The Heritage of the Monk') rejected the notion that monks could not play an active role in society and in politics, and favoured the development of the role of the 'political monk' (Malalgoda 1977; Bartholomeusz 1999). This has undoubtedly contributed to the situation in which a number of monks now sit in parliament, the first of these was Baddegama Samitha in 2001 and now as a part of the 'The National Heritage Party', or Jathika Hela Urumaya (JHU) monks hold nine seats in parliament and as of January 2007 form part of the government ('Monk's Party to Join Lankan Govt'). They are a conservative group and have played a role in campaigning against conversions and are firmly against any peace process with the Tamil community ('JHU Press Statements').

South Korea

Buddhism in Korea has been through a number of phases, waxing and waning in influence. In the long term this was apparent in its dominance during the Koryo dynasty (918-1392) followed by its being subject to anti-Buddhist statutes during the Choson dynasty (1392-1910). In the twentieth century Japanese imperialism led to initial liberalisation of laws on Buddhism, followed by heavy state interference in the running of the *sangha*. After 1945 Buddhism was all but wiped out in the North under the regime of Kim Il Sung but has flourished in South Korea.

The tradition of government control of Buddhist monasteries and temples was further entrenched by the 1961 law on control of Buddhist property in the republic of South Korea. Under the government of Park Chung Hee from 1962 to his assassination in 1979 Buddhism was seen as supporting the regime and was supported by the regime. However, aspects of the relationship that were problematic were highlighted by issues such as the conscription of monks into the armed forces, which is clearly against the monastic code of conduct. In yet another turn in fortune, the next leader, Chun Doohwan, was a staunch Christian who withdrew support from Buddhism and tried to attack it wherever possible. In a move reminiscent of Chinese current policies Chun turned monasteries and temples into national parks and took control of their lands and began to develop them as tourist resorts. By 1980 this led to open conflict between the *sangha* and the state. Arrests and repression of Buddhist monks continued and culminated in the popular uprisings of 1986 which led to the first democratic elections in South Korea. The dominant Chogye order tries to maintain order within the diverse groups of monks in temples, monasteries and renunciate orders that make up its membership. At times this has boiled over into actual fighting, as happened in 1994 at the main Chogye Temple in Seoul, for control of the order (Sorensen 1999). In another incident at Chogye Temple in 1998 over a hundred monks barricaded themselves in the Temple in protest over the control of funds by another faction of monks and in the end the occupation had to be broken up by riot police ('Monks Charged Over Temple Violence'). As well as Buddhists fighting with Buddhists in South Korea there is also a history of Christian attacks on Buddhist monasteries, sites, monuments and individuals which has been going on since 1982. Christians even burned down

19

a number of Buddhist temples in northern Seoul in 1996 (Tedesco 1999). In view of the ways in which the South Korean government has taken an active part in the management of the *sangha* and its property since 1945 it is also evident that these conflicts cannot be seen in isolation from political struggles in South Korea over wealth, property and the rights of different communities.

Taiwan

There has been an extraordinary proliferation of Buddhist new movements in Taiwan such as the Fo Guang Shan, Tzu Chi and Dharma Drum Mountain which has given rise to questions about the relationship between traditional Buddhism, business and politics. The Fo Guang Shan movement, also known outside of Taiwan as the 'Buddha's Light International Association' (BLIA) is an excellent exemplar of this. It was founded in 1967 by the Ven. Hsing Yun and has become prominent as it has founded many temples around the world. These include the Nan Tien Temple in Wollongong, Australia, and the Hsi Lai Temple in California, USA. It is also actively engaged in educational and charity work ('Fo Guang Shan'). It is the largest Buddhist organisation in Taiwan and extremely wealthy. It is not surprising, therefore, that it should be courted by political leaders as essentially such a large organisation cannot but be seen as a potential vote bank in any democratic system. Ven. Hsing Yun has also at times been labelled a 'political monk' as he has made comments on Chinese reunification, supported the Tibetan cause and has been implicated as involved in a scandal involving Al Gore where the BLIA Hsi Lai Buddhist Temple in California raised funds for the Al Gore campaign, despite it being illegal for a registered charity to support a political candidate (Sperry 2000).

There is also considerable overlap in Taiwan itself between the government and the *sangha*. In particular, a number of religious leaders have played active roles in politics which has led to a blurring of the line between religion and politics (Laliberte 2004: 42–43).

Cambodia

After the devastation of religious culture during the Pol Pot regime era (1975-79) Cambodia has seen an extraordinary rebirth of Buddhist culture which highlights the way that diaspora community members are able to interact with their own countries of origin. Since 1989, when the People's Republic of Kampuchea started lifting restrictions on religions, large numbers of monasteries have been rebuilt and the number of monks and nuns has increased enormously (Gutherie 2005). The *sangha* is today, though, largely a supporter of the government and its leader Hun Sen (Stuart-Fox 2006: 13). That there are other possibilities is shown by the work of Maha Ghosananda, an exiled Cambodian monk who now lives in the USA. In 1992 he started a practice of *dhammayatra* ('peace walks'). His ideas have included such notions as organising meditations by monks and nuns with the aim of influencing the creation of a 'just constitution' for Cambodia in 1993 (Poethig 2004).

India

India has a population of perhaps around seven to ten million Buddhists out of a total population of around a billion; in other words, Buddhists are a very small minority. Despite this they are a vocal minority in certain states and Buddhism is a factor in the politics of Maharashtra and Uttar Pradesh. This is due to its influence amongst the *dalits*, or oppressed, peoples, also formerly known as untouchables. In 1956, B.R. Ambedkar, the leader of the untouchable communities in Maharashtra and in some areas of Uttar Pradesh, encouraged his followers to convert to Buddhism (Omvedt 2003). This is now known as the Ambedkarite Buddhist community. Ambedkar's followers also established a political party to represent their interests, the Republican Party of India, but it was not successful in becoming a major force in Indian politics. The *dalit* vote has been courted by various parties as numerically the lower caste and *dalit* voters often represent the majority of voters in some areas, and during the 1980s a number of state governments came to power which organised coalitions of these communities to seize power from the previous ruling parties. In Uttar Pradesh the Bahujan Samaj Party led by Mayavati courted the Buddhist vote and organised a coalition based around the *yadav* and *dalit* communities.

A proportion of the inhabitants of Ladakh and Himachal Pradesh form an Indian Buddhist community whose culture is closely related to that of Tibet. Following the Indo-Chinese war of 1962 Ladakh and the border areas of China became militarised zones, and tension with China continues to this day. Due to this, the politics of these Buddhist border areas of India is very sensitive to security concerns related to China. India–China relations during the period when the BJP government was in power in the 1990s were dominated by Prime Minister Atal Bihari Bajpayee taking a conciliatory line on matters related to China, and the defence minister George Fernandez taking a hard line on China-related issues

Under the Congress-led coalition government that came to power in 2004 a similar balanced strategy seems to be in operation. The implication of this is that neither does the Indian government completely support the Tibetan government in exile in all areas for fear of offending China, nor yet does it suppress the exile Tibetan community as it does not want

to be seen to be following a pro-Chinese line. At the moment India is enthusiastically trying to increase pilgrimage by Chinese Buddhists to India. Part of its promotional materials for tourism also draws on the appeal of the Dalai Lama, and as such is not acceptable to the Chinese government. In 2007, a delegation from China representing pilgrims walked out of a showing of a film about Buddhism in India due to the inclusion of footage of the Dalai Lama in the film (Yadav 2007). This points to the tightrope that India walks in dealing with China and suggests that Buddhism has an influence on Indian politics both because of the Ambedkarite Buddhist community's influence and also because the presence of the Tibetan community in India affects India's relationship with China.

Western countries

Despite the growing interest in and popularity of Buddhism in Western countries the number of Buddhists there is not high, and where it is it is mostly due to immigration from Buddhist countries. A current estimate (2004) by the BBC of active Buddhists in the UK put their number at 150,000 ('BBC - Schools - Buddhist Festivals'). Another way of looking at it is that according to the 2001 census of England and Wales the percentages of Buddhists were 0.3% in England and 0.2% in Wales ('Ethnicity and Religion').

In Australia in 2001 the number of Buddhists was about 357,000 (1.9% of the population) according to the ABS. The majority of these were immigrants from Vietnam, Cambodia or China or their children. In the USA there are estimates that there are around three million Buddhists (1% of the population) and that something like three-quarters of these people are from Asian countries ('Buddhism in the United States'). Despite the relatively small numbers of Buddhists in Western countries their influence is substantial as they often represent the visible face of Buddhism for Western cultures. For instance, the Nan Tien temple near Wollongong in Australia, which was opened in 1995, is said to be the largest Buddhist temple in the southern hemisphere and is regarded as a major driver of tourism to the area (Nan Tien 2007). Figures such as the Dalai Lama also can attact audiences of thousands to public meetings in Western countries and generate considerable revenue for charitable works, half a million dollars recently being generated by a single visit to Madison, Wisconsin (Roby 2007). It is indeed increasingly apparent that their influence is much greater than their small numbers might suggest.

The future

Current trends in the development of the relationship between Buddhism and politics suggest that two conflicting patterns are emerging. One is of localised shifts towards increasing diversity; the other is of a global trend towards increasing uniformity. In a sense there is nothing new in this; Buddhism has always adapted to local circumstances and continues to do so, but what is new is the way that globalisation is leading to the possibility of crossing the boundaries between the localised traditions.

An extremely clear case of how politics and Buddhism are interacting is apparent in the USA where a movement called 'Mindful Politics' has been developing. It aims to introduce Buddhist perspectives into the debate over moral and political issues. In part this is a response to the Christian-right lobby in US politics (McLeod 2006). However, whereas the Buddhists sit in some degree of harmony with the humanitarian lobby on some issues, they are closer to the Christian right on others. For instance, the implications of non-violence as a guiding principle are on the one hand that Buddhists oppose war, which puts them at odds with the Christian right, but on the other hand they oppose abortion, which puts them in the same camp as Christian pro-life advocates.

A second issue in the development of global Buddhist perspectives is the extent to which Buddhist traditions come into conflict with other religions and political systems. Two entrenched examples of this are the Buddhist–Hindu dimension to Sri Lankan politics and the emerging Buddhist–Muslim conflict in Thai politics. Obviously in each case it could be argued that the conflict is not really religious, but social, political and economic, but in each case the longer the conflict lasts the greater chance that the religious label will gain an independent life as an indicator of the conflict. Indeed, in the case of Sri Lanka it is hard to see how the conflict cannot now be seen as being drawn on religious lines. Nor yet does there seem to be any hope of a realistic settlement of the conflict in the near future. At present the conflict in southern Thailand between insurgent groups who identify themselves as Muslim and the Buddhist central government seems to be getting further entrenched. The possibility of the perception from the Islamic extremist perspective of an alignment of Buddhism and the forces of the enemies of Islam cannot bode well for future of Islamic–Buddhist relations.

One further scenario needs to be considered, I suggest, in relation to future conflictual relationships in which Buddhism might be involved. In 2007 there were conflicts featuring tensions between Buddhists and Hindus and Buddhists and Muslims. What are the prospects for conflicts between Buddhists and Christians? There are already fundamentalist American Christian groups which campaign against Buddhist influences in the USA ('Sonrise Center for Buddhist Studies'). Whilst in Buddhist countries such as Sri Lanka there are movements against Christian missionary activity where the Sri Lankan government drafted a law in 2004 against offering inducements to convert or making conversions by force which was clearly aimed at combating Christian missionary activity.

Another area in which all Buddhists are unlikely to agree is whether Buddhist ideas should be used to legitimise non-democratic governments. On the one hand in China, Myanmar and other states the notion of Buddhist values as an element in 'Asian values' is seen as supporting non-democratic government. On the other hand, engaged Buddhists in many countries argue that Buddhist values support democratic government and there is no contradiction between Asian values and democracy.

A final, and paradoxical, source of conflict in Buddhism is the very attempt to develop a common platform for global Buddhism. The very notion of 'World Buddhism' highlights this paradox. Chinese Buddhist groups in the PRC and Burmese and Thai groups are keen on the notion of 'World Buddhist conferences'. Yet neither the Thai government in 2000 nor the Cambodian government in 2002 would let the Dalai Lama attend their 'World Buddhist' conferences due to pressure from the PRC (Dechard 2002). In addition, in 2006 the Chinese World Buddhist Conference not only did not invite the Dalai Lama but included in his place their candidate for Panchen Lama, which was a provocative move in diaspora Tibetan eyes as the Panchen Lama was traditionally regarded as the second most important Lama in Tibet, but the Chinese-sponsored Panchen Lama is regarded by many Tibetans as simply a puppet of the Chinese government ('China Hosts First Buddhism Forum'). Moreover, it is difficult to imagine the Myanmar government welcoming engaged Buddhist human rights activists from Asia or the West. Finally, I cannot imagine groups like the Sokka Gakkai or many Pure Land schools actually

finding a common platform with many other Buddhist traditions on some issues.

So in terms of the future relationship between Buddhism and politics it is hard to imagine the development of a Global Buddhism, in the sense of a unified Universal Buddhism, and I doubt such a thing will ever exist. But it is clear that in the future the diverse Buddhist traditions of the world will increasingly interact on a national and international level with each other and with political groups, and this is likely to highlight not only their shared aims, but also their differences.

Bibliography

Books and articles

Bartholomeusz, T. (1999) 'First amongst Equals: Buddhism and the Sri Lankan State' in Harris, I. (ed.), *Buddhism and Politics in Twentieth-century Asia*, London and New York: Continuum, pp. 173–193.

Do, T. (1999) 'The Quest for Enlightenment and Cultural Identity: Buddhism in Contemporary Vietnam', in Harris, I. (ed.), *Buddhism and Politics in Twentieth-century Asia*. London and New York: Continuum, pp. 254–284.

Flood, G. (1988) *An Introduction to Hinduism*, Delhi: Cambridge University Press.

Gombrich, R. (1971) *Precept and Practice: Traditional Buddhism in the Rural Highlands of Ceylon*, Oxford: Clarendon Press.

Gutherie, E. (2005) 'Rebuilding Cambodian Buddhism Anew: Modernity at a Cost or Khmer Renaissance?', Conference paper presented at the Australasian Association for Buddhist Studies, Sydney.

Hardacre, H. (2006) 'State and Religion in Japan', in Swanson, P. and Chilson C. (eds), *Nanzan Guide to Japanese Religion*, Honolulu: University of Hawai'i Press, pp. 274–288.

Harris, I. (ed.). (1999) *Buddhism and Politics in Twentieth-century Asia*, London and New York: Continuum.

Horner, I. (trans.) (1970) *The Book of the Discipline* (Vinaya-pitaka), Vol. 1 (Suttavibhanga), London: Pali Text Society.

Horner, I. (trans.) (1982) *Sacred Books of the Buddhists,* Vol. 30, *The Book of the Discipline* (Vinaya-pitaka) Vol. 4 (Mahavagga), London: Pali Text Society.

Houtman, G. (1999) *Mental Culture in Burmese Crisis Politics*, Tokyo: ILCAA. Study of Languages and Cultures of Asia and Africa Monograph Series, no. 33, publication of the Institute for the Study of Languages and Cultures of Asia and Africa, Tokyo University of Foreign Studies.

Keay, J. (1988) *India Discovered*, London: Collins.

Khosla, S. (1989) *The Historical Evolution of the Buddha Legend*, Delhi: Intellectual Publishing House.

King, S. (1996) 'Thich Nhat Hanh and the Unified Buddhist Church', in Queen, C. and King, S. (eds), *Engaged Buddhism, Buddhist Liberation Movements in Asia*, New York: State University of New York Press, pp. 321–364.

Laliberte, A. (2004) *The Politics of Buddhist Organisations in Taiwan*, London: Routledge-Curzon.

Lopez, S. (1999) *Prisoners of Shangri-la*, Chicago: Chicago University Press.

Lopez, S. (ed.) (2002) *Modern Buddhism*, London: Penguin Books.

McLeod, M. (ed.) (2006) *Mindful Politics: A Buddhist Guide to Making the World a Better Place*, Boston: Wisdom.

Malalgoda, K. (1977) 'Buddhism in Post-independence Sri Lanka', in Oddie, G. (ed.), *Religion in South Asia: Religious Conversion and Revival Movements in South Asia in Medieval and Modern Times*, London: Curzon Press, pp. 183–189.

Mathews, B. (1999) 'Buddhism and the Nation in Myanmar', in Harris, I. (ed.), *Buddhism and Politics in Twentieth-century Asia*, London and New York: Continuum, pp. 26–53.

Miller, J. (2006) 'The Opium of the People: Religion, Science and Modernity', in Miller, J. (ed.), *Chinese Religions in Contemporary Societies*, Santa Barbara: ABC-CLIO, pp. 31–56.

Miller, J. (ed.) (2006) *Chinese Religions in Contemporary Societies*, Santa Barbara: ABC-CLIO.

Norman, K. (1997) *A Philological Approach to Buddhism*, London: School of Oriental and African Studies.

Omvedt, G. (2003) *Buddhism in India, Challenging Brahmanism and Caste*, Delhi: Sage Publications.

Phongpaichit, P. and Baker, C. (2004) *Thaksin: The Business of Politics in Thailand*, Chang Mai, Thailand: Silkworm Books.

Poethig, K. (2004) 'The Transnational in Cambodia's Dhammayatra', in Marston, J. and Guthrie, E. (eds), *History, Buddhism, and New Religious Movements in Cambodia*, Honolulu: University of Hawai'i Press, pp. 197–212.

Queen, C. (ed.) (2000) *Engaged Buddhism in the West*, Boston: Wisdom.

Queen, C. and King, S. (eds). (1996) *Engaged Buddhism, Buddhist Liberation Movements in Asia*, New York: State University of New York Press.

Rahula, W. (trans. Wijayasureeendra, K.) (1974) *The Heritage of the Monk* (translation of second edition *Bhikshuvage Urumaya* of 1948), New York: Grove Press.

Rahula, W. (1974) 'Wrong Notions of Dhammata (Dharmata)', in Cousins, L. (ed.), *Buddhist Studies in Honour of I.B. Horner*, Dordrecht, Holland: D. Reidel Publishing Company, pp. 181–191.

Rahula, W. (1985) *What the Buddha Taught*, London: Gordon Fraser.

Reynolds, F. (1972) 'The Two Wheels of Dhamma', in Smith, B. (ed.), *The Two Wheels of Dhamma*, Chambersburg: American Academy of Religion, pp. 6–30.

Snodgrass, J. (2003) *Presenting Japanese Buddhism to the West*, Chapel Hill and London: University of North Carolina Press.

Sorensen, H. (1999) 'Buddhism and Secular Power in Twentieth-century Korea', in Harris, I. (ed.), *Buddhism and Politics in Twentieth-century Asia*, London and New York: Continuum, pp. 127–152.

Strong, J. (1983) *The Legend of King Asoka*, Princeton: Princeton University Press.

Thapar, R. (2000) *Asoka and the Decline of the Mauryas*, Delhi: Oxford India.

Walshe, M. (1987) *Thus Have I Heard: A New Translation of the Digha Nikaya*, London: Wisdom.

Wells, H. (1936) *A Short History of the World*, London: Penguin.

Yin, J. (2006) 'Buddhism and Economic Reform in Mainland China', in Miller, J. (ed.), *Chinese Religions in Contemporary Societies*, Santa Barbara: ABC-CLIO, pp. 85–99.

Internet references

'BBC – Schools – Buddhist Festivals', 2004, on *BBC.CO.UK*. at http://www.bbc.co.uk/

schools/religion/buddhism/ accessed: 28 April 2008.

'Buddhism in the United States', 2007, on *Wikipedia*, at: http://en.wikipedia.org/wiki/Buddhism_in_the_United_States, accessed: 28 April 2008.

'China Hosts First Buddhism Forum', 13 April 2006, on *BBC NEWS,* at: http://news.bbc.co.uk/2/hi/asia-pacific/4905140.stm, accessed: 13 February 2007.

Decherd, C., 'Dalai Lama Barred from Cambodia Buddhist Conference at China's Request', 2002, on *WorldWide Religious News*, at: http://www.wwrn.org/article.php?idd=12429&sec=52&con=16, accessed: 13 February 2007.

'Ethnicity and Religion', 2003, on *National Statistics Online*, at: http://www.statistics.gov.uk/census2001/profiles/commentaries/ethnicity.asp, accessed: 28 April 2008.

'Fo Guang Shan', 2007, in *Wikipedia,* at: http://en.wikipedia.org/wiki/Fo_Guang_Shan, accessed: 28 April 2008.

'JHU Press Statements', on the *Jathika Hela Urumaya* website at: http://www.jhu.lk/e_press.html, accessed: 28 April 2008.

Kitiarsa, P., 'In Defense of the Thai-style Democracy,' 2006, at: http://www.ari.nus.edu.sg/showfile.asp?eventfileid=188, accessed: February 2007.

'Monks Charged Over Temple Violence', 24 December 1998, on *BBC NEWS*, at: http://news.bbc.co.uk/1/hi/world/asia-pacific/241066.stm, accessed: 28 April 2008.

'Monk's Party to Join Lankan Govt', in *Hindustan Times*, 31 January 2007, at: http://www.hindustantimes.com/news/7598_1916135,000500020002.htm, accessed: 28 April 2008.

'Nau Tien Temple', nd, on: *Tourism Wollongong* at: http://www.tourismwollongong.com.au/recreation/recDetails.asp?recNo=59, accessed: 11 May 2007.

'New Komeito's Views on Politics and Religion in Japan', 2004, at: http://www.komei.or.jp/en/about/view.html . accessed: 28 April 2008.

Roby, B., 'Dalai Lama Brings in Cash', 10 May 2007, on *The Badger Herald*, at: http://badger-herald.com/news/2007/05/10/dalai_lama_brings_in.php, accessed 11 May 2007.

'Sonrise Center for Buddhist Studies', 2005, on Sonrise Center for Buddhist Studies, at: http://www.sonrisecenter.org/, accessed: 28 April 2008.

Sperry, P., 'Gore Had 15 Chances to Escape Temple of Doom', 2000, in WorldNetDaily, at: http://www.worldnetdaily.com/news/article.asp?ARTICLE_ID=20676, accessed: 28 April 2008.

Stuart-Fox, M., 'Buddhism and Politics in Laos, Cambodia, Myanmar and Thailand 2004', paper presented at the ANU Cambodia, Laos, Myanmar and Thailand Summer School, ANU, online at: ww.anu.edu.au/ThaiOnline/BUDDHISM%20AND%20POLITICS%20IN%20SOUTHEAST%20ASIA.pdf, accessed: 19 July 2007.

Tedosco, F., 'Questions for Buddhist and Christian Cooperation in Korea', 1999, on the website of *The International Association for Religious Freedom*, Oxford, at: http://www.geocities.com/~iarf/tedescol.html, accessed: 28 April 2008.

'The Largest Buddhist Communities', 2005, on www.adherents.com, at: http://www.adherents.com/largecom/com_buddhist.html, accessed: 28 April 2008.

'UBCV Patriarch Thich Huyen Quang Declines to Meet Thich Nhat Hanh in Binh Dinh', 2005, on *Que Me: Action for Democracy in Vietnam*, at: http://www.queme.net/eng/e-news_detail.php?numb=397, accessed: 28 April 2008.

Yadav, J., 'When Dalai Lama Stopped a Patna Show for Chinese Pilgrims', 13 January, 2007, in *The Indian Express*, at: http://www.indian-express.com/story/20815.html, accessed: 28 April 2008.

25

3

Christianity

Protestantism

Paul Freston

Why study global Protestant politics?

I was once invited to the United States to observe a meeting of scholars who studied Christianity and politics in that country. I soon realised that scholars of Catholicism perceived the comparative dimension of their work, that Catholicism and American politics had to be studied in the light of Catholicism and politics elsewhere. But scholars of Protestantism showed no such awareness; it was as if an important contemporary relationship between Protestantism and politics existed only in the USA.

This belief is probably shared by most people in the developed West. But it misunderstands not only the reality of Protestantism but of religion and politics globally. While belief in the inevitable decline of religion's public importance has now largely been replaced by awareness of Islam and the American religious right, there is still much ignorance of the political dimensions of global Christianity.

By the most widely accepted estimate (Barrett *et al.* 2001), Protestants represent around 11% of world population. Two factors enhance their importance. Firstly, they are heavily practising; nominal adherence is high in Europe but low in areas of recent Protestantisation. Secondly, they have a truly global spread which is due to conversion rather than migration.

Protestantism has done especially well in sub-Saharan Africa, Latin America and the Chinese and Korean worlds. After the USA, the countries with most practising Protestants are now Brazil, China and Nigeria. Many of these are not connected with institutions founded in Europe or North America, but with pentecostal denominations founded in Latin America, or 'African Independent Churches', or 'unregistered' Chinese groups. On some restrictive definitions of 'Protestant' (e.g. Bastian), these are not Protestants. But they are reasonably orthodox, trinitarian Christians who are not Catholic or Eastern Orthodox, and who claim to base their faith on the Bible. They are the grassroots Protestants of the global South, and often more numerous than those linked with the old mission churches. This expansion (mainly post-colonial) has been largely due to indigenous initiatives. Global Protestantism is predominantly non-white and distant from power and wealth.

These characteristics give it considerable political importance. In addition, it helps us re-examine the historical correlation between Protestantism and democracy. Is that a spurious correlation, dependent on other factors in the West which might not exist in the global South? What is the weight of religious traditions versus the importance of circumstances? We should be wary of ideas such as 'Protestantism is essentially democratic' or 'Islam is essentially undemocratic'. Religions are always diverse and mutable. Yet changing social contexts do not explain everything. Each religious tradition has a unique approach to law, territory, religious organisation and religion–state relations, and this may well influence how believers behave in particular circumstances.

Protestantism as heir to the Western Christian tradition

Protestantism's spread into economically and culturally distinct societies has increased the variability of its relationship to politics which stems from Christianity's origin as a persecuted sect, the lack of 'law' in its scriptures and its emphasis on cultural and linguistic adaptation. Christ never gave a 'law' comparable to the Law of Moses or sharia. While Moses and Mohammad governed communities, early Christianity was distant from political responsibilities. Its politics has generally been less sure of itself. Although the Hebrew scriptures were incorporated into the Christian Bible, political appeal to Mosaic Law has usually been regarded with suspicion. While many Christians speak of a worldview and political *principles*, few find in the Bible a full-fledged political *programme*.

Protestantism is a 'purer' Christian monotheism (rejecting Catholic dilution of the sacred in the saints). Perceptions of its relationship to politics are therefore coloured by perceptions of monotheism in general. For some scholars, monotheistic religions tend to arrogance and intolerance, unless constrained by extraneous factors (Bruce 2003: 225). But distinctions must be made. Monotheism does not necessarily imply belief that only our group holds the truth. Monotheists are not always epistemologically arrogant, as Protestantism well illustrates. And mass voluntarist monotheism has different implications from elite or state monotheism.

Many scholars also argue for differences *between* monotheistic religions which transcend their current contexts. While Christianity started on the margins of an existing empire, Islam became the centre of a new empire and is not carried by a 'church'. The Islamic monist ideal differs from the normative dualism of church–state relations in Christianity, the notion of two 'cities' to which Christians belong and between which critical distance should be maintained. Islam also emphasises a religiously sanctioned body of laws, which gives it a greater tendency to be theocratic. Another contrast is in Islam's stress on territoriality. Christianity thus lacks an original connection with power, law and territory. But no religion is frozen in time; Christianity later acquired territoriality and became Christendom.

Protestantism, born largely within the Christendom model, nevertheless accentuates these characteristics. Especially in its evangelical form, it sees itself as a return to the early church. It thus tends to seek justification for its political positions in the New Testament. However, early Christianity was a discriminated sect which soon became a cross-cultural voluntary community. Instead of imposing a religious law, it spoke of a law 'written on the heart' and a 'kingdom not of this world', which at once enabled believers to belong to any earthly kingdom ('render unto Caesar') but also relativised all of them. Lacking a definite political recipe, a variety of postures towards the state could be adopted, from eschatological indifference through prophetic critique to conformist legitimation. Early Christianity also lacked a concept of territoriality. But this voluntarist, non-legalist and non-territorial model faced enormous resistances which partially distorted it. The marginalised faith later became the official cult and partly reverted to the Old Testament programme. But from early modern times, differentiation reactivated its original status as a voluntary group (Martin 1997: 106–117).

Thus, Protestantism's relationship to politics is born two-pronged. Firstly, it 'protests' against accretions to scriptural faith. Thus, Christianity's circumstances when its scriptures were written are vital. Luke's late first-century 'Acts' describing the expansion of the politically powerless faith becomes authoritative scripture, whereas Eusebius' fourth-century works lionising the newly converted emperor Constantine do not. But secondly, Protestantism also inherits the Western Christian tradition.

A key part of that tradition is 'dualism'. This stems from prophetic Old Testament religion, which led to a refusal of the state-cult, a tendency to pacifism and eschatological relativisation. But 'dualism' also refers to the political development of the West, where the church acquired institutional importance after the collapse of the Western empire. Later (with the eleventh-century reforms of the Roman Church), dualism was sharpened by the struggle between pope and emperor, laying the groundwork of institutional pluralism for the gradual development of civil society and democracy (Berger 2004). In contrast to Byzantine 'caesaropapism' (subordination of clerical to secular power), the normative doctrine of the West became the 'two swords', recognising secular authority but denying it jurisdiction over the church, and asserting the right of the church to challenge the secular power.

However, both Western and Eastern Christianity were heirs of the fourth-century shift from being a popular movement supported by its members to an elite organisation supported by the state. This is a second element of the Western tradition that will influence Protestantism. A third element is the thirteenth-century revival of the Aristotelian notion of a self-sufficient polity, undergirding the emergence of national monarchies and weakening papal political claims.

The politics of early Protestantism

The Western tradition did not bequeath to Protestantism a uniform approach. Its variety was accentuated by the circumstances of the early modern world, as well as its own organisational and doctrinal diversity. Protestantism reflects primitive Christianity's political disadvantages. Primitive Christian thought, said Tocqueville, lacked the idea of moral citizenship and created a dangerous political void (Siedentop 1994: 134). Since Tocqueville's time, this void has been minimised in Catholicism by a social magisterium, whereas it has continued in (increasingly evangelical) Protestantism with its 'primitivist' return to origins. Since Christianity's origins were distant from the state, perhaps the abiding 'temptation' for evangelicalism is not theocracy but apoliticism.

Protestantism has become the natural home of the *sect* tendency, one of the possible sociological outworkings of primitive Christianity. The *church*, in Troeltsch's (1931: 461) conception, is an institution endowed with grace, able to receive the masses and adjust itself to the world. It becomes an integral part of the social order. The *sect*, however, is a voluntary association, usually connected with the lower classes or those opposed to the state.

It aspires to personal perfection, which usually means renouncing the idea of dominating the world (though it may oscillate between indifference, hostility and tolerance). For Troeltsch, the key idea is Christian universalism. The Kingdom of God cannot be realised in this world apart from compromise. Eschewing universalism through *churchly* compromise, the *sects* occasionally appeal to force or more usually to eschatology (postponement until the end of time).

The Reformation, says Troeltsch, was 'immediately confronted by this fateful question: church or sect? It has deliberately held firmly to the church-type' (Troeltsch 1931: 382). Writing in the early twentieth century, he sees *sectarian* influence as limited mainly to ascetic Calvinism's 'attempts to restore holy community' within the world. But that scarcely did justice to Anglophone Protestantism; and since then its global expansion has increased influence of the 'sect-type' and of the *denominational model* in which universalism is 'spiritualised' by explicit acceptance of organisational pluralism.

The sixteenth-century Reformation was divided into Lutheran, Calvinist and Anglican branches, plus the Anabaptist 'radical Reformation' (and later voluntarist offshoots of Anglicanism such as Baptists and Quakers). Their political consequences are very diverse. But one emphasis in common is the sovereignty of God (as distinct from pope or emperor), understanding sovereignty as not only a royal metaphor which can legitimate tyranny, but also a prophetic metaphor which debunks claims to absolute power. Another is the notion of some degree of consent in theories of government, stressing the priesthood of all believers. The right to read the scriptures prepared for the discovery of the person as subject and the right to freedom of conscience (De Gruchy 1995: 72). But Protestantism's lack of a magisterium or canonical sanctions

meant a 'secularisation of political life' (Mehl 1965: 270), linked to its weaker communal dimension (compared to Catholicism and Orthodoxy). The more a religion sees God relating to individuals, the more difficult it becomes to sustain notions of a 'holy commonwealth'.

Lutheranism attempts to retain universalism by Christianising the Decalogue and equating it with Natural Law. Catholicism's 'two-stage' ethics is transformed into the contrast between 'person' and 'office'. The 'two swords' theory is replaced with 'two kingdoms'. All political authority is left to the prince, to whom the ageing Luther increasingly turns to oversee the church (Berman and Witte 1987: 492; O'Donovan and O'Donovan 2000: 555). In effect, the universal church is replaced by the territorial church, in line with the rise of the nation-state. The Peace of Augsburg in 1555 strengthened this 'Erastian' subordination of church to secular ruler by decreeing that 'the ruler's religion prevails in his territory' (*cuius regio, eius religio*). Conformity or exile were the individual's only options. Not surprisingly, the stereotypical Lutheran came to be characterised by obedience towards officialdom. Lutheran orthodoxy insisted religion and politics not be mixed. With its conviction of the incorrigibility of the world and autonomy of the state from gospel norms, Lutheranism is historically weak in generating political activism (Madeley 1994: 145) or rational reformism.

Calvinism is very different: it adopted the sect-ideal of 'holy community' and applied it to a national church. The Anabaptists deemed this impracticable, but Calvin believed the spiritually 'elect' were a majority. In the end, though, the attempt made a breach in the state–church system. As 'the second great Christian social ideal [of] comprehensive historical significance', the other being medieval Catholicism, Calvinism penetrated political movements. Making an ethic of sanctification the basis of the state, using Old Testament principles rather than the love ethic of the Sermon on the Mount, Calvinism everywhere attempted 'a systematic endeavour to mould the life of society'. The result is commonly called 'this-worldly asceticism' and its connection with modern capitalism has been exhaustively debated. It 'accepts the basis of the modern economic situation without reserve', while still stressing that property-owners are God's stewards (Troeltsch 1931: 647).

Calvin's concept of government is variously described as authoritarian (Smith 1998: 94), aristocratic (O'Donovan and O'Donovan 2000: 665) or 'essentially positive' rather than merely repressive (Biéler 1959: 283). Certainly, his view of the religion–state relationship differed from other Protestant branches. It hovered between a 'two swords' doctrine and a subjection of temporal authority to spiritual (O'Donovan and O'Donovan 2000: 556). It desired ecclesiastical independence but appealed to civil coercion in religion. The church, meanwhile, reminds governments of their God-given tasks. Through the idea of 'covenant', this soon led to justification for violent rebellion as a last resort and sovereignty of the people (albeit not in modern terms) as the ultimate court of appeal against an ungodly regime. On an analogy with Israel, Scots and Dutch Calvinists and English Puritans understood their world in covenantal terms and defended international interventionism. Covenant theology and contract theories of politics show clear parallels, but it is difficult to decide, says Hill (1993: 178), as to cause and effect.

Calvinism's attempt to combine *sectarian* 'holy community' with *churchly* religious unity did not survive the seventeenth century. Thereafter, the ideal of conformity was set aside. But radical Protestants had abandoned it long before. Mystical groups stressed religious experience and freedom of conscience. And the sects wanted voluntary communities divorced from the state; in fact, the Anabaptists ('rebaptisers', rejecting infant baptism and its link to church membership as ascribed identity) regarded governmental functions as off-limits. Despite occasional revolutionary violence (Münster 1534), they were generally pacifist and held it was impossible to implement the Christian ethic in the world.

Theocracy, nationalism, religious freedom and pacifism in early Protestantism

In the early seventeenth century, the first English-speaking Baptists pioneered a new approach to religion–state relations which would transcend their direct influence. Rejecting the Anabaptist refusal to participate in the state, they retained the demand for separation of church and state. This contrasted with the theocratic experiments of early Calvinism (Geneva and Massachusetts, both small and young states unsaddled by tradition). Some question whether Geneva was a theocracy (Biéler 1959; De Gruchy 1995), but Calvin clearly got state support for church discipline. In the English Revolution of the mid-seventeenth century ideas of 'rule of the saints' came to the fore, often accompanied by the idea that morality must be enforced on the unbelieving masses to avoid divine punishment upon the whole community. Despite the harshness of such concepts, they also contain democratic possibilities in their negating of social rank (Hill 1993: 274).

Protestantism's dalliance with theocracy was easy to abandon; a religion that 'requires individual conscience cannot serve as justification for theocracy' (Bruce 2000: 122). However, it did seem to justify nationalism. Hastings (1997) traces nationalism to the impact of the Bible and vernacular literature in creating a politically stable ethnicity. Biblical Israel is a mirror for national self-imagining; as a religion of translation, Christianity has been a shaper of nations. But Christianity remained politically ambivalent between nation-state and world empire. In Protestantism, this tension seemed to be resolved in favour of the former. Yet it was established churches subordinate to the state (Anglican, Lutheran) that were most nationalist in practice. Non-state churches have frequently combined a universalist spiritual loyalty with a particularist political loyalty; yet it is from them (Mennonites, Quakers) that the most creative efforts to free Protestantism from nationalist bondage have come. Early Protestantism's link with rising nation-states fed into the Protestant–Catholic 'wars of religion'. The Treaty of Westphalia (1648) introduced the bases of modern international society, including increasing privatisation of religion and the right of each ruler to dictate the religion of his realm.

But eventually the Protestant emphasis on freedom to interpret the Bible undermined religious uniformity. Even mainstream Protestantism promoted tolerance because it weakened all human instances for resolving religious disputes and often stressed the individual's inner state. In addition, radical Protestantism by the 1640s was breaking the 'Augustinian consensus' on religious coercion. And it was doing so from religious conviction, not scepticism. Even sectarians who were intolerant in polemical or ecclesiastical contexts were often supporters of civil tolerance. The 'principled pluralist' position of early Baptists and Levellers was possible because their understanding of the relationship between Old and New Testaments allowed them to overcome any godly/ungodly division of the political world. Their conception of toleration and a non-confessional state rested on theological conviction.

Religious freedom is connected to broader human rights. Historically, Protestantism had a closer relationship to human rights than other major religions. Jellinek's classic study (1895) argued that human rights had historically centred on the demand for religious freedom by dissident English-speaking Protestants. Recent authors reaffirm this. Johnson says 'a principled position of toleration and freedom happened more quickly in the Protestant camp', but eventually more systematically in Catholicism (Johnson 1996: 69). For Witte, the right to choose religion was 'patristic, pragmatic and Protestant in initial inspiration' (Witte 2001: 745).

Early seventeenth-century Protestant radicals made a principled defence of pluralism on theological grounds. An English Baptist wrote in 1614: 'Let them be heretics, Turks, Jews or whatsoever it appertains not to the earthly power to punish them.' Rhode Island implemented this; its founder Roger Williams stated it was God's will that (since the coming of Jesus) 'a permission of the most Paganish, Jewish, Turkish or Antichristian consciences and worships be granted to all men in all nations'. For Williams, the state is not Christian but merely 'natural, human and civil'. These early tolerationists 'envisaged a multi-faith society governed by an impartial secular state' (Coffey 2000: 57). Some of them were theological fallibilists (such as one Baptist's dictum that 'all truth is not among one sort of men', since only God and the Bible were infallible); but they were not sceptics. And three seventeenth-century New World colonies established by Protestant dissenters passed the 'power test'.

Some Protestants were also principled pacifists. Pacifism was probably predominant in the early church, but by medieval and early Protestant times the 'just war' tradition was dominant. But the proto-Protestant Waldenses of the twelfth century and some Anabaptists returned to pacifism, and in 1661 the Quakers became 'the first organised body to proclaim pacifism as a principle' (Hill 1993: 422).

They and Mennonites (of Anabaptist origin) have since become renowned for their 'peace testimony'.

This has never been the mainstream Protestant position, however. Lutheran and Anglican state churches have generally striven to adjust *raison d'état* to 'just war' doctrine. Calvinism in besieged cultures (early North America, South Africa, Northern Ireland), replete with myths of promised land and ethnic chosenness, at times resurrected the link between territory, ethnicity and 'holy war', elaborating an ideological bedrock for oppression of native populations. Later Calvinism, however, besides reverting to Calvin's 'just war' stance, sometimes even led the 'ethical movement against war' (Troeltsch 1931: 652). One interpretation of this trajectory (Martin 1997) is in terms of the recovery of Christianity's original peaceableness as a cross-cultural voluntary movement. The clergy thus became distanced from the agencies of violence. Since the seventeenth century, the involvement of religion in wars has been largely as one marker of national identity; nevertheless, such reversals to violence were only partial. For Martin this was true also in domestic politics, agreeing with Halévy's opinion that evangelical conversion assisted peaceful cultural evolution rather than violent revolutionary upheavals.

Protestantism and democracy

Of major religions, Protestantism has the longest historical links with democratisation. Even today, predominantly Protestant countries are more likely to be democratic: in 2002 the Freedom House ratings from 1 (very free) to 7 (very unfree) gave them the best ranking (1.65), followed by mixed Protestant–Catholic countries (1.83) and Catholic (1.83), followed at some distance by other religions (Anderson 2006: 205). Until the Second Vatican Council, the Protestant lead would have been even greater.

The question is how to characterise the link. For Anderson, it is 'at the very least a particularly "suitable" religion for democracy' (Anderson 2006: 196); Protestant countries disproportionately avoided the authoritarian embrace in the twentieth century. Berger goes further, talking of an 'inherent affinity' (Berger 2004: 78). Hastings specifies that 'countries where democracy, even if limited in scope, first flourished are almost all Calvinist' (Hastings 1998: 140). And in the 1830s Tocqueville emphasised the Calvinist (Puritan) heritage of Anglo-America and its capacity to combine religion with freedom. Political innovation was possible because Puritanism had internalised authority. While never directly involved in government, it was nevertheless the first of American political institutions. In addition, popular Protestantism democratised through its vibrant associational life and its ability to combat the democratic temptations of envy and short-term thinking. And all this was possible, thought Tocqueville, precisely because the clergy stayed out of party politics (Tocqueville 1987; Siedentop 1994; Mitchell 1995).

Yet 'none of the leading Reformers were democrats', which leads Anderson (2006) to doubt whether the connection 'goes beyond simple correlation'. On the contrary, for Hill, Calvinist doctrines of human depravity led 'logically' to authoritarian theories (Hill 1993: 174). One can point to the 'enlightened absolutism' of Lutheran Germany and Scandinavia, the dictatorship of Cromwell, and more recent Protestant backing for apartheid and Third World authoritarianisms, and indeed the Ku Klux Klan. Berger (2004) therefore stresses that the best situation 'is where the church is most clearly a voluntary association', which is reminiscent of P.T. Forsyth's remark that 'Calvin could not have fathered democracy without an Anabaptist mother' (in De Gruchy 1995: 85).

There is a middle course between portraying democratisation as intended or as merely the result of religious division and stalemate in the wars of religion. There were other contributions (intended and unintended) besides organisational pluralism. Elements of Protestant teaching and organisational life also assisted democratisation: the de-sacralisation of religious authority, which aided the de-sacralisation of political power and the autonomy of the political; the 'priesthood of all believers', with implied right to individual dissent; the emphasis on sinfulness and its implied notions of accountability and distribution of powers; congregational governance (in some churches) as prototype for political democracy; Protestant organisational forms as templates for trades unions, pressure groups and political parties; congregational life as training in leadership, organisation and public speaking; and encouragement of economic development through general approval of market relations and incentive to literacy (De Gruchy 1995; Anderson 2006a; Bruce 2004; Witte 1993; Willaime 1997; Berger 2004). And Protestant diversity went far beyond Bruce's portrayal of sects which only turned to toleration after failing to impose their own agenda. 'Principled pluralism' was one of the early Protestant postures towards the state. Old Testament Israel was seen as exceptional; today, the state should be non-confessional. The Levellers went further: their 1647 programme is 'the first modern political movement organised around the idea of popular sovereignty', universal male suffrage and inalienable rights. Where did such ideas come from? From the Leveller leaders' location on the lower fringes of the social and educational elite and in London, where anonymous market relations made independent expression easier (Wootton 1991).

History does not support Bruce's opinion that 'religion taken seriously is incompatible with democracy' because the godly/ungodly dichotomy denies that all people are of equal worth (Bruce 2003: 245; 2004: 18). Not only through bitter experience, but also through theological principle and practical contributions, Protestantism became the first major religion to demonstrate its 'compatibility' (and more) with democracy. Nevertheless, early Protestantism included also the 'Christian nation' idea of the state promoting true religion and morals, and the apolitical 'rejection' of the state. Protestantism has often been undemocratic at diverse levels: in its internal life, in its attitudes towards other religions, and in its association with undemocratic regimes or with undemocratic political actors.

Protestantism and revolution

Protestantism ran straight into a revolutionary situation: the Peasants Revolt in 1520s Germany. Luther rejected the peasants' political appeal to his theology, but Lutheran pastor Thomas Müntzer embraced it, leading Engels to conclude that Protestantism, although generally bourgeois, could at times be revolutionary, albeit unrealistically. But Calvinism is often mentioned as contributing to modern revolutionary politics. For Walzer (1965), it did so by shifting the focus of political thought from the prince to the 'saint'. It also encouraged Bible reading, which Hill (1993) sees as the main cause of the English Revolution.

Much sectarian revolutionary impulse came from millennialism, the belief in a future divine utopia on earth. The Fifth Monarchists' revolt of 1661 was 'the last attempt to prepare the way for the Kingdom of God by means of the sword' (Troeltsch 1931: 709); at least in the West. Elsewhere, Protestant millennialism still inspired revolts, as in the nineteenth-century Taiping Rebellion in China. But in Western revolutionary thought, secular and even anti-Christian themes

33

replaced biblical ones, and Protestantism (especially the evangelical revival) came to be seen as adversarial to revolution, thus contributing to Britain's 'extraordinary stability' (in Halévy's 1949 view) or crushing the spirit of the new proletariat (for Thompson 1963).

Protestantism and imperialism

Although Protestantism initially cared little for worldwide mission, that changed from the late eighteenth century with the invention of the 'voluntary society'. Missions henceforth would be done by civil society, without state support. This distanced missionaries from soldiers and traders; only partially, of course, but enough to ensure the British Empire did not become Anglican as the Spanish had become Catholic (Martin 2004: 274). In post-colonial times, declining European involvement has been replaced by initiatives from Asia, Africa and Latin America. Increasingly, Protestant missionaries are non-whites from formerly colonised countries (Freston 2004a), an ironic development in view of the common impression that missions were the ideological arm of imperialism.

The relationship between Protestant missions and imperialism dates at least from the English colonies in North America. Yet religious motivations did not mean a uniform position regarding the natives. Richard Baxter believed a Christian nation might be obliged to rule some nations by force and compel them to admit missionaries; but Joseph Hall considered force unlawful. John Eliot felt conversion involved introducing Indians to European civilisation; but Roger Williams railed against 'monstrous and inhumane conversions', comparing religious compulsion to rape and questioning colonists' right to take Indian land (Hill 1993: 137–138; Gaustad 1991: 32).

The Dutch and British empires were long run by chartered companies concerned only with profitability. Until the 1830s, British missions struggled to gain entrance. When Company rule was abolished, Victoria's coronation speech as empress of India disclaimed the 'desire to impose our [religious] convictions on ... our subjects'. Political control was paramount, even if it meant favouring, for example, Muslim interests in northern Nigeria. And administrators' and settlers' opposition to missionaries might be based not on respect for natives but on disdain; Christianisation gave them 'ideas above their station', whether intellectually, economically or politically.

But imperial governments did generally encourage missions for their educational and health work. Sometimes, missions depended on imperialism to gain entrance, as in China. But often missions preceded empire. How they regarded empire's subsequent advance varied; even approval might be for diverse reasons. Mid-nineteenth-century evangelical missions were generally interventionist (against slavery) but not annexationist, envisaging internal transformation of African societies through legitimate trade and local Christian leadership (Walls 2002: 96). Later, however, some lobbied for pre-emptive British annexation, as in the missionary vision of Nyasaland as protected from white (Rhodesian or Portuguese) settlement.

In the heyday of imperialism (1880–1930), most missionaries were influenced by the conventional wisdom regarding European superiority (Porter 2003: 13). Colonialism expanded their territorial scope, but at the price of less 'embeddedness' in local populations. Colonial-era missionaries were less ready than their predecessors to put Africans in charge. Many Christians escaped mission control by joining African Independent Churches.

Most missionaries were ambivalent about imperialism, accepting it as a historical process but often criticising actual policies (as harmful to native interests or as discouraging missions). In general, missionaries were weak agents of cultural imperialism. They had limited resources, depended on indigenous cooperation and their message was constantly filtered and turned to local advantage (Porter 2004: 317–322). Most nationalist leaders in sub-Saharan Africa were educated in mission schools, finding in mission education (and sometimes in the faith itself) the resources for their anti-colonial struggle.

Protestantism and human rights

Despite Calvin's condemnation of slavery, Protestantism was largely indifferent to the phenomenon in Protestant colonies. The first abolitionist tract in the British colonies was written by a Puritan in 1700 and Quaker John Woolman pressed for abolition from the 1750s, but it was only in 1776 that Philadelphia Quakers prohibited slave-owning. Other denominations were even slower, but activists and clergy eventually became the spine of the American Anti-Slavery Society. This led in most denominations to a North–South schism, with southern clergy developing theological defences of slavery. In Britain's evangelical revival, Whitefield viewed slavery as a necessity, whereas Wesley campaigned for abolition. From the 1780s, the group of elite (Anglican and nonconformist) evangelicals known as the Clapham Sect led abolitionism in the British Empire. As Stark says, it was largely Bible-quoting Protestants who persuaded the political class to embrace voluntary 'econocide' (Stark 2003: 352–353).

The mid-nineteenth century marked the high point of evangelical social reform, connecting traditional humanitarian concern for the vulnerable with a rights frame focused on the individual (Keck and Sikkink 1998: 76). But it was hard to transfer abolitionist enthusiasm to tackling the ills of industrial capitalism, since evangelical individualism obscured the structural dimensions.

As for the twentieth-century human rights movement, the Protestant connection is well documented (Stackhouse and Hainsworth 1999; Nurser 2005). The emerging ecumenical movement clearly affirms religious freedom and human rights. This leads to the Commission of the Churches on International Affairs campaigning for the UN Charter of 1945 and the Universal Declaration of Human Rights of 1948. Nearly every denomination marked the UDHR with a commemorative pronouncement. Since the 1960s, mainline denominations and ecumenical bodies have included human rights promotion in their global ministry (Stackhouse and Hainsworth 1999: 227). And by the late twentieth century Traer could speak of a growing Christian consensus (including evangelicals) on the importance of human rights advocacy (Traer 1995: 85–92).

Nevertheless, an irony of the contemporary human rights movement is the relative silence of Protestants (Witte 2001: 725). Having pioneered the way, Protestantism's contribution must now be compared with post-conciliar Catholicism, with its sophisticated theological statements, official magisterium and global articulation. Protestantism's divisions, which once helped it to be in the vanguard, are now a disadvantage. And Protestantism has changed in global location and social composition; it is now concentrated in poorer and less educated sectors in Third World countries. At the same time, traditional churches in the old heartlands have shrunk. Thus, in Latin America for example,

35

burgeoning Protestantism has taken a back seat in human rights to the Catholic Church. This is partly because of lack of cultural resources and vulnerability to repression. Exceptions have been mostly historical Protestants with ecumenical affiliations. Another option has been to work with international Protestant organisations such as the Mennonite Central Committee or World Vision. The exception to this pattern of international connections is from Peru, where an unusually representative National Evangelical Council has spawned a Peace and Hope Commission (Freston 2001: 238–241).

Protestantism in the advanced societies in the age of mass politics

Tocqueville saw denominational Protestantism as peculiarly suited to maintaining freedom in a democratic age. By separating church and state and voluntarily keeping clergy out of partisan politics, it represented a presence in civil rather than political society. However, one branch of Protestantism led the way in forming Christian parties based on broad suffrage: nineteenth-century Dutch neo-Calvinism. Talking of 'sphere sovereignty' and 'common grace', neo-Calvinism rejected the Christendom model of churchly supervision of societal spheres. The world was thus free from the church but not from God. In opposition also to strict separationism, neo-Calvinism taught a symbiosis of church and state. This paved the way for Protestant parties based on acceptance of multiparty competition, religious freedom and a non-confessional state (Freston 2004b).

Protestantism's relationship to multiparty democracy differed from Catholicism's. Denominationalism was readier to embrace the competitive party model, with its adherents dispersed across the party spectrum. However, in the Netherlands a variety of Protestant parties developed from the 1870s. The first one can even be considered the first 'Christian Democratic' party in the world. Scandinavian Protestant parties were founded from the 1930s. Subsequently, the model has extended to the former communist world and the 'global South'.

There are currently about fifty such parties. Most are small, but the Scandinavian parties have been in coalition governments, and the Norwegian has been in power. The Dutch ARP formed numerous governments between 1888 and its merger with another Protestant party and a Catholic one in 1980, after which the new CDA has headed most governments. The circumstances most favouring such parties are proportional representation and perceived marginalisation in society and existing parties. Church hierarchs are usually cautious, since they represent rival power structures.

Parties can represent a range of 'projects': defence of ecclesiastical interests; divine right to rule; identity politics; ethnic defence; broad political and economic concerns. Some are neoliberal, others preach a 'social market' and a few are anti-capitalist. The newer Third World parties are sometimes fundamentalist, whereas the maturer parties of Northern Europe talk of justice, solidarity and stewardship, and support foreign aid and environmental protection.

In inter-war Europe, churches faced the challenge of fascist regimes. Catholic-majority countries (with the Vatican's suspicion of democracy and support for corporatist ideologies) were more susceptible to fascism than Protestant ones, the exception being religiously mixed Germany where Protestants were more favourable to Nazism (Anderson 2006: 194). Hitler at first encouraged the 'German Christians' (an Aryanised version of Christianity); in protest, the 'Confessing Church' broke away.

However, the Lutheran doctrine of state autonomy reduced the level of opposition. In some occupied countries, Protestant churches protested the deportation of Jews, but the German churches made a post-war confession of guilt for collusion with the regime.

The other great challenge was communism. Some marginal seventeenth-century Protestants had experimented with models of communism; and there had been socialist currents in Protestantism since the nineteenth century. But all this counted for little in the face of Marxist-inspired post-war regimes. The only Protestant-majority areas in the Soviet bloc were East Germany, Latvia and Estonia. The East German church (weakened by secularisation and Lutheran deference to state power) developed an accommodationist stance called 'the church in socialism'. But the 'church from below' gave space to opposition tendencies, and churches became refuges for gestating the regime's peaceful overthrow. Uniting ethnicity and Reformed Protestantism, ethnic Hungarians in Romania also played a catalysing role; while in Latvia, sectors of Lutheranism were important in the independence movement.

Post-war Western Europe experienced growing marginalisation of public religion, due to individual secularisation and the churches' loss of functions under the welfare state. Nevertheless, from the 1980s churches once more voiced political concerns as neoliberal policies accentuated social divisions and lifestyle and identity issues achieved political prominence.

Although Protestants and Catholics have come closer religiously, old divisions still colour even secular views on European integration. There are no Protestant equivalents of the role of socially minded Catholics in integration since the 1950s. This is partly due to the link between Protestant ecclesiologies and sovereign states, allied to linguistic particularities

(Philpott and Shah 2006). Protestant Norway and Iceland remain outside the EU, while Denmark, Sweden and Britain have sought to limit aspects of integration. Although the Conference of European Churches supports integration, individual Protestants are less supportive than Catholics or secular people. Sectarian Protestants (often influenced by interpretations of biblical prophecy) are the most opposed (Hanson 2006: 142).

The United States: civil rights and the religious right

The United States was founded on 'no establishment' and 'free exercise of religion'. This resulted in denominationalism and civil religion. While democracy became secularised in Europe, it became tied to revivalist Christianity in America (De Gruchy 1995: 105). Separation meant churches did not compete with the state and religious people could enter politics with abandon. And, not having to compete politically with churches, politicians felt free to draw their imagery from religion (Hammond 1980).

The major recent cases of Protestant involvement have been the civil rights movement and the religious right. In the civil rights campaign of the 1950s and 1960s, black clergy provided leadership and churches furnished networks and an ethos for non-violent mobilisation. The religious right of the 1980s onwards, however, is a different form of politicisation which appeals essentially to the evangelical community alone.

Various factors favoured such involvement: the federal polity, which allows strong subcultures and multiple entry points to the system; low turnouts in most elections; parties which are coalitions of interest groups. But why did the religious right emerge when it did? As Marsden (2006) stresses, fundamentalist militancy typically arises when a once-dominant religious culture feels threatened by broader cultural trends. These included greater federal intervention; judicial decisions affecting gender, family and sexual behaviour; and perceived secularist attempts to eliminate religion from public life. Involvement was encouraged by non-religious conservative politicians, and facilitated by church growth and increased regional affluence.

Today, verdicts on the movement's achievements are mixed. On the one hand, it has been key in the shift to the Republican Party. In 2004, 78% of white evangelicals favoured Bush. The religious right has had more space in the Bush administration than in previous ones. Many respected evangelical voices blessed the invasion of Iraq. Just after the invasion, 87% of white evangelicals supported it (Marsh 2006). Many church leaders viewed it as creating space to evangelise Muslims. Evangelicals' influence on foreign policy is perhaps strongest in support for Israel. This is due to Christian Zionism which believes much of the Middle East belongs in perpetuity to the Jewish people.

Yet in other ways the religious right has achieved little. It has failed to end abortion, curtail the participation of mothers in the workforce, prevent the advance of gay rights or impose the teaching of 'creation science'. It has not expanded much beyond its religious–ethnic base (83% of black evangelicals voted for Kerry in 2004). And its religio-political zealotry has disadvantages: it resists politics as the 'art of the possible'; it has difficulty tolerating internal differences; and it quickly becomes disillusioned (Bruce 2000: 88).

Protestantism was the original home of the term 'fundamentalism', but today the concept is applied broadly and is heavily determined by Islamic phenomena. Thus, use of the term for the American religious right obscures important characteristics.

Bruce talks of a differential propensity of belief systems to fragment and produce fundamentalist wings (Bruce 2000: 98). The Catholic Church is relatively immune to schism, but Protestantism and Islam are vulnerable because they suppose authoritative knowledge to be democratically available. And fundamentalism is more common when a religion lacks an international bureaucracy and can express local reactions to immediate circumstances. Nevertheless, Protestant and Islamic fundamentalisms are different. The latter is communal whereas the former is individual. And American fundamentalism reacts to local change, whereas Islamic fundamentalism also reacts to 'Westernising' forces. Also, the religions themselves are different. Almost all American fundamentalists accept democratic rules. They are shaped by the ideals of the American Revolution, as well as by the Baptist heritage of separation of church and state and the American Enlightenment heritage of individual choice. This combination means they are wary of governmental coercion nationally, but often uncritical of the coercive use of American power internationally (Marsden 2006).

Protestantism, violence and peacemaking

The leading contemporary cases of militant Protestantism in the developed world are the US and Northern Ireland, where the Rev. Ian Paisley rose to power. How does his anti-Catholic evangelicalism relate to the violence there? Some accuse him of links with the Protestant paramilitaries; for others, he has incited terrorism or at least created an atmosphere in which violence could flourish. Bruce feels the latter charge is the most compelling, although Paisley explicitly rejects violence (Bruce 2003: 211). But Juergensmeyer judges that 'paramilitaries have received spiritual sustenance and moral encouragement from Paisley's statements' (Juergensmeyer 2001: 41).

Protestantism can, evidently, be used to justify violence; like many religions, it offers images of cosmic war which absolutise conflicts. It has been used to justify the absolutising 'war on terror'. But Bruce insists American Protestants have eschewed violence; the few attackers of abortion clinics have been marginal to their own faith communities.

But not committing or condoning violence is not the same as peacemaking. Notwithstanding noble exceptions, it is often felt churches in Northern Ireland fell short in this respect. Nevertheless, peacebuilding by religious NGOs (and by now-secular NGOs started by religious people) has grown worldwide, including Protestant examples such as the Mennonite International Conciliation Service and its Christian Peacemaker Teams, exemplifying the evolution of this Anabaptist denomination from quietism to active peacemaking (Appleby 2000: 145).

Protestantism in the global South

Compared to Western Protestantism, the Third World version is more evangelical and pentecostal. For those caught in the traumas of globalisation, it can appeal both to the disappointed and to those who need moral reinforcement and new skills to seize opportunities. Conversion often has economic effects, helping the disorganised get greater control over their personal circumstances. Evangelicalism challenges adherents to see themselves as agents rather than victims. It combines individual experience of the divine with participation in a moral community. Evangelicals are disproportionately city-dwellers in contexts of migration and violence. They offer supportive communities, and their emphasis on healing appeals

greatly in contexts bereft of social services. Even though the language often sounds patriarchal, their reconciliation of gender values serves the interests of poor women, who are numerically preponderant in the churches.

Global Protestantism is institutionally divided and usually over-represented among the poor (though South Korea is different). It is not a state religion; in a few countries it is discriminated against. It usually lacks strong institutions and its cultural and educational resources are limited. Transplanted foreign denominations are now usually nationally run; but many denominations are founded locally.

Autonomous appropriation has enabled Protestantism to transcend associations with colonialism. Most African expansion has been post-colonial; Korea never was a Western colony; and Protestantism was barred from colonial Latin America. However, one interpretation of this globalisation of Protestantism is that it is American fundamentalist neo-imperialism, 'contributing mightily to the Americanization of global culture' and promoting acceptance of American global hegemony (Brouwer et al. 1996: 270–271). But although American missions are numerous and well resourced, most growth comes from indigenous initiatives. American tele-evangelists should not be believed when they trumpet their global importance. It is 'globalisation from below' which is more determinant. This globalisation is largely conversionist rather than diasporic. Large-scale conversion provides a new dimension to existing conflicts (Nigeria and North-east India) or sparks a transition to a new religion–state relationship (Latin America).

Political positions adopted by Protestants have been diverse and the record mixed (Freston 2001). Active Protestants have become presidents of several global southern countries. Sometimes Protestants have achieved a significant presence in legislative or lower executive levels. Parties of Protestant inspiration have been formed. Protestants have been hegemonic in ethnic separatist rebellions (Burma, India, Sudan). Churchgoers have been key in pro-democracy movements (Kenya). While concern for human rights and democracy predominates among some actors, others merely seek state resources for church aggrandisement. Some talk of a divine right of evangelicals to govern. But fragmentation means their political impact is always smaller than hoped or feared.

Brouwer *et al.* (1996) allege that most pentecostal churches in the global South form part of an exported American fundamentalism, supportive of capitalism, authoritarianism and intolerance, and identifying God's interests with those of the United States. It is true many pentecostals are unreflective fundamentalists, but more interested in the experience of spiritual gifts. Unlike Islamists, they do not seek an organic relationship between law and faith. Instead, they are part of the transformation of religion towards an achieved identity. The dynamic of conversion gives pentecostalism a different relationship to global processes from fundamentalism. For pentecostalism, pluralism is advantageous, whereas fundamentalisms constitute its most serious barrier. Most accounts of American fundamentalism emphasise peculiarly American factors. As a reinvention of white Bible-belt religion, there is little reason for it to characterise evangelicalism the world over. The Fundamentalism Project of the early 1990s examined Guatemalan pentecostalism, but concluded it really did not fit their definition of 'fundamentalism' (Almond *et al.* 1995: 414).

Fundamentalism is often associated nowadays with violent politics. What is global Protestantism's record on this? Despite the context of poverty and geopolitical humiliation, there is so far no Protestant version of religiously justified geopolitical violence. There has, however, been violence (in self-defence, they would allege) against Muslims in Nigeria and Indonesia, where the state is weak or conniving. Elsewhere, Protestantism has fused with ethnic separatist rebellions in postcolonial states (Freston 2001: 82–83, 88–91, 94–100, 116–118). There was some Protestant involvement in the Rwandan genocide; and there are a few pentecostal vigilante groups in Central America, in a context where such groups are proliferating. However, a recent book on religious terrorists (Stern 2003) mentions only three evangelical phenomena. Two are in the US: the racist 'Identity Christians' (not exportable to the Third World); and the extreme anti-abortionists (potentially exportable, if most of the Third World were to legalise abortion on demand). The third group are Christian militias in eastern Indonesia, which emerged as the transmigration of Javanese Muslims and the activity of Muslim militias upset the local religious and ethnic balance.

What about state violence? Guatemala had the ferocious anti-insurgency strategy of the pentecostal general Ríos Montt, president in 1982–83. Ríos was not repressive because he was pentecostal (there have been many similar Central American regimes); but pentecostalism did not *prevent* him being repressive, since he was highly regarded by his church. And the tendency of many pentecostals to demonise their religious rivals is worrying in regions where democratic norms are shaky. Nevertheless, the 2006 Pew Forum survey of pentecostals in nine countries of the global South paints a more encouraging portrait. To the question whether it is important that there be freedom for religions other than one's own, pentecostals everywhere were at least as affirmative as the general population of their countries.

In short, popular Protestantism in the global South has some connection with violence, but nearly always related to self-defence in the absence of the state, or to ethno-regional separatism. These Protestants do not have Islamic concepts of honour of a sacred community (*umma*) and defence of sacred territory (*dar-al-islam*). Nor do they have the geopolitical influence of American evangelicals. And pentecostalism's insistent promotion of a discourse of 'winning' is opposed to the discourse of victimhood that generally undergirds political violence.

In fact, pentecostalism is perceived as a bulwark against urban violence in the peripheries of megacities. In the absence of the state, pentecostalism provides escape-routes from criminality, prostitution and drug addiction. Its individual transformative power is efficacious against privatised violence, in contrast to the advantage of transnational and hierarchical Catholicism in combating state violence (Birman and Leite 2000; Corten 2005). While pentecostals are adept at personal transformation, they are less so at the complex task of societal transformation.

Does the globalisation of evangelicalism mean similar politics to that of American evangelicals? So far, American-style 'culture wars' have not been repeated (except perhaps in South Africa). Most societies (and legal systems) are opposed to easy abortion and gay marriage. In addition, most Protestants are on the edge of survival. As they reconstruct the family amidst unemployment, violence and anomie, they are little attracted to occasional efforts by denominational leaders to involve them in single-issue 'values' politics.

The Pew survey asked whether abortion is ever morally justified. In all southern countries surveyed, a high percentage of pentecostals answered no. But that usually reflects or slightly reinforces the national average. When asked whether government should interfere with a woman's ability to have an abortion, nuances appear. Pentecostals in South Korea are far more

favourable to anti-abortion legislation than their national average, but elsewhere they reflect national opinion and in four countries are below the average! Little over a third of Guatemalan pentecostals favour anti-abortion legislation.

On economic policy, pentecostals generally reflect national opinion regarding a market economy (from 89% favourable in Nigeria to 47% in Chile). However, on welfare (whether government should guarantee food and shelter to every citizen) pentecostals everywhere are slightly more favourable than their general populations.

To what extent does global Protestantism conflate American interests with those of God? Attitudes towards the 'war on terror' and the war in Iraq suggest not very much. Studies show a gap between evangelical attitudes in much of the global South and in the USA. A World Evangelical Alliance statement shortly before the invasion of Iraq merely said war 'is almost always the worst solution' (www.worldevangelical.org). But the Baptist World Alliance called the invasion 'a great sin' (20 March 2003, http://www.internationalministries.org/updates/bwa_war2003.htm).

The leading Brazilian interdenominational magazine *Ultimato* strongly opposed the war, seeing it as a pretext for a new world order. It denounced the tendency of American evangelicals to defend huge military spending and an exacerbated nationalism. Similarly, a television programme with Brazilian evangelical congressmen discussed the issue. However conservative their parties and 'unconventional' their churches, they were unanimous in condemning the imminent invasion. For Spanish-speaking Latin America, Padilla and Scott (2004) discovered not a single denomination in favour, even in countries whose governments supported President Bush.

A South African political party based mostly among charismatic churches, the African Christian Democratic Party, strongly opposed the invasion and condemned 'American civil religion that says America is predestined by God to save the world' (Freston 2004a: 96). In China (personal communication from Kim-Kwong Chan), virtually all Christians followed the standard Chinese sentiment that the USA was bullying the world in its own national interest. In the Philippines, however (personal communication from David Lim), many leading evangelicals are pro-Bush, albeit less strongly than before. It should be remembered that Filipinos are one of the few peoples who would have re-elected Bush in 2004 (Freston 2007).

The Pew survey asked whether respondents favoured 'the US-led efforts to fight terrorism'. In all countries surveyed, pentecostals are similar to the national average, except (obviously) in the religiously divided country of Nigeria. Only there (71%) and the Philippines (76%) do pentecostals support the 'war on terror' as much as in the USA (72%); both these countries suffer internal tension between Muslims and non-Muslims. But in Latin America and South Africa, only around one-third of pentecostals support the 'war on terror', and in South Korea only 16%. In all Latin American countries surveyed, pentecostals are actually slightly less favourable than their general populations; so much for the idea of global pentecostalism as 'global American fundamentalism'.

Does the globalisation of evangelicalism mean more support for Christian Zionism? Not necessarily. Intensity of prophetic interest depends on other priorities; for poor people, survival takes precedence, and the idea of national blessing depending on support for Israel is not as cogent. They feel no post-Holocaust guilt, have little contact with Jews and feel less threatened by terrorism. Some denominations cultivate links with the 'Holy Land', but usually emphasise 'where Jesus walked' rather than current issues.

The Pew survey asked whether respondents sympathised more with Israel or the Palestinians. Everywhere, pentecostals are above national average in sympathy for Israel, especially in the Philippines. But the sum of the three replies which preclude a Christian Zionist position (sympathy for the Palestinians, both or neither) is telling. Only 18% of American pentecostals come in those categories, versus 56% of pentecostals in Chile, followed by five countries between 46% and 52%.

One prediction regarding global Christianity is of a new wave of Christian states (Jenkins 2002: 12). Is there any evidence for this?

In Africa, anti-colonial nationalism did not stress Christianity. But by the 1990s hopes of rapid development had evaporated, while Christianity had grown and become central to civil society. At this point 'Christian nationalism' emerges. Zambia is declared a 'Christian nation' in 1991 and Madagascar in 2007. The Malawian president refers to his country as a Christian nation. But, partly due to the denominational patchwork, this takes the form of exalting Christianity in general rather than creating a state church or legally discriminating against non-Christians, much less instituting a Christian 'sharia law'.

When asked (in the Pew survey) whether there should be a 'Christian country' or separation of church and state, pentecostals prefer a 'Christian country' in Nigeria (58-35) and South Africa (45-37). Elsewhere, they reject the idea, notably in Chile (23-62) and Brazil (32-50). However, everywhere except Chile pentecostals are more favourable to it than other believers.

Global Southern Protestantism is not yet solidly in the democratic camp, and it often operates in contexts where few other political actors are wholehearted democrats either. Woodberry and Shah (2004), however, allege that the historical correlation between democracy and Protestantism does hold in the global

South. However, the effect may be smaller than before, as other religions adopt its characteristics; and some strains of pentecostalism may be less useful than historical Protestantism (in part, for their lesser emphasis on education).

Different types of Protestantism are better at different things. For opposing dictatorships, it is better to be a hierarchical, transnational church with elite connections, rather than a local and lower-class pentecostal church, deprived of intellectual resources and vulnerable to repression. However, in democratic consolidation, pentecostals might be more useful because they are anti-fatalistic and instill skills of leadership and public speaking. But there is no guarantee either type of church will in fact perform these functions. Some pentecostals now say believers should govern countries in the name of God. Others use electoral democracy merely to strengthen their own institutions. It is hard to develop a universalist reflection on public life such as characterises Catholic social doctrine. In some countries the churches' public image has declined through association with political naivety, and sometimes with corruption and hunger for power.

However, in the Pew survey pentecostals everywhere are affirming of the importance of honest multiparty elections, similar to or above national averages. When asked whether, to solve the country's problems, it would be better to have a more participatory government or a strong leader, pentecostals always prefer a participatory government. In seven countries, they are less favourable to a strong leader than their general populations, so in this respect pentecostal attitudes strengthen democracy.

Evangelicalism's emphasis on individual freedom is inherently pluralist. The results for democracy are paradoxical. Totalitarian regimes and non-Christian religious nationalisms are resisted, but authoritarianisms which do not impinge on evangelicals

may not be. Evangelicalism is too fissured to undergird national movements advocating major political change in whatever direction.

The future of Protestant politics

Protestantism is curiously advantaged and disadvantaged in contemporary politics. It was the first major religion to accept (and even encourage) a secular state and an independent civil society. Its variety of ecclesiastical forms and its individualism accentuate its political diversity and innovativeness. But the complexity of modern politics is a challenge, especially to Protestants, since they cannot achieve the economies of scale necessary to develop coherent political philosophies and practices. Paucity of dialogue between pentecostal and mainline churches impoverishes both sides. Rapid growth in the global South places market pressures on church leaders which are unfavourable to ethical reflection. And, since Christian origins were times of powerlessness, the search for scriptural purity does not produce clear-cut political proposals or the consensus for effective action. Thus, Protestantism is disadvantaged vis-à-vis Catholicism and Islam.

When Protestantism was largely Western, its diversity was already evidenced in classical sociologists' evaluations: a domesticating ideology serving the bourgeoisie or an unrealistic popular revolutionary movement (Engels); an unwitting vanguard of the iron cage of capitalist rationality (Weber); a buzzing hive of democratic associational life (Tocqueville). Its shift to the global South could only bring further diversification, which cannot be understood within a 'clash of civilisations' framework.

Evangelical political effervescence in the global South is reminiscent of mid-seventeenth-century England, when restraints on Protestant pluralism had weakened and it boiled over into diverse manifestations at all social levels. But the result, as Hill stresses, was that no new agreed political philosophy could emerge from popular readings of the Bible, which ultimately ceased to be used as a guide to political action (Hill 1993: 145). Similarly, African politics may 'outgrow' its current phase in which Christianity provides a commonly accepted idiom.

Evangelicals have not long been politically active in the global South, and they are beginning a steep learning curve. Growing involvement in social projects sometimes leads to political involvement oriented more to the common good. No religion is frozen in time, and certainly not evangelicalism.

Yet there are foreseeable problems. Each religion has political dilemmas that stem from its tradition and not just from its current context. Christianity's problems include how to incorporate the Hebrew Scriptures with their notion of 'holy commonwealth'. Different approaches to relationship between the Testaments suggest different political postures. It is hard to develop Christian justifications using only the Old Testament. However, if Christian politics relies purely on the New Testament it falls under Tocqueville's strictures about the lack of a civic ethic. Primitive Christianity alone is deficient for a democratic age which needs active citizens. Catholics have an ongoing magisterium, and the Reformed tradition (at times) has used a concept of 'unfolding'. But many Protestants are bound to 'primitivist' concepts of return to original purity, which in Christianity was distant from the state, leading to the 'default danger' of apolitical conformism exploitable by authoritarian regimes.

Tocqueville stresses the importance of Christianity to democracy, but only in the right relationship (separate from the state and partisanship, yet undergirding politics) and only if performing some necessary tasks. Envy and difference are perils for democracy. Christianity can redress the first by averting the soul's gaze towards heaven, and the second by insisting upon underlying unity. Democracies need long-term thinking to balance the democratic impulse toward the short term; and that is best provided by religion (Mitchell 1995).

Global pentecostalism has not done well in maintaining distance from the vicissitudes of democratic politics, or in averting people's gaze from materialistic envy, or in balancing democratic impulsiveness with long-term thinking. The pentecostal self-belief that assists personal transformation is a liability in politics. And the charismatic ritualism that produces results at the micro level (especially in largely ungoverned and crime-ridden communities) does not function at the macro level.

A key challenge for global Protestantism will be to combine institutional plurality with some means of achieving political impact at national and global levels. How much, for example, will it be able (as a faith which straddles global divides) to offer a different vision of our global future?

In Latin America, rapid numerical growth will one day stop, leading to more stable membership and bringing demands for different relations with public life. In Africa, Christianisation has accompanied a worsening of the economic, political and health situation. Will the historic correlations between Protestantism, democracy and development still hold? China may be the next cultural powerhouse of Christianity. If, as some believe, it becomes the new centre of numerical growth and eventually achieves greater freedom, then it will constitute the greatest challenge yet to the remaining Western hegemony within the Christian world. This will have political implications. By the time China is a great power, how large and influential will its Christian community (which is mainly Protestant) be? But as Hanson points out, China's 'Great Awakening' under conditions of state hostility is just as likely to result in another Taiping Rebellion as in a liberal democracy (Hanson 2006: 169). In the United States at the time of writing (early 2008), there are signs of tiredness with the limited agenda of the religious right and a modest resurgence of a more 'progressive evangelicalism'. But caution is necessary; the demise of the religious right has been forecast for the last twenty years! In Europe, Protestantism's prospects may be tied to immigration. Muslim immigration may encourage (and open space for) a rebirth of public Christianity; all forms of Christian politics (not only reactive anti-Islamic ones) may benefit. Also, many immigrants are practising Protestants. The globalisation of Protestantism may yet play a part in renewing its political importance in the region of its birth.

Bibliography

Almond, G., Sivan, E. and Appleby, R. Scott (1995) 'Fundamentalism: genus and species', in M. Marty and R. Scott Appleby (eds.), *Fundamentalisms Comprehended*, Chicago: University of Chicago Press, pp. 399–424.

Anderson, J. (2006a) 'Does God matter, and if so whose God? Religion and democratization', in J. Anderson (ed.), *Religion, Democracy and Democratization*, London: Routledge.

Anderson, J. (ed.) (2006b) *Religion, Democracy and Democratization*, London: Routledge.

Appleby, R. Scott (2000) *The Ambivalence of the Sacred*, Lanham: Rowman and Littlefield.

Barrett, D., Kurian, G. and Johnson, T. (eds.) (2001) *World Christian Encyclopedia*, 2nd edn, New York: Oxford University Press, 2 vols.

Bastian, J.-P. (1993) 'The metamorphosis of Latin American Protestant groups: a sociohistorical perspective', *Latin American Research Review*, 28, 2, pp. 33–61.

Berger, P. (2004) 'The global picture', *Journal of Democracy*, 15, 2, pp. 76–80.

Berman, H. and Witte, J. (1987) 'Church and state', in M. Eliade (ed.), *Encyclopedia of Religion*, vol. 3, New York: Macmillan, pp. 489–495.

Biéler, A. (1959) *La Pensée Économique et Sociale de Calvin*, Geneva: Georg.

Birman, P. and Leite, M. (2000) 'Whatever happened to what used to be the largest Catholic country in the world?', *Daedalus*, 129, 2, pp. 271–290.

Brouwer, S., Gifford, P. and Rose, S. (1996) *Exporting the American Gospel: Global Christian Fundamentalism*, London: Routledge.

Bruce, S. (2000) *Fundamentalism*, Cambridge: Polity.

Bruce, S. (2003) *Politics and Religion*, Cambridge: Polity.

Bruce, S. (2004) 'Did Protestantism create democracy?', *Democratization*, 11, 4, pp. 3–20.

Coffey, J. (2000) *Persecution and Toleration in Protestant England: 1558–1689*, Harlow: Pearson.

Corten, A. (2005) 'Peur et religion: de la violence d'État à la violence privatisée', paper presented at the 27th Conference of the Société Internationale de Sociologie des Religions, Zagreb, 18–22 July.

De Gruchy, J. (1995) *Christianity and Democracy*, Cambridge: Cambridge University Press.

Freston, P. (2001) *Evangelicals in Asia, Africa and Latin America*, Cambridge: Cambridge University Press.

Freston, P. (2004a) 'Les dynamiques missionnaires internationales du pentecôtisme Brésilien', in S. Fath (ed.), *Le Protestantisme Évangélique: un Christianisme de Conversion*, Paris: Brepols, pp. 123–143.

Freston, P. (2004b) *Protestant Political Parties: A Global Survey*, Aldershot: Ashgate.

Freston, P. (2007) 'Evangelicalism and fundamentalism: the politics of global popular Protestantism', in J. Beckford and N. J. Demerath III (eds.), *The Sage Handbook of the Sociology of Religion*, London: Sage, pp. 205–226.

Freston, P. (2008) 'The changing face of Christian proselytizing: new actors from the global South transforming old debates', in R. Hackett (ed.), *Proselytization Revisited*, London: Equinox.

Gaustad, E. (1991) *Liberty of Conscience: Roger Williams in America*, Grand Rapids: Eerdmans.

Hálevy, E. (1949) *A History of the English People in the Nineteenth Century*, 2nd edn, London: E. Benn.

Hammond, P. (1980) 'The conditions for civil religion: a comparison of the United States and Mexico', in R. Bellah and P. Hammond, P. (eds.), *Varieties of Civil Religion*, San Francisco: Harper and Row, pp. 40–85.

Hanson, E. (2006) *Religion and Politics in the International System Today*, Cambridge: Cambridge University Press.

Hastings, A. (1997) *The Construction of Nationhood: Ethnicity, Religion and Nationalism*, Cambridge: Cambridge University Press.

Hastings, A. (1998) 'Christianity', in R. Wuthnow (ed.), *The Encyclopedia of Religion and Politics*, Washington: Congressional Quarterly, pp. 131–142.

Hill, C. (1993) *The English Bible and the Seventeenth-century Revolution*, Harmondsworth: Penguin.

Jellinek, G. (1895) *Die Erklärung der Menschen- und Bürgerrechte. Ein Beitrag zur modernen Verfassungsgeschichte*, Munich.

Jenkins, P. (2002) *The Next Christendom*, New York: Oxford University Press.

Johnson, L. (1996) 'Religious rights and Christian texts', in J. Witte and J. van der Vyver (eds.), *Religious Human Rights in Global Perspective: Religious Perspectives*, The Hague: Martinus Nijhoff, pp. 65–95.

Juergensmeyer, M. (2001) *Terror in the Mind of God*, Berkeley: University of California Press.

Keck, M. and Sikkink, K. (1998) *Activists Beyond Borders*, Ithaca: Cornell University Press.

Madeley, J. (1994) 'The antinomies of Lutheran politics: the case of Norway's Christian People's Party', in D. Hanley (ed.), *Christian Democracy in Europe: A Comparative Perspective*, London: Pinter, pp. 142–154.

Marsden, G. (2006) *Fundamentalism and American Culture*, 2nd edn, New York: Oxford University Press.

Marsh, C. (2006) 'Wayward Christian soldiers', *New York Times*, 20 January.

Martin, D. (1997) *Does Christianity Cause War?*, Oxford: Clarendon Press.

Martin, D. (2004) 'Evangelical expansion in global society', in D. Lewis (ed.), *Christianity Reborn*, Grand Rapids: Eerdmans, pp. 273–294.

Mehl, R. (1965) *The Sociology of Protestantism*, London: SCM Press.

Mitchell, J. (1995) *The Fragility of Freedom*, Chicago: University of Chicago Press.

Nurser, J. (2005) *For All Peoples and All Nations*, Geneva: WCC Publications.

O'Donovan, O. and O'Donovan, J. Lockwood (eds.) (2000) *From Irenaeus to Grotius: A Sourcebook in Christian Political Thought*, Grand Rapids: Eerdmans.

Padilla, C. R. and Scott, L. (2004) *Terrorism and the War in Iraq*, Buenos Aires: Kairos.

Philpott, D. and Shah, T. (2006) 'Faith, freedom and federation: the role of religious ideas and institutions in European political convergence', in T. A. Byrnes and P. J. Katzenstein (eds.), *Religion in an Expanding Europe*, Cambridge: Cambridge University Press, pp. 34–64.

Porter, A. (2003) 'Introduction', in A. Porter (ed.), *The Imperial Horizons of British Protestant Missions 1880–1914*, Grand Rapids: Eerdmans, pp. 1–13.

Porter, A. (2004) *Religion versus Empire?*, Manchester: Manchester University Press.

Siedentop, L. (1994) *Tocqueville*, Oxford: Oxford University Press.

Smith, G. Scott (1998) 'Calvinism', in R. Wuthnow (ed.), *The Encyclopedia of Religion and Politics*, Washington: Congressional Quarterly, pp. 93–97.

'Spirit and Power' (2006) Washington: Pew Forum on Religion and Public Life.

Stackhouse, M. and King Hainsworth, D. (1999) 'Deciding for God: the right to convert in Protestant perspectives', in J. Witte and R. Martin (eds.), *Sharing the Book*, Maryknoll: Orbis, pp. 201–230.

Stark, R. (2003) *For the Glory of God*, Princeton: Princeton University Press.

Stern, J. (2003) *Terror in the Name of God*, New York: Ecco.

Thompson, E. P. (1963) *The Making of the English Working Class*, Harmondsworth: Penguin.

Tocqueville, A. de. (1987) *A Democracia na América*, 3rd edn, Belo Horizonte, Itatiaia; São Paulo, Edusp.

Traer, R. (1991) *Faith in Human Rights*, Washington, DC: Georgetown University Press.

Troeltsch, E. (1931) *The Social Teaching of the Christian Churches*, Chicago: University of Chicago Press.

Walls, A. (1994) 'The Evangelical revival, the missionary movement, and Africa', in M. Noll, D. Bebbington and G. Rawlyk (eds.), *Evangelicalism*, New York: Oxford University Press, pp. 310–330.

Walls, A. (2002) *The Cross-cultural Process in Christian History*, Maryknoll: Orbis.

Walzer, M. (1965) *The Revolution of the Saints*, Cambridge, MA: Harvard University Press.

Willaime, J.-P. (1997) 'La contribution du Christianisme à la modernité politique', in F. Lenoir and Y. Tardan-Masquelier (eds.), *Encyclopédie des Religions*, 2nd edn, Paris: Bayard, vol. 2, pp. 2079–2088.

Witte, J. (2001) 'A Dickensian era of religious rights: an update on religious human rights in global perspective', *William & Mary Law Review*, 42, 3, pp. 707–770.

Witte, J. (ed.) (1993) *Christianity and Democracy in Global Context*, Boulder: Westview Press.

Woodberry, R. and Shah, T. (2004) 'The pioneering Protestants', *Journal of Democracy*, 15, 2, pp. 47–61.

Wootton, D. (1991) 'Leveller democracy and the Puritan Revolution', in J. H. Burns and M. Goldie (eds), *The Cambridge History of Political Thought 1450–1700*, vol. 2, Cambridge: Cambridge University Press, pp. 412–442; paperback edn 1995.

Wootton, D. (1992) 'The Levellers', in J. Dunn (ed.), *Democracy: The Unfinished Journey 508 BC to AD 1993*, Oxford: Oxford University Press, pp. 71–89.

4

The Catholic Church and Catholicism in global politics

Allen D. Hertzke

The oldest institution on earth, the Roman Catholic Church sustains a far-flung flock whose one billion adherents comprise one-sixth of the globe's population. This alone ensures political import, but equally crucial is the Church's deep tradition of engagement with worldly affairs – a comfortableness with politics not shared by all religious faiths. Such size and tradition, combined with the legacy of John Paul II, ensure the visibility and impact of the Church in world politics.

The Catholic Church, however, defies easy political categorization. On the one hand it remains a quintessentially conservative body with a hierarchical organization designed to preserve traditional theological teachings. This impulse produces conservative stances on sexual morality, abortion and marriage, and puts the Church in alliance with other religious traditionalists, including Muslims. On the other hand, Catholic teachings on the dignity of the human person and the authenticity of the common good produce concern for the poor in the global economy and, especially in recent decades, advocacy of religious freedom, human rights and democratic governance (Huntington 1991; Philpott 2005). Thus the Church stands in seeming equipoise between contending impulses of tradition and modernity.

Despite this strategic position the Church faces challenges that blunt its political impact.

First, a shortage of priests and women religious in some places means that Church leaders must devote energies to institutional maintenance, to the potential detriment of social engagement. Second, with the cutting edge of growth in developing nations the Church must sustain its core practices amidst the syncretic influences of local cultures, desperate poverty or opposition by hostile governments. Thus, as we will see, Catholic politics varies enormously by region, context and issue.

This chapter begins with a review of the theological and historical context of Catholic engagement with politics, paying particular attention to the evolution of Catholic social teaching. It will then examine Vatican diplomacy, with emphasis on the papacies of John Paul II and Benedict XVI. This is followed by a discussion of Catholic politics in different regions of the world. The chapter concludes by examining issues that loom large on the horizon. The exploration of Catholicism, consequently, will provide a window into the broader and ever-dynamic relationship between religion and politics in the contemporary world.

Theological and historical context

From its inception the Catholic Church has been enmeshed in worldly affairs. Popes raised armies, formed alliances and anointed political rulers. The Church sought to wield the two swords of spiritual and temporal authority to perpetuate its vision of a united Christendom. In the West this vision was shattered first by the Protestant Reformation and then by republican revolutions that attacked the Church's official role in political governance. In Italy this meant the loss of the papal states in 1870, the last major vestige of the Church's temporal power.

To understand the logic and rationale of contemporary Catholic politics one must trace how the loss of this temporal position led the Church to think afresh about its place in the world. We see this in the dramatic transformation of the Church in the century between the two Vatican councils (1869 and 1962–1965). Faced with the challenge of antagonistic political movements and governments, the Church's first response was reactionary. Pope Pius IX not only convened the first Vatican Council, which promulgated the doctrine of papal infallibility, he also issued his infamous Syllabus of Errors in 1864. In that document the pontiff condemned modernism, liberalism, religious freedom, the idea of progress and separation of church and state.

Such a position was not tenable in the face of inexorable forces of modernization, and Pius's successor, Pope Leo XIII, began in earnest the long rapprochement of the church to the 'new things' of the world. His encyclical Rerum Novarum (1891) argued that the Church must bring to bear gospel values in addressing the crises of the

industrial age – untrammelled capitalism, child labour, mass suffering and Marxist revolutions. This encyclical, to which Pope John Paul II often referred, inaugurated modern Catholic social teaching and set the stage for the transformation of the Church at Vatican II. In the words of John Paul II, it gave the Church 'citizenship status' to replace its previous temporal ambitions (Centesimus Annus 1991).

Anchoring Rerum Novarum and subsequent social teaching is the idea of 'Dignitatis Humanae' – the dignity of the human person. Made in the image and likeness of God and equal in his sight, all people are invested with a 'surpassing dignity' ('Gaudium et Spes' 1965) Such a dignity demands that the organization of society foster conditions for human flourishing and justice. Desperate poverty and exploitation violate the gospel message of love and require appropriate political responses, particularly the payment of just wages and provision of leisure time for worship and family succour. Capital owners, therefore, are bound by transcendent duties to treat their workers not as mere instruments of production or 'bondsmen' but as moral persons endowed with priceless worth and nobility.

This language of human personhood also implies that people are social creatures, embedded in families and organic communities that should be supported, not supplanted, by the state. This doctrine of 'subsidiarity' – that is, the need to nurture subsidiary institutions of society – contrasted both with the radical individualism of classical liberalism and the collectivism of Marx. Thus church teaching sought a middle way between laissez-faire capitalism and state socialism.

Although the church sought to lift the yoke on workers in Rerum Novarum, it did not yet accept central tenets of liberal democracy. Just eight years after his encyclical on the condition of workers Pope Leo XIII condemned 'Americanism', which among other things meant the 'false' doctrine of religious toleration (Jelen 2006: 75). In Catholic countries the Church sought state privilege and the attendant limitation of the rights of non-Catholics. In a symbiotic relationship authoritarian regimes happily granted such privilege in return for the legitimacy the Church could provide. With the rise of fascism in the twentieth century the Church endeavoured to preserve its position by signing infamous Concordats with Hitler's Germany and Mussolini's Italy. The legacy of fascism, instrumental in the devastation of Europe during World War II, shocked the Church into a deeper reflection on the proper governance of society. In his Christmas Message of 1944, for example, Pope Pius XII articulated a detailed endorsement of democracy. In opposing the 'concentration of dictatorial power' as contrary to 'the dignity and liberty of citizens', the Pope speculated 'that had there been the possibility of censuring and correcting the actions of public authority, the world would not have been dragged into the vortex of a disastrous war'. To be sure, the Pope, in Aristotelian fashion, qualified his endorsement of democracy by arguing that it depended on citizens properly guided by natural law and socialized to seek the common good ('Democracy and a Lasting Peace' 1944).

Despite this embrace the Church continued to resist a key tenet of pluralist democracy – that all religious groups should enjoy freedom of worship and organization. As Alfred Stepan has argued, liberal democracy depends on 'twin tolerations': the state protects the freedom of churches to operate in civil society and churches in turn do not seek to use the powers of the state to enhance their prerogatives or limit competitors (Stepan 2005). As late as the 1950s, however, the Church's official position was that since 'error has no rights', Catholicism, as the true faith, should alone be sanctioned by the state.

And the Church enforced that view on its clergy and scholars. The celebrated American theologian John Courtney Murray made a Catholic case for religious freedom, pluralist forms of church–state relations, and ecumenical cooperation. But he was reproached and silenced by the Church in the 1950s (Wills 2002: 214–221).

Understanding this background helps us see the significance of the Second Vatican Council (1962–1965), especially its later documents. In its 'Pastoral Constitution on the Church in the Modern World', 'Gaudium et Spes' (1965), the Church developed its most systematic theological defence of democratic governance, human rights and economic succour. Claiming no earthly ambition the document instead proclaimed the Church's solidarity with suffering humanity and offered its insight on human dignity as a guide to the development of wholesome social institutions, egalitarian political structures and just economic organizations.

But it was the companion document on religious freedom that would complete the Church's transformation. Tellingly, its 'Declaration on Religious Liberty' was titled 'Dignitatis Humanae' (1965), and the rationale for protecting the free pursuit of spiritual truth was anchored in the 'sublime' dignity of humanity. Two individuals would be pivotal drafters of this historic document: John Courtney Murray, who brought with him the American experience of Catholic participation in a pluralist democracy, and one Bishop Wojtyla of Poland, whose defence of the faith against the totalitarian tyrannies of Nazism and Communism forged a fierce commitment to free churches as bulwarks of civil society and resistance to oppression. As pontiff, of course, he would be placed in a pivotal position to implement this vision.

When the Church stopped relying on temporal power to pursue its spiritual mission it was freed to challenge the legitimacy of authoritarian regimes, and with a few exceptions it did just that. Indeed, like a great ocean liner that turns slowly but with tremendous force in its new direction, the Church became a powerful engine of democracy in the last quarter of the twentieth century. As Samuel Huntington documents, the last great wave of democratization was largely a Catholic wave. In 1974 three-quarters of all Catholic countries were ruled by authoritarian regimes; by 1990 all but a few were democracies (Huntington 1991).

The dramatic transformation of the Spanish Church helped inaugurate this great wave of democratization. From an institution tied for centuries to the crown and reactionary authoritarianism, the Church became by the 1960s a major source of opposition to the Franco regime, undercutting its legitimacy over the next decade (Casanova 1994: ch. 4). Thus after 'rising' in Spain (and Portugal) in 1975, 'the Catholic wave then surged across Latin America, carried democracy to the Philippines, and crested in Poland with the first of several East European revolutions against communism' (Philpott 2005: 32).

Pivotal to this story was the papacy of John Paul II, who 'seemed to have a way of showing up in full pontifical majesty at critical points of the democratization process' (Huntington 1991: 83–84). Perhaps the most dramatic illustration were his trips to Poland, which electrified the people and spawned the Solidarity movement that helped undermine communist rule (Weigel 1999). As we will see, however, the Church has enjoyed only mixed success in Africa where conditions of destitution and tribalism continue to frustrate democratic consolidation.

Vatican diplomacy and political activism

The Catholic Church is a unique multifarious institution. Headquartered at Vatican City, the Holy See retains remnants of state sovereignty, including an elaborate diplomatic structure that sends and receives ambassadors (Allen 2004). But the Church's myriad institutions also function as interest groups or non-governmental organizations (NGOs) that lobby governments or have observer status at the United Nations (Ferrari 2007). Indeed, the Catholic Church encompasses a vast array of national or regional episcopal conferences, religious orders, relief and development organizations, charities, hospitals and educational associations enmeshed in politics and government. Finally, as Vatican II declared, the Church is also the 'people of God' (Philpott 2005: 36). Thus to understand Catholicism and civic engagement one must include the laity who populate Catholic organizations or participate as citizens in nearly two hundred nations. This section explores the first of these roles, as captured under the rubric of Vatican diplomacy. Later sections will examine the civic initiatives of Catholic institutions and lay members in select regions of the world.

As a transnational actor the 'Holy See directs a truly global church' (Ferrari 2006). Thus it has both tangible interests to defend and religious values to promote at different times and in different settings. This brief overview looks at the constellation of issues that have engaged the Pope and the Vatican in the diverse contexts the Church encounters.

One of the signal thrusts of Pope John Paul II was human rights, with special focus for the first decade of his papacy on communist countries (Weigel 1999). With the collapse of the Soviet empire the emphasis expanded more generally to authoritarian nations and the Islamic world, along with the communist remnant. In particular, the Pontiff became the globe's most visible promoter of religious freedom. For example, in a widely cited speech before the Vatican diplomatic corps in 1996 he sounded the clarion call against communist and militant Islamic regimes that 'practice discrimination against Jews, Christians, and other religious groups'. The Pope condemned such persecution as an 'intolerable and unjustifiable' violation 'of the most fundamental human freedom, that of practicing one's faith openly, which for human beings is their reason for living' ('Annual Message to Diplomatic Corps' 1996).

Especially animating the Vatican has been the waxing of militant Islamist movements, making the lives of Catholic minorities in the Muslim world more vulnerable to harassment and persecution. This includes democratic countries like Indonesia, where violent attacks by Islamic radicals have terrorized the Christian population. And it also involves allies of the West like Pakistan, where anti-blasphemy laws have been exploited to attack Catholic religious leaders and laity (Hertzke 2004: ch. 2).

While John Paul II criticized some Islamist regimes, he also sought to build bridges by engaging in extensive dialogue with Islamic leaders. He travelled to Turkey in 1979 and then, after an unprecedented invitation from King Hassan, to Morocco in 1985. Thousands of enthusiastic college students in Casablanca heard the pontiff proclaim that 'we believe in the same God, the one God, the living God' (Filteau 2005).

Pope Benedict XVI, on the other hand, took a more aggressive stance toward the Islamic world. As Joseph Bottum observes, 'as communism was to Pope John Paul II, so radical Islam is to Pope Benedict XVI' (Bottum 2006). His Regensburg speech on 12 September 2006, in which he quoted a fourteenth-century Byzantine emperor's statement that Islam brought 'things only evil and inhuman', created a firestorm in Muslim nations ('Vatican asks Muslims to help defeat terrorism' 2006). Massive demonstrations, riots and violent reprisals stunned the pontiff, who issued

an apology and assured Muslims that the quote did not reflect his views. In an apparent concession Benedict reversed his opposition to Turkey's entrance into the European Union (Fisher and Travernise 2006). But Benedict did not back down on his demand for 'reciprocity', that Christians in Muslim nations be afforded the same rights to religious freedom that Muslims enjoy in the West, including the right 'to propose and proclaim the Gospel' to Muslims (Kahn and Meichtry 2006). This position reflected an agreement among the cardinals of the Church, whom Benedict had summoned on 23 March 2006, that persecution of Christians in the Islamic world required a sustained diplomatic push (Allen 2006).

As the Vatican sought meaningful dialogue with Muslim leaders, so it also strove to build links to the Jewish community. This included an unprecedented visit to a synagogue by Pope John Paul II, then a trip to Israel. In a move that Jews worldwide celebrated, the Vatican also established diplomatic relations with Israel ('Pope shares pain of Palestinian people over Arafat' 2004). Because Pope Benedict has taken a more assertive posture toward the Islamic world, where anti-Semitism is on the rise, some Jewish leaders hope for even more initiatives.

The most critical issue for the Vatican in Asia concerns China, whose communist government created an official body, the Patriotic Catholic Association, that is forbidden to be in communion with Rome. Wanting to unite both state-sanctioned and 'underground' Catholics (who pledge fealty to the Pope), the Vatican has engaged in a delicate minuet of negotiations. In May 2006 it signalled that it might end diplomatic relations with Taiwan and establish them with Beijing, in return for the authority to appoint or approve Chinese bishops. But shortly thereafter Chinese authorities appointed two bishops without consulting the Vatican.

In turn, Pope Benedict elevated Joseph Zen of Hong Kong, an outspoken proponent of democracy and religious freedom, to cardinal, a move that China condemned as a 'hostile act' (Mitchell 2006). In an apparent concession China allowed the ordination of a priest who enjoyed papal approval ('New ordination' 2006).

Concern about the plight of the world's destitute has led the Vatican to champion efforts to ameliorate poverty and provide succour to refugees. Agencies like Catholic Relief Services work in some of the harshest places on earth, such as Darfur refugee camps, and funnel information and policy recommendations to the Vatican. An example of one broad policy initiative concerns debt relief, which is particularly pressing in poor African countries whose debt service payments crowded out expenditures for education, healthcare and economic development. In highly visible gestures Pope John Paul II endorsed the 2000 'Year of Jubilee' campaign to write off such debts and even met with rock star Bono, the signal celebrity working for debt relief.

Another notable foray into global politics concerned war. While the Church is known for having the most fully articulated 'just war' doctrine, it has moved toward a greater scepticism about the use of force in international relations. As Drew Christensen observes, 'with Pope John XXIII's landmark encyclical Pacem in Terris (1963)', the Church began developing a concept of peace as more than 'the absence of war'. This trend accelerated from 1991 onward, as John Paul II promoted social justice as an antidote to war and lauded 'nonviolence and forgiveness in international politics'. Increasingly, the Pope questioned whether modern warfare could meet the criteria of just war, and erected a high moral threshold for the use of force (Christensen 2006). This posture was demonstrated during the run up to the US-led war against Iraq in 2003.

Both in private conversations and public pronouncements the Pope inveighed against the war, and his nuncio to the US joined the American bishops in challenging its justification (Allen 2004: ch. 7).

If the Church has taken 'progressive' positions on human rights, poverty and war, it remains a traditional body when it comes to the constellation of issues surrounding abortion, human sexuality, AIDS prevention, population control, contraception and the family. The Church takes issue with the 'condom message' of AIDS activists, for example, pointing to abstinence and fidelity in marriage as the only sure ways to prevent the spread of the disease ('Pope rejects condoms for Africa' 2005). Because the Vatican has observer status at the United Nations and its NGOs attend AIDS summits, the Church is an active lobbyist for this position. On the other hand, the Church has joined the AIDS community in calling for more spending on medical treatment and succour for AIDS orphans, and its own agencies have such programmes.

On artificial contraception the Vatican's most visible initiatives have involved the issue of birth control for minors. Whereas a host of liberal and feminist NGOs seek to provide 'sexual and reproductive health information and care' to adolescents, the Church has emphasized the rights and responsibilities of families. Church officials fear that the approach of liberal NGOs undermines traditional morality and promotes sexual permissiveness that leads to the abuse of girls and women (Crossette 1994). Thus both in international population summits and on the ground Catholic representatives have fought against bypassing parents in dispensing contraception, and they have opposed certain kinds of sex education programmes ('UN General Assembly highlights: International Conference on Population and Development' 1994). On the other hand, some critics of the Church, including some lay Catholics, argue that since the doctrinal prohibition against artificial means of contraception emerged before the global population explosion, the Church should 'reassess the official Catholic positions' (Schwarz 1998).

By far the most vigorous lobbying on the constellation of population issues involves abortion. This was vividly displayed at the highly publicized United Nations International Conference on Population and Development, held at Cairo, Egypt, in September of 1994, which sought strategies to stabilize the global population. Vice-President Al Gore, representing the Clinton Administration, promoted language in conference documents that advocated 'reproductive choice' and wide access to all forms of birth control, including abortion. This position was widely backed by an alliance of western nations, other countries, feminist groups, and many NGOs.

But Church envoys fought tenaciously against abortion language, in effect 'filibustering' for changes. Frustrated delegates negotiated with Catholic representatives and agreed to altered wording that often drew fine distinctions (Cowell 1994). The Church went so far as to enlist allies among Muslim nations, including Islamist states, such as Iran and Libya. Not only was this initiative successful in getting several countries to denounce abortion provisions, but leaders of Al Azhar Islamic University in Cairo, 'a foremost center of Islamic learning', condemned 'the proposed United Nations document as offensive to Islam' (Tagliabue 1994). In the end the Church, having gained concessions but still declining to sign on to abortion provisions, endorsed other parts of the report in a move that some saw as a subtle shift in the Church's posture toward population control (Cowell 1994). Overall, what makes this episode striking is that the Catholic Church – acting both like a state and an NGO – was the only

religious body with delegates engaged in actual negotiations over UN population recommendations.

This prominence ensures the Church a hearing on related issues. The Church in fact has found diverse allies in its condemnation of forced sterilisation and infanticide, China's harsh one-child policy, and the widespread abortion of females in some countries (resulting in severe imbalances between men and women). Church agencies also promote access for girls and women to education, medical treatment, and economic opportunity as efficacious means of stabilizing populations. At UN summits on women, Vatican envoys have especially championed female education in developing nations.

With its seat in the heart of Europe the Vatican has focused considerable energies defending the Church and its values on the continent. After the collapse of communism this meant battling secularizing trends. When John Paul II returned to democratic Poland, for example, he chided the people for rising consumerism and materialism. Throughout Europe the Vatican also fought (largely unsuccessful) battles against socially liberal policies, such as legal abortion, same-sex marriage or civil unions, stem cell research and euthanasia. This has put the Vatican at odds with Italian governments, particularly the centre-left coalition of the former prime minister Romano Prodi. After meeting with Prodi in the autumn of 2006 Pope Benedict XVI urged Catholics to fight 'with clarity and determination' any legislation seeking to redefine the traditional family or compromise the 'sanctity' of human life (Nouaille 2006).

Another level of engagement with Europe, as well as the rest of the advanced world, is an intellectual one. In the strikingly philosophical encyclical 'Fides et Ratio', on 'Faith and Reason', John Paul II challenged post-modern thought that undermines timeless verities. The Pope began by asserting that faith and reason 'are like two wings on which the human spirit rises to the contemplation of truth'. He then challenged intellectual trends that call into question the objectivity of truth, and suggested that only faith can rescue the good, the true and the beautiful from postmodern relativism ('Fides et Ratio' 1998). Cardinal Ratzinger (now Pope Benedict XVI) in turn challenged the 'subjectivism' of cultural studies in making the case for a uniquely Catholic concept of inculturation – of instantiating gospel truths in diverse cultural settings around the world (Ratzinger 1999).

The spectre of a seemingly inexorable secularization took on amplified significance when Cardinal Ratzinger became Pope Benedict XVI in 2005. In an address specifically aimed at Europe the pontiff denounced 'the dictatorship of secularism' and called upon Europeans to return to their Christian roots. This took tangible form in deliberations over the constitution of the European Union, in which the Vatican backed language that would explicitly acknowledge the Christian heritage of Europe, but only gained watereddown reference to its religious roots.

We now turn to the diverse examples of political engagement by the Church in different regions of the world.

Europe

Europe was once the Catholic heartland and the Church played a large role in statecraft. That has changed, as church growth has shifted to the developing world of the 'global South'. But it is useful to highlight briefly the contributions of Catholicism to the political scene of Europe.

One of several signal contributions involved the formation of the Christian Democratic parties that played a crucial, if unheralded, role in building stable democracies in Western Europe after World War II. Inspired by Catholic social teaching on

human dignity, lay intellectuals and activists in Europe pressed for democracy and human rights, in some cases pushing the envelope farther than the Church's official position. A leading figure was Jacques Maritain (1882–1973), who helped lay the intellectual foundations for the Christian Democratic movement. In particular, he developed the doctrine of 'Thomistic personalism', a view of the human person as naturally embedded in organic institutions of society, such as family, church, community or guild (Maritain 1943, 1947). Although not explicitly planned by the Church, the emergent Christian Democratic parties drew heavily upon the doctrine of subsidiarity – that the state should support, not supplant, these natural societal institutions. Guided by this vision, Christian Democratic parties enacted family and church-friendly social welfare policies. Thus while often depicted as the main 'conservative' opposition to social democratic parties, the Christian Democratic movement in fact represented a distinct blend of traditional and progressive elements. A genuine international movement, Christian Democratic parties went on to help consolidate democracy in several Latin American nations (Papini 1997; Kalyvas 1996).

In Eastern Europe the story of how the Church helped undermine communism is well known (Weigle 1999). Not only in Poland, but in Czechoslovakia and elsewhere in Eastern Europe congregations became places where people could begin to freely express themselves. This shielded religious and secular dissidents alike, who developed trust and solidarity through religious rituals that took on political significance (Havel et al. 1990).

With the collapse of communism and massive migrations into Europe new issues now confront the Church. An emerging focus is the restive Muslim population. With high birth rates, Muslims are growing relative to a shrinking proportion of (mainly traditional Christian) Europeans, whose fertility rates in many places are below replacement levels. Concerned about this dynamic, Pope Benedict has called for the re-evangelization of Europe. In this he is aided by the incorporation into the European Union of intensely Catholic nations like Poland, which may infuse 'renewed religious vitality into European political and social life' (Katzenstein and Byrnes 2006: 679).

The fear of Muslim militancy has brought Benedict some unlikely allies. Indeed, the pontiff actively courted secular intellectuals, who are concerned that Europe was losing its roots. In an allusion to the Islamic challenge, Benedict said that societies that 'abandon' their roots are unable 'to dialogue with other cultures where religion is a much stronger presence'. The Pope's remarks apparently had special resonance in Italy, where some prominent atheists have embraced the Church as the 'repository of European values' in the face of an unassimilated Muslim presence (Nouaille 2006). Intensely religious Muslims, ironically, may help prod other Europeans to re-evaluate their secularism, to the benefit of the Church.

The United States

The Catholic Church represents 'a distinct voice' in American politics (M.O. Steinfels, 2003). It joins conservatives in opposing abortion and gay marriage, or in supporting educational vouchers and public displays of religion. But it unites with liberals in backing humanitarian foreign aid, healthcare for the poor, social welfare spending, increases in the minimum wage, humane treatment of immigrants, and opposition to the death penalty.

Because of this unique ideological blend Catholics have become the quintessential swing voters in American politics, a strategic voting bloc assiduously courted by both political parties. One-fourth of the US electorate, Catholics comprise the median voting group whose movement often provides the decisive margin of victory in national elections.

Catholics in America also operate an impressive array of institutions, including the nation's paramount parochial school system, a large hospital network, extensive charities and adoption agencies, diverse religious orders, along with national and state Catholic conferences. This institutional presence provides Catholic lobbies with expertise and heft on a host of issues.

As citizens of the globe's dominant economic and military power American Catholics find themselves in a position of potentially unique international influence. The United States Conference of Catholic Bishops, for example, provided pivotal backing for the International Religious Freedom Act, debt relief legislation, and other humanitarian and human rights initiatives.

Add to these features the depth and sophistication of Catholic social teaching and it is not surprising that one analyst wrote that 'the Catholic moment' had arrived in America (Neuhaus 1990). Unfortunately, the Catholic moment was stifled by the devastating revelations of priest sex scandals in what has come to be called the 'long lent' of 2002. Not only did the scandal damage the Church's credibility, it drained millions of dollars from church coffers to provide restitution to victims. Thus what took immigrant communities decades to build was often wiped out by the negligence of Church leaders. Remarkably, the Church has endured and continues to play a quiet political role, especially at the state level where fewer actors have the institutional resources to make a difference (Yamane 2005).

In a sense Catholic Americans came of age with the election of John Kennedy in 1960, which along with the prominent participation by priests and women religious in the landmark civil rights struggle gave the community a certain cachet in American society. The shock of the Supreme Court's 1973 *Roe v. Wade* decision legalizing abortion in turn spurred an extensive pro-life network in the Church, which continues to provide the most vigorous institutional support for limits on abortion and its funding by government. A growing critique of public schools, especially their perceived failure to adequately serve the poor, led to increased attention to the ways parochial schools compensated for family deficits (Coleman and Hoffer 1987), producing alliances with both home-schooling evangelicals and inner-city blacks for various 'school choice' initiatives. The bishops' visibility and clout seemed to crest in the 1980s, as they aligned with liberals in producing pastoral letters critical of nuclear arms and certain capitalist structures, and in opposing Reagan Administration military initiatives in Central America (Byrnes 1991).

Thus the Church has become a key ally of both liberals and conservatives, depending on issue. This is illustrated by recent developments. When the gay marriage issue burst on the scene in this decade the Church joined with conservative evangelical groups in affirming the legal status of traditional marriage. In turn, some bishops thrust the Church into the midst of the 2004 election when they threatened to withhold communion to Democratic presidential candidate John Kerry, in protest of his pro-choice position on abortion. But Church agencies, heavily involved with the growing Hispanic population in the USA, also fought against conservative attempts to crack down on undocumented immigrants.

Although the Church suffered from the failure of bishops to deal with sexually abusive priests, a political development, the devolution of power to the states, provided new life to Catholic civic engagement.

The so-called 'New Federalism' has given state governments more policy-making authority. As recent scholarship shows, this has enhanced the role of state Catholic conferences, which are permanent agencies composed of dioceses but 'usually headed by a lay executive director' (Yamane 2005). In the majority of states these conferences are often the most well established and influential religious advocacy group – but in characteristic fashion blending culturally conservative stands with economically progressive positions (Yamane 2005; Cleary and Hertzke 2006). On balance this advocacy, as Yamane concludes, 'contributes [positively] to American democracy' (2005).

Latin America: democracy and development

Latin America contains the largest regional Catholic population, comprising some 44% of all the world's Catholics (Barrett *et al.* 2001). For nearly five centuries the Catholic Church backed authoritarian regimes and economic oligarchs in Latin America. This makes the transformation of the Church following Vatican II especially noteworthy. In a number of instances bishops, priests, and women religious opposed dictatorships and shielded dissidents. Papal nuncios in turn provided international legitimacy of such efforts, helping to lead a wave of democratization in the last few decades.

An excellent example is Brazil, by population the largest Catholic country in the world. For centuries the Church tied itself to wealthy landowners and authoritarian rulers who granted it vast privileges. But by the 1960s a progressive episcopate embraced the aspirations of the poor and offered the most prominent challenge to despotic military rule. By providing space for civil society and undermining the legitimacy of the regime, the Church helped midwife democratization (Casanova 1994; Huntington 1991).

To be sure, democratization in Latin America was uneven, and Church support for authoritarianism endured until recently in a few countries, such as Argentina, Honduras and Uruguay. One possible explanation for this variability is that the Church changed the least where it faced little competition, either from Protestant growth or secular movements (Gill 1998).

Closely linked to its democratic role was the Church's embrace of justice for rural peasantry and urban poor. Vatican II highlighted the enormous inequalities in the global economy and questioned the justice of destitution amidst unprecedented wealth. This theme was developed at meetings of the Latin American Bishop's Conference (CELAM) in Medellin in 1968 and Pueblo in 1979. Church leaders articulated the widely influential idea that public policies should be guided by a 'preferential option for the poor'.

This idea, of course, was bolstered by liberation theology, which applied the analysis of class conflict to press for radical changes in societal structures that would end exploitation of the destitute (Gutierrez 1973). While many bishops may not have embraced the 'Marxist methodology of liberation theologians', as Anthony Gill observes, 'they could not but help to reflect upon their critiques of Latin American society and perhaps arrive at less radical, but still progressive conclusions' (1998: 45). So whether influenced by Vatican II, CELAM conferences, or liberation theology, Church leaders in many cases became champions of the dispossessed.

Of course, the Marxist dimension of liberation theology troubled the Catholic hierarchy. By the 1980s Cardinal Joseph Ratzinger had condemned liberation theology as a 'fundamental threat' to the Church (Reel 2005) and silenced Brazilian friar Leonardo Boff, a leading figure in the

movement (Rother 2005). Pope John Paul II in turn appointed more conservative bishops in Latin America. Despite this assault, liberation theology lingers among a cadre of priests and lay Catholics, who seek structural changes in confronting desperate poverty (Reel 2005).

In addition to skittishness on the part of the hierarchy, the progressive impulse has limits for other reasons. The Church faces a dramatic shortage of priests in Latin America, which weakens its influence relative to the rapidly growing Pentecostal churches with their abundance of lay evangelists. This competition has induced Catholic bishops to lobby for governmental assistance, leading them to a 'greater accommodation with the political and economic elite'. Thus while concern for the poor remains, reliance on government support in some countries blunts the Church's agitation for progressive reforms (Gill 1998: 173).

African struggles

During the twentieth century the Catholic Church experienced dramatic growth in sub-Saharan Africa, from a tiny population in 1900 to nearly 125 million by 2000 (Barrett et al. 2001). At least four African nations are at or near majority Catholic population while a substantial Catholic presence is found in several others (www.cia.gov/library/publications/the-world-factbook/index.html). But the vast African continent confronts the Church with diverse challenges, from tribalism to poverty, civil war to AIDS, Islamic militancy to dictatorship and corruption. Thus Catholic politics varies enormously, with the Church's impact differing radically from nation to nation.

As an independent sector of civil society the Church promoted democratization, to a greater or lesser extent, in a number of countries. In Malawi, for example, the Catholic bishops distributed a pastoral letter that criticized the one-party rule of Hastings Kamuzu Banda, which was the 'turning point' in that nation's democratization. Moreover, 'the Church led popular opposition movements against authoritarianism' in Kenya, Zambia, and Ghana (Philpott 2005: 110–111). In war-torn Congo (with approximately half of its population Roman Catholic) Church leaders have striven to provide a forum for reconciliation as a means of promoting peace and democratic transition. Though initial mediation efforts failed to end civil war, the Church's efforts have helped solidify a tentative peace and a move toward democracy (Elenga 2006). In other countries, however, such as Rwanda, Cameroon and Uganda, 'Catholics proved ineffective as brokers of democracy' (Philpott 2005).

The Church often provides vital educational and health services where governments are either ineffective or corrupt. In Angola the Church transformed itself from a virtual appendage of Portuguese colonizers into a truly independent force. As the nation recovered from civil war in the new century the Church became a 'surrogate state', managing a network of schools and charities and operating the country's premier radio station. As one scholar concluded, the Church 'weathered a devastating civil war and substantial ideological attacks to emerge as a potent prophetic and political leader in an independent Angola' (Heywood 2006).

The Church's international connections also serve as a resource for popular struggle. The most dramatic illustration of this is Sudan. There an Arab Islamist regime waged a 20-year scorched-earth war (1983–2003) against the nation's ethnic Africans of the south, comprised mostly of Christians and tribal religionists. The war, declared genocidal by the administration of George W. Bush, resulted in 2 million deaths and displaced another 5 million. For a long time

this was Africa's 'forgotten war', until western Christians and Jews took up the cause of the southern Sudanese. A leading figure who raised international awareness of the plight of the besieged Africans of Sudan was Catholic Bishop Macram Gassis. With a diocese larger than Italy Bishop Gassis took frequent forays into war-torn areas, maintaining the Church's spiritual, educational and charitable institutions. Equally important, he travelled extensively in Europe and the United States, publicizing atrocities against his people. He was a key figure in pressing the US Congress to pass the Sudan Peace Act in 2002, which ultimately pressured the government of Khartoum to sign a peace treaty with southern rebels. Though fragile, the peace brought international aid to rebuild the shattered nation and enabled refugees to return. When war subsequently broke out in the west of the country, leading to another round of ethnic cleansing, Bishop Gassis took on the cause, this time of African Muslims in Darfur (Hertzke 2004: ch. 7).

Uganda is another nation in turmoil. Here the Church serves as a popular champion of people of the north terrorized for years by the Lord's Resistance Army (LRA). A bizarre marauding band, the LRA for years killed adults and abducted children to serve as its troops and concubines. Catholic leaders publicized the crisis in northern Uganda, particularly the thousands of refugees, especially children, who fled their homes. The Church provided centres of refuge for these children and operated places where former child soldiers of the LRA could be reintegrated into society.

While the above illustrations show the Church's influence, Rwanda, whose population is majority Roman Catholic, represents an example of abject failure to overcome tribal conflicts. The roots of this failure lie in the fact that the Church colluded with Belgian colonizers, who employed a deliberate policy of playing the Tutsis and Hutus against each other. Indeed, Catholic missionaries initially 'chose the Tutsi hierarchy as their tool for evangelization'. Then the Church switched allegiance to the Hutus, which exacerbated ethnic divisions in Rwandan society (Rutagambwa 2006: 176).

This had devastating consequences in 1994 when Hutu forces inaugurated a genocidal campaign against Tutsis and moderate Hutus. Not only did the Church not systematically protest the genocide, but some Catholic priests actually participated in the atrocities, their sanctuaries becoming killing fields. Even after the slaughter ended, Rwandan Catholic leaders continued to downplay the massacres and refused to acknowledge their complicity and failure. Though some observers hold out hope that the Church can still engage in truth and reconciliation processes, its mission has been seriously discredited (Rutagambwa 2006). Thus the way may be opened for evangelical Protestant competitors to move into the social and moral void.

Asia: a quest for civil society

With its huge population and geographic reach Asia presents a multifarious setting for Catholic political engagement. Despite diverse nationalities and forms of government, however, the quest to carve spaces for itself in civil society is a consistent thread throughout the region.

For example, with a growing Catholic population in Taiwan and South Korea, the Church nurtured dissent against authoritarian regimes and helped to encourage democratization in the two states. Remarkably, in South Korea, Catholic Kim Dae-jung, who fought a lifelong democracy campaign, used Church settings to arouse the citizenry against South Korea's military dictatorships.

He was twice imprisoned and even sentenced to death in 1980. The intervention of the United States led to his release and exile; his subsequent return to South Korea intensified pro-democracy forces. He was elected in 1997 and earned the Nobel peace prize in 2000 for his role in democratizing the nation.

Similarly, in the Philippines the Church fostered the central opposition to the authoritarian rule of Ferdinand Marcos. This began in earnest in the early 1980s with a series of pastoral letters from the Bishops Conference critical of the regime, which prepared the ground for the 'people power' revolution of 1986. Under pressure from the Church, Marcos called a 'snap election' designed to 'throw the opposition off balance'. But Cardinal Jaime Sin and other bishops frustrated Marcos by in effect backing the candidacy of Cory Aquino, wife of the assassinated opposition leader Ninoy Aquino. The bishops then condemned widespread voting fraud that initially gave the election to Marcos. Finally, in one of the most dramatic episodes in Philippine history, the Church called out hundreds of thousands of Filipinos to flood the streets and protect with their bodies military officers who joined the Aquino forces. Under pressure from the Church and the US government, Marcos resigned and Aquino assumed the presidency (Wooster 1994). The Church continues to play an active role in the nation, supporting initiatives for the poor and challenging corruption.

Another example of where the Church became tied up in a people's cause was East Timor. For centuries the Church served the colonial power, but the invasion by Indonesia in 1975 severed the Church from the government and ironically freed priests to lead the popular struggle against occupation. As the interests of the Church and the indigenous population merged, affiliation with Catholicism mushroomed.

In 1973 less than a third of the population was Catholic; by 1990 that figure was an astonishing 90%. Under international pressure Indonesia agreed to a referendum on independence in 1999. Its passage resulted in violent reprisals by Indonesian military troops and militia, in which some priests and nuns were killed. This brought new pressure on the Indonesian government, which ultimately withdrew its troops and recognized East Timor independence. The Church now focuses on rebuilding community structures shattered by occupation and war (Lyon 2006).

Asia contains most of the remaining communist states: China, Vietnam, Laos and North Korea. North Korea, which crushed religion with some of the worst persecution in the world, is *sui generis,* and there the Church barely clings to life. Internationally, however, Catholics have taken up the cause of refugees who have fled the totalitarian regime of Kim Jong Il, putting pressure on China to cease deporting or exploiting them.

Elsewhere in Asia the Church strives for independence from communist authorities, who seek to keep power by controlling nascent civil society. In China, with an estimated Catholic population of 12 million, this has produced a persecuted and divided church. Underground Catholics who pledge fealty to Rome risk arrest by the authorities, and they often disdain those who worship in state-sanctioned 'patriotic' congregations. The failure of Vatican diplomats to reach some kind of détente with the regime has perpetuated such divisions, which inhibit church growth and hamper the Church's ability to foster independent civil society (Madsen 1998; Reardon 2006). Church leaders hope that international exposure of China's repression of religion will come with the 2008 Olympics, forcing the regime to loosen its control.

Conclusion: to the future

As this discussion indicates, the Catholic Church will remain a strategic actor in national and global politics. Its effectiveness, however, will depend on its vitality as a religious institution, and that will vary from region to region, nation to nation. Attracting more people to religious vocations and socializing more youth to stay active in church will be key indicators to watch for the renewal of congregational life.

The Church will also face new issues. Advances in the bio-genetic engineering, for example, will present a major challenge to basic theological understandings of the unique giftedness of persons made in the image and likeness of God. Though hardly on the radar of many religious communities, genetic engineering poses profound questions about the dignity of human life, even about the definition of human life itself. Cloning, foetal farming, patenting life-forms, designer babies engineered with specific traits, even the chimera of human-animal–hybrid combinations used to harvest organs mark the horizon. If the abortion controversy hinged on when human life begins, the genetic revolution thrusts forward such questions as 'What is a human being? Who decides? What about new creations?' This new technology may also widen the gap between the poor and the affluent, who are most likely to engineer advantageous traits in their offspring. This prospect also raises the further question of how society will perceive (or welcome) the imperfect (Cameron 2003).

Although Catholic theologians have begun focusing on these profound questions, it will take a massive educational campaign for the Church to provide a moral lead in the debates to come. Again, its capacity to provide moral guidance in this revolutionary era will hinge in part on whether the Church remains a vigorous spiritual institution around the globe.

Bibliography

Allen, Jr., J.L. (2004) *All the Pope's Men: The inside story of how the Vatican really thinks,* New York: Doubleday.

Allen, Jr., J.L. (2006) 'A challenge, not a crusade', *The New York Times,* 19 September.

'Annual Message to Diplomatic Corps' (1996) Pope John Paul II.

Barrett, D., Kurian, G. and Johnson, T. (eds) (2001) *World Christian Encyclopedia,* New York: Oxford University Press.

Bottum, J. (2006) 'Benedict meets Batholomew: the real reason for the pope's visit to Turkey', *The Weekly Standard,* 11 December, pp. 14–15.

Byrnes, T.A. (1991) *Catholic Bishops in American Politics,* Princeton, NJ: Princeton University Press.

Cameron, N.M. (2003) 'Evangelicals and bioethics: an extraordinary failure', in Cromartie, M. (ed.), *A Public Faith: Evangelicals and civic engagement,* Lanham, MD: Rowman & Littlefield.

Casanova, J. (1994) *Public Religions in the Modern World,* Chicago: University of Chicago Press.

Centesimus Annus (1991) Encyclical letter of Pope John Paul II.

Christiansen, D. (2006) 'Catholic peacemaking, 1991–2005: the legacy of Pope John Paul II', *Review of Faith and International Affairs,* 4(2), pp. 21–28.

Cleary, E.L. and Hertzke, A.D. (eds) (2006) *Representing God at the Statehouse: Religion and politics in the American states,* Lanham, MD: Rowman & Littlefield.

Coleman, J.S. and Hoffer, T. (1987) *Public and Private High Schools: The impact of communities,* New York: Basic Books.

Cowell, A. (1994) 'How Vatican views Cairo', *The New York Times,* 18 September.

Crossette, B. (1994) 'Vatican holds up abortion debate at talks in Cairo', *The New York Times,* 7 September.

'Democracy and a lasting peace' (1944) Christmas message of Pope Pius XII, 25 December.

'Dignitatis Humanae' (1965) *Vatican Council II,* Flannery, A. (ed.) (1975), Collegeville, MN: Liturgical Press.

Elenga, Y.C. (2006) 'The Congolese Church: ecclesial community with the political community', in Manuel, P.C., Reardon, L.C., and Wilcox, C. (eds), *The Catholic Church and the Nation-state: Comparative Perspectives,* Washington, DC: Georgetown University Press, pp. 245–57.

Ferrari, L.L. (2006) 'The Vatican as a transnational actor', in Manuel, P.C., Reardon, L.C., and Wilcox, C. (eds), *The Catholic Church and the Nation-state. Comparative perspectives,* Washington, DC: Georgetown University Press.

'Fides et Ratio' (1998) Encyclical Letter of Pope John Paul II.

Filteau, J. (2005) 'Pope made important overtures to non-Christian religions,' Catholic News Service, www.catholicnewscom/jpii/stories/story04htm.

Fisher, I. and Tavernise, S. (2006) 'In reversal, pope backs Turkey's bid to join European Union: gesture is an effort to repair a rift with Muslims', *The New York Times,* 29 November.

'Gaudium et Spes' (1965) *Vatican Council II,* Flannery, A. (ed.), 1975. Collegeville, MN: Liturgical Press.

Gill, A.J. (1998) *Rendering unto Caesar: The Catholic Church and the state in Latin America,* Chicago: University of Chicago Press.

Gutierrez, G. (1973) *A Theology of Liberation: History, politics, and salvation,* Maryknoll, NY: Orbis Books.

Havel, V. *et al.* (1990) *The Power of the Powerless: Citizens against the state in Central-Eastern Europe,* Armonk, NY: M.E. Sharpe.

Hertzke, A.D. (2004) *Freeing God's Children: The unlikely alliance for global human rights,* Lanham, MD: Rowman & Littlefield.

Hertzke, A.D. (2005) 'Roman Catholicism and the faith-based movement for global human rights', *Review of Faith and International Affairs,* 3(3), pp. 19–24.

Heywood, L. (2006) 'The Angolan Church: the prophetic tradition, politics, and the state', in Manuel, P.C., Reardon, L.C. and Wilcox, C. (eds), *The Catholic Church and the Nation-state: Comparative perspectives,* Washington, DC: Georgetown University Press, pp. 191–206.

Huntington, S. (1991) *The Third Wave: Democratization in the late twentieth century,* Norman, OK: University of Oklahoma Press.

Jelen, T.G. (2006) 'The American Church: of being Catholic and American', in Manuel, P.C., Reardon, L.C. and Wilcox, C. (eds), *The Catholic Church and the Nation-state: Comparative perspectives,* Washington, DC: Georgetown University Press, pp. 69–87.

Kahn, G. and Meichtry, S. (2006) 'A tumultuous world tests a rigid pope', *The New York Times,* 25 November.

Kalyvas, S.N. (1996) *The Rise of Christian Democracy in Europe,* Ithaca, NY: Cornell University Press.

Katzenstein, P.J. and Byrnes, T.A. (2006) 'Transnational religion in an expanding Europe', *Perspectives on Politics,* 4(4), pp. 679–94.

Lyon, A.J. (2006) 'The East Timorese Church: from oppression to liberation', in Manuel, P.C., Reardon, L.C., and Wilcox, C. (eds), *The Catholic Church and the Nation-state: Comparative perspectives,* Washington, DC: Georgetown University Press, pp. 131–48.

Maritain, J. (1943) *The Rights of Man and Natural Law,* New York: Scribner's Sons.

Maritain, J. (1947) *The Person and the Common Good,* Notre Dame, IN: University of Notre Dame Press.

Mitchell, T. (2006) 'Angry Beijing acts against Zen approach to freedom', *The Financial Times,* 8 May.

Neuhaus, R. J. (1990) *The Catholic Moment: The paradox of the church in the postmodern world,* New York: HarperCollins.

'New ordination does not mean better China–Vatican ties' (2006) *Agence France Presse,* 8 May.

Nouaille, M. (2006) 'Pope courts intellectuals in defense of Europe's Christian values', *Agence France Presse,* 19 October.

Papini, R. (1997) *The Christian Democrat International,* translated by Robert Royal, Lanham, MD: Rowman & Littlefield.

Philpott, D. (2005) 'The Catholic wave', in Diamond, L., Plattner, M.F., and Costopoulos, P.J. (eds), *World Religions and Democracy,* Baltimore: Johns Hopkins University Press, pp. 102–16.

'Pope rejects condoms for Africa' (2005) *BBC News,* 10 June.

'Pope shares pain of Palestinian people over Arafat' (2004) *Agence France Presse,* 11 November.

Ratzinger, C.J. (1999) 'Culture and truth: reflections on *Fides et Ratio*', *Origins,* 28(36), 25 February.

Reardon, L.C. (2006) 'The Chinese Catholic Church: obstacles to reconciliation', in Manuel, P.C., Reardon, L.C., and Wilcox, C. (eds), *The Catholic Church and the Nation-state: Comparative perspectives,* Washington, DC: Georgetown University Press.

Reel, M. (2005) 'An abiding faith in liberation theology', *Washington Post,* 2 May.

Rerum Novarum (1891) Encyclical letter of Pope Leo XIII.

Rother, L. (2005) 'Pope Benedict XVI: developing nations', *The New York Times,* 20 April.

Rutagambwa, E. (2006) 'The Rwandan Church: the challenge of reconciliation', in Manuel, P.C., Reardon, L.C. and Wilcox, C. (eds), *The Catholic Church and the Nation-state: Comparative perspectives,* Washington, DC: Georgetown University Press, pp. 173–89.

Schwarz, J.C. (1998) *Global Population from a Catholic Perspective,* Mystic, CT: Twenty-third Publications.

Steinfels, M.O. (ed.) (2003) *American Catholics and Civic Enagement: A distinctive voice,* Lanham, MD: Shed & Ward.

Steinfels, P. (2003) *A People Adrift: The crisis of the Roman Catholic Church in America,* New York: Simon & Schuster.

Stepan, A. (2005) 'Religion, democracy, and the "twin tolerations"', in L., Diamond, Plattner, M.F., and Costopoulos, P.J. (eds), *World Religions and Democracy,* Baltimore: Johns Hopkins University Press.

Tagliabue, J. (1994) 'Vatican seeks Islamic allies in UN population dispute', *The New York Times,* 18 August.

UN General Assembly Highlights: International Conference on Population and Development, Cairo, Egypt, 5-13 September 1994.

'Vatican asks Muslims to help defeat terrorism' (2006) *Daily Mail,* London, 21 October.

Weigel, G. (1999) *Witness to Hope: The biography of Pope John Paul II,* New York: HarperCollins.

Weigel, G. (2005) *The Cube and the Cathedral: Europe, America, and politics without God,* New York: Basic Books.

Wills, G. (2002) *Why I Am a Catholic,* New York: Harper Perennial.

Wooster, H. (1994) 'Faith at the ramparts: the Philippine Catholic Church and the 1986 revolution', in Johnston, D. and Sampson, C. (eds), *Religion, the Missing Dimension of Statecraft,* New York: Oxford University Press, pp. 153–76.

Yamane, D. (2005) *The Catholic Church in State Politics: Negotiating prophetic demands & political realities,* Lanham, MD: Rowman & Littlefield.

5

Confucianism, from above and below

Michael D. Barr

Confucianism notionally began in the sixth century BC with the teachings of an obscure Chinese scholar and occasional government adviser called *Kongfuzi* (Confucius). This picture, however, is slightly misleading because Confucius was himself drawing upon traditions, ideals and cosmologies that were already ancient. He was in fact calling for a revitalisation of these traditions in an attempt to bring an end to the chaos that had engulfed China in his own day. He reaffirmed the traditional Chinese notion that virtue, morality, humaneness and harmony are all heavenly realities waiting to be discovered through education and the adoption of 'proper' relationships between members of families and members of society. In the hands of his disciples and generations of their successors his teaching gave rise to an ethical code that assumed a status akin to that of a state religion (Turner 2006: 212) in China, Korea, Japan and Vietnam, providing a central basis of regime legitimacy for many generations of imperial dynasties. As a state religion and as a system of governance Confucianism is now dead, but at the level of the lived experience of ordinary people, it continues to act as a religion, imposing patterns of social cognition that provide a reasonably consistent social underlay across Chinese and other East Asian cultures. The divergent elements separating 'Confucian' cultures (China, Taiwan, Japan, Korea, Vietnam and the overseas Chinese of Southeast Asia, including those in Singapore) are legion, but the common elements are also very firmly established.

Confucianism makes no claim to absolute or revealed truth, but its proponents believe that it brings to light natural and innately known truths (Ng 1999: 169). They regard it as a philosophy and praxis that provides a logical and time-honoured method of ordering society for the common good by cultivating virtue in everyone from the highest political authority to the most menial commoner, with the ruler and his advisers setting the highest standard: a 'virtuocracy'. Indeed its classical statecraft was premised on recognition of the absolute power of the emperor, but sought to direct that power for the common good by cultivating virtue in the heart of the emperor and by surrounding him with wise, virtuous and scholarly advisers. The ideal Confucian is a 'cultured gentleman' (*junzi*) and a 'humane person' (*ren*) as opposed to a 'mean/small person' (*xiao ren*).

The two central elements that we find in common in societies influenced by Confucianism include:

- a heavily relational, hierarchical and conservatively ordered view of society, whereby society is regarded substantially as an extension of a patriarchal family; and
- respect for scholarship and virtue, with an implicit assumption that the latter is derived from the former.

In its classical form Confucianism also sees virtue as being properly expressed through rites and rituals (*li*) that ensure everyone in society operates in a proper fashion according to his or her place in the social hierarchy. Although the formal rituals are no longer widely practised, even today social intercourse still tends to follow somewhat ritualised patterns that can seem obsequious to outsiders. Central to the relational and hierarchical perspective of classical Confucianism are two sets of relationships. The first is the 'five relationships' that govern Confucian thought: ruler over minister/subject; father over son; husband over wife; elder brother over younger brother; and friend and friend. Friendships are the only apparently non-hierarchical relationship in the Confucian order, but in practice friends tend to model their behaviour on the older brother/younger brother relationship (de Bary 1998: 17–18). The second set of relationships is the traditional hierarchy of occupations, whereby scholars are almost venerated, farmers are accorded considerable respect, workers are held in lower regard, and merchants are at the bottom of the pile. It is a sign of the flexibility of contemporary Confucianism that the subservient role of women is generally dismissed (at least at levels of official policy), and that merchants are held in high regard in many 'Confucian' societies.

Described in broad terms, Confucianism can appear to be a monolithic social force and an uncompromising force for conservatism, but such an assessment ignores the heterogeneity that is found in 'Confucian' societies. Perhaps the most stark and public point of difference today is in political outcomes, whereby Confucianism finds itself being conscripted to the side of authoritarian established orders in China and Singapore, even as radical and apparently successful experiments in democracy are taking place in the 'Confucian' societies of South Korea and Taiwan. The conservative claims rest upon classical Confucianism's elitism, the high value it places on social order and its promotion of deference towards those in positions of authority. Advocates of democracy do not generally justify their positions with reference to Confucianism at all, but when they do they are more likely to point to the inherent humaneness of Confucianism, the obligation upon scholars to be fearless when advising leaders, and the obligation of the classical Confucian emperor to retain the support of his subjects (expressed by mystical allusions to retaining the 'Mandate of Heaven') (see, for example, Xu 2006; Ackerly 2005).

Confucianism: a religion?

The residual life of Confucianism as a grassroots mode of social cognition should be sufficient to establish a *prima facie* case that, regardless of any quibbles over whether it is technically a religion, it is worthy of being treated as a religion for the purposes of understanding its relationship to politics because it has the capacity to exercise social power comparable to that of a religion. Indeed, in its pre-modern, classical form it was, as Turner (2006: 212) articulates, primarily a state religion, though one that also conveyed an expression of 'a sense of human dependency on the spiritual realm'. It has now been thoroughly deposed from exercising direct state power, but it still retains elements of both the public and the private dimensions of its original character. It is true that in both spheres it is substantially subservient to other religions and worldviews (e.g. communism, capitalism, democracy), but then this is only a variation of the historical theme, since Confucianism has always found itself in ambiguous relationships with rival religions and ideologies: hence the prevalence of syncretism in East Asia, with variously Legalism, Daoism, Buddhism, Shinto and Shamanism sharing social and political hegemony with Confucianism in different times and places.

There are many elements of Confucianism as a religion that are worthy of study, but if we consider it precisely as it articulates with modern politics we can reasonably restrict ourselves to three elements that are identified by Fox (2001: 61–7) as specifically relevant to International Relations:

- religion as a direct influence on policy-makers;
- religion as an indirect influence on policy-makers because of:
  - the expectations of their constituents;
  - the expectations generated by the 'political and cultural mediums' created by the religion; and
- religion as a tool of legitimation for governments and for those who oppose them.

Fox's interest is in religion as a phenomenon rather than Confucianism itself, but the same cannot be said of Tu Weiming. Tu is a Harvard-based scholar of Confucianism who, since the early 1980s, has also been a tireless international advocate of Confucian ethics and philosophy,

having been intimately involved in both the Singaporean and PRC Confucianism campaigns. During his advocacy in Singapore he argued that there are three distinct but related forms of Confucianism at work in the modern world:

- Confucianism as an ideology;
- Confucianism as a mode of scholarship; and
- Confucianism as a system of personal ethics (Tu 1984: 204).

To study the role of Confucianism in modern politics I suggest that we need a framework based essentially upon Tu's, but which is more open to answering the questions raised by Fox.

With these parameters in mind I propose to interrogate the relationship between Confucianism and modern politics through three conceptual prisms:

- Confucianism as a tool for manipulation by political elites;
- Confucianism as a subject of study by scholars of Confucian texts, ethics and philosophy, and any scholars who are wont to become participants in state-sponsored Confucian revivals; and
- Confucianism as a generic term for the many traditional East Asian forms of social cognition related to family, education, scholarship, society and governance that – despite significant variations between them – can be loosely described as 'social Confucianism'.

At all three levels, Confucianism continues to influence the conduct of politics in Chinese and East Asian societies. This can be seen most clearly in the recent history of China and Singapore, where the elite manipulation of Confucianism for political ends and legitimation is most overt, but it is also apparent in the 'informal' politics of South Korea, Taiwan, Japan and Vietnam because of the strength of social Confucianism. I postulate that Confucianism at all three levels will continue to influence Chinese and East Asian societies, but its impact on politics will not be simple or uncontested because the stakeholders (elites, scholars and the various 'Confucian' societies) have differing and to some extent contradictory interests, and no one stakeholder – not even the political leadership of China or Singapore – has sufficient moral or political force to monopolise even a single national agenda, let alone the international discourse.

Political elites

The most obvious point of articulation between Confucianism and politics is in the way the leaders of China and Singapore have tried to market Confucianism as a basis of state and political legitimacy. In each case the resurrection of Confucianism was prompted by the collapse of a previously useful basis of legitimation, and – probably not coincidentally – by the emergence of new domestic political threats.

In the case of Singapore, which had its 'Confucian' heyday in the 1980s, the particular triggers were the forced withdrawal of Singapore from the Socialist International in 1976 (Barr 2002: 30–1), and the electoral resurgence of opposition parties in the early 1980s. Yet behind both these immediate causes lay a more remote one: then-Prime Minister Lee Kuan Yew's Chinese 'turn', whereby he apparently 'discovered' his Chinese roots and set out to make 'Chineseness' the centrepiece of his personal life, his statecraft and Singapore's successful pursuit of economic growth (Barr 2000: 164–74; Barr and Low 2005). He saw the public promotion of 'Confucianism' in schools, in the media

and in social welfare, family and housing policy – along with speaking Mandarin, and celebrating 'Chinese culture' and history – as central to this re-articulation of the Singapore national project (Barr and Low 2005). Housing policy was amended to include incentives for traditional three-tier families to live near each other, ignoring the fact that their separation was engineered by the government's housing policies in the first place (*The Straits Times*, 1 March and 30 April 1982; Tremewan 1994: 59–60). Health and social security policies were reconfigured on principles intended to encourage 'filial piety' and personal and family responsibility, sometimes forcing adult children to assist aged parents with money (Barr 2001). Singapore's Confucian experiment had slipped to the background of the broader Sinicisation project by the late 1980s, but it continues at a less intensive level. Overt references to 'Confucianism' and kindred concepts (such as 'filial piety', 'meritocracy', deference to those in authority), are now thoroughly integrated into most mainstream public discourses in Singapore.

The resurgence of officially sponsored Confucianism in China had tentative beginnings in 1983 (with the restoration of Confucius's tomb), came fully into the open in 1989 (the first year in which Confucius's birthday was celebrated in the People's Hall in Beijing), and emerged officially in 1994 (the year in which the International Confucian Association was launched with a gala international conference in Beijing). During this period Deng Xiaoping's embrace of capitalism was in full force throughout Eastern China (thus making a mockery of the claim the country was still being run according to communist principles), the widespread unrest of 1989 (culminating in the Tiananmen Square massacre) was a fresh memory, and China was facing severe diplomatic-cum-trade pressure from the United Nations and the United States over its human rights record (Barr 2002: 51–63). More recently the regime has been acutely worried about new waves of unrest across China, with the Ministry of Public Security reporting 87,000 'mass incidents' in 2005, up from 74,000 in 2004 and 58,000 in 2003. These figures represent a 600 to 900 per cent increase on the rate of public order disturbances involving 'obstruction of justice, gathering of mobs and stirring up of trouble' compared to the first half of the 1990s (*The Times*, 20 January 2006). In March 2005 the National People's Congress publicly declared this increase in public protests as a primary reason for the renewed emphasis on the Confucian virtue of 'harmony' (*Xinhua News Agency*, 8 March 2005). According to research conducted by the Chinese Academy of Social Sciences Institute of Rural Development, the main cause of these disturbances was seizure of land (*Xinhua News Agency*, 8 March 2005) – that is, confiscation of real estate by officials and government-linked entrepreneurs scrambling to acquire a share of the wealth to be had by participating in China's burgeoning economic 'development'. Regardless of the direct cause, the accumulation of challenges from these disturbances was indicating a new crisis of legitimacy for the government because the rate of peasant disturbances has always been taken as a prime indicator of the level of legitimacy enjoyed by Chinese regimes (a direct legacy of the Confucian myth of the 'Mandate of Heaven'), so either the rapaciousness of entrepreneurs needed to be curbed, or the people needed to be taught to be more quiescent.

Former President Jiang Zemin responded to these challenges by overtly promoting Confucianism *per se* as a stabilising factor that would provide a new rationale for the legitimacy of the regime. His efforts culminated in his 2001 call for the study of Confucian classics in Party schools, and his publicly voiced aspiration to see the imposition of a 'rule of virtue' in China to complement the widespread but half-hearted campaign to introduce the rule of law (*South China Morning Post*, 20 February 2001). A sceptic might interpret this as Jiang calling for the existing ruling elite to be recognised as virtuous, thereby bestowing Confucian-inspired legitimacy on the regime. The response of his successor, Hu Jintao, extended and refined Jiang's approach: he made a strategic decision even before taking over the full reins of the leadership to make 'harmony' the key concept of his rule so that he was able to launch his strategy in his nationally televised acceptance speech immediately after being elected President of the PRC (*Xinhua News Agency*, 17 March 2003; *BBC*, 18 March 2003). Since then his promotion of 'harmony' and a 'harmonious society' has become ubiquitous, with Hu's speeches and those of other members of the political elite containing so many references to these concepts that it would be tedious to cite them individually. Suffice to say that the promotion of a 'harmonious society' quickly became the officially designated top priority of the Chinese Communist Party (CCP) (*Xinhua News Agency*, 20 February 2005). By October 2006 'harmony' had been listed as a direction for the country, on a par with the quest for prosperity, democracy and a civilised society (*South China Morning Post*, 12 October 2006). In strictly Confucian terms this was perhaps an odd choice of concept because Confucian 'harmony' is not so much a virtue to be practised or a state to be imposed, but a good outcome to be applauded. 'Harmony' is the social benefit derived from rule by virtue and the proper functioning of society, but here it is being presented as the precondition, not a result, of a good social order (Hu, quoted in *Xinhua News Agency*, 27 June 2005).

Confucianism was the explicit inspiration of the rhetoric in both Singapore and the PRC, but the rhetorical result was more like a parody of Confucian ideals, which accounts for Tu Wei-ming's lament in a 1989 newspaper interview that the prospective rejuvenation of Confucianism in China was 'a mixed blessing' because he feared that 'another politicisation of Confucianism is in the offing' (*San Francisco Chronicle*, 19 April 1989). The Singaporean version was mapped out in explicit detail in a series of 'Confucian Ethics' textbooks designed for use in Singaporean schools (Grosse 1985a, 1985b, 1985c and 1985d) and was reinforced by continual rhetoric from the political elite. The messages were constant and quickly became predictable: the ideal of the *junzi*; the importance of education and meritocracy; the virtues of a supposed 'Confucian work ethic'; the central role of 'filial piety' and the importance of the extended, three-tier family; 'family values'; social responsibility; the need for consensus, cooperation and political restraint from sectional and political interests; social harmony; respect for elders; and deference to those in positions of authority (*The Straits Times*, 1980–5).

The cynicism with which this rejuvenation of Confucianism was approached was indicated in a research interview that I conducted with Goh Keng Swee, Singapore's former Deputy Prime Minister and the man who founded the research institute that spearheaded the Confucianism revival of the 1980s. I asked him whether Lee Kuan Yew was really a 'Confucian gentleman'. He replied:

[Lee Kuan Yew] is not a Confucian. He can't be a Confucian gentleman. But he did say that societies that were under a Confucian theory have certain attributes – Japan, Korea, China, and overseas Chinese – and these attributes were useful. Like saving money, working hard and education.

(Author's interview with
Goh Keng Swee, 1 October 1996)

The spirit of the regime's approach is revealed in an anecdote that this same Goh Keng Swee – then speaking as Deputy Prime Minister – recounted in 1972:

Recently I had an interesting after-dinner discussion with a widely travelled American banker. ... He asked what my choice would be if I had to recommend one single prescription to solve the economic problems of a poor country. I said I would recommend that the population be converted to some demanding, narrow-minded, intolerant form of the Protestant religion, such as one of the more extreme Calvinist sects. This would bring about the end of easy-going thrift-less habits among the populace and the beginning of scrupulous honesty in public administration.

This fanciful idea puts, in an extreme way, the view that a firm moral order need be established in a society which seeks economic progress.

(Goh 1977: 46)

Converting Singapore to Calvinism was never an option, but Confucianism was clearly considered to be a viable substitute.

Singapore's experiment with a Confucian revival reached its most public and official zenith in the country's five official 'Shared Values', which were adopted by Parliament in 1991. The final version of the values reads:

1 nation before community and society before self;
2 family as the basic unit of society;
3 community support and respect for the individual;
4 consensus, not conflict; and
5 racial and religious harmony.

The 'Shared Values' were consciously designed through the prism of Confucianism, which is indicated by the fact that the government White Paper that paved the way for their adoption explicitly invoked the Confucian ideal of 'government by honourable gentlemen *junzi*' (Government of Singapore 1991). Yet the political intent of these 'values' is revealed in another episode in their gestation. At one point the government considered, but rejected, a proposal to amend Shared Value 1 to read 'harmony or balance between individual and community interests' (Mauzy and Milne 2002: 63). This change would have weakened the conceptual supremacy of the state over the individual and community, and so was rejected by the government.

The PRC leadership's version of Confucianism has changed significantly with the change of leaders. Jiang Zemin was particularly concerned with the rhetoric of a 'new ethical standard' based explicitly on Confucianism but without having any clearly directed political end beyond promoting a perception, including a self-perception, that the political elite was operating from high ethical principles (*South China Morning Post*, 20 February and 20 December 2001) and was therefore worthy of deference, respect and support. His successor, Hu Jintao, has thus far refrained from invoking Confucianism by name, and yet has strengthened and refined his appropriation of 'Confucianism' for political purposes. From his first speech upon being elected President of China, Hu began expounding his Confucian vision in explicit detail, the essence of which was an instruction to:

- learn from and foster the noble moral characters of the country's older generations of leaders; and
- impose strict self-discipline, keep honest and clean in performing public duties, always maintain a modest, prudent and industrious

style of work, and work hard and selflessly night and day for the country and the people (*BBC*, 18 March 2003).

Thus we have the essential message of conservative Confucianism: the populace is to defer to their leaders because they are wise and virtuous, and the leaders are to be worthy of their place by being wise, virtuous and diligent. Beyond this the role of 'harmony' was introduced explicitly as a device to legitimise and sustain the CCP leadership: the Party leadership, the people, and the rule of law were to be brought into 'organic harmony' in a context in which the Party leadership was 'upheld' without compromise. Hu also placed 'the interests of the state [embodying the collective interests of "the people"] above anything else'.

Such sentiments are typical of those enunciated by authoritarian dictatorships the world over, but they are of particular interest to this study because they are couched in explicitly Confucian terms. The leadership must be sustained but not adulated. Rather, the people are to learn from the leaders because of their noble moral character, their modesty, prudence and industriousness. These are the characteristics of a good Confucian ruler: of a *junzi*. Since this speech in 2003, Confucian themes have become increasingly nuanced, with 'harmony' and 'harmonious society' emerging as the key rhetorical tenet of Hu's reign. In July 2006, five specific areas of concern were identified by a spokesperson for the United Front Work Department of the Party (*BBC*, 2 September 2006). These were 'relations between political parties, nationalities, religions, social strata, and compatriots at home and abroad'. Each of these items has such an immediate political implication that cynics might suspect ulterior motives in the 'harmony' agenda. The concern about harmony between political parties, for instance, can only refer to relations between the CCP and the political parties of Hong Kong and Taiwan, since there are no other parties in the country. 'Nationalities' is the standard term for China's ethnic minorities, and concern about religions refers not to generic religious tolerance – of which China has very little – but to China's troubled relations with the Vatican, its Muslim minorities, the Buddhists of Tibet, and the Falun Gong movement. The reference to 'social strata' reflects the Party leadership's impotent concern about the growing wealth gap and rising tide of protests referred to earlier. 'Compatriots at home and abroad' refers not only to generic Chinese expatriates and investors, but specifically to the governments and people of Taiwan and Hong Kong. On top of these concerns, there have been pronouncements linking 'harmony' to the fight against corruption, and expressing concern for 'harmony between population, resources and [the] environment' (*China Daily*, 12 March 2004). Harmony at all these levels is, of course, desirable by any measure, but the distinctive feature of Hu's version of 'harmony' is that in order to be consistent with his proclamations upon his election as President, it must be a 'harmony' that upholds Party leadership and brings the rest of society into harmony with the centre.

At this point it is worth noting that Lee Kuan Yew, Jiang Zemin and Hu Jintao are not the only rulers of 'Confucian' societies to conscript Confucianism for their own ends. In the 1930s the Kuomingtang leadership of Nationalist China overtly invoked Confucianism under the banner of the New Life Movement, and as recently as 2004, South Korean President Roh Moon-Hyun donned classical Confucian garb (literally) and very publicly withdrew from public life in the style of a Korean emperor of old as part of his strategic (and successful) response to impeachment proceedings initiated by the

parliamentary opposition parties (*The Straits Times*, 2 April 2004). These examples of overt political usage of Confucianism demonstrate the latent potential for this type of exploitation across East Asia, but in most countries of the region the role of Confucianism in politics is much more subtle and takes the forms that are more properly explored in the section on 'Social Confucianism', below.

Effect on the elite?

It is difficult to measure the effectiveness of these efforts, but judging by the Singaporean experience it seems to provide some tangible benefits for ruling elites. While popular resentment and grievances against the Singapore government has not dissipated because of the Confucianism campaign (or its thinly disguised successors, the 'Asian values' and 'Chinese values' campaigns), the regime has successfully used the trope of Confucianism to build a Gramscian hegemony. It has generated popular acceptance of a language of legitimacy based on Confucianism that makes it very difficult for domestic critics and opposition politicians to mount a sustained critique of the regime. The impact of this trope is seen most strongly at the level of the elite, which self-consciously operates on various principles drawn straight from the Confucian worldview: a meritocratic Mandarinate (at least in form if not in practice – see Barr 2006a); hierarchical and highly personal power relationships (Barr 2006b); a culture of honest, incorruptible and selfless public service within the elite (using a definition of corruption that ignores corruption for political objectives as opposed to corruption for personal gain); and deference to those in positions of authority.

A very public practical outcome of this culture can be found in the mode by which the ruling People's Action Party (PAP) selects its parliamentary candidates, Cabinet and Prime Minister. To display ambition is a negative in Singapore politics. As Deputy Prime Minister Wong Kan Seng described it in the lead-up to the 2006 General Elections:

> We don't go for jostling of powers to compete for positions because we believe that in order to run our system, we need a process in which everybody understands what his or her role is. That makes us different from other countries where there is a lot of personal interest and gain in wanting to achieve certain leadership positions.
>
> (*Reuters*, 5 May 2006)

At this point we find ourselves moving from a consideration of the impact of state-sponsored Confucianism on the populace to its impact on the behaviour of the political elite itself. Perhaps the most poignant observation of this aspect of the matter was made by Chua Beng Huat in 1995, when he wrote:

> [although] the PAP leadership has not succeeded in inscribing Confucianism into the ideological system of Singapore ... it may be said to have 'Confucianised' itself by prescribing for itself a code of ethics, that of the *junzi* or honourable individual. ... This 'self-Confucianisaton' does not mean that the PAP leadership will not behave like other politicians to win votes and stay in power. This desire is, however, rationalised in terms of the public interest which provides the warrant for their actions.
>
> (Chua 1995: 193–4)

In fairness to the advocates of political Confucianism, it should be acknowledged that although I am treating this as a secondary effect, such impacts on the behaviour of the political elite are and always have been an intended and primary effect of Confucianism: fostering virtue and inculcating a sense of public service in the hearts of rulers and their advisers.

In China it is doubtful that the introspective impact of political Confucianism on the political elite is having much overt effect beyond providing a strong conceptual weapon in the anti-corruption campaign, but this could be because the ruling elite is already so inculcated with the Confucian worldview that the impact of this highly constructed 'Confucianism from above' is obscured (see under 'Social Confucianism' for elaboration). Nevertheless, overt examples of the use of 'harmony' as a tool in intra-Party intrigue are already starting to emerge. Perhaps the first victim of this pattern was the fall of Hong Kong's first Chief Executive Officer, Tung Chee Hwa, in 2006. Towards the end of his troubled reign, Tung began articulating his role in terms of achieving 'harmony' (*China Daily*, 13 January 2005) and when his downfall was imminent the criticism being offered from his superiors was couched explicitly in terms of his failure to achieve 'harmony' (*South China Morning Post*, 1 February 2005). Beyond such expediencies, it remains to be seen whether the rhetoric of Confucianism-cum-harmony in China will significantly affect approaches to environmental issues, religious freedom, or dealings with Taiwan.

Scholars

Scholars play a ubiquitous but uncomfortable role in political Confucianism. Ubiquitous because scholars and scholarship are and always have been intrinsic to Confucianism, to the point where Confucian revivals cannot achieve any level of credibility without the cooperation of scholars. Uncomfortable because modern Confucian scholars are generally well-meaning humanists who believe that Confucianism, properly understood, can be an active agent for humanistic virtue and civility among rulers and ruled alike (and who generally argue that Confucianism is compatible with democracy and human rights), but who routinely find themselves as the handmaidens of authoritarian regimes. Take the case of Tu Wei-ming and the other North American Confucian scholars who were brought to Singapore in the 1980s to facilitate the government's Confucian revival. They came; they wrote and delivered scholarly papers; they took part in televised discussions and gave advice to the government; but the crucial task of writing the Confucian Ethics textbooks and workbooks went to a team of Singaporeans, none of whom has any record of scholarship or publication on Confucianism outside the confines of the Singapore 'Confucianism' project.[1] The final product of these courses was didactic and conservative, predictably emphasising the social hierarchy of the Confucian worldview and projecting society as a conflation of the family (Grosse 1985a: 101, 102; Grosse 1985b: 124). The Secondary Three Confucian Ethics textbook described the relationship between the ruler and the ruled using Confucius's analogy:

> The grass must bend when the wind blows across it. ... In other words, just as healthy green grass sways naturally and gracefully with the breeze, so good citizens will spontaneously respond to the good policies of virtuous leaders.
>
> (Grosse 1985a: 124)

The Secondary Four textbook goes further: 'Fulfilment begins with the cultivation of the individual self. ... The leaders must show the way. That is why the virtuous and able are elected to office' (Grosse 1985b: 92). No wonder Tu Wei-ming now disassociates himself from the revival movement that he helped to start (*Asian Wall Street Journal*, 28 May 1993).

The scholars of the PRC's revival find themselves in a similar position, with the added complication that some of them have academic positions in the PRC itself, which means that they cannot question, among other things, the leading role of the Party in China. These academics, whether from Asia, North America or Europe, have played crucial and very direct roles in the Confucian revival in China. Hu Jintao's strategic decision to use 'harmony' as the central conceptual tenet of his regime was itself the result of representations over a long period of time by Confucian scholars and 'think tanks' operating from within Chinese academic institutions.[2] Today scholars remain crucial to the development and perceived legitimacy of the Confucian revival, and scholars within China are routinely coopted into the government's overtly political Confucian programme. This involves not just scholars of Confucianism and related topics attending conferences on Confucianism and themes related to 'harmony' (of which there are many), but the whole academic community. The scope and dimensions of this programme was indicated in March 2005 when the city of Beijing announced that its eleventh Five-Year Plan would downplay economic growth for the first time in years, and would instead 'strive to achieve harmonious development' (*China Daily*, 31 March 2005). This shift of focus, together with the 'preliminary investigations' needed to begin giving distinct shape to this vague new direction involved over 600 researchers from 57 institutions: not just scholars of Confucianism and the humanities, but, according to *China Daily* (31 March 2005), specialists covering 'a wide range of local social and economic development issues, including industrial development, communications network construction, environmental protection, heritage preservation and social security'. This academic involvement is a form of cooption, but in saying this I do not wish to imply passivity or unilateral submission on the part of these academics. Whether they are scholars of Confucian ethics or Harvard-trained civil engineers, the academics that are proactively contributing to Hu Jintao's 'harmonious society' are generally operating self-consciously from a desire to contribute to the common good. They see themselves in the mode of the classical Confucian scholarly advisers to government, and insofar as they have an agenda to influence government, it is most likely to be one that idealises a humane, beneficent government. The fact that an authoritarian regime is able to cherry pick its way through this academic discourse to find the bits that suit its own agenda is generally accepted with equanimity.

Social Confucianism

The aspects of Confucianism that have been canvassed thus far are easily the most public and quantifiable elements of Confucianism as a factor in politics, but perhaps the most significant in terms of endurance, consistency and profundity is the more mercurial aspect of Confucianism's impact on the political cultures of the countries that come under its influence: aspects that are identified by Lowell Dittmer, Haruhiro Fukui and Peter N.S. Lee (2000) as the 'informal politics' of East Asia, and described in their volume as 'interpersonal activities stemming from a tacitly accepted, but unenunciated, matrix of political attitudes existing outside the framework of legal government, constitutions, bureaucratic constructs and similar institutions (the latter being the domain of formal politics)' (Pike 2000: 281). It is remarkable, for instance,

how easily the resonance of Confucianism can be identified in the familial and social actions of generations of nationalist, communist and post-communist Chinese, who have tended to remain locked in Confucian patterns of thought and habit, often despite their conscious intentions. Even in matters of statecraft, the legacy of Confucianism still flourishes just below the surface throughout East Asia. In Vietnam, not only has the politics of the educated Mandarinate been reproduced under the guise of the Leninist bureaucratic state, but centuries-old Vietnamese classics on the art of Confucian statecraft have been re-published and have enjoyed a major resurgence (Woodside 1999). Even during the worst barbarities of Mao Zedong's rule, Maoist political rituals and education replaced only the dogma of Confucianism: it retained the template in which the dogma lived. The Confucian emphasis on personal virtue [de] was retained, but it was aligned according to 'redness' and revolutionary purity, rather than to the virtues of the Confucian gentleman (Shirk 1982: 1–23). And when the concept of 'good' and 'bad' class replaced that of lineage, one's class was still determined by the traditional method: patrilineal descent (Stockman 2000: 83–134). A strong, almost tangible tribute to Confucianism's perseverance is the fact that China's modern student-dissidents of the 1980s and 1990s, who grew up decades after Confucianism's supposed eradication, constructed their dissent according to classical Confucian precepts, and operated substantially according to Confucian expectations of how scholarly dissidents should act. This included presenting deferential petitions to the rulers, and holding their worker and merchant allies in contempt (Perry and Fuller 1991: 667–71). Perhaps it is just as extraordinary that the Communist Party leadership also followed Confucian patterns of action when dealing with these students: receiving students' petitions relatively graciously, and showing relative leniency towards the scholar-dissidents, but attacking worker-dissidents savagely. On one occasion Jiang Zemin (then Mayor of Shanghai) apologised for police brutality against a student, explaining that police had mistaken the student for a worker (Perry 1992: 155).

A survey of the rest of East Asia elicits a similar picture, though without the extremes found in China. In Korea, Japan, Taiwan, Hong Kong and Singapore, the formal study and practice of Confucianism died during the twentieth century, as it variously faced the challenges of modernity, Christianity, capitalism and communism. Yet in all these cases the low cultural influence of Confucianism is overt and inescapable at all levels of society and governance – though admittedly it is sometimes difficult to distinguish between the influences of Confucianism *per se* and Confucianism's various accommodations with local cultures. It is surely not a coincidence that China, Vietnam, Japan (at least as it operated until 1993) (Koh 1989) and Singapore are all governed by Mandarinates that are basically distorted versions of the traditional Confucian Mandarinates of old. One of the differences between the old Mandarinate and the new is that today the personnel staffing the Mandarinates and advising governments are generally not *junzi*, schooled in Confucian humanism as verified in Confucian examinations, but engineers, scientists, lawyers, doctors, town planners and other professionals.

Let me be clear that I am not attempting to paint a two-dimensional picture of supposedly 'Confucian East Asians' reacting in Pavlovian fashion to stimuli according to an equally two-dimensional view of 'Confucian culture'. Hopefully such distorted pictures died with the 'Asian Values' discourses of the early 1990s. I am actually arguing a much more modest case: that popular, grassroots assumptions of 'good' that have survived persecution and attacks

from a myriad of modern and pre-modern enemies continue to inform constituencies at all levels of these societies. This affects how these constituencies expect members of their societies to behave – including their political leaders, their students and their academics. Not only are political leaders influenced directly by the same expectations, but they also have an incentive to be seen to be meeting those expectations.

Most of this chapter has focused on authoritarian uses of political Confucianism, but at the level of social Confucianism, 'Confucian' democracies need also to be considered. Scholarly opinion is severely divided over how social Confucianism is affecting the development and stability of democracies in East Asia, with some, such as Park and Shin (2006), arguing from the results of sociological surveys conducted in South Korea, that the Confucian influence is on balance a negative one. Specifically, they identify Confucianism's hierarchical view of social relations, its emphasis on social harmony, and its privileging of the group over the individual and on social unity and order ahead of pluralism and diversity as aspects of Confucianism that mitigate against democratic processes. They argue that these factors discourage criticism of leaders and encourage meek compliance with authority and that the key to the entrenchment of democracy in South Korea is the diminution of the influence of Confucianism.

Yet even these critics acknowledge that those surveyed who are attached to such values are generally 'supportive' of democracy and speculate that perhaps they merely have a 'conception of democracy [that] differs from the notion of Western-style democracy', and that they might 'equate democracy with good governance [which to them] seems not so much liberal as communitarian' (Park and Shin 2006: 360–1). Chung Oknim (1999: 105–6) argued precisely this point in the early years of South Korea's experiment with democracy:

> [The South Korean] notion of what is 'humane', 'just' and 'moral' is still governed by Confucianism. The family orientation witnessed in the business practices of *chaebol* [conglomerates], formalistic decision-making, and emphasis on 'moral politics' rather than democracy based on self-interest, compromise, and the rules of the game – these are all Confucian as well as South Korean ideals.

Hence, South Koreans, despite thinking and talking of liberal democracy as their governing principle, actually behave in accordance with the Confucian influence of the past.

L.H.M. Ling and Chih-yu Shih argued the same case, using newly democratic Taiwan as their example:

> Politicians may hinge their moral leadership on appearance more than fact, rhetoric more than action. But mass and elite alike demand a ritualized demonstration of selflessness for the common good as the critical standard for public office.
>
> (Ling and Shih 1998: 69)

Given the hierarchical, elitist, communitarian and conservative character of Confucianism, it does seem likely that Park and Shin will be proved correct when they argue that Confucianism's influence on democracy is unlikely to be a positive one, but there is nevertheless ample evidence that democracy can accommodate itself to Confucian societies, and vice versa, producing forms of democracy that are genuinely democratic while still being distinctively 'Confucian' in character. The experience of post-war Japan provides a strong piece of evidence in this regard.

Japan has been a democracy of sorts since the Americans ended their post-war occupation. From very soon after its inception it was based on rule by a dominant, hegemonic party (the Liberal-Democratic Party, LDP) that monopolised the networks of patronage and which employed an easily manipulated electoral system that rivalled England's old 'rotten boroughs'. In 1993 democracy took a step forward when a split in the ruling party forced a change of government, but even then it was only a year before the LDP was back as the dominant party in a new coalition. Since then the LDP's hegemony has been maintained substantially by a system of patronage underpinned by largess dispensed through the Post Office Savings Bank, but even this has been dismantled by former Prime Minister Koizumi Junichiro, confirming a pattern of systematic, if slow, improvement in the quality of the country's democracy. So despite being in a substantially Confucian culture, Japan has maintained a recognisable, if flawed, system of democratic governance for half a century. Furthermore this Confucian society has improved its system of democracy, gradually removing sources of systemic abuse. One can reasonably doubt whether Confucianism played any active part in this developmental process, but it is unquestionably evidence of the compatibility of democracy and a Confucian culture.

The adaptation of democracy into a Confucian culture is neither mysterious nor profound. Just as different Western cultures have developed different democratic cultures that reflect, for instance, a spirit of individualism (such as in the US) or a culture of consensus (such as in Scandinavia), East Asian democracies are acculturating democracy to suit the proclivities of their societies. This is in the nature of democracies. If constituencies in a democracy expect, for instance, the Confucian virtues of consensus, harmony and deference to those in authority, then of course politicians will be seen to be trying to deliver it (Barr 2002: 64–71).

Conclusion

In this survey we set out to examine the role of Confucianism in politics through the prisms of the political elites, scholars and social Confucianism. Through this tripartite approach we hoped to find answers to the questions that Fox (2001: 61–7) asked about religions more generally: religion as a direct influence on policy-makers; religion as an indirect influence on policy-makers; and religion as a tool of legitimation for governments and for those who oppose them. It is clear that in all three forms, Confucianism continues to influence the conduct of politics in Chinese and East Asian societies. This can be seen most clearly in the recent history of China and Singapore, where the elite manipulation of Confucianism for political ends and legitimation is most overt, but it is also apparent in the 'informal' politics of South Korea, Taiwan, Japan and Vietnam because of the strength of social Confucianism. Political rulers of all hues can be expected to continue their efforts to exploit Confucianism for their own ends, though it seems to be authoritarian rulers who find the most sustenance in Confucianism – reflecting its conservative, elitist roots. Yet despite its anti-democratic tendencies, scholars, democratic politicians and the grassroots of Confucian societies find Confucianism and democracy to be companionable bedfellows, able to live comfortably in the one culture and the one polity.

Notes

1 The list of project participants is available in Grosse (1985a, 1985b, 1985c and 1985d).

2 This information was conveyed in private correspondence by a Confucian scholar from a Chinese university, confirming what he had earlier indicated in an academic workshop in Hong Kong in June 2006. At the request of the organisers of the workshop I am not at liberty to give more details at this stage.

Bibliography

Ackerly, B. (2005) 'Is liberalism the only way toward democracy? Confucianism and democracy', *Political Theory*, 33(4), pp. 547–76.

Barr, M. (2000) *Lee Kuan Yew: The Beliefs Behind the Man*, Richmond: Curzon.

Barr, M. (2001) 'Medical savings accounts in Singapore: a critical inquiry', *Journal of Health Politics, Policy and Law*, 26(3), pp. 707–24.

Barr, M. (2002) *Cultural Politics and Asian Values: The Tepid War*, Routledge Advances in Asia–Pacific Studies, 6, London and New York: Routledge.

Barr, M. (2006a) 'The charade of meritocracy', *Far Eastern Economic Review*, October, pp. 18–22.

Barr, M. (2006b) 'Beyond technocracy: the culture of elite governance in Lee Hsien Loong's Singapore', *Asian Studies Review*, 30(1), pp. 1–17.

Barr, Michael D. and Jevon Low (2005) 'Assimilation as multiracialism: the case of Singapore's Malays', *Asian Ethnicity*, 6(3), pp. 161–82.

Chua Beng Huat (1995) *Communitarian Ideology and Democracy in Singapore*, London and New York: Routledge.

Chung Oknim (1999) 'Values, governance, and international relations: the case of South Korea', in Han Sung-Joo (ed.), *Changing Values in Asia: Their Impact on Government and Development*, Singapore: Institute of Southeast Asian Studies; Tokyo and New York: Japan Center for International Exchange, pp. 76–111.

de Bary, W. (1998) *Asian Values and Human Rights: A Confucian Communitarian Perspective*, Cambridge, Massachusetts, and London: Harvard University Press.

Dittmer, L., Haruhiro Fukui and P. Lee (eds) (2000) *Informal Politics in East Asia*, Cambridge: Cambridge University Press.

Fox, J. (2001) 'Religion as an overlooked element of International Relations', *International Studies Review*, 3(3): 53–73.

Goh Keng Swee (1977) *The Practice of Economic Growth*, Singapore; Kuala Lumpur; Hong Kong: Federal Publications.

Government of Singapore (1991) *White Paper: Shared Values*, Singapore: Singapore Government.

Grosse, P. (ed.) (1985a) *Confucian Ethics: Textbook Secondary Three*, Singapore: EPB Publishers.

Grosse, P. (ed.) (1985b) *Confucian Ethics: Textbook Secondary Four*, Singapore: EPB Publishers.

Grosse, P. (ed.) (1985c) *Confucian Ethics: Workbook Secondary Three*, Singapore: EPB Publishers.

Grosse, P. (ed.) (1985d) *Confucian Ethics: Workbook Secondary Four*, Singapore: EPB Publishers.

Koh, B.C. (1989) *Japan's Administrative Elite*, Berkeley; Los Angeles; Oxford: University of California Press.

Ling, L.H.M. and Chih-yu Shih (1998) 'Confucianism with a Liberal face: the meaning of democratic politics in postcolonial Taiwan', *Review of Politics*, 60(1), pp. 52–82.

Mauzy, D. and R.S. Milne (2002) *Singapore's Politics under the People's Action Party*, London and New York: Routledge.

Ng, On-cho (1999) 'Negotiating the boundary between hermeneutics and philosophy in early Ch'ing Ch'eng-chu Confucianism: Li Kuang-ti's (1642–1718) *Study of the* Doctrine of the Mean (*Chung-yung*) *and* Great Learning (Ta-hsueh), in Kai-wing Chow, On-cho Ng and John B. Henderson (eds), *Imagining Boundaries*, Albany, NY: State University of New York Press, pp. 165–93.

Park, Chong-min and Doh Chull Shin (2006) 'Do Asian values deter popular support for democracy in South Korea?', *Asian Survey*, 46(3), pp. 341–61.

Perry, E. (1992) 'Casting a Chinese "democracy" movement: the roles of students, workers, and entrepreneurs', in J. Wasserstrom and E. Perry, *Popular Protest and Political Culture in Modern China: Learning from 1989*, Boulder: Westview Press, pp. 146–64.

Perry, E. and E. Fuller (1991) 'China's long march to democracy', *World Policy Journal*, 8, pp. 663–85.

Pike, D. (2000) 'Informal politics in Vietnam', in L. Dittmer, Haruhiro Fukui and P. Lee (eds), *Informal Politics in East Asia*, Cambridge: Cambridge University Press, pp. 269–89.

Shirk, S. (1982) *Competitive Comrades: Career Incentives and Student Strategies in China*, Berkeley: University of California Press.

Stockman, N. (2000) *Understanding Chinese Society*, Cambridge: Polity Press.

Tremewan, Christopher (1994) *The Political Economy of Social Control in Singapore*, London: Macmillan Press; New York: St Martin's Press.

Tu Wei-ming (1984) *Confucian Ethics Today: The Singapore Challenge*, Singapore: Curriculum Development Centre of Singapore and Federal Publications.

Turner, B. (2006), 'Religion and politics: nationalism, globalisation and empire', *Asian Journal of Social Science*, 34(2), pp. 209–24.

Woodside, A. (1999) 'Exalting the latecomer state: intellectuals and the state during the Chinese and Vietnamese reforms', in A. Chan, B. Kerkvliet and J. Unger (eds), *Transforming Asian Socialism: China and Vietnam Compared*, Sydney: Allen & Unwin, pp. 15–42.

Xu, Keqian (2006) 'Early Confucian principles: the potential theoretical foundation of democracy in modern China', *Asian Philosophy*, 16(2), pp. 135–48.

6

Hinduism

James Chiriyankandath

Introduction: the uniqueness of Hinduism

As a religion Hinduism stands out. Of all the great world faiths, Hinduism is the one that is the most geographically focused, both in terms of its sacred topography and the concentration of its adherents in the Indian subcontinent. All the sacred sites of Hinduism are located within the subcontinent as are over 98 per cent of Hindus (O'Brien and Palmer 1993: 24–25). In this respect it is profoundly unlike the great monotheist and universal faiths of Semitic origin, Christianity and Islam. Yet it also does not possess either the singularity of their precursor, Judaism, with which it shares the sense of a specific sacred homeland, or its geographical dispersion (the majority of the world's Jews continue to live outside Israel).

In claiming no single founder and possessing no scriptural canon, Hinduism is different from Zoroastrianism, the other living religion of Indo-Aryan origins, as well as later Indic religions founded by great teachers or *gurus* – Buddhism, Jainism and Sikhism – or the religious traditions associated with Taoism or Confucianism. While it might resemble traditional African, American, Australian and other aboriginal belief systems in its variety, it is set apart by factors such as its written traditions and the overarching subcontinental unity imparted by the hierarchically complex social institution of caste. In this sense it is not so much a religion as a body of philosophy, ritual and social practice that has evolved in a particular geographical region and come to be interpreted in a world of religions as one.

An important distinction between Hinduism and the other contemporary world religions is what has variously been described as its 'inclusiveness' (Lannoy 1971: 227) or its uniquely 'capacious' character (Sen 2005: 49). This uniqueness is significant in considering the relationship of Hinduism to politics because it endows it with features that are peculiar to the Indian situation. On the one hand, its bewildering variety can make the political influence of Hinduism seem pervasive. Yet, paradoxically, its very plurality appears to limit its capacity to dominate politics. The modern politics of 'Hindutva' (Hindu-ness) can thus be seen as an attempt to overcome the historically well-established 'broad and generous' Hinduism (Sen 2005: 49) that has been seen as an obstruction to the kind of unilinear social and institutional development witnessed in the West (Lannoy 1971: 227; Saberwal 1996: 3).

This chapter shall explore the changing political role of Hinduism. It will begin by examining how it came to be recognised as a religion and its significance in pre-colonial India. Subsequent sections will consider the use of 'Hindu' identity in post-independence India, the impact it has had on contemporary Indian politics and the future for Hinduism in politics.

The construction of 'Hinduism'

Hinduism may be defined and understood as denoting the spiritual beliefs and rituals associated with the Indian subcontinent rather than as a singular, organised religious system. While its origins predated the Indo-Aryan invasion of the Indus Valley in the northwest early in the second millennium BCE, it was Aryan religion that imparted to it the characteristics now most distinctly associated with what the philosopher Sarvepalli Radhakrishnan, the second President of the Republic of India, called the 'Idea of Hinduism' (Radhakrishnan 1937: 256). The *Rig Veda*, the oldest of the four main *Vedas* (from the Sanskrit *vid*, to know), or collections of most sacred knowledge in the Indic tradition, was composed more than a millennium before the time of Christ. It is therefore the oldest of the religious scriptures of any living religious tradition, a point of pride for contemporary Hindu nationalists.

The *Upanishads* followed the *Vedas* and are therefore also known as *Vedanta* – the end of the *Vedas*. Numbering over a hundred texts concerned with the ultimate dual search for the eternal self (*atman*) and the eternal universe (*brahman*), they represented the end of the *sruti*, literally hearing (the eternal word heard by the sages of antiquity) and were followed by the more amorphous *smrti*, or texts of memory. The latter include the philosophic *Sutras*, books on *dharma* (maintaining the natural order of the universe), the *Puranas* (mythologies extolling one or other great deity) and the well-known epics of the *Mahabharatha* and the *Ramayana*. The *Mahabharatha* relates the story of the victory of the Pandavas over the Kauravas in a struggle involving all of India and includes the *Bhagavad Gita* (Lord's Song), a dialogue on righteous action between Arjuna, the Pandava warrior, and Krishna, his charioteer and the incarnation of the Vedic god Vishnu. The *Ramayana* narrates the story of Ram, the righteous heir to the throne of the kingdom of Ayodhya who in the Sanskrit rendition of Valmiki heroically rescues his kidnapped wife Sita and defeats Ravana, the demon king of Lanka, to return to his kingdom in triumph.

The responsibility of the ruler to protect the *dharma* became central to the Indian idea of kingship – an idea until very recent preserved in neighbouring Nepal where the 1990 Constitution defined it as a Hindu kingdom of which the monarch is 'an adherent of Aryan culture and the Hindu religion' (http://www.nepalgov.gov.np/sambhidan/6.pdf). Indeed, scholars such as K.M. Panikkar discern in the dualism between *dharma* and *artha* (worldly wisdom) the basis for a Hindu conception of 'a purely secular theory of state of which the sole basis is power' (Panikkar quoted in Murty 1967: 136). Yet in India in the past century the phrase Ram *rajya* (the rule of Ram) has acquired a religious connotation, being widely used in politics – from Mahatma Gandhi in the campaign for Indian independence to Hindu nationalists today – to denote just and righteous government. (That the Ram story retains a powerful resonance was dramatically illustrated in the 1980s and 1990s by the political reverberations set off by the campaign to construct a Ram temple at his legendary birthplace in Ayodhya, and the 1991 general election manifesto of the Hindu nationalist Bharatiya Janata Party (BJP) was entitled 'Towards Ram Rajya'.)

Nevertheless, the alternative versions of the *Ramayana* that exist emphasise the plural character of Hinduism, a feature that has inhibited its utility as a basis for modern Hindu nationalism. This is not to gainsay the crucial role played by the Indic religious tradition in imparting a sense of unity to the subcontinent, one particularly notable from the perspective of the Brahmanical Hinduism associated with Shankara, the ninth-century CE religious teacher who founded the school of *Advaita* [non-dualist or monist] *Vedanta* and the four great *mathas* (seminaries), each headed by a Shankaracharya who continues to command widespread respect and authority. Significant in embedding that authority has been the social institution that India is best known for: caste.

Even though the hierarchical ancient Aryan Vedic classification of Indian society was based on *varna* (Sanskrit – colour), it was the Portuguese who, from the fifteenth century CE, applied the Spanish–Portuguese word *casta* (pure or chaste), used by the Spanish to refer to race, to describe the social divisions encountered on the subcontinent. Over the past five hundred years the idea of caste has changed. It has acquired new meanings and significance and shed old connotations.

Two related concepts that are central to unravelling caste are *varna* and *jati*. The Vedic division of society into four *varnas* first encountered in the *Rig Veda* – Brahmins (priests), *Kshatriyas* (warriors/rulers), *Vaisyas* (merchants) and *Sudras* (cultivators) – reflects a notional ideal typology. What actually operates locally throughout the subcontinent is *jati* (Hindi – birth group) and there are thousands of endogamous *jatis*, based on a variety of elements, most notably kinship and occupation. The position of the latter is not static – *jatis* can move up and down the *varna* hierarchy over time, depending on wealth and control over resources (especially land), and through the process the sociologist M.N. Srinivas called 'Sanskritisation', achieving upward mobility by changing ritual and social practices (1969: 6). The intensification of spatial communications (roads, railways etc.), and the spread of a subcontinental administrative system, helped consolidate local *jatis* into regional *jatis*, usually based on linguistic areas. The most important element in bringing this about was the British colonial preoccupation with classifying and ordering *jatis*, a concern that matched the stress laid on differentiating between followers of different religions and manifested in ethnographical surveys, census reports and administrative classifications. In post-independence India the role of caste as the basis for political mobilisation has been further reinforced by the conjunction of mass democratic politics with the official recognition accorded it in terms of the reservation of seats in legislatures, administrative jobs and educational places for historically disadvantaged low castes.

In many ways it was the European 'discovery' of Hinduism that created the modern idea of it as one religious tradition to be interpreted and understood as such – 'a Hinduism in their own image' (Marshall 1970: 43). This perception influenced subsequent Indian thinkers but they were also more aware of the difference between the legacy of Hinduism and that of the great monotheist religions. For instance, Radhakrishnan not only interpreted Jainism, Buddhism and Sikhism as reform movements 'from within the fold of Hinduism' but added that 'Zoroastrianism, Islam, and Christianity have been so long in the country that they have become native to the soil and are deeply influenced by the atmosphere of Hinduism' (Radhakrishnan 1937: 259). The fact that the perception and operation of caste is found in some form among people of almost all religious backgrounds in India is the most striking testimony to this.

Paradoxically, the persistence, prevalence and mutation of caste represent a formidable obstacle to the attempt to create a singular Hindu nationalism on the basis of Hinduism. It might even be argued that it is the overarching phenomenon of caste that has made possible the modern Indian adaptation of liberal-democratic government. It has provided a common frame of reference for social groups right across the hierarchy, from the Brahmins at the apex to the so-called Untouchables (now commonly referred to as Dalits) at the bottom, to progressively mobilise to access the novel institutions of democracy. So, despite its intrinsically anti-democratic nature, the history and consciousness of caste created a shared sense of a bounded social universe within which people from competing groups competed to appropriate the democratic institutions to their needs and purposes. The six decades since India's independence have thus seen the country's democracy undergo a messy process of democratisation – a 'silent revolution' in the making, transferring power from upper-caste elites to the traditionally underprivileged (Jaffrelot 2003: 494).

'Hindu' identity and modern politics

The idea of Hinduism developed in parallel with that of nationalism in India through the nineteenth and twentieth centuries. The Hindu social reform movements that arose in British India, beginning with Raja Ram Mohun Roy's Brahmo Samaj founded in Bengal in 1828, helped form the intellectual climate in which a nascent western-educated predominantly upper caste and urban middle class began to inculcate notions of national political identity and self-government. One movement that gave this process a more militant edge was the Arya Samaj, founded by Dayanand Saraswati in Punjab in 1875, less than two decades after the 1857 uprising against the spread of British dominion. Unlike the Brahmo Samaj, which derived much of its inspiration from combining Christian ethics and rationalist ideas with the philosophy contained in the

Upanishads, the latter aggressively asserted the need to return to the *Vedas* to create a rejuvenated Hinduism free of alien accretions, able to effectively counter Christian and Muslim proselytisation and yet modern in its organisation, methods and commitment to education.

The overlap of Hindu reform and nascent Indian nationalism was visible in the membership and leadership of the Indian National Congress that held its first meeting in Bombay in 1885. Leading personalities in the pre-First World War Congress such as Mahadev Ranade and Gopal Krishna Gokhale in the Bombay Presidency, the Brahmo Samajist Bipin Chandra Pal in Bengal and the Arya Samajist Lala Lajpat Rai in Punjab all began their public careers as social reformers. Others, most notably Bal Gangadhar Tilak in Bombay, combined a robust defence of what they perceived as orthodox Hindu *sanatana dharma* (eternal religion) – the caste system, child marriage and *purdah* (the seclusion of women) – with militant nationalism. However, the lines of political divisions did not necessarily coincide with social attitudes. For instance, when Congress temporarily split between 'Moderates' and 'Extremists', Chandra Pal and Lajpat Rai were found together with Tilak in the latter camp, the consequence, at least in part, of the regional social and political differences between western India and Punjab and Bengal.

The way in which religious sentiment imbued the more radical manifestations of Indian nationalism was seen in the adoption of *Vande Mataram* (Hymn to the Mother), a poem composed by Bankim Chandra Chatterjee and first published in his novel *Anandamath* in 1881, as the political cry of the movement against the British partition of Bengal in 1905. After independence the Indian Constituent Assembly eventually made it the national song. That it did not become the national anthem – Rabindranath Tagore's 'Jana gana mana' was preferred – was due to the longstanding objections of many Muslims and others that its evocation of India as motherland was idolatrous and distinctly Hindu in tenor:

In the arm thou art might, O Mother,
In the heart, O Mother, thou art love and faith,
It is thy image we raise in every temple.
For thou art [the goddess] Durga holding her ten weapons of war.
(Bhattacharya 2003: 101)

The poem continues to stir political passions. In 1998 the general election manifesto of the BJP highlighted *Vande Mataram* in deprecating what it described as the post-independence tendency to reject pre-independence values and symbols based on ancient Indian wisdom as 'unsecular and unacceptable' (BJP 1998). Shortly afterwards the BJP state government in Uttar Pradesh issued a directive, later withdrawn after public protests, requiring the daily recitation of the poem in government-aided schools.

With the rise of Mahatma Gandhi to the leadership of Congress in the years immediately after the First World War, the connection between religion and Indian nationalism found its most striking embodiment. The transformation of Congress into much more of a mass movement over the next decades was marked by his use of the language and symbolism of religion to imbue it with a popular character. While this was not exclusively Hindu (Congress under Gandhi adopted the Indian Muslim Khilafat movement to defend the status of the Ottoman Caliph in 1920–22), it came to be widely perceived as predominantly so, especially by Muslims. Gandhi's own proclaimed personal commitment to the equality of all religions (Gandhi 1980: 84) – he regularly read texts from the Bible, the Koran and the Sikh Granth Sahib, as well as from the *Bhagavad Gita*, in the daily prayer meetings held in his ashram – and the fact that his close followers included people from diverse religious backgrounds, could not dispel this impression.

The Gandhian approach to politics and religion was actively opposed by radical campaigners against the oppression and discrimination of the caste system such as Dr B.R. Ambedkar, for nearly three decades the leading champion of the cause of the outcaste Untouchables who constituted close to an eighth of the population, and Ramaswamy Naicker, who launched the anti-Brahmin Dravidian (Tamil) Self-Respect Movement in south India in 1925. While Gandhi himself vigorously opposed the stigmatisation and discrimination associated with the observance of caste distinctions, calling the Untouchables '*Harijans*', or people of God, he nevertheless accepted the fourfold *Varnashrama dharma* as Vedic and 'inherent in human nature' (Gandhi 1980: 15). Another perspective from which the Gandhian position came under criticism was from secular modernisers such as Jawaharlal Nehru, independent India's first prime minister from 1947 to 1964, who felt that organised religion produced 'narrowness and intolerance, credulity and superstition, emotionalism and irrationalism' (Nehru 1961: 513).

Nehru was conscious that his was a minority viewpoint not only within the country but also within Congress, where Gandhians and Hindu majoritarians of various shades were far more common. But the most uncompromising Hindu chauvinists were found outside the capacious folds of the Congress cloak. Two organisations in particular sought to promote a distinctly Hindu nationalism. The first was the *Hindu Mahasabha*, initiated mainly by Punjabi Arya Samajists in 1915 and including among its early leaders prominent Congressmen like Lajpat Rai and Madan Mohan Malaviya. Its chief ideologist was Veer Damodar Savarkar, its president from 1937 to 1943. A onetime follower of Tilak, in 1923, while exiled by the British to a penal colony in the Andaman Islands, he published *Hindutva. Who Is a Hindu* which defined a Hindu as a person who 'looks upon the land that extends ... from the Indus to the Seas ... as his Fatherland (*Pitribhu*) ... as his Holyland (*Punyabhu*), as the land of his prophets and seers, of his godmen and gurus, the land of piety and pilgrimage' (Savarkar quoted in Gottlob 2003: 154–155). Politically no match for the National Congress, the Mahasabha was banned after the assassination of Gandhi in 1948 by a onetime member, Nathuram Godse. Despite the subsequent acquittal of Savarkar of complicity, it then effectively disappeared as a political force with many of its members joining the Bharatiya Jana Sangh (Indian People's Organisation) founded in 1951.

The second organisation, the *Rashtriya Swayamsevak Sangh* (National Volunteer Organisation) (RSS), was started in 1925 in Nagpur in what is now the state of Maharashtra in western India and proved more resilient and significant. Founded by K.B. Hedgewar, a Brahmin doctor, and led for more than three decades during its formative phase by his successor, M.S. Golwalkar, known as *Guruji* (teacher), it concentrated on a wide spread of cultural and social activity and what it saw as building up a distinct, strong, martial Hindu ethos. Closely associated with the Mahasabha in the 1930s and 1940s, it was not uncommon to find men, like Gandhi's assassin, who had been members of both. However, while also temporarily banned in 1948–49, the distance it kept from direct involvement in party politics facilitated its steady growth into what by the 1980s was a formidable force in Indian public life. At the beginning of the 1990s it claimed over three million members, organised in thousands of *shakhas* (branches) across India guided in each region by

pracharaks (celibate full-time propagandists), as well as a network of linked organisations known collectively as the *sangh parivar* (organisational family). The latter included the second biggest national students and labour federations, as well as a multiplicity of political, religious cultural, intellectual, social service, cooperative, peasants and women's bodies.

The independence of India in 1947, in the wake of the traumatic partition of the subcontinent and the creation of Pakistan as a separate homeland for Muslims, left aspirations for a distinctly Hindu nationhood unrealised. Despite the Hindu sympathies of many Congressmen, the 1950 Constitution was, in large measure, couched in secular terms, notwithstanding features such as statutory provisions reserving seats in legislatures and shares in public jobs and educational institutions for low-caste people, and empowering the state to open all Hindu religious institutions to all classes of Hindus. It was against this backdrop that the Jana Sangh was launched in 1951 with the object of 'the rebuilding of Bharat [India] on the basis of Bharatiya "*Sanskriti*" [culture] and "*Maryada*" [rectitude]' (Graham 1993: 51).

RSS activists formed the bulk of the leadership and activists of the new party and over the next twenty years it was mainly in the Hindi-speaking states of central and northern India, where the RSS and the Hindu Mahasabha had a history of strength, that it made the greatest electoral inroads, campaigning on issues such as the banning of the slaughter of cows, sacred to Hindus, the promotion of Hindi as India's sole official language, the appeasement of minorities and the Indian claim to Kashmir. The Jana Sangh registered a high-water mark of 35 of 520 parliamentary seats and 9.4 per cent of the vote in the 1967 general election (Graham 1993: 261–262). In 1977 it merged with a broad range of other non-communist opposition parties opposed to form a *Janata* (People's) coalition that defeated the Congress Party but the merger was short-lived with controversy over the RSS connection resulting, following the Janata defeat in 1980, in the exit of most of the erstwhile Jana Sangh group to form the new BJP.

Hindu nationalism in India since 1980

The BJP faced the same challenge as its predecessor – how to translate the notional overwhelming Hindu majority in India into the electoral basis for a Hindu nationalist takeover of the state? According to the 2001 census, 80.5 per cent of the more than a billion Indians were Hindu, 13.4 per cent Muslim, 2.3 per cent Christian, 1.9 per cent Sikh, 0.8 per cent Buddhist and 1.1 per cent others. Hindus are not in the majority in only 6 of the 28 states and only in 6 others do non-Hindus even constitute as much as a quarter of the population. Yet despite a century of effort at developing a distinct Hindu political identity, Indians remain stubbornly plural in their political, religious and social identities.

Not only are Hindus differentiated by language, region and attachment to particular local deities, as well as by other significant social markers such as class and education, the Indian Constitution actually recognises a third of Hindus separately as belonging to the Scheduled Castes – the erstwhile Untouchables or *Dalits* (oppressed) (16 per cent of the total population) or Scheduled Tribes (8 per cent). The remainder can also be variously grouped as upper caste (17 per cent) or Other Backward Classes (OBC), another administratively recognised category (43 per cent) (Mandal 1980). When taken together with the complex system of locally or regionally discrete *jatis*, this represents a formidable obstacle to the creation of a singular Hindu political identity. However, in the space of less than a decade

the BJP succeeded in moving from the political periphery to becoming the main party in a coalition government that ruled India for six years. This section shall discuss how it was able to do so and what this tells us about the contemporary political significance of Hinduism.

Several factors made the theme of giving a more distinctly 'Hindu' hue to national identity central to Indian politics in the 1980s and 1990s. First, there was, after Indira Gandhi's return to power in 1980, the increasing exploitation by the Congress Party of the ambiguity of Indian secularism for the political use of religion, especially in the form of populist invocations of a majority Hindu identity. This was manifested in the use of the mass media, particularly television, to cultivate a more homogenised national ethos – a Hinduism redefined as 'an ideology for modernization' (Thapar 1989: 23). The trend continued under Mrs Gandhi's son and successor, Rajiv Gandhi. Most strikingly, in 1988 and 1989, Doordarshan, the state television network, broadcast hugely popular soap operas based on essentially Brahminical versions of the Hindu epics of the *Ramayana* and *Mahabharatha*.

One reason for the movement away from the more secular attitude espoused by Mrs Gandhi's father, Jawaharlal Nehru, lay in the steady decline of Congress as a mass political institution at a time when its authority was under increasing challenge not only from the Hindu right but also low-caste and regional parties – the outcome of the process of the steady 'democratisation' of the Indian polity previously referred to, with the rise of social groups and regions hitherto not directly represented in the political arena. The political and personal insecurity, which had pushed Mrs Gandhi towards reforming Congress into a personality-based vote-gathering machine, facilitated such a shift. One factor was the increasingly strident, even violent, separatist demands on the part of some non-Hindus in peripheral regions, which culminated in the descent into effective civil war of border states like Assam, Punjab and Kashmir. This was itself to some degree the consequence of short-term Congress stratagems involving the exploitation of communal divisions. For instance, in Punjab Congress leaders initially promoted the radical Sikh preacher and inspiration for the Khalistani separatists, Sant Jarnail Singh Bhindranwale, in order to undermine its chief rival, the Akali Dal, the Sikh regional party.

Another element fostering the growth of Hindu nationalism at this stage in India's development was the liberalisation of the economy, initiated in half-hearted fashion in the 1980s and adopted more wholeheartedly by the minority Congress government of P.V. Narasimha Rao in the wake of the balance of payments crisis of 1991. Some of the repercussions of the economic changes initiated by liberalisation facilitated the growing appeal of a kind of 'syndicated Hinduism' (Thapar 1990: 31) upon which Hindu nationalism could draw, especially among the burgeoning sector of urban middle-class consumers who have been the primary beneficiaries of India's recent economic growth. As one commentator put it, the 'overlap between the narratives of communal and consumer identity formation' (Rajgopal 1996: 341), together with the rapid expansion of electronic communication (the proliferation of satellite television channels, TV advertising and the spread of the internet) allowed for the emergence of a kind of retail Hindu identity that the Hindu nationalists were able to turn into a valuable political resource. At times, such as during the explosion of anti-Muslim violence in Gujarat in early 2002, it could become a powerfully malign force:

For the first time, persons of middle class background, including women, well dressed and driving from bazaar to bazaar, cooperated in the looting of Muslim-owned shops and businesses, providing cover for those breaking open television stores and cloth shops to take goods away. Revealed suddenly was the expanding urban middle class base for the majoritarian definition of the nation.

(Frankel 2005: 744)

It was the unprecedented mass mobilisation of Hindus in a movement launched in 1984 to construct a temple on the disputed site of a disused sixteenth-century mosque, the Babri Masjid, claimed as the legendary birthplace of the Ram in Ayodhya in the northern state of Uttar Pradesh, that was the most important factor in highlighting the appeal of Hindu nationalism. After having spent the first half of the 1980s in the political doldrums, the preparedness of the BJP to exploit the movement catapulted the party to centre stage. Despite being the product of the ructions in the shortlived Janata coalition over the association of the Jana Sangh group with the RSS, the BJP had begun as a party apparently less closely tied to the apron strings of the *sangh parivar*. It initially adopted the deliberately ill-defined concept of 'Gandhian Socialism' as its guiding philosophy but, following a dismal performance in the 1984 general election when it won just two of 542 parliamentary seats, this was effectively jettisoned. Under Lal Krishan Advani, who succeeded Atal Bihari Vajpayee as party president in 1986, the party drew closer to the RSS.

Before the 1989 general election the party's National Executive endorsed the Ram Janmabhoomi (Ram's birthplace) campaign, launched five years earlier by the Vishwa Hindu Parishad (VHP; the World Council of Hindus). (The VHP had been founded in 1964 on the initiative of the RSS's *Sarsanghchalak* (Supreme Guide), M.S. Golwalkar, in order to organise religious leaders to consolidate and strengthen Hindu society.) Advani and other BJP leaders attended Ram *shila pujas*, ritual ceremonies held across India to consecrate bricks to be used in building the Ram temple. On the eve of the November 1989 general election, a foundation-laying ceremony took place in Ayodhya. The communally vitiated atmosphere engendered by the Ram *shila* processions, together with widespread disenchantment with the Congress government and an electoral accommodation reached by the BJP with the other main non-communist opposition party, the Janata Dal, played a significant role in contributing to the remarkable advance recorded by the party.

It won 86 seats and 11.5 per cent of the popular vote, increasing this to 120 seats and 20.1 per cent in the subsequent mid-term poll in 1991 when the BJP assumed the position of the official opposition to the ruling Congress. In between the two polls Advani undertook a six-week, 10,000-kilometre Ram *rath yatra* (chariot journey) to Ayodhya in a van decorated in the style of the chariot of Arjuna in the *Mahabharatha* television serial. As with the Ram *shila* processions, the *rath yatra* sparked off an epidemic of communal rioting in which hundreds died. Again there was a striking correlation between where the BJP enjoyed greatest electoral success and the spread of communal violence (Chiriyankandath 1992: 68–69, 73).

The Ayodhya campaign sought to transcend caste and regional distinctions in emphasising a common Hindu, indeed national, objective. The BJP's 1991 manifesto, entitled *Towards Ram Rajya*, affirmed the construction of the Ram temple as a 'vindication [*sic*] of our cultural heritage and national self respect'. Yet the continuing significance of caste in Indian public life was highlighted by another controversy that came to a head in 1990. The shortlived National Front government of Prime Minister V.P. Singh adopted the

1980 Report of the Backward Classes Commission chaired by B.P. Mandal which had recommended the reservation of more than a quarter of all public service jobs for the OBC, the numerically large low castes not included in the Scheduled Castes and Tribes categories already guaranteed reserved jobs through constitutional provisions. This was strongly opposed by people from other castes, especially educated youth, who feared the impact on their own job prospects, and there was a wave of public protest including a rash of self-immolations by youths. Advani's *rath yatra* was designed in part to deflect the potential for embarrassment for the BJP in how to respond to Mandal without alienating either its bedrock support among upper-caste, educated, urban Hindus or the OBC who represented the single largest category of Hindus.

Communal tensions reached a fever pitch in December 1992 when Hindu militants unrestrained by the BJP state government of Uttar Pradesh, and in the presence of party leaders including Advani, destroyed the Babri Masjid. The nationwide communal violence that followed was the worst since partition, claiming at least two thousand lives, and led to both the RSS and VHP being temporarily banned. Although the intensity of the passion whipped up by the Ayodhya confrontation had hitherto paid rich political dividends for the BJP, in the years that followed the BJP's political strategy, recognising the logic of India's political demography, shifted steadily towards building a network of alliances with regional parties. This aimed at outflanking Congress by gaining strength in areas of the country, notably the south and east, where Hindu nationalism remained a peripheral force. The strategy proved remarkably successful. Despite continuing to trail Congress in the popular vote, adding merely 5 per cent to its share – still only a quarter of the electorate, it emerged as the largest single party in parliament in three successive elections (1996, 1998 and 1999), with 183 of 543 seats by 1999. This provided the platform for six years of BJP-led coalition government (the 1999–2004 National Democratic Alliance was supported by as many as 24 parties) from 1998 until its unexpected defeat at the hands of a rival Congress-led combination in 2004.

In government, the BJP under Prime Minister A.B. Vajpayee, like Advani a veteran of the RSS and a founder-member of the Jana Sangh, proved much more restrained than their rhetoric and agitational strategy of the early 1990s might have led observers to expect (Adeney and Saez 2005). For instance, controversial longstanding party manifesto commitments such as those to do away with separate Muslim and Christian personal law in favour of a uniform civil code, the pledge to build the Ram temple at Ayodhya and to revoke the special constitutional status of Jammu and Kashmir, were not acted upon. In addition, although early in the NDA's period of office there was a spate of attacks on Christian churches and missionaries by Hindu extremists and the BJP state government in Gujarat was widely censured for permitting a veritable anti-Muslim pogrom to take place in March 2002 in which some two thousand people died, much of India did not witness the kind of communal violence seen in the early 1990s. This apparent moderation may in part be ascribed to the need to retain the support of its regional coalition partners, many of which were sensitive to the reaction of their Muslim and other supporters. A desire not to alienate moderate voters, as well as foreign investors and business interests, by embarking on controversial policies that risked jeopardising both social stability and India's healthy economic growth may also be surmised to have played a role.

However, there were areas of policy where the Hindu nationalist agenda did make an impression on government policy. Most dramatic was India's public emergence as a nuclear power with the underground tests carried out in May 1998, just weeks after the BJP-led government had taken office (Chiriyankandath and Wyatt 2005). This represented the realisation of a long-held aim of the BJP and its precursor, the Jana Sangh, considered by the chief RSS ideologue, M.S. Golwalkar, to be a national imperative (Golwalkar 1980: 429). Yet, Vajpayee, after appearing to lead the country to the brink of war with Pakistan over cross-border attacks by Kashmiri Muslim militants in 2001 and 2002, ended his premiership by initiating a peace process with Pakistan.

Domestically, the main focus of Hindu nationalist attempts to bring about significant change came in the field of education under the direction of Murli Manohar Joshi, like Advani and Vajpayee a former president of the BJP who had been a member of the RSS since before independence. RSS members or sympathisers were appointed to leading positions in many national educational institutions and a wide-ranging programme of revising school textbooks, especially in history and the social sciences, in line with the Hindu nationalist narrative was attempted (Lall 2005). That it made only limited progress was not for want of trying but down to the difficulties of imposing such changes from the centre in the face of resolute opposition from the majority of state governments controlled by parties opposed to the Hindu nationalist agenda.

The 2004 defeat of the BJP-led coalition government was partly the consequence of its perceived indifference to people, especially among India's rural majority, who felt left out of the rapid growth of India's liberalised economy (the NDA's ill-advised campaign slogan, 'India Shining' appeared to reflect this indifference).

As one observer pithily put it, 'Among these "ordinary" citizens, the notion of "India Shining" only illuminated the darkness in which they lived' (Frankel 2005: 783). In the months after its election defeat the BJP demonstrated little of the discipline or cohesion associated with the RSS. Its veteran leaders, Vajpayee and Advani, both came under attack from more militant Hindu chauvinists and in 2005 Advani, who had succeeded Vajpayee as parliamentary leader and party president after the election, resigned from the latter post. This followed outspoken attacks on him by VHP and RSS leaders after a visit to Pakistan during which he controversially praised a 1947 speech in which Mohammed Ali Jinnah, the founder of Pakistan, had upheld secular principles. Although Advani remains the BJP's leader in parliament, and therefore its projected prime ministerial candidate in the next general elections, he is now (2008) already over 80 and the party lacks any younger leaders of national stature with a significant power base except for Narendra Modi, the controversial Chief Minister of Gujarat who presided over the 2002 massacre of Muslims in the state.

The future of Hinduism in politics

The political salience of Hindu nationalism and the rise of the BJP in the 1980s and 1990s belied the image of Hinduism as tolerant and pluralistic. Yet the latter perception of Hinduism was always based on a superficial grasp of the nature of Hindu religion. In pointing out Hinduism's 'ability to encapsulate almost any religious or cultural entity without admitting any genuine dialogue or possibility of interaction' (Embree 1990: 25), Ainslie Embree touched upon an aspect that modern Hindu nationalist discourse exploited in its endeavour to transform the bewildering variety of Hindu beliefs and deities into a supple political resource for the creation of a sub-continental ethno-religious nationalism.

Still, the BJP's failure to significantly expand its electoral base, after an initial surge in the early 1990s, underscored the difficulties inherent in trying to reconcile the hierarchy and amorphousness of Hindu religion with a modern ideology of nationalism. This was especially the case within a context of deepening mass democracy. While religious groups that possessed a distinct non-Hindu identity were, understandably, strongly antipathetic to the Hindu nationalist project, newly politically mobilised people belonging to low castes were also profoundly suspicious of what they saw as its Brahminical Hindu bias. Both factors go a long way towards explaining the limits of the Hindu nationalist advance and in 2007 contributed to the upset election victory of the Bahujan Samaj Party (BSP) led by a Dalit woman, Mayawati, in state elections in India's most populous state, Uttar Pradesh, which saw the BJP relegated to a distant third place in a state that they had ruled until 2002. The fact that nearly a third of the winning BSP candidates were Brahmins or other upper-caste people was also significant, indicating the waning appeal of Hindu nationalism even among its traditional supporters.

There can be little doubt that Hinduism, broadly defined as the distinctive culture of Indian religion and encompassing deeply entrenched social institutions like caste, will continue to influence Indian politics. With the BJP having now been one of the two major political parties in India for the best part of two decades, Hindu nationalism as an organised political force remains powerful enough to be a serious contender for power at the national level at the head of another coalition government after the next general election, due in 2009. However, although over the past century the evolving ideology and praxis of Hindu nationalism has left a deep imprint on Indian public life, the spread of the Hindu nationalist project appears likely to continue to be delimited by Hinduism's most significant legacy to contemporary Indian politics – the potency of caste. In this sense the diversity and plurality of Hinduism has proved an effective antidote to the attempt, through the ideology of 'Hindutva', to make all Hindus embrace a singular political identity.

Bibliography

Adeney, K. and Saez, L. (eds) (2005) *Coalition Politics and Hindu Nationalism*, London: Routledge.

Bayly, S. (1999) *Caste, Society and Politics in India: From the Eighteenth Century to the Modern Age*, Cambridge: Cambridge University Press.

Bhattacharya, S. (2003) *Vande Mataram: The Biography of a Song*, New Delhi: Penguin.

BJP (1998) *BJP Election Manifesto '98*. Available at http://www.bjp.org/manifes.html, accessed 23 March 2000.

Chiriyankandath, J. (1992) 'Tricolour and Saffron: Congress and the Neo-Hindu Challenge', in S.K. Mitra and J. Chiriyankandath (eds), *Electoral Politics in India: A Changing Landscape*, New Delhi: Segment, pp. 55–79.

Chiriyankandath, J. and Wyatt, A. (2005) 'The NDA and Indian Foreign Policy', in K. Adeney and L. Saez (eds), *Coalition Politics and Hindu Nationalism*, London: Routledge, pp. 193–211.

Dumont, L. (1980) *Homo Hierarchicus: The Caste System and Its Implications*, Chicago: University of Chicago Press.

Embree, A.T. (1990) *Utopias in Conflict. Religion and Nationalism in Modern India*, Berkeley: University of California Press.

Frankel, F. (2005) *India's Political Economy 1947–2004*, 2nd edn, New Delhi: Oxford University Press.

Gandhi, M.K. (1980) *The Spirit of Hinduism*, New Delhi: Pankaj Publications.

Golwalkar, M.S. (1980) *Bunch of Thoughts*, Bangalore: Jagarana Prakashana.

Graham, B. (1993) *Hindu Nationalism and Indian Politics*, Cambridge: Cambridge University Press.

Hansen, Blom T. (1999) *The Saffron Wave: Democracy and Hindu Nationalism in Modern India*, Princeton: Princeton University Press.

Jaffrelot, C. (1996) *The Hindu Nationalist Movement: 1925 to the 1990s*, London: Hurst & Co.

Jaffrelot, C. (2003) *India's Silent Revolution: The Rise of the Lower Castes in North India*, London: Hurst & Co.

Lall, M. (2005) 'Indian Education Policy under the NDA Government', in K. Adeney and L. Saez (eds), *Coalition Politics and Hindu Nationalism*, London: Routledge, pp. 153–170.

Lannoy, R. (1971) *The Speaking Tree: A Study of Indian Culture and Society*. Oxford: Oxford University Press.

Mandal, B.P. (1980) *Report of the Backward Classes Commission*, New Delhi: Government of India Press.

Marshall, P.J. (1970) 'Introduction', in P.J. Marshall (ed.), *The British Discovery of Hinduism in the Eighteenth Century*, Cambridge: Cambridge University Press, pp. 1–44.

Nehru, J. (1961) *The Discovery of India*, Bombay: Asia Publishing House.

O'Brien, J. and Palmer, M. (1993) *The State of Religion Atlas*, New York: Simon & Schuster.

Panikkar, K.M. (1967) 'The Hindu Conception of the State' (from *The State and the Citizen*, Bombay, Asia Publishing House), in K. Satchidananda Murty, *Readings in India History, Politics and Philosophy*, London: George Allen & Unwin, pp. 135–138.

Radhakrishnan, S. (1937) 'Hinduism', in G.T. Garratt (ed.), *The Legacy of India*, Oxford: Oxford University Press, pp. 256–286.

Rajagopal, A. (1996) 'Communalism and the Consuming Subject', *Economic and Political Weekly*, 10 February, pp. 341–347.

Saberwal, S. (1996) 'Enlargement of Scales, Plural Traditions, and Rule of Law', *Review of Development & Change*, 1(1), pp. 1–19.

Savarkar, V.D. (2003) 'Hindutva' (from *Hindutva: Who is a Hindu?*, 6th edn, Delhi, Bharti Sahitya Sadan, 1989), in M. Gottlob (ed.), *Historical Thinking in South Asia: A Handbook of Sources from Colonial Times to the Present*, New Delhi: Oxford University Press, pp. 153–157.

Sen, A. (2005) *The Argumentative Indian: Writings on Indian Culture, History and Identity*, London: Penguin Books.

Srinivas, M.N. (1969) *Social Change in Modern India*, Berkeley: University of California Press.

Thapar, R. (1989) 'Epic and History: Tradition, Dissent and Politics in India', *Past and Present*, 125 (November), pp. 3–26.

Thapar, R. (1990) 'The Politics of Religious Communities', *Seminar*, 365 (Jan.), pp. 27–32.

Zaehner, R.C. (1962) *Hinduism*, Oxford: Oxford University Press.

Zavos, J. (2003) *The Emergence of Hindu Nationalism in India*, Delhi: Oxford University Press.

7

Islam and Islamism

*Andrea Teti
and Andrea Mura*

Introduction

One of the most common misunderstandings about Islam is that it contains some kind of essential 'core' which dictates the fundamental nature of political movements adopting its banner. Such misunderstandings are nowhere more obvious than in Western reactions to the 1979 Iranian Revolution and to Khomeini's followers, who eventually dominated the post-revolutionary government, which saw frenzied talk of a 'Green Peril' rising in the East, describing the Islamic Republic and its regional sympathisers as new and unprecedentedly dangerous 'Pan-Islamic' revolutionary movement, state terrorism without boundaries, which was somehow quintessentially 'Islamic'. However, during the revolution, slogans such as 'neither East nor West, [only] an Islamic Republic', or the adoption of religious symbols such as veiling, were straightforward and highly visible ways of protesting against the US-backed Shah's policies and the superpowers' twin attempts at 'imperialist' influence as well as a claim for greater cultural authenticity. Even then, religion as the hijacked banner for politics was not a new phenomenon. In its 'modern' guise, it has its roots at least a century earlier, at the

peak of European imperial influence, when throughout the Ottoman Empire debates raged about whether religion could provide a solution to the Empire's weakness. In the twentieth century, religion provided a rallying point for opponents of authoritarian regimes, both monarchic and 'secular' nationalist. The Iranian Revolution simply thrust these movements to the forefront of the West's political attention.

These kinds of misunderstandings arise in relation to both Sunni and Shi'a Islam, so although this chapter looks at key theological and legal aspects of Islam, and to its practical historical manifestations, with a particular focus on Sunni Islam, a similar analysis can be carried out in relation to the Shi'a world. The idea that Islam – whether Sunni or Shi'a – is somehow inherently political, and perhaps inherently violent, has been central to Western debates about Middle Eastern politics, and more recently also to Western states' domestic politics. An overview of the connection between 'Islamist' movements and the political context within which they emerge, however, shows that the nature of these movements has little to do with religion in itself. Rather, it reflects a politicisation of religion by which Islamist movements oppose a *status quo* which adherents believe is inherently unjust.

Principles of Islam

Islam is one of the three 'Abrahamic' religions, along with Judaism and Christianity. While Christianity sees itself as a 'refinement' of Judaism, Islam sees itself as the final revelation in that line. For Muslims, the Prophet Muhammad is the 'Seal' of a long line of prophets starting with Adam and including most of those recognised by Judaism and by Christianity. Beliefs and rules of behaviour in Islam are based on three sources: holy scripture (*Qur'an*), stories (*hadith*) about the Prophet's life (which, combined, constitute the *Sunna,* or tradition), and the extensive body of Islamic legal scholarship (*shari'a*). The fundamental elements of the faith, known as the 'Five Pillars', are:

1   *Shahada*: Recognising the oneness of God, and that Muhammad is His Prophet;
2   *Salat*: Prayer five times a day;
3   *Zakat*: An 'alms tax' to care for the poor;
4   *Hajj*: Pilgrimage to Makkah once in one's lifetime, if possible;
5   *Ramadan*: Daytime fasting and spiritual reflection during this holy month.

Beyond this, however, Islam's principles have been interpreted in widely different ways, and the practices carried out by Muslims themselves have varied just as much as those of any other 'world religion' (see Figure 7.1). Indeed, shortly after the Prophet's death (632 CE), a schism occurred between two groups, Sunni and Shi'a, over who should be his rightful successor – Abu Bakr (Muhammad's uncle) or 'Ali (his son-in-law) – and how succession should

---

While the main beliefs in Islam – the five pillars – have remained constant, legal and theological interpretations, as well as practices, have varied across regions/states and over time. Saint-worship, for example, is associated with traditional popular Islam, but was challenged by modernist Salafism (the label for radical reformism) in early twentieth-century North Africa.

- *Purdah* (modesty): Dress in public should be 'modest' (for both men and women). For women, this has taken various forms: loose scarves of the Sudan; *chador* in Iran; *burqa* in Afghanistan and parts of Pakistan; Turkey, non-provocative dress but no *hijab*.
  - There is no Qur'anic injunction specifying how women should dress. What 'modesty' entails has been interpreted differently over time and in different places (e.g. urban/rural, Gulf/Levant).
- *Marriage*: Technically, men can take up to four wives. This was a provision related to a specific historical context in which there were many widows (largely legally unprotected before Islam), a paucity of men and no means for most women to earn a living. Given women's weak position at the time, it was useful for them to be protected in this way. Most Muslims today see this as arcane. Moreover, this right is legally subject to men being able to look after all wives *equally* – but, as the Qur'an itself points out, this equality is impossible to achieve in practice.

Overall, diversity of interpretations of Islam and its real-world practices induce a scepticism regarding suggestions that there is but one unique or unchanging 'essence' of Islam. Just how much Islamic discourses and practices in politics have changed over time becomes evident in an overview of its political history.

Figure 7.1 Practices

be determined (by consultation or by family line). Today, Sunnis are the majority in North Africa, the Eastern Mediterranean, most of the Arabian peninsula, and in Asia, while there are Shi'a majorities in Iran, parts of Central Asia and in some Sunni-ruled Gulf states. Within Sunni Islam, there are four major theological and legal schools – Hanafi, Hanbali, Maliki, Shafi'i – alongside which Sufism (mysticism) must also be mentioned.

One of the many poorly understood aspects of Islam is its jurisprudence. *Shari'a* is a body of scholarship on the basis of which legal codes can be drawn up. *Shari'a* is therefore *not* a specific legal code; it is, if anything, 'Islamic legal studies'. For most Sunnis, *shari'a* is based on the Qur'an and *hadith*: through *qiyas* (analogy) and *ijma* (consensus) the body of Muslim scholars (*ulama*) arrives at the principles which any law must respect. *Ijtihad* (interpretation) is the exercise of judgement necessary to apply principles and precedents to new cases. After the rule of the Prophet's Companions, the 'Rightly Guided Caliphs', as the community of Muslims moved farther away from the spirit of those times, the 'door of *ijtihad*' was closed, theoretically preventing 'innovation' in Islamic jurisprudence.

Traditional concepts constituting the Islamic heritage have often been reformulated to legitimise change and present political aspirations. For instance, in order to help the Empire regain its position of strength in relation to Europe, during the nineteenth century the Ottomans reinvented the tradition of the Caliphate which had remained merely nominal following the decline of Arabs after the Abbasid age (750–1258). Other debates – which became particularly important during the nineteenth century – centred on traditional concepts such as *dhimma, shura* and *ijtihad*.

Dhimma is a formulation allowing non-Muslim 'people of the Book' (Jews, Christians, Sabeans and Zoroastrians) to live freely in Muslim states in their own communities, governed by their own laws, by paying a small tax. This system, known as *millet* under the Ottomans, allowed the peaceful coexistence of different faiths on the same land. For Sunnis, *shura* (consultation) is an important principle in selecting a leader: the community as a whole should agree on a choice. Shura was particularly emphasised in response to the need, felt by some, to lessen the absolutism of the Ottoman Empire. Finally, some argued that the problems of the time were unprecedented and therefore not covered by the existing body of jurisprudence, thus requiring the elaboration of new rules for this new era. But re-opening 'the door of *ijtihad*' generated understandable controversy.

Early history and expansion

In 610 CE, Muhammad receives his first revelation, and in 622 CE started public preaching. Gradually, Islam became a political force, and, after encountering opposition in Makkah, the first community undertook the *hijra* ('emigration') to Medina in 627/28 CE where it achieved political power through an alliance with the local Jewish majority. The so-called 'Constitution of Medina', which regulated relations between religious communities, is the first written historical document of Islam, and still remains central to many contemporary debates. One such debate concerns under what conditions Muslims may live under non-Muslim authority, and the fact that the Constitution of Medina did not establish a theocracy but a religiously pluralist city-state is highly significant.

The period going from the classical age of Arab expansion under the Umayyad (661–750) and Abbasid (750–1258) Caliphates to the intervention of European forces in the eighteenth century saw various ethnic groups assuming the lead and expansion of 'Islamic' empires, emphasising their inclusive, universal character. In addition, different ethnic groups found themselves leading parts of the Islamic world through different dynasties, including Turks, Berbers, Iranians and Mongols. This produced various dynasties, such as the Seljuks, Almoravids, Ayyubids and Mamlukes. Between the fifteenth and sixteenth centuries, the Muslim world found itself divided into various empires: the Sunni Ottoman Empire (Middle East, Balkans and Northern Africa); the Shi'a Safavid Empire in the Caucasus and West Asia; and the Mughul Empire, occupying most of the Indian subcontinent. This range of different ethnic groups and dynasties was mirrored in a great diversity of cultural expressions, including: Hellenistic traditions, Persian (Indo-Iranian) culture, and Turkish influences. This contributed to development of highly refined literatures, artistic expressions, architectures, philosophy and sciences (e.g. Moorish Spain, or Safavid Isfahan). It was through this heritage that many classical Greek texts were later 'rediscovered' in Europe during the Renaissance.

Moreover, throughout the Empire's expansion, Islamic jurisprudence recognised the legitimacy of various kinds of political system. It is important to stress that since its earliest times, Islam has been used by 'temporal power' to consolidate itself. This affected both theology and jurisprudence: scholars close to the Empire developed theories of 'jihad' which allowed the political leadership to justify expansion into richer lands to the north of Arabia.

The political and cultural climate subsequent to the early conquests favoured the emergence of legal interpretations which provided key examples of religious and ethnic pluralism, often by drawing on the notion of *dhimma*. The closest comparison in Europe was Frederick II's Sicily, itself largely based on the model of the island's earlier Muslim rulers.

Next, our discussion focuses on the period following the encounter with European colonial powers in the nineteenth century in the Sunni Arabophone Middle East since it provides major paradigms explaining further developments in the history of Muslim countries.

Late nineteenth- and early twentieth-century political debates

Throughout the nineteenth century, the Ottoman Empire's economic and military weakness in relation to Europe became increasingly clear. This strongly coloured political debate within the Empire, eliciting two kinds of responses: first, some argued that the Islamic community – which is what, after all, the Ottoman Empire at least nominally claimed to be the Sunni incarnation of – had weakened because it had abandoned its original spirit, and that therefore it should rediscover that spirit by going back to the original purity of Islam. The second response was that the Empire was faced with an unprecedented threat, which should be dealt with at least partly by adapting technical knowledge and institutions from Europe. This led to the Ottoman *tanzimat* (reform) laws, and other local reforms within the Empire (notably in Egypt). Three religious scholars, Jamal al-Din al-Afghani, Muhammad Abduh and Rashid Rida, are the central figures of late-nineteenth-century debates over the reform of (Sunni) Islamic law to meet the challenge of European imperialism, the 'fathers of Islah' (reform) to whom both moderates and radicals today trace their intellectual roots, and whose heritage they claim.

Al-Afghani (1838–1897), dreamt of a reinvigorated Caliphate unifying the entire

Muslim world under one political and spiritual leadership. Despite his very limited political success, he is important firstly, for his influence on later figures like Rashid Rida and Hasan al-Banna, the founder of the Islamist movement 'Muslim Brotherhood' (al-khwan al-Muslimun); secondly, because he was the first major intellectual to react against European penetration by formulating a political opposition based on innovative religious grounds; and finally, because to do so he looked back to a supposed 'Golden Age' of early Islam – a move which, albeit historically rather 'creative', has since then marked virtually all attempts to think about burning issues such as the relationship between Muslim communities and secular states.

Muhammad 'Abduh (1849–1905) came from a wealthy family, and taught at Cairo's prestigious al-Azhar University. He was a gradualist reformer, advocating adaptation of some European institutions. Supporting the need for consultative government, 'Abduh argued that rather than 'importing' from Europe, Muslims should rediscover *shura*. He also called for re-opening the 'door of *ijtihad*' in order to meet the unprecedented challenges of European imperialism.

Rashid Rida (1865–1935), who was a student of both 'Abduh and al-Afghani, and edited the political magazine *al-Manar*, marks a turning point in Islamist thought and in the attitudes of intellectuals towards Europe. Writing during the British occupation of Egypt (1882–1922), he advocated *active resistance* to imperialist encroachment by arguing that (defensive) *jihad* should be widened to include defence against political as well as religious oppression, its more conventional understanding.

To understand why these developments took place at this particular time, it is necessary to note that in Egypt at the time the main political problem was – and, until 1952, remained – independence from British occupation. Following Egypt's

declaration of bankruptcy, Viceroy Ismail was deposed in 1875 and the Franco-British 'Dual Control' over Egyptian state finances established. After Ismail, Egyptian rulers were mostly compliant to British interests. Like the British, they felt threatened by nationalist opposition, and cooperated with the former in curtailing nationalists' access to power. Following a coup in 1880 by a nationalist – Colonel 'Urabi – the British invaded, heralding seventy years of military and political presence. Other features, such as parallel courts for Egyptians and for foreigners, gradually established a system of discrimination which contributed to radicalise both nationalist and religious opposition.

From peaceful reform to armed resistance in early twentieth-century Egypt

The continued presence of the British helped to radicalise political ideologies and practices across the political spectrum. Two events epitomised the impact of British imperialism: declaration of a British Protectorate over Egypt during World War I, effectively allowing the former to occupy the country; and the refusal to admit an Egyptian delegation demanding national independence to the post-World War I peace negotiations at Versailles. The establishment of a Mandate following the war reflected a further Western betrayal of the 'democratic nationalism' which was supposed to inform the Versailles settlements. Even when, in 1922, after three years of unrest, the British unilaterally recognised Egyptian 'independence', they retained control over areas such as foreign policy and the right to a military presence and to political intervention which effectively emptied 'independence' of any meaning: Egypt remained a *de facto* colony.

Paralleling trends in Europe, the 1920s and 1930s saw the emergence of extremist politics across the entire political spectrum, from socialist and communist movements, to Islamism and radical Egyptian nationalism. Meantime, although the popular nationalist Wafd was regularly voted into power, the British collaborated with the Egyptian king – as they did with the Hashemite monarchs in Syria, Iraq and Arabia – in consistent attempts to discredit the Wafd. In practice, this helped undermine Egyptian nationalism, creating the context for alternative ideologies – e.g. Islamist, Arabist and Socialist – to challenge the Wafd's 'liberal nationalism', and facilitating a generalised political radicalisation.

In this context schoolmaster Hassan al-Banna (1906–1949) established the Muslim Brotherhood in 1928 as an organisation providing welfare services, aiming to encourage and defend morality, Islamising society 'from below', rather than through revolution. The Muslim Brotherhood was soon drawn into politics, developing explicit political goals. The increasingly troubled political context favoured the radicalisation of the Brotherhood's political philosophy and tactics – just like its 'secular' counterparts' – and, like these, the Brotherhood soon developed an armed wing. However, its main focus remained education from below and the infiltration of political and social institutions. The combination of its welfare services, its religious credentials, the government's increasing authoritarianism, and the progressive discrediting of the Wafd, soon made the Muslim Brotherhood Egypt's largest political organisation.

It is important to understand that the Brotherhood, despite its own rhetoric, was not a manifestation of traditional Islamism. On the contrary, it was a prime example of a *modern* political organisation: mass-based, populist, supported mainly by the urban middle and lower classes, using a cell-based structure, and embracing religious reformism. Finally, the Brotherhood prioritised Egypt: it wished to reform primarily *Egyptian* politics, not the universal Islamic community, struggling first and foremost for Egyptian independence. Like the nationalists, it wanted 'Egypt for the Egyptians'.

The radicalisation of Islamism in the Sunni world

Sayyid al-Mawdudi (1903–1979) was an influential Islamic thinker and the founder of the Sunni Islamic political movement *Jamaat-e-Islami*. He elaborated most of his radical theories during the political turmoil preceding the separation of Hindu-majority India, and Muslim-majority Pakistan. Al-Mawdudi thought Islam was *inseparably* faith and state (*din wa-dawla*), arguing sovereignty cannot rest with the people but only with God, and that a religious state cannot simply be Muslim-majority, it must be governed not only according to his vision of 'true Islam' but also only by 'true Muslims'.

Another separate and distinctive approach – Wahhabism – also emerged as a conservative movement based on normative and literalist approaches to Scripture. As for many such movements of its time, in Wahhabism, tradition is perceived as a fixed set of values that must be protected from the assaults of religious innovations (*bid'ah*). However, many critics argue that the Wahhabi stylisation of the past is both nostalgic and passive: the past is taken to offer a refuge from the moral corruption of the present rather than a potential set of resources to be managed in order to promote an assertive Islamic answer to change. Wahhabi clergy – both doctrinally and politically – had supported the ruling family of Sa'ud in Arabia in their rise to power during the eighteenth century. During the rejuvenation of Islamism in the 1970s, Wahhabism provided the Saudi family with an alternative ideological platform to spread its 'political' influence, in concurrence with the great international resonance of the (Shi'a) Islamist Iranian Republic. Like Mawdudi, Banna and the 'fathers of Islah', Wahhabism represents a political response to a historical context of European expansion.

During the 1950s and 1960s, the Egyptian Muslim Brotherhood took a radical turn. Having helped him come to power and to consolidate his rule, under Nasser the Brotherhood was not only heavily repressed by the state but also marginalised politically by Arab nationalism. Nasser's single party coopted, marginalised or repressed his main rivals: the Brotherhood, large land-owners and the Communists. This radicalised the Brotherhood, as evidenced by the history of the involvement of Sayyid Qutb (1906–1966). Qutb joined the Brotherhood in 1951, following two years in the USA, and effectively took over leadership soon after al-Banna's death (1949) despite the fact he was never Supreme Guide. Arrested in 1954 under Nasser and executed in 1965, while in prison Qutb personally experienced the harshness of Nasser's repression. There, he wrote his most important tract, *Milestones*, which argued for a radical new definition of *jihad* as: 'destroying the kingdom of man in order to bring about the kingdom of God [*hakimiyya*] [...] Those who understand the true nature of this religion will realise the absolute necessity for the Islamic movement, as well as and effort by preaching, [of including] armed struggle, and that this should not be understood as purely defensive'.

For Qutb, the depth of contemporary corruption was such that society should be regarded as being in a state of *jahiliyya* (pre-Islamic ignorance), and therefore to be rejected in its entirety, requiring a radical overhaul to be imposed 'from above'.

What links the ideas of all these movements is not theoretical unity or even agreement about goals and methods of political struggle, but the simple fact that the radicalisation of Islamist discourse and practices (in our case Sunni) occurred as a response to a specific political context, namely the combination of internal repression and growing 'Western' interference.

The question of jihad

The notion of 'jihad' is central both to the political theory of radical Islamists, and to many Western (mis)representations of Islam. This section offers a brief review of the classical notion of jihad and its evolution (in Sunni jurisprudence) in Egypt during the late nineteenth and early twentieth centuries, outlining the influence of the experience of European imperialism in its radicalisation.

In mainstream Islamic thought, conventional interpretations of 'jihad' are far from its common – and erroneous – translation, especially but not exclusive in the West, as 'holy war'. 'Jihad' translates as 'striving', but the historical theorisation of this struggle, still by far the most dominant today, could hardly be farther from that of a 'holy war'. Nor is *jihad* central to Islamic political theory, as is often claimed. In the Qur'an, organised violence is referred to as *ghazwa* (raid), *harb* and *qital* (war) – not *jihad* – using terms with roots *qtl* and/or *hrb*, not *jhd*. Indeed, verses in which *jhd* appears rarely directly and exclusively link it to armed conflict, but *always* to personal effort (e.g. hence *ijtihad*, the effort of exegetic interpretation). Just how misleading interpretation can be is clear when considering verses containing the term jihad and substituting the two different meanings. Take for example: 'Fear God and attempt to move closer to Him and His religion, and fight on His path' (Qur'an V, 35). Here one finds *jhd*, not *hrb* or *qtl*, and replacing 'fight' with 'strive' changes the apparent meaning of the verse entirely.

So what *is* jihad? Conventional interpretations distinguish between at least two kinds of jihad: the 'greater jihad' entails striving against one's own negative inclinations, behaving piously. The 'lesser jihad', or 'jihad of the sword', permits the use of force to defend the faith only when Muslims are actively prevented from practising their religion (if there has been a *fatwa*, a legal opinion issued by legitimate religious authorities). This shows how marginal armed resistance, let alone aggression, is in conventional jurisprudence. The interpretation by modern radicals is very different: exclusive, aggressive and through a language of 'defending the faith' and 'individual duty,' aims towards 'Islamising' state and society. It is also more central to modern radical theories, to the point that it is sometimes considered to be 'the neglected duty', the 'Sixth Pillar' of Islam (recall that Islam's only imperative duties are the Five Pillars).

Such a stark difference between classical and contemporary radical notions, such a movement from a spiritual meaning to a duty of revolution begs an explanation. The gradual evolution of the concept of *jihad* into an attempt to justify *armed* struggle against *political* oppression cannot be divorced from the historical context of a hundred and fifty years or so of European (neo)imperial pressure: it is a response in both political discourse and in practices to (1) authoritarian governments at home, and (2) the impact of imperialism. The Egyptian case clearly illustrates a spiral of authoritarian governments, foreign interference and radicalisation.

From armed struggle to elections: contemporary Islamism in Egypt

It should not be assumed that the only or indeed dominant translation of Islam into politics is violent. Indeed, in the Middle East and elsewhere Islamist groups have emerged to political prominence, even power, which are not violent or particularly radical. Turkey, Jordan, Morocco and Egypt all provide cases in point. In Jordan and Morocco, Islamists have been coopted into a political process dominated by an authoritarian monarchy, in Turkey an Islamist party was voted into power in 2002, while in Egypt Islamists have provided the only credible, mass-based opposition to authoritarian regimes since the 1970s.

The emergence of this complex range of Islamist politics is rooted in external political influence in the Middle East, in the failure of Arabism and of 'developmental' nationalism, and in the authoritarianism of regimes throughout the region. Again, Egypt's experience typifies these trajectories.

Arab nationalism was severely damaged by its defeat in the 'Six-Day War' (June war or *naksa*) of 1967, shifting power towards the conservative and more pro-Western monarchies led by Saudi Arabia. However, it was Sadat's negotiations with Israel after the October War (Yom Kippur or Ramadan War) of 1973, culminating in the Camp David Accords, which finally broke Arab nationalism's back. After that, although Arab identity remained important, religion has increasingly been used to justify government policy and to hold governments to account for failing to fulfil their promises, for protesting corruption, immorality, etc.

Sadat became President upon Nasser's death in 1970, but no one expected his succession to last. This supposedly innocuous vice-president, however, oversaw a momentous shift in Egyptian politics which frames the relationship between regime and Islamist opposition to this day. Initially politically weak, Sadat consolidated his power by doing two things. First, he went to war with Israel. This brought them to the negotiating table, and Sadat won not only a public opinion coup but also got the Sinai peninsula and the Suez

Canal back. It also allowed him to offer his allegiance to the US, as he disliked the Soviets. Secondly, he isolated Nasser's single party, the Arab Socialist Union (ASU) by using the Muslim Brotherhood as a domestic counterweight.

This tactical choice had far-reaching strategic implications. The Brotherhood's leadership had been radicalised by prison, some extreme sections splintering into groups like *al-Gama'at al-Islamiyya* or *al-Jihad*. The price of Sadat's international realignment was a peace with Israel which left his Arab counterparts badly weakened, a personal trip to Israeli-occupied Jerusalem, and a speech to the Knesset for which he would never be forgiven. Economic liberalisation (*infitah*) required by the USA and sadat's bourgeois allies also badly hit the poor, causing extensive riots. Along with his periodical crackdowns on opposition, his political and economic reforms proved his undoing: Sadat found he ultimately could not control the forces he had unleashed and was assassinated at a military parade in 1981.

Hosni Mubarak, who also 'inherited' the Presidency, continued the alternating cycles of liberalisation and repression his predecessor used to manipulate domestic politics. He immediately declared a state of emergency which has been renewed to this day, and while he allowed elections, he made sure the National Democratic Party (NDP) stayed in power, thereby guaranteeing his Presidency. He maintained the ban on the Muslim Brotherhood, preventing their participation in elections, and met armed resistance with brutal repression. The Brotherhood, however, engaged in innovative political strategies: they entered into electoral alliance with weakened secular parties, allowing Brothers to run for office. By the late 1990s, Brotherhood candidates were standing as 'independents', and rapidly became the largest opposition 'party' in parliament. Moreover, migrant labour returning from the Gulf brought back more conservative social attitudes, Brotherhood supporters rose through the ranks of professional associations, and the state's continued weakness as a welfare provider contrasted starkly with the array of social services provided by the Muslim Brotherhood.

Political Islam: a failure?

The pattern noted in the section above – Islamists adapt to government oppression while developing ability to build and consolidate mass support – provides important indications not only regarding political developments throughout the Middle East generally but also in relation to Islamism. Since the 1970s, the economic and political crisis of postcolonial development projects stimulated the growth of a diverse political opposition. The oil-related economic slump of the mid-1980s increased pressure on the already struggling economies of non-oil-producing states, highlighting their economic difficulties and – given their general crackdowns on opposition – just how thin the veil of 'democracy' covering these regimes was. The 1990s increased such pressures, as the end of the Cold War on the one hand undermined the need for limited liberalisation to combat Soviet influence (as well as US aid), while on the other hand democratic discourse became unassailably central to international politics. The second Gulf War, following the breaking of another Arab nationalist taboo, the invasion of one Arab state (Kuwait) by another (Iraq), also stoked the embers of anti-Americanism as it was widely perceived to be a 'war for oil'. This weakened Washington's allies' domestic position, with opposition movements accusing them – with more than some justification – not only of being in Washington and Riyadh's pockets, but also of not practising the democracy they preached.

Some have argued that 'political Islam' has failed to produce successful revolutions, living up to its supposed universalist ideals, or indeed modernising reforms (Roy 1994). This underestimates the influence, either directly in government or indirectly in opposition, which increasingly popular Islamist movements have had. Some parties have been allowed to participate in elections, and, as in Turkey or Palestine, have won. In other cases, governments have tried to pre-empt such electoral success through a combination of police harassment (e.g. Egypt, or the Algerian extreme of an Army coup suspending elections, leading to a bloody civil war), legislative obstacles, and an at least superficial pandering to a conservative religious agenda.

Islam and revolution?

In the light of the above, can we say that there is a link between 'Islam' and revolution or political violence generally? This question has often been raised, particularly since the Iranian Revolution. It should be clear from the remarks above that the answer is negative. The Iranian Revolution provides a case in point: this was not, as many incorrectly state, an 'Islamic' revolution, but an uprising by a wide range of forces across all Iranian society – from the Shi'a clergy to the Communists to the Kurds – reacting to an authoritarian monarchy which was perceived as being 'in the pocket of the USA', and whose imbalanced 'modernisation' project placed enormous strain on society. Only afterwards did Islamists gain primacy among other factions. The role of Islam during the revolution was that of a symbol of opposition to arbitrary 'modernisation', which felt too much like a wholesale abdication of a proud millennia-long identity in favour of narrow materialism, consumerism and subjection to foreign interests. The Ayatollah Khomeini (1900–1989),

religious authority and the political leader of the Iranian revolution, significantly called this 'Westoxification,' and, again significantly, one of the Islamists' slogans was 'Neither East nor West, [only] an Islamic Republic' – a token of how oppressively the superpowers' presence was felt during the Cold War.

Thus, *religious principles* did not bring about revolution: political oppression and enormous inequalities which clashed with a discourse of development and democracy – these were the motors of the Revolution. 'Islam' was simply its banner. So much so, that the significance of the revolution was felt across the Sunni/Shi'a and Arab/Persian divides. Iran became a model not for doctrinal reasons, but because for the first time it demonstrated the feasibility not only of a revolution, but of a culturally 'authentic' political system: it appeared to throw off the yoke of imperialism, both material and cultural, completely and definitively.

Islamist nationalist' movements such as Hizballah and Hamas provide analogous cases: for these movements, the independence of a national community is even more important than the 'Islamisation' of society. Indeed, both happen to be responses to the Israeli presence in South Lebanon and in the Occupied Territories respectively. It is also no coincidence that these movements rose to prominence once their earlier 'secular' counterparts were perceived to be failing.

Islam(ism) and democracy

Another supposed 'failure' of Islam in its relation to politics is Huntington's (1993) argument that Islam in its 'essence' constitutes a 'civilisation' inherently different from, and more violent than, any other. This supposedly explains why the Middle East did not democratise after the end of the Cold War, as did Eastern Europe. This argument, however tempting such simple answers might be, ignores the causes of the emergence of radical ideologies and violent practices and the relationship between political oppression and radical politics generally (not just religious radicalism). In the Middle East, it is clear that what has radicalised the opposition is the inability and/or unwillingness of local regimes and their international counterparts to accept the consequences of genuine pluralism.

In Western debates, questions about the relationship between Islam and violence are virtually symbiotic with doubts about its 'compatibility' with democracy. The argument is often heard that while democracy requires secularism, openness and the acceptance of non-religious state authority, Islam by its nature – and therefore any 'Islamist' politics – demands a theocratic state in which there can be no debate about right and wrong, or about appropriate social order, because its aim must be 'to bring about the rule of God'. It should be clear by now that this is historically and jurisprudentially wrong.

Nonetheless, there has been considerable debate about the scope for liberalising Middle Eastern politics. Ghassan Salamè et al. (1994) point out that, aside from a few notable examples, what 'democratisation' there has been in the Middle East has been largely cosmetic, putting in place institutions, but undermining their democratic potential by curtailing their remit or bypassing them (e.g. skewing electoral law in favour of ruling parties, or rigging the results). Laura Guazzone (1995) points to an 'Islamist Dilemma': if allowed to run for elections, Islamists may win and cancel elections once in power, but preventing them from running undermines democracy. On the other hand, allowing real pluralism may give more moderate voices a chance to meet popular political demands, thus preventing wider socio-political marginalisation and radicalisation.

Such debates about the relationship between Islam and violence, democracy, etc., are significant not so much for their intellectual depth, but because they illustrate a certain way of thinking about Islam, particularly in the West. As Said (1995) and others point out, much Western public discourse about the 'Orient' suggests a Manichean representation of the West as advanced, progressive, democratic, egalitarian, secular, rational and peaceful, and of the East as backward, stagnant, authoritarian, discriminatory, religiously dogmatic, fanatical and violent. This representation is supported by the histories of neither Western states nor Middle Eastern ones, but it has historically enabled policies such as colonialism, or the Mandate system, which would have been difficult to justify had non-Western cultures been accorded equal dignity to those of the West. Overall, recent Islamist political responses throughout the Middle East and North Africa are neither specifically *Sunni* nor even particularly *Islamic*. Instead, they are inherently *political*, responses to authoritarian political systems and continuing foreign meddling.

Islamism in theory and in practice

It should be clear by now that Sunni 'Islamist' movements – much like their confessional counterparts – are primarily political phenomena, and that beyond the language they use to articulate their goals, they cannot be said to stem from some 'essence' of Islam. Islam is not Islamism. Not only is Islam's 'intrinsic nature' a historical myth, but both supporters and opponents use it for political purposes. The historical variety of 'political Islam' shows that a great variety of phenomena fall under this label – a range within which violent extremism is a minority position. 'Islamism' is simply a set of political and social movements aiming to 'bring Islam back' into politics and society. Islamists aim for some kind of 'Islamisation' of the state and/or of society, meaning essentially a return to a more socially and morally just life. In contemporary political contexts, this translates into demands for changes in the law, changes in political leadership, and changes in foreign policy. In social terms, this means demands for a more conservative morality and for changes in education. But on specifics, there is little agreement between such movements.

Moreover, in some countries, Islamists have come to power following sometimes violent revolutions or coups (Shi'a Iran, Sunni Sudan), while in others they have been allowed to run for election – albeit with mixed results. In Turkey an Islamist political party achieved power (AKP), while the FIS in Algeria were denied electoral victory by a military coup, which plunged the country into an infamously bloody civil war. In most Middle Eastern countries, mainstream Islamist parties aim to participate in the political process and achieve power peacefully. Some groups, often small splinter organisations, use violence, as did some Egyptian and Algerian groups in the 1990s, or Hamas and Hizballah today, although larger groups never use violence exclusively.

Whatever political outcomes, Islamist groups have adapted to state pressure by innovatory political tactics. In some cases, larger groups with greater popular support have been able to achieve a variety of goals, such as pushing for changes in the law to meet their interpretation of *shari'a*. Since the 1980s, these tactics have allowed their influence – whether in power or in opposition – to grow throughout the region (e.g. Turkey, Egypt, Morocco, Jordan). In several cases, for example, *shari'a* is acknowledged in constitutions as 'one' of, or even 'the', principal source of law. Also, religious courts have often been allowed to rule on 'personal status' issues (e.g. divorce or inheritance). Moreover, the restrictions on participation in electoral politics has often led Islamists on the one hand to promote precisely the democratic and pluralist discourse they are accused of wanting to undermine (e.g. Turkey), and on the other hand to attempt to infiltrate those professional associations which act both as access to, and channels of, patronage (e.g. lawyers' and judges' guilds, medical associations, etc.).

Perhaps Islamists' most important function, however, is as charitable organisations, providing welfare services which many states seem incapable of supplying – a weakness often exacerbated by economic liberalisation. This role, for both principled and pragmatic purposes, has given Islamist groups considerable political weight (e.g. Egypt's Muslim Brotherhood) and has provided a vital bedrock of support for those organisations which also have paramilitary wings (e.g. Hamas or Hizballah).

The slogans such as 'Islam is the solution' or 'Neither East Nor West but Islam' are therefore indicative not of some purported 'essence' of Islam, but of Islam*ism*'s populist roots. Religiously inspired political discourses since the late nineteenth century have emphasised lack of corruption, culturally and religiously 'authentic' values, political empowerment, fairer distribution of national income, and resistance to foreign meddling. Despite their currently waning popularity, it is important to note that this emphasis precisely mirrors that of nationalist and socialist groups, and it is no coincidence that all these movements, despite their ideological differences, emerged in opposition to both authoritarian regimes domestically and the interference of great powers internationally.

The role of Islamism as a sway of articulating political demands is clear not only from Islamist movements, but also from states' reaction. Several states, notably Morocco, Jordan, and Egypt under Sadat, have attempted to appropriate religious symbolism to legitimise their own rule. Sadat portrayed himself as the 'Believer President', while Moroccan and Jordanian kings have used their lineage – which they trace back to the Prophet Muhammad's family – to legitimise their rule. Also, the Saudis and other ruling Gulf families combine traditional and religious symbols to legitimise their rule.

How important is 'Islam'?

Does Islam set the Middle East apart from other regions? If so, is this difference purely one of degree, or is it unique, utterly different? The answers to these questions are vital: answering in the affirmative raises the spectre of a 'clash of civilisations' between 'Islam and the West', while a negative answer sweeps away the very foundations upon which such arguments stand.

Islam is seen as 'more political' than other religions. Yet, other religions are also highly political, as even cursory overviews of the history of Buddhism, Hinduism, Christianity or Judaism show. Moreover, like others, Islam leaves room for interpretation concerning the relationship between religion and politics.

Islam has been used as a vehicle for conferring political legitimacy, and has been made to 'serve' authoritarianism, monarchy and democracy. In this, it is in no way dissimilar to its counterparts, as clearly in most countries – Western as well as non-Western – religion plays an important part, both directly as a party-political force, and indirectly as an influence upon morals. Not all Western states, for example, have a strict separation of Church and politics (UK, Japan), and even in those which do – e.g. Spain, Germany, France or Italy – clearly Christianity, its Churches, and the parties which subscribe to their values play a considerable role. In North America, most US Presidents have been active Christians, while Israel is an explicitly religious state.

Given the connection between authoritarianism and radical politics, it seems more plausible to explain the manifestation of extremism in relation to local authoritarian contexts. Moreover, while the most 'media-friendly' images are those conjured by violent extremism, the fact remains that most Muslims and most Islamist politics remain non-violent and desirous of more, not less, democracy.

Islam, globalisation and the internet

The idea that in principle religion can and should be separated from politics, and that they are separate in fact, is a staple of political debate in the 'West' and of Western representations of itself. However, the lines of demarcation between such domains are neither precise nor self-evident, whether in historical contexts, in current practices of Western democracies, or in the theories underpinning them, as evidenced by recent debate on 'civil unions' in Spain and Italy or on the *hijab* in France or Britain. This demarcation is not clear in either the 'West' or in the 'East', nor is it clear in Christianity, in Islam, or in other religions. Indeed, the notion of religion itself might vary significantly in different religious settings, challenging Western societies' 'commonsensical' beliefs about themselves and about their global counterparts.

In an Islamic setting, the debate about the role of religion in individual and social life has produced an enormous variety of opinions and practices combining religion and politics in different ways, sometimes overlapping through the notion of 'Islamic order' (*al-Nizam al-Islami*), other times maintaining separation of some sort. As noted above, Islamic jurisprudence legislates on a variety of topics (marriage, inherited property, social duties, etc.) which would, from a Western perspective, be generally considered non-religious, but which some Muslims perceive to be strictly religious affairs.

Others might be aware of and accept this distinction, but may choose to challenge society's specific arrangements of a given social institution – e.g. divorce or banking – through the language of a critique based on religious principles. Religious precepts thus provide a self-conscious way of articulating and pursuing political aims. Indeed, throughout the history of Islam, religion has often helped legitimise what from a Western perspective may appear purely 'political' decisions.

Another interesting pattern is illustrated by groups which appeal to the much misunderstood Islamic conflation between religion and politics, but contribute to the very process of 'secularization' (Roy 2004). When suggesting Islam is a 'system' (*minhaj*) of life they sometimes reduce it to a set of religious precepts, radically isolated from cultural, political, economic and other spheres (Eickelman and Piscatori 2004).

Western societies have equated religion with the private sphere, and politics with the public for historical reasons essentially tied to the emergence of bourgeois nationalism and its struggle against the 'old powers' of the Monarchy and the Church. Rejecting the 'dogmatism' of religion and asserting individual rights allowed the bourgeoisie to prevent interference in their economic affairs, while giving them a voice in politics and undermining the privilege of aristocracies. This, however, did not mean religion did not have an impact on politics. Indeed, even today in supposedly secular Western states, from the professed faith of its leaders to the stance of religious authorities on issues from abortion to (civil) marriage, the signs of the importance of Christianity in public life are obvious.

Equally obvious are the ways in which religion and politics mix, voluntarily or otherwise, explicitly or implicitly, in dress codes, in music and film, in education, in labour relations (e.g. public holidays and prayer times), in literature or indeed in public honours (as the 'Rushdie affair' reminds us). Consider a wedding: whether in a Western or Middle Eastern setting, although technically a private event, it may acquire recognised public relevance, especially when speeches given during the celebration spread significantly via word of mouth or videotape (Eickelman and Anderson 2003).

The notion of two clearly distinct and separable domains, public/political and private/religious, is problematic: there are clearly a whole range of phenomena which inherently bridge these dimensions. By further blurring these borders and hierarchies, by increasing possibilities of cross-cultural encounters, and by stimulating cross-border migration, globalisation has increased the number and 'visibility' of these hybrid spaces, accelerating and intensifying the degree of interconnection between the public and the private. These unprecedented cultural challenges, alongside mass education and the emergence of new media, have contributed to reshape these supposedly independent spheres, redefining the space from which ideas on community and selfhood – Islamic, but not only – are discussed.

These challenges have also eroded the privileged position of both traditional religious authorities and of political establishments, whose ability to control the elaboration and broadcast of ideas has decreased drastically. Significant in this sense has been the appearance of the internet as a medium through which the monopoly over traditional religious interpretations has been challenged.

Traditional media such as the printed press, television and radio, were based on a centralised, top-down model of communication in which the sender controlled the elaboration and diffusion of messages, while audiences passively received it. Audiences did attempt to bypass government control of such media through alternative vehicles of new ideas. In the Middle East, this led to the diffusion of audio- and videotapes by which religious teachings and cultural forms of expression – including the politically subversive North African musical genre, *ra'i* – have bypassed strict state control (Eickelman and Anderson 2003: 9).

In this sense, the internet represents the most important vehicle in the articulation and dissemination for alternative doctrinal, social and political viewpoints about Islam. The net has been increasingly used in very different contexts and for very different purposes.

As an instrument for political action, the methods and uses to which it has been put have varied. Despite fears it would be used to carry out cyber attacks, cyber wars and cyber terrorism, these remain quite rare. Many websites discuss the implementation of 'e-jihad' (*jihad* on/via the internet), some provide military training, and in a handful of cases bomb-making instructions. Nonetheless, the risk of online 'amateur' jihadism remains virtually non-existent. 'Hacktivism', attacks carried out by hackers, require a sophistication which is still rare among the numerous websites of a possible jihadist online infrastructure. Furthermore, internet-based recruitment is currently insignificant, given the still prominent role played by personal contacts. Nonetheless, the internet represents a low-cost and effective tool to mobilise domestic political actors, disseminating ideas and messages which would otherwise be censored by the state.

In some cases, movements from Muslim countries attempt to address the international community by providing information on local political contexts or by explaining their political objectives. Islamic organisations sometimes resort to websites in English and Arabic to address different audiences. For instance, whilst the Arabic-language website of the London-based Saudi Movement for Islamic Reform in Arabia (MIRA) emphasises its Islamic dimension, its English-language version presents MIRA as an organisation fighting human, civil and political rights violations.

Similarly, where the official websites of the Egyptian and Jordanian Muslim Brotherhoods focus on doctrinal issues to avoid censorship, unofficial English-language websites and newsletters openly level political criticism at their respective regimes. (See www.miraserve.com; also compare the Arabic-language www.daawa-info.net with the English-language www.ikhwanweb.com (Egyptian Muslim Brotherhood).)

The internet also enables a much more immediate mass debate over the role of Islam, bypassing historical monopolies of state and *ulama*, and increasingly challenging the doctrinal and socio-political role of classically trained religious scholars. Both the language and the scholarly traditions upon which many new 'experts' – often engineers or doctors – draw, is much more popular (and populist) and finds inspiration in non-traditional areas such as science or popular culture.

A worldwide Islamic community (*ummah*) previously fractured into national, political and doctrinal particularities seems to be increasingly replaced by a new, innovative, rich and complex space in which voices and ideas bypass previous structural limits of geography, politics and confession. For some, this promises a new age of global unity, a global 'virtual *ummah*' which will finally (re)unify the Muslim community.

Within the virtual *ummah*, complex networks of websites, chat forums, newsletters, blogs, MUD directories (multi-user dungeon/domain/dimension), bulletin boards etc., give voice to an incredible exchange of opinions and information about every aspect of a Muslim's life. Sharing information and community-building are two frequently and explicitly articulated aspirations. Participants may endeavour to build virtual communities of like-minded individuals sharing the same views on Islam and on the problems of living in the modern world. Sometimes the internet is used simply to convey the difficulty of sharing communitarian feelings in real life. In Western countries this may be a consequence of Muslims being a minority within societies in which many of them do not feel fully integrated – indeed, many such European websites are based on a sense of religious and social solidarity, reducing Western Muslims' sense of isolation, and reinforcing identities and self-confidence. This is true of both second- and third-generation Muslims, and of newly arrived and more obviously isolated migrants. Moreover, the very fact of living in Western countries stimulates discussions about the best way to reconcile religious precepts with a secular environment. This may also be true for Muslims living in 'Islamic' societies.

A common feature of Christianity and Islam in fact seems to be that of conceiving the religious community as a 'minority' in face of a global scenario which is perceived as a secularised one. Discussing Islam in relation to a specific milieu entails that a certain degree of mutual criticism arises between traditional and new interpreters. Some of the most popular websites such as Islam Online (www.islamonline.net), IslamiCity (www.islamicity.com) and Fatwa-Online (www.fatwa-online.com) feature not only news and general information on Islam, health, culture, art, and many other topics, but also links to archives of fatwas issued by contemporary and historical scholars and 'experts' (Bunt 2003). Where for instance Fatwa-Online reveals the influence of Saudi Arabian scholars, Islam Online has featured many fatwas issued by Yusuf al-Qaradawi, an Egyptian religious scholar whose modern style and alternative views on specific issues (not necessarily progressive) have encountered strong criticism by more traditional interpreters.

Another new and significant phenomenon is internet use by young Muslims, who also express their views on Islam, debate issues from alternative viewpoints and build virtual communitarian ties. Many claim the importance of Islam in their everyday life, yet its celebration is conducted in 'progressive' ways. Religion and politics come to be filtered by an alternative multidimensional vision of Islam which often radically rebels against traditional views on Islam. Blogs and chat forums – very popular in networking services such as MySpace, Facebook and Bebo – allow users to easily create an interactive, user-submitted network of friends. Groups discuss issues such as the defence of male and female homosexuality, women's emancipation, youthful rebellion, distinctive fashion, DIY attitudes, and a variety of anti-establishment perspectives.

Blogs and forums also spread and develop innovative cultural movements, such as Islamic hip-hop and Islamic Punk. Hip-hop is one of the most important forms of protest against social and political discrimination, racism, lack of education, and all sources of social disquiet over the last few decades. Spreading beyond its original African-American context, Muslim rappers have been central to its evolution. Many rappers, from Mos Def to JT the Bigga Figga, stress its importance in spreading the faith, bridging the gaps between Muslim Black communities, and creating a global hip-hop *ummah*.

Hip-hop's popularity as a vehicle for social reflection and protest is in part due to the immediacy of a rhyme scheme by which considerable amounts of information can be easily delivered and memorised (see, for example, Cooke and Lawrence 2005). The internet's ability to popularise Muslim rappers' lyrics has been crucial in bringing it to a wider audience, in turn providing an Islamo-hip-hop melting pot, with Islam being celebrated by new rappers like Vinnie Paz (an Italian-American convert), the European Muslims Aki Nawaz (Fun-Da-Mental, UK), Natacha Atlas (Transglobal Underground, UK), and Akhenaton (IAM, France), as well as the Egyptian MBS and Arabian Knightz, the Algerian Intik, Hamma and Le Micro Brise Le Silenc, etc. Nor has this phenomenon gone unnoticed by traditionalists: www.muslimhiphop.com, for example, criticises rebellion among Muslim rappers, offering a counter-selection of morally conservative artists.

'Islamopunk' is another trend encompassing punk, hard rock and hip hop influences. Initially spreading particularly among American-Asian Muslims, it was rapidly reflected by the publication of Michael Muhammed Knight's (2004) novel, *The Taqwacores*. The author, an American of Irish-Catholic descent who converted to Islam, proposes the adaptation of *taqwa*, an Islamic concept of love and fear of Allah, to Hardcore, a punk subgenre. In his view, what relates Islam to punk is that both 'smash idols' such as materialism and dogmatism, thereby also contesting conservative establishments. A wide range of intellectual activities and music groups inspired by Islamic punk and, partly, by this book, gave rise to several forums and blogs. Among the most popular groups – with MySpace profiles – are *Vote Hezbollah*, *Al-Thawra*, and above all, *The Kominas*, whose song, 'Rumi Was a Homo', controversially attacks Siraj Wahhaj, a prominent Brooklyn imam accused of homophobia.

Finally, recent increasing popularity of virtual worlds such as 'Second Life' (SL) has also seen the emergence of virtual Islamic settlements. With over 7 million residents (as of June 2007), SL is a user-created 3D virtual reality enabling its 'virtual citizens' to participate to the creation of this virtual world, to communicate through movable avatars, organise individual and group activities, and buy virtual goods and services. The presence of religious groups was first reported in 2004 when a virtual Catholic mass was organised. Subsequently, Buddhist, Jewish,

Muslim and several Christian groups have settled, triggering long discussions on Second Life's forums. Interestingly, several Islamic groups and mosques and even a research centre, the Tanseem Projects, have recently been settled, reflecting a considerable diversity of scholarly and political views.

Conclusion

This chapter suggests two key conclusions: first, that Islam – here we have focused particularly on the Sunni Middle East – has often been moulded for political goals by both rulers and their opposition; and, second, that such manifestations, in all their 'extremist', 'conservative' or 'progressive' diversity, must be understood as a product of their political contexts, not of some religious 'essence'.

What exercises political attention particularly in the West after '9/11', is the idea of 'Islam' as an inescapably radical and violent political force. The history of the development of 'Islamism', however, reveals a wide range of ideologies and political practices responding to specific problems, such as corruption, oppression or foreign interference. In this sense, the similarities between the political origins and trajectories of these movements and their nationalist counterparts are more significant than their differences.

As Halliday (2003) and Esposito (1999) show, the notion that Muslim cultures must necessarily have a confrontational relationship with others, is a myth. Similarly, notions of a 'Green Peril' are not new, dating back to the Iranian Revolution. Along with the idea of 'Islamic terrorism' as an unprecedented – and unprecedentedly dangerous – threat, both these ideas were criticised already in the early 1990s for being a thinly veiled attempt to look for new enemies after the end of the Cold War. The idea that Islam *per se* presents a threat is therefore not only historically wrong, but also far from new: the heat generated by the events of 11 September, 2008 is the latest version of this idea. The fact remains that violent Islamists are a small minority, and that the wider anti-Western centre of gravity in Middle Eastern politics has much more to do with the corrupt and socially ineffective regimes – eager to receive Western support in the name of a 'democracy', but reticent to translate it into practice – than it does with religion. The real challenge, therefore, is to understand and deal with the underlying issues of political representation, accountability and welfare which generate Islamist movements.

In this context, Islamism remains the most potent opposition to authoritarian regimes. Moreover, the presence of Islamists in power in Turkey shows that Islamists are not necessarily anti-democratic, or anti-Western. National and international attitudes can help bring such groups into the political fold, or radicalise them.

This chapter has covered considerable territory, necessarily ignoring much that falls under the rubric of 'Islam and Politics'. There has been no in-depth discussion of 9/11 and its aftermath, or of the relationship between Muslim immigrants and their European host societies, their impact on debates about asylum and immigration, or of the development of 'European Islam(s)'.

An implicit over-simplification which we tried to avoid is, however, common to many treatments: in their political engagement, Muslims are implicitly represented as either middle-of-the-road democrats, secular and absorbed into mainstream Western societies; or as radical and violent extremists, probably bearded and dressed in *galabiyyas*. The last section, in particular, hopefully challenges such over-simplifications. What is important about those phenomena is that they directly and innovatively intervene in a public debate about Islam and about politics in a way which transcends conventional dualisms – secularism/public, religion/private, moderate/radical and geographical boundaries. What it means to be 'Muslim' continuously finds new expressions, all of which are equally valid ways of articulating the relationship between 'Islam' and 'Politics', just as in the relationship between politics and other religions. Moreover, in their geographical, cultural and political hybridity, they explode the myth of 'Political Islam' as either modernist or anti-modern.

This diversity of Muslims' contemporary politics is at least as important as the historical, theological and jurisprudential diversity of the movements outlined above. The point about 'Political Islam' is not that it is 'Islamic', but that it is political.

Bibliography

Ahmad, A. (1984) *Islam in the Era of Postmodernity*, London: Palgrave Macmillan.
Ayubi, N. (1997) *Political Islam*, London: Routledge.
Beinin, J. and Stork, J. (eds) (1997) *Political Islam: Essays from Middle East Report*, Berkeley: University of California Press.
Bunt, G. (2003) *Islam in the Digital Age: E-jihad, Online Fatwas and Cyber Islamic Environments*, London: Pluto.
Choueiri, Y. (1990) *Islamic Fundamentalism*, London: Continuum.
Cooke, M. and Lawrence, B. (eds) (2005) *Muslim Networks from Hajj to Hip Hop*, Chapel Hill: University of North Carolina Press.
Eickelman, D. and Anderson, J. (2003) 'Redefining Muslim Publics', in D. Eickelman and J. Anderson (eds), *New Media in the Muslim World: The Emerging Public Sphere*, Bloomington, Ind.: Indiana University Press.
Eickelman, D. and Piscatori, J. (2004) *Muslim Politics*, 2nd edn, London: Princeton University Press.
Esposito, J. (1999) *Islamic Threat: Myth or Reality?*, New York: Oxford University Press.
Esposito, J. and Voll, J. (1996) *Islam and Democracy*, Oxford: Oxford University Press.

109

Guazzone, L. (ed.) (1995) *The Islamist Dilemma: The Political Role of Islamist Movements in the Contemporary Arab World*, Reading: Ithaca Press.

Halliday, F. (2003) *Islam and the Myth of Confrontation*, London: I.B. Tauris.

Hourani, A. (1983) *Arabic Thought in the Liberal Age*, Cambridge: Cambridge University Press.

Hourani, A., Khoury, P. and Wilson, M. (eds) (1993) *The Modern Middle East*, Berkeley: University of California Press.

Knight, M. Muhammad (2004) *The Taqwacores*, New York: Autonomedia. (Telegram's 2007 UK edition was heavily censored in the wake of the 'Danish cartoons' affair.)

Roy, O. (1994) *The Failure of Political Islam*, London: I.B. Tauris.

Roy, O. (2004) *Globalized Islam: The Search for a New Ummah*, London: Hurst.

Sadowski, Y. (1997) 'The New Orientalism and the Democracy Debate', in J. Beinin and J. Stork (eds), *Political Islam: Essays from Middle East Report*, London: I.B. Tauris.

Said, E. (1995) *Orientalism: Western Conceptions of the Orient*, revd edn, London: Penguin.

Said, E. (1997) *Covering Islam: How the Media and the Experts Determine How We See the Rest of the World*, 2nd edn, London: Vintage.

Salamè, G. *et al.* (eds) (1994) *Democracy without Democrats?*, London: I.B. Tauris.

Salvatore, A. (1999) *Islam and the Political Discourse of Modernity*, Reading: Ithaca Press.

8

Shiism and politics[1]

Mohammad Nafissi

Shiism represents Islam's largest minority branch with up to 15% of the world's 1.5 billion Muslims. Like the majority Sunnis, the Shia further divide into several sects of which the Imami or Twelver Shias are the largest and politically the most significant. This has not always been the case. If this account had been written almost any time in Islam's first millennium, the Ismaili or Sevener sect, the founders and rulers of the Fatimid empire in the eleventh and twelfth centuries and several other states in later periods, would have formed its main focus. But this being the twenty-first century and a short chapter, I concentrate on Imami Shiism and discuss its political impact with reference to Iran, its main home since the Safavids made it the religion of the empire they founded in the sixteenth century. After Iran's revolution in 1979, the country's status as Shia Islam's core state was further enhanced by the establishment of Islam's first and only full fledged (clerical) theocracy.

In part thanks to the resonance and resources of the Islamic republic (IR), since the 1980s political Shiism has gained momentum in most states with a significant Shia population. States with 10% or more Shia include Azerbaijan (approximately 75% of total population), Bahrain (70%), Iraq (60%), Lebanon (the largest group at 35%), Yemen (40%), Kuwait (35%), Pakistan (20%), Afghanistan (18%), UAE (15%), Oman (10%), Qatar (10%) and Saudi Arabia (10%). Not only variations in the size of Shia community but also other differences, including institutional capacity and sociological composition of Shia sects, geo-political factors and relative significance of other sources of identity, contribute to significant variations in the impact of the so-called Shia revival (Nasr 2006; cf. Nakash 2006). Note, however, that consequential to their geo-political distribution and cultural resources, Shias' political influence has historically been greater than their numbers and this is certainly so today.

The first part of this chapter discusses the sacred foundations of Shiism with reference to which all subsequent significant Shia approaches to politics, quietist and revolutionary, theocratic and pluralist, have developed. These foundations were laid during a period where the 'proto-Shia' lost battles to achieve, retain or renew 'the rightly guided' form of governance. The second part is devoted to the period characterised by the quietist rejection of politics and the consolidation of 'private jurisprudence' (Kadivar 1997: 13). The period between Shiism's emergence from semi-clandestine conditions as the official religion of the new Safavid state and Iran's Constitutional Revolution (1905–11), which divided the Shia hierocracy for and against democracy, is discussed in the third part. The fourth part examines the development of democratic and theocratic Shiism under the 'modernising' Pahlavi monarchy which targeted Islam as a developmental hindrance. The ascendancy since 1979 of Khomeini's theocratic Shiism and its contradictory realisation in an Islamic theo-democracy is the focus of the fifth part. The chapter concludes with remarks on the broader politics and prospects of Shiism.

Islam's sacred foundations and the rise of Shiism

Although signifying a diverse, changing, tradition, 'Islam' is understandably considered the political religion *par excellence*. As the 'final' re-formation of the Abrahamic tradition, Mohammad's political fusion of temporal and spiritual authority realised the millenarian Jewish longing for the age when Israelites were united under a single prophet king. Judaism, as Weber observed, 'never in theory rejected the state and its coercion but, on the contrary, expected in the Messiah their own masterful political ruler' (Weber 1978: 594). Mohammad fulfilled this expectation by extending, in line with Christian universalism, Yahweh's immediate constituency to humanity as a whole. In the process, he founded a holy state and resolved the Christian problem of the Saviour's postponed return and the prolonged separation of secular and religious realms. It is thus not surprising that the rise of Shiism is traced to succession conflicts following Mohammad's death in 632 AD.

The followers ('*shia*') of Ali, the Prophet's cousin and son-in-law, lost the battle of succession in the community's consultative council to Abubakr, another companion of the Prophet and his father-in-law, and his proto-Sunni followers. Following the consolidation of Shiism as a distinct branch of Islam, this dispute came

to be seen as the first of a series of acts of injustice committed by 'usurpatory' (*al-jae'r*) caliphs against the Prophet's true 'deputies', i.e. Ali and his 'infallible' off-spring. To avoid martyrdom, the fate believed to have been visited on every one of his forefathers, the last and twelfth Imam went into occultation in 874 CE (Momen 1985: 165). Like Jesus Christ, who will accompany him along with other Imams, Imam Mahdi will return to restore the just order before the Judgement Day.

Although this primordialist (re-) construction of the Sunni–Shia split is understandable in the retrospective light of the schism itself, it is not supported by a critical scrutiny of scanty (and contested) historical evidence or indeed the mytho-historical accounts that have functioned as facts in shaping the actions of generations of believers. The salient observation here is that however unhappily, Ali himself accepted the consensus of the community notables and went on to be elected as the fourth caliph and included by the future Sunnis (who considered the actual order of succession legitimate) as the last of the especially venerated 'rightly guided caliphs'. The consecration of these caliphs took place when the participatory basis of their polity was replaced by the dynastic principle and the armed might of the Umayyad clan. This and other evidence all point to the rise of Umayyad's caliphate that ended the retrospectively sacred era of democratic politics as the decisive turning point to which the Sunni–Shia divide should be traced.

All notable branches of Islam were consolidated in response to the question posed by the Umayyad's forcible seizure and transformation of the mighty guided caliphate into a hereditary institution: how to reconcile the separation of the sword and the word with their self-appointed role as the trustees of the sacred era's unity of the sword and the word represented by the Prophet's divine appointment and his successors' democratic mandate? (Nafissi 2005).

Both Shia and Sunni solutions were crucially influenced by the example of Ali's sons, the realist Hassan and the idealist Hussein, the second and third Shii Imams. Elected the fifth caliph after his father's assassination amidst the Umayyad's armed rebellion against Ali, Hassan gave it up in favour of the rebellious Muawiyyah 'since I considered whatever spares blood as better than whatever causes it be shed' (Madelung 1997: 323). In return, it was agreed that the new caliph allowed the 'community' (umma and its notables) to choose his successor. Instead, Muawiyyah appointed his 'depraved' son, Yazid, as his successor without consultation, causing Hossein's uprising (1997: 322). Invited by the people of Kufa to lead them against Yazid and then abandoned in the face of the overwhelming force dispatched by the new caliph, Hossein refused to escape or surrender and was martyred along with his closest companions. Hossein's martyrdom is seen as Shiism's most identifiable and commemorated hallmark, a militant counterpart to the passion of Christ.

In view of the double failure of these and other attempts to restore the 'rightly guided caliphate' even after the success of the 'Abbasid revolution' in overthrowing the Umayyads in 750 CE, both Shii and Sunni political theologies developed via two versions of 'quietism', which may be distinguished as oppositional and accommodationist or 'realist'. Repelled by the divisiveness and futility of opposition to ruling caliphs, and committed to guarding Islam's sacred legacy from their despotic reach, the emerging Sunni hierocracy developed an ingenious 'second-best' solution that dominated until western modernity intervened. Sanctifying and drawing on the Prophet's at least partly fabricated words and deeds (tradition/sunna), 'traditionist' scholars developed the Islamic law (Shari'a) that effectively replaced the Quran as the Muslim's ultimate guide. This enabled them to (1) extend and resolve the Quran's limited and ambiguous legal content, and (2) trump all living claimants to Islam, including caliphs, Shia Imams, rationalist theologians and Sufi masters, with the legacy of the dead prophet. Thus armed with the Shari'a, the men of the word struck a compact with the wielders of the sword which separated political and religious realms but masked it in view of the sacred era's unified legacy. Accordingly, the caliphs retained the title of 'commander of the faithful' but had very little to do with matters of faith, and the religious establishment, although projecting a comprehensive and binding Shari'a, left the political sphere to the rulers and did not follow or develop original Islam's political legacy. Western modernity eventually highlighted the debilitating costs of this ideological conflation of the ideal and actual in Sunni Islam, including its 'closure of the gate ijtihad' (rational development of Islamic traditions) and the associated failure to develop a church-like agency, able to respond effectively to new developments. From this perspective, Shiism presents a contrasting, evolutionary, case, even though it appeared to have lost the battle of hegemony for good, 'Islamic', even proto-modern reasons: insistence on caliphate as the preserve of Ali's offspring undermined the case for opposing the ruling dynasties and minimised the role of community (umma) and consultation (shura); the insistence on divine sanction and holiness of Imams contradicted Mohammad's position as God's last messenger. The full explanation of this paradox requires a comparative account of the Sunni developments (Nafissi 2005); here only a brief overview of the Shia trajectory can be provided.

Shiism and political principles

Emerging in response to injustices suffered by Ali and the Prophet's 'family' (ahl- al Bayt) at the hands of usurping caliphs,

113

Shiism centred around the ideal of justice and opposition to ruling caliphs (Sachedina 1988; Manzoor al-Adjdad 2002). In addition to Islam's three universal principles that there are no gods but God (the principle of *tawhid* or unity), that Mohammad is his (last) messenger (*nabbovat* or prophecy) and resurrection (*ma'aad*), Shia Muslims asserted two other related principles. These are justice (*adl*) and divinely guided leadership (*imamate*) confirmed in the longer Shia call to prayer enjoins the community to act justly (*hayya ala khayr al-amal*) and, in some versions, attests to Ali's divine appointment as Muslims' ruler-guide (*wali*). The major Shia sects originally divided over the leadership and organisation of the struggle for just governance. Ismailis built a centralised missionary organisation around the offspring of Ismail, the predeceased eldest son of the Sixth Imam, eventually establishing the Fatimid empire in North Africa. For a period, this revolutionary–hereditary fusion of Imamate and caliphate posed the gravest threat to the Abbasid caliphate and its allied sultanates. Eventually, however, it proved unsustainable as Caesaropapism retarded the work of Ismaili missionaries and left the empire with a majority Sunni population open to the restoration of Sunni rule, and a political order threatened by incompetent hereditary rulers, patrimonialsim, and sibling rivalry (Hodgson 1974: 25–8; Daftary 2007).

In contrast, the Imami hierocracy's capacity for evolutionary development was enhanced by a quietist delegation of the struggle for justice to an indefinite future marked by the return of the Saviour. The idea of occultation cleared the ground for four major evolutionary developments. First, it maintained the universal Shia claim that God never leaves the world without a living guide, while minimising its debilitating institutional and political consequences by making him invisible. Thus imamate was removed as a source of politico-religious schism, as was reliance on inherited personal charisma that blocked the institutional development of other Shii sects.

Second, the occultation completed the differentiation of the religious field itself by withdrawing the only legitimate agent for restoring the original sacred unity of political and religious authorities. As the last Imam was made invisible to protect himself, so too his followers had a collective obligation of self-protection until his return. This sanctioned the practice of dissimulation (*taghiyyeh*) of one's true beliefs as a means of shielding the Shias from persecution by Sunni rulers and clergy. The corollary of this double occultation and distance from the existing political order was reliance on the community and its resources. In giving up any claim on government or any hope of reforming or replacing it, the Shia community thus started a limited form of self-governance which in time led to the rise of a hierocracy with an autonomy and agency exceptional in the Muslim world and elsewhere with the exception of western Christianity.

Third, occultation left a massive void at the heart and head of the Shia community that could no longer be legitimately filled in patrimonial fashion by an Imam, or a Caliph–Imam. Following the Sunni lead and borrowing heavily from the more developed Sunni schools of law, the Shia developed their own version of the Shari'a. Although seriously limiting in many intellectual and creative respects, the legalistic turn was important in providing a basis for a stable and systemic institutional identity and action.

Fourth, adding traditions of the dead Imams as the distinguishing source of Shii law did not satisfy Shias' demands for living guidance which had initially led them to follow the Imams. This was addressed not only by waiting for the Imam's return but also by allowing the gradual assumption of his 'prophetic' functions by the clergy whose higher ranks, the *mujtahids*, retained, in contrast to mainstream Sunni jurists, the independent use of 'reason', *ijtihad*. Although this presumed delegation was extended centuries later to the Imam's political functions in Khomeini's reform in Iran, the depoliticised–legalist Shiism has remained influential, both in its own right and, ironically, as a legitimising source of its politicised theocratic variants.

Nevertheless, it is unlikely that these advantages would have added to an evolutionary breakthrough without the forceful, and theologically precluded, patronage of the Safavid state that inaugurated the third period in the evolution of Shiism. Notwithstanding the many claimants to the mantle of Mahdi since the tenth century, evidently he remains in occultation. Yet, the rise of the Safavids in the sixteenth century and the installation of Imami Shiism as their imperial religion, not only removed the threat of Sunni persecution, the main reason for the double occultation of Imam and community, but also led to the conversion of the Sunni majority by coercion as well as persuasion. This development entailed the reconsideration of the Shia approach to political authority and ended the period of so-called private jurisprudence stretching between the occultation (874 CE) and the coronation of the first Safavid Shah in 1501.

For over two centuries, the Shia hierocracy served the Safavid empire until Afghan invasions led to its collapse in the eighteenth century. In the process, Iran was transformed into an irreversibly Shia society. Although the Safavids had entrenched the Shia scholars to ensure their own longevity, they ended up by serving the latter both when in power and then by losing power. As the only society-wide institution to maintain continuity in the face of reassertion of centrifugal tendencies between the collapse of Safavid state in 1721 and the crowning of the first Qajar monarch in 1795, the hierocracy emerged in the nineteenth century with its prestige, self-confidence and power enhanced absolutely and relative to the state.

The Qajar dynasty lacked the religious credentials of the Safavids or the 'national' reach that the hierocracy had achieved some three centuries before the Qajars turned themselves from a tribal formation into Iran's ruling dynasty. In this context the hierocracy was compelled to reconsider its role beyond its classical conception as 'the Imam's deputy', engaging in charitable distribution of religious taxes, supervising care of orphans and disabled, and ensuring the correct implementation of religious rituals. At the hands of the hegemonic (*Usuli*) faction, this led to a clear division of the members of the community into a mass of followers or imitators and a few senior *mujtahids* or *maraj'a taghlids* (sources of imitation, SI). The latter were so qualified by virtue of their knowledge of the Islamic law and principles (certified by their predecessors and demonstrated in their own catechism and commentaries on scriptures), and justice in the practice of law and piety (*taghva*). However, instead of taking this to its hierarchical conclusion of establishing a supreme authority, a Pope or a quasi-Imam, the choice of one or other SI to 'imitate' was left to the potential followers themselves. Consequently, the hierocracy has remained a multi-centred network, only occasionally engendering, without any formal mechanism, an SI with paramount authority (Cole 1983). The influence of the SIs to this day varies with their sense of 'leadership' (*riyast*) as indicated by the size of their voluntary following among the clergy and lay believers (Amanat 1988: 99–111). The followers provide the religious leaders with the social and financial resources (including the religious taxes) with which the Sources of Imitation support the junior clergy who in turn transmit their rulings and promote their views.

The hierocracy's association with the state as its official religion was thus complemented by its role as the society's representative agency with growing capacity for collective action in opposition as well as in support of the state (Algar 1967). The resulting dynamic dialectic was reflected in the so-called theory of bipolar governance. Bipolarity refers to the division of the political domain and functions overseen by the Sultan/Shah (*saltanat*) and the religious domain and the 'prophetic' functions guided by the SIs, the Sultan's counterparts. Although sometimes conflictual, this relationship was primarily a partnership based on mutual need and distinct ideological, social and politico-military resources that powered the clergy and the crown. Iran's constitutional revolution forced the clergy to choose between continuing this partnership or the one it had forged with the increasingly rebellious nation and thus help create a new type of society.

Between the state and the nation: autocratic versus democratic Shiism

The governor of Tehran's public flogging of two respected merchants, the civil society's leading lay strata and the main source of religious taxes and donations was a catalyst for the Constitutional Revolution (1905–11). The anti-despotic camp that sprang into action had already had its dress rehearsal during one of the world's first and most widely observed consumer boycotts ever. The 'Tobacco Rebellion' of 1891–2, stopped the consumption of tobacco until the monopoly concession awarded to a British subject, Major G. Talbot, to produce and sell the country's entire tobacco crop for fifty years, was cancelled (Keddie 1966). Driven by reformist clergy and intelligentsia and the merchants, the mass mobilisation was made possible by an edict from

(or attributed to) the paramount SI calling for the boycott. Forced to cancel the concession and apparently overcompensate Talbot, the big loser in this landmark battle was the clergy's original benefactors, the Shia crown, while the hierocracy consolidated its social ties and political position.

Again driven by the bazaaris and modernist clerics and officials, but primarily fronted by mainstream *mujtahids*, the first, generally peaceful, phase of the Constitutional Revolution was victorious after a relatively short campaign (1905–6). Royal ascent was given to a liberal constitution largely based on that of Belgium. The revolution entered its second longer and far bloodier phase with the enthronement of Mohammad Ali Shah, a committed autocrat who bombarded the parliament and was met with the resistance of the revolutionary forces in a civil war that only ended in 1911 with the Shah's escape to Russia.

It is in this phase that for the first time Imami-Usuli Shiism divided openly and violently over the question of just order. Now standing opposed as leaders of the revolutionary camp or apologists of the autocracy, the Shia jurists were compelled to articulate their polarised political agendas directly and publicly rather than as derivative, truncated and obscure legal commentaries. In the period between the Tobacco protest and the execution of the leader of the autocratic faction, Sheikh Fazlollah Nouri, Shia political theology developed to make sense and/or legitimise its own surprising political power. Among the many often rushed, confused or weathervane pronouncements, two generally and mutually illuminating treatises may be singled out, Nouri's *Illegitimacy of Constitutionalism* (1907) and Ayatollah Mohammad Hossein Naini's *Government from the Standpoint of Islam* (1907) in defence of the constitutionalism and what may be called democratic Islam.

In contrast to Khomeini's *Islamic Government* (1970), the foundation stone of IR, both Nouri and Naini recognised the classical Shia separation of religion and state. The central political difference between the opposed camps was whether autocratic rulers should remain clergy's partners and in charge of the political domain. For Nouri, the answer was 'yes', whereas the constitutionalist turned to the nation and its elected representatives. Anticipating Khomeini theologically, though not politically, Nouri's fundamental objection to constitutionalism rested on the claim that 'Islam has no gap for somebody to fill' through democratic legislature. To assume so, he claimed, 'is pure heresy' and entails capital punishment whilst praying for the success of the autocratic monarch (Nouri 1907: 167).

Perhaps more acutely than his rivals, Nouri sensed the threat democracy posed to traditional Islam or the 'nation' (1907: 165). Yet, he was undermined by leaving two important questions unanswered. First, if the nation was not immunised against the anti-Islamic tendencies, the Russian-backed crown was evidently even more susceptible to such forces. Second, if the clerical–sultanate status quo ante was to be renewed, then its coincidence with the evident decline of Shia Iran and its subordination to 'Christian' powers had to be explained. This of course is the question yet to be faced by Muslim traditionalists and fundamentalists until today.

In contrast, Naini's tract opens with identifying precisely the 'despotic' regime and religion defended by Nouri as primary causes of Muslim societies' backwardness and traces the European ascendancy to having got rid of both earlier (Naini 1907: 1–17). From this perspective, the actually existing Islam had many urgent gaps to fill. This entailed not only learning from Europe but also acknowledging the merit of Sunnis' original emphasis on consultation in the choice of caliphs rather than relying on sacred lineage. Naini thus followed reformers such as Sayyid Jamal, enhancing the universalist basis of their pan-Islamism by authenticating democracy as internal to Islam's sacred, proto-modern, heritage (Bellah 1970). Although lacking the absolute justice dependent on the Saviour's return, democracy was its closest human approximation.

Anti-Islamic modernisation and the rise of theocratic Islam

Following the revolution of 1905–11, democratic constitutionalism appeared as an irreversible evolutionary advance. It was the (more) 'rightly guided' culmination of a progressive path through tyrannical Sunni rule and the far more congenial tyranny of Shia dynasties. As deputies of the Imams, the Shia clergy had realised what had eluded their Imams and their Sunni counterparts: the (democratic) fusion of state and community, a true Islamic nation-state. In the next fifteen years, however, this account, too, became redundant as the revolutionary coalition, its main vehicle, collapsed. Violent factionalism pitting moderates (including most religious leaders) against radicals (mainly revolutionary social democrats and secularist nationalists) broke out, exacerbated by tribal and regional centrifugal forces unleashed by several developments: the revolution, the First World War, and semi-colonial interventions of the British and Russian empires. This paved the way for the emergence of a new type of autocracy. Reza Shah, the founder of the Pahlavi dynasty in 1925, viewed Islam as a major hindrance to his mission of revitalising–modernising the nation. Shunning backward Islam, Pahlavis promoted ethnic nationalism centred on the glorification of ancient Persia whose Aryan people provided the modernising link with the glorious contemporary Western Aryans.

In this context, quietist, depoliticised Shiism managed to reclaim its predominance. Unlike the pre-Safavid period, however, this revival took place within a generally shrinking religious field, except in one important respect which broadened the range of Shia voices. The graduates of the newly established Tehran University and the scholarship students sent to Europe as part of the modernisation drive articulated their own liberal and socialist variants of Islam and broke the hold of clergy as monopoly suppliers of Islam. These developments become visible when Iran entered another anarchic–democratic interregnum following the Allied invasion and forced abdication of the pro-German Reza Shah in 1941. The years before the new Shah regained autocratic power thanks to the CIA-engineered coup in 1953, saw the rise of political groups such as God Worshipping Socialists and various professional associations, with lay Muslims playing leading roles. For example, Mehdi Bazargan, the first Prime Minister of IR was a leading member of the Association of Engineers and went on a decade later to set up the Freedom Movement, the major liberal Islamist party that included many influential lay and clerical leaders of IR as members or supporters (Chehabi 1990). On the theocratic side, the Devotees of Islam, an organisation inspired by the example of the Muslim Brotherhood, achieved notoriety with several high-profile assassinations including Prime Minister Razmara and the country's most notable historian (and critic of Shiism), the former cleric Ahmad Kasrvai (Akhavi 1980). Khomeini was associated with this movement and his first book-length contribution is an uncompromising defence of Shia orthodoxy against the charges of backwardness raised by Kasravi and others (Khomeini 1947).

At the time, in contrast to both theocratic and democratic Islamists, the religious leadership was resigned to further loss of ground under the Pahlavi modernisation which was considered less damaging than the agendas of the liberal and leftist opposition. This explains its general support for the royalist camp against the alliance of religious and secular liberals and socialists in the conflict over the powers of the monarch and the nationalisation of oil. However, the second Pahlavi monarch rewarded the religious leaders for their support by pursuing a more corrupt variant of his father's combination of militant secularism and oppressive modernisation which in turn fuelled the rise of revolutionary Shiism in both theocratic and quasi-Marxist forms.

The decisive turning point came a decade after the 1953 coup that restored the Pahlavi autocracy. To gain legitimacy, especially in the eyes of the fast growing educated, urban stratum, the regime started its own 'White Revolution' by appropriating the many demands of the left and liberal opposition that the Shah, along with Western (and Soviet) social scientists and advisers, considered his regime's main threat. Instead, the crown not only lost its traditional mainstays, but failed to gain a reliable constituency among the emerging modern sectors. The extension of women's rights alienated the mainstream clergy, and the land reform effectively eliminated the landlords as a socio-political force, whilst increased oppression and dependence on the USA discredited the reform package as a whole (Katouzian 1981; Abrahamian 1988).

Khomeini's rise as a national leader is traceable to this moment. He was the youngish SI who issued an edict banning 'Taghiyyeh' and thus ditching quietism in what he considered an existential struggle against the state (Moin 1999: 96). On 5 June 1963, hundreds of (mainly) Khomeini followers were killed in an aborted rising against the 'White Revolution' in what was soon described as another Ashura, the day of Hossein's martyrdom. However, one telling difference this time was that the martyred were the ordinary followers while their leader was eventually sent to the safety of exile in Iraq whence he made his triumphant return in 1979 to assume the title and authority of the last Imam. In the intervening period, Khomeini reformed his corner of the hierocracy into a revolutionary network linking his supporters in mosques, seminaries, bazaars, charitable associations and several clandestine organisations engaged in activities ranging from assassination to distribution of his edicts and collection of religious taxes. In retrospect, and after many aborted claims and fallen claimants, Shiism was about to find its own Luther, Pope and Constantine, not to mention Lenin, rolled into one.

Democratic revolution and theo-democratic republic

According to Mohsen Kadivar, Khomeini was the first among the Shia jurists to have used the term Islamic government and to have theorised it politically as an absolute theocracy (Kadivar 1997: 24). This position, however, not only still remains that of a minority of senior clerics, but was also only one among several championed by Khomeini himself (Kadivar 1998: 160–204). Khomeini's writings and pronouncements feature four different approaches to Islamic governance: the traditional bipolar theory whereby the state respects or at least does not publicly flout the Shari'a (1947); theocratic governance of the jurisconsult (*faqih*) according to which an SI presides over the Shari'a's implementation (1970); democratic bipolarity championed by Naini and his modern descendants (1978–9); and theo-democracy of IR (1979–) whose theological and political basis was radically undermined by the time of Khomeini's death (1988).

As the legitimating source of the theocratic–military (Revolutionary Guard Corps and Basiji Militia) axis dominating IR, however, the series of lectures published as *Islamic Government* (IG) *or The Governance of the Jurisconsult* [*Velayat-e Faqih*] (1970), remains Khomeini's most influential political contribution. The distance between the revolutionary theocratic Khomeini of IG and the still widespread, traditional, Shia ideal of governance may be gauged by the following passages. In his first major work on Shiism and politics he leaves no doubt about bipolar governance: 'We do not say that government is the task of the jurist. But we say government should be run in accordance with divine law which is in the interest of the country and the people. And this cannot be undertaken without the supervision of the clergy as stipulated in the Constitution' (1947: 222). Contrast this with what he says about the same issue in IG: 'If the ruler adheres to Islam, he must necessarily submit to *faqih*, asking him about the ordinances of Islam in order to implement them. This being the case, the true rulers are *fuqaha* [jurisonculs] themselves, and rulership ought officially to be theirs' (Khomeini 1970/1981: 60) At the time, merely a utopian theory, this shift laid the ground for the profound transformation of Shiism.

Underpinning his practical revolutionary stance against the Pahlavi regime, this political theology was crucial in turning Khomeini's hierocratic network into a party machine dedicated to the seizure of political power. The Shia community is now re-imagined in its pre-Safavid situation where all 'non-Shia', i.e. all existing political orders, are 'systems of *kufr*' or anti-Islamic/Shia (48), but where the believers – and here's the major advance – no longer have to wait the return of the Imam for the establishment of the just 'Islamic government defined as governance of the just jurists with the same authority given to the Prophet and the [12th] Imam' (Algar 1981: 26). In time, of course, Khomeini returns as Imam Khomeini.

Despite some 'vigorous criticism' from senior SIs (Moin 1999: 158–9), this revolutionary, if not heretical, reform did not marginalise Khomeini within the hierocracy; nor did its totalitarian–theocratic agenda lead to his isolation among the rest of the opposition. This was, firstly, because of the historically decentralised flexibility of the Shia hierocracy where the autonomy of individual *mujtahids* was entrenched and geo-politically dispersed. Secondly, Khomeini's position enhanced the powers of the clergy overall and appeared as the evolutionary culmination of a century of institutional, theological and political development. Third, he presented it at a time when his fellow clerics shared his particular concerns over the anti-Islamic direction of the autocracy. Fourth, Khomeini's revolutionary clericalism replete with attacks on imperialism resonated widely in the 1960s and 1970s, coinciding with the rise of new radical agendas throughout the world in a variety of Third Worldist, neo-Marxist, Maoist, Guevaraist and liberationist-clerical guises. In this context, rather than losing support for his break with traditional Shiism, his theocratic militancy attracted a large contingent of energetic junior clerics enhancing his links with other 'anti-imperialist' and even liberal movements. Fifth, whereas every other political agenda (with the partial exception of the Shah's own suicidal one) had an exemplar in Western democracies, Soviet Union, Cuba, China or Iran's own brief periods of constitutional monarchy, Khomeini's was truly novel and untested. This gave it an appealing, utopian quality that seduced many into overlooking its otherwise problematic features.

Khomeini thus represented a potential second-best option for most other members of the emerging coalition that eventually overthrew the Shah. The revolution, let alone 'the Islamic revolution', however, would not have taken place without the Shah's own self-destructive moves that blocked the possibility of a reformist resolution of his regime's deepening crisis. Nor would Khomeini's position as the leader of the widest revolutionary front in the modern era have been assured without the groundwork laid by pluralist Shias of both reformist and revolutionary variety.

In the late Pahlavi era, liberal-reformist Shiism was represented by the Freedom movement led by the aforementioned Mehdi Bazargan and Ayatollah Taleghani, both ardent supporters of the secular nationalist Mossadeq and most prominent Muslim opposition leaders of their generation (Chehabi 1990). The armed People's Mujahedin Organisation represented radical Islam and was led by Masood Rajavi who, following the Organisation's failed attempts in the 1980s to overthrow IR, has presided over its cultish decline (Abrahamian 1989; Banisadr 2004). Associated with both movements, but remaining an independent thinker with the greatest influence in renewing Islam in Iran, was Ali Shariati who died in 1977, a year before the revolutionary process became visible. Shariati has been singled out as 'probably the only twentieth-century Iranian intellectual who created a socio-political momentum which gave birth to a social movement, culminating in a social revolution' (Rahnema 1998: 370; Bazargan 1984: 103), albeit one that engendered an order which exhibited many traditionalist elements that he had characterised and thoroughly rejected as 'Safavid Shiism' (Shariati 1998).

Eclipsed by Khomeini's triumphant legacy is the fact that the overall share of this broad tendency in Iran's second revolution was at least as great as that of the former and his followers. Notwithstanding their significant differences, Bazargan,

Taleghani, Rajavi, Shariati and their clerical and lay associates may all be distinguished as pluralists in the sense that they reached critically beyond the totalitarian and theocratic accounts of Islam and Shiism. Their Islams openly drew on liberalism, Marxism and other non-Shia, non-Islamic traditions. Through renewing Islam's marginalised tendencies of rational, universalist, inquiry, they effectively questioned the narrow legalism of the clerical establishment and released the evolutionary potential of the concept of *ijtihad*. Thanks to the pluralists, Islam regained its appeal amongst the educated and especially the young without whom there would not have been an Islamic revolution or republic.

By the time of the revolution, Khomeini had, as discussed above, already developed his preferred, theocratic, option. In the course of the revolution, however, either as a result of genuine conversion as some of his democratic followers believed, or pragmatic recognition of 'the objective conditions', Khomeini himself gave every impression that he favoured a democratic republic that respected Islamic norms or an Islamic republic that respected democratic norms (Bazargan 1984: 49–55; cf. Homayoun 2000). Crucially, he never once referred to the government of jurisconsult and specifically rejected any suggestion that he would have an executive role, assume the powers of the monarch, or directly intervene in the affairs of the state (Kadivar 1998: 172–5). In short, Khomeini's public posture and that which consolidated his position as the leader of the revolutionary coalition coincided with 'the best option' of the religious and lay democrats led by veterans of the Mossadeq movement such as Bazargan, and Karim Sanjabi, the leader of the secular National Front, all of whom were committed to implementing the essentially liberal constitution of Iran's first revolution.

Khomeini's position resembled that of the influential authoritarian left whose constituent groups generally saw liberal democracy as a transitional stage to some idealised version of Soviet, Chinese, Cuban or even Albanian socialism (Behrooz 1999). The liberal agenda, however, united the opposition to the Pahlavi monarchy not only because democracy is the default discourse of all modern oppositions to autocratic regimes. It also reflected 'the objective conditions' after seven decades of modernisation since it was first advanced in Iran's first revolution (Katouzian 1981; Abrahamian 1988). After all, the terminal decline of the Pahlavi regime may be dated to the period in the mid-1970s when rather than democratic reform, the Shah declared the country a one-party, totalitarian state.

Beyond the articulation of a generally democratic Islamic vision, Khomeini's recognition of this scenario was indicated by the appointment of Bazargan as the revolution's prime minister presiding over a cabinet whose members all came from lay liberal religious and secular ranks of Freedom Movement and National Front. Equally telling, Bazargan's appointment was followed by the election of Abolhassan Banisadr as the first president of the republic who belonged to the same camp and was elected with Khomeini's tacit blessing. Finally, the draft constitution was written in the main by Hassan Habibi of Freedom Movement and was based on the French presidential system with no mention of theocratic governance that became the centrepiece of the eventually approved constitution.

By the revolution's second anniversary in the winter of 1981, Bazargan had been replaced by a hardline lay theocrat leading a cabinet with a sizeable clerical membership. President Banisadr was well on his way to being impeached by a parliament dominated by a new theocratic party and would soon go into exile in France. An 'Assembly of Experts', replete with Khomeini's theocratic supporters, had concluded its job as a surrogate Constituent Assembly, enshrining the most momentous development in Shiism since the Safavid period. As a result, the turban was enthroned in place of the crown (Amir Arjomand 1988), while the newly anointed 'Imam Khomeini' reversed the promises of the revolutionary period by assuming the position of the supreme head of the state. Twelver Shiism had its first Caliph–Imam since Imam Ali, except that, as the popular joke went, on any reasonable count, he must be the Thirteenth Imam.

The new constitution did not so much abandon the democratic demands of the revolution as subordinate it to the normative agenda of its dominant faction. Khomeini's republic thus approximated to the ideal of a theo-democracy most clearly articulated by the influential Sunni theorist, Abolala Mawdudi, but yet to be realised in any other Muslim country precisely because, among other things, all lacked a hierocratic organisation with the authority and evolutionary capacity to complete such a project.

A potent brew of mass adulation, radicalising logic of the revolution, and historical fear may have persuaded Khomeini to assume or, as his Shia opponents would say, usurp the title as well as the powers of the Twelfth Imam. As Khomeini remarked on the assassination of his closest disciple and the chair of the revolutionary council, Ayatollah Mottahari, by a dissident Shia group in the early days of the revolution: 'They want to sideline the clergy just as they did after the Constitutional period. They killed Nouri and diverted the path of the nation. They have now the same plan; they have killed Mottahari and perhaps it is my turn tomorrow' (cited in Moin 1999: 223). Khomeini's fear was informed by the fact

that those who intended to 'sideline' the clergy included many of the highest ranking clerics who considered theocracy a step too far in appropriating the unique privileges of the last Imam. Grand Ayatollah Shariatmadari even permitted his followers to establish the Muslim People's Republic Party to fight the ruling theocratic Islamic Republic Party on a democratic platform, before being forced to recant on state television. This and other coercive measures against senior clerics overturned a central plank of Shiism underlined by Khomeini on his way to absolute power: 'the *fuqaha* do not have absolute authority over all other *fuqaha* of their own time, being able to appoint or dismiss them. There is no hierarchy ... endowing one with more authority than another' (Khomeini 1981: 64).

By the time of Khomeini's death in 1988, IR had survived many challenges, including an eight-year war against Iraq, several coup attempts and a US-led economic boycott, and a civil war. In the process, all groups, Islamic or otherwise, opposed to the 'governance of the jurist' were violently suppressed, banned or otherwise excluded from electoral politics. The main threat to theocracy, since then, has instead come from reformist tendencies evolving out of the original theocratic camp. This reflects the nature of IR whose institutional configuration, national and international contexts, ideological goals, and socio-economic roots dramatically exemplify characteristics of a 'torn state'. The country's constitution effectively frames and safeguards this condition by its dual theocratic and democratic conceptions of sovereignty. Theocratic tendency's foremost guardian, 'the supreme leader of the World Muslims', is appointed by an Assembly of Leadership Experts (Islam's first formal 'college of cardinals') which in turn is elected by popular vote, but from a restricted list filtered by the unelected Guardian Council. In addition to 'the supervisory' function 'over the proper execution of the general policies of the system', article 110 of the new constitution gives the leader the power to appoint or dismiss the following:

- Clerical members of the Guardian Council;
- Supreme judicial authority of the country;
- Head of the radio and television network;
- Chief of joint staff;
- Commander of the Islamic Revolution Guards Corps;
- Supreme Commanders of the armed forces.

Among many other notable sources of unaccountable power, the leader also appoints the heads of vast semi-public 'charitable' foundations, and has 'special emissaries' variously 'guiding' the otherwise formally accountable-bureaucratic rational ministries and public organisations inherited from the Pahlavi period. Yet, according to article 107: 'The leader is equal with the rest of the people of the country in the eyes of the law' and article 6 of the Constitution stipulates that 'the affairs of the country must be administered on the basis of public opinion expressed by means of elections'. True to these articles and compelled by its internal divisions, IR must have held more competitive, if highly restricted, elections than any other modern totalitarian or authoritarian state. This contradictory insistence on theocracy and democracy has engendered, on the one hand, a crisis-prone, factionalised state incapable of articulating any viable conception of the 'national interest', and on the other hand, contested domains and democratising tendencies that dispute theocratic domination and may have paradoxically helped ensure its resilience.

Between theo-democracy and theo-autocracy

Ironically, Khomeini's theocracy has survived at the cost of the collapse of the theocratic case that originally underpinned it. This is most obviously attested to by the defection of its once most credible champions, from the Grand Ayatollah Montazeri, now the most senior SI and the chair of the Assembly that drew up the Republic's theo-democratic constitution, to Abdul Karim Soroush, the country's foremost Islamic philosopher and a one-time member of the Council of the Cultural Revolution that presided over the closure and purge of the universities' non-conformist staff (see Soroush, 2007). The depletion of the regime's religious legitimacy became fully evident over the choice of Khomeini's successor and current supreme leader. The current president of the republic, Ali Khamenei, was a relatively junior cleric, lacking certified mastery of religious law, the single most important qualification for the job. His appointment by the Assembly of Experts (filled with politically dominant but theologically minority clerics) showed the extent to which politics had come to trump religion, the first and ultimate justification of Khomeini's theocracy.

This outcome was anticipated in Khomeini's last years. In order to overcome recurring stalemates between the elected and appointed agencies often acting in the name of scientifically informed 'national interest' (e.g. land reform) and religiously fixed principles (sanctity of private property), Khomeini created yet another agency, the Assembly for Determination of the Interests of the Islamic Republic. Rather than addressing the key contradiction between democracy and theocracy, he attempted to bypass it by ruling that Islamic principles and laws may be suspended for an indefinitely renewable period as and when required by the 'interest' of the

Islamic state which were to be determined by the supreme leader's appointees in the new Assembly (Shirazi 1997: 229–44; Zubaida 2003: 182–219). As to be expected from any crisis-ridden programme, ad hoc attempts to patch things up were doomed to failure. In this case, the assembly deepened the difficulty of determining the republic's interest by adding another collective and internally divided agency showing, *contra* Khomeini's assumption of evident and unitary self-sufficiency of Islamic law, that: (1) there was more than one legitimate conception of Islamic governance and 'Islam' even among his own loyal supporters; (2) the question of 'interest' had to be constructed and negotiated rather than read off some text, however holy and everlasting it may be; and (3) the interest of the Islamic state, if defined in terms of clear objectives such as social justice, material welfare, or economic and military power entailed mediation of social sciences and debates over land reform, level of taxation and nationalisation of foreign trade, matters outside the religious jurists' competence. Ironically the democratic framework required for addressing these questions had been the platform on which IR's first prime minister and first president as well as secular democrats had opposed Khomeini's theocratic turn.

Following Khomeini's death, there were two major attempts to end the Republic's transitional character through pragmatic economic liberalisation, and reformist political opening respectively championed by former Presidents Rafsanjani (1989–97) and Khatami (1997–2005). In neither case, however, could Iran's institutionally gridlocked political economy be sufficiently loosened to sustain such seemingly evolutionary advances. By exacerbating the regime's endemic economic and political crisis, President Ahmadinejad's 'populist' fundamentalism (2005–) is seen by some as the last – albeit necessarily doomed – attempt at a theocratic resolution of the regime's

contradictory trajectory. It is however unlikely that he will be able to put Iran on a theocratically governed path of growth and development. Yet, contrary to the 'optimists', democratic reform will not necessarily follow. An equally plausible outcome is acceleration of the developing autocratic–military colonisation of the theo-democracy – already exemplified by the open backing (and vote rigging) of the Revolutionary Guards and Militia without which Ahmadinejad would have been eliminated in the first round of the 2005 presidential election. The Islamic Republic's prolonged transitional period may thus close not with democracy but with a military dictatorship allied to a clerical faction, a theo-autocracy and a Shia variant of Zia-ul-Haq's Pakistan, a truly macabre conclusion to a thousand years of religious evolution and two great revolutions.

This takes us back to the disputes over Mohammad's succession and the rise of the tyrannical caliphate that ended the rightly guided era. In successfully reforming Shiism to give the theocratic jurists the full authority hitherto reserved for the Prophet and Imams, Khomeini founded another tyrannical state in the sense understood by himself in a long line going back to the common foundations of both Shia and Sunni Islam: a state whose actions are ultimately determined not by 'Islamic norms' or the consent of the community, but by its 'interest' as defined by caliphs, sultans or shahs who attained or retained power primarily through the power of the sword. Such 'Islamic' states were of course precisely those against which both quietist and revolutionary Shiism as well as various Sunni schools rose in the first place.

Concluding remarks: the Shia revival and the Islamic Republic

The Islamic Republic has lasted longer than most predicted and in the process has achieved the negative promises of one of its major revolutionary slogans: 'Neither West, nor East, Islamic Republic is the best'. The challenges of Western- and Eastern-inspired Islamic and secular 'liberals' at home have been seen off, and the republic has survived the Soviet collapse to become the most vocal opponent of the American hegemon. Yet, the negative objectives of the revolution have been achieved through an intrinsically unstable, and altogether inefficient, oppressive and particularistic model of governance that could not retain majority support at home, let alone be replicated elsewhere in the Muslim world as was attempted with liberal, social democratic and socialist models.

To judge Iran's position by reading the international press or even academic journals, however, things could not be better. The country's most immediate and important regional and security objectives have been achieved on its behalf by the Anglo-American armies in Afghanistan and Iraq. In this process, the US has also contained the power that Iran considers its number one global enemy, namely the US itself. Whilst the US is stuck in Afghanistan and Iraq, and forced to reconsider its master plan for the Middle East and its decadent Saudi and Egyptian allies, Iran and its Syrian, Lebanese and Palestinian allies seem revived. Although centred on Imami Shiism, the Iranian regime's defiant message resonates among the long oppressed and humiliated Sunnis in the Muslim world not seen since the days of Nasser.

Yet, these advances and their hyped projection by both the Iranian regime and its US, Israeli and Arab opponents should not be allowed to occlude the Republic's central failure: the Iranian revolution has not and will not spread to a single state beyond its borders despite the advances made by the recipients of its revolutionary/oil revenue largess in Iraq, Lebanon and Palestine.

Consonant with Islam's universalist ambitions, 'Khomeini believed that the existing world order should emulate his version of the Islamic state paradigm' (Ramazani 2001: 214). Three decades on, 'political Islam' has certainly outlived the announcements of its 'failure' (Roy 1994; cf. 2004: 74–5), but in highly differentiated forms that range from the Turkish AKP, the initiator of the most extensive programme of democratic reforms in recent Turkish history, to Afghanistan's Taliban representing the most regressive face of Islamism. All these movements in one way or the other may have been energised by the Iranian revolution, but the cardinal point is that none presides over, or aspires to, or is active under conditions that allow the establishment of a clerical theocracy or theo-democracy.

This is the case even in Iraq, Lebanon and Bahrain where the Shia form the largest and most oppressed social groups in unstable states still or until recently dominated by Sunni (or Christian) minorities. Theocracy is ruled out in each case not only because of regional geo-political factors and the balance of domestic power. The collapse of the theological justification for the Iranian theocracy and its rejection by most SIs removes the one agency without which another theocratic IR could not be established. Inside Iran these SIs remain persecuted and marginalised. This has helped extend the reach of the grand Ayatollah Sistani outside and even inside Iran: 'Shias in Lebanon, Bahrain and Saudi Arabia have all watched developments in Iraq with great interest. They all embraced Sistani's pragmatic approach to politics and were quick to echo his call for "one man, one vote". They all looked to gain from following in the footsteps of Iraqi Shia in adopting democracy to turn the tables on the Sunnis' (Nasr 2006: 231, 250).

Vali Nasr exaggerates the extent of Shia–Sunni divide on the question of democracy on two counts, even if the discredited

Sunni autocracies continue using the fear of Shia revival to shore up support as they have done for so long with the Palestine–Israel conflict. First, all Sunni majority states in the Middle East are oppressive and would be overthrown if 'one man, one vote', let alone 'one person, one vote' were to be attempted. Democracy and constitutional government, as Naini recognised, could unite rather than divide Sunnis and Shias. If there is a problem, it arises, on the one hand, from the democratic demands of many Islamist (and secular) movements facing oppressive rulers, and, on the other, from doubts about their own democratic credentials especially when it comes to the implementation of the anti-democratic elements of the orthodox Shari'a.

Secondly, Sistani's position highlights deep divisions within Shiism more than signalling the exacerbation of the Shia–Sunni conflict. Rather than simply uniting the Shia against the Sunni, Sistani's inclusive agenda is threatened by, and threatens, the ruling theocratic faction in Iran, as well as the increasingly powerful militias mobilising in the name of Shiism (and Sunnism) but acting out warlordist scenarios in conditions of lawless insecurity. The theocratic–military axis in Iran may have the power to block the consolidation of secular democracy in Iraq as it has done in Iran itself. But it does not seem to have any viable alternative for Iraq, especially one that would not in some form exacerbate its own multifaceted ideological, political and economic crisis. In the longer term, Iraq will disintegrate or achieve some kind of democratic stability. This means that notwithstanding the current euphoria in Tehran and the fears in Arab capitals about the rise of the Shia arc, the recent developments in the region are on balance working to exacerbate IR's contradictions.

From this perspective, the chief legacy of Khomeini's failed reformation may prove to be the renewal of the case for democratic Shiism (and Islam), first argued

at length by Naini in the course of Iran's first revolution, and by Bazargan and other pluralist Muslims in the revolution of 1979 and ever since. Whether and when the contemporary democratic Shia, together with their secular and Sunni counterparts in the Muslim world and beyond are able to overcome the unholy alliance of Jihadists, theocratic and traditionalist fundamentalists, and the Middle Eastern autocracies and their Western backers of course remains to be seen (Bayat 2007; Nafissi 2007).

Note

1 I thank Jeff Haynes, Farhad Nourbaksh, Najma Yousefi and Sami Zubaida for suggestions that both enhanced my argument and reduced its size to the required limit.

Bibliography

Abrahamian, E. (1988) *Iran between the Two Revolutions*, Princeton: Princeton University Press.
Abrahamian, E. (1989) *Radical Islam: The Iranian Mojahedin*, London: Tauris.
al-Adjdad Manzoor, *S.M.H. Imami Shiism in the Age of Seljuqs* (PhD thesis in Persian) Tehran: Tarbiyat Moddares University.
Akhavi, S. (1980) *Religion and Politics in Contemporary Iran: Clergy–State Relations in the Pahlavi Period*, Albany, NY: SUNY Press.
Algar, H. (1967) *Religion and State in Iran, 1785–1906*, Berkeley: University of California Press.
Algar, H. (1981) 'Editor's introduction', in *Islam and Revolution*, Berkeley: Mizan Press.
Amanat, A (1988) 'In between the Madrasa and the marketplace: the designation of clerical leadership in modern Shi'ism', in S.A. Arjomand (ed.), *Authority and Political Culture in Shiism*, Albany, NY: SUNY Press.
Arjomand, S. (1988) *The Turban for the Crown: The Islamic Revolution in Iran*, New York: Oxford University Press.
Banisadr, M. (2004) *Masoud: Memoirs of an Iranian Rebel*, London: Saqi.
Bayat, A. (2007) *Making Islam Democratic*, Stanford: Stanford University Press.

Bazargan, M. (1984) *Iran's Revolution in Two Movements* (in Persian), Tehran: Freedom Movement.

Behrooz, M. (1999) *Rebels with a Cause: The Failure of the Left in Iran*, London: Tauris.

Bellah, R. (1970) 'Islamic tradition and the problems of modernisation', in R. Bellah, *Beyond Belief*, Berkeley: University of California Press.

Chehabi, H. (1990) *Iranian Politics and Religious Modernism: The Liberation Movement of Iran under the Shah and Khomeini*, London: Tauris.

Cole, J. (1983) 'Imami jurisprudence and the role of the Ulama: Mortaza Ansari on emulating the Supreme Exemplar', in N. Keddie (ed.), *Religion and Politics in Iran*, Yale: Yale University Press.

Daftary, F. (2007) *The Ismailis: Their History and Doctrine*, Cambridge: Cambridge University Press.

Hodgson, M. (1974) *The Venture of Islam*, Vol. 2, Chicago: University of Chicago Press.

Homayoun, D. (2000) *Yesterday and Tomorrow* (in Persian), Bethesda: Ibex Publishers.

Kadivar, M. (1997) *Theories of State in Shia Jurisprudence* (in Persian), Tehran: Ney.

Kadivar, M. (1998) *Velaii Government* (in Persian), Tehran: Ney.

Katouzian, H. (1981) *The Political Economy of Modern Iran: Despotism and Pseudo Modernism 1926–79*, Basingstoke: Macmillan.

Keddie, N. (1966) *Religion and Rebellion in Iran: The Tobacco Protest of 1891–2*, London: Frank Cass.

Khomeini, R. (1947) *Kashef al-Asrar* (in Persian), no publisher.

Khomeini, R. (1970/1981) *Islamic Government*, in H. Algar, translator and editor, *Islam and Revolution*, Berkeley, Mizan Press.

Madelung, W. (1997) *The Succession to Muhammad*, Cambridge: Cambridge University Press.

Moin, B. (1999) *Khomeini: The Life of the Ayatollah*, London: Tauris.

Momen, M. (1985) *An Introduction to Shii Islam*, New Haven: Yale University Press.

Nafissi, M. (2005) 'Reformation, Islam and democracy: evolutionary and antievolutionary reform in Abrahamic religions', *Comparative Studies of South Asia, Africa, and the Middle East*, 25, 2.

Nafissi, M. (2007) 'Before and beyond the clash of civilisation', *ISIM Review*, 19.

Naini, M.H. (1907/1955) *Government from the Standpoint of Islam* (in Persian), Tehran: Enteshar.

Nakash, Y. (2006) *Reaching for Power: The Shia in the Modern Arab World*, Princeton: Princeton University Press.

Nasr, V. (2006) *The Shia Revival*, New York: Norton.

Nouri, F. (1907/1998) 'The illegitimacy of constitutionalism', in Gh. Zargarinejad (ed.), *Treaties on Constitutionalism* (in Persian), Tehran: Kavir.

Rahnema, A. (1998) *An Islamic Utopian: A Political Biography of Ali Shari'ati*, London: Tauris.

Ramazani, R.K. (2001) 'Reflections on Iran's foreign policy: defining the national interests', in J.L. Esposito and R.K. Ramazani (eds), *Iran at the Crossroads*, New York: Palgrave.

Roy, O. (1994) *The Failure of Political Islam*, London: Tauris.

Roy, O. (2004) *Globalised Islam*, London: Hurst.

Sachedina, A. (1988) *The Just Ruler in Shiite Islam*, Oxford: Oxford University Press.

Shirazi, A. (1997) *The Constitution of Iran*, London: Tauris.

Soroush, A. (2007) www.drsoroush.com.

Weber, M. (1978) *Economy and Society*, Berkeley: University of California Press.

Zubaida, S. (2003) *Law and Power in the Islamic World*, London: Tauris.

9

Judaism and the state

Shmuel Sandler

The relationship between religion and politics has always been complex. It is especially challenging in the contemporary era when contrary to academic expectations, especially among social scientists, religion has made a comeback to play a role in world politics. It is also particularly challenging to study Judaism and politics. After almost two millennia of Diaspora existence Judaism is now acting in world politics as both a state and an identified worldwide community. Because of the magnitude of the subject, the purpose of this chapter will be narrowed down to highlight only the intersection between Judaism and state with a special emphasis on the contemporary era.

Indeed, to some, only the establishment of the State of Israel implied the return of the Jewish people to the world's political history, from which it had been absent since the Destruction of the Second Temple and the collapse of the kingdom of Judaea (Harkabi 1985: 44). To others, the whole mix between statehood and Judaism as a religion is not conceivable (Leibowitz 1975; Belfer 1991: 302–326). The working assumption of this essay is that a Jewish political tradition in both domestic and international affairs has existed since the inception of the Jewish people, and in contrast to the above views some of these norms and institutions continue to influence Israeli politics and foreign policy.

Daniel J. Elazar, created the concept known as 'the Jewish Political Tradition'. By developing the concept of the Jewish community as a political player, he provided an extremely relevant paradigm for a theoretical school, which attempts to break out of the narrow confines of the nation-state. In addition, Elazar developed the concept of the 'Jewish polity' both in his work as the founder of the academic study of the Jewish political tradition, as well as in his studies of the behaviour of the world Jewish community. This concept was meant to expand the Jewish political structure beyond limitations of place and of time (Elazar 1989). By so doing, Elazar developed a constellation of political concepts that included both state and Diaspora.

Whereas the covenant is the basis for a political regime according to Elazar (1995) and this will be developed at the outset of this chapter, both the state and the nation need a territorial base. The second section will concentrate on the special bond between Judaism and the Land of Israel. Whether in their homeland or in the Diaspora the Jews had to interact also with external forces. These realities added another dimension – which I define as a Jewish foreign policy (Sandler 1987: 115–121). The link between the foreign relations of the Jewish people over the generations with foreign policy and international politics principles is intended to uncover an additional dimension of the Jewish political tradition, which extends over thousands of years. My intention is that unveiling the international Jewish dimension will contribute to a better understanding of Israel's foreign policy as a Jewish state. The latter sections of this chapter will be devoted primarily to this concern.

The Jews and the state

The Jewish political tradition discloses a multifaceted attitude to the state: a mixture of respect and contempt for state power. In retrospect, the relationship between the Israelites and the state has not been simple. It starts with apprehension. The first acquaintance of the founding father Abraham with an organised polity was with the Egyptian Empire. The foremost impression one gets from the Forefathers' interactions of the Israelites and Egypt is the built-in tension between Pharaoh, the earthly ruler of the empire who represents bondage, and the rule of God which frees. The exodus from Egypt appears repeatedly throughout the Bible as the formative event of both Judaism as a religion and the Israeli/Jewish nation. Moreover, God links his presence and special relationship with the Israelites in the first of the Ten Commandments with the exodus from Egypt: 'I am the Lord thy God, which have brought thee out of the land of Egypt, out of the house of bondage' (Exodus 20:2). The Empire of Egypt is being portrayed as the inverse of God who stands for the ideal regime.[1]

The alternative to the Egyptian regime on earth is the Covenant. Abraham and God contract the Covenant after the former's return from Egypt. It is during this holy scene that Abraham is informed about the forthcoming enslavement of his descendants in Egypt and their eventual exodus.

God again contracts a binding agreement at Sinai between Him and the Israelites after the exodus from Egypt. The Covenant can be seen as a basis of 'consent theory', the opposite of the regime of slavery they had left behind (Wildavsky 1984: 93; Walzer 1993: ch. 3). There are no doubt uneven power relations between the Almighty and human beings. However, according to interpretations in the Rabbinic literature for the Covenant to be binding the people must consent (Walzer et al. 2000: 7–8). Accordingly, Elazar sees the Covenant idea as a form of constitution building (Elazar 1989: 2). Over time, of course, the notion of limitation of power has become a key basis of all democratic regimes. The concept is deep-rooted in this ancient idea of Covenant – where the omnipotent God takes it upon himself not to exercise all His powers and the Israelites take it upon themselves to live according to His norms (Elazar 1989: 98–99).

Indeed, upon entering Canaan the disdain of the Israelites for imperial Egypt resulted in a decentralised confederacy of tribes. This structure, described in the book of Judges was, perhaps, ideal as it conformed to the revolutionary idea rejecting the centralised model of the 'Egyptian house of bondage' (Walzer 1993: 17–45). Even following the establishment of the monarchy the non-centralised tribal structure was preserved in the Israelite kingdom. Likewise during the Second Temple the Hasmonean ascendance to power was primarily a religious rebellion and expressed itself in the exploitation of patriotic sentiments, but never in the building of a powerful state (see below).

Another pillar in the decentralisation of power was a tradition of separation of powers that had presumably developed since the establishment of Priesthood in the desert. Moses was the leader, but not a priest, and alongside him were the Zekenim (the sages). Following the entrance to the

Land of Israel the political leadership parted from the prophets. However, throughout the biblical era both the Israelite and the Judaean kings encountered prophets – such as, Nathan, Isaiah, Jeremiah and Elijah – who denounced the king and the nation for what they saw as their iniquitous behaviour. Similarly the power of the Priesthood was kept apart from the political leadership. King Uzziah entered the Temple to perform functions preserved for the High Priest and thereafter was penalised with leprosy (2 Chronicles 27:16–22). A major factor in the Hasmonite rulers' difficulty in being perceived as legitimate was that while they were priests (*Kohanim*), they sought to combine two institutions (monarchy and priesthood), which were against the Jewish political tradition. Another source of tension was over authority. One example of this tension was the hostility between King Yanai and the Sanhedrin (council of sages). The latter claimed its authority in an assumed chain of a *halakhic* (Jewish law) tradition going back to Moses (Avot I: 1). In short, during the second Temple we find three institutions competing against each other: Priests, Kings and the Sages. With the destruction of the second Temple in 70 CE the Priesthood lost its power and the institution of the sages that had existed since the Desert took over. The separation of powers among the crowns of Kingdom, Priesthood, and Torah (the written and oral law), according to Stuart Cohen (1997: 54–55), was only recognised formally with the emergence of the Rabbinic era (around 100 BCE). This diffused structure according to Elazar and Cohen (1997), accompanied the Jewish polity right through to contemporary Israel.

With political authority moving to the Diaspora around the third century the Jews found it necessary to replace the territorial component with other constituents. The overall structure was what came to be known as the Kehila (the Community). Significantly, the Jewish polity kept, also in the Diaspora, its diffused structure. For their security they developed a strategy of relying upon the local rulers or the host state. For example, according to Salo Baron, the Jews later integrated themselves within the corporative structure of medieval Europe and thus created a special status in the eyes of the local rulers who needed their services (Baron 1928: 515–526). The special status implied Jewish autonomy as a polity with full powers of running its public affairs (Elon 1997: 220–222).

But the central element in safeguarding the Jewish subsistence was the Torah – in both written (Five books of Moses) and oral (Talmud) forms – in effect becoming a constitution. In response to dispersion, Judaism developed a combination of both a centralised authority of judicial decision-making and local interpretation. For example, in the sixteenth century the Jewish polity was in effect divided between two communities: the Sephardim, concentrated around the Mediterranean, and the Ashkenazim, living in central and Eastern Europe. Both accepted the Joseph Karo Code (Shulchan Aruch) that came from Zefat in Palestine as the basic religious code. However, while the Sephardi communities accepted the code wholesale, Ashkenazim adopted the modifications of the Karo Code formulated by an East European Halachic authority, Rabbi Moses Iserlish. In this way the overall structure of the constitution was kept while also being moulded to the local customs that had developed over the years. In addition, the enormous literature – comprising commentaries, codification, and 'responsa'[2] – kept the Jewish polity while lacking a territorial base.

This structure of autonomous Communities and a central code that served as a constitution started breaking up with the advance of modernity especially following the French Revolution. On the one hand, modernity brought with it secularisation that weakened the role of the religious code. On the other, the modern nation-state was unable to tolerate a separate Jewish identity within itself. Emancipation for the Jews came with a demand that in exchange for equality the Jews must abandon their separate national identity (Sacher 1976: 3). At the same time, religious anti-Jewishness was reincarnated in the form of modern anti-Semitism. Consequently, it was considered that survival during the nation-state era required territoriality. Having been influenced by the rise of modern nationalism, the Jews developed their own national movement opting for a return to Zion. It was against this background that a new type of Community (Kehila), a territorial one, started developing in Palestine.

Significantly, the Jewish settlement in Palestine under the rule of the British Mandate during the first half of the twentieth century, known as the *Yishuv*, developed a consociational political system – characterised by cooperative association as well as power sharing between groups – in contrast to the Westminster model. Both institutional branches of the *Yishuv* – the World Zionist Organisation and the Jewish Agency – as well as the Territorial Knesset Israel, developed consociational mechanisms, such as elections conducted via the principles of proportional representation and grand coalitions that encompassed almost all the ideologically distinct parties in the Yishuv and the Jewish Diaspora (Horowitz and Lissak 1977: 317–318). The federated political structure of the World Zionist Organisation and the consociational political regime that emerged in Palestine illustrates how the democratic culture of the Jewish polity – followed from 1948 by the Jewish state – did not emerge from a vacuum: the Jewish political tradition influenced the Israeli political culture (Dowty 1990: 60–61).

Following independence, the Jewish state retained proportional representation and broad coalition governments thus belonging to the category of consociational democracies rather than a Westminster democracy practised by Britain, the Mandatory power (Horowitz and Lissak 1990: 26–27). In addition, there has commonly been power-sharing arrangements between the religious and secular sectors; only rarely during the political history of Israel has there been a government that did not include a religious party – even when an alternative secular majority was available (Don-Yehiya 1975). In sum, power sharing in the contemporary state of Israel has a long political tradition supporting diffusion of power of over two millennia both in the Diaspora and in ancient Israel.

Alongside its diffusion, the Jewish polity that emerged in Palestine also developed an institutional centre that gave rise to a political centre. The former was composed of the national institutions – the World Zionist Organisation and the Jewish Agency – alongside the territorial institutions of Knesset Israel. Following the establishment of the state, the Israeli Government took over many of the functions and services that had until then been dispersed among the parties and ideological camps of the Yishuv. Paramilitary formations, educational ideological streams, as well as social services, were integrated into the state system. In parallel, political centrism implied that despite the ideological diffusion only the politically centrist parties could form the government. David Ben-Gurion, Israel's first prime minister, understood this very early as head of the newly formed MAPAI (Labourers Party in the Land of Israel) party in the 1930s, and positioned the predecessor of the Israeli Labour party in the centre (Horowitz and Lissak 1977: chs 3 and 8). The result was that MAPAI ruled Israel from 1948 until 1977.

131

Menachem Begin, the head of the Irgun organisation who turned into the head of a legitimate right-wing party named Herut (Freedom), thus learned the lesson of being ideologically dogmatic in the wastelands of opposition and consequently initiated a strategy of alliances with parties that were at the centre of the political map, like the Liberal party, eventually forming the Likud party (which in Hebrew stands for unity) (Goldberg 1986: 146–169). The Likud party moved further to the centre following its electoral victory in 1977. Over the following years, the two major parties ruled alternatively or jointly. Eventually, however, in 2006, Prime Minister Sharon, who had roots in both camps, pushed aside the two veteran parties and positioned his newly formed Kadima party at the hub of the Israel political system. Despite the absence of Sharon because of a stroke, Kadima as a centrist party still won the election and tried to preserve power sharing with the religious sector by including three religious candidates on its list. In addition, the coalition that emerged following the 2006 election included the Sephardic religious party SHAS even though Prime Minister Ehud Olmert could have put together a secular majority government with other parties.

Finally, to comprehend the full disposition of decentralisation of power in the Jewish state we must look at the rise in power of the Supreme Court under the leadership of Chief Justice Aharon Barak who as President of the Supreme Court between 1996 and 2006 promoted the status of court vis-à-vis the other branches of government. Barak regarded every issue as adjudicable implying that the Supreme Court had a voice on every social or political dispute. To justify his approach Barak used Jewish phrases with religious tones. Mimicking the biblical expression 'the whole land is full of His glory', Barak coined the expression 'the whole land

is Law'. Significantly, it was primarily the religious sector that objected to this legal revolution since the Supreme Court is more elitist and does not represent Israeli pluralism like the Knesset (Neuer 2007). Since the court under Barak adopted a policy that it had the right to abolish Knesset legislation that it did not find constitutional, the struggle moved to the legislative process of the evolving Israeli constitution. Thus, for instance, in the early 1990s two basic laws were amended. In 'Basic Law: Human Dignity and Liberty', and 'Basic Law: Freedom of Occupation', a paragraph was added stating that its purpose was 'to anchor in the Basic Law the values of the State of Israel as a Jewish and democratic state' (Ha'aretz 1993: A4).

In sum, the Israeli political system that emerged in the mid-twentieth century, although influenced by the European origins of many of the immigrants into Palestine and by the British pre-state Mandatory regime in Palestine, was also predisposed to the Jewish political tradition that can be traced over two millennia. It was this combination that ultimately has been contained in the emergence of the definition of Israel as a 'Jewish and Democratic State'.

Territoriality

The relationship between Judaism and the state cannot be comprehended without the territorial component, namely the role of the Land of Israel in Jewish political norms and behaviour. Jewish religious bonds to a particular land have been associated with a sense of common origin (Abraham as the nation's ancestor), as well as a common history. Both a nation and state need a territory to qualify as such. It is the ethnic element that binds a nation to a particular territory, while it is the territory that binds a nation to the state and through it to international relations. A.D. Smith asserted that 'modern concepts of national mission and national destiny are linear descendants of the ancient beliefs in ethnic election, with their emphasis on the privileges and duties of the elect before God' (Smith 1999: 350). With the birth of modern nationalism, replacing to some extent religion as a source of identity, ethno-religious communities became ethno-national communities (Smith 1981: 87). However, despite the linkage between ethno-nationalism and the state via the territory there is not always congruence between the two. More than two ethno-national groups may have claims to the same territory and hence the interest of the state and the nation are not identical (Connor 1972: 319–355).

The Jewish narrative starts with the migration of Abraham from Mesopotamia to the Land of Canaan upon God's order. Subsequently, God contracts a Covenant in which He promises the land to Abraham's ancestors. It is this land the Children of Israel head to after the exodus from Egypt. After being exiled to Babylonia they return to this land upon an imperial decree of the Persian monarch King Cyrus (Chronicles II, chap. 36: 22–23). During the second temple, despite the existence of a Diaspora in Babylonia and later on around the Mediterranean, they clung to this land. The Diaspora started to become religiously significant (for example, establishment of religious academies and the editing of the Babylonian Talmud) only after the dwindling of the Jewish settlement in Palestine (the new name given by the Romans to the Land of Israel following the two Rebellions). But even after the transition of the centre from Palestine, the Land of Israel still remained the focus of Jewish religious ritual. Hence, for example, prayers for rain in the Diaspora were accorded with the seasons in the land of Israel as were the harvest festival and other agricultural celebrations. In their prayers Jews requested God's return to Zion. The land enjoyed divine attributes only when reunited with its people. Only in the Land of Israel could prophecy take place. Following the expulsion of the Jews from their land, mystical Judaism's view was that God's presence on earth (the *Shechina*) was also in exile (Vital 1975: 5).

During the middle ages and into the modern era religion motivated some Jewish migrations to Palestine. Rabbinical authorities like Maimonides and Nachmanides as well as Joseph Karo arrived in Palestine and were buried in the Holy Land. In 1700 one thousand Jews led by Rabbi Judah the Pious immigrated to the Land of Israel. This migration differed from the previous ones, as they wanted to hasten redemption despite the Sabbatai Zevi Messianic débâcle. In the next two centuries rabbinical sages and cabbalists immigrated and established what came to be known as the Old Yishuv (settlement) (Dinur 1969: 90–95). It was only during the last decades of the nineteenth century that secular Zionists started immigrating to Palestine and established what came to be known as the New Yishuv (also called the Jewish polity in Mandatory Palestine) (Horowitz and Lissak 1977).

The strength of the Land of Israel in Zionism came to the fore during what came to be known as the Uganda debate. Despite the formal victory of Theodor Herzl, head of the Zionist Congress, in the debate at the Zionist Congress, to investigate the possibility of a temporary Jewish settlement in Eastern Africa, it is agreed that in effect it was a defeat. This was because the Zionist movement could not foresee – despite the gravity of the Jewish condition in the Diaspora – even a *temporary* detour from the Land of Israel (Vital 1982: chs 9–10). In 1937, when the Royal Peel Commission suggested the partitioning of Palestine into two segments, with a Jewish state on one part and an Arab on the other, the debate again almost tore apart the Zionist movement. This time the leadership of the Yishuv won and accepted partition because of both the gravity of the Jewish condition and the fact that the Jewish state would be established on part of the Land of Israel. The Religious Zionists objected to the proposal because of the divine promise of the whole Land of Israel for the Jewish people (Gorny 1985: 350–352). In 1947 following the UN partition decision of 29 November, the religious parties again demanded the whole of the Land of Israel on religious grounds (1985: 395–396).

The issue of the entire Land of Israel was dormant in Israeli politics between 1948 and 1967, that is, from Israeli Independence to the Six Day War. During this time, the National Religious Party (NRP), the political organ of religious Zionism, was a loyal partner of the ruling Labour party elite in foreign and national security affairs. Following the June 1967 war when Israelis came into renewed contact with territories (Judaea and Samaria) that had constituted the heartland of Biblical Israel, a new wave of ethno-religious feelings poured out. Foremost in this awakening was the old city of Jerusalem where the Western Wall – the last remnant of the Temple – was still standing. Indeed, three weeks after the conquest of the Old City the government formally annexed it. The West Bank encompassed other holy towns like Hebron and Bethlehem, where the Patriarchs and the Matriarchs had been buried, and their tombs traditionally were prayer places to Jews. Places like Shiloh and the tomb of Joseph were identified and so were dozens of other religious sites. Significantly, the religious parties did not become active on the issue of the Land of Israel until the mid-1970s. It was after the 1973 war that the religious Zionists founded a settlement movement named Gush Emunim (Block of the Faithful) that defied the government perception of the

territories as collateral to be exchanged for peace. In 1977, following the electoral defeat of Labour, the NRP had no difficulty in switching loyalties to nationalist Likud, the party most identified with the ideology of the Land of Israel.

Nevertheless, despite the ascendance to power of the right-wing Likud, the settlement drive brought out the conflict between settling of the Land of Israel and the State of Israel. The peace process with Egypt and the autonomy plan to the Palestinians brought in its wake the establishment of what was known as 'the Jewish Underground' in the early 1980s. The most extreme group among the underground movement headed by Yehuda Etzion wanted to remove the Dome of the Rock mosque, an event that would induce tumultuous reactions in the Arab world. The Likud government under nationalist Prime Minister Yitzhak Shamir arrested the underground leaders in 1984. In an attempt to stop the Oslo Peace process that would lead to partition of the Land of Israel in 1994, a supporter of extremist Rabbi Meir Kahane massacred 29 Palestinians in the Patriarch's Tomb in Hebron. On 4 November 1995 a religious student assassinated Prime Minister Yitzhak Rabin. Ten years later, religious settlers clashed with the Israeli defence forces when Likud Prime Minister Ariel Sharon implemented the disengagement of the Israeli state from the Gaza Strip.

For religious Zionists, however, the struggle against the state of Israel posed a theological dilemma. Many of the leaders of Gush Emunim were influenced by the teachings of Rabbi A. Y. Kook as interpreted by his son, Z. Y. Kook. For both the state of Israel was as holy as the Land of Israel. In contrast to Ultra-Orthodox Jewry who had theological difficulties in cooperating with secular Zionism, Rabbi Kook basing his theology on cabbalistic tradition that an inner divine spark propels Jews, even those who are not religiously observant saw

Zionism as the beginning of redemption (Yaron 1974: 87–89). Jewish efforts in redeeming the Land of Israel through agriculture and physical labour revealed this spark, while blooming of the land and restoration of the state of Israel were seen as vivid indications that the redemption has started. Historic events, like the Balfour Declaration in 1917, the United Nations vote in 1947 to establish a Jewish state, and the Six Day War in 1967, were all signals to the religious Zionists that the Messianic Era has dawned and that the state of Israel was an integral part of this process (Ravitzky 1993: ch. 3).

The theological schism that confronted Religious Zionism is an interesting example of a conflict between religion and state. Two sanctified ideals collided: the Land of Israel versus the State of Israel. Objecting violently to the orders of the Israeli government in evacuating settlements in the Land of Israel has put the theology of religious Zionism in a dilemma. This is a challenge that Religious Zionism has not faced since its inception. It represented a more complicated problem than the traditional dilemma of who prevails: the law of God or the law of the state? For religious Zionism, both the state of Israel and the Land of Israel encompass religious connotations. Moreover, the territorial issue confronted Religious Zionism with the need to formulate their positions in an arena they had abstained from between 1948 and 1967, the area of foreign policy. The linkage between the state and foreign policy, as we shall see, has been inherent in the Jewish political tradition.

Jewish foreign policy and the state

The request for state building in the Jewish political tradition goes back to Biblical Israel and is clearly related to external threats (Judges 8:10). The demand of Samuel that he anoint a king is made 'so that we also may be like all the nations and that our king ... go out before us and fight our battles' (1 Samuel 8:20). Significantly, Maimonides, the twelfth-century Halachic authority and philosopher, entitled the section of his Code relating to Monarchy as 'Laws of Kings and Their Wars' (Blidstein 1983: 214). In other words, the building of a state with central institutions was deemed necessary for amassing strength against external threats. Moreover, the unique status of David, the founder of the monarchy, and the one to whom eternal kingship was promised, speaks to the fact that he built a Jewish centralised state and defeated the enemies who had threatened the Jewish people since they entered the land.

External needs might create a powerful state in both domestic and external senses even if this goes against a society's initial philosophy and its political tradition. For example, the institution of the American presidency grew in power over the course of time in light of the international needs of the United States and vice versa the imperial presidency served an imperial America (Schlesinger 1974). Jewish history is not replete with instances of imperial domestic institutions and Empire building. With the exception of the era of Kings David and Solomon, during the First Commonwealth, a strong state does not exist, in the étatist sense that is likely to develop imperial aspirations. Following the death of Solomon in 928 BCE a split occurred, thus terminating the attempt to build a powerful monarchy (Mazar 1965: 207–209). Despite the constant external threats the Judaean kingdom did not become a strong state, neither in the sense of strong institutions and bureaucracy nor in that of external power. The Israelite kingdom in effect returned to a non-centralised tribal structure. The instability of the monarchy and the frequent transformation of power *did* not reflect a potent central state. With the emergence of the Assyrian empire, the kingdom of Israel was defeated and sent into exile. Subsequently, the kingdom of Judah – also not noted for strong ruling institutions, despite the fact that its rulers enjoyed the legitimacy of belonging to the Davidic dynasty – could not stand up to the empires on the Nile or the Euphrates. One hundred and forty years after its northern sister, in 586 BCE the Babylonian empire defeated the Judaean kingdom and exiled its inhabitants.

Likewise, during the period of the Second Commonwealth Judaea did not emerge as a strong state with external powers. Judaea after the Return of Zion (516 BCE) was a province of the Persian empire and, subsequently, part of Alexander's empire. The Hasmonean's religious rebellion though also a patriotic uprising, despite external threats, did not proceed into the building of an empire. Even those Hasmonean kings, particularly Alexander Yannai, who had statecraft ambitions, gave up on these plans for internal reasons. The Pharisees struggled with Alexander Yannai for religious reasons as they were not impressed by his state-building efforts and aggrandisement of his external rule.

Being weak and lacking a desire to aggrandise dictated supporting law and order. Michael Walzer, in a lecture entitled 'Universalism and Jewish Values', which was dedicated to the memory of Hans Morgenthau, identified four examples of Jewish universalism (Walzer 2000: 9–32). The first two originate in the Bible and were articulated by the prophets, while the latter two are derived from rabbinic literature. The first example is a rebuke by the prophet Amos to the neighbouring nations for their failure to keep international agreements and their responsibility for what would today be termed 'war crimes'. Walzer argues that, in practice, the prophet is calling for the adoption of what we might define today as international law.

The second example is found in the parallel prophecies of Isaiah and Micah concerning the end of days, which may be best described as reflecting a vision of world peace, based upon a pluralistic international system. The third example is the Talmudic statement that 'the law of the Kingdom is law'. This statement refers to the relations of Jews to their host state, and therefore belongs to the area of Jewish foreign policy. According to Walzer, since we have here the recognition of the law of the state by the *halakhic* legal system, we find here an example of international law being adapted to the needs of a Diaspora. The fourth example is provided by the Seven Noahide Code. The acceptance by the non-Jewish nations of the normative system that was given to the world (in the sense of the cosmos) even prior to the giving of the Torah to the Jews facilitates co-existence between Jews and non-Jews. It provides a *modus vivendi* for non-Jews living in a Jewish state, as well as for Jews living in a non-Jewish state. The common denominator of all four examples is that they reflect the support of the normative Jewish approach for international order. Support for international order is usually the lot of imperial powers, who wish to establish their rule within their own sphere or that of small nations, who are the first to be harmed by imperial struggles. The Jews, as we have seen, did not belong to the first category, and so the second category is more appropriate for them.

International politics also regularly entails alliance politics. In general, the normative Jewish approach towards alliances is negative. It is an attitude reflective of the apprehension of alien cultural influences, as well as the implied lack of trust in God. Moreover, there is a certain antagonism between God's covenant with Israel and international alliances (Greenberg 1984: 187, n. 11). The prophets Hosea and Jeremiah warned primarily against the dangers involved in regional alliances with Egypt and Assyria, together with reliance upon them (Isaiah 30:1–7, 31:1–3; Hosea 7:11, 8:9, 13; Jeremiah 16–19). In fact, there were alliances, starting with King Solomon and Hyram King of Tyre and ending with the alliance between Judah the Hasmonean and the Romans during the second Temple. But the main dilemma in alliance politics during the biblical era was related to the geo-political situation of the Israelite polities (approximately 1200–586 BCE).

Early Jewish history was deeply influenced by the geo-political location of the Israelite tribes and the kingdoms of Israel and Judah between the Egyptian empire and those empires that lay to the north. The Land of Israel also became a battlefield during the power struggles between the Persians and the Greeks, between the latter and the Romans, and finally between the Romans and the Parthians. Also, in the middle ages the Jews were caught in requests for identifying their political identity during periods of conflicts between empires. At times the Jews found themselves in the middle of power struggles between empires, the most striking of which was the religio-civilisational conflict between Islam and Christianity.

Another dilemma occurring during the middle ages was the Jewish position as subordinates of the aristocracy and monarchs who provided them with protection. The strategy of relying upon the state or local rulers, as identified by Ginsberg (1993), may be seen as an offshoot of the concept of the vassal treaty, which is a form of alliance. However, the peasantry and other serfs tended to perceive the Jews as agents of the oppressors, tax collectors, interest sharks and hence as enemies of the general populace (Baron 1996: 87–89). Many of the Jewish massacres occurred against this background.

How do we detect these Jewish attitudes towards the state and foreign relations in the post-independence State of Israel? In fact, the appearance of Zionism, in its various varieties, was intended first and foremost to ensure survival. To be sure, the forebears of Zionism, as they are called by Jacob Katz (1983: 263–285), were greatly influenced by the rise of nationalism in nineteenth century Europe and the 'spring of nations' surrounding them, but political Zionism was primarily motivated by the physical threat to the Jews and hence demanded a Jewish state. Perhaps the most significant figure as far as a state as a shelter was concerned, was Rabbi Jacob Reines, the founder of Religious Zionism, who was prepared to go to East Africa in order to establish a Jewish colony as a 'night refuge' (Vital 1987: chs 7, 10; Vital 1982: 223). For Rabbi Reines, who was devoted to the Land of Israel (Schwartz 1997), establishment of a colony in Africa was necessary for Jewish survival.

But also the State of Israel's foreign policy carried on with some of the characteristics of traditional Jewish alliance politics. From its inception the secular Zionist movement, as well as the post-independence secular State of Israel, continued in many regards the Jewish foreign policy of courting powerful actors. The search of an international charter that had appeared in Herzl's, *The Jewish State*, was implemented in his diplomatic activity at the dawn of the twentieth century (Herzl 1946: 95–96; Sandler 1994: 28–29). During World War I and its aftermath, Haim Weitzman, president of the World Zionist Congress adopted a pro-British orientation (Rose 1996: ch. 13) Later, however, Israel's founding father and first Prime Minister, David Ben-Gurion, followed the shift in the global balance of power by switching to a pro-United States orientation (Brecher 1972: 262–269), while trying to mobilise the support of at least one great power such as Great Britain and France in 1956. Despite the cost of being perceived as an emissary of the colonial powers, the Jewish state preferred the support of the great powers rather than to try to improve its image among its Middle Eastern neighbours and/or within the developing world more generally (Brecher 1974: 118–152). Similarly, by identifying with the colonial powers and the United States, the Jewish state was criticised by some of the developing countries, notably from within Africa, often at the United Nations. Another similarity with Ancient Israel and the middle ages was the Jewish position between imperial struggles. Salo W. Baron has drawn an analogy between this problem and the dilemmas that confronted the nascent State of Israel, which from the beginning of its path was forced to identify with one of the two sides in the global struggle between East and West (Baron 1996: 39–42). Today, as well, some would argue that the Jewish state finds itself in the midst of a 'clash of civilisations'. That is, being located in the Middle East but Western in its orientation and political culture it became a target of attacks by radical Islam.

The Jewish state and world Jewry

The establishment of a Jewish state did not prevent conflicts of interests between the interests of the state of Israel and those of the Jewish people or those of the local Jewish community. For example, Israel's interest in international recognition involved diplomatic recognition by the new states of black Africa from the 1960s. However, such recognition was pending on Israel's vote in the United Nations and economic boycott against South Africa. The Pretoria government exerted pressure on the local Jewish community to exert their influence on Jerusalem to refrain from anti-South African steps. Apartheid was also contrary to Israel's self-proclaimed image of 'Light to the Nations'. Another example

was the kidnapping of World War II Nazi criminal Adolph Eichmann motivated *inter alia* by Israel's interests of being acknowledged as the historical heir of the Jewish people. This act, however, conflicted with the interests of the Jewish community in Argentina, as the government saw its sovereignty harmed by the operations of a foreign government within its territory (Brecher 1972: 229–244).

There were several other occasions where the Jewish and the Israeli interests did not coincide. Salient among them were the emigration of Algerian Jewry and Soviet Jewry. The interests of Israeli-Franco relations did not always correspond to those of Algerian Jewry (Mualem: 2004: 229–241). In the case of Soviet Jewry, the government of Israel during the 1950s did not protest the persecution of the 'Jews of silence' due to its own political interest (Blum 1985: 131–139). In the 1970s the government of Israel wished to limit the struggle for immigration from the Soviet Union to those Jews who intended to come to Israel, while American Jewry demanded an overall struggle unrelated to the destination of Russian emigration.

Overall, it would be accurate to say that in cases where there was no existential threat to the State of Israel, the Jewish state took world Jewish interests into account. By contrast, in national survival incidents the Israeli interest always prevailed (Inbar 1990: 165–183). Israel did not dare to challenge the Soviets regarding their treatment of Soviet Jewry without American backing. Israel only began to raise this subject on the world agenda in the 1970s, when Washington stood behind it. On the issues of Algerian Jewry, Israel's interest in receiving a supply of Mirage fighter planes from France, and the completion of the construction of the atomic reactor in Dimona, was stronger than the needs of the local Jewish community (Mualem 2004: 229–244).

However, the priority given to considerations of survival for the Jewish state, above general Jewish interests did not contradict the values found in the Jewish tradition. Jewish survival has been a basic impulse in the Jewish value system. To be sure, every state within the international system accords priority to survival and in the case of Israel, there were both valid objective and subjective reasons for the search after broad margins of security. Moreover, Ben-Gurion, the founding father of the state, laid the foundation to the conviction that the fate of world Jewry was pending on the survival of the State of Israel (Brecher 1972: 256). This was a far-reaching claim that closed a cycle that had started over three thousand years earlier when the first Jews encountered the state. After a Diaspora experience of almost two thousand years in which they embraced the state where they were residing, they now clinched a Jewish state.

Conclusion

The state has played a central role in Judaism from its inception. Ideally the regime that the Jewish political tradition inspired to establish was the inverse of the centralised ancient Egyptian empire. At the basis of this ideal polity was the covenant tradition which could be seen as the origin of the idea of a contractual relationship and constitutionalism. When the loosely confederated tribal structure evolved into a monarchy the Israelites did not construct a lasting centralised polity. It was this mixture of central authority and competing institutions that evolved during Jewish history, including the Jewish Community (Kehilah) in the Diaspora. Significantly, despite its secular character, the contemporary Jewish state has in effect preserved some elements from the Jewish political tradition. The definition of Israel

in the evolving constitution is as 'a Jewish and democratic state'.

A second feature in the Jewish relationship with the state is the bondage with an ancient sacred territory. To be sure, the Jewish political tradition helped keep Judaism alive during the Diaspora, while the Jews crucially lacked a territorial element. The birth of the nation state in nineteenth-century Europe and modern anti-Semitism culminating in the Holocaust in the mid-twentieth century induced the Jews to re-constitute a national state in the land of their ancestors. This restoration of the Jewish state in the Land of Israel resulted in a protracted conflict whose solution cannot be seen on the horizon. For the religious national sector in the country on certain occasions an inherent contradiction has emerged between two sacred maxims: the State of Israel and the Land of Israel.

The tension between statecraft demands and religious principles was also felt in foreign affairs. Most of the history of both the Israelite and Judaean kingdoms was one of a defensive doctrine against their neighbouring imperial powers. The prophets strived to advance an international order based on norms, an approach that fits the needs of a small nation. This approach was also suitable for a national or religious minority in exile that constantly felt threatened. Another facet of this reality in the Diaspora was an alliance policy with the ruling political elite resulting on several occasions in the hostility of the subordinate classes. This policy of alignment with the leading power was maintained also by modern Israel that developed a foreign policy of searching for the support of the great powers. This policy contributed to hostility from the Third World.

Finally, despite the almost full support of the Jewish Diaspora to the Jewish state, the interests of both the organs of the state and of world Jewry have not always coincided. On certain occasions of which only a few have been outlined in this chapter, the overall Jewish national interest was split between the Jewish state and local Jewish communities. In most cases it was the national state interest that prevailed but definitely not in all instances. Nevertheless, despite these occasional disputes and despite the fact that the relationship between religion and state has so far not been resolved, the State of Israel defines itself as a Jewish and democratic state.

Notes

1 I take the Bible literally and assume that the Jewish narrative influenced its approach to the state.
2 Responsa is the Latin plural of *responsum*, meaning, literally, 'answers'. The responsa literature, known in Hebrew as *Sheelot U-teshuvot* ('questions and answers'), is the body of written decisions and rulings given by rabbis in response to questions.

Bibliography

Armstrong, J. (1976) 'Mobilized and proletarian diasporas', *American Political Science Review*, 70, 2, pp. 393–408.

Baron, Salo W. (1928) 'Gheto and emancipation: shall we revise the traditional view?', *Menorah Journal*, 14, pp. 515–526.

Baron, Salo W. (1996) *The World Dimensions of Jewish History*, Jerusalem: Zalman Shazar Centre for Jewish History.

Bavli Talmud, *Trachat Ketubot. Ketubot* is one of the tractates in Jewish law that deals with marital contracts.

Belfer, E. (1991) 'The Jewish people and the kingdom of heaven', in D. Elazar (ed.), *People and Community: The Jewish Political Tradition and its Implications for our Day* (Hebrew), Jerusalem: Reuven Mass, pp. 302–326.

Ben-Gurion, D. (1962) 'Uniqueness and destiny', in *Vision and Path*, vol. 2 (Hebrew), Tel-Aviv: Am Oved.

Biale, D. (1986) *Power and Powerlessness in Jewish History*, New York: Schocken.

Blidstein, G. (1983) *Political Concepts in Maimodean Halakha*, Ramat-Gan: Bar-Ilan University Press.

Blum, Y. (1985) 'A Jewish state among the states', *Hagut, Between Israel and the Nations* (Hebrew), Jerusalem: Ministry of Education and Culture, pp. 131–139.

Brecher, M. (1972) *The Foreign Policy System of Israel*, London: Oxford University Press.

Brecher, M. (1974) *Decisions in Israel's Foreign Policy*, London: Oxford University Press.

Cohen, S.A. (1997) 'The concept of three Ketarim: their place in Jewish political thought and implications for studying Jewish constitutional history', in D.J. Elazar (ed.), *Kinship and Consent*, New Brunswick: Transaction Publishers, pp. 47–76.

Connor, W. (1972) 'Nation building or nation destroying?', *World Politics*, 24, 3, pp. 319–355.

Dinur, B. Zion (1969) *Israel and the Diaspora*, Philadelphia: Jewish Publications Society of America.

Don-Yehiya, E. (1975) 'Religion and coalition: the National Religious Party and coalition formation,' in A. Arian (ed.), *The Elections in Israel – 1973*, Jerusalem: Jerusalem Academic Press, pp. 255–284.

Don-Yehiya, E. (1983) 'Ideology and policy formation in religious Zionism: the ideology of Rabbi Reines and Mizrahi policy under his leadership', *Haziyonut*, 3, pp. 105–146.

Dowty, A. (1990) 'Jewish political traditions and contemporary Israeli politics', *Jewish Political Studies Review*, 2, 3–4, pp. 55–84.

Elazar, D.J. (1989) 'The themes of the Jewish Political Studies Review', *Jewish Political Studies Review* 1, pp. 1–5.

Elazar D.J. (1995) *Covenant and Polity in Biblical Israel*, New Brunswick: Transaction Publishers.

Elazar D.J. and Cohen, S. (1997) *The Jewish Polity*, Jerusalem: Jerusalem Center for Public Affairs.

Elon, M. (1997) 'On power and authority: the Halalchic stance of the traditional community and its contemporary implications', in D.J. Elazar (ed.), *Kinship and Consent*, New Brunswick: Transaction Publishers.

Ephron, J. (1980) *Studies in the Hasmonean Period* (Hebrew), Tel Aviv: Hakibbutz Hameuhad.

Fox, J. and Sandler, S. (2004) *Bringing Religion into International Relations*, New York: Palgrave.

Freeman, G. (1997) 'The Rabbinic understanding of the Covenant', in D. J. Elazar (ed.), *Kinship and Consent*, New Brunswick: Transaction Publishers, pp. 77–105.

Ginsberg, B. (1993) *The Fatal Embrace*, Chicago: University of Chicago Press.

Goldberg, G. (1986) 'The struggle for legitimacy: Herut's road from opposition to power', in S.A. Cohen, and E. Don-Yehiya (eds.), *Conflict and Consensus in Jewish Political Life*, Ramat Gan: Bar-Ilan University Press, pp. 146–169.

Gorny, Y. (1985) *The Arab Question and the Jewish Problem*, Tel Aviv: Am Oved.

Greenberg, M. (1984) *On the Bible and Judaism* (Hebrew), Tel Aviv: Am Oved.

Ha'aretz: (1993) 29 November, p. A4.

Harkabi, Y. (1985) 'Jewish ethos and political positions in Israel', *Forum*, 56, pp. 43–52.

Herzl, T. (1946) *The Jewish State*, New York: American Zionist Emergency Council.

Horowitz, D. and Lissak, M. (1977) *The Origins of the Israeli Polity*, Tel Aviv: Am Oved.

Horowitz, D. and Lissak, M. (1990) *Trouble in Utopia*, Tel Aviv: Am Oved.

Inbar, E. (1990) ' "Jews" "Jewishness" and Israel's foreign policy', *Jewish Political Studies Review* 2, 3 and 4, pp. 165–183.

Katz, J. (1983) *Jewish Nationalism* (Hebrew), Jerusalem: Zionist Library.

Kaufmann, Y. (1958) 'The revealed son of David and the hidden son of David', *Molad* (Hebrew), 56, pp. 197–203.

Leibowitz, Y. (1975) *Judaism, the Jewish People and the State of Israel* (Hebrew), Jerusalem and Tel Aviv: Mossad Bialik.

Mazar, B. (1965) 'Israel's wars with Aram', in J. Liver (ed.), *Military History of the Land of Israel in Biblical Times* (Hebrew), Tel Aviv: Ma'arakhot pp. 206–220.

Mualem, Y. (1999) 'The Jewish dimension in Israel's foreign policy: between political realism and pan-Jewish goals' (Hebrew), dissertation submitted to the Bar-Ilan University, Tel Aviv.

Mualem, Y. (2004) 'Between Israeli foreign policy and Jewish foreign policy: the exodus of the Jews of Algeria in 1958–1962', in M. Orfali and E. Hazan (eds), *Renewal and Tradition: Creativity, Leadership and Processes of Culturization of North African Jewry* (Hebrew), Jerusalem: Bialik Institute, pp. 229–241.

Neuer, H. (2007) 'Aharon Barak's revolution'. Available at www.daat.ac.il/DAAT/ezrachut/english/hillel.htm.

Ravitzky, A. (1993) *Messianism, Zionism and Jewish Religious Radicalism* (Hebrew), Tel Aviv: Am Oved.

Rose, N.A. (1996) *Chaim Weizman*, Jerusalem: Keter.

Sacher, H. (1976) *A History of Israel: From the Rise of Zionism to Our Present Time,* Jerusalem: Steimatzky.

Sandler, S. (1987) 'Is there a Jewish foreign policy?', *Jewish Journal of Sociology*, 24, 2, pp. 115–121.

Sandler, S. (1994) *The State of Israel, the Land of Israel, the Statist and Ethnonational Dimensions of Foreign Policy*, Westport: Greenwood Press.

Schlesinger, A. M. Jr. (1974) *The Imperial Presidency*, New York: Popular Library.

Schwartz, D. (1997) *The Land of Israel in Religious Zionist Thought* (Hebrew), Tel Aviv: Am Oved.

Shilo, S. (1975) *The Law of the Land is the Law* (Hebrew), Jerusalem: Jerusalem Academic Press.

Smith, A.D. (1981) 'States and homelands: the social and geopolitical implications of national territory', *Journal of International Studies*, 10, 3, pp. 187–202.

Smith, A.D. (1999) 'Ethnic election and national destiny: some religious origins of nationalist ideals', *Nations and Nationalism*, 5, 3, pp. 331–355.

The Holy Scriptures: A Jewish Bible According to the Masoretic Text (1971) Tel Aviv: Sinai.

Vital, D. (1975) *The Origins of Zionism*, Tel-Aviv: Am Oved.

Vital, D. (1982) *Zionism: The Formative Years*, Tel Aviv: Oxford University Press.

Walzer, M. (1993) *Exodus and Revolution*, Tel Aviv: Papirus.

Walzer, M. (2000) *Universalism and Jewish Values*, New York: Carnegie Council.

Walzer, M., Lorberbaum, M. and Zohar, N.J. (eds) (2000) *The Jewish Political Tradition,* New Haven: Yale University Press.

Wildavsky, A. (1984) *The Nursing Father, Moses as a Political Leader*, Alabama: University of Alabama Press.

Yaron, Z. (1974) *The Philosophy of Rabbi Kook* (Hebrew), Jerusalem: WZO.

Part II

Religion and governance

10

Secularisation and politics

Steve Bruce

Introduction

Since at least the middle of the nineteenth century the religion that once dominated European societies and most of their colonial offshoots has been in decline. The liberal democracies of the west are now markedly less religious than they were in 1900 or at any point in the previous ten centuries. The description and explanation of that change is 'the secularisation thesis'. Given its complexity, 'paradigm' might be more appropriate than 'thesis' but social scientists are agreed on this: although 'secularisation' initially meant the deliberate removal of property or functions from the religious to the secular sphere (and still has that sense in Francophone social science), the explanation of secularisation owes more to the unintended consequences of diffuse social changes than to the deliberate actions of people promoting a secularist agenda.

The details of the decline in the power, popularity and prestige of religion vary from society to society but that decline has been general and unrelenting. Different indexes of religiosity decline from different starting points but they point the same way. Remarkably, societies with very different histories of church–state relations end up in a similar place. For example, in France the dominant religion, being Catholic, was relatively immune to

internal fragmentation. Because the Catholic Church had firmly allied itself with the ancien regime, the progressive political forces of the eighteenth century became anti-clerical. When the revolutionaries triumphed they imposed secularity on the state and its institutions. In contrast, in Britain, where the dominant Protestant tradition divided into many different churches, denominations and sects, social conflict could be expressed as variations within Christianity. Rising social classes associated with particular sects opposed the privileges of the established churches but they did not oppose religion as such; there was no significant anti-clerical spirit. Once the state churches had been stripped of their real advantages, their competitors stopped pressing for change and left a great deal of formal religion in the public sphere. But though their histories have been very different, the current position of Christianity in France and in Britain is similar: the majority of the population have little knowledge of Christianity, take no part in its rituals, pay no attention to the churches' social and moral teachings, and do little to ensure the survival of the faith.

Not only is the decline general, it is also regular. None of the great upheavals of the nineteenth or twentieth centuries produced significant religious revivals. Membership of the Methodist churches in the UK (useful

145

to the social scientist for the rigour of their record-keeping) shows only one tiny increase over the twentieth century and that reflected a change in data collection.

The spread and regularity of secularisation suggests that it cannot be explained either by idiosyncratic features of particular cultures or by the particular failings of certain churches. Nor is secularisation a consequence of particular features of religious markets. We find the same decline in the highly competitive situation in England (where by 1851 half of those who attended church did so other than in the state-established Church of England), in the Lutheran monopoly of Sweden, and in the Catholic monopolies of Italy and France.

Further evidence that secularisation is a general social process is provided by the failure of alternatives to the Christian churches. It is certainly true that the decline in the power of the Christian churches to stigmatise alternatives as dangerously deviant has allowed an enormous variety of imports and new inventions but non-Christian religions, the new religious movements of the 1970s, and the many diffuse forms of 'New Age' spirituality common in the 1990s, have all failed to make significant inroads into the very large European populations now free from a Christian attachment. To give just one datum, a very detailed study of an English provincial town found that only 1.6 per cent of the population was involved in any form of 'New Age' or 'holistic milieu' activity in 2001 and half of those involved declined to describe their interest in yoga, aromatherapy, meditation and the like as 'spiritual' (Heelas and Woodhead 2005).

The history of church–state relations in those countries that were dominated by communism is very different to that of western Europe. With varying degrees of enthusiasm, communist states deliberately suppressed organised religion, replaced church leaders with people loyal to the communist party, and attempted to remove the demand for religion by creating secular alternatives to religious rites of passage. When communism collapsed in the late 1980s and early 1990s many expected that Christianity would recover. There was institutional restoration: churches regained property, acquired the freedom to operate as they wished and, in many cases, regained the rhetorical status of honoured representative of the titular nationality. Some nationalist politicians sought to have the Christian nature of their countries established in their new constitutions. But there has been little or no 'bounce back' in popular involvement in the churches. Kääriäinen (2001) finds some increase in Russian church attendance post-communism: the percentage who said they attended 'several times a year' increased from 8 in 1991 to 21 in 1999 but 'at least once a month' attendance barely changed. It fluctuated between 6 and 7 per cent over the decade. Borowik noted of Russians in 2002: 'their connections with the Orthodox Church are somewhat theoretical' (2002: 500). And in countries where the Catholic Church had previously benefited from its oppositional role (Poland and Lithuania, for example) the achievement of national independence was followed by a decline in popular involvement as the church came to be seen as just one interest group among others.

In retrospect the success of state-led secularisation in most of Communist Europe is no surprise. Enforced secularisation may not have changed the minds of any of the first generation but it seems to have effectively prevented the transmission of the cultural product to the second and third generations.

This point may be premature but the liberalisation of the religious market in eastern Europe has been no more effective for the overall levels of Christian belief and observance (or to the popularity of religion overall) than it has been in the west. Despite being well-funded by western organisations, most innovations have made little impact. If we stretch the definition of Christian to admit the Mormons, we can see the point. There were no Mormons in Russia in 1991; there are now 46 groups. This is impressive but the likely 500 members vanish in the Russian population of 149 million.

To recap, the fact that, despite great difference in church–state relations, the trajectory of change in Christianity across Europe has been similar, suggests that secularisation is to be explained by general social processes rather than by idiosyncratic features of particular settings.

The general causes of secularisation

The secularisation paradigm which presents features of modernisation as causes of the decline in the plausibility of religion is complex. An extensive synoptic treatment I offer elsewhere (Bruce 2002) has 22 variables. In this summary I will concentrate on a few of the major considerations.

Structural and social differentiation

Modernisation entails structural differentiation: as societies grow and become more elaborate they evolve specialised roles and institutions are created to handle specific functions previously embodied in one role or institution (Parsons 1964). The family was once a unit of production as well as the institution through which society was reproduced. With industrialisation, economic activity became divorced from the home. It also became increasingly informed by its own values. At work we are supposed to be rational, instrumental and pragmatic. We are also supposed to be universalistic: to treat customers alike, paying attention only to the matter in hand. The private sphere, by contrast, is taken to be expressive, indulgent and emotional. Such specialisation

directly secularised many social functions which were once performed by the church: education, healthcare, welfare and social control. This was particularly the case where increased diversity of religious culture made it difficult for the state to regard a particular religious affiliation as an essential element of citizenship.

As society fragments, so do the people. Economic growth created an ever-greater range of occupation and life-situation which, because it was accompanied by growing egalitarianism, led to class avoidance. In feudal societies, masters and servants could live in close proximity because the gentry had no fear that the lower orders would get ideas 'above their station'. As the social structure became more fluid, those who could afford to do so replaced the previously effective social distance with literal space.

The plausibility of a single moral universe in which all people have a place depends on a stable social structure. With new social roles and increasing social mobility, communal conceptions of the moral and supernatural order fragmented. As classes became more distinctive they created salvational systems better suited to their interests. The religious pyramid of pope, bishops, priests and laity reflected the feudal social pyramid of king, nobles, gentry and peasants. Independent small farmers or the rising business class preferred a more democratic religion; hence their attraction to such Protestant sects as the Presbyterians, Baptists and Quakers.

Individualism

Martin noted a major effect of the Reformation when he wrote that 'The logic of Protestantism is clearly in favour of the voluntary principle, to a degree that eventually makes it sociologically unrealistic' (1978: 9). Belief systems differ greatly in their propensity to fragment. To simplify, some religions claim a unique truth while others allow that there are many ways to salvation. The Catholic Church claims that Christ's authority was passed to Peter and then fixed in the office of Pope. It claims control of access to salvation and the right to decide disputes about God's will. If those claims are accepted, the Church is relatively immune to fission. As to depart from Rome goes to the heart of what one believes as a Catholic, such departures are rare and are associated with extreme upheavals, such as the French Revolution. As Catholic countries modernise they split into the religious and the secular: so in the twentieth century Italy, Spain and France had conservative Catholic traditions and powerful communist parties.

Protestantism was vulnerable to schism because it rejected institutional mechanisms to settle disputes. Asserting that all can equally well discern God's will invites schism. Tradition, habit, respect for learning or admiration for piety restrained but could not prevent division. The Reformation produced not one church purified and strengthened but competing perspectives.

Individualism gradually developed an autonomous dynamic as a vague egalitarianism. The link between modernisation and inequality is paradoxical. Industrialisation produced both greater social distance and egalitarianism. The Reformers were not democrats but they inadvertently caused a major change in the relative importance of community and individual. By removing the special status of the priesthood and the possibility that religious merit could be transferred (by, for example, saying masses for the souls of the dead), they re-asserted what was implicit in early Christianity: that we are all equal in the eyes of God. That equality initially lay in our sinfulness but the idea could not indefinitely be confined to duty. Equal obligations eventually became equal rights.

That was made possible by changes in the economy (Gellner 1983, 1991).

Economic development brought change and the expectation of further change. And it brought occupational mobility. As it became more common for people to better themselves, it also become more common for them to think better of themselves. However badly paid, the industrial worker was not a serf. The serf occupied just one role in an all-embracing hierarchy and that role shaped his entire life. A tin-miner in Cornwall in 1800 might be oppressed at work but in the late evening and on Sunday he could change clothes and persona to become a Baptist preacher: a man of prestige. Such alternation marked a crucial change. Once social status became task-specific, people could occupy different positions in different hierarchies. That made it possible to distinguish between the role and the person who played it. Roles could still be ranked and accorded very different degrees of power or status but the people behind the roles could be seen as in some sense equal: the basis for our modern culture of human rights.

Societalisation

Societalisation is the term Wilson gives to the way in which 'life is increasingly enmeshed and organised, not locally but societally (that society being most evidently, but not uniquely, the nation state)' (1982: 154). If social differentiation and individualism are blows to small-scale communities from below, societalisation is the attack from above. Close-knit, integrated, communities gradually lost power and presence to large-scale industrial and commercial enterprises, to modern states coordinated through massive, impersonal bureaucracies, and to cities. This is the classic community-to-society transition delineated by Tönnies (1955).

Wilson argues that religion draws its strength from the community. The church of the Middle Ages baptised, christened, married and buried. Its calendar of services mapped on to the seasons. It celebrated and legitimated local life. In turn it drew strength from being frequently re-affirmed by the local people. In 1898 almost everyone in my village celebrated the harvest by bringing tokens of their produce to the church. In 1998, a very small number of people in my village (only one of them a farmer) celebrated by bringing to the church tinned goods (many of foreign provenance) bought in a multinational supermarket. Instead of celebrating the harvest, the service thanked God for all his creation. Broadening the symbolism of the service solved the problem of relevance but removed direct contact with the lives of those involved. When the all-embracing community of like-situated people working and playing together gives way to the dormitory town or suburb, there is little left in common to celebrate.

Differentiation and societalisation reduced the plausibility of any single overarching moral and religious system and thus allowed competing religions. While each may have had much to say to private experience, none could have much connection to the performance of social roles or the operation of social systems because they were not society-wide. Religion, now 'privatised', retained subjective plausibility for some, but lost its objective taken-for-grantedness. It was now a preference, not a necessity.

Again it is worth stressing the interaction of social and cultural forces. The Reformation's fragmentation of the religious tradition hastened the development of the religiously neutral state. A successful economy required a high degree of integration: effective communication, a shared legal code to enforce contracts, a climate of trust, and so on (Gellner 1991). This required an integrated national culture. Where there was consensus, a national 'high culture' could be provided through the dominant religious tradition. The clergy could continue to be the school teachers, historians, propagandists, public administrators and military strategists.

Where there was little consensus, the growth of the state was secular.

Social and cultural diversity

Diversity created the secular state. Modernisation brought with it increased cultural diversity in three ways. Peoples moved and brought their language, religion and social mores into a new setting. Second, the expansive nation-state encompassed new peoples. Third, especially common in Protestant settings, economic modernisation created classes which created competing sects. Hence the paradox: at the same time as the nation-state was trying to create a unified national culture out of thousands of small communities, it was having to come to terms with increasing religious diversity. The solution was an increasingly neutral state. State-established churches were abandoned altogether (the United States) or neutered (the British case). While freedom from entanglements with secular power allowed churches to become more clearly spiritual, their removal from the centre of public life reduced contact with, and relevance for, the general population.

Separation of church and state was one consequence of diversity. Another was the break between community and religious worldview. In sixteenth-century Europe, every significant event in the lifecycle of the individual and the community was celebrated in church and given a religious gloss. The church's techniques were used to bless the sick, sweeten the soil and increase animal productivity. Testimonies, contracts and promises were reinforced by oaths sworn on the Bible and before God. But beyond the special events that saw the parish troop into the church, a huge amount of credibility was given to the religious worldview simply through everyday interaction and conversation. People commented on the weather by saying 'God be praised' and on parting wished each other 'God Speed' or 'Goodbye' (an abbreviation for 'God be with you').

Diversity also called into question the certainty that believers could accord their religion (Berger 1980). Ideas are most convincing when they are universally shared. The elaboration of alternatives provides a subtle but profound challenge. Believers need not fall on their swords when they find that others disagree with them. Where clashes of ideologies occur in the context of social conflict or when alternatives are promoted by people who need not be seriously entertained, the cognitive challenge can be dismissed (Berger and Luckmann 1966: 133). Nonetheless diversity undermines the sense of inevitability.

Compartmentalisation and privatisation

Believers may respond to pluralism by supposing that all religions are, in some sense, the same. Another possibility (and they are not incompatible) is to confine one's faith to a particular compartment of social life. With compartmentalisation comes privatisation: the sense that the reach of religion is shortened to just those who accept the teachings of this or that faith. As Luckmann puts it:

> This development reflects the dissolution of *one* hierarchy of significance in the world view. Based on the complex institutional structure and social stratification of industrial societies different 'versions' of the world view emerge. ... With the pervasiveness of the consumer orientation and the sense of autonomy, the individual is more likely to confront the culture and the sacred cosmos as a 'buyer'. Once religion is defined as a 'private affair', the individual may choose from the assortment of 'ultimate' meanings as he sees fit.
>
> (1970: 98–9)

Casanova (1994) argues that differentiation need not cause privatisation. The major churches, having now accepted the rules of liberal democracy, can regain a public role. They achieve this not by the old model of a compact between a dominant church and the state, but by acting as pressure groups in civil society. This is true but it misses the point that religious interest groups are now forced to present their case in secular terms. For example, abortion is not opposed as unbiblical but because it infringes the universal human right to life.

The secular state and liberal democracy

Social innovations, once established, can have an appeal that goes far beyond the initial motive to innovate. Secular liberal democracy evolved as a necessary response to the egalitarianism made possible by structural differentiation, and to the social and cultural diversity created by the interaction of the fissiparousness of Protestantism and social differentiation. But it became attractive in its own right to social groups within hegemonic religious cultures. By the late nineteenth century societies that had no great need for them introduced the same principles as part of wider political reforms. Despite dissent being largely confined to differences of observance and emphasis within the Lutheran tradition, the introduction of representative democracy and the weakening of the monarchy (or Grand Duchy) in the Nordic countries was accompanied by a weakening of the national churches (which retained some social functions only by presenting them universally as secular social services).

Rationality

All of the above variables are concerned with social structures: they concern the environment for the preservation and promotion of a particular religious worldview. There is another strand of the secularisation paradigm that focuses more on the content of dominant patterns of thought. The worlds of science and of magic are not absolutely discrete but there is an obvious difference between the models of causation popular in parts of Africa, for example, where witchcraft is still a powerful force in the explanation of misfortune (Gifford 2004) and in the United Kingdom, where superstitions are rare and at best 'half-believed-in' to use Campbell's depiction (Campbell 1996). Not only has the supernatural largely disappeared from the secular parts of Europe: the mainstream Christianity of the West has little space for the demonic. Hence one strand of the secularisation paradigm is concerned with the decline of the supernatural and the corresponding rise of a rational scientific worldview.

A zero–sum notion of knowledge, with rational thought and science conquering territory from dark superstition was carried into sociology by Comte and Marx among others but it is not part of the modern secularisation paradigm. We know that modern people are quite capable of believing untruths and hence that the decreasing plausibility of religion cannot be explained simply by the presence of some (to us) more plausible ideas. The crucial connections are more subtle and complex than those implied in a science v. religion battle and rest on nebulous consequences of assumptions about the orderliness of the world and our mastery over it. More important than science was the development of effective technologies. Religion is often practical. Holy water cures ailments and prayers improve crop quality. Technology secularises by reducing the occasions on which people have recourse to religion. Farmers did not stop praying to save their sheep from maggots because the invention of an effective sheep dip persuaded them

that God was not well-informed. But as the accumulation of scientific knowledge gave people insight into, and mastery over, areas that had once been mysterious, the need and opportunity for recourse to the religious gradually declined.

More generally, as Martin puts it, with the growth of science and technology 'the general sense of human power is increased, the play of contingency is restricted, and the overwhelming sense of divine limits which afflicted previous generations is much diminished' (1969: 116).

In exploring the psychology of modern work, Berger et al. (1974) argue that, even if we are unaware of it, modern technology brings with it a 'technological consciousness' that is a poor foundation for an expectation of supernatural intervention. An example is 'componentiality'. Modern work assumes that the most complex entities can be broken down into parts that are infinitely replaceable: any one mass-produced component can be replaced by any other. Likewise actions (such as welding together a car body) can be reduced to elements that can be indefinitely repeated with identical results. This attitude is carried over from manufacture to the management of workers (a style known after its heroic promoter as 'Fordism') and then to bureaucracy generally. While there is no obvious clash between these assumptions and the teachings of most religions, there are serious incompatibilities of approach. There is little space for the eruption of the divine or the demonic in the world of computerised internet sales.

To summarise, the effects of science and technology on the plausibility of religious belief may be misunderstood. Direct clash is less significant than subtle undermining. Science and technology have not made us atheists but the underlying rationality – orderliness, rule-following, research, controlled experiment – makes us less likely than our forebears to entertain the notion of the divine.

Relativism

All of the above combines in a significant new attitude that weakens religion: relativism. The Christian Church of the Middle Ages was firmly authoritarian and exclusive in its attitude to knowledge. There was a single truth and it knew what it was. Increasingly, social and cultural diversity combined with egalitarianism to undermine all claims to authoritative knowledge. It is difficult to live in a world which treats as equally valid a large number of incompatible beliefs, and which shies away from authoritative assertions, without coming to suppose that there is no one truth. We may continue to prefer our worldview but we find it hard to insist that what is true for us must also be true for everyone else. The tolerance which is necessary for harmony in diverse egalitarian societies weakens religion by forcing us to live as if we could not be sure of God's will or as if God himself was not sure of his will. The consequence, visible over the twentieth century in liberal democracies, was a decline first in the commitment of, and then in the number of, church adherents.

We can clarify the point by following a common biographical pattern. A young Catholic girl is raised in the east end of Glasgow in 1910. Her entire extended family are pious Catholics and she attends a Catholic church school. What she knows of Protestants is filtered through a series of negative stereotypes. But in 1915 she leaves home for Gretna to work in the enormous explosives factory built by the government to supply the troops in the First World War. There in a rapidly constructed new town of 30,000 people she mixes with people from all over Britain (and many from abroad). Her faith is no longer re-affirmed in countless acts of everyday interaction. The official organisations do not endorse her beliefs. Indeed the Ministry of Munitions has shown its impartiality by funding the construction of

three churches: Presbyterian, Episcopalian and Catholic. At work, in her shared lodgings and at the local dances, she discovers that Presbyterians and Methodists and people of no particular faith can be as pleasant and attractive as the members of her former community. She falls in love with and marries an English Methodist. With children comes the difficult decisions of choice of schooling and of religious socialisation. Even if the parents raise their children as Catholics or Methodists (and half of such parents will do neither) the children will be aware that their parents once did not agree. The common consequence of positive interaction with people of a different faith (and none) is for the believers to shift from a dogmatic certainty to a vague relativism: all forms of Christianity are equally valid. If all faiths (and none) offer a road to God, if there is no hell for heretics, there is no need to ensure the transmission of orthodoxy. The children's generation will sit looser to its faith than the previous one.

Countervailing forces

The above explains 'the process by which sectors of society and culture are removed from the domination of religious institutions and symbols' and the associated increase in the number of people 'who look upon the world and their own lives without the benefit of religious interpretations' (Berger 1969: 107–8).

To stop there would be to create a false impression. Secularisation theorists have also written extensively about settings where religion remains seriously implicated in the central operations of economies, polities and societies, and continues to play a major part in shaping people's lives. The case can be summarised as saying that religion diminishes in social significance, becomes increasingly privatised, and loses personal salience *except where it finds work to do other than relating individuals to the super-natural.* Such work can be described under two broad headings: cultural defence and cultural transition. As we will see, there is a slight difference in the relationship of each to modernisation. While both sources of religious vitality involve responding to current conditions (and in that sense are modern), the cultural defence role of religion requires one 'pre-modern' element.

Cultural defence

What many settings where religion remains a powerful social force have in common is that religion is implicated in group identity, primarily of an ethnic or national character. Where culture, identity and sense of worth are challenged by a source promoting either an alien religion or rampant secularism and that source is negatively valued, secularisation will be inhibited. Religion often provides resources for the defence of a national, local, ethnic or status group culture. Poland and the Irish Republic are prime examples. We can go back over the basic elements of the secularisation thesis and note how ethnic conflict can inhibit their development. Consider structural differentiation. My account assumed that there were no obstacles to the increasing autonomy of social functions but clearly hostility between religio-ethnic groups can prevent or retard the process. For example, where it has been unable to dominate a national culture, the Catholic Church has insisted on maintaining its own school system and has often generated parallel versions of secular institutions such as trade unions and professional associations. Though a minority can rarely evade the state's social control systems, it may still prefer to pre-emptively exercise its own church-based controls on the behaviour of members.

In the classic model of functional differentiation, the first sphere to become free of

cultural restraints is the economy. Yet even in this pre-eminent site for rational choice, ethnic identification may inhibit rationality. In Northern Ireland attempts to impose rationality on the world of work (through 'fair employment' legislation) have largely failed to prevent the exercise of religio-ethnic preferences (especially in small firms that do not depend on the state for contracts and thus cannot be easily controlled). People also exhibit their ethnic identity in personal consumption. Small towns will often support one Protestant and one Catholic enterprise, each only marginally viable, where the market can profitably sustain only one. Especially at times of heightened tension, Protestants and Catholics boycott each other's businesses and travel considerable distances to engage in commerce with their own sort.

Consider societalisation. A beleaguered minority may try to prevent the erosion of the community. Deviants who attempt to order their lives in the societal rather than the community mode may be regarded as disloyal and treacherous and punished accordingly. For example, in the ethnic conflicts in Bosnia and Northern Ireland, those who marry across the divide have been frequent targets for vigilantes keen to clarify and maintain their boundaries.

Finally, ethnic conflict mutes the cognitive consequences of pluralism because the power of invidious stereotypes allows alternative cultures to be thoroughly stigmatised. Relativism as a way of accommodating those with whom we differ is only necessary if we take those people seriously. If we have good reason to hate them, such consideration is neither necessary nor desirable. Where religious differences are strongly embedded in ethnic identities, the cognitive threat from others is relatively weak.

It is important to note that all major cultural defence cases involve religion (or the church) *continuing* to play a role as the embodiment of collective identity. None of them are examples of religion acquiring this role after it has been lost. Where church has become separated from state, and religion has become privatised because of the press of cultural diversity in an egalitarian culture that respects individualism, no amount of social pressure can restore the close bond. For example, the initial British hostility to Irish immigrants in the early nineteenth century, when most Britons had a Protestant church connection, was often religious. But the successful integration of that immigrant block, increasing religious toleration, and the secularisation of the culture meant that opposition to Muslim migrants a century later was secular racist and made no appeal to religious identity. The point is obvious and can be seen very clearly in comparing the resistance to communism of the three Baltic states. Lithuania, which was overwhelmingly Catholic, was better able to maintain its sense of identity vis-à-vis Russian communism than was Estonia which was religiously diverse. Religion can only serve as a major component in cultural defence if the people share the same religion. As there is no sign of major religious revivals reuniting religiously diverse populations, we can reasonably see the historical change as being one-way.

This does not mean that all religio-ethnic movements are merely survivals of pre-modern structural arrangements; they are also reactions to troublesome aspects of modernisation. We do not need to consider much detail to appreciate that the Iranian revolution of 1979, for example, was in large part a reaction to western exploitation of Iran and to the failure of the Shah's attempts to impose western culture. To use the terms advanced above, there was considerable forced differentiation and the intention of the Iranian revolution was to roll that back. In that sense, 'de-differentiation' may be possible where the original change was artificially imposed.

However, the crucial point is that religion could only play the role of cultural defence in Iran because the vast majority of Iranians shared the same religion and such differentiation as had occurred had been short-lived, unpopular and imposed from outside, rather than emerging slowly and 'naturally' from indigenous social development (Bruce 2001).

To put the case formally, the relative absence of the sort of differentiation that occurred in most parts of the stable democracies of western Europe is a necessary condition for movements of cultural defence.

Cultural transition

Where social identity is threatened in the course of major cultural transitions such as migration, religion may provide resources for negotiating such transitions or asserting a new claim to a sense of worth. Ethnic religious groups can ease the transition between homeland and new identity. The church (or temple, gurdwara or mosque) offers a supportive group which speaks one's language but which also has experience of, and contacts within, the new social and cultural milieu.

To summarise, it is not an accident that most modern societies are largely secular. Industrialisation brought with it a series of social changes – the fragmentation of the life-world, the decline of community, the rise of bureaucracy, technological consciousness – that together made religion less arresting and less plausible than it had been in pre-modern societies. My account differs from the classic sociological treatment only in the stress I give to diversity. Where others have begun their explanation for the decline of religion with the increasingly neutral state, I have attended to the cause of that neutrality. The idea that citizens should not have their rights constrained by religious affiliation became sufficiently well established as part of liberal and democratic discourse by the middle of the nineteenth century that it became part of democratic reform; but it was born out of necessity. The cultural diversity created by the interaction of the fragmenting religious culture and structural and social differentiation pushed religious identity (and with it all but the blandest religious affirmations) out of the public arena and into the private sphere. The removal of support at the level of social structure has a corresponding effect on the social psychology of belief. The dogmatic certainties of the church and sect are replaced by the weak affirmations of the denomination and the cult.

However, there are counter-trends that retard or prevent secularisation. The secularising impact of diversity depends to a very great extent on an egalitarian culture and a democratic polity. In their absence, diversity may heighten racial and ethnic conflict and deepen commitment to a communal religious identity.

Is secularisation inevitable?

It is difficult to imagine a reversal of secularisation in western liberal democracies. Its consequences are so firmly entrenched that when pious believers enter the political arena to campaign for values that have a religious basis, they have to argue in secular terms. The New Christian right in the USA argues against abortion on the basis of the human rights of the foetus and campaigns against divorce or gay rights on the apparently neutral functional ground that the stable nuclear family offers the best environment for child-rearing. It is certainly difficult to imagine any liberal democracy according pride of place to a particular religion or accepting that rights should be tied to religious affiliation. It is equally difficult to see cultural diversity being reversed or people volunteering to give up individual autonomy.

If we accept the above explanation of secularisation, it is probable that it is irreversible.

But that is not to say that it is inevitable. The secularisation paradigm is, in the first place, an explanation of the past of the 'First World'; we should expect a similar outcome elsewhere only if all the necessary conditions are in place. What makes extrapolation from the past of the West difficult is that later modernising societies develop in a very different environment: an environment dominated by the existence of the First World and by the need to respond to it. Secularisation is no longer just an abstract description of the past: it is encumbered by reactions to it and to the actions of its carriers.

It is an artificial distinction but we can try to divide intrinsic and extrinsic sources of change (which often coincide with popular versus elite modernisation). In the extrinsic or 'top-down' form of modernisation, religious toleration, the separation of church and state, the freedom of citizenship rights from religious affiliation are heavily promoted, and sometimes imposed, by western powers. Other societies may imitate aspects of the western model. For example, Kemal Ataturk (and subsequent leaders in post-Ottoman empire states such as the Shah of Iran) decided that economic progress required a secular state, even though the religious culture was sufficiently homogenous for many people to think secularity unnecessary. In the case of India, religious diversity created an intrinsic need for state secularity but large parts of India were sufficiently homogenous that the underlying corrosive effects of pluralism (inter-marriage and positive interaction between carriers of different faiths leading to religious relativism) were absent. Hence the tension between the secularity of the state and powerful local movements for religio-ethnic solidarity. Furthermore, largely secular disputes such as the objection of many Muslim states to US foreign policy can readily generate opposition not just to the Christianity of the west (as we see when Islamists label western powers as 'Crusaders') but also to secularity. Whatever potential for secularisation may be generated by indigenous social change in Muslim societies may be retarded by reforms being branded as bowing to the will of the Great Satan.

But to concentrate on indigenous forces that make secularisation unlikely, it is first worth noting that many developing countries are relatively homogenous in their religious complexion (and the many civil conflicts in such countries have made them more so by driving out minorities and subdividing states along religio-ethnic lines). The USA was too diverse to have a state religion; Iran and Pakistan are not.

In addition, the secularisation paradigm concerns societies that had sufficiently strong states to effectively provide society-wide social functions. Although many of the new states established in the twentieth century were either founded on the basis of secular nationalism or soon adopted it (for example, the Baathist ideology of Syria and Iraq) the subsequent failure of those states to provide effective government left gaps that were filled by popular grassroots religious organisations. The success of the Muslim Brotherhood, Hezbollah and similar organisations in some Muslim states and the popularity of Christian churches in many African countries owes much to the simple fact that religious institutions are more effective than secular ones.

However, secularising forces are not entirely absent. The comparative international World Values surveys organised by Inglehart (1997) show a weak but clear general connection between increasing prosperity and secularisation. Even in religiously homogenous cultures, political stability and rising prosperity are associated with weakening commitment to the dominant religion. It seems to be universally the case that when the crises that force people to rely on extended family, clan and tribe abate, people will desire increased personal freedom and autonomy and that often takes the form of wishing to decide for themselves to what extent they will conform to their traditional religious culture.

What is not yet clear is the extent to which science and technology will erode supernaturalism. If we generalise from the western experience we should expect that after a generation or two, those Indians heavily involved in modern science-based technologies such as computer programming should gradually give up the many religious and spiritual acts associated with their Hindu tradition.

Conclusion: the political consequences of secularisation

The political consequences of secularisation can be divided in two: for secular and for religious societies. Secularisation fundamentally changed the political environment for western societies by removing one of the major constraints on individual liberty. The very notion of 'human rights' requires the absence of entitlement characteristics and for most societies for most of human history having the right religion was an entry qualification for any sort of right. Pre-modern societies varied in the extent and the details of the toleration they extended to (or denied) people who worshipped the wrong God but they expected people to belong to a religious 'bloc' and they accorded rights and privileges to blocs. Modern western societies treat people as individuals whose religious identity, if they have one, is a private matter. We no longer accord the vote, or the right to own property, or the right to legal due process to only those who share our religion. Our legislatures and constitutions are still adorned with fragmentary reminders of the past (opening parliamentary sessions with prayers, for example) but no western legislature will refuse to pass an Act on the grounds that it is contrary to the will of God. Our legislators will be required to swear allegiance to the state or to the monarch; they will not be subject to religious tests. We accept a distinction between law (what the state can require) and morality (what our faith may require) and do not expect the former to be the same as the latter. On all three counts, Iran now and Britain in 1900 were different.

For many developing countries, secularisation is not a background cause of aspects of the political environment: it is a contentious political issue. It is not the product of slow and gradual erosion of the power, persuasiveness and popularity of religious beliefs: it is a choice. It is an agenda item to which people must react. Turkey, for example, is radically divided. There are those who see the secularity of the state and the public sphere as not just a social benefit, a desired instance of personal freedom, but also as a necessary condition for economic prosperity. And there are those who wish to restore Islam to the centre of public life. While almost every member state of the United Nations pays lip-service to the notion of human rights, many, in practice, do not accept that citizenship should be faith-blind.

Bibliography

Berger, P. L. (1969) *The Social Reality of Religion*, London: Faber and Faber.

Berger, P. L. (1980) *The Heretical Imperative: Contemporary Possibilities of Religious Affirmations*, London: Collins.

Berger, P. L. (1983) 'From the crisis of religion to the crisis of modernity', in M. Douglas, and S. Tipton, (eds), *Religion and America: Spiritual Life in a Secular Age*, Boston: Beacon Press, pp. 14–24.

Berger, P. L. and Luckmann, T. (1966) 'Secularization and pluralism', *International Yearbook for the Sociology of Religion*, 2, pp. 73–84.

Berger, P. L. and Luckmann, T. (1973) *The Social Construction of Reality*, Harmondsworth: Penguin.

Berger, P. L., Berger, B. and Kellner, H. (1974) *The Homeless Mind*, Harmondsworth: Penguin.

Borowik, I. (2002) 'Between Orthodoxy and eclecticism: on the religious transformation of Russia, Belarus and Ukraine', *Social Compass* 49, pp. 497–508.

Bruce, S. (1999) *Choice and Religion: A Critique of Rational Choice Theory*, Oxford: Oxford University Press.

Bruce, S. (2000) 'The supply-side model of religion: the Nordic and Baltic states', *Journal for the Scientific Study of Religion*, 39, pp. 32–46.

Bruce, S. (2001) *Fundamentalism*, Oxford: Polity Press.

Bruce, S. (2002) *God is Dead: Secularization in the West*, Oxford: Blackwell.

Campbell, C. (1996) 'Half-belief and the paradox of ritual instrumental activism', *British Journal of Sociology*, 47, pp. 151–66.

Casanova, J. (1994) *Public Religions in the Modern World*, Chicago: University of Chicago Press.

Gellner, E. (1983) *Nations and Nationalism*, Oxford: Blackwell.

Gellner, E. (1991) *Plough, Sword and Book: The Structure of Human History*, London: Paladin.

Gifford, P. (2004) *Ghana's New Christianity: Pentecostalism in a Globalising Economy*, London: Hurst.

Heelas, P. and Woodhead, L. (2005) *The Spiritual Revolution*, Oxford: Blackwell.

Inglehart, R. (1997) *Modernization and Postmodernization: Cultural, Political and Economic Change in 43 Societies*, Princeton: Princeton University Press.

Kääriäinen, K. (2001) 'Lowest church attendance rates in Europe', *East–West Ministry Report*, 9(3), p. 10.

Luckmann, T. (1970) *The Invisible Religion: The Problem of Religion in Modern Society*, New York: Macmillan.

Martin, D. (1969) *The Religious and the Secular*, London: Routledge and Kegan Paul.

Martin, D. (1978) *A General Theory of Secularization*, Oxford: Blackwell.

Parsons, T. (1964) 'Evolutionary universals in society', *American Journal of Sociology* 29, pp. 339–57.

Tönnies, F. (1955) *Community and Association*, London: Routledge and Kegan Paul.

Wilson, B. R. (1966) *Religion in Secular Society*, London: C. A. Watts.

Wilson, B. R. (1968) 'Religion and the churches in America', in W. McLoughlin and R. N. Bellah (eds), *Religion in America*, Boston: Houghton Mifflin, pp. 73–110.

Wilson, B. R. (1975) 'The debate over "secularization"', *Encounter*, 45, pp. 77–83.

Wilson, B. R. (1976a) *Contemporary Transformations of Religion*, Oxford: Oxford University Press.

Wilson, B. R. (1976b) 'Aspects of secularization in the west', *Japanese Journal of Religious Studies*, 3, pp. 329–76.

Wilson, B. R. (1982) *Religion in Sociological Perspective*, Oxford: Oxford University Press.

Wilson, B. R. (1988) 'The functions of religion: a re-appraisal', *Religion*, 18, pp. 199–216.

Wilson, B. R. (1990) *The Social Dimensions of Sectarianism: Sects and New Religious Movements in Contemporary Society*, Oxford: Oxford University Press.

Wilson, B. R. (1992) 'Reflections on a many-sided controversy', in S. Bruce (ed.), *Religion and Modernization: Sociologists and Historians Debate the Secularization Thesis*, Oxford: Oxford University Press, pp. 195–210.

Wilson, B. R. (2000) 'Salvation, secularization and de-moralization', in R. Fenn (ed.), *The Blackwell Companion to the Sociology of Religion*, Oxford: Blackwell, pp. 39–51.

11

Religious fundamentalisms

Jeffrey Haynes

Contemporary manifestations of religious fundamentalism are an aspect of a more general religious resurgence in most but not all parts of the world, with western Europe an exception to the general trend (Hadden 1987; Shupe 1990; Bruce 2003; Norris and Inglehart 2004). It is useful to think of the various manifestations of contemporary religious fundamentalism as a counter-movement often militantly opposed to what followers perceive as the inexorable onwards march of secularisation, leading to political and public marginalisation and privatisation of religion. To many observers and 'ordinary' people, a further defining characteristic of any form of religious fundamentalism is its social and political conservatism. Socially, religious fundamentalism is regarded as backward looking, anti-modern, inherently opposed to change. Note, however, that if this was actually the case it would be very difficult satisfactorily to explain the sometimes *revolutionary political demands and programmes* of some religious fundamentalist thinkers and activists. Some aim, particularly Islamists in the Middle East and elsewhere in the Muslim world, to overthrow regimes that they regard as un- or anti-Islamic and replace them with more authentically Islamic governments. On the other hand, some Christian fundamentalists in the United States – people who believe in the inerrancy of the Bible

and subscribe to a modern form of millenarianism (that is, the teaching in Christianity that Jesus will rule for a thousand years on earth) may seem to fit more closely conventional wisdom. This is because they are often linked to conservative political forces, for example in the USA, whose aim is to seek to undo what they judge to be symptoms of unwelcome liberalisation and the relaxation of traditional social and moral mores characteristic, they believe, of secularisation (*Religion and Ethics News Weekly* 2004).

Explaining religious fundamentalism

According to Woodhead and Heelas, religious fundamentalism is a 'distinctively modern twentieth-century movement' albeit with 'historical antecedents' (Woodhead and Heelas 2000: 32). Conceptually, the term has been widely employed since the 1970s to describe numerous, apparently diverse, religious and political developments around the globe (Caplan 1987). However, the term was first used a century ago by conservative Christians in the USA to describe themselves: they claimed they wanted to get back to what they saw as the 'fundamentals' of their religion, as depicted in the Bible. Such people typically came from 'mainline' – that is, established – Protestant denominations, not usually the Roman Catholic Church. Now, however, the label 'religious fundamentalism' has become a generic term, widely applied to a multitude of groups from various religious traditions, comprising people who share a decidedly conservative religious outlook (Simpson 1992).

Generally speaking, both the character and impact of fundamentalist doctrines are located within a nexus of moral and social concerns centring on state–society interactions. In some cases, the initial defensiveness of 'religious fundamentalists' came from a belief that they were under attack from modernisation and secularisation and/or the intrusion of alien ethnic, cultural or religious groups. Sometimes this developed into a broad socio-political offensive to try to redress the situation, in particular targeting political rulers and lax co-religionists for their perceived inadequacies and weaknesses. Informing their religious and political outlooks, religious fundamentalists turn to core religious texts – such as the Christian Bible or the Quran – to find out God's 'opinion' on various social and political topics, often through the use of selected readings which may form the basis of programmes of reform (Marty and Appleby 1991).

Contemporary religious fundamentalisms are often said to be rooted in the failed promise of modernity, reactive against perceived unwelcome manifestations of modernisation, especially declining moral values or perceived undermining of the family as a social institution (Haynes 2003). To many religious fundamentalists God was in danger of being superseded by a gospel of technical progress accompanying sweeping socio-economic changes. Around the world, the pace of socio-economic change, especially since World War II, everywhere strongly challenged traditional habits, beliefs and cultures, and societies were under considerable and constant pressure to adapt

to modernisation. Not least, in an increasingly materialist world one's individual worth was increasingly measured according to secular standards of wealth and status; religion seemed ignored, belittled or threatened. Thus to many religious fundamentalists unwelcome social, cultural and economic changes were the root cause of what they saw as a toxic cocktail of religious, moral and social decline.

Religious fundamentalism: definitional issues

It is time to confront a significant analytical problem. It is sometimes suggested that 'religious fundamentalism' is an empty and therefore meaningless term. It is said to be erroneously and casually employed, primarily 'by western liberals' in relation 'to a broad spectrum of religious phenomena which have little in common except for the fact that they are alarming to liberals!' (Woodhead and Heelas 2000: 32). This view contends that the range of people and groups casually labelled 'fundamentalist' is so wide – from the revolutionary political Islamism of the Iranian ideologue, Ali Shariati, the Egyptian Sayyid Qutb, the Pakistani Maulana Maududi, and the Saudi Arabian, Usama bin Laden, through to socially conservative Christians in the USA, such as Pat Robertson and the late Jerry Falwell – that the term lacks clarity, precision and meaning. As a consequence, Hallencreutz and Westerlund aver, the broad use of the term 'religious fundamentalism'

has become increasingly irrelevant. In sum, viewed as a derogatory concept, tied to Western stereotypes and Christian presuppositions, the casual use of the term easily causes misunderstandings and prevents the understanding of the dynamics and characteristics of different religious groups with explicit political objectives.

(Hallencreutz and Westerlund
1996: 4)

We shall turn later to the various political objectives of religious fundamentalists. For now, we can note that, despite such criticisms, the term 'religious fundamentalism' is commonly found in both academic and popular discourse. Numerous journal articles and books on the topic have appeared, including important volumes in the 1990s by Marty and Appleby (1991, 1993a, 1993b, 1994, 1995) and Lawrence (1995), which used the term analytically. Thus by no means all analysts and observers reject the use of the term. Those accepting its analytical and explanatory relevance do so because they perceive contemporary religious fundamentalist thinkers and movements around the world – albeit encompassing very different religious traditions – as having some important features in common, including: core beliefs, norms and values. These include:

- a desire to return to the fundamentals of a religious tradition and strip away unnecessary accretions
- an aggressive rejection of western secular modernity
- an oppositional minority group-identity maintained in an exclusivist and militant manner
- attempts to reclaim the public sphere as a space of religious and moral purity
- a patriarchial and hierarchical ordering of relations between the sexes.

(Woodhead and Heelas 2000: 32)

Drawing on data compiled from studies of numerous religious fundamentalist groups from several religious traditions in different parts of the world, Marty and Scott Appleby arrive at the following definition of religious fundamentalists. They are people who hold a 'set of strategies, by which beleaguered believers attempt to preserve their distinctive identity as a people or group'. They see themselves acting in response to a real or imagined attack from those who, they believe, want to draw them into a 'syncretistic, areligious, or irreligious cultural milieu' (Marty and Scott Appleby 1993a: 3). Following an initial sense of defensiveness as a result of perception of attack from unwelcome, alien forces, fundamentalists may well go on to develop an offensive strategy aimed at altering radically prevailing socio-political realities in order to 'bring back' religious concerns into public centrality.

In sum, it can be stated that religious fundamentalists have the following in common:

- They fear that their preferred religiously orientated way of life is under attack from unwelcome secular influences or alien groups.
- Their aim is to create traditionally orientated, less modern(ised) societies
- As a result, many pursue campaigns in accordance with what they believe are suitable religious tenets in order to change laws, morality, social norms and – in some cases – domestic and/or international political configurations.
- Many are willing to contest politically with ruling regimes in various ways if the latter's jurisdiction appears to be encroaching into areas of life – including education, gender relations and employment policy – that religious fundamentalists believe are integral to their vision of a religiously appropriate society, one characterised by a certain kind of 'pure' moral climate
- They may also actively oppose co-religionists who they believe are excessively lax in upholding their religious duties – as well as followers

of rival or opposing religions who they may regard as misguided, evil, even satanic.

Even those rejecting the general use of the term 'religious fundamentalism' might accept that it has relevance in one specific context: self-designated Christian fundamentalists in the United States. Emerging over a century ago, such people – believing implicitly in the inerrancy of the Bible – sought to resist what they saw as the unacceptable inroads of secular modernity. Until the 1970s, US Christian fundamentalists were often apolitical, even in some cases excluding themselves from the public realm. Over time, however, many began to realise that retreating from the world was actually self-defeating – because as a result they could not hope to alter what they saw as catastrophically unwelcome developments intrinsically linked to modernisation and secularisation. In recent years, Christian fundamentalists in the USA have become increasingly vociferous, an influential political constituency. Leaders of the movement have included the late Jerry Falwell, founding leader of the organisation Moral Majority (formed in 1979, dissolved in 1989), as well as two recent but unsuccessful presidential candidates: Pat Robertson and Pat Buchanan. However, usage of the term has been rather flexible, sometimes used in reference to the broad community of religious – mostly Christian – conservatives and at other times to denote a small subset of institutionalised organisations pursuing explicit goals of cultural and economic conservatism. Many Christian fundamentalists in the USA coalesce in a movement known initially when it was founded in the 1970s as the 'New Christian Right'; now it is referred to as either 'the Christian Right' or 'the Religious Right', with the latter term implying that other religious traditions are also present. In short, the Religious Right is an important

religious/social/political movement in the USA, not exclusive to but generally linking conservative American Christians (Bruce 2003; Dolan 2005).

The use of the Bible by the Christian conservatives in the USA draws attention to the fact that religious fundamentalists generally use holy books as a key source for their ideas. However, drawing on the example of American Christian conservatives, many analysts who employ the term religious fundamentalism suggest that it is only properly applicable to Christianity and the other 'Abrahamic' religions of the 'book': Islam and Judaism. This is because Christian, Islamic and Jewish fundamentalists all take their defining dogma from what they believe to be the inerrancy of God's own words set out in their holy books. In other words, singular scriptural revelations are central to each set of fundamentalist dogma in these three religions.

'Islamic fundamentalism'/ Islamism

Bealey defines religious fundamentalism in terms of a

> religious position claiming strict adherence to basic beliefs. This frequently results in intolerance towards other beliefs and believers in one's own creed who do not strictly observe and who do not profess to hold an extreme position. Thus Protestant fundamentalists scorn Protestants who fail to perceive a danger from Catholicism; Jewish fundamentalists attack Jews with secularist leanings; and Muslim fundamentalists believe that they have a duty to purge Islam of any concessions to cultural modernisation. *A political implication is the tendency of fundamentalists to turn to terrorism.*
>
> (my emphasis; Bealey 1999: 140)

While the Muslim world, like the Christian universe, is divided by religious disputes, it is also the case that many Muslims would accept that they are linked by belief, culture, sentiments and identity, collectively focused in the global Muslim community, the *ummah*. It is also the case that there were clear international manifestations of what we might call 'Islamic resurgence', especially after the humbling defeat of the Arabs by Israel in the Six-day War of June 1967 and the Iranian revolution a dozen years later.

Like their Jewish and Christian counterparts, Islamic fundamentalists (or Islamists, the term many analysts prefer), take as their defining dogma what are believed to be God's words written in their holy book, the Quran. In other words, singular scriptural revelations are central to Islamic fundamentalist dogma. We have also noted that a defining character of all religious fundamentalisms is social conservatism. As already noted, however, this does not imply a corresponding political conservatism, characterised by an unwillingness to countenance significant political changes. But what of Bealey's most contentious claim, that religious fundamentalists, including Islamic fundamentalists, are noted for a political 'tendency' to 'turn to terrorism'?

Let's start by noting that Islamist groups work to change the current social and political order by the use of various political means. These include incremental reform of existing political regimes by various means, including, if allowed, taking part in and winning elections through the auspices of a political party, as well as the use of political violence or terrorism *in some circumstances*. But what might these circumstances be? And is this course of action linked to the very nature of their fundamentalist beliefs? As a way of answering these questions, it is useful to refer to some of the ideas expressed by several noteworthy twentieth-century Islamist thinkers: Maulana Maududi, Sayyid Qutb, Ali Shariati and Ayatollah Khomeini.

Born in India, Maulana Maududi (1903–79) was one of the most influential Muslim theologians of the twentieth century. His philosophy, literary productivity and tireless activism contributed immensely to the development of Islamic political and social movements around the world. Maulana Maududi's ideas profoundly influenced Sayyid Qutb of Egypt's *Jamiat al-Ikhwan al-Muslimun* (the Muslim Brotherhood), another leading Muslim philosopher of the twentieth century. Together, Maududi and Qutb are considered the founding fathers of the global Islamist movement. Maududi's ideas about the Islamic state are widely regarded as the basic foundation for the political, economical, social and religious system of any Islamic country that wishes to live under Islamic law (*sharia*). This is an ideological system that, while intentionally discriminating between people according to their religious affiliations, in no way prescribes the acceptability of political violence, much less terrorism.

Sayyid Qutb (1906–66) was an Egyptian, a prominent Islamist and member of the Muslim Brotherhood, the Arab world's oldest Islamist group, which advocates an Islamic state in Egypt. Qutb's political thinking was deeply influenced by the revolutionary radicalism of a contemporaneous Islamist, Maulana Maududi. Qutb's ideological development fell into two distinct periods: before 1954, and following a sojourn in the United States, from 1954 until his execution by the Egyptian government in 1966, after imprisonment and torture by the secularist government of Gamal Abdel Nasser. Following an attempt on Nasser's life in October 1954, the government imprisoned thousands of members of the Muslim Brotherhood, including Qutb, and officially banned the organisation. During his second, more radical, phase, Qutb declared 'Western civilisation' the enemy of Islam; denounced leaders of Muslim nations for not following

Islam closely enough; and sought to spread the belief among Sunni Muslims that it was their duty to undertake *jihad* to defend and purify Islam. Note however that in this conception *jihad* does not necessarily imply anti-western conflict; instead, it refers to an individual Muslim's striving for spiritual self-perfection.

Ayatollah Ruhollah Khomeini (1900–89) was Iranian Shi'ite leader and Head of State in Iran from 1979 until his death in 1989. He was arrested (1963) and exiled (1964) for his opposition to Shah Muhammad Reza Pahlavi's regime. He returned to Iran on the Shah's downfall (1979) and established a new constitution that gave him supreme powers. His reign was marked by a return to strict observance of the Islamic code. Iran's revolution was divided into two stages: the first saw an alliance of liberal, leftist and Islamic groups oust the Shah; the second stage, often named the 'Islamic Revolution', saw the ayatollahs come to power. During the second stage Khomeini achieved the status of a revered spiritual leader among many Shi'a Muslims. In Iran he was officially addressed as Imam[1] rather than as Ayatollah. Khomeini was also a highly influential and innovative Islamic political theorist, most noted for his development of the theory, the 'guardianship of the jurisconsult'.

The Iranian, Dr Ali Shariati (1933–77), was another influential Islamist. Shariati was a sociologist, well known and respected for his works in the field of the sociology of religion, including *Mission of a Free Thinker* and *Where Shall We Begin?* (http://www.shariati.com/). He was strongly influenced by the work of the West Indian author and revolutionary, Franz Fanon (1925–61). Shariati urged Muslims to 'abandon Europe' and 'end the impossible task of acting as intermediaries between them and the forces at work in the colonisation project'. In this respect Shariati's ideas reflect similar concerns in Asia, the Middle East and Africa, that echoes and reflects what

might be called a shared 'Third World consciousness' and a growing resentment at the outcomes of current and historical episodes of western involvement and interaction (Milton-Edwards 2006: 81).

In sum, the various concerns expressed by Maududi, Qutb, Khomeini and Shariati reflect in somewhat different ways a shared focus on Islamist 'growth, exploration and generation of discourse of protest against the West' (Milton-Edwards 2006: 81). What they have in common, in other words, is a shared sense that the West – because of its expansionism and perceived disdain for religion in general and Islam in particular – is a key problem for Muslims around the world.

This concern with inequality and injustice, with its perceived roots in a historical Western hegemony manifested in an earlier period by colonialism and imperialism and now via global capitalist economic control, is said to be a key factor encouraging the growth of Islamism throughout the Muslim world (Akbar 2002). The end of World War I in 1918 coincided both with the demise of the Turkish Ottoman empire and the onset of Arab nationalism. Throughout, the Middle East nations began to demand political freedom from *de facto* British or French colonial rule that, as a result of League of Nations mandates, replaced Ottoman power. The nationalist struggle was also informed by the extent to which emerging, predominantly Muslim, states in the Middle East should seek to employ the tenets of Islamic law (*sharia*) in their legal and political systems. The issue of the Islamicisation of polities in the Middle East had a precedent in some parts of the Muslim world in the form of anti-imperialist and anti-pagan 'holy wars' (*jihads*) which had periodically erupted from the late nineteenth century, especially in parts of West Africa and East Asia (Akbar 2002). These were regions where conflicts between tradition and modernisation, and between Islam and

Christianity, were often especially acute, frequently fuelled by European colonialism and imperialism.

Going further back, to the emergence of Islam fourteen hundred years ago, Muslim religious critics of the status quo have periodically emerged, opposed to what they perceive as unjust, unacceptable forms of rule. Contemporary Islamists can be seen as the most recent examples of this trend. This is because they characterise themselves as the 'just' involved in a *jihad* ('holy war') against the 'unjust', primarily but not exclusively their own domestic political rulers. Sometimes, as with the current Al-Qaeda campaign, a key enemy is located internationally (Haynes 2005a, 2005b). Overall, there is a dichotomy between the 'just' and the 'unjust' in the promotion of social change throughout Islamic history that parallels the tension in the west between 'state' and 'civil society'. In other words, 'just' and 'unjust', like 'state' and 'civil society', are mutually exclusive concepts where a strengthening of one necessarily implies a weakening of the other. The implication is that the 'unjust' inhabit the state while the 'just' look in from the outside, seeking to reform political and social systems and mores that they regard as both corrupt and insufficiently Islamic. Contemporary Islamic fundamentalists regard themselves as the Islamic 'just', striving to achieve their goal of a form of direct democracy under the auspices of God and *sharia* law. In some conceptions of Islamic rule, a religious and political ruler, the *caliph*, would emerge, a figure who would use his wisdom to settle disputes brought to him by his loyal subjects and rule the polity on God's behalf (Fuller 2003: 13–46).

Shared beliefs, relating to culture, sentiments and identity, link Muslims in the global *ummah*. As a result, it is unsurprising that certain international events appear to influence the contemporary Islamic resurgence – of which Islamism is an important although not the only aspect (Milton-Edwards 2006). Among them, we can note two: the humbling defeat of Arab countries by Israel in the calamitous Six-day War of June 1967 and the Iranian revolution (1979). The sense of inferiority and defeat that the Six-day War engendered was to some extent lightened by the Iranian revolution a dozen years later (Saikal 2003). Since then, a lethal combination of often poor government, high unemployment and apparently generalised social crisis in many Muslim countries has interacted with growing inequalities and injustices at the global level to encourage Islamist movements throughout much of the Muslim world (Akbar 2002). This development can also be associated more generally with widespread, failed attempts at modernisation and the impact of globalisation, Western hegemony and American domination (Milton-Edwards 2006).

Islamists are of course also concerned about domestic political, social and economic issues. Throughout the Middle East many rulers appear content to receive large personal incomes from the sale of their countries' oil for US dollars – with little in the way of beneficial development effects for the majority of their citizens. In addition, many such leaders do little to develop more representative polities, plan successfully for the future, or seek means to reduce un- and underemployment. In short, there has been a skewed modernisation process featuring, on the one hand, urbanisation and limited industrialisation and, on the other, growing numbers of dissatisfied citizens, some of whom turn to Islamist vehicles of political change to reflect their strong opposition to incumbent rulers and their developmental failures (Nasr 2001; Esposito 2002).

The contemporary Islamic revival, of which Islamism is a key aspect, is generated primarily in urban settings (Esposito 2002; Juergensmeyer 2000). The key issue is what can Islam do for Muslims in the contemporary world? Can the faith rescue communities and societies from decline, purify them and help combat both internal and external forces of corruption and secularisation? For many Islamic radicals the Iranian Revolution of 1979 was a particularly emblematic event in this regard (Saikal 2003: 69–88). This is because the revolution enabled Ayatollah Khomeini, after the revolution the supreme political, religious and spiritual authority, to put into place and enforce *sharia* law as the law of the land, to pursue a proclaimed commitment to social justice, and to try begin to roll back western hegemony at the international level with its economic, political and cultural influences. Over time, however, despite western fears, while the revolution undoubtedly energised Islamic radicals throughout the world, it was not followed by a consequential revolutionary wave affecting the Muslim world. Instead, governments in many Muslim-majority countries – such as Algeria, Egypt and Libya – responded to real or perceived Islamist threats with a variable mixture of state-controlled re-Islamicisation, reform and coercion (Husain 1995). In response, many grassroots Islamist movements turned attention to local social and political struggles, with the overall aim of a re-Islamicisation of society 'from below', focusing on the requirement for personal and social behaviour necessary to be Islamically 'authentic', in line with religious tradition. Political violence was not rare, although not eschewed, for example in Algeria and Egypt, if judged necessary by the radicals for their community's 'purification'. In addition, from the 1980s and 1990s, movements within countries sought to develop transnational networks that were often difficult for states to control, contributing to conditions of social, political and economic instability in many Muslim societies (Voll 2006; Casanova 2005).

An interesting example comes from Algeria. There was much western concern in the early 1990s as it appeared that Algeria was about to be taken over by Islamic fundamentalists who, it was believed, were about to win parliamentary elections. This fear led the governments of France and the United States to support a successful military coup d'état in early 1992 to prevent this feared outcome. The assumption was that if the radical Muslims achieved power they would summarily close down Algeria's newly refreshed democratic institutions and political system as they had earlier done in Iran. Following the coup, the main Islamist organisations were banned, and thousands of their leaders and supporters incarcerated. A civil war followed which finally fizzled out in the early 2000s; over its course an estimated 120,000 Algerians died (Volpi 2003).

While the political rise of radical Islam in Algeria had domestic roots, it was undoubtedly strengthened by financial support from patrons such as the government of Saudi Arabia. In addition, there were the mobilising experiences of Algerian *mujahideen* ('holy warriors'), who served in Afghanistan during the anti-Soviet war in the 1980s. On returning home, many such people were no longer content to put up with what was regarded as an un-Islamic government. There was also a large cadre of (mostly secondary) school teachers from Egypt working in Algeria at this time. Many were influenced by the ideas of the Egyptian Muslim Brotherhood or its radical off-shoots, and they were believed to have introduced similar radical ideas to Algerian youth (Volpi 2003; Tahi 1992).

The overall point is that the emergence and consolidation of Islamism since the 1970s has had both domestic and international causes. On the one hand, in many countries its domestic appearance was often linked to failures of modernisation to deliver political and developmental promises. As a result, Etienne and Tozy argue, the Islamic resurgence of the 1980s and 1990s carried within it Muslim 'disillusionment with progress and the disenchantments of the first 20 years of independence' (Etienne and Tozy 1980: 251). Faced with a state power that sought to destroy or control formerly dominant Muslim communitarian structures and replace them with values, norms, beliefs and institutions focusing on the concept of a *national citizenry* – based on the link between the state and the individual – popular (as opposed to state-controlled) Islamist movements emerged in many Muslim countries. In short, the Muslim political 're-awakening' expressed in various expressions of Islamism can usefully be seen primarily in relation to its *domestic* capacity to oppose the state: 'It is primarily in civil society that one sees Islam at work' (Coulon 1983: 49). In addition, there are significant international issues that have also encouraged Islamist worldviews, notably the perceived unjust impact of globalisation and western economic and cultural power.

Christian fundamentalism

We have seen that for some Muslims, poverty and declining faith in the developmental and political abilities of their governments led to their being receptive to Islamist arguments. In such circumstances, poverty and feelings of hopelessness may be exacerbated by withering of community ties – especially when people move from the countryside to the town in a search for paid employment. When traditional communal and familial ties are seriously stretched or sundered, religion-orientated ones may replace them, often appealing to the poor and dispossessed. In the United States, on the other hand, Christian fundamentalists are found among all strata of society – including affluent, successful people (Wald 1991: 271). Clearly, it would be absurd to argue that poverty and alienation explain the widespread existence

of Christian fundamentalists in the USA. In fact, as we noted earlier, Christian fundamentalism in the USA is quintessentially modern, offering a response to contemporary conditions and events.

It is not however only in the United States that one finds significant groups of people that are classified as 'Christian fundamentalists'. Africa has millions of such people who, like their Muslim counterparts, see a religious fundamentalist worldview as a necessary corrective to failed modernisation. In regard to Africa, some scholars link the failed developmental promises of independence in the 1960s to the rise of Christian fundamentalism several decades later (Gifford 2004; Haynes 1996). In such views, Christian fundamentalism is reactive against unwelcome manifestations of modernisation – such as poverty, marginalisation and insecurity. In addition, in some cases, such as Nigeria, a turn to Christian fundamentalist worldviews has coincided with a perception that many local Muslims are increasingly belligerent and assertive (Isaacs 2003).

The recent growth of Christian fundamentalism in various parts of the developing world, notably Latin America and Africa, is said to be the result of a merging of two existing strands of Christian belief – pentecostalism and conservative Protestantism (Gifford 1990). American television evangelists, such as Pat Robertson, Jim and Tammy Bakker, Jimmy Swaggart and Oral Roberts, were instrumental in bringing together the two strands in the 1970s and 1980s. Such people often call themselves 'born again' Christians. They may either remain in the mainline Protestant denominations (for example, Episcopalian, Presbyterian, Methodist, Baptist and Lutheran), or in the Catholic Church (where they are known as 'charismatics'), or who worship in their own denominational churches (Gifford 1991).

Generally, 'born again' Christians stress religious elements associated with pentecostalism: that is, experiential faith, the centrality of the Holy Spirit, and the spiritual gifts of glossolalia ('speaking in tongues'), faith healing and miracles. Such people are 'fundamentalist' in the sense of wishing to get back to the fundamentals of the faith as they see them. The 'born again' worldview is embedded in certain dogmatic fundamentals of Christianity, with emphasis placed on the authority of the Bible in all matters of faith and practice; on personal conversion as a distinct experience of faith in Christ as Lord and Saviour (being 'born again' in the sense of having received a new spiritual life); and, evangelically, in helping others have a similar conversion experience.

To this end, some churches sponsor missionaries who are required to look to 'God alone' (by way of followers' contributions) for their financial support. They may believe that their church is a lone force for good on earth, locked in battle with the forces of evil; the latter may even manifest itself in the form of Christians who do not adhere to the 'born again' worldview. Unsurprisingly, such 'born again' conservatives are often strongly opposed to the ecumenical movement – because of its more liberal theological views, which may include a concern for social action in pursuit of developmental goals, in tandem with spiritual concerns.

'Born again' Christians typically seek God through personal searching rather than through the mediation of a hierarchical institution. The aim is to make beneficial changes to one's life spiritually and life chances through communion and other interaction with like-minded individuals. To this end, groups may come together to pray and to work for both spiritual redemption and material prosperity, sometimes perceived as inseparable from each other. When the latter goal – that of material prosperity – is seen as paramount, this can lead to charges that it is in fact little more than a 'mindless and self-centred appeal to personal well-being' (Deiros 1991: 149–50).

In sum, 'born again' Christians may see themselves as offering converts two main benefits: worldly self-improvement and ultimate salvation, within a context of what are perceived as Christian 'fundamentals', including a strong belief in the perceived inerrancy of the Bible.

Some accounts suggest that members of such 'born again' groups are politically more conservative than those in the mainstream churches and that such people are willing to submit, rather unquestioningly, to those in authority (Moran and Schlemmer 1984; Roberts 1968). In addition, they are said to assimilate easily to the norms of consumer capitalism which helps further to defuse any challenges to the extant political order (Martin 1990: 160). In addition, in theological and academic debates they are often judged in relation to two other issues: their contribution to personal, social and political 'liberation', and their potential or actual role as purveyors of American or other foreign cultural dogma in non-western parts of the world. It is also claimed that the 'born again' doctrine may offer converts hope – but it is a hope without practical manifestation in the world of here and now; it does not help with people's concrete problems nor in the creation of group and class solidarities essential to tackle sociopolitical concerns (Martin 1990: 233). The reason for this political conservatism, it is alleged, is that conservative evangelical churches collectively form an American movement of sinister intent (Gifford 1991).

Cognisant of such concerns, the spread of conservative American-style 'born again' churches in Africa, Latin America and elsewhere was greeted with concern by leaders of the established Protestant and Catholic churches, who saw their followers leaving for the new churches in large numbers. Often sponsored by American television evangelists and local churches, thousands of born-again foreign crusaders were seen to promote American-style religion and, in some cases, conservative politics from the 1980s. Ardently anti-communist, they worked to convert as many ordinary people as possible to a conservative Christian faith and in the process, it is argued, to promote America's political goals (d'Antonio 1990).

It was also alleged that a new religio-political hegemony emerged as a result of the impact of American fundamentalist evangelicals. Pieterse asserts, for example, that the so-called 'faith' movement gained the cultural leadership of Christianity in many parts of the 'developing' world, largely because of its social prestige and ideological persuasiveness (Pieterse 1992: 10–11). It was said that norms, beliefs and values favourable to the interests of the USA were disseminated among the believers as a fundamental part of religious messages. What this amounts to is that individuals who converted to the American-style evangelical churches were, it was claimed, victims of manipulation by this latest manifestation of neo-colonialism; the objective was not, as in the past, to spirit away material resources from colonial areas, but rather to deflect popular efforts away from seeking necessary political and economic structural changes, in order to serve American strategic interests and those of American transnational corporations.

Jewish fundamentalism

Since the establishment of the state of Israel as a homeland for the Jews in 1948, there has been intense controversy in the country over whether the state should be a modern, western-style country – that is, where normally religion would be privatised – or a *Jewish* state with Judaist law and customs taking precedence over secular ones. Luckmann noted several decades ago that the state of Israel was characterised by a process of bureaucratisation along

rational business lines, reflecting for many Jewish Israelis, he argued, accommodation to an increasingly 'secular' way of life (Luckmann 1969: 147). According to Weber's well-known classificatory schema, Israel would be judged a 'modern' state, that is, with a powerful legislative body (the Knesset) enacting the law; an executive authority – the government – conducting the affairs of the state; a disinterested judiciary enforcing the law and protecting the rights of individuals; an extensive bureaucracy regulating and organising educational, social and cultural matters; and with security services – notably the police and the armed forces – protecting the state from internal and external attack (Weber 1978: 56).

Yet, to many people, Israel is not 'just' another western state. This is largely because in recent years religion seems to have gained an increasingly central public role. Religious Jews warn of the social catastrophes that they believe will inevitably occur in their increasingly secular, progressively more 'godless', society, while many non-religious Jews see such people as intolerant religious fanatics: Jewish fundamentalists. Such matters came to a head in November 1995. The then Prime Minister, Yitzhak Rabin, was assassinated by Yigal Amir, a 25-year-old Jewish fundamentalist, because of Rabin's willingness to negotiate with the Palestine Liberation Organisation (PLO) to end its conflict with the state of Israel. Rabin's murder led some Israelis to fear that violence would increasingly characterise the already tense relationship between religious and secular Jews. Yet what appeared initially to some observers to be the onset of a religious war among the Jews eventually only had a limited impact in Israel, a setting where, despite much intense political and social conflict, religious interests were not consistently powerful enough to determine major issues of public policy (Sandler 2006: 46–7).

169

On the other hand, the murder of Rabin by a Jewish fundamentalist appeared to be a clear manifestation of the willingness of 'Jewish fundamentalists [to] attack Jews with secularist leanings' in pursuit of their religious and political agendas (Bealey 1999: 140). The killing of Rabin also served to focus attention on the growing polarisation in Israel between, on the one hand, non-religious or secular Jews, and, on the other, highly religious or 'fundamentalist' Jews. The latter are characterised by a determination personally to follow the 'fundamentals' of Judaism as they see them – and work towards getting them observed in both public and private life (Silberstein 1993; Ravitsky 1993). Contemporary Jewish fundamentalism – manifested by organisations such as Gush Emunim – is believed, in part, to be a result of the impact of Israel's victory over the Arabs in the 1967 war (Sprinzak 1993). For many religious Jews this was a particular triumph as it led to the regaining of the holiest sites in Judaism from Arab control, including Jerusalem, the Temple Mount, the Western Wall, and Hebron. This was taken as a sign of divine deliverance, an indication of impending redemption. Even some secular Jews spoke of the war's outcome in theological terms.

Jewish identity has long been understood as an overlapping combination of religion and nation. Put another way, the Jews of Israel tend to think of themselves as a nation inhabiting a *Jewish* state created by their covenant with God (Ravitsky 1993). The interpretation of the covenant and its implications gave rise to the characteristic beliefs and practices of the Jewish people. Vital to this covenant was the promise of the land of Israel. Following their historical dispersions under first the Babylonians and then Romans, Jews had prayed for centuries for the end of their exile and a return to Israel.

However, except for small numbers, Jews lived for centuries in exile, often in separate communities. During the Diaspora while awaiting divine redemption to return them to their homeland, many Jews' lives were defined by *halacha* (religious law), which served as a national component of Jewish identity. The Jews' historical suffering during the Diaspora was understood as a necessary continuation of the special dedication of the community to God. In sum, Jewish fundamentalist groups in Israel are characterised by an utter unwillingness to negotiate with Palestinians over what they see as land given by God to the Jews for their use in perpetuity. In addition, especially since the Israeli government cleared the Gaza strip of Jewish settlements in August 2005, there has been another issue of massive importance to many Jewish fundamentalists. Sandler puts it like this: 'Who or what prevails? Is it the law of God or the law of the State?' (Sandler 2006: 47). For Jewish fundamentalists, the issue is especially significant and difficult to resolve as both the contemporary State of Israel and the biblical 'Land of Israel' have important religious associations.

Conclusion

The concept of popular religious interpretations, including religious fundamentalist ones, is not new; there have always been opponents of mainstream religious interpretations. What is novel, however, is that in the past manifestations of popular religion were normally bundled up within strong frameworks that held them together, serving to police the most extreme tendencies, as in the Christian churches, or were at least nominally under the control of the mainline religion – as with popular sects in Islam. In the contemporary era, however, it is no longer possible to keep all religious tendencies within traditional organising frameworks. This is primarily a consequence of two developments: (1) widespread, destabilising change after World War II – summarised here as modernisation and secularisation; and (2) religious privatisation, in both the developed and developing worlds.

Religious fundamentalism is particularly associated with the Abrahamic 'religions of the book' (Islam, Christianity and Judaism). Scriptural revelations relating to political, moral and social issues form the corpus of fundamentalist demands. Sometimes these are markedly conservative (most US or African Christian fundamentalists), sometimes they are politically reformist or even revolutionary (some Islamist groups), and sometimes they are xenophobic, racist and reactionary (some Jewish fundamentalist groups, such as Gush Emunim, Kach and Kahane Chai, and various Islamist groups).

While secularisation is the 'normal' – and continuing – state of affairs in most societies away from western Europe, the various fundamentalist groups examined in this chapter tend to share a disaffection and dissatisfaction with established, hierarchical, institutionalised religious bodies; a desire to find God through personal searching rather than through the mediation of institutions; and a belief in communities' ability to make beneficial changes to their lives through the application of group effort. This desire to 'go it alone', not to be beholden to 'superior' bodies, tends to characterise many of the groups we have examined. For some, religion offers a rational alternative to those to whom modernisation has either failed or is in some way unattractive. Its interaction with political issues over the medium term is likely to be of especial importance, carrying a serious and seminal message of societal resurgence and regeneration in relation both to political leaders and economic elites.

Note

1 The term Imam means a male spiritual and temporal leader regarded by Shi'ites as a descendant of Muhammad, divinely appointed to guide humans.

Bibliography

Akbar, M. J. (2002) *The Shade of Swords: Jihad and the Conflict between Islam & Christianity*, London: Routledge.
d'Antonio, M. (1990) *Fall From Grace: The Failed Crusade of the Christian Right*, London: Deutsch.
Appleby, R. Scott (2000) *The Ambivalence of the Sacred: Religion, Violence and Reconciliation*, Lanham, MD: Rowman and Littlefield.
Bealey, F. (1999) *The Blackwell Dictionary of Political Science*, Oxford: Blackwell.
Berger, P. (ed.) (1999) *The Desecularization of the World: Resurgent Religion in World Politics*, Grand Rapids/Washington, DC: William B. Eerdmans/Ethics & Public Policy Center.
Bruce, S. (2002) *God Is Dead: Secularization in the West*, Oxford: Blackwell.
Bruce, S. (2003) *Politics and Religion*, Cambridge: Polity.
Callaghy, T. (1993) 'Vision and politics in the transformation of the global political economy lessons from the Second and Third Worlds', in R. Slater, B. Schutz and S. Dorr (eds), *Global Transformation and the Third World*, Boulder, CO: Lynne Rienner, pp. 161–258.
Caplan, L. (ed.) (1987) *Studies in Religious Fundamentalism*, Albany, NY: State University of New York.
Casanova, J. (2005) 'Catholic and Muslim politics in comparative perspective', *Taiwan Journal of Democracy*, 1, 2, pp. 89–108.
Coulon, C. (1983) *Les Musulmans et le Pouvoir en Afrique Noire*, Paris: Karthala.
Deiros, P. (1991) 'Protestant fundamentalism in Latin America', in M. Marty and R. Scott Appleby (eds), *Fundamentalisms Observed*, Chicago: University of Chicago Press, pp. 142–96.
Dolan, C. (2005) *In War We Trust: The Bush Doctrine and the Pursuit of Just War*, Aldershot: Ashgate.

Dorr, S. (1993) 'Democratization in the Middle East', in R. Slater, B. Schutz and S. Dorr (eds), *Global Transformation and the Third World*, Boulder, CO: Lynne Rienner, pp. 131–57.

Esposito, J. (2002) *Unholy War*, Oxford and New York: Oxford University Press.

Etienne, B. and Tozy, M. (1981) 'Le glissement des obligations islamiques vers le phenomene associatif à Casablanca', in Centre de Recherches et d'Etudes sur les Sociétés Méditerranénnes, *Le Maghreb Musulman en 1979*, Paris, pp. 235–51.

Fuller, G. (2003) *The Future of Political Islam*, New York and Basingstoke: Palgrave Macmillan.

Gellner, E. (1983) *Nations and Nationalism*, Oxford: Blackwell.

Gellner, E. (1991) *Plough, Sword and Book: The Structure of Human History*, London: Paladin.

Gifford, P. (1990) 'Prosperity: a new and foreign element in African Christianity', *Religion*, 20, 3, pp. 373–88.

Gifford, P. (1991) *The New Crusaders: Christianity and the New Right in Southern Africa*, London: Pluto Press.

Gifford, P. (1994) 'Some recent developments in African Christianity', *African Affairs*, 93, 373, pp. 513–34.

Gifford, P. (2004) *Ghana's New Christianity: Pentecostalism in a Globalising African Economy*, London: Hurst and Co.

Hacker, J. and Pierson, P. (2005) *Off Center: The Republican Revolution & the Erosion of American Democracy*, New Haven and London: Yale University Press.

Hadden, J. (1987) 'Towards desacralizing secularization theory', *Social Forces*, 65, pp. 587–611.

Hallencreutz, C. and Westerlund, D. (1996) 'Anti-secularist policies of religion', in D. Westerlund (ed.), *Questioning the Secular State: The Worldwide Resurgence of Religion in Politics*, London: Hurst, pp. 1–23.

Halper, S. and Clarke, J. (2004) *America Alone: The Neo-Conservatives and the Global Order*, Cambridge: Cambridge University Press.

Haynes, J. (1993) *Religion in Third World Politics*, Milton Keynes: Open University Press.

Haynes, J. (1996) *Religion and Politics in Africa*, London: Zed.

Haynes, J. (2002) *Politics in the Developing World*, Oxford: Blackwell.

Haynes, J. (2003) 'Religious fundamentalism and politics', in L. Ridgeon (ed.), *Major World Religions: From their Origins to the Present*, London: RoutledgeCurzon, pp. 324–75.

Haynes, J. (2005a) 'Al-Qaeda: ideology and action', *Critical Review of International Social and Political Philosophy*, 8, 2, pp. 177–91.

Haynes, J. (2005b) 'Islamic militancy in East Africa', *Third World Quarterly*, 26, 8, pp. 1321–39.

Husain, M. Zohair (1995) *Global Islamic Politics*, New York: HarperCollins.

Ibrahim, Y. (1992) 'Islamic plan for Algeria is on display', *The New York Times*, 7 January.

Isaacs, D. (2003) 'Islam in Nigeria: simmering tensions', BBC News online, 23 September. Available at http://news.bbc.co.uk/1/hi/world/africa/3155279.stm). Accessed 1 December 2005.

Jervis, R. (2005) 'Why the Bush doctrine cannot be sustained', *Political Science Quarterly*, 120, 3, pp. 351–77.

Juergensmeyer, M. (1993) *The New Cold War? Religious Nationalism Confronts the Secular State*, Berkeley and London: University of California Press.

Juergensmeyer, M. (2000) *Terror in the Mind of God: The Global Rise of Religious Violence*, Berkeley and London: University of California Press.

Lawrence, B. (1995) *Defenders of the Faith: The International Revolt Against the Modern Age*, South Carolina: University of South Carolina Press.

Luckmann, T. (1969) 'The decline of church-oriented religion', in R. Robertson (ed.), *The Sociology of Religion*, Baltimore, MD: Penguin, pp. 141–51.

Martin, D. (1990) *Tongues of Fire: The Explosion of Protestantism in Latin America*, Oxford: Basil Blackwell.

Marty, M. E. and Scott Appleby, R. (eds) (1991) *Fundamentalisms Observed*, Chicago: University of Chicago Press.

Marty, M. E. and Scott Appleby, R. (eds) (1993a) *Fundamentalisms and Society*, Chicago: University of Chicago Press.

Marty, M. E. and Scott Appleby, R. (eds) (1993b) *Fundamentalisms and the State*, Chicago: University of Chicago Press.

Marty, M. E. and Scott Appleby, R. (eds) (1994) *Accounting for Fundamentalisms*, Chicago: University of Chicago Press.

Marty, M. E. and Scott Appleby, R. (eds) (1995) *Fundamentalisms Comprehended*, Chicago: University of Chicago Press.

Milton-Edwards, B. (2006) *Islam and Violence in the Modern Era*, Basingstoke and New York: Palgrave Macmillan.

Moran, E. and Schlemmer, L. (1984) *Faith for the Fearful?*, Durban: Centre for Applied Social Studies.

Nasr, S. Vali Reza (2001) *Islamic Leviathan: Islam and the Making of State Power*, Oxford: Oxford University Press.

Norris, P. and Inglehart, I. (2004) *Sacred and Secular: Religion and Politics Worldwide*, Cambridge: Cambridge University Press.

Pieterse, J. (1992) 'Christianity, politics and Gramscism of the right: introduction', in J. Pieterse (ed), *Christianity and Hegemony. Religion and Politics on the Frontiers of Social Change*, Oxford: Berg, pp. 1–31.

Ravitzky, A. (1993) *Messianism, Zionism and Jewish Religious Radicalism*, Tel Aviv: Am Oved.

Ray, A. (1996) 'Religion and politics in South Asia', *Asian Affairs*, 1, 1, pp. 9–12.

Religion and Ethics News weekly (2004) 'Interview: Leo Ribuffo' [Ribuffo is a historian of conservative Christianity in the USA], 23 April. Available at: http://www.pbs.org/wnet/religionandethics/week734/interview3.html. Accessed 17 March 2005.

Roberts, B. (1968) 'Protestant groups and coping with urban life in Guatemala City', *American Journal of Sociology*, 73, pp. 753–67.

Saikal, A. (2003) *Islam and the West: Conflict or Cooperation?*, New York and Basingstoke: Palgrave Macmillan.

Sandler, S. (2006) 'Judaism and politics', in J. Haynes (ed.), *The Politics of Religion: A Survey*, London: Routledge, pp. 37–47.

Shupe, A. (1990) 'The stubborn persistence of religion in the global arena', in E. Sahliyeh (ed.), *Religious Resurgence and Politics in the Contemporary World*, Albany, NY: State University of New York Press, pp. 17–26.

Silberstein, L. (1993) 'Religion, ideology, modernity theoretical issues in the study of Jewish fundamentalism', in L. Silberstein (ed.), *Jewish Fundamentalism in Comparative Perspective: Religion, Ideology, and the Crisis of Modernity*, New York and London: New York University Press, pp. 3–26.

Simpson, J. (1992) 'Fundamentalism in America revisited: the fading of modernity as a source of symbolic capital', in B. Misztal and A. Shupe (eds), *Religion and Politics in Comparative Perspective: Revival of Religious Fundamentalism in East and West*, Westport and London: Praeger, pp. 10–27.

Sprinzak, E. (1993) 'Fundamentalism, ultranationalism, and political culture: the case of the Israeli radical right', in L. Diamond (ed.), *Political Culture and Democracy in Developing Countries*, Boulder and London: Lynne Rienner, pp. 247–78.

Tahi, M. S. (1992) 'The arduous democratisation process in Algeria', *Journal of Modern African Studies*, 30, 3, pp. 400–20.

Thomas, S. (2005) *The Global Resurgence of Religion and the Transformation of International Relations: The Struggle for the Soul of the Twenty-first Century*, New York and Basingstoke: Palgrave Macmillan.

Voll, J. (2006) 'Trans-state Muslim movements in an era of soft power', paper prepared for the Conference on New Religious Pluralism in World Politics, Georgetown University, 17 March.

Volpi, F. (2003) *Islam and Democracy: The Failure of Dialogue in Algeria*, London: Pluto.

Wald, K. (1991) 'Social change and political response: the silent religious cleavage in North America', in G. Moyser (ed.), *Religion and Politics in the Modern World*, London: Routledge, pp. 239–84.

Wallis, R. and Bruce, S. (1992) 'Secularization: the orthodox model', in S. Bruce (ed.), *Religion and Modernization*, Oxford: Clarendon Press, pp. 8–30.

Weber, M. (1978) *Economy and Society*, Berkeley: University of California Press.

Wilson, B. (1992) 'Reflections on a many sided controversy', in S. Bruce (ed.), *Religion and Modernization*, Oxford: Clarendon Press, pp. 195–210.

Woodhead, L. and Heelas, P. (eds) (2000) 'Introduction to chapter two: religions of difference', *Religion in Modern Times*, Oxford: Blackwell, pp. 27–33.

173

12

Religion and the state

John Madeley

There is, it seems, no Archimedian point from which the relationships between religion and the state can be observed. While in the early twenty-first century the modern state is the key template for political organization across the globe, its form and function remain matters of ongoing dispute. Responsibility for the management of affairs affecting the physical and material security of citizens is generally accepted but on wider issues – including how it should relate to religious concerns – radicals, liberals, conservatives and reactionaries of various hues continue to engage in seemingly unresolvable controversy. The liberal democratic option of ruling that such concerns are no proper business of the state and should as far as possible be kept off the political agenda has failed to attract general agreement even in the more prosperous parts of the first world (Madeley 2003a). Elsewhere, where material conditions are much less favourable, issues of state–religion relations often appear to occupy centre stage. The existence of different worldviews encapsulated in, or extrapolated from, contrasting religious traditions continue to make for incommensurable and, even, non-compossible standpoints on important issues.

Any survey of the relations between religion and the state has to take account of the enormous variety of traditions,

institutional forms and ethical drives to be found in each of the two spheres. Even operating with mainstream Western conceptualizations of the principal terms the range of combinations identifiable across world history is as vast as it is in detail complex. Traditionally, most treatments have reduced the scope and range of these complexities to manageable proportions by addressing them through the Western lens of 'church–state relations' where the term church is taken to represent all religious bodies and organizations (and so, in addition to actual churches: denominations, sects, cults, religious orders etc.) and the term state is assumed to represent instances of the modern state conceived in Weberian terms as based on successful claims to territorial sovereignty. However, this foreshortening of focus with its distinctly ethnocentric underlying assumptions as to what counts as religion and the state systematically underestimates the actual range of variation to be found in the other parts of the world and at other times.

Within political science attention to the contemporary political significance of religious traditions and how they relate to different forms of the state has been a relatively recent phenomenon. When in the 1950s the field of comparative politics was extended from a concentration on Western political systems to address the major changes occurring in the then newly independent states of the developing world, the subject remained peripheral. This peripherality was reinforced by that fact that one of the principal organizing concepts which came to dominate comparative politics at the time was modernization, understood crudely as the process whereby 'traditional' societies became 'modern'. Modernization theory rested on evolutionary assumptions which postulated that interlinked trends of economic, social, cultural and political development combined to make for the differentiation of structures and specialization of functions thought to be characteristic of modern societies.

Some attempted to refine the evolutionary scheme which underlay modernization theory by identifying stages which could explain the observed variety of different cultures in terms of their having stabilized at different stages. Thus Bellah developed a classification of five stages of religious development: primitive, archaic, historic, early modern and modern, each marked by combinations of distinct features of belief, ritual practice and organizational type (Bellah 1964). A particularly important threshold in this developmental sequence was seen to have occurred between the so-called archaic and historic phases. Prior to this transition the beginnings of priesthood could be found as specialists in healing and shamanistic practices began to emerge. With the shift to the historic stage, however, religion became increasingly transcendental in its reference as the gods and the sacred realm were understood more and more as separate from the natural world and a more elevated concern with salvation took hold. Coincidentally the emergent institution of a priesthood achieved a degree of autonomy, the political and religious spheres tended to become distinct and the possibility arose for the first time of tensions and conflict between holders of authority in the two spheres. This change appears to correspond to what Karl Jaspers identified

as the great Axial Shift, occurring across much of the globe from about the sixth century BCE (Eisenstadt 1986).

For all its relevance to the emergence of separate spheres of religion and the state and the relation between them, evolutionary conceptual schemes of this sort suggested that variations between the different religious traditions of the world arose principally from the level of development each attained. For Weber, however, many important variations could not be explained in this fashion (Gerth and Mills 1948). Thus his key distinction between the traditions of Oriental mysticism and Occidental asceticism could not be taken to imply that the other-worldly salvationist orientation of Hinduism, for example, indicated that it had developed to a higher level than the this-worldly asceticism which emerged within the context of Judaism and some branches of Christianity. Despite the evolutionary bias of the modernization paradigm some texts produced from within it attempted to take account of these dimensions of difference. Thus D.E. Smith in 1970 examined the connections between religion and 'political development' in the context of the process of modernization understood characteristically as 'fundamentally one of differentiation, by which integralist sacral societies governed by religiopolitical systems are being transformed into pluralist desacralized societies directed by greatly expanded secular polities' (Smith 1970: 1). Despite the claimed commonality of sacral political systems as recently as 1800 however, Smith also pointed to important ideational and structural contrasts to be found between Hindu, Buddhist, Muslim and Catholic traditions and how these contrasts made for distinctive orientations towards the state.

A growing appreciation of the significance of qualitative contrasts contributed to the virtual abandonment of modernization theory and directed attention instead

175

to the role of episodic change occurring around critical discontinuities in the history of particular societies, cultures and traditions. Weber's analogy comparing decisive historical junctures with the points on railway tracks which send trains off in one direction or another (with unavoidable 'path-dependent' consequences) highlighted the importance of these discontinuities for explaining contrasting patterns of institutional and cultural change, not least in the area of relations between religion and the state (Gerth and Mills 1948). Taking the case of Christianity, the variety of state forms with which it has been confronted over its two millennia of existence as a distinct tradition has spanned Roman colonial administration in first-century Palestine, to pagan empire, to Christian empire(s) of contrasting types, to feudal lordships, city-states, principalities (both civil and ecclesiastical), papal states, republics, kingdoms, authoritarian dictatorships, both sympathetic and antagonistic, and to a variety of forms of (liberal) democracy. In some of these formations, particular Christian traditions have been marginal and actively persecuted and in others overwhelmingly dominant and influential, while in most they have been located somewhere in between – and in each case attitudes toward, and linkages with, the temporal authorities have varied markedly. Certainly, with regard to the Christian case it is difficult to argue that there has been a uniform trend of development from some undifferentiated pristine community cult towards its current condition in most of the West, as an enclave of religiosity in otherwise largely secular environments. Rather, the picture is one of cyclical movement through many phases, starting from: sectarian separation and persecution, rising to imperial church, then claimant to supreme source of all authority temporal and spiritual, followed by a decline into serving as an instrument of temporal authority under the early-modern state

and, finally in the modern era, being made serially to relinquish its claims to exercise authority anywhere except within its own increasingly circumscribed religious jurisdiction. The trend line of the development of the state can also be seen as cyclical only in the obverse to that of the church(es): when state power has waned, as at various times in the middle ages, the religious institution's claims to authority waxed and vice versa.

One important strand of evolutionary modernization theory has maintained a stubborn – if more and more embattled – resistance among sociologists of religion: secularization theory. According to José Casanova (1994), by the 1960s secularization theory had achieved the rare feat in the social sciences of attaining virtual paradigm status. Nor have its continuing rearguard defenders been lacking, despite retractions from some of its most distinguished expositors, such as Peter Berger (1999), while other analysts have adopted more nuanced stands. In 1978 David Martin presented a dense analysis which was one of the first systematically to stress the role of critical historical junctures in bringing about, deflecting and occasionally reversing secularization trends in the territories of particular states (Martin 1978). In 1994 Casanova argued in similar vein that secularization theory should not be treated as a coherent set of propositions but as three distinct ones, only one of which (secularization as differentiation) could be defended as the valid core proposition.

For many normative theorists of liberal democracy separation of religion and state (reflecting the differentiation between the two spheres) was until recently a matter of widespread consensus: a system that did not institutionalize this basic requirement could scarcely qualify as a liberal democracy at all. The ongoing resurgence of the religious factor in politics across the world has, however, led to a re-examination of the empirical link between church–state separation and liberal democracy. For example, Alfred Stepan points out that 'virtually no Western European democracy now has a rigid or hostile separation of church and state' (Stepan 2001: 222). Normative disagreements about state–religion separation in the liberal democracies is, however, as a distant echo compared to the din heard elsewhere in parts of the world, especially following the impact of such 'frame-setting events' as the 1979 Iranian revolution and September 11, 2001 ('9/11'). As Halliday put it, the Iranian revolution posed a particular challenge to observers of world affairs, that of explaining how for the first time in modern history (that is, since the great French revolution of 1789), 'a revolution took place in which the dominant ideology, forms of organization, leading personnel and proclaimed goal were all religious in appearance and inspiration' (Halliday 1995: 43). Although the Iranian revolution did not, as feared by many and hoped by some, spread widely to other countries, as had occurred in the wake of the French revolutionary wars two centuries earlier, it did occur at a time when the resurgence of the religious factor in politics was evermore evident in many places around the world.

Pippa Norris and Ronald Inglehart (2004) have shown convincingly that secularization, understood as the progressive decline in levels of belief and observance in the principal mainstream forms of organized religion, has clearly progressed only in the world's most economically developed countries, except for the United States. However, since these societies currently account for a decreasing proportion of the population of the planet and other, less well-favoured, societies generally exhibit a resurgence of religious belief and observance, it can be said that overall the world is becoming in an important sense more, not less, religious. In this context the political mobilization of fundamentalist forms of many of the world religions,

including Christianity, has made the issue of state–religion relations increasingly one of practical concern as well as academic interest. What the French call the 'integralism' of fundamentalist movements stands witness to the continuing possibility that trends of secularization (whether as decline, differentiation or privatization) can under certain circumstances be stopped dead in their tracks and reversed by projects of radical de-differentiation, even on occasion under the literal 'presidency' of religious figures and institutions, as in Iran. In this context it is interesting to examine the case of Europe: in most of its Western part, one of the most secular parts of the globe and yet, as noted by Stepan (2001), one marked by sets of religion–state relations across all its fifty-odd territories which the Supreme Court of the USA with its separationist rule would not tolerate in even one of its fifty constituent states.

Religion and the state in modern Europe

The record of the relations between religion and the state over time and space in Europe illustrates perhaps better than any other, the decisive role critical junctures have played in marking the shifts between often radically contrasting patterns of state–religion relations. While it can be claimed that it was in the USA that the constitutional format of the secular state was invented, it was in medieval Europe that the underlying distinction between the religious and the secular was first elaborated (Ward 2000). From the time of its birth as a distinctive religious tradition, Christianity famously distinguished between what was due to Caesar and to God, something which it was easier to do for as long as Caesar was both pagan and, occasionally, an author of persecution. When the Emperor became the supporter and enforcer of the Christian cult, however, the distinction became progressively blurred – only to reassert itself when the papacy in the eleventh-century bid for recognition as the fount of all power on earth; this occurred when Pope Gregory VII reiterated the long-standing claim to the precedence of papal over royal authority at a time when it seemed there was, at least briefly, the possibility of making a reality of this pretension. It was arguably at this time that the concept of the distinction between secular and religious took a decisive form, becoming fixed in a way which identified the church with a superordinate religious and spiritual sphere and the state with the subordinate secular and temporal sphere (Badie and Birnbaum 1983: 87). One of the perversities arising from this invidious distinction is that the state itself could no longer be seen as a subject of secularization because of the declaration that it was definitionally secular – and could not therefore itself be subject to secularizing trends. Yet it is obvious that the instrumentalities of state power and authority can – and indeed often have been – dedicated to and utilized for religious ends in Christian Europe as much as in other parts of the world: in other words, that states have at times been and in a number of cases remain in some non-trivial sense religious.

In the West European case during the middle ages when the papacy attempted to assert its claims to feudal precedence, monarchs were routinely consecrated at their coronations by high church officials, usually archbishops, bishops, metropolitans or even, as in the case of Charlemagne, by the pope in Rome. Church involvement in these ceremonies was transparently intended, *inter alia*, to ensure by the administering of oaths that the crowned monarchs would undertake to recognize the authority of the popes and support the church in its divine mission. While the church was itself always careful to distinguish the separate spheres of the spiritual *sacerdotium* from the temporal *regnum*, and

to assert its claim to sole jurisdiction in the former, it also maintained the duty of the temporal authorities to aid it in serving its religious ends, however indirectly. Nor did the Reformation, despite the seismic changes which it wrought in church–state relations in the sixteenth century, put an end to the notion that the temporal authorities had religious as well as temporal responsibilities. Indeed, on one view, the Reformation can be seen in the countries where it became institutionalized as greatly extending the scope of religious duties to all holders of public office. From a Catholic point of view it represented the disastrous triumph of the secular over the religious sphere: 'If before, it was the religious realm which appeared to be the all-encompassing reality, within which the secular realm found its proper place, now the secular sphere will be the all-encompassing reality, to which the religious sphere will have to adapt' (Casanova 1994: 15). The alternative view, stressed by Weber (Gerth and Mills 1948), was that the removal of the barriers between religious and secular spaces had the effect of releasing the religious impulse from its previous confines, thereby allowing it to permeate the wider society, so that, for example, the idea of God-given vocations was extended to cover all legitimate roles in society – to ploughmen and princes, as much as to priests and prelates. This radical shift was all the more significant since it coincided with and contributed (not least by the transfer of church property and wealth to the coffers of the state authorities) to the emergence of the modern state. In both ideological and material terms this particular critical juncture was, it is interesting to note, both modernising and radically de-differentiating.

The emergent pattern of the modern state was in fact from its beginnings in sixteenth-century Europe a confessional institution committed to its favoured religious tradition. The birth of the modern state system, which is conventionally dated from the 1648 Peace of Westphalia, did require the signatories henceforth to desist from attempts by diplomacy or war from changing the religious adherence of target populations but this secularizing requirement only affected the external relations between states. Internally by contrast, Westphalia buttressed the prohibition against religious war by insisting on the sovereign right of the state authorities of a given territory to impose a particular confession on their subject populations on the basis of the *cuius regio eius religio* rule (literally, whose the region, to him the religion), inherited from the 1555 Treaty of Augsburg and now, finally, set in stone. In fact, from 1648 onwards, recognition of the exclusive authority of the state in matters of religion led to a new and decisive phase in the consolidation of church settlements aimed at enforcing conformity to the locally established religion and penalizing or expelling those who refused to conform. This process of the 'confessionalization' of populations continued after 1648 for a long time, signified by such notorious episodes as the Revocation of the Edict of Nantes, which ended the toleration of Protestantism in France in 1685, and the expulsion of many thousands of Protestants from the archbishopric of Salzburg in the 1720s. As Rémond points out under the *ancien régime* governments which ruled over most of the European Continent until the French Revolution of 1789, a so-called regalist tradition obtained virtually regardless of confessional differences: 'It asserted the superiority of the secular power over the churches. ... It did not necessarily proceed from animosity towards the church; the same power that closely controlled the clergy held them in honour and showed consideration and respect for religion. *Ancien régime* governments shared the conviction, then generally held, that society was unable to do without religion and that the state had authority and responsibilities in the matter' (Rémond 1999: 79–80).

More than a century after the 1789 French Revolution had made the first decisive departure from the entrenched tradition of state confessionalism in Europe, it is remarkable that church establishment of one sort or another remained firmly in place across most of Europe. In 1900 as Table 12.1 illustrates, despite the progressive de-linking of citizenship from church membership, the largest churches almost everywhere continued to benefit from advantageous arrangements with the state authorities. This was most particularly the case in the three mono-confessional blocs which occupied the Lutheran northern, Roman Catholic southern and Orthodox eastern parts of Europe (Madeley 2003b; Knippenberg 2006). Even in Italy, where since 1870 the Vatican had refused to accept the loss of the Papal Territories and recognize the legitimacy of the then newly-united Kingdom of Italy, the Catholic Church's overwhelmingly dominant position persisted. In the multi-confessional belt which spanned from Ireland in north-western Europe through Britain, the Netherlands, southern Germany, Switzerland, Bohemia and Hungary all the way into the Transylvanian part of Romania, relations between the different religious institutions and the state were complex not least because of the coexistence within many individual territories of substantial populations of different confessional adherence. Even in those territories, however, the predominant pattern was one of establishment of the historically dominant confession twinned with the more or less *de facto* toleration of the principal religious minorities.

In addition to their confessional affiliations the actual forms of establishment varied a great deal. In France, where the Roman Catholic Church had been restored under the terms of the 1802 Concordat and the associated Organic Articles, Catholicism was recognized not as a – or the – state religion but as the religion of the great

Table 12.1 The religiosity of states in Europe (*de jure*), 1900–2000

Empire groups as of 1900	National territories	I: 1900	II: 1970	III: 2000	IV: Absolute conf. majority % in 2000
	Andorra	RC	RC	RC	RC: 89
	Belgium	R	R	R	RC: 81
	Denmark	RL	RL	RL	RL: 86
	Iceland	RL	RL	RL	RL: 99
	France	R	S	S	RC: 70
	Germany	R	R	S	No abs. maj.
	Greece	RO	RO	RO	RO: 93
	Italy	RC	RC	RC	RC: 85
	Liechtenstein	RC	RC	RC	RC: 80
	Luxembourg	RC	RC	RC	RC: 97
	Netherlands	S	S	S	No abs. maj.
	(Poland)	R	A	RC★	RC: 92
	Portugal	RC	RC	RC	RC: 97
	Romania	RO	A	RO★	RO: 77
	Spain	RC	RC	RC	RC: 99
	Sweden	RL	RL	R★★	RL: 84
	Norway	RL	RL	RL	RL: 95
	Switzerland	R	R	R	No abs. maj.
	(Yugoslavia)	R	A	RO★	RO: 60
United Kingdom	*Britain*	RA	RA	RA	RA: 53
	Ireland	RC	RC	R	RC: 92
	Malta	RC	RC	RC	RC: 91
Russian Empire	*Russia*	RO	A	S	RO: 52
	Armenia	OO	A	OO	OO: 92
	Azerbaijan	RI	A	RI	RI: 95
	Belarus	RO	A	RO	RO: 70
	Ukraine	RO	A	RO	RO: 54
	Estonia	R	A	S	No abs. maj.
	Finland	RX	RX	RX	RL: 89
	Georgia	RO	A	RO	RO: 75
	Latvia	RO	A	S	No abs. maj.
	Lithuania	RO	A	S	RC: 85
	Moldova	RO	A	RO	RO: 70
Austria-Hungary	*Austria*	R	S	S	RC: 78
	Czech Rep.	R	A	RC	No abs. maj.
	Bosnia-Herz.	R	A	RI	No abs. maj.
	Croatia	RC	A	RC	RC: 89
	Hungary	R	A	S★	RC: 58
	Slovakia	R	A	S	RC: 67
	Slovenia	RC★★	A	RC★★	RC: 76
Ottoman Empire	*Turkey*	RI	S	S	RI: 100
	Albania	RI	A	S	RI: 65
	Bulgaria	R	A	RO★	RO: 82
	Cyprus	R	R	R	RO: 78/RI: 99
	Macedonia	RO	A	RO	RO: 59

Sources: Barrett *et al.* (1982) and Barrett *et al.* (2001) supplemented by *2005 Annual Report on International Religious Freedom: Europe and the New Independent States* (US Dept of State, Sept. 2005); Inglehart and Norris dataset for the last column.

Notes: ★ These attributions changed (from A) on the basis of information culled from the more recent source (see below). ★★ Changed attribution: formal disestablishment of the Lutheran church occurred in January 2000. ★★★ Corrected attribution (in Barrett (2001) listed as RO).

Codes: A Atheistic; R Religious (unspecified); RA Anglican; RC Roman Catholic; RI Islamic; RL Lutheran; RO Orthodox; RX (Finland only) Lutheran and Orthodox; OO (Armenia only) Oriental Orthodox; S Secular.

majority of the French nation. Alongside it, furthermore, Protestants and Jews each received official recognition and state support. In the United Kingdom the Anglican state church retained full and formal established status in England and Wales and the Presbyterian Church of Scotland remained the officially recognized national church. Other systems of multiple establishment could be found at or below state level in the multi-confessional territories – in Switzerland, for example. Finland, which stood at the northern end of a second multi-confessional belt running north–south along the border between Eastern Orthodoxy and the other confessions, a unique system of dual establishment – Lutheran and Orthodox state churches alongside each other over the same undivided territory – existed. In those parts of Europe where the eighteenth-century Enlightenment had impacted either through the action of the so-called Enlightened Despots such as Frederick the Great in Prussia, Joseph II in Austria and Catherine the Great in Russia or through the later, and more forceful, intervention of the French revolutionary armies, systems of religious establishment had on the whole made a successful, if partial, return after 1815. In the case of Austria, for example, the 1855 Concordat with the Vatican abandoned the policy which has been inaugurated by Joseph II and removed all Catholic education from state control, placing it again under the exclusive jurisdiction of the bishops. Around 1900 in Eastern Europe the trend was also towards reinforcing the principle of religious establishment; in the Russian Empire, for example, under the influence of the reactionary Konstantin Pobedonostsev (Overprocurator of the Holy Synod from 1880 to 1905) Russian Orthodoxy was ruthlessly promoted even in the peripheral territories where Lutheranism (in the northern Baltics) Catholicism (in Poland) and Armenian Orthodoxy (in Armenia)

had previously enjoyed a measure of toleration and even privilege.

As Table 12.1 indicates, in 1900 all but one of Europe's 45 territories were occupied by states which could still be judged *de jure* 'religious'; that is, officially committed in one way or another to the support of either a particular religion or religions (31 cases) or to religion in general (14 cases). The one exception identified is the Netherlands which is labelled *de jure* 'secular'. In that country a series of constitutional and other enactments in the nineteenth century had progressively extended the reach of individual and corporate religious freedoms. The Dutch Reformed Church had been disestablished in the 1790s but this had not ushered in full religious freedom; the 1801 Constitution required, for example, that at the age of 14 every independent person of either sex must register with a church denomination (Bijsterveld 1996: 209). In 1815, when the United Kingdom of the Netherlands incorporated the southern Catholic provinces (until 1830), the previous state church was not re-established; instead, the principle that the state should not interfere in the internal affairs of religious organizations was laid down. In 1848 when constitutional amendments opened the way for the Roman Catholic Church to restore its hierarchy, a new article was adopted which allowed religious processions only under a set of restrictive provisions which effectively amounted to a *de facto* ban (Bijsterveld 1996: 211). Other marks of state secularity in 1900 were the ban on clergy celebrating a religious marriage prior to a mandatory civil marriage and the facts that no concordat had been negotiated with the Vatican and that no specific ministry for religious affairs had existed since 1871. The state did however continue to make a contribution to the salaries and pensions of church ministers and maintained theological faculties in the state universities in addition to subsidizing a number of free theological colleges.

The foundations of the inherited systems of church establishment, which still survived across almost all of Europe, were by 1900 nonetheless under threat. In most countries religious freedoms had expanded, albeit at different paces and occasionally with reversals, so that establishments could rely for their maintenance less on the negative penal disciplines with which state authorities had once supported them. In France where tensions between clericals and anticlericals had run especially high in the 1890s, as reflected for example in the storm around the Dreyfus affair, matters came to a head soon after 1900 and issued in a decisive change which made France Europe's first *laïciste* (or *secularist*, as opposed to merely *secular*) state. The Law of Separation of 1905 proclaimed that henceforth the Republic would neither recognize nor subsidize, any religious confession or cult whatsoever, thereby *inter alia* unilaterally annulling the Concordat of 1802 (Rémond 1999: 149). In Britain at around the same time non-conformist agitation for Anglican disestablishment in Wales was rising on the back of a dispute about the funding of religious education, a classic issue wherever church–state tensions arose, and in 1914 the decisive vote was taken to disestablish, something which finally came into effect in 1920.

If the principle of formal church establishment was already being pegged back in parts of Western Europe before 1914, the First World War and its outcome acted as a major 'extinction event', especially in Eastern Europe where the great land empires were finally broken up. In Russia the Orthodox Church was disestablished three months after the Bolsheviks seized power in late 1917; it was thereby reduced to the status of a mere religious association with no corporate personality and thus prevented from owning property. Accordingly, all lands and buildings which

had previously belonged to it were nationalised. In Georgia and Armenia the Orthodox churches were also disestablished after a brief experiment with independence from the Soviet Union but in the parts of the Russian Empire which succeeded in gaining their independence around this time (Finland, Estonia, Latvia, Lithuania and Poland) establishment of the locally dominant confession was either confirmed or reinforced. The end of the Austro-Hungarian Empire in 1918 also spelt the end of church establishment in Austria itself, Hungary, and the territories which became part of the 'Kingdom of the Serbs, Croats and Slovenes' (from 1921 Yugoslavia). Similarly in Germany the Weimar constitution of 1919 formally disestablished the state church while allowing for cooperation in matters of religious education in the public schools, the raising of the *Kirchensteuer* (a church tax collected by the state tax authorities), and military chaplaincies (Robbers 1996: 58). And, finally, at the south-eastern corner of Europe after the collapse of the Ottoman Empire the Kemalist regime not only abolished the caliphate in 1923 but also launched a radical campaign of state-enforced secularization which prohibited the use of conspicuous religious dress (including the *hijab* for women and the fez for men) in public, while subjecting all religious bodies to close state control under a Ministry of Religious Affairs.

Some contemporary commentators concluded that all these developments indicated that church establishment had finally been consigned to the dustbin of history (Wyduckel 2001: 169). Its survival in different confessional guises in the Nordic countries, the Iberian peninsula, and the Orthodox states of the continent's south-east were seen as anomalous and likely soon to suffer the same dismal fate as the necessary lessons of modernity were finally absorbed. In Catholic thinking state churches – despite their virtual existence in the small overwhelmingly Catholic states of Liechtenstein, Malta and Monaco – had never been fully legitimate institutional forms, often having come into existence on the back of an unwelcome entanglement with the local temporal authorities. The arrangement preferred by the Vatican was instead friendly cooperation between church and state within a particular territory on the basis of Concordats, that is, treaties which were negotiated to protect the autonomy of the church within the spiritual sphere and to provide favourable conditions for its mission within civil society. It was on such a basis that relations between the Vatican itself and the Italian state were finally settled with the Lateran Pact of 1929 – a series of Concordat agreements which also finally regularized the existence of Europe's only remaining church–state: the State of Vatican City. Four years later major concordat agreements were also signed in 1933 with Germany and Austria. In Spain, where the Latin pattern of clerical–anticlerical confrontation was starkly exemplified in a series of violent political oscillations, 1931 saw the establishment of a Second Republic, the separation of church and state, the nationalization of church property, the abolition of state support, the secularization of the education system and the expulsion of the Jesuits. By the end of the decade, however, after three years of bitter civil war, Franco's authoritarian regime had reversed the situation once again and firmly entrenched a system of National Catholicism.

Following World War II in 1945, a wave of democratization swept Western Europe as complete disenchantment with the authoritarian and totalitarian alternatives of fascism, Nazism and communism set in. Christian Democratic parties were among the beneficiaries of this rejection of both extremes of left and right alternatives on the continent and it was largely under governments dominated by them that post-war reconstruction was taken forward. Aside from the critical economic revival over which they presided they were also responsible for ensuring conditions favourable to the principal religious institutions in their several countries. Unlike in 1918 and largely because of the strength of the Christian Democratic parties, there was no appetite for further measures of disestablishment. Instead, in Western Europe churches tended to be restored to their former places of honour and privilege. In Germany and Italy the interwar concordats remained in force while in Franco's Spain, a new concordat in 1953 reinforced the system of National Catholicism. In Eastern Europe the end of the world war produced radically different outcomes as Soviet-installed regimes introduced strict controls on the churches and other religious bodies and the state atheism which had been pioneered in Russia after the Bolshevik takeover in 1917 was imposed – thus, in Poland, for example, the government abrogated the concordat. This occurred more often than not in the context of constitutional provisions which ostensibly guaranteed religious freedom in accordance with the Universal Declaration of Human Rights of 1948 and other international legal instruments (Boyle and Sheen 1997). By 1970 however, as Table 12.1 indicates, all 22 countries of Central and Eastern Europe which lay behind the Iron Curtain could be designated Atheistic *de jure*, committed in Barrett's terms to 'formally promoting irreligion'. This meant typically that while the state was ostensibly separated from all religions and churches, it was also 'linked for ideological reasons with irreligion and opposed on principle to all religion', claiming the right 'to oppose religion by discrimination, obstruction or even suppression' (Barrett 1982: 96). Separation in these states meant exclusion from public life and the cutting-off of most of the resources required for religion to flourish;

183

it emphatically did not mean that the state was debarred from interfering in the field of religious provision – rather that, as in Turkey, the state and its organs should exert maximum control and surveillance. In the extreme case of Albania, finally, the attempt was openly made from 1967 to 1991 to abolish religion altogether.

In very different ways the decades after 1945 can be seen then as a time when the connections between, and mutual involvement of, religion and the state was actually reinforced in both Western and Eastern Europe.

Thirty years on however, Europe's third wave of democratization began with the April 1974 military overthrow of Portugal's authoritarian regime and the transition to democracy which followed shortly afterward upon the death of Franco in neighbouring Spain. This wave spread to Latin America and parts of Asia before washing back across Eastern Europe in the late 1980s, finally putting an end to the communist or state socialist regimes. Churches and religious groups were in some of these countries, for example and most notably in Poland, of considerable significance in the campaigns for liberalisation and democratisation which – along with the withdrawal of Soviet guarantees – precipitated the shift to more open democratic regimes. As Table 12.1 indicates, by 2000 all the states which were coded as Atheistic in 1970 had either returned to the category of *de jure* Religious states providing support to the locally dominant religious tradition (15 cases) or had opted to be *de jure* Secular (7 cases: Russia, the three Baltic states, Hungary, Slovakia and Macedonia), that is, officially promoting neither religion nor irreligion.

It is remarkable how little Europe's confessional geography has changed despite the turbulence and violence of the twentieth century. Column IV of Table 12.1 illustrates how the division of Europe along confessional lines which was inherited from the

Latin-Orthodox schism and, in Western Europe, from the period of Reformation and Wars of Religion, was still evident in the proportion of countries' populations which retained confessional or denominational identities. Of the 45 countries listed, fully 38 (84%) continued in 2000 to exhibit single-confession absolute majorities, 33 (72%) had super-majorities (that is, populations where more than two-thirds shared a single confessional identity), while in 12 countries (27%), more than 90% of people shared a single religious identity. However crude, these figures can be taken to demonstrate that the early-modern confessional state continues to throw a long shadow across contemporary Europe.

In 1999 canon lawyer Silvio Ferrari presented the thesis that despite surface, legalistic differences there actually existed a common model of relationship between the state and religious faiths in Western Europe. He argued that the conventional focus on 'outmoded' typologies of church–state relations, which stressed, for example, the differences between separatist, concordat-based and national (or state–church) systems, obscured the existence of real commonalities at the level of 'legal substance'. The model was characterized first by a common commitment to the recognition of individuals' rights to religious liberty. Anomalies in this area – such as the continuing constitutional ban in Greece on proselytism – were gradually being eliminated, although novel problems in connection with the toleration of unconventional 'cults' such as the Church of Scientology or the Moonies continued to pose a challenge. What distinguished Ferrari's common European model, however, was its deliberate privileging of religion:

A religious sub-sector is singled out within the public sector. This may be understood as a 'playing field' or 'protected area'. Inside it the various collective religious subjects (churches, denominations, and religious communities) are free to act in conditions of substantial advantage compared to those collective subjects that are not religious.

(Ferrari 1999: 3)

One question-begging feature of Ferrari's model centres on what he saw as the essentially secular nature of the modern state: 'the fundamental principles of the common European model of relationships between the state and the religious communities ... are quite rigid. ... [They] have been summed up in the formula "the secular state"' (Ferrari 1999: 11). A glance at the data presented in Table 12.1 suggests, however, that what distinguishes the European model is not so much state secularity as state religiosity, particularly when contrasted with the separationist model in the USA (Krislov 1985). This is a point that emerges even more clearly from the analysis of Jonathan Fox's large worldwide data collection mapping church–state connectedness (Fox and Sandler 2005; Fox 2006). If the secularity of the state is to be seen as a fundamental principle of the European model, then, it is surely one more honoured in the breach than the observance (Barro and McCleary 2005).

The record in Eastern Europe is instructive. None of the eight former Communist countries of Central and Eastern Europe that joined the EU in May 2004 (in alphabetic order: the Czech Republic, Estonia, Hungary, Latvia, Lithuania, Poland, Slovakia and Slovenia) formally adopted a state–church model after the end of the Cold War; nor, on the other hand, did any of them adopt a rigid separation model either despite the claim of some that it constitutes a *sine qua non* of liberal democracy. Most instead chose 'benevolent separation' or 'cooperation' models and all, including those that did not have significant Catholic populations, negotiated

some kind of concordat settlement with the Vatican. This is all the more remarkable since of the 15 previous EU members only 5 (Austria, Germany, Italy, Portugal and Spain) had existing concordats. In Germany the fall of the Wall in 1989 also led to a new wave of church–state treaties, as the Eastern *Länder* were again opened for free religious activity.

Beyond Europe: contemporary religion–state relations in the rest of the world

In the red dawn of the third millennium of the Common Era it is a nice irony that debates about secularization continue unabated; the rising trend line of controversy itself would seem to mock the very idea that religion is declining in political significance. As in the case of Europe, indications reflecting the mutual entanglements of states and religion across the world point Janus-like in both directions: while the parliament of Tuvalu in 1991 approved legislation establishing the [Congregationalist] Church of Tuvalu as the state church, at the end of 2007 Nepal's provisional parliamentary assembly voted to abolish the monarchy whose kings were held to be reincarnations of the Hindu god Vishnu. With the development of the Fox (2006) dataset measures for the different components of state–religion relations between 1990 and 2002, it is now possible to review the contemporary situation using empirical indicators for all states of one million or more inhabitants.

As was noted above in the case of Europe, secularizing trends, have failed to make for anything like a clear separation between state and religion, even in those countries where critical political changes had for much of the previous century placed anti-religious elites in power. As Table 12.2 indicates, the hostile pattern of state–religion juxtaposition had in fact by

2002 become a rarity across the whole globe. The number of remaining cases of regimes judged by Fox (2006) to be either 'hostile' or 'inadvertently insensitive' to religion had reduced to only five; these were respectively Vietnam and Cuba, and China, North Korea and Laos. An equally remarkable finding is the failure of separationism to have made significant headway: only nine states in 2002 could be counted as having separationist regimes – in Europe, only France and Azerbaijan, and, in the Americas, only Mexico and Uruguay.[1] Fully 92% of all cases (161 out of 175 countries) were coded as having state–religion regulatory regimes which ranged from full religious establishment to 'accommodationism' (understood as involving a posture of benevolent neutrality towards religion).[2]

The largest single category, accounting for over a quarter of all countries, is the one which most positively favours not just religion in general but a particular religion – or, as in the anomalous cases of the United Kingdom and Finland, two particular religions: this is the category of countries which still maintained systems of Established Religion(s). As Table 12.2 indicates, this pattern is to be found in all confessional traditions, although it is most common in those countries where Islam has been historically dominant, where it accounts for almost 60% of all cases. In traditionally Catholic countries the most common state–religion regulatory regime is that of Endorsed Religion where there is an official acknowledgement that Roman Catholicism has a special place in the country's traditions, as for example in the cases of Ireland, Spain, Portugal, Poland and Croatia. Finally, among the countries where 'Other Christian' – mainly Protestant and Orthodox – confessional traditions have been historically dominant, Accommodationist regimes are found to be most common.

While Table 12.2 provides a summary overview of state–religion relations in terms of alternative models it cannot show the range of variation in scope and intensity of the regulatory relationships which are to be found within and across the individual categories (Fox 2006: 538). For example, cases of the Established Religion(s) model are found in Catholic Malta, Protestant United Kingdom and Muslim Saudi Arabia, yet even without quantitative measures to demonstrate the fact it is evident that the 'weight' of religious establishment, as it is expressed in regulatory arrangements affecting the established religion itself and other religions, varies widely between these three cases. Similarly the fact that both France and Azerbaijan are coded as cases of separationist regimes obscures vast

Table 12.2 State–religion regimes in 2002, by historically dominant confession

	Catholic	Other Christian	Muslim	Other	Totals
Established religion(s)	7 (16.3%)	6 (14.1%)	27 (57.4%)	4 (12.5%)	46 (26.2%)
Endorsed religion(s)	18 (41.9%)	10 (18.9%)	6 (12.8%)	2 (6.3%)	36 (20.6%)
Cooperationist	9 (20.9%)	14 (26.4%)	5 (10.6%)	10 (31.3%)	38 (21.7%)
Accommodationist	6 (14.0%)	20 (37.7%)	5 (10.6%)	10 (31.3%)	41 (23.4%)
Separationist	3 (7.0%)	1 (1.9%)	4 (8.5%)	1 (3.1%)	9 (5.1%)
Insensitive/hostile	0	0	0	5 (15.6%)	5 (2.9%)
Total	43 (100%)	53 (100%)	47 (99.9%)	32 (100.1%)	175

Notes: I have chosen to adapt Cole Durham's (1996) original labelling for this table, shortening his coding by combining the Cooperationist (T = 35) and Supportive (T = 3) and the Inadvertent Insensitivity (T = 4) and Hostile (T = 1) categories. The source of the data is Fox (2006).

differences in their internal arrangements. Fox's government involvement in religion (GIR) index, however, provides a useful summary indication of these variations.[3]

Table 12.3 shows the banded scores for GIR in 2002 across all 175 countries arranged by world region. In many respects the picture which emerges is unsurprising. The fact that the mean GIR score for the countries of the Middle East and North Africa, which are overwhelmingly Muslim (the exceptions being Israel and Lebanon) is much the highest (over 50) is consistent with the finding in Table 12.2 that a large majority of countries where Islam has been historically dominant have systems of religious establishment. Equally, the fact that Saudi Arabia (78) and Iran (67) score first and second in this measure of governmental regulatory weight in the sphere of religion accords with what is widely known about their theocratic or hierocratic systems of government given their treatment of certain

Table 12.3 Government involvement in religion scores in 2002, by region

GIR score deciles	Western democracies	Former Soviet bloc	Asia	M. East and N. Africa	Sub-Saharan Africa	Latin America	Totals
0.00>9.99	USA Netherlands Australia Canada	Estonia Albania	Taiwan S. Korea Mongolia Solomon Is. Philippines Japan		Congo-B. Lesotho Namibia Benin Angola Burkina-F. Burundi, Gambia S. Africa Zaire Swaziland Liberia Senegal Malawi Mozambique Ghana Botswana Rwanda	Guyana Ecuador Bahamas Brazil Barbados Trinidad & Tobago Suriname Uruguay	38 (21.7%)
10.00>19.99	Luxembourg New Zealand Sweden Italy Ireland Gk Cyprus Tk. Cyprus Germany	Tajikistan Slovenia Bosnia-H. Yugoslavia Latvia Lithuania Czech Rep. Kyrgyzstan Slovakia Ukraine	Fiji Papua NG Vanuatu		Mauritius Guinea-B. Sierra L. Gabon Cape Verde Togo Cameroon Mali Zimbabwe Tanzania Central Af. Rep. Madagascar Niger Uganda Ivory Coast	Mexico Jamaica Guatemala Nicaragua Colombia	41 (23.4%)

Continued

187

Table 12.3 Continued

GIR score deciles	Western democracies	Former Soviet bloc	Asia	M. East and N. Africa	Sub-Saharan Africa	Latin America	Totals
20.00>29.99	Switzerland Portugal France Andorra Austria Belgium Malta Norway Denmark Liechtenstein UK, Spain Iceland	Poland Croatia Hungary Romania Macedonia	Thailand India Nepal Cambodia Singapore	Lebanon	Ethiopia Guinea Nigeria Chad Equat. Guinea Kenya Eritrea Zambia	Belize Chile Paraguay Honduras Haiti Peru Venezuela El Salvador Panama Domin. Rep.	42 (24.0%)
30.00>39.99	Finland Greece	Russia Azerbaijan Kazakhstan Moldova Georgia Belarus Bulgaria Turkmenistan	Sri Lanka Bangladesh Laos	Israel Bahrain	Djibouti Somalia	Argentina Costa Rica Bolivia	20 (11.4%)
40.00>49.99		Armenia Uzbekistan	N. Korea Bhutan Indonesia Burma China Afghanistan	Syria Oman Kuwait Turkey Libya Yemen W. Sahara	Comoros Mauritania	Cuba	18 (10.3%)
50.00>59.99			Pakistan Brunei Vietnam Malaysia	Morocco Qatar Algeria Iraq Tunisia UAE	Sudan		11 (6.3%)
60.00>69.99			Maldives	Jordan Egypt Iran			4 (2.4%)
70.00>79.99				Saudi Arabia			1 (0.6%)
Mean scores	19.17	24.24	30.71	50.82	15.82	17.88	175 (100.1%)

Source: The source of this data is the RAS (Religion and State) dataset developed by Jonathan Fox. A full description is available in J. Fox, *A World Survey of Religion and the State*, Cambridge: Cambridge University Press, 2008) and from the Religion and State project website: http://www.biu.ac.il/soc/po/ras/

religious minorities, their patterns of regulation of the majority religion, and their privileging of religious legislation. Israel's GIR score (37) which is by contrast low for the Middle East/North Africa region is shown also to be relatively high in a world context. The overall GIR score for the Western liberal democracies with a mean well under half that of the Middle East/North Africa is considerably lower. Here the interesting point to note is, however, that when all the elements of governmental involvement in the sphere of religion are taken into account only four out of 27 score under 10 and only the USA scores zero, reflecting its history until recently of strict separationism. Interestingly, the median case is Portugal (22), where as Table 12.1 indicated 97% of the population are, formally at least, Roman Catholic and Catholicism has been the established religion throughout the twentieth and into the twenty-first century.

This brief statistical survey of state–religion institutional arrangements can take little account of the turbulent struggles which have revolved, and in many parts of the world continue to revolve, around them and been involved in constructing them. Thus, Islamists following the line marked out by radicals including the Egyptian Sayyid Qutb (1906-66) and the Pakistani Sayyid Abul Ala Mawdudi (1903-79) regard many of the political regimes, which incorporate forms of Islamic religious establishment in, say, Egypt or Algeria or Saudi Arabia, as corrupt, in practice anti-Islamic and worthy only of violent overthrow. And contemporary Islamists' sometimes-violent campaigns against such regimes and those in the West who are seen to support them, such as the USA and Britain, have tipped much of the world into the turmoil of the so-called War on Terror. In those countries where Islamists have, for a time at least gained power – Iran, Afghanistan and Sudan, for example – and attempted to

craft fully Islamic polities with the state under the authority of religious officials, the resulting struggles have been no less turbulent, while in others where the contest between rival factions remains undecided – Somalia, Iraq and Pakistan, for example – the threat or reality of state failure with the complete breakdown of the state's ability to rule is present. While the world of Islam presents the most dramatic attempts by religious forces to assert their precedence in the exercise of state powers it is not alone. In India and Sri Lanka, for example, Hindu, Sikh and Buddhist fundamentalists also struggle to reorder on religious lines the political arrangements set in place at the time of independence.

Conclusion

Located in a world context, the situation in Europe is increasingly seen as exceptional. In spite of – or, perhaps, because of – the maintenance there of important state–religion linkages, the secularity of European societies and cultures has seemed to resist the sacralizing trends evident elsewhere. Even in the USA such trends are evident, although in one manifestation they can be seen as pressing for changes which would bring state–religion relationships closer to those obtaining in Europe (Monsma and Soper 1997). Europe is far from immune to the trends, however (Byrnes and Katzenstein 2006). Nor is it clear that the European state–religion model of benevolent neutrality will prove sufficiently robust to accommodate and so 'domesticate' the more difficult challenges that face it (Madeley 2006a, 2006b). Olivier Roy has argued that 'neofundamentalist' Islam, which, he avers, increasingly appeals to Europe's rootless and materially disadvantaged Muslim youth, is associated in one of its forms with support for the militancy of extreme groups such as Al-Qaeda. Even in less threatening variants, which typically seek reassertion of strict or 'pure' Islamic values within the minority communities, deterritorialized Islam can be seen as embracing multiculturalism – principally as a means of resisting, rather than easing, integration into the European host societies (Roy 2002: 1). Both cases, however, would appear to represent a radical integralist challenge to both state and society in Europe, and place a large question mark over secularization as differentiation. The violent events of 2004 in the Netherlands, including the murder of the film director, Theo van Gogh, by an avowed Islamist, stand as a cautionary tale from modern Europe's first largely secular state and the site of many of its most progressive social experiments: 'What happened in this small corner of northwestern Europe could happen anywhere, as long as young men and women feel that death is their only way home' (Buruma 2006: 262).

Notes

1 The others so identified were Tajikistan, Kyrgyzstan, Niger, Eritrea and Singapore.
2 It is particularly noteworthy in this context that the USA, the world's first state to introduce church–state separation, was judged to have ceased to count as separationist and ranks instead as accommodationist. In line with the Fox finding, Cole Durham points out that many scholars, McConnell for example, argue that the USA is now to be regarded as accommodationist rather than separationist not least because '[a]s state influence becomes more pervasive and regulatory burdens expand, refusal to exempt or accommodate shades into hostility' (Cole Durham 1996: 2).
3 The index scores represent an overall measure of GIR obtained by combining six narrower-gauge measures for: (1) state support for one or more religions either officially or in practice; (2) state hostility toward religion; (3) comparative government treatment of different religions, including both benefits and restrictions; (4) government restrictions on the practice of religion by religious minorities; (5) government regulation of the

majority religion; and (6) legislation of religious laws. The figures given are simply summations of the number of positive instances of GIR.

Bibliography

Badie, B. and Birnbaum, B. (1983) *The Sociology of the State*, London: University of Chicago Press.
Barrett, D. (ed.) (1982) *World Christian Encyclopaedia: A Comparative Study of Churches and Religions in the Modern World AD 1900–2000*, New York: Oxford University Press.
Barrett, D., Kurian, G.T. and Johnson, T.D. (eds) (2001) *World Christian Encyclopaedia: A Comparative Study of Churches and Religions in the Modern World AD 1900–2000*, 2nd edn, New York: Oxford University Press.
Barro, R.J. and McCleary, R. (2005) 'Which countries have state religions?', *Quarterly Journal of Economics*, 4, pp. 1331–70.
Bellah, R.N. (1964) 'Religious evolution', *American Sociological Review*, 29, pp. 358–74.
Berger, P. (ed.) (1999) *The Desecularization of the World*, Washington, DC: Ethics and Public Policy Center.
Bijsterveld, S.C. van (1996) 'State and church in the Netherlands', in R. Robbers (ed.), *State and Church in the European Union*, Baden-Baden: Nomos Verlag.
Boyle, K. and Sheen, J. (eds) (1997) *Freedom of Religion and Belief: A World Report,* London: Routledge.
Buruma, I. (2006), *Murder in Amsterdam: The Death of Theo van Gogh and the Limits of Tolerance*, London: Atlantic Books.
Byrnes, T. and Katzenstein, P. (eds) (2006) *Religion in an Expanding Europe*, Cambridge: Cambridge University Press.
Casanova, J. (1994) *Public Religions in the Modern World*, Chicago: University of Chicago Press.
Cole Durham, W. (1996) 'Perspectives in religious liberty: a comparative framework', in J.D. van der Vyver and J. Witte (eds), *Religious Human Rights in Global Perspective,* The Hague: Martinus Nijhoff Publishers, pp. 1–44.
Ehler, S. and Morrall, J.B. (1954) *Church and State through the Centuries*, London: Burnes and Oates.
Eisenstadt, S. (1986) *The Origins and Diversity of Axial-age Civilizations*, Albany, NY: SUNY Press.

190

Ferrari, S. (1999) 'The new wine and the old cask: tolerance, religion, and the law in contemporary Europe', in A. Sajo and S. Avineri (eds), *The Law of Religious Identity: Models for Post-Communism*, The Hague: Kluwer Law International, pp. 1–15.

Fox, J. (2006) 'World separation of religion and state into the 21st century', *Comparative Political Studies*, 39, 5, pp. 537–69.

Fox, J. and Sandler, S. (2005) 'Separation of religion and state in the 21st century: comparing the Middle East and Western democracies', *Comparative Politics*, 37, 3, pp. 317–35.

Gerth, H.H. and Mills, C.W. (1948) *From Max Weber: Essays in Sociology*, London: Routledge & Kegan Paul.

Halliday, F. (1995) *Islam and the Myth of Confrontation*, London: I.B. Tauris.

Klausen, J. (2005) *The Islamic Challenge: Politics and Religion in Western Europe*, Oxford: Oxford University Press.

Knippenberg, H. (2006) 'The political geography of religion: historical state–church relations in Europe and recent changes', *GeoJournal: An International Journal on Human Geography*, 67, pp. 253–65.

Krislov, S. (1985) 'Alternatives to separation of church and state in countries outside the United States', in J. E. Wood (ed.), *Religion and the State: Essays in Honor of Leo Pfeffer*, Waco, TX: Baylor University Press, pp. 421–40.

Madeley, J.T.S. (2003a) 'European liberal democracy and the principle of state religious neutrality', in J. Madeley and Z. Enyedi (eds), *Church and State in Contemporary Europe: The Chimera of Neutrality*, London: Frank Cass, pp. 1–22.

Madeley, J.T.S. (2003b) 'A framework for the comparative analysis of church–state relations in Europe', in J. Madeley and Z. Enyedi (eds), *Church and State in Contemporary Europe: The Chimera of Neutrality*, London: Frank Cass, pp. 23–50.

Madeley, J.T.S. (2006a) 'Still the century of antidisestablishmentarianism?', *European Political Science*, 5, 4, pp. 395–406.

Madeley, J.T.S. (2006b) 'Religion and the state', in P. Heywood, E. Jones, M. Rhodes and U. Sedelmeier (eds), *Developments in European Politics*, London: Palgrave, pp. 237–55.

Martin, D. (1978) *Toward a General Theory of Secularization*, London: Robertson.

Modood, T. (ed.) (1997) *Church, State and Religious Minorities*, London: Policy Studies Institute.

Monsma, S. and Soper, C. (eds) (1997) *The Challenge of Pluralism: Church and State in Five Democracies*, Oxford: Rowman and Littlefield.

Norris, P. and Inglehart, R. (2004) *Sacred and Secular: Religion and Politics Worldwide*, New York: Cambridge University Press.

Rémond, R. (1999) *Religion and Society in Modern Europe*, Oxford: Blackwell.

Richardson, J.T. (ed.) (2004) *Regulating Religion: Case Studies from around the Globe*, London: Kluwer Academic/Plenum.

Robbers, R. (ed.) (1996) *State and Church in the European Union*, Baden-Baden: Nomos Verlag.

Roy, O., (2002) *Globalized Islam: The Search for a New Ummah*, London: Hurst.

Schanda, B. (2005) 'Church and state in the new member countries of the European Union', *Ecclesiastical Law Journal*, 8, 37, pp. 186–98.

Smith, D.E. (1970) *Religion and Political Development*, Boston: Little, Brown.

Stepan, A. (2000) 'Religion, democracy, and the "twin tolerations"', *Journal of Democracy*, 11, 4, pp. 37–56.

Stepan, A. (2001) *Arguing Comparative Politics*, Oxford: Oxford University Press.

Ward, K. (2000) *Religion and Community*, Oxford: Clarendon Press.

Wilson, B. (1990) 'New images of Christian community', in J. McManners (ed.), *The Oxford Illustrated History of Christianity*, Oxford: Oxford University Press, pp. 572–601.

Wyduckel, D. (2001) 'Die Zukunft des Staatskirchetums in der Europäischen Union', in P.-C. Müller-Graff and H. Schneider (eds), *Kirchen und Religionsgemeinschaften in der Europäischen Union*, Baden-Baden: Nomos Verlagsgesellschaft, pp. 169–85.

13

Does God matter, and if so whose God?

Religion and democratisation[1]

John Anderson

The question of how, or if, religious traditions might affect the possibility of successful democratisation has been hotly debated for several decades. During the immediate post-war years many writers stressed the importance of political culture in explaining the success or otherwise of democratisation and some focused on the ways in which religious traditions fed into the making of any country's political culture. More recently a 'new orthodoxy' has emerged which concentrates on institutional or economic factors in the making of democracy and tends to see the impact of cultural factors as marginal or irrelevant. Few authors analysing the 'third wave' give much space to religion, except in discussing countries such as Poland where institutional religion played a role in undermining authoritarian regimes. Juan Linz and Alfred Stepan, analysing the East European experience, suggest that religion is a hypothesis that one can do without because other factors are sufficient to explain the differential results of democratisation in the region (Linz and Stepan 1996: 452–453). In similar vein Fred Halliday argues that the barriers to democracy in Islamic countries have to do with 'certain other social and political

features that their societies share. ... Though some of these features tend to be legitimised in terms of Islamic doctrine, there is nothing specifically "Islamic" about them' (Halliday 1996: 116). By way of contrast Samuel Huntington has seen religion as crucial in defining the civilisational blocs into which he claims the world is divided and has argued that religious tradition does have an impact upon the likely success of democratisation efforts (Huntington 1991, 1996).

This chapter offers a brief review of the key debates and points to the main arguments of the new orthodoxy which stress: the impossibility of essentialising religious traditions, the multi-vocal nature of all religious discourses which can provide resources for both supporters and opponents of democracy, and the secondary nature of cultural factors in explaining successful or failed democratisation. This chapter accepts many of these arguments but simultaneously argues that religion is not entirely irrelevant to understanding the evolution of democratic experiments. In particular, it suggests that religious traditions do have core elements – just as does democracy, contrary to cultural relativist critiques; that religious traditions may, in Stepan's words be multi-vocal (Stepan 2001: 252–253), but that at any point in time the dominant voices within them may prove more or less receptive to pluralistic development; and that intertwined religious and cultural traditions as expressed through public discourse and in the positions adopted by key religious actors, though not decisive, may have some marginal impact upon the success or otherwise of democratic consolidation. In other words, the (rather weak) argument is not that religion determines political outcomes, or that religious emphases cannot change, or that the world is divided into inevitably clashing civilisational blocs – though my focus (for reasons of space) on Islam and Eastern Orthodoxy as partially problematic traditions may superficially appear to support such an approach – but simply that religion is not irrelevant to evaluating the prospects for democratisation.

The debate

The Protestant connection

Many of those writing about the preconditions for democracy in the decades following 1945 noted that the first countries to democratise tended to have a Protestant religious tradition – the USA, Great Britain, Scandinavia, Holland – whilst, as Steve Bruce notes in his contribution to this collection, these were also the countries that avoided the authoritarian embrace during the twentieth century. Of course there were exceptions – intermittently in some Latin American countries and in India after independence – so there was no suggestion that Protestantism was a necessary condition, but the argument was made that there were elements within this religious tradition that were more suited to the emergence of pluralist politics. For some this affinity lay in economic developments within these countries, for others democracy stemmed from certain ideological features of the Protestant tradition, whilst yet others saw democracy as a largely 'accidental' by-product of certain aspects of the Reformation process.

Those who focused on the economic connection tended to see democracy as a consequence of economic modernisation and, because the most developed countries tended to be Protestant in tradition, it was perhaps inevitable that democracy should emerge first in these countries. Max Weber's *The Protestant Ethic and the Spirit of Capitalism* had suggested that certain psychological conditions contributed towards the creation of the modern capitalist system, and that these were created in large part by religious change. Here he linked the urge to accumulate to the peculiarly Calvinist notions of 'calling' and 'predestination' which gave birth to a 'worldly asceticism' that encouraged the pursuit of wealth so long as it was not used for worldly pleasure (Weber 1930: chs 4, 5). Needless to say, Weber was far too sophisticated to posit a deterministic relationship, warning that 'we have no intention of maintaining such a foolish and doctrinaire thesis as that the spirit of capitalism … could only have arisen as a result of certain effects of the Reformation, or even that capitalism as an economic system is a creation of the Reformation … we can only proceed by investigating whether and at what points certain correlations between forms of religious beliefs and practical ethics can be worked out' (Weber 1930: 91). Equally, it should be stressed that he was not at this point making an argument about democracy as such, though some of the implications of his thesis have been extended to suggest a connection between Protestantism and democracy. In particular, it has been argued that the Reformation helped to break down the traditional cultural barriers to economic modernisation which in turn created a growing division of labour and a degree of egalitarianism.

193

The link to democracy was also seen in the ideological nature of Protestantism with its emphasis on the individual's relationship with God, an idea that was inherently egalitarian in nature. At the heart of Luther's vision was the notion of the priesthood of all believers which, at least in the spiritual sphere, made no distinction between prince or pauper when it came to one's relationship with God. Similarly Calvin's 'calling' was something that could come to any member of a society and on paper his congregational politics could be seen as a prototype of democratic forms of governance. Of course, in practice none of the leading Reformers were democrats in the modern sense of the word. Luther stressed the naturalness of the given social order, relied heavily on princes for the defence of the new teachings, and vigorously denounced the peasants who rose against their masters (for a general survey of Luther's thinking on politics, see Cargill 1984). Equally, Calvinist congregational polities were often heavily dominated by their pastors and Calvin's own experience of struggling with Geneva's notionally representative assembly rendered him sceptical about the conformity of any particular form of government to the divine ideal (Kingdom and Linder 1970; Wuthnow 1989: 126–128).

Nonetheless, there emerged out of Reformation discourse several ideas that were to contribute to the emergence of democracy in the modern sense: the notion of rule as a covenant between rulers and ruled, the acceptability of resistance to rulers under some circumstances, and the idea of tolerance. During the latter half of the sixteenth century various writers explored the question of when it might be acceptable to resist tyranny and who had the right to overthrow evil rulers. By and large, the reformers were conservative but by the end of the century there had begun to emerge an emphasis on rule as the product of a covenant between people and monarch, an idea perhaps best set out in the Calvinist-inspired *Vindicae contra tyrannos* (1579). Here it was suggested that should the prince flout God's law he would lose divine approval and the mutual obligation implicit in the covenant would be undermined. In such circumstances the community had a right to encourage a change in behaviour and in the last resort to remove an erring leader (Kingdom 1991).

With regard to tolerance, this was not a virtue initially much discussed by the Reformers and religious liberty was often seen in terms of 'freedom in Christ' or freedom from the 'mire of Catholicism' (Benedict 1996: 69–93). In consequence they generally advocated acceptance of their own right to differ from Catholic orthodoxy but were often unable to accept difference within communities and states that they ruled. Yet perhaps inevitably the religious fragmentation that followed on from the Reformation helped to undermine the notion of a single-faith community dominating the political order. This was certainly not the intent of the Protestant reformers but, in Steve Bruce's words, an inadvertent by-product of the social and theological changes they initiated. In particular, rising prosperity attendant upon economic modernisation, the changing relationship between the individual and the community, and the rise of religious diversity helped to break the organic connection of religion and community and to push religion into the private sphere. With increasing religious diversity, enforcing orthodoxy became more expensive for emerging nation states and in consequence they organised their activities with decreasing reference to religious institutions or ideas (Bruce 2003: 144–254). Thus the acceptance of religious diversity which gradually emerged following the Reformation contributed to a wider acceptance of diversity and the need for consent in constructing the political order, which was later institutionalised in liberal-democratic forms.

'Undemocratic' religions

If Protestantism was seen as a key contributor to the emergence of democratic orders or at the very least a particularly 'suitable' religion for democracy, nearly all other religious traditions tended to be viewed as in some sense incompatible with pluralist politics. Initially, much of the discussion focused on Roman Catholicism which historically had been deeply hostile to democratic ideals and which, during the first half of the twentieth century, seemed to find it easy to live with authoritarian political systems. The fact that democracy had largely emerged within the Protestant world meant that for some time the Roman Catholic Church did not have to engage directly with democratic forms of rule. The excesses of the French Revolution, ostensibly committed to giving citizens the right of political participation, reinforced the Church's view that democracy was in some sense associated with chaos, anarchy and hostility towards true religion. Moreover, the very notion of popular sovereignty appeared to contradict the sovereignty of God, whilst genuine tolerance was viewed as threatening to the Church's ideological hegemony. In consequence, Gregory XVI was quick to condemn the erroneous concept of 'freedom of conscience' whilst the Syllabus of Errors (1860) rejected the view that the Church should compromise with 'progress, liberalism and modern civilisation' (Sigmund 1987: 530–548). Though Leo XIII's encyclical *Rerum Novarum* (1891) promoted a vision of social Catholicism, the Vatican clung to its rejection of democratic politics till the perceived threat of communism led it to re-think its position. Even then Catholic hierarchies in practice continued to remain ambiguous in their relationships with authoritarian regimes, whether the fascist rulers of Central Europe during the 1930s or the corporatist leaders of Iberia and Latin America

during the post-war years. And, as Sigmund notes, the Vatican's view of all political order as provisional and its willingness to adapt to all regimes so long as they did not directly threaten the Catholic conception of the common good encouraged a tendency to accept the status quo (Sigmund 1987: 531).

It was the experience of the Iberian and Latin American countries from the 1930s through the 1960s that led some scholars to suggest the incompatibility of Catholicism and democratic governance. So long as these regimes protected the institutional interests of the Church, whose bishops often came from the same social groups as the political elite, there was little reason for clergymen to oppose authoritarian rulers. In most cases such regimes provided legal support for Catholic hegemony, promoted Catholic education in education and permitted the censorship of works critical of religious teaching. More importantly, there were key elements within the Catholic organisational and ideological tradition that chimed in well with the authoritarian and paternalistic political traditions of these states. These included its monarchical and hierarchical structure, its emphasis on submission to the authority of the clerical estate, and its intolerance of diversity within predominantly Catholic states. Dealy points out that in North America the founding fathers sought to disperse power, whereas in Latin America the rulers who broke away from Spain and Portugal sought to unify power, and he sees the roots of this monistic vision in the common Catholic culture of the region and springing out of the Catholic notion of the common good, something which is distinct from the sum of many private interests and tends to view the pursuit of particular interests as invariably divisive (Dealy 1992: 40–60). Thus elements within the Catholic tradition reinforced and strengthened Iberian–Latin American predispositions towards hierarchy, paternalism and authoritarianism.

195

The primary focus of academic discussion in the 1950s and 1960s was the Catholic Church, and the limited attention paid to other religions suggested that few scholars took seriously the possibility that they might prove supportive of democratic development. Many scholars focused on 'Islam' and 'Confucianism' as religions that contained elements within them that sat uneasily with democracy. With regard to Islam it was suggested that reliance on a fixed religious text and quasi-legal ordinances, the emphasis on divine sovereignty, and the supposed lack of distinction between the religious and the political realms, all worked against democratic development. Moreover, in practice democracy had by and large, and with the partial exceptions of Turkey and Pakistan, failed to take root in any predominantly Muslim country in the decades following the war (Vatikiotis 1987; Kedourie 1992). In similar vein several writers argued that the Confucian culture that dominated parts of East Asia, with its emphasis on hierarchy, order and consensus also worked against democracy (on Confucianism, see Pye 1985). Other religions barely rated a mention in these early discussions, the assumption perhaps being that Eastern Orthodoxy with its long tradition of dependence upon the state (Koyziz 1993: 267–289) and Buddhism with its alleged passivity offered few resources to would-be democratisers. More interesting is the relative absence until recently of any significant discussion of Judaism, or of Hinduism whose plurality of divinities and broad tolerance of religious difference in an earlier period might have been seen as underlying India's unlikely adoption of democratic governance post-independence. Conversely it might be noted that the attempt of Hindu nationalists to develop a more coherent 'scriptural' model of Hinduism has been accompanied by a partial rejection of the post-independence pluralist model of political order (Hansen 1999; Batt 2001).

The thesis revised

The suggestion that certain religious traditions were more suitable for democracy came under increasing attack from the early 1980s onwards with criticism taking two forms. The first argued that in practice the position adopted by political actors in pushing for democratisation was generally decisive and culture largely irrelevant or secondary – if external pressures, political elite activity or bottom-up pressure was such as to encourage or compel authoritarian leaders to stand down then democratisation was more likely to happen. A second approach argued that culturalist theories over-emphasised the role of religion in shaping contemporary political cultures and equally that they had too static a view of religious tradition which made no allowance for resources within religious traditions that might be supportive of democracy.

Nonetheless, several authors continued to focus on the *suitability* of different religions for democratic development, albeit revising the thesis in the process. Perhaps the most notable revision was put forward by Samuel Huntington in his book on democratisation's 'third wave'. Here he argued that changes in five independent variables during the 1960s and 1970s had made possible the new democratic wave, and that these included religious change, most notably within the Catholic Church. Huntington starts by noting the ongoing relationship between democracy and Protestantism, quoting a 1960s study which suggested that, in 91 countries studied, the greater the proportion of Protestants the higher the level of democracy. Moreover, he argued that to some extent this relationship still held, pointing to the experience of South Korea as the one country where Christianity in general and Protestantism in particular had expanded rapidly during the 1960s and 1970s, with Christians making up about 1% of the population in 1945 and maybe 25% by the mid-1980s. In turn, Christianity created 'a surer doctrinal and institutional basis for opposing political repression' by promoting ideas of equality and respect for authority beyond that of the state (Huntington 1991: 73–74). Later discussions of the rapid expansion of Pentecostal Christianity in Latin America have also revolved around the question of whether this might reinforce a Protestant work ethic that would contribute to economic development and a deepening of democratisation, though Gill's contribution to this collection suggests the need for caution in suggesting a distinctive Protestant contribution to socio-political life (Martin 1990).

Of greater significance, however, was the fact that according to Huntington around three-quarters of the countries undergoing transition prior to 1991 had a predominantly Catholic tradition – this factor appears to have been less significant in the wave of the 1990s. By then most predominantly Protestant countries were already democratic and therefore any new democratisations had to be in countries with another religious tradition, but why Catholic? Though Huntington saw this as in part a product of the fact that these countries had higher rates of economic growth than traditionally Protestant countries, he also suggested that changes within the Catholic Church itself were of crucial importance. Prior to the 1960s the Church and its national hierarchies generally proved supportive of authoritarian orders but from that time onwards the institution as a whole became increasingly critical of such regimes. At the global level this stemmed from the changes in Catholic social teaching and theological 'style' emanating from the Second Vatican Council held in the early 1960s which led the Church to defend human rights and promote democracy. At the local level a new generation of priests, often with European education but also with more experience of working amongst the marginalised within their own societies, came to see their role in terms of defending the interests of their flock against the economically and politically powerful. All this was reinforced in the late 1970s by the election of John Paul II who, though sceptical about the radicalisation of the clergy, remained committed to the defence of the dignity of the individual and supported those national hierarchs who promoted human rights or got involved in mediating between regimes and political opposition. All this not only changed the position of a key institutional actor but also had an impact upon regional political by promoting a more participatory and less hierarchical vision of the political order (Martin 1990). Hence the thesis of religious influence was effectively modified with Huntington suggesting that it was not Protestantism that was crucial in the present period but Western Christianity more generally – or even maybe any religious tradition so long as it became 'Protestantised' by reducing hierarchical elements and focusing more on the individual. Others have been more sceptical of this argument with Jeff Haynes, for example, suggesting that in Africa senior religious leaders jumping on the democratic bandwagon to preserve their own ideological hegemony within society (Haynes 1996: 104–133).

Much of the voluminous literature on religion in Latin America tended to support the view that the Catholic Church had by and large shifted its position in favour of a more pluralistic vision of the ideal polity, though rational-choice analysts such as Anthony Gill thought this had more to do with responses to ideological and organisational competition – primarily from expanding Protestant communities – than ideological shifts within the Catholic Church (see, for example, Sigmund 1994; Kleiber 1998; Gill 1998). Linz and Stepan, who generally reject explanations rooted in religion, argue that the Catholic Church's ability to promote pluralism in authoritarian and especially totalitarian countries comes from

> its transnational base. The papacy can be a source of spiritual and material support for groups that want to resist monist absorption or extinction. ... This source of higher international power is not available in a political system (such as Bulgaria, Romania or the former Soviet Union) which has Orthodox churches that are national but not transnational in scope and that historically have accepted a form of 'caesaropapism'. ... It is also not available in a predominantly Islamic society because Islam as a religion is a community of believers in which all believers can be preachers and where there is no transnational hierarchy.
> (Linz and Stepan 1996: 260–261)

In his 1991 book Huntington appeared to accept that cultural constraints on democracy were not fixed for ever and that just as Catholicism changed so might other religious traditions that help to shape regional political cultures. Yet in the later *Clash of Civilisations* (1996) he appears to take a much stronger view which sees Islam in particular as providing infertile ground for the development of democratic institutions, especially in a global context where democracy is associated with Western dominance. And in analysing post-communist Europe he argued that:

> The most significant dividing line in Europe, as William Wallace has suggested may well be the eastern boundary of Western Christianity in the year 1500. ... The peoples to the north and west of this line are Protestant or Catholic; they shared the common experiences of European history – feudalism, the Renaissance, the Reformation, the Enlightenment, the French Revolution, the Industrial Revolution: they are generally economically better off than the peoples to the east; and they may now look forward to increasing involvement in a common European economy and to the consolidation of democratic political systems. The peoples to the east and south of this line are Orthodox and Muslim: they historically belonged to the Ottoman or Tsarist empires and were only lightly touched by the shaping events in the rest of Europe; they are generally less advanced economically; they seem much less likely to develop stable democratic political systems.
> (Huntington 1996: 105)

In somewhat less deterministic fashion Inglehart has posited the existence of cultural zones that have been shaped in part by religious differences. In his view this has less to do with present religious affiliations than with the legacy of the past which means, for example, that even in countries such as the Netherlands or Germany which now have as many Catholics as Protestants value systems tend to be 'typically Protestant' (Inglehart and Carballo 2000: 341). Consequently, though religious tradition does not determine democratic outcomes, these authors restated the argument that belief systems may create a value and even structural bias that can work for or against successful democracy building at the present moment in time.

The thesis challenged

By the late 1980s and early 1990s approaches which sought to explain political transition in terms of political culture and religious tradition were coming under sustained attack. 'Transitologists' increasingly questioned the 'pre-conditions' approach which suggested that democracy could only be constructed where the conditions were 'right' and argued that in principle democratisation could take place in varying circumstances. The experiences of the 'third wave' – and some would say 'fourth wave' – pointed to the possibility of creating democratic governance in virtually every corner of the globe, though the Muslim countries of the Middle East and Central Asia appeared to be lagging behind, and in a variety of cultural settings. This led a succession of scholars to emphasise the importance of agency. In consequence the focus of study was less on cultural and economic pre-conditions than on the choices made by key social and political actors. There was, however, an awareness of the need to separate out the causes of democracy – why it emerges – from what makes it flourish, a distinction I will suggest later creates an opportunity to bring religion back into consideration (see, for example, Potter 1997).

Leaving aside the actor focus, much criticism was levelled at the way in which religion had been used in explaining political development. For Beetham, the trouble with all such 'negative' hypotheses about religion and democratisation is that they treated 'religions as monolithic, when their core doctrines are typically subject to a variety of schools of interpretation; and as immutable, when they are notoriously revisionist in the face of changing circumstances and political currents' (Potter 1997: 29). In a wide-ranging essay published in 2001 Alfred Stepan suggested that all religious traditions were multi-vocal, containing organisational and intellectual resources that could be called upon in support of democratic forms of governance. Thus, whilst Singapore's leaders might utilise 'Asian values' in defence of authoritarianism, Kim Dae Jung in South Korea could appeal to those same values in seeking to promote democratisation.

At the same time he noted that even political orientations that have sometimes been seen to work against democratisation can, on occasion, work the other way, as in the case of the Greek Orthodox Church whose tradition of subservience to the political authorities led it to become supportive of democracy once the political elite opted for pluralism (Stepan 2001) – though as we shall note later the attitude of that Church towards genuine pluralism is, on occasion, rather ambiguous even today.

Much of the discussion, however, has focused on Islam in response to the observation that the Muslim-dominated regions of the world have proved particularly resistant to democratisation. Whereas authors such as Huntington and Francis Fukuyama have stirred up considerable public debate with their tendency to see the religious and civilisational aspects of Islam as barriers to the inauguration and development of democracy, many scholars of the Middle East remain sceptical about the role of Islam (Huntington 1996; Fukuyama 1992: 44–45). For Fred Halliday,

> to be drawn into an argument about any necessary incompatibility, or for that matter compatibility, between Islam and democracy, is to accept precisely the false premise that there is one true, traditionally established 'Islamic' answer to the question, and that this timeless 'Islam' rules social and political practice. There is no such answer and no such 'Islam'. …
> If there are in a range of Islamic countries evident barriers to democracy, this has to do with certain other social and political features that their societies share. … Though some of these features tend to be legitimised in terms of Islamic doctrine, there is nothing specifically 'Islamic' about them.
>
> (Halliday 1996: 16)

Ray Hinnebusch (2000) takes a similar view in arguing that developments in political economy provide much better explanations for the failures of democratisation in the Middle East than appeals to cultural exceptionalism.

For many writers, there is no such thing as a single Islamic political tradition (Filali-Ansary 1999), and they suggest that within the varying Islamic traditions there were ample intellectual resources for those seeking to promote democratic governance. Though Ernest Gellner argued for a 'Muslim exceptionalism' he also recognised that 'by various obvious criteria – universalism, scripturalism, spiritual egalitarianism, the extension of full participation in the sacred community, not to one, or some, but to all, and the rational systematisation of social life – Islam is, of the three great Western monotheisms, the one closest to modernity' (quoted in Bromley 1997: 233) and, by implication therefore, the one closest in principle to democracy. Esposito and Voll point out that democracy was a contested term in the West, and it might well be possible to draw on Islamic traditions that were loyal to the core concern of democracy with participation whilst allowing it to take into account the specific concerns of Muslims for recognition of 'special identities or authentic communities' (Esposito and Voll 1996: 17). Like others, they pointed to the concepts of *shura* (consultation), *ijma* (consensus) and *ijtihad* (independent reasoning) as providing some intellectual basis for the development of Muslim democracies (Esposito and Voll 1996: 27–32). That such debates are not confined to the academy is demonstrated by recent political developments in Iran where during the 1990s a number of respected imams have joined leading academics in arguing that the politicisation of religion and its association with authoritarianism have only undermined the spiritual essence of Islam with its emphasis on righteous living by the individual, the promotion of justice by the

state and the right of all to participate in political life (Menashri 2001). One might also note the variety of organisational forms within Islamic societies, some of which have allowed for degrees of popular consultation, or point out that up to 40% of the world's Muslims do in fact live in countries that are more or less democratic – often as minorities – and that this might well encourage a more positive view of the democratic model (Stepan 2001: 236–237).

This more critical approach had almost become a new orthodoxy by the late 1990s. For Bromley, 'the very idea that religious belief can operate as an insuperable obstacle to a particular kind of politics, democracy, has been challenged on the grounds that all religions require interpretation to give them meaning in specific contexts. In this sense religious belief is socially and politically contingent, it does not and cannot determine or prescribe a certain kind of politics' (Bromley 1997: 321–344). In such circumstances, even if a specific religious tradition had historically helped to shape a particular country's political culture, one could not make assumptions about whether this was likely to favour or hinder democratisation. And this argument tied in with the growing assumption of many 'transitologists' that political culture was unhelpful in explaining anything, tended to serve as a 'residual' explanation for developments that institutional analysis or political economy had failed to comprehend. In other words, even if there were problematic elements within religious traditions, which few now accepted given the existence of 'positive' as well as 'negative' elements in each tradition, these were largely irrelevant to the outcomes of democratisation processes.

Correlations and explanations: the debate re-opened

In view of this critique, is there any sense in trying to factor religion into explanations of democratic outcomes? Clearly, there are problems with the thesis that certain religious traditions in themselves are more or less likely to contribute to transition processes or democracy promotion during the transition phase. Whilst religious groups have contributed to the undermining of authoritarian regimes, there are always counter-examples to be found, as in the support given to Central American dictators by some Protestant groups, or the fact that democratisation took place in Argentina and Chile despite the fact that the Catholic hierarchies in the two countries adopted very different positions with regard to military rulers. Contingent factors often play a key role, as in the Iberian peninsula where a highly conservative and anti-democratic Spanish Church, initially horrified by the outcome of Vatican II, underwent considerable personnel change as a result of the intervention of the papacy and the resident nuncio. In consequence, numerous auxiliary bishops sympathetic to liberalisation were appointed during the 1960s and went on to play a key role in shifting the Church away from its uncritical support for the Franco regime. By way of contrast, the papal nuncio in Portugal sympathised with the traditionalist approach of the hierarchy and the Catholic Church was largely marginalised during the events of the 1970s. There is also a certain mechanistic feel to the argument about any necessary link between religious adherence and democratisation, rather like Adam Przeworski's caricature of the position that universal suffrage was achieved in Western Europe when the proportion of the labour forces outside agriculture reached 50% and that such a social development might have similar consequences elsewhere (Przeworski 1986: 48). The religious corollary of this might be to suggest that the best ways to advance democratisation was via a renewal of the Crusades so as to promote Western Christianity.

Equally problematic are culturalist explanations which focus less on the immediate activities of religious groups than on the overall contribution of religious traditions to political cultures which may reinforce or undermine old authoritarian ways of doing politics. Even those who retain the view that political culture matters have problems isolating the ways in which religion may have contributed to its historical development. Did religion, particularly through the medium of a lettered clerisy, serve to shape the culture and ways of a nation, or was it religion that was shaped by the culture within which it found itself – or, more likely, both? For example, according to the Russian chronicles, Prince Vladimir of Kiev went looking for a religion that suited the character of the people of Rus' – and promptly rejected Islam because Russians like to drink! And even if religion was central to the formation of a country's political culture, to what extent is it relevant today, especially in those countries where religious adherence and participation has declined dramatically?

And yet, whilst it remains impossible to speak of some linear causal relationship between religious tradition and successful democratisation, there remains a nagging doubt that the seeming connection between religious inheritance and the success of democratisation goes beyond simple correlation. That there is a correlation is not in question. Though it is far too early for definitive conclusions, an impressionistic view of the post-communist world, for example, shows that as a general rule those countries with an Orthodox Christian or Islamic tradition have found it harder to consolidate their democratic experiments than those with a Western Christian inheritance. A more substantial analysis might be offered utilising the democracy ratings offered by Freedom House over recent years. Using their 2002 report I have divided countries into a variety of

Table 13.1 Religions and freedom

Religious tradition (no. of countries)	Freedom House score
Protestant (23)	1.65
Catholic (50)	1.83
Mixed: Prot.–Cath. (12)	1.83
Orthodox (12)	3.25
Hindu (2)	3.25
Mixed: Asian (12)	3.96
Mixed: African (30)	4.12
Buddhist (4)	4.63
Islam (39)	5.39

religious categories – inevitably my assignments will be contestable – assuming a single dominant tradition where over 60% of the population nominally adheres to a single-faith community. Inevitably, some of the categorisations are problematic – for example, in Africa the combinations vary considerably and include Catholicism, Protestantism, Islam and indigenous religious traditions in a variety of mixes – and the results are crude but they produce the results shown in Table 13.1, where the lower the score the freer the country.

Whilst it is difficult to disagree that democracy is strongest in countries of a Western Christian tradition and that it is generally weakest in those of a majority Islamic tradition, the question remains as to whether there is any causal relationship at work. As already noted, most writers have taken the view that:

- all religious traditions are multi-vocal and that would-be democrats and authoritarians can find or interpret elements within the tradition to support their own political preferences. Thus, just as Catholicism has adapted to democracy over recent years so might other traditions in areas of the globe currently under authoritarian rule;
- in any case religion is secondary in explaining democratisation to a host

of other factors. For example, in post-communist Europe the Orthodox and Islamic countries have found transition problematic but they are also the countries in which communism was most secure, where civil society was weakest and economic development lagged behind that of 'Western Christian' Central Europe – though equally it might be argued that the reason they 'lagged' was because of their cultural traditions;

- that the argument is predicated on a model of democracy created within Western society and built on assumptions about individualism and value-free politics which might be inappropriate in areas of the world where religious worldviews predominate.

The argument here, however, is that:

- democracy in general (as well as Western liberal democracy in particular) does have core meanings and that some religious traditions may have problems reconciling themselves to these;
- religions are indeed multi-vocal but that at any point in time there may be a dominant discourse and practice that renders them more or less supportive of certain patterns of political development;
- though critics are right in arguing that religious tradition is not central or determining, indeed often marginal, religion is not irrelevant to outcomes, and that in the short term what tradition is dominant in a country may – subconsciously or as deliberately fostered by religious and/or secular leaders – help to shape the outcome of democratisation processes.

Democracy for all occasions

Esposito and Voll (1996) remind us that democracy is a contested concept in the West and that therefore it should in principle be possible for other types of society, in particular Muslim, to come up with participatory schemes that allow for the recognition of 'special identities and authentic communities'. Moreover, in Western systems of liberal democracy there are tensions between the liberal and democratic elements that are reflected in some Muslim writings. Whilst most Muslim thinkers would accept some notion of the rule of law, fewer would be happy about the notion of those laws being created by the will of a majority in a democratically elected legislature. Or if permitted there would be, as remains the case in contemporary Iran, some provision for the religious elite to over-rule the legislature by retaining control over candidacies or the effective right to veto undesirable legislation – though arguably the US Supreme Court does the same thing with reference to America's own foundational documents.

So, of course, the Western model is not the only possible line of development for forms of democratic governance. Nonetheless, democracy does have some core meanings and a dangerous conceptual stretch may creep in, allowing virtually any political order to be described as in some sense democratic. All understandings of democracy have at their heart notions of participation, competition, consent and the protection of individual and minority rights. How these are organised or structured may not matter but that they are present in some form does. In all existing democracies this raises dilemmas, but it may create far more in some cultural and religious contexts than others. Hence it may be possible to find structural forms that recognise communal identities, but if these are accompanied by restrictions on the rights of other communities or groups or individuals it is not clear that this is compatible with a meaningful evolution of democracy in the long term. And if those with a direct line to the divine, which in principle should be all believers in traditional Protestantism and Islam but in practice is often limited to a clerical (often male) elite, claim the right to 'trump' democratic decision-making then we have a problem. This is a discussion for another context, but clearly whilst the possibility of an Islamic model of democracy should not be ruled out, it becomes meaningless, as in Soviet-style 'socialist democracy', if its practice blatantly contradicts the core elements of liberal democracy in denying participation or rights to sections of the population.

The limits of religious multi-vocality

Many authors have stressed that all religious belief systems contain within them resources that can be used to promote different visions of the most appropriate political order, with Bromley noting that all religions require interpretation 'to give them meaning in specific contexts' (Bromley 1997: 333). In Stepan's words all religious traditions are multi-vocal and contain intellectual and organisational resources that might be used to promote political pluralism. Though correct, such arguments tend to focus on 'theological' debates or rely on interviews on religious leaders out of power and as such offer only a partial aid. In the political 'real' world one has to deal with 'actually existing' systems and ideological tendencies, not the interpretations of a handful of 'liberally' inclined intellectuals. During the Cold War there were those who argued that Marxism had never been tried properly, which may or may not have been true, but the bottom line was that virtually all of the functioning 'Marxist' systems had ended in authoritarianism of one form or another. What was important was not whether these were false applications of the theory, but the fact that these were the type of political orders that had actually emerged in these societies. In just the same way we have first to deal with 'actually existing' Protestantism, Catholicism, Orthodoxy, Islam, Judaism, Confucianism etc. As Halliday points out in the case of Islam, there is no monolithic system that one can isolate but, as Bruce has countered, there are surely core elements that help to differentiate one religious tradition from another (Bruce 2003: 216–218). In consequence – and without denying the possibility of major changes, as happened within Catholicism during the post-war years - we have to look less at what might be than at what in practice are the dominant themes or arguments within a religious tradition at any particular time and how these might impact upon the political order. For reasons of space our focus here will be on Eastern Orthodoxy and Islam.

We have already suggested that in the post-communist world democratic governance has struggled to take root in those countries with an Orthodox tradition, and several writers have argued that there are elements within the Orthodox tradition that sit uneasily with democratic politics, and that have thus prevented Orthodox Churches from making a significant contribution to democratisation. With a theology geared more towards liturgy than social practice, and towards heaven rather than earth, the Orthodox Church has tended intellectually (if not always in practice) to treat the social order with a degree of disdain – the troubles of this time are as nothing when compared to the centuries in which the Church thinks. Consequently, Orthodox churches have been able to adapt to a variety of political

regimes, from the Ottoman Empire of the past to the communist regimes of the twentieth century.

In the Russian case the Orthodox Church on the eve of the revolution still lacked many of the 'potentialities' enjoyed by the Western churches. Social theology was weakly developed and, as Richard Sakwa has pointed out, the core notion of 'sobornost', with its implicit rejection of the distinction between separate spheres of state and society – an absence that some would argue is also found in much Muslim social thought – worked against the creation of a liberal-democratic ideology (Sakwa 1994). The Church also lacked the wide array of clerical and lay institutions and associations that underlay the creation of Christian social movements in Western Europe at the end of the nineteenth century. In 1917, as today, the Russian Orthodox Church had a mass nominal following, but was largely cut off from the broad current of social change and found it hard to mobilise would-be adherents. And then, as later, the Church's reputation had been weakened by past compromises with the state order. During the communist period the Church was forced by circumstances to fall back on liturgical celebration and the struggle for survival in the face of a hostile regime. Despite some involvement with the ecumenical movement, the East European Orthodox churches had limited opportunities to develop a social theology and there was no equivalent of Vatican II to galvanise the church into rethinking its relationship with the world in the modern era. The 1918 Church Council (Sobor) might have served that purpose but this possibility was removed by the Bolshevik revolution. Thus the religious component of Russian and Balkan political culture experienced little change, and was perhaps reinforced by the hierarchic, authoritarian and collectivist nature of communist rule which in turn developed quasi-religious rituals for its own mobilising and legitimising ends. At the same time, Soviet rule destroyed the last opportunities for religious influence over political development and created an extremely defensive church. The institution that survived through 1991 in many ways remained rooted in the past, hierarchical and paternalistic, and suspicious of diversity (Anderson 1994). This is not to deny the difficulties that the church faced or the presence of reformist trends within the institution, but to note that the dominant voices within the Orthodox churches of Russia and the Balkans remained wary of the new order being created and its consequences for themselves. This stemmed in large part from an ideological suspicion and critique of the consequences of pluralism and liberalism which were seen as in some sense undermining Orthodoxy's very 'way of being' (Witte and Bourdeaux 1999: 19–20).

Such reactions were not confined to the post-communist Eastern churches, for in Greece religious identity questions again sprang to life at the turn of the century. Despite Stepan's comments about the adaptation of the Greek Orthodox to democracy (Stepan 2001: 247–250), the reaction of leading hierarchs and church organisations to issues of religious liberty, the removal of the religious question from Greek identity cards, and debates over the European Union during the 1990s and beyond (Anderson 2003), indicate that the Church remains defensive and wary of some of the consequences of democratic politics. What all this suggests is that whilst Orthodoxy social teaching does not preclude or oppose democratisation, there are elements within its actual outworkings at the present moment – focusing on the unity of society, the necessary link between faith and nation, distrust of difference – that are not always helpful for democratic development.

In many respects similar things can be said about the role of Islam in societies where it remains the sole or dominant religious tradition. As noted earlier, many scholars have argued that there is no single, monolithic or essentialist Islam to which one can refer and that Islamic teachings contain resources that could be used to promote pluralistic politics. Islam has all too often been coopted by authoritarian leaders for their own ends – and Ayubi points out that, historically, Muslim regimes were built on the remnants of the authoritarian empires they conquered and that this inheritance, rather than Islam, accounts for the type of political orders that emerged in much of the Middle East (Ayubi 1991: 32). At the same time, pluralism of a sort has emerged in a number of predominantly Muslim states – most notably Turkey, Indonesia and, to some extent, in Iran. Quite rightly such authors point to various red-herrings utilised to promote the view of Islam as inherently anti-democratic, notably the idea that Islam has no tradition of the separation of the religious and the political sphere which tends to underlie contemporary democratic orders. Nonetheless, it might still be argued that there remain elements within 'actually existing Islam' – within the tradition as presently constituted and realised in the world – that are problematic for democratic development.

At the ideological level there remain features of contemporary Islam that may be unhelpful for processes of democratisation. For Steve Bruce, one fundamental problem lies in the focus on way of life rather than theology, on orthopraxy rather than orthodoxy:

> Rule bound religions are *inevitably* more conservative than ones that do not embed divine revelation in a legal code. This follows simply from the fact that rules were written in the past. ... Putting it bluntly ... a society governed by rules written ten centuries ago will be less pleasant than a society that can evolve. ...

The centrality of shariah to Islam does not prevent interpretation but it does restrict it. In contrast Christianity has no choice but to be metaphorical about its teachings.

(Bruce 2003: 243–238)

This distinction is perhaps too facile, insofar as medieval Catholicism and New England Puritanism could be pretty unbending towards those who transgressed moral rules as well as theological orthodoxy, but it does isolate a structural feature of many, though not all, variants of the Islamicist vision. Many such movements claim to be seeking a 'restoration' of an idealised past where sharia rules dominated and where, unlike in the New Testament, there is as much emphasis on what one should do as on what one should not do.

There is also some suggestion that the greater emphasis given to the community over the individual may be problematic for, whilst democratic governance can encompass forms of communal or group representation, defining which groups should be represented remains fraught with difficulty. Of particular concern to most observers of Islamic thought and practice are issues relating to individual and minority rights. Whatever the arguments of liberal Muslim thinkers, there remain deep ambiguities about the extent to which minority rights are guaranteed and protected in those countries where Islam dominates. This is not just a case of authoritarian leaders utilising Islam to justify their own abuses but something more fundamental. As Ann Mayer has shown, many of the major thinkers who have influenced emerging Islamicist movements as well as the constitutions and proclamations of Muslim states on human rights issues tend to hedge guarantees to right with qualifications when it comes to issues relating to gender, minorities and religious difference. Whilst the populations of these countries generally aspire

to human rights protection, those who rule or aspire to rule, and many within the 'clerical' elite, would argue that so-called universal principles of rights are being imposed from a Western cultural context and have to be adapted to local circumstances and value systems (Mayer 1995). This may well be, but liberal democracy as commonly understood requires not just participation and competition but, crucially, protection of the rights of minorities and individuals. Whilst there may be legitimate debate about the boundaries of rights in different cultural contexts, the general assumption of international declarations and mainstream democratic thought is that rights should be extended even to those who the majority find alien or even abhorrent. So whilst many Muslims may aspire to democracy and intellectuals may find supportive elements within the tradition, the dominant ideological trends at present remain problematic and tend not to offer strong support for democratic change – which is not to say they might not do so in the future.

There may also be problems at the political level in the weakness of those forces committed to democracy within the Muslim countries. Recent years have seen the emergence of human rights groups in a number of these countries and a number have liberalised to some degree, allowing the appearance of an embryonic civil society if not full political participation (Norton 1995, 1996). But the reality remains that these groups are weak in most cases and 'liberal' intellectuals generally have limited influence, especially when they find themselves in competition with more radical groups. Formally many Islamicist opposition groups claim to be committed to a more genuinely democratic order than currently exists in their own countries though, as suggested above, ambiguities remain when explaining how their visions will affect those who dissent or differ – and the experience of the three purportedly Islamicist states (Iran, Sudan and Afghanistan) has not been positive in this respect. More important may be the fact that they often reject the implantation of political forms created in a West they increasingly despise for both its corrupt lifestyles and perceived negative impact upon their own region or countries. In so doing they repeat the mistakes of those socialists during the immediate post-war years who in legitimately criticising the failures of 'bourgeois democracy' neglected the importance of the civil rights guaranteed by such orders. Instead, they look to an idealised past. At the same time writers such as Graham Fuller have suggested that in the long term recognition of the limits of revolutionary adventurism as well as participation within partially liberalised political orders may in some sense 'tame' Islamicist groups or, as has happened in Iran, demonstrate that the guarantees of liberal democracy are not without positive benefit for their respective causes and populations (Fuller 2003: 193–213).

Where does religion make a difference?

Even if at certain points in time the dominant voice in a religious tradition is more likely to promote or inhibit democratisation does this really matter given religion's marginality in most democratisation processes? After all, most sources see transition coming as a result of changes in elite configurations and perceptions, as a product of socio-economic development, or in response to crises. Religious communities or leaders may play a role in undermining authoritarian regimes but their activism may in turn come as a response to wider social change, or arise from the need to protect their economic, class or institutional interests. So whilst one can argue that specific religious groups made contributions to democratisation in some

circumstances (Poland, the Philippines, or perhaps Brazil and Chile) this tells us nothing about the impact of broad traditions rather than specific organisations or hierarchies. Even the Catholic contribution to the 'third wave' has to be treated with some caution because, whilst many Catholic hierarchies took a prominent role as critic of authoritarian regimes and defender of civil society, some (e.g. in Argentina) adopted an ambiguous position in relation to authoritarian regimes. Though a majority of these transitions took place in 'Catholic countries', this may have had more to do with their similar levels of economic development and place in the world economy than the fact that they were 'Catholic'. Nonetheless, it is the case that the 1960s and 1970s witnessed significant changes in Catholic thinking on the political order and pluralist politics which led to changes in the relationship between national hierarchies and the state in many Catholic countries and which in turn may have impacted upon local political cultures. In many those cultures were predominantly hierarchical and authoritarian, a tendency reinforced by pre-Vatican II-style Catholicism. Changes within the religious institution and its more 'democratic' way of functioning – at least at lower levels – may have contributed towards an undermining of political cultures which had long inhibited, though in themselves prevented, democratic political change.

Conversely, in virtually no countries where Eastern Orthodoxy or Islam predominated – with the possible exception of Indonesia – have religious establishments or oppositions emerged as prominent promoters of democratisation. In the Orthodox case, a few individual priests or bishops may have spoken out about human rights abuses or called for the observance of human rights under the communist regime, but leaders of these churches generally collaborated in suppressing such voices and did not publicly argue for liberalisation. In the Islamic context, various groups have promoted their own visions of the good society but they have not generally been prominent actors in stressing transition to more pluralistic political orders as amongst their key priorities. In other words, we would appear to have some of Weber's 'correlations between forms of religious beliefs and practical ethics'.

The significance of these 'correlations' is harder to assess. It does appear to be the case the religious tradition, as it has evolved at certain points in history, plays some role in determining whether 'ecclesial' actors will actively promote democracy, sit on the side lines or actively oppose democratisation – though it does not guarantee that they will do the same in every case. It is perhaps more important to pursue the notion that specific traditions, as opposed to particular institutions or individuals, may have more of an impact on the 'consolidation' phase. Though there are many other factors at work in explaining the problems of democratisation in some of the post-Soviet countries – economic decline, poor institutional design, lack of elite commitment – historical and cultural inheritances often make the task harder. To the extent that religious tradition has contributed to the formation of that inheritance, religion may continue to have an influence even in societies where religious practice and political influence are significantly diminished. Assessing the role of political culture is always problematic, as is evaluating religion's contribution to that culture, but arguably both Eastern Orthodoxy and Islam in most of the countries of the former Soviet Union and Balkans have reinforced communalist and authoritarian traditions that are wary of social and religious pluralism. And the behaviour of religious elites since 1990 – in seeking to curtail religious freedom, acquire political

influence or engage in rather dubious economic activities – has tended to reinforce these older patterns rather than those that might be supportive of democratic development. It is not that practising believers – who in these countries generally make up a small minority of the population – are less favourably disposed to democracy than other citizens (White, *et al.* 1994; Vorontsova and Filatov 1994; Fletcher and Sergeyev 2002), but that the way in which religion has fed into the wider political culture over time has up to now tended to favour the 'wrong' elements within the political culture of some of these countries.

My argument, therefore, has not been that religious tradition determines the likelihood of democratisation or its successful implementation in any specific country or region, nor do I deny that in most cases other factors are far more important in explaining both transition and the success or otherwise of democratisation. Instead it has been to suggest that the 'correlations' that do exist are not purely accidental and that, though religious traditions are multi-vocal, at any one point in time the dominant voices and practical political circumstances may work more or less in support of democratisation efforts. That this is still a live debate is evident in the continuing and often heated discussions over the role of Islam in inhibiting democratisation but also in recent debates over the likely impact of Protestant–Pentecostal expansion in Latin America, Africa and Asia. For David Martin, it may be the case that this new 'enthusiastic' religion 'will perform a service akin to Methodism in preparing working and lower middle class people for the frugal enjoyment of prosperity, polite public discourse and democratic citizenship' (Martin 1990) – though Gill (1998) sees little attitudinal difference between Catholics and Protestants on public issues. Others are more wary, seeing the circumstances as very different from those of late eighteenth-century Britain, and stress the deeply 'conservative' political style of the neo-Pentecostal movements (Brouwer, et al. 1996: 230). Here is not the place to explore this particular debate but it serves as a useful reminder that there are still interesting problems that need further examination in assessing whether particular religious traditions do impact upon the prospects for successful democratisation and, if so, how. For the time being, the rather weak conclusion of this chapter is that religious tradition still matters, albeit often indirectly, and does so as much by ruling out certain ways of 'doing politics' or setting cultural constraints on politicians seeking to advance the cause of democratisation as by prescribing any specific political form. Religious tradition cannot determine outcomes, but when the factors working for or against democratisation are finely balanced, then whose god is prevalent may just make a difference.

Note

1 First published in *Democratization*, 11, 4 (2004).

Bibliography

Anderson, J. (1994) *Religion, State and Society in the Soviet Union and the Successor States*, Cambridge: Cambridge University Press.

Anderson, J. (2003) *Religious Liberty in Transitional Societies: The Politics of Religion*, Cambridge: Cambridge University Press.

Ayubi, N. (1991) *Political Islam: Religion and Politics in the Arab World*, London: Routledge.

Batt, C. (2001) *Hindu Nationalism: Origins, Ideologies and Modern Myths*, Oxford: Berg.

Benedict, P. (1996) 'Une roi, ine loi, deux fois', in O.P. Grell and B. Scribner (eds), *Tolerance and Intolerance in the European Reformation*, Cambridge: Cambridge University Press, pp. 69–93.

Bromley, S. (1997) 'Middle East exceptionalism', in D. Potter (ed.), *Democratization*, Cambridge: Polity, pp. 321–44.

Brouwer, S., Gifford, P. and Rose, S. (1996) *Exporting the American Gospel: Global Christian Fundamentalism*, London: Routledge.

Bruce, S. (2003) *Politics and Religion*, Cambridge: Polity.

Cargill Thompson, W.D.J. (1984) *The Political Thought of Martin Luther*, Brighton: Harvester.

Dealy, G. (1992) 'The tradition of monistic democracy in Latin America', in H. Wiarda (ed.), *Politics and Social Change in Latin America: Still a Distinct Tradition?*, Boulder: Westview Press, pp. 40–60.

Esposito, J. and Voll, J. (1996) *Islam and Democracy*, Oxford: Oxford University Press.

Filali-Ansary, A. (1999) 'Muslims and democracy', *Journal of Democracy*, 10, 3, pp. 18–32.

Fletcher, J. and Sergeyev, B. (2002) 'Islam and intolerance on Central Asia: the case of kyrgyzstan', *Europe–Asia Studies*, 54, 2, pp. 251–7.

Fukuyama, F. (1992) *The End of History and the Last Man*, London: Penguin Books.

Fuller, G. (2003) *The Future of Political Islam*, New York: Palgrave.

Gill, A. (1998) *Rendering unto Caesar: The Catholic Church and the State in Latin America*, Chicago: University of Chicago Press.

Halliday, F. (1996) *Islam and the Myth of Confrontation*, London: Tauris.

Hansen, T. (1999) *The Saffron Wave: Democracy and Hindu Nationalism in Modern India*, Princeton: Princeton University Press.

Haynes, J. (1996) *Religion and Politics in Africa*, London: Zed Books.

Hinnebusch, R. (2000) 'Liberalization without democratization in "post-populist" authoritarian states', in N. Butenschon, U. Davis and M. Hassassian (eds), *Citizenship and the State in the Middle East*, New York: Syracuse University Press, pp. 123–45.

Huntington, S. (1991) *The Third Wave: Democratization in the Late Twentieth Century*, Norman: University of Oklahoma Press.

Huntington, S. (1996) *The Clash of Civilizations and the Remaking of World Order*, New York: Simon & Schuster.

Inglehart, R. and Carballo, M. (2000) 'Does Latin America exist? (And is there a Confucian Culture?): a global analysis of cross-cultural differences', in L. Crothers and C. Lockhart (eds), *Culture and Politics: A Reader*, New York: St Martin's Press, pp. 325–47.

Kedourie, E. (1992) *Politics in the Middle East*, Oxford: Oxford University Press.

Kingdom, R. (1991) 'Calvinism and resistance theory', in J.H. Burns (ed.), *The Cambridge History of Political Thought, 1450–1700*, Cambridge: Cambridge University Press, pp. 193–218.

Kingdom, R. and Linder, R. (eds) (1970) *Calvin and Calvinism: Sources of Democracy*, Lexington: D.C. Heath.

Kleiber, J. (1998) *The Church, Dictatorship and Democracy in Latin America*, New York: Orbis Books.

Koyziz, D. (1993) 'Imaging God and his kingdom: Eastern Orthodoxy's iconic political ethic', *Review of Politics*, 55, pp. 267–89.

Linz, J. and Stepan, A. (1996) *Problems of Democratic Transition and Consolidation: Southern Europe, South America and Post-Communist Europe*, Baltimore: Johns Hopkins University Press.

Martin, D. (1990) *Tongues of Fire: The Explosion of Protestantism in Latin America*, Oxford: Blackwell.

Mayer, A. (1995) *Islam and Human Rights*, Boulder: Westview.

Menashri, D. (2001) *Post-Revolutionary Politics in Iran: Religion, Society and Power*, London: Frank Cass.

Norton, A. (ed.) (1995, 1996) *Civil Society in the Middle East*, 2 volumes, Leiden and New York: E.J. Brill.

Potter, D. (1997) 'Explaining democratization', in D. Potter (ed.), *Democratization*, Cambridge: Polity, pp. 1–40.

Przeworski, A. (1986) 'Some problems in the study of transitions to democracy', in G. O'Donnell (ed.), *Transitions from Authoritarian Rule: Comparative Perspectives*, London: Johns Hopkins University Press, pp. 47–63.

Pye, L. (1985) *Asian Power and Politics: The Cultural Dimensions of Authority*, Cambridge: Harvard University Press.

Sakwa, R. (1994) 'Christian democracy and civil society in Russia', *Religion, State and Society*, 22, 3, pp. 273–304.

Sigmund, P. (1987) 'The Catholic tradition and modern democracy', *Review of Politics*, 49, 4, pp. 530–48.

Sigmund, P. (1994) 'Christian democracy, liberation theology and political culture in Latin America', in L. Diamond (ed.), *Political Culture and Democracy in Developing Countries*, Boulder: Lynne Reinner, pp. 211–28.

Stepan, A. (2001) 'The world's religious system and democracy: Crafting the "twin tolerations"', in A. Stepan, *Arguing Comparative Politics*, Oxford: Oxford University Press, pp. 213–53.

Vatikiotis, P. (1987) *Islam and the State*, London: Routledge.

Vorontsova, L. and Filatov, S. (1994) 'The changing pattern of religious belief: perestroika and beyond', *Religion, State and Society*, 22, 1, pp. 73–96.

Weber, M. (1930) [1904] *The Protestant Ethic and the Spirit of Capitalism*, London: George Allen and Unwin.

White, S., McAllister, I. and Kryshtanovskaya, O. (1994) 'Religion and politics in post-communist Russia', *Religion, State and Society*, 22, 1, pp. 73–88.

Witte, J. and Bourdeaux, M. (eds) (1999) *Proselytism and Orthodoxy in Russia: The New War for Souls*, New York: Orbis.

Wuthnow, R. (1989) *Communities of Discourse: Ideology and Social Structure in the Reformation, the Enlightenment and European Socialism*, London: Harvard University Press.

14

Religion and political parties

Payam Mohseni and Clyde Wilcox

Political events in the 1980s reminded social scientists of the power of religion to influence parties and social movements. The Iranian revolution showed that a religious movement could overthrow a regime once seen as the exemplar of secularization in the region (Brumberg 2001; Siavoshi 2002). The rise of the Christian Right in the United States showed how religious movements can evolve along with political parties (Wilcox 2007a), changing both in the process. The role of the Pope and the Catholic Church in supporting Solidarity in Poland showed the power of religious groups to mount movements and parties that challenge non-democratic regimes; the Church's more complex role with post-independence political parties in Poland showed that democracy does not simplify the relationships between religious institutions and parties (Byrnes 2002).

Modernization and secularization theories which predicted that the importance of religion on politics would decline failed to explain the resurgence of religion in many political systems, and have channelled scholarly attention away from religious politics (Gill 2001; Wald and Wilcox 2006). Although secularization has clearly occurred in many countries (Norris and Inglehart 2004), there has been a substantial revival of religion in many parts of the globe (Finke and Stark 1992; Stark 1999). The impact of religion on politics has not

declined but, rather, changed in complex ways (Bruce 2003; Casanova 1994), while the separation of religion and state has paradoxically decreased with higher socio-economic development throughout the world (Fox 2006).

In this chapter, we consider the relationship between religion and political parties. Although there are a number of studies of religion and parties in particular nations, there is less comparative analysis, in part because of the complex variety of relationships in play. Consider just a few examples:

- In officially secular India, the Hindu nationalist party BJP came to power after staging a 10,000-kilometre march that sought to destroy an ancient mosque that was alleged to be built on the remains of Rama's temple (Sahu 2002).
- In the United States, known for separation of church and state, candidates of both parties make speeches from church pulpits. Today candidates from both parties speak openly of their faith and its implication for their policies.
- In Turkey, a secular state with a large Muslim majority, parties that are insufficiently secular are banned (Koçak and Örücü 2003). The ruling party – the Justice and Development

Party (AKP) – is mildly Islamist, but balances its rhetoric with the secular goals of many national actors.

- In the Netherlands, three confessional parties once represented distinctive pillars of politics. These three parties merged in 1980 but their strength declined with secularization (Lacardie 2004). By 2002, a new party that focused anger toward Muslim immigrants became for a time the largest party (Van Holsteyn and Irwin 2003).
- In Japan, a secular society where citizens mix elements of Buddhism and Shinto, one faction of the ruling LDP is especially open to Shinto nationalism. The internal party cleavage is symbolized by visits of the Prime Minister to a shrine to the war dead (Toyoda and Tanaka 2002).

These cases obviously differ greatly along many dimensions. Some feature religious parties, in other cases religious citizens are factions in a party, or secular citizens react to immigration by those of another faith. We do not seek here to offer a comprehensive theory of religion and political parties. Instead, we begin with a discussion of the various ways that religion and political parties can intersect, and then consider three sets of cases that have provoked considerable scholarship in recent years – Christian Democratic parties in Europe, religion and parties in the United States, and Islamic parties in the Middle East.[1]

Religion and political parties: a theoretical overview

Any comparative discussion of religion and political parties is complicated because of conceptual difficulties with both terms. Religious institutions can include hierarchical bodies like the Catholic Church,

which can negotiate separate agreements with political leaders in different countries (Byrnes 2002; Manuel et al. 2006), and institutions in more decentralized traditions such as Sunni Islam and evangelical Protestantism. Institutions can mean the top leadership of denominations, or specific congregations (Wald et al. 1988; Wald et al. 1990).

But religion is more than institutions. Religious bodies and traditions can spawn an 'associational nexus' that support religious parties (Rosenblum 2003). Lay activists in the Catholic Church in Europe created civil society organizations that were linked to the Church in various ways, and this in turn led to the formation of Christian Democratic parties, sometimes against the opposition of Church leaders. In the US, social and political groups channel religious enthusiasm toward political parties, and in India Hindu social groups rather than religious institutions sparked the rise of the BJP. On the other hand, religious parties can also create their associational nexus, as Hezbollah has done in Lebanon (Deeb 2006; Harb and Leenders 2005).

Finally, religion can provide the energy to social movements that seek to change the assumptions, values and routines of society (Wilcox 2007b). These social movements can spark political parties, but parties can also help to spark social movements by channelling resources. These social movements can cut across religious institutions, and they can occur without active support from religious leaders – indeed they can occur despite their strong opposition.

Political parties might appear at first to be easier to define. Scholars generally agree that parties create programmes and ideological packages that articulate societal goals, aggregate and articulate societal interests, mobilize the public and recruit elites who stand for the party in elections (von Beyme 1996: 135; Harmel and Robertson 1985). But in practice, parties are more difficult to distinguish from other political groups. In many multi-party systems, minor parties form and dissolve as quickly as other political organizations (Norris 2005), while religious social movements may recruit candidates and support them within parties to try to win office (Rozell and Wilcox 1996). In many countries, religious groups act as 'indirect parties' (Duverger 1963).

Moreover, recognizing religious parties is more complex than it might initially seem. Although many political parties have standing programmes that can be analysed, increasingly parties are using these programmes as electoral vehicles to attract votes and thus using secular language to state their goals (Budge *et al.* 2001). Many religious parties have secularized over time, while officially secular political parties have developed a stronger tie with religious groups (Vassallo and Wilcox 2005). In some countries, such as Turkey, explicitly religious parties are barred, but some secular parties nevertheless make implicit and explicit religious appeals. And even explicitly religious parties frequently win power with non-religious appeals, including those based on class and economic policy: the Front Islamique du Salut (FIS) in Algeria used economic class appeals to win votes (Chhibber 1996), the Bharatiya Janata Party (BJP) in India won power in part by its critique of ruling party economic policies (Chhibber 1997), and religious parties in Israel frequently win votes through policies toward school, housing and other issues (Sharkansky 2000). Meanwhile, secular parties may compete for the votes of religious citizens by couching their programmes in moral language, even using specifically religious language in narrowly cast communications (e.g. through mail or phone) (Wilcox and Robinson 2007a).

Religious parties may vary in their support for democratic institutions and practices, and thus some may be conceived as

not parties, but rather vehicles for the elimination of parties. Some Catholic parties in the inter-war period in Europe sought to end democratic governance (Bruce 2003), and there is a lively debate today over whether Islamic parties will be supportive of democratic processes if or when they win power (Jenkins 2003; Kalyvas 2000).

But religious influence on parties does not end with religious parties. Sometimes religious bodies and associations stand outside the party system to pressurize all parties, trying to structure the constitution or the political debate as a societal force, as has been the case in Poland (Byrnes 2002). In other cases, political parties may align with different religious groups, and/or compete for the allegiance of some religious voters, as has been the case in the United States (Layman 2001; Wilcox and Robinson 2007c).

Moreover, religion can influence party systems whereby explicitly secular parties are created in opposition to religious forces. This has been true in southern Europe, in Turkey, and to a certain extent in the United States, as the evangelical mobilization into politics has pushed seculars to the Democratic side (Bolce and DeMaio 2007). And many right-wing parties in Europe have adopted anti-Muslim slogans (Rydgren 2004). In summary, the relation between religion and political parties is complex because of the multiple ways in which religion can be analysed – doctrinally, institutionally and socially – and the diverse configurations that can form between religion and political parties. Therefore, an analytical framework is needed in order to approach this topic more theoretically in a comparative perspective.

A framework for the study of religion and political parties

Most research on religion and political parties has centred on Western Europe, and in other Western liberal democracies. This work has frequently focused on the way that political parties develop to compete along the main social divisions, or cleavages, in a country. Lipset and Rokkan (1967) suggest that there are four main cleavages in Western societies that are sources of conflict: the centre–periphery divide, the church–state divide, the land–industry cleavage, and the divide between the capitalists and workers. They argue that the class cleavage is most important and predict that class will gain in importance as other pre-modern cleavages, such as religion, disappear. Some observers have reported declining salience of religion for voting in Europe, although evidence is clearly mixed (Dalton 2002; Dogan 1995; Kotler-Berkowitz 2001; Norris 2004).

The view of religion as one of several social cleavages remains the dominant model for political party analysis, particularly in democratic polities (Lijphart 1999). Yet Rosenblum (2003: 30) argues that 'The standard thesis on party formation simply assumes that where religious cleavages are politically salient, religious-based parties will arise. This leaves the black box of party-formation unopened.' The standard thesis may not be helpful in understanding the rise of the BJP in India at a time when religious cleavages were not especially high (Chhibber 1997), or the emergence of two parties representing Shi'ite religious interests (Amal and Hezbollah) in Lebanon. And it does little to help us understand the prominence of religious actors in Republican party politics since the 1980s in the USA.

Several key factors must be considered in order to fully understand the relationship between religion and political parties:

Regime type

Although most work on religion and political parties has focused on liberal democracies for obvious reasons, religious parties also operate in secular competitive authoritarian regimes that hold elections, such as Jordan and Yemen. They exist in theocratic regimes that hold elections, such as Iran, and do not in sultanistic religious regimes, such as Saudi Arabia and Afghanistan under the Taliban. Parties may perform different tasks in non-democratic systems, but recognizing them as parties allows us to broaden our thinking about parties and religion.

Religious marketplace

Religious cleavages come from religious differences, but nations differ in the type of religious differences that might be politically relevant. Many nations (such as Shi'a Islamic Iran and Catholic Poland) have overwhelming religious majorities, but voters divide on how much direct influence religious institutions should have on politics (Byrnes 2002; Siavoshi 2002). In other countries, such as Turkey, an overwhelming majority of religious citizens share a particular faith, but there are strong anti-clerical elements in politics, and a religious–secular divide. In other countries such as Belgium and Brazil, a religious majority is challenged by a new faith, either via conversion or immigration (Fetzer and Soper 2005; Gill 1998). Elsewhere, for example in India and Japan, different religious traditions may compete or cooperate (Sahu 2002; Toyoda and Tanaka 2002). And in a few countries such as the US, there are many competing religious traditions vying to define the dominant values of the society.

Religious institutional structure

Some religious institutions are in a better position to bargain with political parties than others. In particular, scholars have argued that the Catholic Church as a hierarchical (and non-democratic) institution is better situated to negotiate the realm of democratic politics than more decentralized faiths such as Protestant evangelicalism and Islam (Jelen and Wilcox 2002; Kalyvas 2000). Some scholars have even portrayed the Catholic Church as a rational actor negotiating with the state, constrained by paths previously taken in national history (Warner 2000). Kalyvas (2000) argues that Islamic parties, such as the Islamic Salvation Front (FIS) in Algeria, are less likely to be able to integrate into a democratic polity because of the less hierarchical nature of Islamic religious institutions.

The associational nexus of religion and political parties

Religious institutions generally create a host of associations that are involved in community and charitable work, that help to organize social life, and provide a supplement to religious activities. Churches, temples and mosques sponsor schools, sports associations, prayer groups, hospitals, service organizations to the poor and elderly and special ministries. Religious enthusiasts may create social movements with related associations that try to change societal views and policies.

It is from these lay groups that religious parties typically spring (Kalyvas 1996), and it is from them that pressure is exerted on existing parties to adopt religiously based policies (Wilcox and Robinson 2007b). The interests of the associational nexus of religion may differ from those of official religious elites, who may oppose the formation of religious parties or the alliance with more secular parties because they will likely lose control of the religious message. By entering into the political process, religious organizations change, with some becoming 'acculturated' to democratic norms. 'By means of the associational nexus religious parties integrate political activity with social and spiritual life. Seen as part of this web of associations with overlapping affiliations, religious parties

appear more like membership groups than other parties' (Rosenblum 2003: 33)

Political parties can create their own associational nexus as well, frequently creating groups specifically to appeal to particular types of voters – including religious ones. There are cases in which religious parties not only establish and institutionalize an associational nexus but also instigate and lead an entire social movement, such as Hezbollah in Lebanon. It is often difficult to distinguish between associations spawned by religious organizations and activists and those created by political parties.

The nature of the party system

Party systems vary across countries, changing greatly the incentives for religious activists and political activists to interact in particular ways. Various electoral rules produce incentives for parties to form, or for interests to work with larger, catch-all parties (Blais and Massicotte 2002; Felsenthal 1992; Norris 2004). Path-dependent trajectories of party development, and party response to minor party encroachment, can also influence the way that religion affects parties. For all of these reasons, religious institutions and activists are more likely to back established parties in some countries, creating factions which support religious agendas, and more likely to form political parties in other countries – and in some cases (e.g. Israel), multiple parties.

The stance of religious groups toward the state and government

Religious organizations vary in their stance toward the state and government. Some early Catholic parties in the inter-war period endorsed an end to democratic elections, and backed authoritarian movements in various European countries. Some Islamic parties similarly endorse Islamic

215

states with theocratic rule (Tamadonfar 2002). History suggests that Catholic parties became viable democratic actors as a result of engagement in the political realm. Whether Islamic parties can similarly accommodate to democratic norms constitutes one of the critical debates in the field of democratization today.

Religious groups that support democratic involvement vary in their prophetic stance against government policies. In many countries, churches and other formal religious institutions are established, funded by the government – and in some cases government has some control over the content of sermons. In other cases, religious parties may define a prophetic critique of government policies when in the opposition, but change their focus when they join a majority coalition. When religious groups form or support a political party, they may lose some ability to critique the party programme. This was evident in the United States, when the Concerned Women for America, a Christian Right women's group that is generally associated with the GOP, took no position on a Republican-sponsored welfare reform bill that forced poor women to get jobs and place their children in childcare, even though this went against one of the group's core principles regarding motherhood (Wilcox and Larson 2006).

Next, we investigate three cases of religion and political parties. We begin with a discussion of Christian Democratic parties and the Catholic Church in Europe. Christian Democratic parties share elements of a common programme but they differ in many ways, in part because of the different associational networks to which they are attached. Once seen as declining because of secularization in Europe, they have enjoyed a revival in recent years. Afterwards, we also look at the USA, where religious discourse in elections is increasing. Social movement organizations seek to link the political parties to groups of religious

voters, and mobilize religion into parties. Finally, we examine Islamic parties in the Middle East. There, popular social movements and religious parties interact in intricate ways within the context of non-liberal polities, supporting and opposing states with planned strategies. See Table 14.1 for major dimensions of religion and political parties in five sample cases.

The Catholic Church and political parties in Europe

In Western Europe, Christian Democratic parties with strong links to Catholic religious institutions and civil society are active in most countries. In Eastern Europe, the church has played an active role in some countries in designing constitutions, but has been less willing to back particular parties. In general, Christian Democratic parties in Western Europe have been less studied than parties on the left, but in recent years a significant amount of scholarship has focused on the relationship of the Catholic Church and political parties (Byrnes 2001; Byrnes and Katzenstein 2006; Hanley 1994a; Kalyvas 1996; Manuel et al. 2006; Van Hecke and Gerard 2004).

Western European nations with Christian Democratic parties share certain characteristics that help to structure the interaction between religion and politics. All are liberal democracies with multi-party systems, interacting with a hierarchical church which has both national and international elements. These countries differ somewhat in the religious marketplace – the Netherlands and Germany have substantial Protestant populations – but overall share a growing secularization and an influx of new Muslim citizens. Their parties are all embedded in networks of associations, which differ slightly from country to country. They are supportive of the state, but their position on church–state issues varies because of varying histories and different sets of state subsidies and limitations.

Table 14.1 Major dimensions on religion and political parties in five sample cases

	Western Europe	United States	Jordan	Yemen	Lebanon
Party	Christian Democrats (and Allies)	Republican Party; Democratic Party	Islamic Action Front	Islah	Hezbollah
Regime type	Liberal democracy	Liberal democracy	Electoral authoritarian: constitutional monarchy	Electoral authoritarian: presidential republic	Consociational system
Electoral system	Mostly proportional representation	First past the post: single-member district	Single non-transferable vote	First past the post: single-member district	Confessional distribution
Associational nexus	Broad; connected	Broad; independent	Cohesive; mixed independence	Fragmented	Hierarchical
Religious institutional structures	Hierarchical	Decentralized	Decentralized	Decentralized	Formal political hierarchy; informal religious hierarchy
Religious marketplace	Catholic majority with sizeable secular population; some with Protestant and Muslim minorities	Diverse; Christian majority	Sunni majority	Muslim majority; Sunni–Shi'a split	Diverse; Muslim majority
Stance towards the state	Pro-state	Pro-state	Mildly anti-state	Pro-state; recent shift to mildly anti-state	Pro-state (since 1992)

The relationship between the Church and parties in Europe is theoretically interesting, for several reasons. First, because early manifestations of Catholic political parties in Europe frequently staked anti-democratic positions, their participation in the electoral process may have implications for the position of Islamic parties in regard to democracy (Kalyvas 2000). Second, the Catholic Church is the most hierarchical religious institution in the world, capable of negotiating concordats with various governments that differ in important ways, and thus allow consideration of the Church as a single rational actor (Warner 2000). Third, distinctive paths that some countries have taken to democracy have also altered the incentives for the Church to back or oppose particular parties (Byrnes 2002; Casanova 1994). Finally, the existence of a family of Christian Democratic parties allows us to consider the various ways that religious and social organization can affect party politics (Dierckx 1994; Kersbergen 1994).

Christian Democratic parties in Western Europe mostly grew out of civil society organizations that were affiliated with the Catholic Church, and with some

Protestant churches as well. These parties shared certain ideological tenets but not a single programme. Christian Democratic parties are generally categorized as centre-right, supportive of the welfare state, federalism and morally conservative policies. The parties have loosely affiliated in the context of the European Union (Hanley 1994b).

The historical paths of these parties differed, and this has affected their relationships to the Church and to other political forces. In Germany, the Church chose to ally itself with a party that combined Catholics and Protestants, rather than with another solely Catholic party that was forming at the same time. With little remaining of the once vibrant Catholic civil society in Germany and a strong regional division of religion, the Christian Democratic Union (CDU) seemed to Catholic and Protestant actors alike a better bet than separate confessional parties. In the Netherlands, separate confessional parties competed for many years, but finally merged in 1980. In Belgium, in contrast, a Christian Democratic party formed early to protect Catholic schools, but later split along linguistic lines.

The parties have developed differently because of their competition in the electoral arena. In some countries, Christian Democratic parties have been seen as the main opposition to leftist anti-clerical parties, whereas in other countries Christian Democrats have had to fend off challenges by nationalist parties of the right. In many cases, the parties historically competed by building ties to civil society organizations. In Italy, Church leaders used available resources, including denial of sacraments, to marshal support for the Christian Democratic party (Warner 2000), but also mobilized the extensive Catholic network of organizations. In France, priests joined unions and used persuasion, and also created new social organizations that were affiliated with the Christian Democrats. The associational nexus of these parties varies – trade unions have been associated with the party in Austria but not Germany, and in Belgium and Italy the party has had official organizations that represented women, students and farmers.

During the 1990s, the vote share of Christian Democratic parties declined in much of Europe as the population became more secular (Dalton 2002; Luther 1999), although there is some evidence of a resurgence in recent years (Gerard and Hecke 2004). Electoral volatility has increased, with new social movement parties and populist parties playing an increased role (Rydgren 2004). Some of these new populist parties have strong anti-Muslim positions in response to immigration.

Christian Democratic parties have reacted to changed political conditions in different ways. Some have sought to coopt support for rightist and populist parties, and staked their identity around the Christian heritage of Europe, while others have opened themselves to Muslims and other non-Christian groups and sought to attract younger voters who are not drawn to the party's religious heritage. Some have broadened their agenda to become 'catch-all' parties of the centre and centre-right, whereas others have criticized neo-liberal economic reforms that have occurred across the continent. All have sought to retain their links to civil society organizations, but in much of Europe these organizations are in decline. Yet it is too early to write off Christian Democratic parties, especially given their renewed success in national and European elections in recent years. Even the diffuse religious identities of Western Europeans may become re-politicized under the right circumstances (Nexon 2006).

Although Christian Democratic parties have formed in most West European democracies, the relationship between religion and parties in the new European democracies has followed a different course. The collapse of communist governments throughout Eastern and Central Europe altered the political balance in the West, but it also created space for new party systems in the recently established democracies. Many of these new countries were heavily secular, but some retained significant Catholic populations and institutions. The Church was strongest in Poland, where it was linked to a rich array of social institutions including the Solidarity Trade Union. The Church provided valuable infrastructure to civil society as it resisted the communist rule, but the transition to multi-party democracy was more complicated.

The Church negotiated with political leaders over the Constitution and protections for religious institutions. Yet when the Solidarity movement split into rival factions and Poland emerged with dozens of political parties, the Church chose not to endorse a political party, including some that were explicitly Catholic in ideology. This path was perhaps different from that in Italy in the post-war period because of doctrinal shifts in the role of the Church in politics (Himes 2007). The complex and rapidly shifting partisan structure of Polish politics also made choosing a party to support problematic, but made choosing which one to oppose far easier. This became more salient as party coalitions formed on the left and right.

In other countries, the Church had a more complex task. In Slovakia, for example, issues relating to Hungarian minorities made it difficult for the Church to become involved in partisan politics, because the Hungarian Church was actively involved in nationalistic expression. The Church has been involved with Christian Democratic party formation, although the rapid formation and mergers of political parties has made any stable alliance problematic.

In summary, religious actors and parties have been critical in the political development of Europe, particularly in the development of democracy in the nineteenth century and in the social movements against Communism in the late twentieth century. Recent declines in religious associational life and the practically non-existence of religious social movements may have left an ideational and associational vacuum for the rise of other political actors. Espousing Christian identity, without religiosity *per se*, nationalism may grow to be an important social movement in many European states, thus altering the political landscape of the continent once again. Across the Atlantic, however, religious associational life and movements remain vibrant in the United States. And while Christian Democratic parties in Europe face an uncertain future, some have argued that in the US the Republican party is now evolving into a Christian Democratic party (Petrocik 1998).

Religion and political parties in the USA

In the US, it is commonly argued that the party system has changed from one where both parties had allies in differing religious traditions, to one in which Christian conservatives support Republican candidates and more secular citizens vote Democratic. Presidential candidates routinely discuss their personal faith, religious experiences, and even in some cases theology publicly, and some churches are actively involved in electoral politics, despite an official separation of church and state.

The US has an increasingly diverse religious citizenry, with a Christian majority that is divided into several blocs and into hundreds of different denominations. Catholics, white mainline Protestants and white Evangelical Protestants each constitute 20% of the population or more, with African-American Protestants at around 11% (Wald and Calhoun-Brown 2007). Although politicians occasionally still declare the country to be a 'Christian nation', today there are Hindu temples, Buddhist meditation centres, mosques, synagogues and other non-Christian houses of worship in all major cities and many smaller towns (Eck 2001).

Although a growing portion of the population is secular, fewer than one in six voters would express no religious affilia-tion – and many of these show some reli-gious sympathies. A substantial majority of Americans report attending church at least once a month; many go more than once a week. Thus secular Americans are insuffi-ciently numerous to form a competitive anti-clerical party, and deeply religious Americans are also too few in number, and too divided by tradition, to command a majority.

With so many religious traditions cooper-ating in some areas but competing to define the dominant worldview of the citizenry, there is no single religious actor that can negotiate with the state. The Catholic Church in the US has sought to exert a unified voice on certain issues such as abor-tion and same-sex marriage, but American Catholics frequently disagree with church teachings, and even the lobbying efforts of various Catholic dioceses differ in their priorities (Larson et al. 2005). Protestant denominations are also divided; issues of gay and lesbian rights divide the Episcopal, Methodist and Presbyterian churches. Evangelical denominations have sought to cooperate within the framework of the National Association of Evangelicals, but they have disagreed publicly about such issues as global warming and torture.

Religious groups have long been a key part of associational life in the USA, spawn-ing a rich array of organizations that serve a variety of spiritual and secular purposes. These associations are often associated with particular religious denominations (e.g. Catholic charities), but are often ecu-menical efforts by religiously motivated citizens (Warren 2001). Churches provide opportunities for their members to acquire political skills, as well as serve the community (Verba et al. 1995).

Moreover, religion has been the impe-tus of many vital social movements that have worked both outside and inside the party system to make substantial changes in American public life (Mitchell 2007). Religion was a major source of mobiliza-tion around abolition, temperance, civil rights and the Christian right. It played a notable role along with other secular forces in the suffrage and labour move-ments. In most cases, these movements started outside of the party system, and were eventually accommodated by changes in the programmers of one or both of the major parties (Wilcox 2007b).

The first-past-the-post system of American congressional and presidential elections has produced the same two major parties for one hundred and fifty years. These political parties frequently build close networks with interest groups and social movement organizations (Berry and Wilcox 2007). Political elites generally seek to exploit cleavages for political gain, not by forming new political parties, but frequently by forming extra-party organ-izations that can mobilize voters – includ-ing many that seek to mobilize religious voters (Leege et al. 2002; Wilcox and Robinson 2007b). These organizations can assist factions within the party in struggles to control nominations and influence the party platform.

Religious groups primarily support the state and are often nationalistic, but they also frequently stake a prophetic stance against particular policies. Religious groups lobby both national and state gov-ernments challenge laws in court, and oth-erwise contest policy in ways very similar to non-religious groups (Brown 2004; Hertzke 1988; Larson et al. 2005).

But tax law limits the ability of religious organizations to endorse candidates, affiliate with parties, as well as to lobby government. Churches can do any of these things, but their status as tax-exempt charities may be at stake. For this reason, churches shy away from explicit endorsements of candidates, although some obey the letter but not the spirit of the law.

Religion and political parties: from denomination to direction?

In the early years of the twentieth century, Democratic leaders began to assemble a religious coalition that included a variety of different groups. Democratic party machines in northern cities welcomed Catholic and Jewish immigrants, and the Republican party opened itself to nativist elements who called for curbs on immigration. Franklin Roosevelt's coalition sought to incorporate African-American Christians, and white evangelicals. White mainline Protestants – who were advantaged in socio-economic resources – constituted the backbone of the GOP.

Yet much of the religious alignment in this period was due to non-religious issues. White evangelicals were mostly southern, and that region was solidly Democratic because of racial politics. Catholic and Jewish immigrants were disproportionately working class, and thus benefited from the pro-labour policies of the Democrats. African-Americans also benefited from Roosevelt's economic policies, especially in northern cities. Religion was important in American life, but was not terribly well mobilized in politics. In 1960, John Kennedy won the presidency not by touting his Catholic faith, but by promising not to let it direct his presidency.

Post-New-Deal religion and party politics

During the 1960s, African–American churches served as a critical infrastructure

for the Civil Rights movement. Black pastors became involved in Democratic party politics, conducting voter registration drives, and inviting Democratic candidates into their churches (Harris 1999). Democratic party operatives cultivated ties to the largest African-American churches across the country.

In the late 1970s, Republican leaders helped conservative white fundamentalists and evangelicals build the Christian right, which was closely linked with the Republican party. The Christian right helped the Republicans woo white evangelical voters with more conservative policies on abortion, education, gay rights and other issues. Republican politicians also helped channel contributions to organizations such as the Moral Majority and later the Christian Coalition, and they in turn helped to register voters and steer them to Republican candidates (Wilcox 2007a).

The Republicans also sought to build support among conservative Catholics, stressing the party's position on abortion and gay rights. Frequently these efforts are coordinated in political groups which receive party support, in other cases they are mounted by individual candidates. In 2004, the Bush campaign sought to mobilize religious voters directly, bypassing social movement organizations. They gathered lists of members from conservative churches, and crafted careful appeals through mail, telemarketing and other private communications to win their votes.

Republican policy-makers have sought to cement their ties to evangelicals and conservative Catholics with public rhetoric on religion – both explicit language that is accessible to all voters, and more carefully worded language that is understood by particular religious communities. In some ways, the Republican party has evolved into a type of Christian Democratic party, with the noticeable absence of support for the welfare state (Petrocik 1998).

Secular Americans, a rapidly growing portion of the population, have moved to the Democrats in response, as have mainline Protestants with moderate to liberal theology (Silk and Green 2007). Journalists frequently argue that the party system is evolving into one pitting a visibly religious party against a secular party.

There is some truth to this claim, for among all three groups of white Christians, the most observant are more likely to vote for the Republicans, and the most secular to support Democrats. Yet among African-Americans, among Muslims, and among certain groups of Jews, the most observant are more likely to support Democrats, and this is true among older Catholics as well. Many religious groups have agendas that intersect with both political parties, including a newly engaged group of moderate evangelicals (Wald and Calhoun-Brown 2007).

Moreover, the two-party system creates incentives for both parties to woo many groups of voters. Catholics and mainline Protestants are currently courted by both parties, whereas African-Americans, Jews, and white evangelicals appear to have formed stable relationships with one or the other party.

In conclusion, the diversity of American religion and its associational life has complicated the relationship between religious groups and the two political parties. The relationship between parties and social movement organizations is a complicated one, and political parties may compete to win the votes of religious groups. Finally, the US case shows that even in long-established democracies the relationship between parties and religion can change. We now turn our attention to Islamic parties and movements in the Middle East, where the importance of both the nature of party–movement relations and the institutional structures of the regime can be made more explicit.

Islamic parties in the Middle East

The Islamic Revolution of 1979 marked a watershed in the ideological discourse of politics throughout the Islamic world, from one of Western secularism as characterized by Kemal Ataturk to that of the religion of Islam as exemplified by Ayatollah Khomeini (Sayyid 1997). Since then, the relationship between Islam and parties has continued to change, for two reasons. First, in the 1970s and 1980s, most Islamists were reluctant to cooperate with the state, seeking instead a broader pan-Islamic revolution (Abootalebi 1999). Second, many regimes banned religious parties, and over time these restrictions have been relaxed in some cases. Today, however, the role and function of parties continue to be much more restricted than those of the other regions of the world due to the illiberalism that characterizes the region (Carothers 2006). Political parties are still banned in Saudi Arabia, Libya and the smaller Persian Gulf states, are limited to *de facto* secular one-party rule in Syria and Tunisia, and are banned in Egypt and Turkey if based on a religious platform.

Scholarly analysis of political Islam has been dominated by two different conceptual approaches. The first places emphasis on discursive, behavioural and ideological analysis, essentializing and presenting Islam as antithetical to Western concepts like democracy (Gellner 1991). Within this group, some further argue that Islamic values are incompatible with modernity, and predict an inevitable clash of civilizations (Huntington 1993; Lewis 1990). Scholars writing in this tradition have largely ignored the role and function of religious organizations and parties.

This view has been criticized for failing to account for differences in Islamic movements and parties, and for having an ethnocentric bias (Said 1978, Sadowski 1993).

Middle Eastern regimes use the 'Islamist threat' as an excuse to limit democratization and ban religious parties. Thus, '[t]he real question is not whether Islamists pose a threat, but what political agendas are served by continuing to paint Islamists as a monolithic, antidemocratic mob' (Schwedler 1998).

Other scholars suggest that Islamic parties may moderate their positions and accept democratic norms as they participate in the democratic process. In this perspective, democratization arises through the strategic interaction of key actors; and ideology and norms may be altered by democratic politics (O'Donnell and Schmitter 1986; Przeworski 1991). Democratic political processes can emerge even among those who lack commitment to democratic norms, hence the phrase 'democracy without democrats' (Salamé 1994). 'Muslim Democracy rests not on an abstract, carefully thought-out theological and ideological accommodation between Islam and democracy, but rather on a practical synthesis that is emerging in much of the Muslim world in response to the opportunities and demands created by the ballot box' (Nasr 2005). As a result, 'change will in turn be the harbinger, not the follower, of more liberal Islamic thought and practice' (2005: 26).

In practice, the ideological positions of Islamic parties and organizations cover a wide spectrum from the conservative application of Shari'a law to more liberal interpretations of religion (Barsalou 2005). Islamic parties may see advantages in participating in elections because 'they generally have far superior organizational support systems, principally through mosque networks, than do secular parties' (Barsalou 2005: 1). Thus, the associational nexus and societal networks of Islamic religious charities, foundations, schools, hospitals and professional organizations form the support base for many, if not all, Islamic parties. But the evidence that Islamic parties moderate when they engage in electoral competition is mixed. Recent academic debates have focused upon clarifying the conceptualization and pinpointing the precise meaning of moderation and change.

A number of scholars have argued that the term 'moderation' oversimplifies the relationship between Islamic movements and democracy. Clark (quoted in Barsalou 2005) argues that some Islamic parties are labelled moderate because of their short-term tactical decisions, ignoring their long-term Islamic agendas. Wickham (quoted in Barsalou 2005) suggests that the relationship between Islamic parties and democracies is complex: some parties may accept some aspects of democracy while rejecting others. Schwedler goes further to argue that '*moderate* and *radical* might be applied to *some positions* on a particular issue, but hold little analytic value as wholesale *categories* of political actors' (Schwedler 2006: 19). This, she holds, leaves the inclusion–moderation hypothesis approach without a clear causal mechanism for explaining moderation.

Therefore, ideological commitments setting the boundaries of justifiable action need to be considered as an important dimension in addition to political opportunity structures and the internal group structures and organizations of parties. Comparing the Islamic Action Front (IAF) party in Jordan with the Islah party in Yemen, Schwedler argues that the IAF was successful in moderating while the Islah was not. In this instance, moderation is defined as the shift from 'a relatively closed worldview to one that is more pluralist and tolerant of alternative perspectives' (Schwedler 2005: 192). In order to see the dynamics of Schwedler's argument empirically and to explain the implications of the six dimensions identified in the introduction, we will present the details of the IAF and Islah parties.

Founded in 1992, the IAF is an offshoot of the Muslim Brotherhood in Jordan. It participates in parliamentary elections, except for a boycott in 1997. Jordan used a bloc voting mechanism that shifted to a single non-transferable vote in the 1990s with a bias towards the rural regions where the Islamic constituency is weaker. Jordan's government is a constitutional monarchy currently headed by King Abdullah II, and the regime has provided room for political parties. The nation is overwhelmingly Sunni with a 6% Christian minority. In addition, more than 50% of Jordanians are Palestinian, and this constitutes one of the important constituencies of the IAF. The party has a mildly prophetic (anti-regime) position described as a 'loyal opposition' by Schwedler, but has links to those in power, including the king. In terms of its structure and organization, the IAF is cohesive with a strong central leadership and is well established in society with clear constituents. Its associational nexus is particularly vibrant. Over time, the IAF has adopted a more democratic discourse, and has justified its cooperation with the left with arguments centred in Islam.

The Islah, or Reform, party was established in 1990 in a secular presidential republic. It has a first-past-the-post electoral system with single-member districts. While predominantly Muslim, Yemen has a Sunni Muslim majority with a substantial Shi'ite minority. Islah is a Sunni party, and has been until recently a coalition partner of the regime. It has a priestly (pro-regime) position characterized by Schwedler as a regime 'coalition partner'. Recently, it suffered a resounding defeat in local council elections at the hands of the ruling party (Longley 2007). Deeply fragmented, the Islah party rests on a constituency based on a weak coalition among diverse social actors who share some common goals. Its associational nexus is relatively weaker and more heterogeneous than that of the IAF.

The important implications of the dimensions identified earlier become evident in Schwedler's analysis of the causal mechanism explaining IAF moderation. Regime type is important, for the uncontested monarchy of Jordan created greater political space for the IAF than the contested presidency in Yemen that limited legitimate competition. Second, the coherent and well-organized structure of the IAF allowed it greater policy-making decisions and adaptations, in contrast to the fragmented Islah party. Finally, the discourse of the IAF became more democratic in nature in contrast to the more conservative discourse of Islah, which suffered from the extremist positions of some of its candidates (Longley 2007). By refining the indicators of moderation to include ideological discourse and looking more specifically at the different dimensions of party context in a comparative perspective, Schwedler makes an important contribution to the study of religion and political parties. At the same time, however, it also raises a few concerns that would be important for future study.

Further research is needed on the form and function of the associational nexus. Schwedler encourages future studies to focus upon questions that 'might explore the dynamics of various publics and the actors who produce them, how narrative spaces shape political practices, and how sites of brokerage facilitate changes in practices as well as ideological commitments' (2006: 215). However, scholars using social movement theory have already accomplished much work on many of these points. Analyses focus upon three elements: resource mobilization bases that exist in society, such as mosques and charities; elites who mobilize and make decisions; and ideology and framing that allows for collective action (Wiktorowicz 2001, 2004a, 2004b). But more work needs to be done on identifying the configuration of political parties with movements and their potential effects on political processes. For example, in her study on Islamic mobilization in Egypt, Wickham (2002) argues that the Muslim Brotherhood is only one part of a larger Islamic movement in the country. Thus, in elections it only receives a part of the total votes that might go to those who support the Islamic movement. In sum, the degree to which an Islamic party can moderate its social constituency may be explained and predicted by the position of the party within the institutional matrix of its respective social movement and the formal and informal structural make-up of the religion itself.

The case of Hezbollah in Lebanon sheds light on the importance of these issues. Lebanon has an ethnically and religiously diverse society managed under a consociational form of democracy that broke down into civil war in 1975 to be re-established in 1990. Officially founded in 1985, Hezbollah, the Shi'a Party of God, became instrumental in the resistance to the Israeli invasion of Lebanon in 1982 (Deeb 2006). Free from the political corruption and patronage politics of Amal, the main party reflecting the Shi'a cleavage within Lebanon, Hezbollah was supported by a growing religious constituency. Two important characteristics allow Hezbollah to serve as an intriguing case on the intersection of religion and political parties. First, the party created the majority of its own associational nexus rather than the other way around. Aided by Iran financially and logistically, the party developed its own organizations involved in the realms of education, reconstruction, health, charity and religion, thus creating a social movement directed by 'holistic and integrated networks' (Harb and Leenders 2005).

As a result, changes in the discourse and agenda of Hezbollah led to broader changes in the constituency of the Shi'a movement in Lebanon, in contrast to the minor effects upon the Islamic movement in Egypt or Jordan with similar changes to the Muslim Brotherhood. This was because Hezbollah managed to achieve hegemony as the definitive organizational leader of the Islamic movement and associational nexus in Lebanon. This contrasts with the Muslim Brotherhood, only a component of a larger social network comprising Egyptian and Jordanian Islamic movements. One example of this change includes Hezbollah's decision to drop its aim of establishing an Islamic Republic in Lebanon and choosing instead to participate in domestic elections (Deeb 2006; Harb and Leenders 2005).

Second, Hezbollah is also interesting in terms of its religious organizational structure and hierarchy. It follows the doctrine of *velayat-e faqih*, or the rule of the jurisprudent, developed by Ayatollah Khomeini and institutionalized in Iran after the revolution. The party followed Ayatollah Ruhollah Khomeini as the Supreme Leader of the Islamic Revolution until 1989 and Ayatollah Ali Khamenei afterwards. In religious emulation, however, individuals choose their own *marja' al-taqlid*, or source of emulation, with many following Ayatollah Fadllalah in Lebanon. Therefore, 'political allegiance and religious emulation are two separate issues that may or may not overlap for any single person' (Deeb 2006: 4). While much more hierarchical than its Sunni counterpart, the religious structure in Shi'ism is still relatively more decentralized than the Catholic Vatican. Despite it links to Iran, Hezbollah is said to act based on its own interests and platform within the Lebanese polity without overtly taking orders from Iran's government (Shaery-Eisenlohr 2004). Is it Hezbollah's greater hierarchical structure that allows it to be successful in leading a social movement and making effective negotiations with other political players? Do hierarchical organizations and religious structures allow for greater democratic accommodation as Kalyvas (2000) claims because of the nature of the hierarchy itself, because of the configuration it develops with an associational nexus and social movement, or both? These are important issues that need to be addressed by future discussions on religion and political parties.

Conclusion

The interaction of religion and political parties takes diverse forms. In Europe, engagement of Christian democrats in democratic processes in the nineteenth century was seen by some as a threat to democracy, but they were able to form legitimate political parties and compete within the system. The centralized hierarchy of the Catholic Church facilitated its ability to guide these parties into democratic politics. In the twentieth century, religious institutions, associations and ideology interacted to form oppositional movements to Communism, particularly in Poland. Yet, the Church did not establish or support a political party, choosing instead to further its interests from the sidelines. With the weakening of religious associational life throughout Europe, an ideological and institutional vacuum has allowed nationalist groups to form and subsume religious discourse as a form of identity politics. These changes quickly altered the landscape of parties because of the proportional representation (PR) systems most European states espouse.

In the US, a vast, diverse and decentralized associational nexus results in differing religious interests and movements, such as the Christian right and the black Protestants. The US two-party system inhibits the formation of a coherent religious party in the face of such diversity. Instead, different religious interests and movements align and support parties in order best to maximize their own interests. Although there has been a socio-moral realignment in US party life, this does not suggest that religious mobilization will necessarily follow a similar pattern in the future. Largely independent of the parties, religious associations can forge their own paths depending on their changing interests and strategies. The Republican party's weak ability to turn moral promises into policy results may undermine their religious associational nexus.

In the Middle East, Muslim religious social mobilization and party politics interact in much starker terms. This is because of their mainly oppositional role – in the context of authoritarian politics and the inadequate number and strength of parties that can successfully articulate societal interests. Different configurations of regime types, party politics and mobilization constitutions alter the way in which religion and political parties interact with one another and, consequently, impact the state.

As a result of this diversity, a parsimonious study of religion and political parties can be a daunting task. We recommend that six dimensions be taken into consideration: regime type, religious marketplace, religious institutional structure, associational nexus, nature of party system, and party and religious groups' stance toward the state. Furthermore, we propose that future studies on religion and political parties undertake greater analysis on the configurations that may occur between religious movements, associational nexus and political parties. The position of these variables towards one another, including their power relationships, and the manner in which they link to each other and help construct one another, is very important in determining the constraints and opportunities that face religious parties and their future trajectories.

Note

1 Generally, the term 'Islamist' acts as a marker for those exposing a non-secular political

agenda while 'Islamic' refers to a denominational category. Since the identification and labelling of parties according to this distinction is a controversial and political task, we use these labels interchangeably in this chapter.

Bibliography

Abootalebi, A. R. (1999) 'Islam, Islamists, and democracy', *Middle East Review of International Affairs*, 3. Available at http://www.biu.ac.il/SOC/besa/meria/journal/1999/issue1/jv3n1a2.html

Barsalou, J. (2005) 'Islamists at the ballot box: findings from Egypt, Jordan, Kuwait, and Turkey', *USIP Special Report*, 144, July.

Berry, J. M. and Wilcox, C. (2007) *The Interest Group Society*, New York: Pearson Longman.

Blais, A. and Massicotte, L. (2002) 'Electoral systems', in L. LeDuc, R. G. Niemi and P. Norris (eds), *Comparing Democracies 2: New Challenges in the Study of Elections and Voting*, London: Sage Publications, pp. 40–69.

Bolce, L. and DeMaio, G. (2007) 'Secularists, anti-fundamenatlists, and the new religious divide in the American electorate', in J. Matthew Wilson (ed.), *From Pews to Polling Places: Faith and Politics in the American Religious Mosaic*, Washington, DC: Georgetown University Press, pp. 251–276.

Brown, S. (2004) *Trumping Religion: The New Christian Right, the Free Speech Clause, and the Courts*, Tuscaloosa: University of Alabama Press.

Bruce, S. (2003) *Politics & Religion*, Oxford: Blackwell.

Brumberg, D. (2001) *Reinventing Khomeini: The Struggle for Reform in Iran*, Chicago: University of Chicago Press.

Budge, I., Klingemann, H.-D., Volkens, A., Bara, J. and Tanenbaum, E. (2001) *Mapping Policy Preferences: Estimates for Parties, Electors, and Governments 1945–1998*, Oxford: Oxford University Press.

Byrnes, T. (2001) *Transnational Catholicism in Postcommunist Europe*, Lanham, MD: Rowman & Littlefield.

Byrnes, T. (2002) 'The challenge of pluralism: the Catholic church in democratic Poland', in T. G. Jelen and C. Wilcox (eds), *Religion and Politics in Comparative Perspective: The One, the Few, and the Many*, New York: Cambridge University Press, pp. 27–46.

Byrnes, T. and Katzenstein, P. (eds) (2006) *Religion in an Expanding Europe*, New York: Cambridge University Press.

Carothers, T. (2006) *Confronting the Weakest Link: Aiding Political Parties in the New Democracies*, Washington, DC: Carnegie Endowment for International Peace.

Casanova, J. (1994) *Public Religions in the Modern World*, Chicago: University of Chicago Press.

Chhibber, P. (1997) 'Who voted for the Bharatiya Janata Party?', *British Journal of Political Science*, 27, pp. 631–639.

Chhibber, P. and Kollman, K. (1996) 'State policy, rent seeking, and the electoral success of a religious party in Algeria', *Journal of Politics*, 58, pp. 126–148.

Dalton, R. (2002) 'Political cleavages, issues, and electoral change', in L. LeDuc, R. G. Niemi and P. Norris (eds), *Comparing Democracies 2: New Challenges in the Study of Elections and Voting*, London: Sage Publications, pp. 189–209.

Deeb, L. (2006) 'Hizballah: a primer', *Middle East Report Online*. Available at http://www.merip.org/mero/mero.html.

Dierckx, G. (1994) 'Christian Democracy and its ideological rivals', in D. Hanley (ed.), *Christian Democracy in Europe: A Comparative Perspective*, London: Pinter Publishers, pp. 15–30.

Dogan, M. (1995) 'Erosion of class voting and of the religious vote in Western Europe', *International Social Science Journal*, 146, pp. 525–538.

Duverger, M. (1963) *Political Parties: Their Organization and Activity in the Modern State*, New York: John Wiley and Sons.

Eck, D. (2001) *A New Religious America: How a 'Christian Country' Has Become the World's Most Religiously Diverse Nation*, San Francisco: HarperCollins.

Felsenthal, D. (1992) 'Proportional representation under three voting procedures: an Israeli study', *Political Behavior*, 14, pp. 159–192.

Fetzer, J. and Soper, J. C. (2005) *Muslims and the State in Britain, France, and Germany*, New York: Cambridge University Press.

Finke, R. and Stark, R. (1992) *The Churching of America: Winners and Losers in our Religious Economy*, New Brunswick: Rutgers University Press.

227

Fox, J. (2006) 'World separation of religion and state into the 21st century', *Comparative Political Studies*, 39, 5, pp. 537–569.

Gellner, E. (1991) 'Civil society in historical context', *International Social Science Journal*, 129, pp. 495–510.

Gerard, E. and Van Hecke, S. (2004) 'European Christian Democracy in the 1990s: toward a comparative approach', in S. Van Hecke and E. Gerard (eds), *Christian Democratic Parties in Europe Since the End of the Cold War*, Leuven: Leuven University Press, pp. 297–318.

Gill, A. (1998) *Render Unto Caesar: The Catholic Church and the State in Latin America*, Chicago: University of Chicago Press.

Gill, A. (2001) 'Religion and comparative politics', *Annual Review of Political Science*, 4, pp. 117–138.

Hanley, D. (ed.) (1994a) *Christian Democracy in Europe: A Comparative Perspective*, London: Pinter Publishers.

Hanley, D. (1994b) 'The European People's Party: toward a new party form?', in D. Hanley (ed.), *Christian Democracy in Europe: A Comparative Perspective*, London: Pinter Publishers, pp. 185–201.

Harb, M. and Leenders, R. (2005) 'Know thy enemy: Hizbullah, terrorism, and the politics of perception', *Third World Quarterly*, 26, pp. 173–197.

Harmel, R. and Robertson, J. (1985) 'Formation and success of new parties: a cross-national analysis', *International Political Science Review/Revue internationale de science politique*, 6, pp. 501–523.

Harris, F. (1999) *Something Within: Religion in African-American Political Activism*, New York: Oxford University Press.

Hertzke, A. (1988) *Representing God in Washington: The Role of Religious Lobbies in the American Polity*, Knoxville, TN: University of Tennessee Press.

Himes, K. (2007) 'Vatican II and contemporary politics', in P. Christopher Manuel, L.R. Reardon and C. Wilcox (eds), *The Catholic Church and the Nation-state: Comparative Perspectives*, Washington, DC: Georgetown University Press, pp. 185–201.

Huntington, S. (1993) 'The clash of civilizations?', *Foreign Affairs*, 72, pp. 22–49.

Jelen, T. G. and Wilcox, C. (2002) 'The political roles of religion', in T. G. Jelen and C. Wilcox (eds), *Religion and Politics in Comparative Perspective: The One, the Few, and the Many*, New York: Cambridge University Press, pp. 314–324.

Jenkins, G. (2003) 'Muslim democrats in Turkey?', *Survival*, 45, pp. 45–66.

Kalyvas, S. (1996) *The Rise of Christian Democracy in Europe*, Ithaca: Cornell University Press.

Kalyvas, S. (2000) 'Commitment problems in emerging democracies: the case of religious parties', *Comparative Politics*, 32, pp. 379–398.

Kersbergen, K. van (1994) 'The distinctiveness of Christian Democracy', in D. Hanley (ed.), *Christian Democracy in Europe: A Comparative Perspective*, London: Pinter Publishers, pp. 31–50.

Koçak, M. and Örücü, E. (2003) 'Dissolution of political parties in the name of democracy: cases from Turkey and the European Court of Human Rights', *European Public Law*, 9, 3, pp. 399–423.

Kotler-Berkowitz, L. A. (2001) 'Religion and voting behaviour in Great Britain: a reassessment', *British Journal of Political Science*, 31, pp. 523–554.

Lacardie, P. (2004) 'Paradise lost, paradise regained: Christian Democracy in the Netherlands', in S. van Hecke and E. Gerard (eds), *Christian Democratic Parties in Europe Since the End of the Cold War*, Leuven: Leuven University Press, pp. 159–178.

Larson, C., Madland, D. and Wilcox, C. (2005) 'Religious lobbying in Virginia: how institutions can quiet prophetic voices', in E. Cleary and A. Hertzke (eds), *Representing God in the Statehouse: Religion and Politics in the American States*, Lanham, MD: Rowman & Littlefield, pp. 55–72.

Layman, G. (2001) *The Great Divide: Religious and Cultural Conflict in American Party Politics*, New York: Columbia University Press.

Leege, D. C., Wald, K., Krueger, B. S. and Mueller, P. D. (2002) *The Politics of Cultural Differences: Social Change and Voter Mobilization Strategies in the Post-New Deal Period*, Princeton, NJ: Princeton University Press.

Lewis, B. (1990) 'The roots of Muslim rage', *Atlantic Monthly*, 266, pp. 47–60.

Lijphart, A. (1999), *Patterns of Democracy: Government Forms and Performance in Thirty-six Countries,* New Haven: Yale University Press.

Lipset, S. M. and Rokkan, S. (1967) 'Cleavages, party systems, and voter alignments: an introduction, in S. M. Lipset and S. Rokkan (eds),

Party Systems and Voter Alignments: Cross-national Perspectives, New York: Free Press.

Longley, A. (2007) 'The high water mark for Islamist politics? The case of Yemen', *Middle East Journal*, 61, pp. 240–260.

Luther, K. R. (1999) 'A framework for the comparative analysis of political parties and party systems in consociational democracy', in K. R. Luther and K. Deschouwer (eds), *Party Elites in Divided Societies*, London: Routledge, pp. 3–19.

Manuel, P. C., Reardon, L. R. and Wilcox, C. (eds) (2006) *The Catholic Church and the Nation-state: Comparative Perspectives*, Washington, DC: Georgetown University Press.

Mitchell, J. (2007) 'Religion is not a preference', *Journal of Politics*, 69, pp. 349–360.

Nasr, V. (2005) 'The rise of Muslim democracy', *Journal of Democracy*, 16, pp. 13–27.

Nexon, D. (2006) 'Religion, European identity, and political contention in historical perspective', in T. A. Byrnes and P. J. Katzenstein (eds), *Religion in an Expanding Europe*, Cambridge: Cambridge University Press, pp. 256–282.

Norris, P. (2004) *Electoral Engineering: Voting Rules and Political Behavior*, New York: Cambridge University Press.

Norris, P. (2005) *Radical Right: Voters and Parties in the Electoral Market*, New York: Cambridge University Press.

Norris, P. and Inglehart, R. (2004) *Sacred and Secular: Religion and Politics Worldwide*, New York: Cambridge University Press.

O'Donnell, G. and Schmitter, P. (1986) *Transitions from Authoritarian Rule: Tentative Conclusions*, Baltimore: Johns Hopkins University Press.

Petrocik, J. (1998) 'Reformulating the party coalitions: the "Christian Democratic" Republicans', Annual Meeting of the American Political Science Association, Boston: APSA.

Przeworski, A. (1991) *Democracy and the Market: Political and Economic Reforms in Eastern Europe and Latin America*, New York: Cambridge University Press.

Rosenblum, N. L. (2003) 'Religious parties, religious political identity, and the cold shoulder of liberal democratic thought', *Ethical Theory and Moral Practice*, 6, pp. 25–53.

Rozell, M. J. and Wilcox, C. (1996) *Second Coming: The New Christian Right in Virginia Politics*, Baltimore: Johns Hopkins University Press.

Rydgren, J. (2004) 'Explaining the emergence of radical right-wing populist parties: the case

of Denmark', *West European Politics*, 27, pp. 474–502.

Sadowski, Y. (1993) 'The New Orientalism and the democracy debate', *Middle East Report*, 183, pp. 14–21, 40.

Sahu, S. K. (2002) 'Religion and politics in India: the emergence of Hindu Nationalism and the Bharatiya Janata Party (BJP)', in T. G. Jelen and C. Wilcox (eds), *Religion and Politics in Comparative Perspective: The One, the Few, and the Many*, New York: Cambridge University Press, pp. 243–268.

Said, E. (1978) *Orientalism*, New York: Vintage Books.

Salamé, G. (ed.) (1994) *Democracy Without Democrats? The Renewal of Politics in the Muslim World*, New York: I. B. Tauris.

Sayyid, B. (1997) *A Fundamental Fear: Eurocentrism and the Emergence of Islam*, London: Zed Books.

Schwedler, J. (1998) 'A paradox of democracy? Islamist participation in elections', *Middle East Report*, 209, pp. 25–29, 41.

Schwedler, J. (2006) *Faith in Moderation: Islamist Parties in Jordan and Yemen*, New York: Cambridge University Press.

Shaery-Eisenlohr, R. (2004) 'Iran, the Vatican of Shi'ism?', *Middle East Report*, 233, pp. 40–43.

Sharkansky, I. (2000) *The Politics of Religion and the Religion of Politics: Looking at Israel*, New York: Lexington Books.

Siavoshi, S. (2002) 'Between heaven and earth: the dilemma of the Islamic Republic of Iran', in T. G. Jelen and C. Wilcox (eds), *Religion and Politics in Comparative Perspective: The One, the Few, and the Many*, New York: Cambridge University Press, pp. 125–141.

Silk, M. and Green, J. C. (2007) 'The GOP's religion problem', *Religion in the News*. Available at http://www.trincoll.edu/depts/csrpl/RIN Vol9No3/GOP'sReligionProblem.htm.

Stark, R. (1999) 'Secularization, R.I.P.', *Sociology of Religion*, 60, 3, pp. 249–265.

Tamadonfar, M. (2002) 'Islamism in contemporary Arab politics: lessons in authoritarianism and democratization', in T. G. Jelen and C. Wilcox (eds), *Religion and Politics in Comparative Perspective: The One, the Few, and the Many*, New York: Cambridge University Press, pp. 141–168.

Toyoda, M. A. and Tanaka, A. (2002) 'Religion and politics in Japan', in T. G. Jelen and C. Wilcox (eds), *Religion and Politics in Comparative*

Perspective: The One, the Few, and the Many, New York: Cambridge University Press, pp. 269–288.

Van Hecke, S., and Gerard, E. (eds) (2004) *Christian Democratic Parties in Europe since the End of the Cold War*, Leuven: Leuven University Press.

Van Holsteyn, J and Irwin, G. A. (2003) 'Never a dull moment: Pim Fortuyn and the Dutch parliamentary election of 2002', *West European Politics*, 26, pp. 41–66.

Vassallo, F. and Wilcox, C. (2005) 'Parties as carriers of ideas', in R. S. Katz and W. J. Crotty (eds), *Handbook of Party Politics*, London: Sage, pp. 413–421.

Verba, S., Schlozman, K. L. and Brady, H. E. (1995) *Voice and Equality: Civic Voluntarism in American Politics*, Cambridge, MA: Harvard University Press.

von Beyme, K. (1996) 'Party leadership and change in party systems: towards a postmodern party state?', *Government and Opposition*, 31, 2, pp. 135–159.

Wald, K. and Calhoun-Brown, A. (2007) *Religion and Politics in the United States*, Lanham, MD: Rowman & Littlefield.

Wald, K. and Wilcox, C. (2006) 'Getting religion: has political science rediscovered the faith factor?', *American Political Science Review*, 100, pp. 523–529.

Wald, K., Owen, D. and Hill, S. (1988) 'Churches as political communities', *American Political Science Review*, 82, 521–548.

Wald, K., Owen, D. and Hill, S. (1990) 'Political cohesion in churches', *Journal of Politics*, 52, pp. 197–215.

Warner, C. (2000) *Confessions of an Interest Group: The Catholic Church and Political Parties in Europe*, Princeton, NJ: Princeton University Press.

Warren, M. (2001) *Dry Bones Rattling: Community Building to Revitalize American Democracy*, Princeton, NJ: Princeton University Press.

Wickham, C. R. (2002) *Mobilizing Islam: Religion, Activism, and Political Change in Egypt*, New York: Columbia University Press.

Wiktorowicz, Q. (2001) *The Management of Islamic Activism: Salafis, the Muslim Brotherhood, and State Power in Jordan*, Albany, NY: State University of New York Press.

Wiktorowicz, Q. (2004a) 'Conceptualizing Islamic activism', *ISIM Newsletter*, 14, pp. 34–35.

Wiktorowitcz, Q. (ed.) (2004b) *Islamic Activism: A Social Movement Theory Approach*, Bloomington: Indiana University Press.

Wilcox, C. (2007a) 'Movements and metaphors', Conference on Evangelicals and Political Action, New York.

Wilcox, C. (2007b) 'Radical dreams and political realities: religion and social movements in the United States', in C. Timmerman, D. Hutsebaut, S. Mels, W. Nonneman and W. Van Herck (eds), *Faith-based Radicalism: Christianity, Islam and Judaism between Constructive Activism and Destructive Fanaticism*, Brussels: P.I.E. Peter Lang, pp. 233–254.

Wilcox, C. and Larson, C. (2006) *Onward Christian Soldiers*, 3rd edn, Boulder, CO: Westview.

Wilcox, C. and Robinson, C. (2007a) 'The faith of George W. Bush: the personal, practical, and political', in M. Rozell and G. Whitney (eds), *Religion and American Presidents*, New York: Palgrave/Macmillan, pp. 215–238.

Wilcox, C. and Robinson, C. (2007b) *Onward Christian Soldiers: The Christian Right in American Politics*, 3rd edn, Boulder, CO: Westview.

Wilcox, C. and Robinson, C. (2007c) 'Prayers, parties, and preachers: the evolving nature of political and religious mobilization', in M. Wilson (ed.), *Religion and Political Mobilization in the United States*, Washington, DC: Georgetown University Press, pp. 1–28.

15

Religion and civil society

David Herbert

Introduction

The term 'civil society' refers to the network of associations and organisations situated between, on the one hand, the state and political society (political associations and parties), and, on the other, kinship networks. It thus includes a vast array of organ-isations, associations and networks, ranging from sports and youth clubs to charities, voluntary organisations and religious groups, newspapers and other independent media producers. Civil society may be regulated but not controlled by the state, and market relations are generally excluded, though this is contested (Gellner 1994; Bryant 1994). Civil society is generally conceived as an area of free association rather than obligation, where individuals choose to join together for a broad range of reasons.

This voluntary basis of participation in civil society has been seen as important for the role that civil society is sometimes ascribed in providing the social preconditions of democracy. This is because it provides a training ground for democratic deliberation and participation, and channels through which grassroots issues can be brought to public attention in the public sphere (Habermas 1996). Civil society and the 'public sphere' – spaces for public debate – are sometimes conflated (Kumar 1993); but as Bryant (1993)

argues, the public sphere may be distinguished as the communicative part of civil society, which also consists of 'association, autonomy, civility' (1993: 498). The voluntary character of civil society is sometimes seen as problematic because it is argued that it presupposes a Western, individualised choosing subject, and hence is unable to reflect adequately the cultural and religious diversity which may in practice support democracy.

Civil society is a contested concept, with arguments centred on its cultural orientation, scope, utility as an analytic concept (given the normative properties associated with it), its relation to democratization, and its compatibility with various religions. In the study of religion and politics, an emphasis on religion in civil society shifts debate away from preoccupations with religious institutions, hierarchies and state, and towards religion's influence in contemporary societies through voluntary organisations and other non-state actors. As such, its use has affinities with broader attempts to re-think the sphere of political activity to include new actors such as social movements, single-issue lobby groups, and environmental pressure groups, all of which may be conceptualised as part of civil society. However, the interaction between civil society and the state remains important.

Like many political concepts, civil society has ancient Greek origins, but its modern sense derives from the Enlightenment. Since European Enlightenment thinkers were often involved in struggles for the emergence of modern progressive politics, in which religion was usually involved in defending the *ancien régime*, religion came to be associated with the legitimisation of the old order and with opposition to civil society. On the other hand, in North America, because religion and church were constitutionally separated from the formation of the new state, religion in civil society fulfilled an important role in integrating a predominantly immigrant society, and was not seen as anti-modern.

Relatively little used in academic or popular circles from the 1840s to the 1970s, for reasons we shall consider below, in the 1980s, the term was popularised by opposition groups struggling against totalitarian regimes in Eastern Europe, Latin America and South Africa, with Christian churches playing a prominent role in some cases. But it was not until the 1990s that religion in civil society began to receive substantial academic attention, heralded by José Casanova's *Public Religions in the Modern World* (1994).

For Casanova, a strong religion–state relationship, whereby religion directly influences state policy and the state intervenes in religious organisations, is incompatible both normatively, and in the long term empirically, with democratic forms of modernity. Therefore, civil society becomes the main locus for religious action in such societies; indeed religions are even able to 'deprivatize', that is, to play an increased public role, especially in protesting against injustices arguably perpetrated by state and/or market. Casanova points to the examples of post-Vatican II Catholicism (with its embrace of human rights and democracy) in Brazil, the United States and Poland in the 1980s and early 1990s, to illustrate the vital public role that religion can play in the civil societies

of quite diverse modern states, both in helping to establish democracy in Brazil and Poland, and in supporting democratic debate in America. Drawing on Habermas's (1987) terminology of 'lifeworld' and 'system', Casanova argues that in these instances religion acts to defend the communicative spaces of the lifeworld against the intrusions of the system.

Others have developed the argument, including applying it to cases more culturally distant from the North American and Western European cultural contexts in which the civil society concept evolved (Enyedi 2003; Herbert 2003). Indeed, in a range of societies from the Middle East to sub-Saharan Africa to South and South East Asia, religion has also come to prominence in spaces and organisations intermediate between kin and state, often providing social and welfare support for marginalised groups in the context of failing states, sometimes criticising states and markets for failing to meet a range of citizens' needs, from democratic participation to food, healthcare and sanitation. However, critics argue that religion (and some religions in particular) is unsuited to these roles – as an example we shall consider below Ernest Gellner's claim that Islam and civil society are incompatible.

The account that follows will outline the history of the concept of civil society, distinguishing between phases in its development and proposing a move which allows both normative and analytic uses of the concept to continue without confusion. It will then consider Poland as arguably the paradigmatic case for the revival of the term in the context of religious mobilisation, its controversial application to Islam and the particular case of Egypt as a lead society in the Arab world, and transformations in the relationship between religion and civil society arguably bringing about changes in the media through which religious images and discourses are communicated.

History and development of the civil society concept

The history of the concept can be traced from Aristotle's *politike koinonia* (political community) through its Roman translation *societas civilis*, to the medieval city state (Cohen and Arato 1992: 84–6). But its modern history begins with Hobbes (1588–1679), Locke (1632–1704) and Montesquieu (1689–1755). Each conceived of civil society as 'an inclusive, umbrella-like concept referring to a plethora of institutions outside the state' (Alexander 1998: 3), which Alexander designates 'Civil Society I' (CSI). It was developed as an attempt to manage a sense of breakdown of the old feudal social order, understood as sanctioned by God, and to defend what the emerging middle classes saw as their civility against the unruly masses. Hence it 'is best interpreted as a social and historical category by which those who have lost, or have been denied, any faith in the natural artifice attempt to explain, confirm and renaturalize ... their social condition' (Tester 1992: 13). The dissolution of the natural artifice was precipitated first by the growth of commerce undermining the power of the nobility, and then by industrialisation and urbanisation, both of which shifted the economic basis of power and created unprecedented social mobility, producing a new social order which needed new sources of legitimisation.

'Horizontal networks of interdependencies' (Habermas 1996) or 'relations of symmetric reciprocity' (Tester 1992) took centre stage in theorising the idea that a range of associations outside the state and apart from the old hierarchical order (including religious hierarchies), can provide the organisational and legitimacy basis of the new order. It should be noted that the CSI deconstruction of patriarchy was limited: the 'horizontal networks' which replaced old hierarchies comprised men of a certain social standing. Thus the patriarchal and elitist construction of CSI, and its attendant concept of a unitary public sphere has been questioned by feminist critics (Fraser 1992).

In respect of religion, not all CSI thinkers were hostile. Visiting America in the 1830s, de Tocqueville saw the churches freed from the ties of state as a key constituent of American civil society and hence democracy. However, soon after de Tocqueville's *Democracy in America* (1840), Karl Marx began a series of writings (1842–5) which linked civil society to capitalist domination. In Marx's understanding:

> Not only is civil society now simply a field of play of egotistical, purely private interests, but it is now treated as a superstructure, a legal and political arena produced as camouflage for the domination of commodities and the capitalist class.
> (Alexander 1998: 4–5)

This marks the beginning of a second historical phase in the concept's development (CSII), a critique so influential that it both largely put the concept out of circulation for a century (Abercrombie *et al.* 1994: 429) and set the pattern for subsequent critiques of CSI, including of its recent revival. Thus recent critics of international donors seeking to build 'civil society' in Bosnia (Chandler 1998) or Africa (Hearn 2000), similarly deconstruct civil society advocates' rhetoric, arguing that it conceals donor self-interest. In this way the role of civil society in channelling private or 'lifeworld' concerns into the public sphere envisaged by Habermas (1996) is blocked or distorted. Can the concept be refined to meet such criticisms?

A distinction may be made between empirical ('actually existing') civil society and normative ('ideal') civil society, enabling normative ideas about how civil society ought to function (e.g. to promote democratisation or defend society against state domination), to be tested against observation of how actually existing civil society performs.

The most influential theorist of civil society in the early twentieth century was Antonio Gramsci (1891–1937). Gramsci re-thought the role of culture in the Marxist tradition, coming to see it as more than mere superstructure, and his ideas have been of continuing influence from Japan in the 1960s to Central America in the 1990s (Keane 1998: 12–14). Gramsci saw civil society as ambivalent: it is both the means by which the state secures authority by non-coercive means, and potentially a site of resistance to it. Gramsci concluded that where the state is entrenched in institutions and the minds of the population through a developed civil society, it cannot be moved by frontal assault – hence the failure during his lifetime of revolutions other than the Russian, where civil society was weak. But the 'trenches' of civil society can also become sites of resistance to the vested interests which control the state – by providing spaces where criticism can be articulated and circulated without state control (Tester 1992: 140–3). Gramsci's insight into the ambivalence of civil society – that it could both be the site of resistance to a repressive state as well as the means of entrenchment of the state – was influential in the revival of the concept in the 1980s (Kumar 1993).

This revival occurred first in Eastern Europe in the early 1980s, followed by its rapid worldwide dissemination to the Middle East (Therborn 1997), Africa (Hearn 2000), China (Strand 1990) and South America (Hudick 1999), where it became a powerful source of mobilisation against repressive states. The idea of the spontaneous self-organisation of society also appealed in a Western context in which the limits of state intervention, especially of the welfare state, seemed to be

increasingly exposed. But the difficulties of post-Communist reconstruction (Skapska 1997), the limitations of Western strategies to promote civil society in developing societies (Hearn 2000) and the problems of applying the concept cross-culturally (Hann 1996), together with criticisms of the CSII kind – that civil society is really a front for vested interests – have produced disillusionment with it. However, Alexander (1998: 6) argues that as these challenges have also led to the emergence of the refined concept 'CSIII', 'more precise and more specific than the all-inclusive umbrella idea of CSI, more general and inclusive[e] than the narrowly reductionist association of CSII', proposing a definition as follows:

> Civil society should be conceived … as a solidary sphere in which a certain kind of universalising community comes gradually to be defined and to a certain degree enforced. To the degree that this solidary community exists, it is exhibited by 'public opinion', possesses its own cultural codes and narratives in a democratic idiom, is patterned by a set of peculiar institutions, most notably legal and journalistic ones, and is visible in historically distinctive sets of interactional practices like civility, equality, criticism, and respect. This kind of community can never exist as such; it can only exist 'to one degree or another'.
>
> (1998: 7)

This normative concept recognises the contingency of the democratising effects of empirical civil society, and overcomes the negative narrowness of CSII, pointing to the potential modes through which civil society may exercise democratising effects. However, it conflates civil society with the public sphere, and problematically locates state institutions – law – in civil society; the issue here is that the space of civil society needs legal protection, but that does not make the law part of civil society.

Alexander's definition illustrates ongoing attempts to refine the concept of civil society in response to criticisms generated by its recent widespread revival, while his delineation of three phases/uses is helpful in guiding discussion. It has also been suggested that a distinction between empirical and normative civil society is helpful to distinguish between potential/imagined and actual effects of the non-state-, non-kinship-based associations, networks and organisations commonly identified with civil society, and that this sphere of activities is worthy of closer observation and analysis, especially as a site of the activity of religious groups, who arguably have been particularly prominent in this sphere since the 1970s. In the following sections we consider some examples of civil society as a site of religious resurgence.

Poland

According to Kumar, 'It was above all the rise of Solidarity in Poland that sparked off the enthusiasm' for civil society in Eastern Europe (1993: 386). With its visibly Catholic symbols – for example in the distribution of holy communion to striking workers at the Gdansk shipyard by Catholic priests in 1981 – Poland was also the most visible instance of the role of religion in the revival of civil society in Eastern Europe. Symbolically, discursively and organisationally, the Catholic Church was crucial to the mobilisation of the Solidarity movement (Kubik 1994; Osa 1997), and demonstrates the politically mobilising power of religion at the heart of Europe, arguably the most secular continent on earth (Bruce 1999: 117). Yet as a paradigm either of the role of civil society in modern politics or of religion in civil society, Poland is highly problematic.

First, there are problems with identifying Solidarity as an example of civil society. Shortly before his death in 1984, Michel Foucault criticised the concept of civil society in relation to Poland:

> when one assimilates the powerful social movement that has just traversed that country to a revolt of civil society against state, one misunderstands the complexity and multiplicity of the confrontations.
>
> (1988: 167)

For Foucault, the civil society label obscures the complexity of social and political relations in a particular, dualistic, kind of way:

> it's … never exempt from a sort of Manichaeism that afflicts the notion of 'state' with a pejorative connotation while idealizing 'society' as a good, living, warm whole.
>
> (1988: 167–8)

While Foucault rarely used the concept of civil society, his work is relevant to its conceptualisation. Foucault argued that much modern social and political theory misunderstands power as centralised in the state. Instead, he saw power as far more diffuse and pervasive, vested in the intellectual 'disciplines' which seek to objectify knowledge (1992), and in the 'disciplinary' practices of modern medical and welfare systems (especially asylums and prisons, 1991). Seen in this way, civil society becomes less a free space for the jostling of diverse groupings giving rise to a public sphere in which a free exchange of views can occur, and more a complex network of power relations, with power being exercised not only through individuals and institutions, but through disciplinary discourses and practices.

However, if one distinguishes between empirical and normative civil society, it is possible to accept these insights without discarding the term. Empirical civil society may always be embedded in the kind of power relations Foucault describes, making its normative (democratising) functions contingent and even fragile; yet the contingency of normative civil society does not preclude its possibility. However, his more specific criticisms in the Polish case of the oversimplification of the complexity of 'confrontations' and of the valorised binary structure of civil society ('good') vs. state ('bad') require some attention.

The coalition of forces brought together under the banner of Solidarity was complex, consisting of groups with very little in common beyond opposition to the state's suppression of independent elements in society. It included labour movements, journalists and groups in the Catholic Church, and its fragmentation after 1989 testifies to its internal incoherence. If civil society is taken to imply a harmonious unity, this is indeed an oversimplification. But if these are seen as elements in an empirical civil society whose character and effects are a matter of empirical enquiry rather than presumption, then the civil society label becomes quite useful.

The strong valorisation of civil society against the state, and the aim of building a parallel society to undermine the state's functional legitimacy, were vital as tactics of opposition to state repression. However, they become dysfunctional in a democratic state. Here, while civil society needs to retain its independence, it is not necessary for it to function as a coherent opposition, and a stance of critical engagement towards different elements within itself and towards the state becomes more appropriate. It has been argued that the conditions under which Solidarity flourished in Poland 'limit its usefulness as a general model' of civil society (Kumar 1993: 387). Instead it seems better to see Poland as a model for what civil society groups

can achieve when they act together under conditions of repressive government, conditions which may now be rare in Europe, but which remain common across the world. Civil society, then, adopts different roles under different conditions.

But how far does the role of the Polish Catholic Church (PCC) in supporting the Solidarity movement provide a paradigm for the role of religion in civil society? As we saw above, Casanova stresses the background to Catholic action in the reforms of the Second Vatican council and its support for human rights and democracy. However, Casanova also recognises the strongly nationalistic character of the PCC, and, writing in the early 1990s set an agenda for steps which the PCC needed to take to complete the transformation from civil society in opposition to civil society in democracy. He argued that the PCC needed to (1) stop 'competing with the state over the symbolic representation of the Polish nation', (2) 'fully accept the principle of separation of church and state, and [hence] … permit public issues to be resolved through institutional democratic channels?' and (3) 'accept the principle of self-organization of an autonomous civil society … [rather than] promote the principle of a homogeneous Polish Catholic community' (1994: 109). We can use these criteria to guide discussion as to how far the PCC can properly be seen as a paradigm of religious action in civil society.

The PCC's actions since 1989 need to be put in context. Since the 1980s democratic politics has become firmly established in Poland. In spite of turbulence in the political system – frequent changes of government and the fission and creation of political parties – all administrations have in practice followed similar economic policies, seen rapid economic growth (though increased disparities of wealth), and achieved full European Union (EU) and NATO membership. However, Poland's accession to the secular-oriented EU has paradoxically been accompanied by the increasing electoral success of religiously nationalist parties, first the League of Polish Families (Liga Polskich Rodzin), formed in 1991, and most recently Freedom and Justice (Prawo i Sprwiedliwosc), who have led the ruling coalition since 2005. In addition, close relationships have developed between elements in the PCC, Freedom and Justice ministers, and the media group responsible for Radio Maryja (a right-wing Catholic radio station, created in 1991) and its related television network (created in 2003) (Burdziej 2005).

This situation has meant that, regarding Casanova's first question (1), the PCC has not generally had to compete with the Polish state to represent the nation, because most governments (including, if less enthusiastically, the post-Communist ones; Brach-Czaina in Burdziej: 169), have been either willing or keen to place the church at the centre of the state's representation of the nation. Concerning (2), the PCC has been unwilling on a number of key issues to 'permit public issues to be resolved through institutional democratic channels'. First, in the immediate post-Communist period (in 1989 and 1993 respectively) on the issues of religious instruction in schools and restriction of Poland's previously relatively liberal abortion laws, the PCC did not seek merely to present its case in public debate and leave the outcome up to the democratic process, but rather to influence government policy by negotiating directly with ministers. In the case of RE the process bypassed the Sejm (Parliament) altogether. Subsequently, on a series of issues including homosexual marriage, further RE related issues and references to Christianity in the Polish and European constitutions, the PCC has continued to influence public policy through direct government contacts rather than by opening up debate to include the wider civil society. As contributors to a debate on the influence of

the PCC in the pages of the daily newspaper *Rzeczposolita* wrote in 2003:

> If we are to be a civil society, various agreements made over the heads of society, for example the decision of the government not to hold a referendum over abortion or the 'back door introduction' of religious education into schools should again be made public.
>
> (Dunin and Sierakowski 2003; also in Burdziej 2005: 169)

The relationship between the PCC, media and government in Poland thus raises doubts about the extent to which the PCC fully 'accept[s] the principle of self-organization of an autonomous civil society'; while there is little evidence that the PCC seeks to stifle free speech, its actions seem more consistent with 'promote[ing] the principle of a homogeneous Polish Catholic community' than actively encouraging the expression of diverse opinions, particularly where such expression might lead to a conclusion contrary to the teaching of the church (Casanova 1994: 109).

However, while the PCC may not be the perfect democratic social actor, it does not seem to behave significantly different with respect to promoting public debate from most other interest groups – like lobby groups or commercial organisations it is primarily concerned with promoting its own agenda, and it will use any influence it legally may – through civil, political society or the state to do so. Problems arise in Poland partly because one religious organisation has such a potentially huge influence, claiming at least the nominal allegiance of some 96% of the population. In contrast, it would be difficult for one religious organisation to obtain so much influence on public policy in a more religiously plural society, such as the United States – although arguably elements of Evangelical Christianity have been able to exercise significant influence on American foreign policy, especially under the administration of George Bush II.

But while there are concerns about the compatibility of religion and civil society raised by the Polish Catholic and American Protestant examples, such concerns have been raised most acutely in relation to Islam. Yet across the Muslim world there has been a large growth in the number and activities of Islamic Private Voluntary Organisations (PVOs), exercising a range of education, health and social welfare functions, which organisationally fit the criteria of empirical civil society, being neither state nor kinship based, nor run for profit. The following sections will first examine some of the objections that have been made to the conjunction of Islam and civil society in principle, and then consider some examples of Islamic PVOs in Egypt.

Islam and civil society

Islam is the main example of a religious tradition widely considered in the West to be in tension if not outright conflict with the normative tradition of civil society (Halliday 1996), perceptions deepened by the events of 11 September 2001. It is therefore more important than ever to consider the evidence for incompatibility. This section will take the form of a critique of the most fully articulated incompatibility argument to date. In his influential *Conditions of Liberty: Civil Society and its Rivals* the late Ernest Gellner claimed that Islam is fundamentally unsecularisable, concluding from this that Islam is also incompatible with civil society, both normatively and empirically (1994: 15). Gellner understands secularisation as the declining social significance of religion – 'in industrial or industrializing societies religion loses much of its erstwhile hold over men and society' (ibid.). Where religion remains

socially significant, argues Gellner, the development of individual autonomy is constrained. This in turn constrains the development of civil society because:

> Individuals, who are not able to act independently of the community of believers, cannot become the building-stones of the kind of intermediary organizations on which civil society is built.
>
> (Özdalga 1997: 74)

This section challenges each stage of Gellner's argument. First, Gellner neglects the different ways in which modernity has been mediated to different regions and hence the consequences of this for modern institutional forms and discourses, including civil society. In particular, modernity was mediated to most Muslim majority societies either through colonial imposition or through indigenous elites responding to external pressures. In either case, for many people, 'everyday life … kept its own laws and customs, though often rigidified by colonial intervention or "indirect rule"' (Therborn 1997: 50), so that new discourses of civil and political rights did not become woven into the fabric of everyday life. Furthermore:

> The key actor [in modernization] is … a modernizing part of the ruling body, trying to adapt both the state and society to external challenge and threat. Cleavage patterns tend to run both between modern and anti-modern parts of the elite and between the former and anti-modernists among the people, with the latter sometimes winning, as in Afghanistan and Iran. In this complex pattern of conflicts and alliances … the meaning of popular rights is ambiguous, not seldom rejected by (large parts) of the people as anti-traditional.
>
> (1997: 51)

Under these conditions, one might antici-pate ambivalent attitudes to modern dis-courses, including civil society: certainly this has occurred with other modern discourses such as democracy and human rights, with Muslims taking up a full range of positions on the compatibility or incompatibility of the relationship between Islam and both democracy and human rights (Goddard 1999; Halliday 1996). This diversity contra-dicts the simplistic essentialist position that Gellner attributes to Islam – the view that Islam insists that all aspects of life should be directly governed by its unchanging pre-cepts. This contemporary diversity is under-scored by the historical diversity of Muslim majority societies, *contra* Gellner. Gellner argues that the differentiation of society necessary for a thriving civil society is con-stantly reigned in by revivals of tribal Islam, bursting in from the nomadic periphery to 'cleanse' and reform 'corrupt' urban Islam (1994: 223). But, as Lapidus argues:

The Middle Eastern Islamic heritage provides not one but two basic con-stellations of historical society, two golden ages, two paradigms, each of which has generated its own reper-toire of political institutions and polit-ical theory. The first is the society integrated in all dimensions, political, social, and moral, under the aegis of Islam. The prototype is the unification of Arabia under the leadership of the Prophet Muhammad in the seventh century. ... The second historical par-adigm is the imperial Islamic society built not on Arabian or tribal tem-plates but on the differentiated struc-tures of previous Islamic societies. ... Thus, despite the common statement that Islam is a total way of life defin-ing political as well as social and family matters, most Muslim societies ... were in fact built around separate institutions of state and religion.

(1992: 14–15)

Furthermore, Muslim thought contains its own resources for distinguishing between religious and secular planes, in the distinc-tion that the *ulama* (religious scholars) in classical period made between *ibadat* (reli-gious duties) and *muamalat* (social relations). As Tariq Ramadan argues:

Many Muslims have continued down through the ages to say for-mulaically, as if they were presenting evidence: 'There is no difference, for us, between public and private, reli-gion and politics, Islam encompasses all areas.' Many orientalists have fallen into step with them. ... But one has the right to ask whether these statements are based on sound evidence. ... The work of categor-ization left by scholars through the ages is phenomenal. ... A careful reading of these works reveals that very precise modes of grasping the sources were set down very early. ... In the area of religious practice (al-ibadat), it was determined that it was the texts that were the only ulti-mate reference because the revealed rites are fixed and not subject to human reason. ... In the wider area of human and social affairs, the established methodology is exactly the opposite: ... everything is per-mitted except that which is expli-citly forbidden in a text (or recognised as such by specialists). Thus the scope for the exercise of reason and creativity is huge.

(2004: 35)

Gellner's account also neglects the central historical factors that have shaped the emergence of modern political Islam – namely the crisis in nationalist ideologies and the failure of both socialist and capitalist development models in many parts of the Muslim world (Ayubi 1991; Binder 1988). In addition, it flies in the face of the fact that where Islamic groups have been permitted to enter the democratic process as legitimate political parties, they have regularly shown themselves both willing and able to follow democratic procedures:

> Beyond the Arab world, Islamists have regularly run for elections in Pakistan, Bangladesh and Turkey since the 1980s. In Indonesia, Malaysia, and the Islamic republics of the former Soviet Union, Islamists have peacefully been engaging in local and municipal politics. ... It is important to note that in three of the biggest Muslim countries (Pakistan, Bangladesh and Turkey) women have recently been elected to the top executive office in the land. ... The important thing in all these cases is that Islamic parties have accepted the rules of the democratic game and are playing it peaceably and in an orderly manner.
>
> (Ibrahim 1997: 41)

Furthermore, other discourses dependent on strong individuation – such as human rights – have also taken firm root in many Muslim societies, such that, in spite of the ambivalence associated with them, they now form part of the terms of public debate. This is illustrated by Dwyer's conversations with intellectuals about human rights in Tunisia, Morocco and Egypt in the late 1980s, many of whom were active in human rights organisations. Tunisia, in particular, provides a good example of a reforming Islamist movement specifically seeking to articulate its vision in terms of human rights without eliding tensions between the valuing individual autonomy and of kinship bonds (Dalacoura 1998). In his study, Dwyer shows the extent to which human rights discourse, contested and polysemous as it is, has penetrated

contemporary Middle Eastern societies. As he concludes:

> Few Middle Easterners I spoke to seem ready to dismiss the idea from their cultural repertoire: they may challenge its foundations, or its provenance, or the content given it by specific groups, but the concept itself has come to constitute a symbol of great power.
>
> (Dwyer 1991: 192)

Thus Gellner essentialises connections between Islam, civil society and democratisation which are in fact contingent. Islam is not necessarily incompatible normatively or practically with structural differentiation (indeed, Muslim tradition contains resources for making distinctions between different spheres of life), and many Muslim societies in practice support both diverse civil societies and democracy, even though, and perhaps unsurprisingly given the manner of their reception of modernity, these discourses remain contested. Given this general situation, we turn next to consider the articulation of religion and civil society in practice in the particular case of Egypt.

Islam and civil society in Egypt

The growth of Islam in the public life of modern Muslim societies is a widespread phenomenon, but Egypt may be regarded as a lead society for several reasons, and hence its use as an example here. Egypt has the largest Arab population of any state, is host to the most influential intellectual establishment in the Sunni Muslim world, the ancient Al-Azhar university (a complex public institution combining the functions of: 'mosque, university, state legitimisation, interpretative authority and centre of Islamic propaganda all in one'; Karam 1997: 158), and is the cradle of the earliest and most influential modern polit-ical Islamic movement, known as *Ikhwan* or the Muslim Brotherhood, founded by Hasan al-Banna in 1928. Not only is this 'arguably the strongest' Islamic movement 'in any Arab, or possibly Muslim country at the present time' (Ayubi 1991: 172), but also its writings and role model have been influential for political Islamic movements across the Muslim world. Fourth, Egypt has more non-governmental organisations than the rest of the Arab world put together, indicative of a diverse and com-plex modern society.

As with communist Poland, the mobil-isation of religion in civil society in Egypt has occurred under conditions of authori-tarian government. The Egyptian parlia-ment 'serves as an instrument of state policy rather than a constraint upon it' (Wickham 1997: 121), and whereas 'civil society ... in its liberal conception ... is not merely a sphere outside government but rather one endowed with a legally mandated autonomy, involving legal rights and pro-tections backed by the law-state', such legal protection is largely absent in Egypt (Wickham 1997: 117). Through the 1990s the Mubarak regime seized control of thousands of private mosques, requiring preachers to conform to government stan-dards (Abdo 2000: 66). It also sought closer control of Al-Azhar and increased the latter's censorship powers, thus seeking to strengthen its hold on public religion. However, there are signs that in spite of a repressive state some Islamic movements are developing Islamic identity as a source of political mobilisation in an inclusive direction: the election of Muslim brothers to the leadership of professional associa-tions (e.g. the pharmacists) while drawing a substantial proportion of the Coptic Christian vote is one small sign of this (2000: 100).

In the absence of a strong independ-ent trade union movement, and forbid-den to form its own political parties, the professional associations have provided a platform on which the Muslim Brotherhood has been able to mobilise politically. These 'syndicates' were originally established by the government as an alter-native to independent trade unions, but, as the Polish case also shows, under certain conditions such bodies can take on an independent life. Their free elections provide a rare opportunity for democracy in a context where government run elec-tions are widely reported to be rigged (Kassem 1999).

Between 1984 and 1992 the Brotherhood had gained control of the Egyptian Bar Association, the Engineers' Association and the Medical Association. Initially, while they were able to gain power in these elite professional bodies, Islamists were less successful in the associ-ations of less prestigious professions. In an Egyptian context, these include the associ-ations of teachers, agronomists and vets, 'sectors characterised by low wages, poor working conditions, and low social status' (Wickham 1997: 128). It may be noted that this greater influence in the elite professions contradicts the stereotype that Islamists recruit mostly from the poorest sections of society. However, by 1997 Islamists had also won control of the agronomists and pharmacists' unions, the latter a particularly notable victory as approximately 30% of pharmacists are Coptic Christians (Abdo 2000: 100).

As the reliance on the Coptic vote in the pharmacists' case suggests, the Brotherhood owes its success less to a stri-dent Islamic political identity than to achievement in delivering services to members, as one Coptic Christian com-ments:

> We can trust the Islamists to work for us, no matter what problems we face. This isn't a syndicate for Muslims. It's a syndicate for pharmacists.
>
> (2000: 101)

The Brotherhood's participation has increased electoral turnout, and some commitment to pluralism has been shown, for example in the decision in 1992 not to contest 5 of the 25 seats on the Medical Association Board in 1992, to allow for other voices: they won the other 20 (Wickham 1997: 126). Islamists have particularly targeted younger members, building on their high profile in most universities, and on the frustrations of graduates qualified beyond the level of work that the public sector dominated economy is able to offer them – hence 'accountants waiting tables ... lawyers ... working the fields' (1997: 122). Even those lucky enough to find an appropriate job find public-sector salaries inadequate to meet their expenses. Hence the Islamist leadership of professional associations have 'initiated projects in the areas of housing, health care, and insurance' (1997: 123). They have come up with creative solutions to practical problems such as providing shared cars for lawyers with meetings all over Cairo but too poor to afford them, and providing loans to help people set up home and get married – huge expenses in Egypt for all but the wealthiest (Abdo 2000: 92).

Beyond the interests of their professional groups, Islamists have sought to build on traditions in these professions of a sense of social responsibility and of acting as advocates for 'the Egyptian people' (al-sha'b) (Wickham 1997: 129). They have taken a stand for democracy and human rights, and in some cases sought to build alliances with secularist opponents (1997: 130). Concretely, after the 1992 earthquake, volunteers from the Medical Association arrived on the scene first in many of the worst-affected areas prompting government suspicion that the Brotherhood was attempting to create 'a state within a state' (1997: 130), a military response and further repressive measures. These have included 'Law 100' (1993), which required a 50% voter turnout in

syndicate elections (or the government nominates the syndicate board itself), and the hirasa laws, which have empowered the government to take the syndicates under direct control, in spite of legal challenges (Abdo 2000: 102–5). However, as Abdo concludes:

> Despite these setbacks, the syndicate movement under the new Islamists has touched Egyptian society in a way few could have imagined. ... In a society bereft of democracy they proved free elections and free debate were in fact possible. In a nation crying out for moral guidance, they successfully married a vision of social justice, rooted in the Koran, with the demands and stresses of modern life. ...
>
> The new leadership raised standards of living for union members, eased pervasive corruption and cronyism, and filled in for an incompetent state that could no longer address the concerns of the middle classes. The syndicates also demonstrated a remarkable degree of democracy, in contrast to the Mubarak regime.
>
> (Abdo 2000: 105)

From the perspective of normative civil society these organisations clearly satisfy the criteria of building trust within the unions and belief in the possibility of change. They also promote diversity in terms of the institutional plurality of Egyptian society, and have proven respectful of equal rights for the Coptic minority within the orbit of a trades union oriented to reaching out into society to improve the lot of its members. In this last respect they have begun to heal some of the wounds inflicted on Coptic–Muslim relations by extremist Islamists. But questions remain on the issue of free speech when it comes to offence to or subversion of religious authority; for example in 1996 after a long battle in the courts Islamist lawyers hounded literary scholar Abu Zaid into exile, accusing him of *riddah* (apostasy) for his materialist reading of the Qur'an (Tibi 1998: x).

Looking to the future: civil society, the public sphere and 'new' media

One feature of the appropriation of public Islam in Egypt by non-state actors has been the dissemination of Islamic discourses by electronic media, including sermons on audio-cassette, desktop publishing, the internet and DVDs. The proliferation of new media has made censorship much more difficult for states, and created and intensified trans-national circuits of communication. These developments have enabled groups to mobilise religious counter-publics against official discourses, thus changing the relationship between religion and civil society. But it is not only where routes to democratic participation are blocked that religious imagery and discourse has become politicised through the appropriation of new media.

India is the largest functioning democracy on the planet, a complex society in which an official state secularism minimised the partisan mobilisation of religious discourses at the level of political society for several decades following independence (1947). However, the early 1990s saw the electoral breakthrough of the overtly Hindu nationalist party the BJP (Bharatiya Janata Party), achieving a consistent period in office from March 1998 (Rajagopal 2001: 275, 326). What relationship does this development have to religion in civil society? Like the Muslim Brotherhood, the BJP and related organisations are active at the grassroots, running education, training and welfare schemes. But intriguingly their electoral breakthrough occurred only after the screening

of two influential Hindu epics on the newly created state national television broadcaster *Doordashan* in the late 1980s and early 1990s. According to some commentators these broadcasts had the unintended political consequence of creating a new political public sphere linked by a 'Hinduized visual regime', both more inclusive and more chaotic than India's linguistically and socially splintered publics had previously been:

> The introduction of a new system of representation, in this case television, set up new circuits of exchange across a split public, thereby casting the existing terms of translation, and the status of the bourgeois public sphere itself, into crisis.
>
> (Rajagopal 2001: 148)

The BJP was able turn the crisis in the bourgeois public sphere and the presentation of an idealised past against which current circumstances could be unfavourably contrasted, to their electoral advantage. Its success also rested on other factors and an uneasy coalition, and its spell in power ended in defeat by the Congress party in 2005. For now their legacy is to have shifted political discourse in a nationalist direction; but beyond the BJP, the mass circulation of Hindu epics may have enduring consequences for Indian civil society:

> Even in the absence of Hindu nationalist domination … we may have in India a Hinduized visual regime, evidenced for example in commodity consumption in daily life, acting as a kind of lower-order claim than national identity and continuing to have force in politics, albeit of a more dispersed, subtle and less confrontational kind, in a kind of capacitance effect whereby social energy may be accumulated and

stored [like an electric charge] via allegiance to such images, to be put to use at some future moment, though in ways that would be hard to predict.

(2001: 283)

This emergence of religion circulated by new media as powerful discourse and imagery in the public spheres of modern societies, is widespread in many post-colonial contexts (Meyer and Moors 2006). But it is not restricted to them; for example in France, arguably one of the most secular countries in the world:

A new socio-cultural configuration is emerging in which the religious, far from appearing in the form of a tradition resisting modernity, appears instead in the form of a tradition that prevents ultra-modernity from dissolving into a self-destructive critique. Increasingly, religion provides identities and offers to individuals the possibility of social integration and direction within individualistic and pluralistic societies. ... It is equally clear, however, that the traditional distrust of religion undoubtedly continues in France.

(Willaime 2004: 375–7)

Such developments are transforming the relationship between religion and civil society, calling into question long established assumptions about secularisation, and creating the potential for new forms of political mobilisation and confrontation.

Bibliography

Abdo, E. (2000) *No God But God: Egypt and the Triumph of Islam*, Oxford: Oxford University Press.

Abercrombie, N., Hill, S. and Turner, B. (1994) *The Penguin Dictionary of Sociology*, 3rd edn, London: Penguin.

Alexander, J. (ed.) (1998) *Real Civil Societies: Dilemmas of Institutionalization*, London: Routledge.

Arato, A. (1981) 'Civil society against the state', *Telos*, 47, pp. 23–47.

Ayubi, N. (1991) *Political Islam*, London: Routledge.

Bruce, S. (1999) *Choice and Religion: A Critique of Rational Choice Theory*, Oxford: Oxford University Press.

Bryant, C. (1993) 'Social, self-organisation, civility and sociology: A comment on Kumar's "civil society"', *British Journal of Sociology*, 44, 3, pp. 397–401.

Bryant, C. (1994) 'A further comment on Kumar's "civil society"', *British Journal of Sociology*, 45, 3, pp. 497–9.

Bundziej, S. (2005) 'Religion and politics: Religious values in the Polish public square since 1989'; *Religion, State & Society*, 33, 2, pp. 165–74.

Casanova, J. (1994) *Public Religions in the Modern World*, Chicago: Chicago University Press.

Chandler, D. (1998) 'Democratization in Bosnia: The limits of civil society building strategies', *Democratization*, 5, 4, pp. 78–102.

Cohen, J. and Arato, A. (1992) *Civil Society and Political Theory*, London: MIT Press.

Dalacoura, K. (1998) *Islam, Liberalism and Human Rights*, London: I. B. Tauris.

Dunin, K. and Sierakowski, S. (2003) 'Jaki Kościół, jaka lewica, jaka dialog?' ['What church, what left, what dialogue?'], *Rzeczpospolita*, 155, 5–6, p. A7.

Dwyer, K. (1991) *Arab Voices: The Human Rights Debate in the Middle East*, London: Routledge.

Enyedi, Z. (2003) 'The contested politics of positive neutrality in Hungary', *West European Politics*, 26, 1, pp. 157–76.

Foucault, M. (1988) *Politics, Philosophy, Culture: Interviews and Other Writings 1977–1984* (translated by A. Sheridan *et al.*), London: Routledge.

Foucault, M. (1991) [1977] *Discipline and Punish: The Birth of the Prison* (translated by A. Sheridan *et al.*), Harmondsworth: Penguin.

Foucault, M. (1992) [1970] *The Order of Things*, London: Routledge.

Fraser, N. (1992) 'Rethinking the public sphere: A contribution to the critique of actually existing democracy', in C. Calhoun (ed.), *Habermas and the Public Sphere*, Cambridge, MA, and London: MIT Press, pp. 109–42.

Gellner, E. (1994) *The Conditions of Liberty: Civil Society and its Rivals*, London: Penguin.

Goddard, H. (1999) 'Islam and democracy', presentation to PSA Politics and Religion Group, Lincoln Theological Institute, Sheffield, 24 February.

Habermas, J. (1987) *Theory of Communicative Action, Vol. 2: Lifeworld and System: A Critique of Functionalist Reason*, Cambridge: Polity/ Oxford: Blackwell.

Habermas, J. (1996) *Between Facts and Norms*, Cambridge: Polity.

Halliday, F. (1996) *Islam and the Myth of Confrontation: Religion and Politics in the Middle East*, London: I. B. Tauris.

Hann, C. (ed.) (1996) *Civil Society: Challenging Western Models*, London: Routledge.

Hearn, J. (2000) 'The "uses and abuses" of civil society in Africa', paper presented to the Review of African Political Economy conference, University of Leeds, April.

Herbert, D. (2003) *Religion and Civil Society*, Aldershot: Ashgate.

Hudick, A. (1999) *NGOs and Civil Society: Democracy by Proxy?*, Cambridge: Polity.

Ibrahim, S. (1997) 'From Taliban to Erbakan: The case of Islam, civil society and democracy', in E. Özdalga and S. Persson (eds), *Civil Society and Democracy in the Muslim World*, Istanbul: Swedish Research Institute, pp. 33–44.

Karam, A. (1997) 'Islamist parties in the Arab world: Ambiguities, contradictions and perseverance, *Democratization*, 4, 4, pp. 157–74.

Kassem, M. (1999) *In the Guise of Democracy: Governance in Contemporary Egypt*, Reading: Ithaca.

Keane, J. (1998) *Civil Society*, Cambridge: Polity.

Kubik, K. (1994) *The Power of Symbols against the Symbols of Power: The Rise of Solidarity and the Fall of State Socialism in Poland*, Philadelphia: Pennsylvania University Press.

Kumar, K. (1993) 'Civil society: An inquiry into the usefulness of an historical term', *British Journal of Sociology*, 44, 3, pp. 375–95.

Kumar, K. (1994) 'Civil society again: A reply to Christopher Bryant's "social self-organisation, civility and sociology"', *British Journal of Sociology*, 45, 1, pp. 375–95.

Lapidus, I. (1992) 'The golden age: The political concepts of Islam', *Annals of the American Academy*, 524, pp. 13–25.

Meyer, B., and Moors, A. (2006) *Religion, the Media and the Public Sphere*, Bloomington, IN: Indiana University Press.

Osa, M. (1997) 'Creating solidarity: The religious foundations of the Polish social movement', *East European Politics and Societies*, 11, 2, pp. 339–65.

Özdalga, E. (1997) 'Civil society and its enemies: Reflections on a debate in the light of recent developments within the Islamic student movement in Turkey', in E. Özdalga and S. Persson (eds), *Civil Society and Democracy in the Muslim World*, Istanbul: Swedish Research Institute, pp. 73–84.

Rajagopal, A. (2001) *Politics after Television: Hindu Nationalism and the Reshaping of the Public in India*, Cambridge: Cambridge University Press.

Ramadan, T. (2004) *Western Muslims and the Future of Islam*, Oxford: Oxford University Press.

Skapska, G. (1997) 'Learning to be a citizen: Cognitive and ethical aspects of post-communist society transformation', in R. Fine (ed.) *Civil Society: Democratic Perspective*, London: Cass, pp. 145–60.

Strand, D. (1990) 'Protest in Beijing: Civil society and public sphere in China', *Problems of Communism*, 34, May–June.

Tester, K. (1992) *Civil Society*, London: Routledge.

Therborn, G. (1997) 'Beyond civil society: Democratic experiences and their relevance to the "Middle East"', in E. Özdalga and S. Persson (eds.), *Civil Society and Democracy in the Muslim World*, Istanbul: Swedish Research Institute, pp. 45–54.

Tibi, B. (1998) *The Challenge of Fundamentalism: Political Islam and the New World Disorder*, Berkeley: University of California Press.

Wickham, C. (1997) 'Islamic mobilization and political change: The Islamist trend in Egypt's political associations', in J. Stork and J. Benin (eds), *Political Islam: Essays from Middle East Report*, London: I. B. Tauris, pp. 120–35.

Willaime, J. (2004) 'The cultural turn in the sociology of religion in France', *Sociology of Religion*, 65, 4, pp. 373–89.

245

Religious commitment and socio-political orientations

Different patterns of compartmentalisation among Muslims and Christians?

Thorleif Pettersson

Secularisation theory assumes religion to have become increasingly differentiated from secular society, privatised and largely irrelevant to public secular issues. In contrast to this view, religious actors in both European and Islamic countries are said to refuse to take the marginal role which secularisation theories have reserved for them. Accordingly, contemporary religion is also assumed to have become increasingly deprivatised and relevant to secular society. Based on similar arguments, recent developments in International Relations (IR) theory also assume religious factors to have become increasingly influential in that discipline.

At the individual micro level, compartmentalisation is said to constitute the psychological parallel to the macro-level differentiation between religious and secular institutions. In this sense, compartmentalisation between religious beliefs and orientations towards secular issues can be thought of as religious differentiation 'in mind'. Accordingly, the privatisation of

religion would be paralleled by increasing levels of compartmentalisation, and deprivatisation by decreasing levels.

Using data from the fourth wave of the World Values Survey, this chapter explores whether the patterns of compartmentalisation between religious commitment and a set of socio-political orientations towards secular issues differ between four Islamic and four European countries. Overall, the empirical findings challenge popular stereotypes of Muslim religiosity as demanding a strong religious impact on politics and as being negatively oriented towards democracy, gender equality, emancipative freedom values, and strong institutions for global governance. In fact, these correlates of religious involvement were often found among the European Catholics. As a consequence, these comparisons of grassroot-level orientations in Christian and Islamic countries *do not support the view of Muslim religiosity as particularly different and challenging.*

Religious commitment and socio-political orientations: different patterns of compartmentalisation among Muslims and Christians?

Religion is said to legitimate both authoritarian and democratic regimes, as well as to divert social grievances into both passive quietism and social activism to demand changes (Williams 1996: 368). However, to explain why religion can show such different faces is a complex task. In particular, there are different dimensions and/or levels of both religious and social systems to consider, and different contexts in time and space to take into account (Jelen and Wilcox 2002a, 2002b). Thus, the many relationships between religion and socio-political issues depend on the internal characteristics of the religious and socio-political systems, their different external socio-economical contexts, and the kinds of religious and political involvement among its followers.

At a very general level, the social consequences of religion are usually analysed from the perspective of secularisation theory. Religious studies have long since been concerned with secularisation as a major factor affecting contemporary society, and almost all of the founding fathers in social and cultural research contributed in different ways to the study of secularisation processes. Therefore, one should not talk about the secularisation theory, but rather of the secularisation paradigm, which includes a number of different interpretations of secularisation (Gorski 2000: 141). However, despite this variation, most secularisation theorists agree that the differentiation between the religious and the secular institutions is a core dimension of secularisation. Most also agree that this differentiation has increased over time, at least in the Western world, and that

specialised roles and institutions have developed in order to handle specific features or functions which were previously carried out by religious institutions. Due to differentiation, 'specialised agencies developed which rested their claims increasingly on technical competence rather than on religiously acclaimed moral authority' (Wilson 1996: 17). As a consequence, religious institutions came to lose many of their previous social functions, no longer the main providers of education, healthcare, social welfare, etc. When secularisation is understood as the differentiation between the religious and the secular institutions, this is just one specific instance of the general process of functional differentiation. In this sense, secularisation can be described as the repercussion of this general development on the religious subsystem (Dobbelaere 1995: 1). Paradoxically, due to this kind of secularisation, the religious subsystem has become more occupied with 'pure religion', unsullied by various this-worldly concerns such as politics and economic matters.

If most secularisation theorists agree on the differentiation thesis, there is more disagreement about the consequences of the differentiation between religion and the secular. Some assume that people's religious involvement has declined over time. Membership rates in churches and denominations are said to have decreased and adherence to religious belief systems to have diminished, especially in Western Europe. Strong evidence for the progressive and apparently still continuing decline of religion is regularly found there (Casanova 1994; Acquaviva 1979). Whether a corresponding decline is also experienced in the US is more debatable (see, for example, Stark and Finke 2000), not to mention the many contexts where Islam is the main religion and levels of religious commitment are usually said to be strong. Others assume that the differentiation between religious and secular institutions primarily leads to the privatisation of religion. As the religious and secular institutions have become differentiated, religion is assumed to have remained more significant to personal and private matters (Turner 1991: 9). Religion has been assigned to the private sphere, understood as the sphere of 'love, intimacy, subjectivity, sentimentality, emotions, irrationality, morality, spirituality … and religion as well as morality became simply matters of individual, private taste' (Casanova 1994: 22).

Recently, however, the privatisation thesis has been seriously questioned. For instance, Jose Casanova's (1994) well-known criticism of the thesis deserves close attention. Contrary to the thesis of an ongoing privatisation of religion, Casanova argues that the Islamic revolution in Iran, the rise of the Solidarity movement in Poland, the role of Catholicism for the Sandinista revolution in Latin America, and the increased political importance of North American Protestant fundamentalism, respectively, demonstrate that the contemporary religions refuse to accept the marginal role which secularisation theory reserves for them. Referring to such developments, Casanova claims that contemporary religions have become *de*-privatised, increasingly important to the public sphere. However, it should be noted that this claim is not part of any absolutist dismissal of secularisation theory altogether. On the contrary, differentiation is seen by Casanova as a key characteristic of modern society, and he regards differentiation between religion and the secular to be the still defensible core of secularisation theory (Casanova 1994: 212). However, to maintain that differentiation *necessarily* must entail the privatisation of religion is according to him no longer defensible (Casanova 1994: 7). Rather, he sees the privatisation of religion more as an option

than as an inevitable structural trend. This view is built on the view that religious privatisation is caused by a number of different factors, which differ between different contexts. Casanova sees religious rationalisation, including pietism, religious individuation and religious reflexivity, as one of the causes of religious privatisation. General structural differentiation which constrains religion into a specific religious sphere is seen as another cause. Liberal categories of thought, which are said to permeate modern Western culture, is said to constitute a third causal antecedent of religious privatisation (Casanova 1994: 215). In addition to these general factors, Casanova also assumes that other circumstances can drive towards the privatisation of religion. For instance, a given religion is said to be less likely to assume public roles, the less it draws on a public collective identity among its disciples. Similarly, the more a religion loses followers, the more likely it is to become privatised. And the less global and transnational a religious tradition, the less probable Casanova finds its impact on public matters (Casanova 1994: 225).

Obviously, normative critiques of the actual boundaries between the private and the public are often forwarded by different religious bodies. This is at the heart of Casanova's claims of public religions at the level of the civic society. What he understands as the deprivatisation of modern religion is the process 'whereby religion abandons its assigned place in the private sphere and enters the undifferentiated public sphere of civil society to take part in the ongoing process of contestation, discursive legitimation and redrawing of boundaries [between the public and the private]' (Casanova 1994: 65ff). By 'crossing boundaries, by raising questions publicly about the autonomous pretensions of the differentiated spheres to function without regard to moral norms or human considerations, public religions may help mobilise people against such pretensions, they may contribute to a redrawing of boundaries, or, at the very least, they may force or contribute to a public debate about such issues' (Casanova 1994: 43).

However, such a strengthened relationship between religion and secular society is primarily assumed to occur at the level of public discourse. Whether the religious actors have a real impact on people's understandings of the differentiation between the public and the private is said to be less important. 'Irrespective of the historical outcome of such a debate, religions will have played an important public role' (1994). Undoubtedly, religious leaders have launched – and in all likelihood will continue to do so - a number of efforts to affect public opinion, for instance concerning governance and democracy, legislation and practice related to reproduction, abortion and euthanasia, aid to developing countries and arms trade, care of the elderly and sick, schooling and cultural programmes, etc. Certainly, such efforts can be said to demonstrate that contemporary religion is still involved in public issues. However, to the degree that such efforts have little impact, and people by and large find them irrelevant, differentiation between religion and secular society seems to be a more adequate feature of contemporary society than de-differentiation. In this sense, the crucial matter is not whether religious spokespeople try to influence public discourse on various matters in secular society, but whether their efforts have a real impact or not. And quite regardless of what one finds to be the crucial matter in this regard, comparative analyses of how ordinary people evaluate the role of religion with regard to politics and public matters would cast additional light on the deprivatisation processes reported by Casanova. This chapter presents such an analysis.

Based on similar lines of thought as Casanova's, contemporary religious factors are also assumed to be increasingly important for international politics (see, for example, Dark 2000; Tibi 2001; Cox 2002). One reason for the contemporary surge of religious factors in world politics is that the end of the Cold War was followed by a number of conflicts which were imbued with religious ingredients. Even if more or less devastating 'clashes of civilizations' (Huntington 1996) need not necessarily occur, tensions between the Islamic and the more or less secularised Western world with its Christian heritage have undoubtedly become more frequent over the last decades. One may refer, for example, to the long and seemingly endless Israel–Palestine conflict, the US war against Iraq in 1990–91, bombings of the American embassies in Tanzania and Kenya in 1998, the al-Qaeda attack against the World Trade Center on 11 September 2001, and the subsequent US attack on Afghanistan and Iraq. The continuing conflict between Russia and Chechnya can also been seen as another indicator of the same tendency. Consequently, there are many reasons to assume religious factors and religiously motivated violence to be increasingly important in international politics (Jurgensmeyer 2000). In these matters, signs of increasing Islamic nationalism are also of interest. 'In the early 90s, Islamic nationalism gained strength in areas far from the Middle East: In Afghanistan, in Algeria and elsewhere in Africa, in Mongolia, in Tajikistan, and in other Central Asian countries of the Commonwealth of Independent States. New leaders rode the crests of power provided by these movements, and they are likely to find in religion a useful support for some years to come' (Juergensmeyer 1993: 194). Obviously, the developments within the Islamic world are certainly of great interest to those who study the relation between religion and the secular, both domestically and internationally.

However, in these regards, one should not readily assume grassroots-level religious and political culture to be more or less homogeneous among either Islamic or Christian societies. The many differences between Protestant and Catholic countries in these regards are well known and documented. In Europe, secularisation is usually assumed to be an uneven process and to have 'affected the major Protestant churches more strongly than the Catholic Church' (Therborn 1995: 274). Because of greater incentives for religious individualism among Protestants, Protestant culture is assumed to be more pluralistic than Catholic, both in terms of lower levels of religious involvement and a weaker impact of religion on various secular spheres. These differences have at least partly been explained by the theological differences between Catholicism and Protestantism. For instance, religious individualism became manifest much earlier in Protestantism (Jagodzinski and Dobbelaere 1995a, 1995b).

Similar heterogeneities are also noticed in the Islamic world. It has proven difficult to assess any distinct and generally shared Islamic pattern, and the different Islamic societies should not be seen as homogeneous in their religious outlooks. For instance, a recent comparative analysis of grassroots religious involvement in Egypt, Jordan and Iran documented noticeable differences. In particular, Iranians placed less emphasis on religion than Egyptians and Jordanians. This was explained by the fact that in Iran, a theocracy dominates the socio-political order, and that opposition groups often are formulated in reaction towards this regime. Therefore, Iranians' (at least partial) withdrawal from religious involvement can be understood as a token of political opposition (Moaddel and Azadarmaki 2003). Among the three countries, Iran also showed the lowest percentage claiming cultural invasion from the West to be a serious problem. Another interesting finding was that in Iran, it was predominantly older people and people with less education who scored highest on religious commitment. Increased education may therefore be an important factor changing Islamic convictions and value priorities. In these regards, the Islamic pattern does not seem to differ much from the Western (especially the Western European) (see, for example, Inglehart 1990; Inglehart and Norris 2003).

In a similar manner, the political culture has not been found to distinguish Islam from the Protestant, Catholic, Orthodox or Hindu worlds; the political cultures within these religious traditions do not demonstrate tradition-specific profiles of political tolerance, support for freedom, participation in or search for alternatives to the democratic system, etc. (Esmer 2003). Another analysis concluded that there is little evidence that Islam and democracy are incompatible (Tessler 2003). And yet another comparative analysis found that 'Islam is not the cause of the lack of democracy in predominantly Muslim countries' (Price 2000: 153). Rather, the difference between Islamic and Western cultures at the grassroots level has been said to concern 'Eros far more than Demos' (Norris and Inglehart 2003).

In summary, it can be concluded that neither the Islamic societies as such, nor the citizens within them, should be regarded as homogeneous in their religious and political attitudes, including their orientations towards global governance. The same conclusion can be made with regard to the Christian context. And yet, at the same time, most secularisation theorists agree that religion has become privatised and increasingly differentiated from secular society, and that this tendency is more pronounced among the highly developed Christian countries as compared to the Islamic world. In order to examine this seeming paradox, it is useful to consider another theoretical perspective.

Individual-level compartmentalisation and societal-level secularisation

Even if neither the Christian nor the Islamic world should be seen as homogeneous with regard to religious culture and relations to secular matters, it is still of great interest to investigate whether in different Islamic and Christian contexts, grassroots-level religious commitments tend to have similar or dissimilar consequences for followers' attitudes towards democracy, how they prefer religion and politics to be linked, what they think about bio-ethical and economical moral issues, how they value emancipative freedom and gender equality, how they view matters of global governance, and so on. In the many comparisons between the Islamic and the Western secularised worlds, this issue is to the best of my knowledge the least investigated. Rather, most analyses on these matters have focused on comparative analyses of aggregated macro-level differences and similarities between Western and Islamic countries. In contrast to such an approach, the key research question of this chapter is to investigate whether regardless of any macro-level cultural differences between a set of Islamic and Western Christian countries, individual-level religious commitment to either Islam or Christianity has similar or dissimilar consequences for the followers' views on secular issues. In order to investigate how Islam and Christianity help shape secular societal values, this issue must also be investigated. Should for instance individual-level commitment to both of these major religious traditions have a similar impact on, for example, dislike for gender equality and preferences for traditional family patterns? It would be difficult to claim that the contemporary macro-level differences between Islam and the West in these regards would primarily be caused by the commitment to the two different religious traditions.

As a theoretical tool for such an investigation, the concept of *compartmentalisation* can be useful (see, for example, Dobbelaere 2002). Compartmentalisation can be thought of as the psychological parallel to macro-level differentiation between religion and the secular, and as 'differentiation-in-mind'. Obviously, differentiation between religious and secular at the societal macro level may drive individuals to isolate and compartmentalise religious orientations from views on secular spheres of life, including politics, gender relations, and bio-ethical issues. However, following both Casanova and Dobbelaere, this need not necessarily be the case. Even if the religious institutions have become differentiated from secular society, the religiously committed believers can still want religion to have an impact, and they can still base their views on secular issues on their religious convictions. Therefore, with regard to compartmentalisation, the key question concerns whether people *prefer*, *think* or *accept* that institutional religion should have an impact on, for example, legal and economical matters. A related question asks whether religious commitment is in fact related to people's views on such secular issues. In these regards, it is not especially far fetched to assume that the higher the level of religious commitment, the more people would prefer a religious impact on secular issues, and the stronger the linkage between their religious convictions and their views on various secular orientations (see, for example, Pettersson 2002; Billiet et al. 2003). It also seems reasonable to assume that these relations should be equally found in both Islamic and Christian contexts.

However, whether people prefer a religious impact on secular domains and deduce their secular attitudes from their religious convictions is also likely to depend on the degree of religious pluralism between religious organisations and movements. When the degree of religious pluralism among churches and religious organisations is high and there are many different denominations and religious movements, the less likely it is that the religiously committed would develop similar orientations towards secular issues (Dobbelaere and Billiet in press). *Ceteris paribus*, the higher the degree of religious pluralism among churches and religious movements, the more likely it is that religious compartmentalisation has developed. Therefore, comparative analyses of the patterns for religious compartmentalisation should take the level of religious pluralism into account.

Analytical strategy

In the following analysis of the patterns of compartmentalisation among Islamic and Christian countries, the findings from four groups of countries will be compared. Two of the groups will be selected from the Islamic world, and two from the Western Christian. The groups from each of the two major religious traditions have been selected to be as different as possible with regard to the special variety of religious traditions which dominates. Since the aim is to find possibly similar patterns of compartmentalisation (see above), this strategy seems appropriate. The first group of Islamic societies contains the Arab Muslim countries of Morocco and Algeria. These two Arab countries are dominated by the Sunni tradition. The second group consists of Iran and Indonesia, two non-Arab Muslim countries. Iran is dominated by Shi'ites, but there are also considerable minorities of Kurds and Sunnites. Indonesia is an Asian country outside the core Islamic region, and in this country Islam is said to harbour a number of non-orthodox Islamic doctrines and to show strong influences, 'not only from the original animistic beliefs but also from Buddhism and Hinduism' (Cederroth 1999: 254).

The first group of Western European countries is composed of Italy and Spain, two of the core Southern European Catholic countries. The second group consists of Sweden and Denmark; two comparatively highly secularised Protestant welfare societies situated in Northern Europe. In a way, this selection of countries follows the 'most different system design' (Przeworski and Teune 1970). Should the level of compartmentalisation be similar among the different groups of countries, it can be concluded that the level of compartmentalisation is *not* affected by the specific characteristics of the different groups. In this regard, it should also be noted that the levels of religious pluralism appear to be at least somewhat similar among the selected countries. Each of them is dominated by a single religious tradition. Therefore, the level of religious pluralism among the four groups is at least partially controlled for. In order to control for other possible contaminating factors, the analytical strategy of this chapter will also seek to control for the impact of political involvement, age, gender, education and household income. By introducing these controls, the 'net' effect of religious involvement on various orientations towards secular issues can be estimated by ordinary multivariate regression analyses, using religious and political involvement, age, gender, education and household income as independent variables, and various orientations towards secular issues as the dependent variables.

As examples of orientations towards secular issues, seven different orientations will be investigated. Of these orientations, two concern orientations towards democracy and the preferred relation between religion and politics. Two other orientations concern views on bio-ethical and socio-economical moral issues, while two other orientations concern preferences for gender equality and emancipative freedom values, respectively. The seventh orientation concerns views on the distribution of vertical power within the United Nations, the leading institution for global governance. The selection of these seven orientations is based on different criteria, for example, data availability, the possibilities of obtaining cross-culturally valid measurements, theoretical considerations, and the contents in popular public discourses on the differences between Islam and the West.

Data

The empirical analyses in this chapter are based on the survey data from the European Value Study/the World Value Surveys. These surveys originally aimed at investigating fundamental value patterns, primarily in the Western world. Large-scale surveys were conducted on representative population samples in a number of European countries in 1981. In order to explore value changes, a second wave of surveys was fielded in 1990. In 1996, a third wave was launched in about 55 countries, many outside the Western world. In 1999/2000, a fourth wave was conducted, this time in 66 countries throughout the world. In the fourth wave, several Islamic countries participated for the first time. More detailed information on field work, response rates, questionnaires, etc., can be found elsewhere (see Inglehart *et al.* 2004). Here, it is sufficient to mention that in each of the 8 countries, a representative sample of the adult population, aged 18 and above, was interviewed. In each country, the sample size was at least 1,000 respondents.

Results

As an introduction to the various analyses of compartmentalisation, the results from

a confirmatory factor analysis which seeks to develop cross-culturally valid measurements of religious and political involvement is presented, followed by a graphical illustration of how the four groups of countries differ on these two kinds of involvement. For the subsequent analyses of compartmentalisation, results for each of the seven orientations towards secular issues are presented in the following order. As a first step, results from a confirmatory factor analysis seek to establish that the various orientations towards secular issues can be validly measured by the same set of items in each of the four groups of countries. In a second step, a graphical illustration shows how the four groups differ on the various orientations towards secular issues. In a third step, the results from a set of multiple regression analyses for each group of countries are reported. The aim of these regression analyses is to explore whether the relationships between religious commitment and the various dependent variables (the orientations towards democracy, gender equality, etc.) are similar or dissimilar among the four groups of countries, also after controls for socio-economic background variables and the level of political involvement. In this way, the answer to the question of whether there are similar or dissimilar patterns of compartmentalisation among Muslims and Christians will be given in terms of a comparative analysis of the multiple regression coefficients for the relation between religious commitment and the various orientations towards more secular issues. The detailed wordings of the items which have been used for the measurements of the various religious and socio-political orientations are found in the Appendix.

Measurements of religious and political involvement

In order to measure the levels of both religious and political involvement, the answers to four questions have been used. The questions ask how important religion and politics are 'in one's life' and the responses are given on a four-point response scale, ranging from 'not important at all' (1), to 'very important' (4). In order to measure the organisational and behavioural component of religious and political involvement, two other questions are used. One asks about a person's confidence in their church or mosque. The responses were given on a four-point response scale, ranging from 'no confidence at all' (1), to 'a great deal of confidence' (4). The second question asks how often one is engaged in political discussions with friends, workmates, etc. The responses were given on a three-point response scale, ranging from 'never' (1), to 'often' (3). Admittedly, one would have preferred other questions on the 'organisational' dimension of political involvement, but these were unfortunately not available for all the countries.

Figure 16.1 show the results from a confirmatory factor analysis, which tests whether the four questions can be used to measure the two kinds of involvement. The results demonstrate that this is the case, and that the four items can be used to obtain comparable and valid measures across the four groups of countries. It should, however, be noted that in this regard, an alternative strategy might be to start from the assumption that religious and political involvement should be tapped by (partly) different indicators in the case of Christianity and Islam. For instance, prayer has a rather different status among Muslims and Christians. Some preliminary checks with such a procedure have, however, indicated that this does not have any major impact on the overall results for compartmentalisation.

Differences in religious and political involvement between the four groups of countries

Figure 16.2 displays how the four groups of countries differ in their mean factor scores for religious and political involvement. Not very surprisingly, the results show that the four Islamic countries score highest on religious involvement and that the European Catholics score higher than the European Protestants. When it comes to the levels of political involvement the results show that the non-Arab Muslims score considerably higher than both the Arab Muslims and the European Catholics.

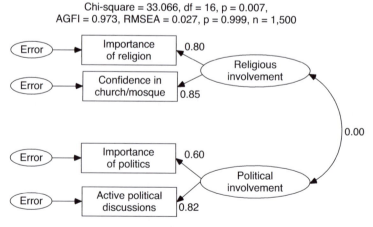

Chi-square = 33.066, df = 16, p = 0.007,
AGFI = 0.973, RMSEA = 0.027, p = 0.999, n = 1,500

Figure 16.1 Results of a confirmatory analysis of four indicators for religious and political involement.
Notes: Data for four Islamic and four Western countries. Test of equivalent factor loadings and covariances between latent variables in four groups of countries.

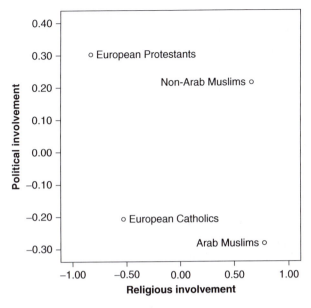

Figure 16.2 Religious and political involvement in four groups of countries.

Given the political situation in Indonesia and Iran, this is perhaps not so unexpected.

Measurements of orientations towards democracy and the political system

Figure 16.3 reports the results from a confirmatory factor analysis of four indicators for views on democracy and the political system. Two indicators tap critical orientations towards democracy. The first indicator summarises the answers to three different questions. These ask whether democracy causes problems for economic growth, for keeping law and order, and for the ability to reach firm decisions. The second indicator taps orientations towards non-democratic alternatives. This indicator summarises the answers to three

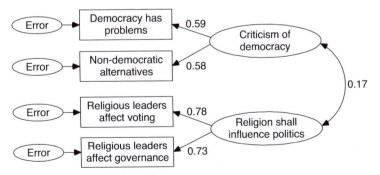

Figure 16.3 Results of a confirmatory analysis of four indicators of views on democracy and the relationship between religion and politics in four groups of Islamic and Western countries.

Note: Test of similar factor structure among the four groups.

other questions. These ask whether it would be better to have a strong leader who need not care about general elections, to let experts rather than politicians decide, and to have the army rule. Two other indicators tap orientations towards the political system, and especially towards the differentiation between religion and politics. One question asks whether religious leaders should affect how people should vote in general elections and the other whether religious leaders should influence government decisions. The results from the confirmatory factor analysis show that the four indicators can be used to obtain cross-culturally comparable measures of the two dimensions of views on democracy and the political system.

Differences in orientations towards democracy and the political system between the four groups of countries

Figure 16.4 displays the mean factor score on the two orientations towards democracy and the political system among the four groups of countries. The two Muslim groups are more critical towards democracy than the two Christian groups. However, when it comes to preferences for a religious impact on politics, the Arab Muslims are considerably more positive than the non-Arab. For example, Indonesia, this is also clearly to be expected (Cederroth 1999). The non-Arab Muslims are even more negative to such an influence than the two European groups.

The impact of religious commitment on orientations towards democracy and the political system

The results displayed in Table 16.1 show that it is only among the European Catholics that the religious involvement is related to critical views on democracy, and that furthermore the regression coefficient is positive. Thus, the more religiously involved among the European Catholics are more critical towards democracy than those who are less

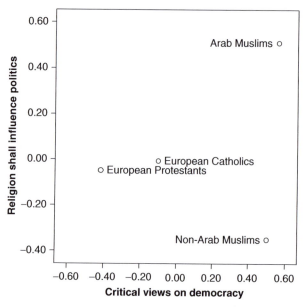

Figure 16.4 Critical views on democracy and preferences for a religious impact on politics in four groups of countries.

Table 16.1 Results from four multiple-regression analyses with critical views on democracy as dependent variable, and religious and political involvement and four SES variables as independent

	Arab Muslims	Non-Arab Muslims	European Protestants	European Catholics
Constant	0.77	0.77	0.10	0.32
Religious involvement	0.07	0.02	0.01	0.08★★
Political involvement	−0.14★★★	−0.04	−0.21★★★	−0.13★★★
Age	−0.01	−0.01★	0.01★	0.01
Gender	−0.04	0.01	0.01	−0.06
Education	−0.02	0.01	−0.09★★★	−0.06★★★
Income	−0.01	−0.02	−0.02★★	−0.03★★

Notes: ★★★$p<0.001$; ★★$p<0.01$; ★$p<0.05$: these figures apply throughout Chapter 16 tables. Entries are unstandardised regression coefficients.

involved in religion! Such a pattern is not found among the other three groups. Even more surprising are the results in Table 16.2 which show that preferences for a religious impact on politics are *negatively* related to religious commitment among the two Muslim groups, but *positively* to religious commitment among the two Christian groups. Thus, the stronger the religious commitment among the Muslims, the stronger the dislike for a religious influence on politics! This pattern is reversed among the Christian groups. There, those who are most religiously committed are more in favour of a religious impact on politics. These findings evidently contradict the often forwarded view that adherence to Islam in contrast to Christianity is especially prone to

become politicised. In contrast to this, the results show that preferences for a differentiation between religion and politics are weakest among the most committed Muslims.

Measurements of moral orientations towards socio-economic and bio-ethical moral issues

In order to measure the moral orientations among the four groups of countries, four questions have been used. Two asked whether the respondents found abortion and euthanasia to be justified or not. Two similar questions asked whether it was justified or not to cheat on taxes and to claim social benefits one is not entitled to.

Table 16.2 Results from four multiple-regression analyses with preferences for a religious impact on politics as dependent variable, and religious and political involvement and four SES variables as independent

	Arab Muslims	Non-Arab Muslims	European Protestants	European Catholics
Constant	0.14	−0.11	−0.22	0.14
Religious involvement	−0.27★★★	−0.16★	0.23★★★	0.22★★★
Political involvement	0.12★★	0.01	0.00	−0.05
Age	0.01★★	0.00	−0.00	−0.00
Gender	0.08	0.03	−0.10★	0.04
Education	0.06★★	−0.03★★	−0.08★★★	−0.03★
Income	−0.04★	−0.01	0.03★★	0.01

Notes: Entries are unstandardised regression coefficients. (For Non-Arab Muslims: only Indonesia.)

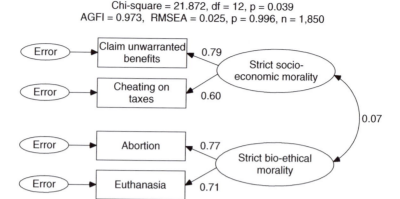

Chi-square = 21.872, df = 12, p = 0.039
AGFI = 0.973, RMSEA = 0.025, p = 0.996, n = 1,850

Figure 16.5 Results of a confirmatory factor analysis of four indicators of bio-ethical and socio-economic morality in four groups of Islamic and Western countries.
Note: Test of similar factor structure among the four groups.

The responses were given on a ten-point scale, ranging from 'always justified' (1), to 'never justified' (10). In this way, higher scores indicate more strict views. The four questions can be assumed to tap two kinds of moral orientations. The first two seem to measure orientations towards bio-ethical moral issues, and the last mentioned two orientations towards socio-economical issues. The results displayed in Figure 16.5 demonstrate that the four items can be used in such a way, and that in this regard they work equally well among the four different groups of countries.

Differences in moral orientations between the four groups of countries

Figure 16.6 reports how the four groups of countries differ on the two moral orientations. In the case of socio-economic morality, it is primarily the non-Arab Muslims who are most permissive, while the three other groups are fairly similar, although the Arab Muslims are most strict. The differences in bio-ethical morality are greater, and the Muslim countries show considerably more strict orientations in this regard. It should also be noted that the

European Catholics are more strict on this dimension than the European Protestants.

The impact of religious commitment on moral orientations

Not very surprisingly, Tables 16.3 and 16.4 show that in each group of countries, the religious commitment is positively related to stricter views on each of the two moral orientations. Thus, regardless whether one is Muslim or Christian, the stronger one's religious commitment, the stricter one's bio-ethical and socio-economic moral orientation. In this regard, there are no differences between the Muslims and the Christians. The level of compartmentalisation between religion and morality appears to be rather similar among these two groups.

Measurements of orientations towards gender equality and emancipative freedom between the four groups of countries

In order to measure orientations towards gender equality and emancipative freedom values, four indicators have been used. In the case of emancipative freedom values,

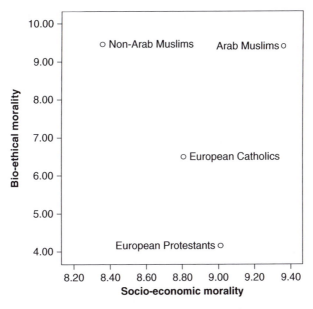

Figure 16.6 Socio-economic and bio-ethical morality in four groups of countries.

one indicator concerns tolerance for having social minorities like immigrants and people of another race as neighbours, and another evaluation of public self-expression values such as individual freedom of speech and having a say on public matters (see Inglehart 1990; Inglehart and Norris 2003). In the case of preferences for gender equality, one question asks whether a working mother damages mother–child relations and another whether both husband and wife should contribute to household income. There are obviously better items for the measurement of preferences for gender equality in the World Values Survey, but unfortunately these items were not included in some of the European countries. Figure 16.7 shows the results from a confirmatory factor analysis of these four indicators. The results demonstrate that the four indicators can be used as predicted and that they allow comparable measurements among the four groups of countries.

Table 16.3 Results from four multiple-regression analyses with strict bio-ethical morality as dependent variable, and religious and political involvement and four SES variables as independent

	Arab Muslims	Non-Arab Muslims	European Protestants	European Catholics
Constant	0.55	0.30	0.74	−0.05
Religious involvement	0.12★★★	0.22★★★	0.26★★★	0.40★★★
Political involvement	−0.04★★	−0.01	−0.08★★★	−0.07★★
Age	0.01★★★	0.00	0.01★★★	0.01★★★
Gender	0.00	0.02	−0.02	−0.10★★
Education	0.00	−0.01	−0.03★★★	−0.03★★
Income	−0.03★★	0.02★★	−0.02★★★	−0.01

Note: Entries are unstandardised regression coefficients.

259

Table 16.4 Results from four multiple-regression analyses with strict socio-economic morality as dependent variable, and religious and political involvement and four SES variables as independent

	Arab Muslims	Non-Arab Muslims	European Protestants	European Catholics
Constant	−0.33	−0.06	−0.46	−0.56
Religious involvement	0.30★★★	0.19★★★	0.06★	0.10★★★
Political involvement	−0.04	−0.17★★★	−0.07★★	0.02
Age	0.00	0.00	0.01★★★	0.01★★★
Gender	0.12★	0.02	0.16★★★	0.07
Education	−0.04★★★	−0.01	0.00	0.02
Income	0.01	−0.04★	0.01	0.02

Note: Entries are unstandardised regression coefficients.

Differences in preferences for gender equality and emancipative freedom between the four groups of countries

Figure 16.8 displays how the four groups of countries differ in their preferences for gender equality and emancipative freedom values. Quite as expected (see Inglehart 1997), the European Protestants are considerably more in favour of gender equality than the remaining three groups. They also score considerably higher on the emancipative freedom values. Even if there is also a similar systematic difference between the European Catholics and the two groups if Islamic countries, these differences are considerably smaller.

The impact of religious commitment on preferences for gender equality and emancipative freedom values

Tables 16.5 and 16.6 show the results from the multiple regression analyses. As expected (cf. Inglehart 1990; Inglehart and Norris 2003), religious involvement is negatively related to emancipative freedom values in all groups, except the Arab Muslims. More surprisingly, it is only among the European Catholics that preferences for gender equality are negatively related to the religious commitment. This kind of relationship would rather be expected for the Muslims. Instead, the level of religious involvement among these

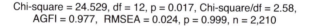

Chi-square = 24.529, df = 12, p = 0.017, Chi-square/df = 2.58,
AGFI = 0.977, RMSEA = 0.024, p = 0.999, n = 2,210

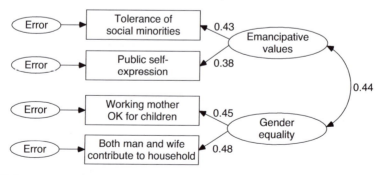

Figure 16.7 Results of a confirmatory analysis of four indicators of emancipative values and gender roles in four groups of Islamic and Western countries.
Note: Test of similar factor structure among the four groups.

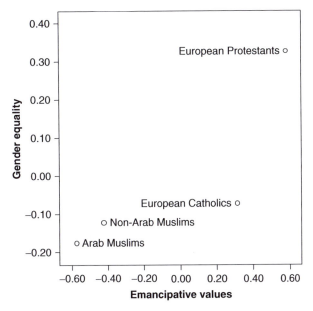

Figure 16.8 Emancipative values and preferences for gender equality in four groups of countries.

is not related to preferences for the emancipation of women.

Measurements of preferences for a centralised vertical power within the United Nations system

One of the most debated issues in the discussions on how to reform the United Nations (UN) concerns the distribution of vertical power within the UN system, and especially whether the UN should be given a more autonomous role in international affairs at the expense of the individual member states. Almost since its foundation, one alternative has been to see the UN as a kind of static conference machinery for resolving conflicts of interest and ideologies, and to be served by a secretariat that represents the interests and ideologies of the member countries. A contrasting approach is to see the UN as a dynamic instrument of governments through which they should seek reconciliation but which

Table 16.5 Results from four multiple-regression analyses with emancipative values as dependent variable, and religious and political involvement and four SES variables as independent

	Arab Muslims	*Non-Arab Muslims*	*European Protestants*	*European Catholics*
Constant	−0.59	0.61	0.10	0.20
Religious involvement	−0.03	−0.48★★★	−0.07★★	−0.11★★★
Political involvement	0.05★	0.11★★★	0.17★★★	0.15★★★
Age	−0.01★★	−0.01★	−0.01★★★	−0.01★★★
Gender	−0.10★	−0.10★★★	0.15★★★	0.09★
Education	0.04★★★	−0.01	0.07★★★	0.08★★★
Income	0.06★★★	−0.03★	0.02★★★	0.01

Note: Entries are unstandardised regression coefficients.

Table 16.6 Results from four multiple-regression analyses with preferences for gender equality as dependent variable, and religious and political involvement and four SES variables as independent

	Arab Muslims	Non-Arab Muslims	European Protestants	European Catholics
Constant	−1.58	−0.05	−0.10	−0.37
Religious involvement	−0.06	0.05	0.01	−0.10★★★
Political involvement	0.08★★	−0.02	0.08★★	0.06★
Age	0.00	−0.00	0.00	−0.01★
Gender	0.57★★★	0.06	0.19★★★	0.22★★★
Education	0.05★★★	−0.02	−0.01	0.01
Income	0.07★★★	−0.01	0.01	0.01

Note: Entries are unstandardised regression coefficients.

should also develop forms of executive action, undertaken on behalf of all members, aimed at both resolving and forestalling conflicts. In current discussions it is often said that the UN needs to be reformed. Parts of this reformation will necessarily concern the redistribution of the vertical power structure within the UN system.

The 2000 questionnaire in the World Values Survey included four questions which asked whether international peacekeeping, aid to developing countries, protection of human rights, and refugee programmes, respectively, would be best handled by the respective national governments, by the national governments working together under UN coordination, or by the UN itself. The questions are coded to give higher marks for preferences for a more autonomous UN in these regards. It should be noted that these four questions unfortunately were not asked in Italy and Denmark. In the analyses of these items, the remaining two European countries (Spain and Sweden) have therefore been collapsed into one group.

The results displayed in Figure 16.9 show that these four items can be used to tap preferences for a centralised distribution of vertical power within the UN system, and that in this regard the items work equally well among the three groups of countries.

Chi-square = 48.625, df = 13, p = 0.000, Chi-square/df = 3.740
AGFI = 0.952, RMSEA = 0.049, p = 0.509, n = 1,100

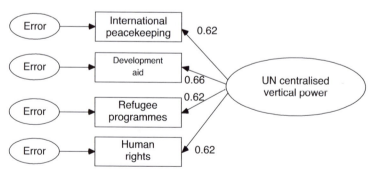

Figure 16.9 Results from a confirmatory factor analysis of four indicators towards a centralised vertical power within the UN system.
Notes: Data for two European and four Islamic countries. Test of a similar one-factor structure in three groups of countries.

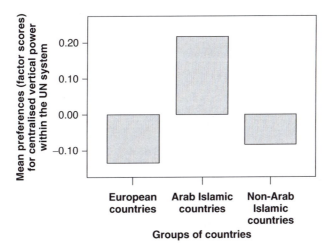

Figure 16.10 Differences in preferences (factor scores) for a centralised vertical power within the UN system.

Differences in preferences for a centralised vertical power within the UN system between three groups of countries

Figure 16.10 shows that Arab Islamic countries are considerably more positive towards a centralised distribution of vertical power within the UN than the remaining two groups. The explanation may be that the Arab countries are more dissatisfied with the way the UN has acted in the Israel–Palestine conflict (Pettersson 2003).

The impact of religious commitment on preferences for a centralised vertical power within the UN system

Table 16.7 reports the relations between religious commitment and preferences for a centralised distribution of the vertical power within the UN system. Interestingly enough, it is only among the Arab Muslims that the religious commitment is positively related to such preferences.

Table 16.7 Results from three multiple-regression analyses with preferences for a centralised vertical power within the UN system as dependent variable, and religious and political involvement and four SES variables as independent

	Arab Muslims	Non-Arab Muslims	European Catholics, Protestants
Constant	0.12	0.08	−0.07
Religious involvement	0.12★★	0.04	0.01
Political involvement	−0.15★★★	−0.02	−0.02
Age	−0.01	−0.04★★★	0.00
Gender	−0.06	0.02	−0.10★★★
Education	0.01★★★	−0.01	0.01★★
Income	0.00	−0.01★	−0.01★

Note: Entries are unstandardised regression coefficients.

Summary and conclusions

In several respects, the results challenge many popular stereotypes of Islamic culture and Muslim religiosity. These challenges can be summarised as follows. The structure of the orientations towards religious, social, political and moral values was found to be the same (or at least similar) in the four groups of countries. This means that cross-culturally comparable measurements of these values can be based on the EVS/WVS data and that one need not assume any specific 'Islamic' response pattern. This finding is an essential requirement for the following conclusions. However, it should also be noted that the measurements which have been developed in this chapter are usually based on only a limited number of indicators. The explanation for this is that the more indicators one wants to include in the measurements, the more difficult it is to obtain cross-culturally comparable measurements. Thus, in order to develop more saturated measurements, which are equally applicable in the various cultural contexts, much work remains to be done.

The results have demonstrated some obvious differences between the countries from the two religious traditions. Taken as a group, the four Muslim countries scored higher on religious involvement, critical orientations towards democracy, a strict bio-ethical morality and preferences for a centralised vertical power within the UN system. These countries also scored lower on preferences for gender equality and emancipative freedom values. In addition to this, there were also obvious differences between the countries from one and the same religious tradition. In several instances, the Muslims from the Arab countries differed from the Muslims from the non-Arab countries. Accordingly, the Islamic countries should not be seen as one homogeneous cultural block. The same conclusion applies for the Catholic and Protestant countries; these countries do not constitute another homogeneous cultural block.

With regard to the patterns of religious compartmentalisation and the impact of religious involvement on the orientations towards the various secular issues, a complex and partly unexpected pattern appeared. In many respects, this pattern challenged several of the popular stereotypes on the correlates of Muslim religiosity. Thus, critical orientations towards democracy were linked to religious involvement among the European Catholics, but not among the Muslims. Among these European Catholics, higher levels of religious involvement were related to more critical evaluations of democracy. This finding undoubtedly contradicts the popular stereotype of Muslim religiosity as especially incompatible with democracy. It was equally surprising to find that the preferences for a religious impact on politics were *positively* related to the religious commitment among both Catholics and Protestants, but *negatively* related among the Muslims. Furthermore, seen as a group, the Muslims were not more in favour of a religious impact on politics than the Europeans. These findings clearly contradict popular stereotypes of Islam as a highly politicised religion.

In the case of orientations towards bio-ethical and socio-economic moral issues, the results showed that religious involvement among both Muslims and Christians was positively related to stricter views. In these instances, the religious involvement among both Muslims and Christians seemed to drive in the same direction and to have similar consequences.

Preferences for gender equality were negatively related to religious involvement among the European Catholics but not among the Muslims. This finding obviously contradicts the popular stereotype that Islam is especially negative towards gender equality. The results also demonstrated that preferences for emancipative freedom values were negatively related to religious commitment among the Catholics, Protestants and non-Arab Muslims, but not among the Arab Muslims. Also this finding contradicts the popular stereo-type that Muslim religiosity is especially negative towards individual emancipative freedom values.

Preferences for a centralised vertical power within the UN system were positively related to religious involvement only among the Arab Muslims. Among the Christians and the non-Arab Muslims, the level of religious involvement was unrelated to the orientations towards the UN. These findings contradict the stereotype that Muslim religiosity should be especially negative towards strong institutions for global governance. To the contrary, the Arab Muslims showed to be most in favour of a development in such a direction.

As a final general conclusion, it can be argued that the findings of this chapter contradict many of the popular stereotypes of Islam and Muslim religiosity. Although the

Muslims scored highest on religious involvement, they were not less involved in politics, and in several other instances the Muslims as a group did not demonstrate the characteristics which are often assumed: for instance, stronger preferences for a religious impact on politics, a much stronger dislike for gender equality, different views on economical moral matters, and more negative views on strong institutions for global governance. Furthermore, the association between religious involvement and orientations towards secular issues was not generally higher among the Muslims than among the Catholics and the Protestants, and in several instances, the correlates of a religious commitment which are usually assumed to be found among the Muslims were instead found among the European Catholics. All in all, these results do not support the view of Muslim religiosity and Islam as a particularly different and challenging religious tradition.

Appendix: Items used for the measurements of the various religious, political, moral, social and international orientations

Religious and political involvement

For each of the following, indicate how important it is in your life. Would you say it is:

	Very important	Rather important	Not very important	Not at all important	Don't know (Do not read out)
Politics	4	3	2	1	−1
Religion	4	3	2	1	−1

I am going to name a number of organisations. For each one, could you tell me how much confidence you have in them: is it a great deal of confidence, quite a lot of confidence, not very much confidence or none at all?

	A great deal	Quite a lot	Not very much	None at all	Don't know
The church/mosque	4	3	2	1	−1

When you are together with your friends, would you say that you discuss politics frequently, occasionally or never?

Frequently	3
Occasionally	2
Never	1
Don't know	−1

Democracy and the political system

I'm going to describe various types of political systems and ask what you think about each as a way of governing this country. For each one, would you say it is a very good, fairly good, fairly bad or very bad way of governing this country?

	Very good	Fairly good	Bad	Very bad	Don't know
Having a strong leader who does not have to bother with parliament and elections	4	3	2	1	−1
Having experts, not government, make decisions according to what they think is best for the country	4	3	2	1	−1
Having the army rule	4	3	2	1	−1

I'm going to read off some things that people sometimes say about a democratic political system. Could you please tell me if you agree strongly, agree, disagree or disagree strongly?

	Agree strongly	Agree	Disagree	Disagree strongly	Don't know
Democracies are indecisive and have too much quibbling	4	3	2	1	−1
Democracies aren't good at maintaining order	4	3	2	1	−1
In democracy, the economy runs badly	4	3	2	1	−1

How much do you agree or disagree with each of the following?

	Agree strongly	Agree	Neither agree nor disagree	Disagree	Strongly disagree	Don't know
Religious leaders should not influence government decisions	1	2	3	4	5	−1
Religious leaders should not influence how people vote in elections	1	2	3	4	5	−1

Moral orientations

Please tell me for each of the following statements whether you think it can always be justified, never be justified, or something in between, using this card.

Claiming government benefits to which you are not entitled
Cheating on taxes if you have a chance
Abortion
Euthanasia: ending the life of the incurably sick

Always justifiable									Never justifiable
1	2	3	4	5	6	7	8	9	10
Don't know = −1									

Emancipative freedom values and gender equality

If you had to choose, which one of the things on this card would you say is most important? And which would be the next most important? (*Code one answer only.*)

	First choice	Second choice
Maintaining order in the nation	2	2
Giving people more say in important government decisions	3	3
Fighting rising prices	1	1
Protecting freedom of speech	4	4
Don't know (*Do not read out*)	−1	−1

On this list are various groups of people. Could you please mention any that you would not like to have as neighbours? (*Code an answer for each.*)

		Mentioned	Not mentioned
V35	People of a different race	2	1
V37	Immigrants/foreign workers	2	1

For the following statements, can you tell me how much you agree? Do you agree strongly, agree, disagree or disagree strongly?

	Agree strongly	Agree	Disagree	Strongly disagree	Don't know
A working mother can establish just as warm and secure a relationship with her children as a mother who does not work.	4	3	2	1	−1
Both husband and wife should contribute to household income	4	3	2	1	−1

Orientations towards the distribution of vertical power within the UN system

Some people believe that certain kinds of problems could be better handled by the United Nations than by the various national governments. Others think that these problems should be left entirely to the respective national governments. I'm going to mention some problems. For each one, would you tell me whether you think that policies in this area should be decided by the national governments, or by the United Nations?

	National governments	United Nations	National governments with UN coordination	Don't know
International peacekeeping	1	3	2	−1
Aid to developing countries	1	3	2	−1
Refugees	1	3	2	−1
Human rights	1	3	2	−1

Bibliography

Acquaviva, S. (1979) *The Decline of the Sacred in Industrial Society*, Oxford: Basil Blackwell.

Billiet, J., Dobbelaere, K., Vilaca, H., Voyé, L. and Welkenhuysen-Gybels, J. (2003) 'Church commitment and some consequences in western and central Europe', *Research in the Social Scientific Study of Religion*, 14, 129–159.

Casanova, J. (1994) *Public Religions in the Modern World*, Chicago: University of Chicago Press.

Cederroth, S. (1999) 'Indonesia and Malaysia', in D. Westerlund and I. Svanberg (eds), *Islam Outside the Arab World*, Richmond: Curzon.

Cox, M. (2002) 'September 11 and the study of international relations', in B Sundelius (ed.), *The Consequences of September 11: A Symposium for the Study of the Implications for the Study of International Relations*, Stockholm: Swedish Institute of International Affairs.

Dark, K. R. (2000) 'Introduction', in K. R. Dark (ed.), *Religion and International Relations*, New York: St Martin's Press, pp. i–x.

Dobbelaere, K. (1995) 'Religion in Europe', in R. de Moor (ed.), *Values in Western Societies*, Tilburg: Tilburg University Press.

Dobbelaere, K. (2002) *Secularization: An Analysis at Three Levels*, Oxford: P.I.E. Peter Lang.

Dobbelaere, K. and Billiet. J. (in press) 'Late 20th-century trends in Catholic religiousness: Belgium compared with Western and Central-European nations', in M. Lamberigts, J. Billiet,

J. De Maeyer and L. Kenis (eds), *The Transformation of the Christian Churches in Western Europe 1945–2000: Proceedings of the Leuven Colloquium 18–21 September 2002*, Leuven, Leuven University Press, KADOC Studies.

Esmer, Y. (2003) 'Is there an Islamic civilization?', in R. Inglehart (ed.), *Human Values and Social Change*, Leiden: Brill.

Gorski, R. (2000) 'Historicizing the secularization debate: Church, state, and society in late medival and early modern Europe', *American Sociological Review*, 65, pp. 138–167.

Huntington, S. (1996) *The Clash of Civilizations and the Remaking of World Order*, New York: Simon and Schuster.

Inglehart, R. (1990) *Culture Shift in Advanced Industrial Society*, Princeton: Princeton University Press.

Inglehart, R. (1996) *Modernization and Postmodernization*, Princeton: Princeton University Press.

Inglehart, R. (2004) *Human Beliefs and Values: A Cross-cultural Sourcebook based on the 1999–2002 Values Surveys*, Buenos Aires: Sieglo XXI Editores.

Inglehart, R. and Norris, P. (2003) *Rising Tide: Gender Equality and Cultural Change around the World*, Cambridge: Cambridge University Press.

Ingehart, R., Basanes, M., Diez-Medrano, J., Halman, L. and Luijkx, R. (eds) (2004) *Human Values and Beliefs: A Crosscultural Sourcebook on the*

1999–2002 Values Surveys, Delegacion Coyocan, Mexico: Siglo XXI Editores, s.s de c.v.

Jagodzinski, W. and Dobbelaere, K. (1995a) 'Secularisation and church religiosity', in J. van Deth and E. Scarbrough (eds), *The Impact of Values,* Oxford: Oxford University Press.

Jagodzinski, W. and Dobbelaere, K. (1995b) 'Religious and ethical pluralism', in J. van Deth and E. Scarbrough (eds), *The Impact of Values,* Oxford: Oxford University Press.

Jelen, T. and Wilcox, C. (2002a), 'Religion: The one, the few, and the many', in T. Jelen and C. Wilcox (eds), *Religion and Politics in Comparative Perspective,* Cambridge: Cambridge University Press.

Jelen, T. and Wilcox, C. (2002b) 'The political roles of religion', in T. Jelen and C. Wilcox (eds), *Religion and Politics in Comparative Perspective,* Cambridge: Cambridge University Press.

Johnstone, R. (1988) *Religion in Society: A Sociology of Religion,* 3rd edn, Englewood Cliffs: Prentice Hall.

Jurgensmeyer, M. (1993) *The New Cold War? Religious Nationalism Confronts the Secular State,* Berkeley: University of California Press.

Jurgensmeyer, M. (2000) *Terror in the Mind of God: The Global Rise of Religious Violence,* Berkeley: University of California Press.

Mayer, E. (1999) *Islam and Human Rights. Tradition and Politics,* 3rd edn, Boulder: Westview Press.

Moaddel, M. and Azadarmaki, T. (2003) 'The worldviews of Islamic publics: The cases of Egypt, Iran, and Jordan', in R. Inglehart (ed.), *Human Values and Social Change,* Leiden: Brill.

Norris, P. and Inglehart, R. (2003) 'Islamic culture and democracy: Testing the "Clash of civilizations" thesis', in R. Inglehart (ed.), *Human Values and Social Change,* Leiden: Brill.

Pettersson, T. (2002) 'Mellan religion och politik', in C. Dahlgren, E. Hamberg and T. Pettersson (eds), *Religion och sociologi. Ett fruktbart möte,* Religio 55, Lund: Teologiska institutionen.

Pettersson, T. (2003) 'Individual values and global governance: A comparative analysis of orientations towards the United Nations', in R. Inglehart (ed.), *Human Values and Social Change: Findings from the Values Surveys,* Leiden: Brill.

Pettersson, T. (2001–2002) 'The United Nations between Islam and the secularised West', *Temenos,* 37–38, pp 163–80.

Price, D. (2000) *Islamic Political Culture, Democracy and Human Rights: A Comparative Study,* London: Praeger.

Przeworski, A. and Teune, H. (1970) *The Logic of Comparative Social Inquiry,* New York: Wiley-Interscience.

Stark, R. and Finke, R. (2000) *Acts of Faith: Explaining the Human Side of Religion,* Berkeley: University of California Press.

Tessler, M. (2003) 'Do Islamic orientations influence attitudes toward democracy in the Arab world? Evidence from Egypt, Jordan, Morocco, and Algeria', in R. Inglehart (ed.), *Islam, Gender, Culture, and Democracy,* Willowdale: deSitter Publications.

Therborn, G. (1995) *European Modernity and Beyond,* London: Sage.

Tibi, B. (2001) *Islam between Culture and Politics,* New York: Palgrave.

Tibi, B. (2002) 'Muslim migrants in Europe: Between Euro-Islam and ghettoization', in M. Al Sayyad and M. Castell (eds), *Muslim Europe or Euro-Islam?,* New York: Lexington Books.

Turner, B. (1991) *Religion and Social Theory,* London: Sage.

Turner, B. (2000) 'Globalization and the post-modernization of culture', in J. Beynon and D. Dunkerly (eds), *Globalization: The Reader,* London: Athlone Press.

Williams, R. (1996) 'Religion as political resource: Culture or ideology?', *Journal for the Scientific Study of Religion,* 35, 4, pp. 368–378.

Wilson, B. (1996) 'Religious toleration, pluralism and privatization', in P. Repstad (ed.), *Religion and Modernity,* Oslo: Scandinavian University Press.

269

Part III

Religion and international relations

17

Integrating religion into international relations theory

Jonathan Fox

Religion and international relations theory have had a unique and interesting relationship. It is arguable that modern international relations, based on the interactions between Westphalian states, had its origin in religious conflict in that the peace of Westphalia was to a large extent motivated by the desire to end international wars over religion. Yet until recently international relations theory – likely at least in part due to the motivations behind the peace of Westphalia – has ignored religion.

The purpose of this chapter is to argue that religion is an important influence on international relations and to discuss how religion can be integrated into international relations theory. A central thesis of the argument presented here is that religion is a multifaceted phenomenon and, accordingly, its influence on international relations is multifaceted. There are numerous ways that religion has influenced multiple aspects of international relations. Any one of these influences, by itself, would be worthy of note and the sum of these influences results in a combined impact that makes it one of the most important intervening variables in international relations. By this I mean that the basic theories of international relations, like realism, liberalism, constructivism, the English school and

Marxism retain their explanatory power and describe important, and even dominant, aspects of international relations but unless they take religion into account they cannot provide a complete explanation for international politics and events.

This chapter proceeds in two stages. First it addresses the history of religion in international relations theory. This brief history is necessary in order to understand why religion was overlooked by this body of theory and why there is a need to integrate religion into it. Second, it discusses a number of distinct but overlapping ways in which religion influences international relations. This part of the discussion to a large extent draws upon literature from other disciplines including political science, history, anthropology and sociology. This is because the lack of attention by international relations scholars to the issue of religion requires that this chapter draw upon the work of those scholars who did address the issue.

Religion in international relations theory: a brief history

For much of the twentieth century, the history of religion in international relations theory, and the social sciences in general, is best described as an absence of religion from these bodies of theory. That is, until recently social science theory in general and international relations theory in particular overlooked religion. On many topics it is difficult to lump American and European social scientists into the same category. But in this case the trend is common among scholars on both sides of the Atlantic and is rooted in predictions by seminal European thinkers including Marx, John Stuart Mill, Weber, Freud, Comte and Durkheim who linked modernity to the demise of religion as a significant social and political force (Appleby 2000; Hurd 2004: 3). These predictions coalesced into more formal bodies of theory known alternatively as modernization theory and secularization theory which predicted the demise, irrelevance and/or privatization of religion.

That being said, this body of theory is by no means monolithic and it is difficult to assess its influence with pinpoint accuracy. However, it is possible to set some bounds. On one extreme, many claim that 'few forecasts have been uttered with more unshakable confidence than [the] belief that religion is in the midst of its final death throes' (Hadden 1987b: 587–588) and that 'the theory of secularization may be the only theory which was able to attain a truly paradigmatic status in the social sciences' (Casanova 1994: 17). However, it is easier to find descriptions of this body of literature as predicting the complete demise of religion than it is to find those who actually made such predictions. Most predictions within this body of literature tended to predict a significant decline in religion's influence or that religion would become privatized – that is, move from the public sphere to the private sphere. Thus, it would remain within society but its influence in the public sphere would decline considerably.

It is clear that most who wrote within this body of literature made some form of the argument that phenomena inherent in modernity would lead to the inevitable decline of religion as a social and political force. In the past religion played an important role in society but this role would be replaced in modern society with science and reason. Religious and moral definitions of proper behaviour would be replaced by a combination of the mental health sciences and secular laws and enforced through surveillance technology. Modern political ideologies, usually some form of connection between government and the will of the people, would supplant religion's role in legitimizing the state. The increased power of the modern state would be able to manufacture social order without resort to religion. Secular institutions would fill roles traditionally held by religion. Also science would usurp religion's role in providing interpretations of the physical universe (Wilson 1982).

This trend was expected to be reinforced by a number of modern processes. Urbanization would weaken the small traditional communities where religion thrived. Universal education and increased literacy rates would undermine religion's monopoly on knowledge and information, allowing individuals to question religious precepts and formulate their own interpretations of religious texts. Science would undermine religion in a number of ways. It would usurp religion's role in solving problems. For example, modern medicine would replace prayer as the solution to medical problems. It would also directly undermine aspects of traditional morality by giving people options that were not previously available. For example contraception has arguably undermined norms of chastity and modesty by eliminating some of the consequences of violating these values.[1]

Thus, while the extreme predications of religion's complete and total demise were rare, there was considerable agreement that significant political, economic and social processes linked with modernization would lead to the decline of religion's public influence. However, when setting the bounds of the influence of this body of theory on the social sciences it is important to note that there have always been elements of the social sciences which did not accept these assumptions. This is especially true of comparativists who focused on specific world regions like the Middle East – a region where religion's influence has remained sufficiently conspicuous to make it difficult to claim that it has or will disappear from the public sphere. There are also some notable exceptions in both American and European scholarship which does focus on the West such as Robert Bellah's work on numerous aspects of religion and society and Rene Girard's work on the intrinsic connection between religion and societal violence. However, these are exceptions to a more general trend that held true at least through the 1980s, when political scientists and sociologists began to question this rejection of religion.

Up to this point the discussion has focused on social science theory and not international relations theory. This is because international relations theory had no analogous body of scholarship to explain why religion was of declining importance. Rather, it generally did not address the topic of religion. That is, instead of explaining why religion was not important, international relations theory simply took religion's irrelevance for granted. In this way, international relations theory can be said to have more profoundly rejected religion than the other social sciences. Whenever international relations scholarship did deal with religion, it was always subsumed into some other category like terrorism or culture. For example, the debate in the 1990s over Samuel Huntington's 'clash of civilizations' theory was essentially over whether future conflict would be between several civilizations that are primarily defined by religion. Yet most of the participants in the debate managed to avoid directly discussing religion (Huntington 1996).[2] The pervasiveness of this phenomenon is demonstrated by a survey of four major international relations journals which shows that only 6 of 1,600 articles published between 1980 and 1999 included religion as a significant element (Philpott 2002).[3] Thus the exceptions to the rule of ignoring religion during the twentieth century were even rarer in international relations than in the other social sciences. Furthermore, this trend began to weaken in the international relations literature only in the twenty-first century, about two decades after it began to weaken in political science and sociology.

There are a number of interrelated reasons that this blind spot for religion is most prevalent in international relations scholarship. The idea that religion is in decline is a particularly Western idea and international relations is arguably the most Western of the social sciences. One would think that a discipline which by definition is international would not be Western-centric, but this is not the case. The core of Western international relations theory as we know it today, especially US international relations theory, evolved from NATO-based national security theories which focused on the Cold War competition between Liberalism and Communism, both secular ideologies.

The longer-term history of the West also played a role. The peace of Westphalia ended the era of international religious wars in the Christian West and the defeat of the Ottomans at the gates of Vienna in 1683 ended the Muslim threat to the West. Thus, centuries of Western historical experience reinforced the notion that religion was not relevant to the relations between states.

Consequently, most major international relations theories, ideas and trends include an anti-religious bias. This bias does not manifest in a specific and overt denial of religion's importance. Rather it manifests as an absence of religion on the list of those phenomena which are considered important. Realism focuses on material power, leaving little room for other motivations for state behaviour. Liberalism and Marxism also focus on rationalist and economic factors. Constructivism posits that all structure is human-made. In principle, Constructivism can accommodate religion as a human-made structure but few if any constructivists do so. Similarly, the English School which focuses on a combination of power politics and international society could also theoretically accommodate religious influences on international relations as an element if international society but until recently none within this school of thought have attempted to do so.[4] Concepts of the nation-state and self-determination focus on a state's ethnic character and its historic mission. If religion is included at all, it is as one part among many of that ethnic heritage and history and not as a motivating force for behaviour. Also, the quantitative branch of international relations scholarship is often accused of ignoring factors that are difficult to measure. This was certainly true of religion until the late 1990s.[5]

Thus, social scientists in general and international relations scholars in particular were arguably blinded by their paradigms which left little room for religion. Consequently, the lion's share of international relations scholarship did not address religion until recently, of defeat and humiliation at Christian hands.

Yet, this failure to notice religion does not mean it was not there. Outside of the West, other paradigms of world politics included religion, sometimes as a central aspect of those paradigms. For example, many Muslims believe that the religious war with the Christian West did not end in 1683. Rather, they see this year as the beginning of centuries of defeat and humiliation at the hands of the Christian West. Russia's conquering of Muslim Central Asia, European colonialism's success in controlling large parts of Muslim South Asia and North Africa, and the conquering of the Muslim Balkans by Greece, Bulgaria and Serbia were all seen as part of this religious war for control of the world. The continuing influence of Western Christian states in the Muslim world, including several recent military interventions like those in Iraq and Somalia, underscore this humiliation of Muslims at Christian hands (Miles 2004).

Thus, on one hand Christian states viewed these events through secular paradigms which focused on power, economics, colonialism and nationalism, particularly until the series of terror attacks on the West by Muslim extremists beginning with those of 11 September 2001. As a result Western powers expected any counter-attacks against their policies to be motivated by these secular factors but did not expect religiously motivated attacks. However, on the other hand, many Muslims continued to view these events through the prism of religion. Consequently, the West had a blind spot with regard to the religiously motivated attacks by groups like Al-Qaeda, which sees its campaign against the West as part of a centuries-old religious confrontation (Miles 2004).

Based on all of this it is arguable that the major shift in international relations in recent years has not been one of substance but one of perception. That is, religion has always been an influence on international relations and the nature of that influence has remained relatively constant over time. What is changing is the lenses international relations scholars in particular and social scientists in general use to view those events. Many like Francis

Fukayama are coming to the conclusion that 'it is, of course, possible to try to give economic or rational explanations for religious and cultural phenomena, and thus to try to fit them into some larger theory of social behavior based on rational choice … But ultimately, these accounts prove to be unsatisfing because they are too reductionist' (Fukuyama 2001: 16–17).

The multiple influences of religion

Arguing that religion is the primary driving force behind international relations is likely going too far, but it is becoming increasingly difficult to deny that it does have an influence. I argue here that religion has multiple influences on international relations. Religion is a multifaceted phenomenon which interacts with politics, society and the economy in multiple ways. This is also true of its interaction with international relations. In this chapter I discuss several ways religion interacts or overlaps with phenomena related to international relations. Any one of these overlaps and interactions by itself would make religion a significant influence on international relations, but the combination arguably makes religion one of the most important intervening factors in international relations.

For the purposes of this chapter, I define religion as a social and political phenomenon that influences aspects of politics, society and the economy. Of course religion is more than this but this definition is sufficient for the purposes of this chapter – to determine religion's influence in the international arena. This is because the discussion below focuses on what religion does and the nature of its influence in the specific context of international relations rather than what religion is.[6]

Legitimacy

Few would dispute that religion is a potential source of legitimacy. Religion can lend legitimacy to governments as well as specific policies followed by governments. Legitimacy can be defined as 'the normative belief by an actor that a rule or institution ought to be obeyed' (Hurd 1999: 381). To convince another that your policy preference is legitimate is to convince them that you are correct, perhaps even morally correct, and that they should support your policies and the actions based on those policies, or at least not oppose them. Religion can be a potent tool in this arena.

Religion is certainly not the only source of legitimacy and there are some set bounds on what is considered legitimate and what is not. For instance, self-defence is near-universally considered legitimate and genocide is not. However, there is a substantial middle ground where debate is possible over the legitimacy or illegitimacy of an action or policy. It is in this grey zone that it is up to policy-makers to convince others – including their constituents, other policy-makers from their own state, policy-makers from other states, and the populations of other states – of the legitimacy of their actions and policies. Religion is one resource that can be tapped to achieve this. Many US presidents have used religious imagery to support their foreign policies. Ronald Reagan called the USSR an 'evil empire'. George W. Bush has repeatedly used religious imagery in his justification for the war in Iraq and the war on terrorism. In fact, 'most American presidents have relied on religious imagery to prepare the nation for war' (Kelly 2005) George W. Bush's view of the world is not unopposed. Numerous Muslim leaders have characterized Bush's policies as a war against all Muslims, invoking religious imagery in order to oppose these policies. In addition, there exist Christian-based challenges to Bush's policies.[7]

The domestic–international nexus

While the role of religious legitimacy has rarely been discussed in the context of international politics, it is often discussed in the context of domestic politics. Until a few centuries ago, it was taken for granted that religion was the basis for the legitimacy of the state itself with the Church, as God's agent, granting rulers the right to rule (Turner 1991: 178–198). In the modern era this is no longer the case with the state's legitimacy resting on multiple sources of legitimacy but 'a strong residual element of religion' continues to exist and continues to perform basic legitimizing functions (Geertz 1977: 267–268). Many argue that this legitimizing function of religion is becoming increasingly important as governments guided by secular ideologies are seen as failing to provide basic needs like security, economic well-being and social justice (Juergensmeyer 1993).

This is particularly relevant to foreign policy because to a great extent all politics, even international politics, are local. Policy-makers operate out of state governments and to differing extents, depending on the nature of the state's regime, need to satisfy domestic constituencies and other policy-makers in their own states that their course of action is correct and legitimate. They also need to convince policy-makers in other states, and often the constituents of those policy-makers, to support or at least acquiesce to those policies. Thus, if religion is a potent source of legitimacy in local politics, it can be the same for international politics.

Religious legitimacy and persuasion

Religion is a complex and versatile tool of persuasion. Most religions are complex with multiple traditions upon which policy-makers can draw to justify different, and often contrasting, policies. For example, most religious traditions can and have been used at various times to justify both policies of war and violence as well as peace and reconciliation (Appleby 2000). It is also in many ways a double-edged sword in that those who wish to oppose a policy can generally also find legitimacy. On one hand, it can be used by foreign policy-makers to support their policies among a number of audiences including other politicians, their constituents, and both policy-makers and citizens from other states. On the other hand, members of all of these audiences can use religion in the same way to oppose a policy or support an alternative policy.

It is important to note that this use of religious legitimacy as a means for persuasion has at least three limits. First, religious persuasion is often limited by cultural and religious boundaries. For example, invoking Jesus is more likely to sway Christians than Muslims or Jews, much less Hindus or Buddhists. Second, not everyone will be swayed by religious arguments. In fact, some people are anti-religious and religious persuasion may make them more likely to oppose a policy. Many secularists in Israel, for example, resent the influence of religious parties on the government and are likely to oppose any policy that is perceived as religious in origin. Finally, religious persuasion is to a great extent dependent on the credentials of the one using it. Someone who is known to be not particularly religious will have more difficulty using religious persuasion than someone with good religious credentials. For example, the Pope or the Dalai Lama will have an easier time invoking religious legitimacy to support a cause than a secular leader widely known to have engaged in immoral behaviour such as Bill Clinton.

Trends in IR literature and legitimacy

There are some trends in the international relations and social science literature which support the argument that religious legitimacy can be potent in international relations. First, many argue that norms are having an increasing influence on international relations.[8] One proof of this is that some groups – including indigenous people - who have very little power in terms of traditional political and economic measures have nevertheless been successful at using international norms to attain their political goals (Wilmer 1993). An example of this is the success of indigenous groups in Canada and Australia at gaining some measure of autonomy and control over their territory and its natural resources. As religion is a source of norms, it also should have this type of influence. Second, the instrumentalist and constructionist literature posits that ethnicity and nationalism are potent forms of persuasion that can be used by politicians. The same reasoning can be applied to religion. Third, religion is a source of identity and many posit that identity is a potent factor in international relations.[9] Finally, the current international laws of war evolved from religious precepts that date back to St Augustine's City of God.

Worldviews

The discussion of legitimacy and persuasion implies that in some cases religion is a tool used cynically by policy-makers, among others, to advance their goals. While this certainly occurs, religion can also act as an independent motivating force. While this insight is not commonly referenced in the international relations literature, the argument that religious beliefs influence people's worldviews and religious motivations influence behaviour is well grounded in the sociological literature and to a lesser extent the political science literature. For instance, Seul (1999: 558) argues that 'no other repositories of cultural meaning have historically offered so much in response to the human need to develop a secure identity. Consequently, religion often is at the core of individual and group identity'. Mark Juergensmeyer (1997: 17) similarly argues that religion 'provides the vision and commitment that propels an activist into scenes of violence, and it supplies the ideological glue that makes that activist's community of support cohere'. This basic argument that religion can strengthen identity and influence behaviour is clearly applicable to the various actors in international relations.

This can influence international relations in two ways. First, religion can influence the worldview or belief system of a policy-maker. To the extent that this is true, religion has the potential to influence that policy-maker's decisions. In cases of religious worldviews this can lead to extreme and intractable policies because 'religion deals with the constitution of being as such. Hence, one can not be pragmatic on concerns challenging this being' (Lausesen and Waever 2000: 719). Thus, religiously inspired views held by policy-makers and the policies based on them can potentially inspire intractable policies which, in turn, can lead to international incidents, including war. On the other hand, religion can also encourage peace and reconciliation (Appleby 2000; Gopin 2000).

There are numerous important international incidents and trends that are clearly influenced by religious motivations. The Iranian clergy which rules Iran feels that its actions are divinely inspired and, therefore, cannot be wrong. This has arguably resulted in, among other things, their defiance of international pressure to stop their nuclear arms programme. The attacks of 9/11 clearly fit into this category. The motivation for these attacks was based at least in part on an extreme version of Wahhabi Islamic theology (an ideology that in and of itself is extreme) (Gold 2003). It also does not fit well into paradigms of international relations which are based on material motivations because the Saudi elites from whom this ideology arose are to a large extent dependent upon US support, thus religious motivation provides a potential explanation for why they acted against their material interests. Also, several studies have found that countries which intervene in ethnic conflicts tend to intervene primarily on behalf of minorities which belong to their religion (Fox 2004; Khosla 1999), which implies that religious affinities are a strong motivation for international intervention.

Be that as it may, it is not necessary that a policy-maker's worldview be completely religious for religion to have an impact. Most people, including religious people, have complex worldviews based on a number of factors including, but not limited to, their upbringing, education, friends, family, cultural heritage, political ideologies and personal history. Nevertheless, even if religion is one among many influences on a worldview, it is still an influence. In fact, it is likely that the most significant influence of religious worldviews on the decisions of policy-makers is not in the more blatant examples like Iran and Al-Qaeda, but, rather, in the cumulative influence of religious aspects of policy-makers' worldviews. That is, leaders of religious states and organizations – who are also a likely influence at least in part by secular concerns – are greatly outnumbered by policy-makers whose worldviews include religion as one of many influences.

The second influence of worldviews on international relations is the constraints placed on policy-makers by widely held religious beliefs among their constituents. Even under autocratic regimes it can be unwise for policy-makers to take an action that runs directly counter to some belief, moral or value that is widely held by their constituents. For example, in the Arab–Israeli conflict, leaders from both sides need to weigh how their populations will react to any agreement. This is particularly true of agreements dealing with the disposition of holy sites like the city of Jerusalem. While there are few large studies which specifically focus on the religious constraints that can be placed on policy-making, several studies show that religion can influence the political and cultural mediums in which policy-makers act. For instance, several studies show that Islam is associated with authoritarian governments (Fisch 2002; Midlarsky 1998).[10] There is also no shortage of studies showing that religious affiliation is associated with political attitudes.[11]

Institutions

Religious institutions clearly play a role in domestic politics. In domestic politics they can be potent agents of political mobilization. Classic mobilization theory[12] holds that any group which has an existing set of institutions which organize them, such as religious institutions, can use those institutions as a basis for mobilization. Thus, the presence of religious institutions can facilitate mobilization for conflict. For instance, if one wants to organize a pro-Israel demonstration in the US, it is far easier to contact as many Synagogues as possible and ask them to help mobilize their congregants than to try to mobilize demonstrators from scratch. This is exactly what happened in mobilizing over 100,000 people for a pro-Israel demonstration in Washington, DC, in April 2002.

This strategy for mobilization is effective because religious institutions tend to have most of the features one would want to have in order to mobilize people for political action. They have meeting places which are regularly used. While these meetings are usually religious and social, making an announcement to congregants at these meetings regarding the desired political activity requires very little additional effort. They also have communication networks that can efficiently contact congregants. People who are active in religious organizations tend to develop organizational and leadership skills that are also useful for political activities. They are also often exposed to mobilization efforts by their religious organizations as well as political and morality messages, which the latter being not so different from political messages. Religious institutions also often have considerable economic assets and good access to the media. In some cases they are part of international networks (Hadden 1987a; Harris 1994; Johnston and Figa 1988; Verba *et al.* 1993).

However, there is also a countervailing trend where religious institutions tend to be conservative and support the status quo. Comparative research shows that when religious institutions benefit from the status quo they tend to support it but when some aspect of the status quo is a threat to these institutions or the religion they represent, they tend to support the opposition. For example, Anthony Gill (1998) asks the question: why does the Catholic Church support the governments of some Latin American states but supports the opposition in others. He finds that in general the Church benefits from a government-supported religious monopoly but in many Latin American states the people's disillusionment with the government and their belief that the Church supports that government is contributing to many Catholics converting to North American-style Evangelical denominations. In the states where this problem is serious the Catholic Church tends to support the opposition because the government-supported monopoly actually hurts the interests of the Church. Put differently,

religious institutions tend to support opposition movements when they feel their institution or religion itself is under threat and one of the main sources of such a threat is when their congregants begin to feel that the institutions are not in sync with their wants, needs and aspirations.[13]

This combination of the mobilization potential of religious institutions, their desire to foster the interests of the institution as well as its religious philosophy, and the desire to remain relevant to congregants all have the potential to influence international politics. Religious organizations often pursue political objectives in the international arena. For example, the World Council of Churches played a key role in supporting the various international divestment and actions which led to the fall of the Apartheid regime in South Africa (Warr 1999). Religious non-governmental organizations are active throughout the world engaging in humanitarian and missionary work as well as supporting political causes (Thomas 2005: 98-115).

Religious conflicts cross borders

While there are not many overtly religious international wars, there is no shortage of local conflicts with religious overtones.[14] These conflicts influence the international arena in a number of ways. First, since the end of the Cold War there has been an increased acceptance of humanitarian intervention in these conflicts. This intervention ranges from humanitarian aid and attempts at mediation to outright military intervention on behalf of an oppressed minority, such as the NATO intervention on behalf of the Albanians in Kosovo. However, the Kosovo case is actually atypical in that when looking purely at the religious identities of those involved, it is an intervention by Christians on behalf of a Muslim minority. As noted earlier, most interventions tend to be along religious lines. That is, when states intervene on behalf of ethnic minorities, over 80% of the time they intervene on behalf of minorities with which they share a religion (Fox 2004).

Second, local conflicts have the potential to cross international borders. Most local conflicts produce refugees which can create problems in neighbouring states. When a group involved in a conflict shares ethnic or religious affinities with a group in a bordering state this can cause the group in the bordering state to become involved in the conflict. It can also inspire a similar conflict in the bordering state. All of this happened in the 1990s in the Former Yugoslav republics.

A conflict in one part of the world can cause conflicts elsewhere both passively and actively. In passive mode, the success of one group can inspire similar groups elsewhere. Many believe that the Iranian revolution had exactly this influence on Muslim opposition movements around the world. In addition, if a religious revolution is successful, as happened in Iran and Afghanistan, those states often actively seek to spread the revolution and support violent opposition movements elsewhere. In the cases of Iran and the former Taliban regime in Afghanistan, this included support for numerous terrorist movements.

Third, the conflicting parties can use international forums in order to further their cause. For example, Arab and Islamic states often use the UN and UN-sponsored conferences as forums to demonize Israel. This is exactly what happened at the UN-sponsored World Conference against Racism, Radical Discrimination, Xenophobia, and Related Intolerance held in Durban, South Africa, in 2001. An effort led by Arab and Muslim states, and supported by a number of human rights organizations engaged in an effort to paint Israel as an 'Apartheid regime' which had

committed 'racist crimes against humanity, including ethnic cleansing and acts of genocide'. Setting aside the specific events of the Arab–Israeli conflict, it is fair to say that there are worse violators of human rights than Israel, including but by no means limited to several of the Arab and Muslim states which led this effort to demonize Israel. That a major focus of this particular international forum was Israel and not the world's worst human rights offenders can be attributed to the calculated use of this forum for political ends by one side in a local religious conflict (Fox and Sandler 2004: 77–79). It can also be attributed to efforts by states who are among the world's worst violators of human rights to deflect attention from themselves.

Fourth, the world is becoming an increasingly smaller place. Interdependence has increased the ability of local events to have an international impact. Economic interdependence means that the local economic disruptions caused by local conflicts ripple across the international economy. Local events are often known and even viewed in real time across the world, placing greater pressure on policy-makers to respond to events that in the past they might have been able to ignore. The attacks of 9/11 demonstrate both of these trends. It is likely that a large percentage of the world's population viewed the second plane hitting the World Trade Center in real time and many more probably saw the video within 24 hours. The attacks strongly influenced the world economy and stock markets due to the uncertainty created.

Of course, all of these avenues through which conflicts spread across borders also apply to non-religious conflicts. Nevertheless, this does not detract from the fact that local religious conflicts do spread across borders and because of this these conflicts influence international relations. Also, since the late 1970s, religious conflicts have been becoming a greater proportion of all conflict. Based on an analysis of the State Failure dataset which provides a list of the most violent domestic conflicts between 1948 and 2004,[15] religious conflicts rose from 25% of all local conflicts in 1974 to 60% in 2004.

Transnational religious phenomena and issues

A number of religious phenomena and issues are becoming increasingly transnational. By transnational I mean that these phenomena and issues are not limited by state borders.

Religious fundamentalism

Perhaps the most prominent transnational religious phenomenon is religious fundamentalism. Both the origins and agenda of religious fundamentalism can be said to be transnational. In brief, religious fundamentalism is a reaction against modernity.[16] As noted earlier, many predicted that processes inherent in modernity would lead to the demise of religion. These predictions were correct in that these modern processes would pose a challenge to religion but failed to foresee that religion would react and evolve to survive and even flourish in its modern environment. Fundamentalism, which is essentially a rejection of many of the values of modernity and the Enlightenment, is one of the results of this process. In fact, a major goal of fundamentalists is to protect their religious identities and traditions from modernity and secularism. They accomplish this through a combination of techniques including a selective reading of religious texts and traditions to the point where they can be said to be engaging in innovation in order to achieve a religious society that is workable in a modern environment. These movements often revolve around

charismatic male leaders and they recruit from the educated unemployed and underemployed – the people who are among the most likely to have a negative attitude toward modernity (Appleby 2000: 87–94). Ultimately many fundamentalist movements, especially Islamic ones, hope to create a worldwide religious society that knows no borders. Thus, for them, transnationalism is very much their goal.

Certainly, few of these movements feel that their ideology is limited by state borders and many of them seek to spread their movement internationally. This is accomplished through a number of strategies. First, many movements seek to take control of or at least influence state and local governments. If they manage to gain control of a state, in addition to enforcing their religious ideals locally, they use the state to spread the revolution worldwide. Iran and Afghanistan under the Taliban regime are prime examples of this. Second, they try to take over religious institutions and become the sole arbiters of religious legitimacy and authority. If they succeed this allows them to use this monopoly of religious legitimacy and authority to portray their goals as moral and correct and paint any who oppose them as evil and subversive. Third, these movements form transnational linkages with other like-minded movements worldwide. These linkages range from the informal to the formal, but clearly represent an effort to form a transnational agenda. Fourth, they make use of the media and international communications both to coordinate activities and spread their message worldwide.

While there are some isolated examples of fundamentalist movements taking over states, it is probably their successes in persuasion and framing public debate and influencing governments (rather than taking them over) which has the greatest influence on international politics. Religious states like Iran and the Talibani

Afghanistan, while having a significant impact on international relations, can be effectively marginalized and countered by the international community. However, the ability of fundamentalist movements to persuade and influence world leaders and, more importantly, the constituents of these leaders of the morality and correctness of their agenda has a less measurable impact, but one that is most likely more significant. Thus, the grassroots efforts of fundamentalists to gain converts to their ideologies will probably have a long-lasting and very important long-term impact on international relations.

Political Islam

Some forms of political Islam can also be characterized as a type of religious fundamentalism, which is perhaps the most visible manifestation of religious fundamentalism on the international scene. As a result, it deserves to be addressed separately. Why is this the case?

First, it is clear that Islam makes no distinction between religion and politics. Secular law is superseded by religious law and many argue that Islam has no concept of separation of religion and state (Dalcoura 2000: 879; Gellner 1992). Second, while many other fundamentalist movements are willing to work within the context of the modern state, Islamic fundamentalists reject modern states as inherently secular and corrupt. Even regimes which are arguably as close to being Muslim religious states as exist in the world today, such as Saudi Arabia, are considered by some Muslim fundamentalists as insufficiently guided by Islam. This is even more true of states which are at least in part guided by Western secular political ideologies, including socialism, communism, fascism and liberalism. The fact that many, if not most, states in the Arab and Islamic world are authoritarian, inefficient and corrupt adds to the ability of Muslim

fundamentalist movements to convince Muslims that their criticism of these states is moral and just.

Third, these movements are particularly visible in the West because they openly reject and oppose the West and Western values. The West is considered by Muslim fundamentalists to be the primary obstacle between them and the achievement of their goal of a pan-Islamic state. That their assessment is at least in part correct adds fuel to this resentment. This trend also draws on popular themes like anti-colonialism and the belief that the West has too much influence on the governments and economies of Muslim states (Fuller and Lesser 1995). The influence of the Western entertainment industry and its ability to undermine traditional morals and values is also a popular complaint.

Fourth, there is a basic incongruity between fundamentalist Islam and Western values like democracy and human rights. Many argue that because Islam is the only legitimate basis for rule, there is no room for democracy, human rights or separation of religion and state. There is also no room for opposing viewpoints or secular authority (Jaggers and Gurr 1995: 478; Lewis 1993: 96–98; Juergensmeyer 1993: 19–23). This argument is not undisputed. Many argue that Islam has within it concepts like consultation, consensus, the equality of all men, the rule of law and independent reasoning all provide a basis for an Islamic democracy (Espositio and Piscatori 1991; Fuller 2002). Others point out that while there are no democracies within the Arab world, about half of all Muslims live in democratic and semi-democratic states (Stepan 2000: 48–49) and that the theory of total religious rule has rarely if ever been put into practice (Haynes 1998: 128–129).

However, the facts on the ground show a tendency toward autocracy among Muslim states and a considerable level of intolerance for religious minorities even in Muslim states that are considered democratic. Existing quantitative studies of Islam and democracy show that Muslim states are clearly more autocratic than non-Muslim states (Fisch 2002; Midlarsky 1998) and that this is particularly true of Middle Eastern states (Jaggers and Gurr 1995).[17] Also, most Muslim states, including democratic ones, legislate aspects of Sharia (Muslim religious) law and Muslim states have the highest average levels of religious legislation (Fox 2006). This leads to poor human rights records for such states since Sharia law, *de facto*, leads to discrimination against members of other religions (Van der Vyver 1996).[18]

Given all of this, it is not surprising that political Islam is the most visible form of religious fundamentalism today, especially from the perspective of many in the West. Nevertheless, it is important to emphasize that despite all of this, Islam is not a monolithic religion. Political Islam is just one of many potential interpretations of the religion. Most Muslim states support interpretations of Islam that support their regimes' legitimacy (Akiner 2000; Haynes 1994: 67–70) and many scholars of Islam think that dialogue with the West is both necessary and healthy for Islam (Esposito and Voll 2000: 617). In fact many Muslims are claiming that jihad – holy war – is not justified against states with good levels of religious freedom, while some reinterpret the concept as a primarily *personal* struggle for self-improvement (Gopin 2000: 82–83; An-Na'im 2002).

Religious terrorism

One of the reasons political Islam has become so prominent is because many who adhere to this interpretation of Islam support terrorism. While religion has always been a justification for terrorism (Rapoport 1984), religious terrorism is becoming the dominant form of terrorism in the world today (Rapoport 2001).

A series of studies has shown that beginning in the 1980s religious terror has become the most prominent form of terror and that most, but certainly not all, terrorist groups formed during and since the 1990s are Muslim groups as well as that most terror from this period onward was perpetrated by these groups (Weinberg and Eubank 1998; Weinberg *et al.* 2002). Despite the prominence of Islam in recent religious terrorism, it is important to note that both currently and historically religious terrorism is not synonymous with Islam.

Religious terror has been prominent in a number of high-profile conflicts such as the Palestinian–Israeli conflict, Chechnya's rebellion against Russia, the Iraq war and the civil war in Algeria. Pan-Islamic terror groups like Al-Qaeda are responsible for high-profile attacks in the West as well as in the Islamic world. It is also present in conflicts that do not involve Muslims, such as the civil war in Sri Lanka.

This phenomenon, in its current form, is related to the growth of fundamentalism. This is true for at least three reasons. First, as noted earlier, fundamentalism is in part a reaction against modernity. Fundamentalists feel the need to alter the political status quo in order to bring the world into alignment with their ideology. Second, fundamentalist movements are often linked with national movements supporting minorities that seek some form of self-determination. Third, as noted earlier, many Muslims resent the encroachment of Western values into their societies.

All of these motivations require political changes in order to accomplish their goals. This, along with the tendency of fundamentalists to want to reorder the world, is a potent combination. However, while most fundamentalist movements would likely prefer peaceful means to accomplish this, peaceful means are often insufficient. Since fundamentalist ideologies are generally absolutist, they are able to justify violence in order to achieve these goals. Why terrorism specifically? Because terrorism is perceived by the fundamentalist movements that use this tactic as the most effective form of violence available to them. Put differently, if these movements were able to achieve their ends peacefully or had military forces comparable to that of the United States, for example, they would not need to use terrorism. But in most cases these movements are involved in asymmetrical conflicts against state forces which have more objective military and police power than them. This leaves terrorism as one of the few options available to them.

In the few cases where Muslim fundamentalists control a state – Iran, Afghanistan under the Taliban, and more recently the Hamas-controlled Palestinian authority – their efforts to spread the Islamic revolution also include terror. This is because engaging in more traditional state warfare is dangerous to those states, especially since those who they consider their primary enemies – the West and Israel – have strong militaries. Thus, engaging in terror through various proxy groups allows them to pursue the violent path but still insulate themselves from retaliation. Though the recent hostilities between Israel and both the Hamas-led Palestinian government and Hizbollah in Lebanon show that this insulation is not complete.

Be that as it may, it is clear that this religious wave of terror has significantly influenced international politics. It has caused the formation or realignment of international alliances between states in order to fight it. It has also led to a recognition that non-state actors can be a potent force which undermine the traditional state monopoly on the use of violence. It has also influenced the foreign policies of many states and will probably continue to do so for the foreseeable future.

Other transnational religious trends, issues and phenomena

There are a number of additional transnational trends, issues and phenomena which overlap with religion that are worthy of note. First, proselytizing is a significant source of international tension. Muslim and Christian groups, among others, send missionaries to states across the world to both find converts to their religions and convince members of their own religion to become more religious or switch allegiance to their particular interpretation of their religion.

These efforts are often unwelcome. In 2002, 77 states placed some form of restrictions on proselytizing, mostly but not exclusively by foreign missionaries. This includes states with Christian, Muslim, Buddhist, Hindu and Jewish majorities and several Western democracies. Twenty-nine states (24 of which are Muslim majority states) restricted conversion away from the dominant religion.[19]

Second, the issue of human and religious rights are increasingly becoming international issues. The issue of human rights in general has become an important element of the foreign policies of many Western states. Also, the issue of religious rights is included in a number of international treaties and documents including the 1948 UN Universal Declaration of Human Rights, the 1948 UN Convention on the Prevention of Genocide, the 1981 UN Declaration on the Elimination of All Forms of Intolerance and Discrimination based on Religion or Belief, the 1950 European Convention for the Protection of Human Rights and Fundamental Freedom, the American Convention on Human Rights, the 1969 African Charter on Human and People's Rights, and the 1990 Cairo Declaration of Human Rights in Islam, among others.

Nevertheless, perceptions of the scope and application of these rights differ along religious lines, especially between the West and Muslim states. One reason for this is that the modern concept of human rights developed in the West and this development was influenced in a number of ways by Christianity (Martin 2005). For example, most Western documents provide a list of specific rights[20] but the Cairo Declaration which represents the Islamic Conference of Foreign Ministers contains only a protection against forced conversion. In fact, the Cairo Declaration goes further in rejecting the international human rights regime by defining Islam as not only the preferred value system for the world's Muslims, but as the only acceptable value system for the entire world (Martin 2005). As human rights violations are increasingly being considered justifications for international intervention, this issue is becoming increasingly important in the international arena.

Third, holy places are a potential source of international tension. The holy places for the three Abrahamic religions which are located in Israel have been an issue of contention. This includes competing claims to the Temple Mount, conflicts among Christians for control of Christian holy sites, and tensions between Christians and Muslims over holy sites in Nazareth. All of these disputes have led to the political involvement of a number of foreign states. Another prominent international incident regarding holy sites was when the Taliban-controlled Afghan government decided to destroy two giant statues of Buddha in Bamiyan Afghanistan. In addition to Buddhist governments and scholars, there was also involvement by UNESCO, and even several Muslim states, in the unsuccessful efforts to stop the destruction of these statues.[21]

Fourth, the issue of women's rights is becoming an increasing source of tension between the West and the non-West. Non-Western states, and especially Muslim states, place many restrictions on women that are incongruent with Western ideas of equality for women. Religion is often used to justify many of these restrictions.

Not all of these sources of tension are inter-religious. One such issue is the (fifth) issue of family planning. In this case the tension is between those with a more secular orientation and those with a more religious orientation as family planning, and especially abortion, is to varying degrees restricted or banned by most interpretations the Abrahamic religions.

Sixth, the issue of stem-cell research also has caused tensions along similar secular vs. religious lines.

Identity

One of religion's many facets is identity. The concept of religious identity overlaps with most of the other ways religion influences international relations that I discuss earlier, but it deserves to be identified and considered separately. That international relations is influenced by various identity issues is probably accepted by many international relations scholars, though there are no doubt many – including realists, neo-realists and Marxists – who would dispute this notion. In short, both the extent and nature of this influence are disputed.

The debate over Samuel Huntington's (1996) clash of civilizations theory illustrates this point well. Huntington essentially argues that the national and ethnic identities which were prominent during the Cold War are becoming less relevant and in the post-Cold War era more macro-level identities, which he calls civilizations, will become the primary form of identity which drives international politics and the primary basis for international conflict. Huntington defines a civilization as

the highest cultural grouping of people and the broadest level of cultural identity people have short of what distinguishes humans from other species. It is defined by both common language, history, religion, customs, institutions and by the subjective self identification of people.

(Huntington 1993: 24)

This definition is essentially the same as most definitions of ethnic and national identity. The primary difference is that the identity groupings he describes are much larger. In fact, Huntington's concept of civilizations is essentially an amalgamation of more narrowly defined ethnic and national identities into a broader identity group based on more generally defined common traits. Furthermore, these amalgamations are largely along religious lines. Most of the civilizations on Huntington's list of civilizations – the Western, Sino-Confucian, Japanese, Islamic, Hindu, Slavic-Orthodox, Latin American and 'possibly' African civilizations – include at least some aspect of religion in their definition and are even named after religions. Other than the African civilization, they are largely religiously homogeneous. Thus, in essence, Huntington argues that religious identity will be the basis for international relations in the post-Cold War era.[22] However, as noted earlier, he buried the religious aspect of this argument in the term civilization, probably because of international relation theory's tendency to avoid directly addressing the issue of religion.

This theory was among the most controversial of the late twentieth century in international relations theory. A number of criticisms emerged to counter the theory. However, few of these criticisms directly denied that identity in general and religious identity in particular now influence international relations, sometimes significantly. In fact many argued that identity would remain important, but it would be the *national* and *ethnic* identities which were the primary forms of identity

in the Cold War era – not religious identities *per se* – which would remain the dominant forms of identity in the post-Cold War era.[23] Thus, to the extent that religion plays a role in national and ethnic identities,[24] religious identity will play a role in international politics.

Due to the sheer volume of the debate over Huntington's theory it is impossible to fully discuss the critics of that theory in this context but a brief listing of the types of criticisms is in order. First, many argue that the previous bases for conflict will remain the bases for conflict in the post-Cold War era. The argument that national and ethnic identities will remain important fit into this category. Second, the world is becoming more interdependent and a single-world identity will form that will make all previous sub-identities irrelevant. This criticism has the distinction of being one of the few that directly argues against the relevance of religious identity. Third, many argue that Huntington ignored or missed some essential factor which makes his theory irrelevant. These factors include conflict management techniques, population and environmental issues, the importance of military and economic power, the processes of modernization and secularization, and the desire of many in the non-West to be like the West. Fourth, many point out that Huntington's description of the facts is inaccurate or even intentionally distorted. Fifth, quantitative studies, which when combined include nearly every domestic and international conflict since World War II, consistently find that civilizational conflicts are a minority of conflicts, civilizational conflict did not increase with the end of the Cold War, and more traditional explanations for conflict have better explanatory power than civilizational factors. Sixth, some argue that Huntington himself does not believe his theory and the reason he presented it was to influence US foreign policy. Seventh, many attach Huntington's methodology for various and often contradictory reasons. Finally, several critics note that Huntington's predictions are potentially self-fulfilling prophecies. That is, if foreign policy-makers come to believe his predictions, especially his prediction of a Muslim versus the West conflict, this will help to make those predictions come true.[25]

Be that as it may, religious identity is certainly a prominent element of conflict and sometimes cooperation. Among domestic conflicts, religious-identity conflicts – conflicts between two groups that belong to different religions or different denominations of the same religion – ranged between 14% and 47% of the total number of conflicts in any given year between 1960 and 2004, with a general trend of a rise in the proportion of religious conflict over time.[26] Also, as discussed earlier, over 80% of international interventions by states in ethnic conflicts are by states which share a religious identity with the minority on whose behalf they are intervening.

Of course it is important to note that not all religious conflicts are religious-identity conflicts. Conflicts like the Iranian revolution, the civil war in Algeria, and numerous others are between members of the same religion but involve important religious issues.

Conclusions

There is a growing realization that international relations theory's blind spot for religion is one of the greatest failings of that body of theory. Many like Samuel Huntington argue explicitly or implicitly that religion has returned to the international scene after having been gone for some undefined period of time. Yet, does it really make sense that religion disappeared then reappeared? Or is it more likely that religion was always present and international

relations scholars were blinded by their paradigms to its existence?

Certainly the influence of many of religion's individual facets waxes and wanes over time. It is also certain that the influence of religion evolves over time. The rise of religious fundamentalism is one example of this. Yet religious fundamentalism's influence on international relations is a new manifestation of an old influence. The idea that religion should guide the state and the desire to spread the influence of one's religion are not new to the relations between states. In fact these influences of religion can be described as ancient. What is new in this case is the specific form of religious ideology. Thus, religious ideologies may change over time, but how they interact with international relations remains more constant. This is true of most of religion's influences on international relations.

Religion is used to legitimate and de-legitimate actions and policies. It influences the worldviews and actions of policy-makers and their constituents. Religious institutions can both mobilize their members for political action and discourage political action. Religious conflicts cross borders. And there exist a number of transnational phenomena and issues related to religion. These general patterns remain constant but their specific manifestations can vary over place and time. Put differently, the specifics of religion's influence on international relations may change over time, but no matter the evolution of these specifics, the general pattern remains relatively constant.

Notes

1 For a more complete discussion of modernization and secularization theory and its critics, see Fox (2002: 31–63).
2 For a review of the debate over this theory see Fox (2004: 155–174).

3 The journals in the study were *International Organization, International Studies Quarterly, International Security* and *World Politics*.

4 For a recent discussion of integrating religion into the English School, see Thomas (2005).

5 For a more detailed discussion of the secularist trends in international relations theory see Hurd (2004), Philpott (2002) and Fox and Sandler (2004: 14–32).

6 For a detailed discussion of how to define religion in the context of the social sciences see Fox (2002: 11–30).

7 See, for example, Laaman (2006). For a more general argument for religious pacifism, see Kimball (2002).

8 See, for example, Cortell and Davis (2000).

9 See, for example, Huntington (1996).

10 These studies look at statistical relationships across large numbers of states. Thus they imply that, on average, Muslim states tend to be more autocratic than non-Muslim states. This does not mean that there are no Muslim states which are also democratic.

11 For a discussion of these studies see Beyerlain and Chaves (2003).

12 See, for example, Mcarthy and Zald (1976) and Tarrow (1989).

13 See also Fox (1999).

14 For an enumeration of local religious conflicts, see Fox (2004).

15 For more information on the State Failure dataset see the project's website at http://globalpolicy.gmu.edu/pitf/. The analysis of that data used here is provided by the author.

16 For a more detailed discussion of the definition of and characteristics of fundamentalism as well as the links between fundamentalism and modernity see Almond *et al.* (2003).

17 These studies look at statistical relationships across large numbers of states. Thus, their findings do not exclude exceptions and show only correlations with authoritarianism which only implies causation but does not prove causation.

18 For a listing of some of the human rights violations by Islamic states, see Fox and Sandler (2004: 96–101).

19 These statistics are based on the Religion and State dataset which contains information on 175 countries and was collected by the author. For more on the RAS dataset, see Fox (2006).

20 For example, see the UN Declaration on the Elimination of All Forms of Intolerance and of Discrimination Based on Religion or Belief at http://www.ohchr.org/english/law/religion.htm.

21 For a more detailed discussion of all of these issues, see Fox and Sandler (2004: 77–79, 108–113).

22 For a more detailed discussion of the overlap between Huntington's civilizations and religious identity, see Fox (2004: 157–159).

23 See, for example, Gurr (1994) and Walt (1997).

24 Prominent scholars of ethnicity and nationalism generally argue that religion is often an essential element of ethnic and national identities. See, for example, Gurr (1993: 3) and Smith (1999).

25 For a full review of these critiques of Huntington's theories, see Fox (2004: 161–165).

26 This is based on an unpublished analysis of the State Failure dataset by this author. The State Failure dataset is available at http://globalpolicy.gmu.edu/pitf/.

Bibliography

Akiner, S. (2000) 'Religion's gap', *Harvard International Review*, 22, 1, pp. 62–65.

Almond, G., Appleby, R. Scott and Sivan, E. (2003) *Strong Religion: The Rise of Fundamentalism around the World*, Chicago: University of Chicago Press.

An-Na'im, A. (2002) 'The Islamic counter-reformation', *New Perspectives Quarterly*, 19, 1, pp. 29–35.

Appleby, R. Scott (2000) *The Ambivalence of the Sacred: Religion, Violence, and Reconciliation*, New York: Rowman and Littlefield.

Beyerlein, K. and Chaves, M. (2003) 'The political activities of religious congregations in the US', *Journal for the Scientific Study of Religion*, 42, 2, pp. 229–246.

Casanova, J. (1994) *Public Religions in the Modern World*, Chicago: University of Chicago Press.

Cortell, A. P. and Davis, J. W. (2000) 'Understanding the impact of international norms: A research agenda', *International Studies Review*, 1, 2, pp. 65 87.

Dalacoura, K. (2000) 'Unexceptional politics? The impact of Islam on international relations', *Millennium*, 29, 3, pp. 879–887.

Esposito, J. and Piscatori, J. (1991) 'Democratization and Islam', *Middle East Journal*, 45, 3, pp. 427–440.

Esposito, J. and Voll, J. (2000) 'Islam and the West: Muslim voices of dialogue', *Millennium*, 29, 3, pp. 613–639.

Fisch, M. Steven (2002) 'Islam and authoritarianism', *World Politics*, 55, 1, pp. 4–37.

Fox, J. (1999) 'Do religious institutions support violence or the status quo?', *Studies in Conflict and Terrorism*, 22, 2, pp. 119–139.

Fox, J. (2002) *Ethnoreligious Conflict in the Late 20th Century: A General Theory*, Lanham, MD: Lexington Books.

Fox, J. (2004) *Religion, Civilization and Civil War: 1945 through the New Millennium*, Lanham, MD: Lexington Books.

Fox, J. (2006) 'World separation of religion and state into the 21st Century', *Comparative Political Studies*, 39, 5, pp. 537–569.

Fox, J. and Sandler, S. (2004) *Bringing Religion into International Relations*, New York: Palgrave Macmillan.

Fukuyama, F. (2001) 'Social capital, civil society, and development', *Third World Quarterly*, 22, 1, pp. 7–20.

Fuller, G. (2002) 'The future of political Islam', *Foreign Affairs*, 81, 2, pp. 48–60.

Fuller, G. and Lesser, I. (1995) *A Sense of Siege: The Geopolitics of Islam and the West*, Boulder: Westview.

Geertz, C. (1977) 'Centers, kings and charisma: Reflections on the symbolics of power', in J. Ben-David and C. Nichols Clark (eds), *Culture and its Creators*, Chicago: University of Chicago Press.

Gellner, E. (1992) *Postmodernism, Reason and Religion*, London: Routledge.

Gill, A. (1998) *Rendering Unto Caesar: The Catholic Church and the State in Latin America*, Chicago: University of Chicago Press.

Gold, D. (2003) *Hatred's Kingdom: How Saudi Arabia Supports the New Global Terrorism*, Washington, DC: Regnery Publishing.

Gopin, M. (2000) *Between Eden and Armageddon: The Future of World Religions, Violence, and Peacemaking*, Oxford: Oxford University Press.

Gurr, Ted R. (1994) 'Peoples against the state: Ethnopolitical conflict and the changing world system', *International Studies Quarterly*, 38, 3, pp. 347–377.

Gurr, Ted R. (1993) *Minorities at Risk*, Washington, DC: United States Institute of Peace.

Hadden, J. (1987a) 'Religious broadcasting and the mobilization of the New Christian Right', *Journal for the Scientific Study of Religion*, 26, 1, pp. 1–24.

Hadden, J. (1987b) 'Toward desacralizing secularization theory', *Social Forces*, 65, 3, pp. 587–611.

Harris, F. (1994) 'Something within: Religion as a mobilizer of African-American political activism', *Journal of Politics*, 56, 1, pp. 42–68.

Haynes, J. (1994) *Religion in Third World Politics*, Boulder: Lynne Rienner.

Haynes, J. (1998) *Religion in Global Politics*, New York: Longman.

Huntington, S. (1993) 'The clash of civilizations?', *Foreign Affairs*, 72, 3 pp. 22–49.

Huntington, S. (1996) *The Clash of Civilizations and the Remaking of the World Order*, New York: Simon and Schuster.

Hurd, E. (2004) 'The political authority of secularism in international relations', *European Journal of International Relations*, 10, 2, pp. 235–262.

Hurd, I. (1999) 'Legitimacy and authority in international politics', *International Organizations*, 53, 2, pp. 379–408.

Jaggers, K. and. Gurr, T. R. (1995) 'Tracking democracy's third wave with the Polity III Data', *Journal of Peace Research*, 32, 4, pp. 469–482.

Johnston, H. and Figa, J. (1988) 'The church and political opposition: Comparative perspectives on mobilization against authoritarian regimes', *Journal for the Scientific Study of Religion*, 27, 1, pp. 32–47.

Juergensmeyer, M. (1993) *The New Cold War?*, Berkeley: University of California Press.

Juergensmeyer, M. (1997) 'Terror mandated by God', *Terrorism and Political Violence*, 9, 2, pp. 16–23.

Kelly, C. (2005) 'With God on his side: Deconstructing the post-9/11 discourse of George W. Bush'. Paper presented at the Annual Meeting of the Australian and New Zealand Communication Association, Christchurch, New Zealand, 4–7 July.

Khosla, D. (1999) 'Third world states as intervenors in ethnic conflicts: Implications for regional and international security', *Third World Quarterly*, 20, 6, pp. 1143–1156.

Kimball, C. (2002) *When Religion Becomes Evil*, San Francisco: HarperCollins.

Laaman, P. (2006) *Getting on Message: Challenging the Christian Right from the Heart of the Gospel*, Boston: Beacon Press.

Laustsen, C. and Waever, O. (2000) 'In defence of religion: Sacred referent objects for securitization', *Millennium*, 29, 3, pp. 705–739.

Lewis, B. (1993) *Islam and the West*, Oxford: Oxford University Press.

Martin, J. Paul (2005) 'The three monotheistic world religions and international human rights', *Journal of Social Issues*, 61, 4, pp. 827–845.

Mcarthy J. and Zald, M. (1976) 'Resource mobilization and social movements: A partial theory', *American Journal of Sociology*, 82, 6, pp. 1217–1218.

Midlarsky, M. (1998) 'Democracy and Islam: Implications for civilizational conflict and the democratic peace', *International Studies Quarterly*, 42, 3, pp. 458–511.

Miles, J. (2004) 'Religion and American foreign policy', *Survival*, 46, 1, pp. 23–37.

Philpott, D. (2002) 'The challenge of September 11 to secularism in international relations', *World Politics*, 55, 1, pp. 66–95.

Rapoport, D. (1984) 'Fear and trembling: Terrorism in three religious traditions', *American Political Science Review*, 78, 3, pp. 658–677.

Rapoport, D. (2001) 'Modern terror: The four waves', *Current History*, pp. 419–425.

Seul, J. (1999) '"Ours is the way of God": Religion, identity and intergroup conflict', *Journal of Peace Research*, 36, 3, pp. 553–569.

Smith, A. (1999) 'Ethnic election and national destiny: Some religious origins of nationalist ideals', *Nations and Nationalism*, 5, 3, pp. 331–355.

Stepan, A. (2000) 'Religion, democracy, and the "twin tolerations"', *Journal of Democracy*, 11, 4, pp. 37–56.

Tarrow, S. (1989) *Democracy and Disorder: Protest and Politics in Italy 1965–1975*, Oxford: Clarendon Press.

Thomas, S. (2005). *The Global Resurgence of Religion and the Transformation of International Relations: The Struggle for the Soul of the Twenty-first Century*, New York: Palgrave Macmillan.

Turner, B. (1991) *Religion and Social Theory*, 2nd edn, London: Sage.

Van der Vyver, J. (1996) 'Religious fundamentalism and human rights', *Journal of International Affairs*, 50, 1, pp. 21–40.

Verba, S., Scholzman, K., Bradey, H. and Nie, N. (1993) 'Race, ethnicity, and political resources: Participation in the United States', *British Journal of Political Science*, 23, 4, pp. 453–497.

Walt, S. (1997) 'Building up new bogeymen', *Foreign Policy*, 106, pp. 177–189.

Warr, K. (1999) 'The normative promise of religious organizations in global civil society', *Journal of Church and State*, 41, 3, pp. 499–523.

Weinberg, L. and Eubank, W. (1998) 'Terrorism and democracy: What recent events disclose', *Terrorism and Political Violence*, 10, 1, pp. 108–118.

Weinberg, L., Eubank, W. and Pedahzur, A. (2002) 'Characteristics of terrorist organizations 1910–2000', presented at the 25th Annual Meeting of the International Society of Political Psychology in Berlin, Germany, July.

Wilmer, F. (1993) *The Indigenous Voice in World Politics*, Newbury Park: Sage.

Wilson, B. (1982) *Religion in Sociological Perspective*, Oxford: Oxford University Press.

Religion and foreign policy

Jeffrey Haynes

It is often considered that religion can have an effect on the way a state acts within the international system. For example, religion is often identified as an organising principle for some Muslim countries, such as Iran or Saudi Arabia. On the other hand, secularism, characterised by separation of state and religion, is said to characterise the foreign policy of many states, including France, the United Kingdom and Russia.

Before the development of increasingly secular international relations, religion was a key source of international competition and sometimes conflict in many parts of the world, including Europe. By the time of the Treaty of Westphalia (1648), such religious activity was an established aspect of Europe's international relations, involving rival religious faiths (both *intra-Christian*, including Protestant and Roman Catholic and Greek Orthodox and Roman Catholic, and *Christianity* versus *Islam*). Over time, however, religion's significance for international relations appeared significantly to decline, linked to the development of politically centralised, increasingly secular states – initially in Western Europe and then via colonialism to much of the rest of the world.

This was reflected in two related processes – modernisation and secularisation. These interrelated concepts carried a shared assumption for international relations analysis: sovereign states are *the* key actors in international relations, characterised by a key attribute, state sovereignty, and a fundamental principle, international non-intervention. Gradually, these notions became embedded in international thinking, manifested in what are known as the 'four pillars' of the Westphalian system. According to Philpott, the Treaty of Westphalia (1648) was 'a structure of political authority that was forged centuries ago by a sharply secularizing set of events and that has endured in its secular guise ever since' (Philpott 2002: 79). Its overall impact was to remove religion as a justification for war. As the salience of religion for international relations declined, it was widely believed that two related developments – secular modernisation and the rise of science and rationality – would combine to put relentless pressure on religious faith, resulting in its steady decay and the emergence – around the world – of decidedly secular polities and societies.

Recently, however, this view has undergone revision, with some seeing a near-global religious resurgence, with only Western Europe not conforming to the trend (Berger 1999; Stark and Fink 2000). This has in turn refocused attention on the 'secularisation thesis', which has undergone sustained and continuing challenge.

Those now attempting to defend the continued veracity of the secularisation thesis, such as Bruce (2002), often interpret

> evidence of burgeoning religiosity in many contemporary political events to mean that we are witnessing merely a fundamentalist, antimodernist backlash against science, industrialization, and liberal Western values ... typically explained away as an isolated exception to unremitting trends of secularization and seldom recognized as part of a larger global phenomenon.
>
> (Sahliyeh 1990: 19)

As the quotation suggests, proponents of the secularisation thesis typically perceive the impact of religion on politics – and by extension international relations – as normatively 'anti-modern', typically associated with the often-pejorative concept of 'religious fundamentalism' (Marty and Appleby 1993). The problem, however, is that to restrict our understanding of religious actors in international relations to such a view means that we would miss important issues that do not fit into the anti-modernist and fundamentalist conception. For example, the Israel–Palestinian conflict – neither anti-modernist nor fundamentalist in orientation – focuses primarily on territorial issues, a concern explicitly linked in recent years with various religious and cultural issues, including who controls holy places of great importance for both Judaism and Islam. In addition, the Iranian revolution (1979) is sometimes regarded as both anti-modernist and fundamentalist in direction – yet its ramifications for international relations include a more general concern with the role of Islam as a revolutionary actor in the service of Iran's foreign policy, a focus that goes way beyond a narrow concern with the revolution's explicitly religious fundamentalist connotations. A third example is provided

by the Roman Catholic Church, which played a leading role in the 1980s and 1990s in relation to democratic transitions in various parts of the world, including Southern Europe, Latin America, Eastern Europe, sub-Saharan Africa and East Asia. There was nothing anti-modern or fundamentalist about this development. A final example comes from the 11 September 2001 ('9/11', New York and Pentagon attacks), 11 March 2003 ('3/11', Madrid bombings) and 7 July 2005 ('7/7', London bombings) outrages perpetuated by various Islamist terrorists against governments and populations in the USA, Spain and Britain. To see these incidents as merely an anti-modernist and fundamentalist reaction against secularisation misses several important points. The bombings collectively raise the question about the ideological assumptions and goals of their perpetrators – given that most of the dead, especially on 9/11, were not Christians or Jews, but Muslims. What were the bombers trying to achieve? What were their ideological assumptions and goals? To dismiss them as simply anti-modernist and as advocates of Islamic fundamentalism leaves us with a narrow focus that does not take into account other important concerns, including the impact of globalisation and of Western, pro-Israel foreign policies.

In addition, various religious actors have taken the view that involvement in politics is essential as a part of their ethics. For example, several religious individuals – including Pope John Paul II (1920–2005) and Archbishops Desmond Tutu (b. 1931) and Óscar Arnulfo Romero y Galdámez (1917–80) – were individually and centrally involved in human rights campaigns in recent years. This is not a new phenomenon: for example, religious actors were centrally involved in the Abolitionist anti-slavery movement in the nineteenth century, the civil rights struggle in the USA in the 1960s, and the anti-apartheid movement in relation to South Africa, concluding with democratisation in 1994.

The overall point is that there are now numerous religious actors in international relations, with various concerns that go beyond a narrow focus on religious fundamentalism and anti-modernism. Some encourage cooperation, 'interreligious dialogue and greater religious engagement around questions of international development and conflict resolution' (Banchoff 2005). Others are more concerned with competition, and occasionally conflict, in relation both to other religious traditions and various secular actors. Finally, religious actors now have a say in foreign policy in some countries, including the USA, India and Iran.

All states have foreign policies ostensibly directed towards achieving a set of national interests and specific goals. A state's foreign policy must be flexible enough to follow the changing contours and dynamics of international politics, while simultaneously preserving and promoting national interests. It is widely agreed that any country's domestic environment has a major role in shaping its foreign policy. For Frankel (1963), foreign policy is to a large extent a reflection of a country's domestic milieu, its needs, priorities, strengths and weaknesses. This suggests that a state's foreign policy is influenced by certain 'objective' conditions – such as history, geography, socio-economic conditions and culture – that interact with the changing dynamics of international politics. For a country to enjoy a successful foreign policy it is necessary to achieve a balance between domestic and external dimensions. In sum, foreign policies of all countries are, to some degree, a product of and interaction between (1) a country's overall power indices (including geostrategic location; economic wealth and health; military strength; and domestic political stability) and (2) the prevailing international environment. Only a few governments have foreign policies and more generally international relations ostensibly or significantly motivated by religion. Below we shall look at the recent foreign policies of the USA, India and Iran – countries where religion is said to play a role in both foreign policy formation and execution.

How and under what circumstances might domestic religious actors influence a state's foreign policy? To answer this question, a useful starting point is to note that as 'religion plays an important role in politics in certain parts of the world' then it is likely that there will be 'greater prominence of religious organizations in society and politics' in some countries compared to others (Telhami 2004: 71). Second, ability of religious actors to translate *potential* ability into *actual* influence on state foreign policies will depend to some degree upon whether they can access and thus potentially influence foreign policy decision-making processes. Third, religious actors' ability to an influence foreign policy is also linked to an ability to influence policy in other ways. For example, the USA has a democratic system with accessible decision-making structures and processes, potentially offering actors – both religious and secular – clear opportunities to influence policy-making, both domestic and foreign (Hudson 2005: 295–7). However, the idea that religious actors must 'get the ear of government' directly is a very limited and traditional understanding of influence. Overall, as Walt and Mearsheimer note, 'interest groups can lobby elected representatives and members of the executive branch, make campaign contributions, vote in elections, try to mould public opinion etc.' (Walt and Mearsheimer 2006: 6).

The USA, India and Iran represent comparatively significant cases. The USA represents a 'deviant' case: the world's most powerful 'modern' society with a high proportion of apparently highly religious people (Norris and Inglehart 2004). Traditionally, while successive US governments have sought to justify foreign policy in terms of Christian morality, it is primarily associated with the secular–universalist rhetoric of democracy, liberty and prosperity. In recent years, however, evangelical Christians have significantly affected foreign policy-making and execution, particularly in relation to: democratisation, human rights and religious freedom (Haynes 2008).

India is another officially secular state, also with a preponderantly religious society. There, two contrasting religious influences have over time influenced the worldviews of foreign policy-makers, paralleling the division between conservative and liberal religious tendencies in the USA. On the one hand, there is the tradition emanating from Gandhian pacifism. On the other hand, a distinctly Hindu religious culture underpins a robust version of Indian nationalism. Over time, however, the impact of these two contrasting traditions on Indian foreign policy has been limited, due to the importance of the overarching tradition of secular Nehruvian nonalignment (Chiriyankandath 2004: 200).

The Iranian state is a revolutionary 'theodemocracy'[1] with regional, sectarian, pan-Islamic and global ambitions. 'Neither East, nor West' was the key revolutionary rallying cry, aiming to transform the USA-dominated global order, through a foreign policy infused with Islamic ideals. Iran's soft power portfolio was, however, both meagre and structurally limited, largely because of the primarily Shia scope of Iran's soft power, which struggled to achieve resonance in a predominantly Sunni Arab Middle East. However, following the US invasion of Iraq in 2003, Iran's ability to project its religious soft power increased.

Religious soft power and foreign policy

'Soft power' refers to the capability of an entity, usually but not necessarily a state, to influence what others do through attraction and persuasion. It covers attributes, including culture, values and ideas, collectively representing different forms of influence compared to 'hard' power, typically involving armed force and/or economic coercion or inducement. Although in the post-9/11 context analysts of international relations can scarcely disregard the international influence of religion, very few scholars (see Haynes 2007: 31–62) have sought to consider soft power in the context of religion and international relations. Joseph Nye (1990), who coined the term some two decades ago, emphasises secular sources of soft power, only noting that 'for centuries, organised religious movements have possessed soft power' (2004: 94). Others who have examined the influence of soft power in international relations – for example, Melissen (2005) – barely give the issue a passing reference.

This chapter addresses this research lacuna in the following way. It seeks to analyse how selected religious organisations and movements, as well as political groups deriving their inspiration from religion, seek to influence foreign policy agendas. It has a comparative focus, examining three religious traditions – evangelical Christianity (USA), Hinduism (India) and Shia Islam (Iran). In each, the core concern is about how different ideological and institutional frameworks, both secular and religious, interact to seek to influence foreign policy formation and execution.

In each country, religious actors[2] seek to influence outcomes by encouraging foreign policy-makers to adopt policies informed by their religious tenets and beliefs. This chapter expands use of the term 'soft power' beyond the common conception developed by Joseph Nye (1990, 2004) that considers soft power to be confined to specific kinds of influence that a government exercises over another government. The intended contribution of this chapter is to demonstrate that the concept of soft power should also include religious actors who pursue their own 'foreign policies', in part by seeking to influence official foreign policy.

But how might a religious actor exercise such influence, and why would they want to influence foreign policy? A starting point is the importance of norms and identity in international relations. Rejecting both neorealism and neoliberalism, Katzenstein (1996) suggests that an adequate explanation of apparently inconsistent or irrational foreign and national security policies depends on factoring in norms, collective identities and cultures of the relevant societies.

USA

While many authors attest to the significance of religion in international relations – with some observers noting a recent widespread global religious resurgence – there is less agreement about *how* religion affects foreign policy-making and execution (see, for example, Fox and Sandler 2004; Thomas 2005; and Haynes 2007).

Religion seems especially, perhaps even exceptionally, prominent in US foreign policy, which to the external observer appears somewhat ironic given that the US Constitution makes it clear that there should be no institutionalised links between religion and the state. This is articulated explicitly in the first amendment of the constitution, 'Congress shall make no law respecting an establishment of religion or prohibiting the free exercise

thereof', thereby restricting the state and religion to separate realms. In addition, unlike several European countries, including Germany, Italy and Sweden, where Christian Democratic parties have been influential for decades, the USA does not have a tradition of political parties with a religious focus.

Still, as James A. Reichley (1986) notes, religion has always played an important part in American politics. Certainly, the republic's founders drew on religious values and rhetoric in forming the new nation, and churches were involved in various moral issues throughout the nation's history, notably controversy about slavery and the resulting Civil War in the 1860s. Later, during the twentieth century, various Christian groups were participants in a number of moral and political campaigns, including: prohibition of the sale of alcohol, enactment of women's right to vote, New Deal measures to increase social welfare in the 1930s, and the passage of laws covering civil rights in the 1960s (Wald 2003).

Today Christian-based social movements are again politically and morally significant in the USA. Evangelical Christians are often noted as especially important in this regard, not least because they significantly influenced the outcomes of the 2000 and 2004 presidential elections, contests that led to the election and re-election of 'one of their own': George W. Bush. More widely, in recent years, evangelicals have been important political and moral voices in relation to various foreign policy issues, especially concerned with human rights (Hertzke 2004; Hehir *et al.* 2004).

The attempt to translate moral and/or religious values into US foreign policy is not a new phenomenon. Indeed, as Table 18.1 indicates, religion has had a strong and continuous influence on US foreign policy over a long period.

Table 18.1 Religion and foreign policy in the United States

Period	Mission	Adversary	Means
Pre-revolutionary colonial America (1600–1776)	Millennium	'Papal antichrist'	Example as 'city on a hill'
Revolutionary and founding era (1776–1815)	Empire of liberty	Old world tyranny, 'hellish fiends' (Native Americans)	Example, continental expansion, without entangling alliances
Manifest Destiny (1815–48)	Christian civilisation	'Savages' or 'children' (Native Americans)	Example, continental expansion, without entangling alliances
Imperial America (1898–1913)	Christian civilisation	'Barbarians' and 'savages' (Filipinos)	Overseas expansion, without entangling alliances
Wilsonian Internationalism (1914–19)	Global democracy	Autocracy and imperialism	International organisations and alliances
Cold War liberalism (1946–89)	Free world	Communism	International organisations and alliances
Bush and neo-conservatism (2001–)	Spread of religious freedom and human rights	International terrorism, often linked to extremist Islam; totalitarian states, such as North Korea	Unilateral action with ad hoc alliances

Source: Judis (2005: 3).

The contemporary prominence of evangelicals has its roots in the late 1970s when evangelicalism began a political resurgence, seeking to pressurise the US government to change policy in relation to certain domestic issues, all of which were concerned with moral and/or religious issues such as abortion, family values and school curricula. As Wessner (2003) argued, from the movement's origin until the present day, evangelicals have 'politicked to take back the Supreme Court, the Congress, the public schools, textbook publishing houses, foreign affairs, and the Executive branch. … [T]heir crusade is as evident as anywhere in the words and deeds of the current Bush Administration'. Note that Wessner is not referring solely to domestic issues; he also avers that evangelicals have sought to be influential in relation to foreign policy.

This expansion of the agenda beyond domestic culture-wars issues to international affairs was encouraged by the accession to power of George W. Bush, who many evangelicals believe is a suitable individual to champion their preferred values in foreign policy. But the broadening of evangelicals' global horizons was established prior to the Bush administration, during the Clinton presidencies (1993–2001). Indeed, as Alan Hertzke details in his important book *Freeing God's Children: The Unlikely Alliance for Global Human Rights* (2004), since the mid-1990s evangelicals have been the most important part of a new human rights movement. This movement helped create a new architecture for human rights monitoring and advocacy in American foreign policy. The 'unlikely alliance' in Hertzke's subtitle refers to the fact that this movement has been one of strange bedfellows. To maximise influence it was essential to develop broad alliances with diverse religious groups (such as the Jewish community and mainline Christian organisations) and with secular entities (including student bodies on college campuses and traditional secular human rights organisations) (Green *et al.* 2003).

The willingness to build coalitions reflects a significant change in the activism of conservative evangelicals, as they leveraged increased lobbying power to mobilise support for an international agenda.

By usual social movement standards, the evangelical-led movement to put various human rights issues on the foreign policy agenda has had remarkable influence in a remarkably short time. Some of the highlights include:

- *The International Religious Freedom Act (1998)*: By establishing an office and an annual international religious freedom report that grades countries on their religious rights, this law made freedom of religion and conscience a core objective of US foreign policy. It was lobbied for by 'a coalition of conservative Christians, Jews, Catholics, mainline Protestants, Tibetan Buddhists and others' (Page 2005).
- *The Trafficking Victims Protection Act (2000)*: The aim was to remove international crime syndicates that dispatch children and women from the developing world into prostitution and sweatshops.
- *The Sudan Peace Act (2002)*: Evangelicals promoted this law, outraged by the Sudanese government's attacks on southern Sudanese Christians and animists. The law and its accompanying sanctions were influential in helping create the road map for Sudan's 2003 ceasefire and the peace treaty in 2004.
- *The North Korea Human Rights Act (2004)*: Evangelicals and Korean Americans lobbied for this bill. The aim was not only to focus US attempts to help North Korean defectors, but also to focus attention on the country's egregious human rights violations and nuclear weapons programme.

These kinds of causes do not conform to culture-war stereotypes of ideological polarisation, and the diverse coalition partners that evangelicals have worked with on these issues is testament to the fact that what is going on here is more than just conventional interest group politics salient only to narrow segments of the population. Furthermore, it is important to reiterate that this movement did not emerge only as a partisan echo chamber for the moralistic foreign policy rhetoric used by the George W. Bush administration. In fact, the movement developed first during the Clinton administration and has persisted through the George W. Bush administration – sometimes as its ally but sometimes as a critic.

The root of evangelicals' persuasiveness is found in a commonplace but crucial fact: unlike all other Western countries, the USA is a highly religious nation (Norris and Inglehart 2004). And, because in America religion plays an important role in political life, there exists 'greater prominence of religious organizations in society and politics' (Telhami 2004: 71). Religions are not mere run-of-the-mill lobby groups, nor are they necessarily monolithic in views, beliefs and expectations. Moreover, while the tangible resources of religious interest groups pales in comparison to corporate lobbies, religion can often wield indirect influence that can be instrumental in helping construct the mindset of policy-makers, including in relation to international human rights in US foreign policy.

During the presidency of Jimmy Carter (1977–81), himself a committed evangelical believer, a progressive evangelical politics became influential as it shared with Carter a focus on human rights and Christian humanitarian values. For some, however, Carter's presidency was notable for a rising tide of pacifist sentiment that not only permeated American critical consciousness at the general level but also the upper levels of the Carter administration (Dorrien 1993: 170). By contrast, Ronald Reagan shared many of conservative evangelicalism's ideals and goals, and encouraged it to develop into a significant lobby group (ibid.) Then during the Clinton era the pendulum swung back toward left-leaning religious activists, who again enjoyed easy access to top administration officials. After George W. Bush's accession to power in 2001, conservative evangelical leaders were once again able to play the part of White House insiders (Page 2005), putting their stamp on administration priorities, including in the area of foreign policy – a shift Howard LaFranchi (2006) refers to as the 'evangelization' of US foreign policy.

In conclusion, a key issue which has informed evangelicals' involvement in foreign policy during the Clinton and George W. Bush administrations is a strong belief that the USA is involved in a continuing international struggle between good and evil. While in the 1980s this struggle was defined by the Cold War, from the mid-1990s evangelical concern focused centrally on various human rights issues – including religious freedom, protection of victims of sex and sweatshops trafficking, repression of non-Muslims in Sudan, and the government of North Korea's egregious suppression of citizens' civil liberties.

India

Hindu nationalism stands at the opposite end of the spectrum from Gandhian pacific universalism. As a non-missionary 'ethnic' religion, Hinduism does not exhibit the global ambitions of Christianity or Islam, although the Hindu nationalists' civilisational compass extends far beyond the borders of India across the Middle East, Southeast Asia and the worldwide Indian diaspora. This section examines the influence of the Sangh Parivar (Hindu nationalist umbrella organisation) on India's foreign policy-making environment, with particular attention to 1998–2004, when the Bharatiya Janata Party (BJP) led the government.

Following independence from British colonial rule in 1947, India was ruled until 1975 by secular Congress Party governments. During that time, India's foreign policy developed according to certain ideological characteristics, especially: non-alignment and 'third worldism'. Demise of Congress Party rule was followed by a period of flux with no one party able to gain ascendancy. It was not until the late 1980s that a new hegemon emerged: the BJP, a party ideologically motivated by *Hindutva* ('Hindu-ness'), an amalgam of nationalist and religious concerns. The case of India under BJP rule indicates both the possibilities and limitations of using religious soft power as an analytical variable in relation to the country's foreign policy: BJP rule was characterised by many continuities in relation to foreign policy when compared to foreign policy under Congress, yet, at the same time, as many observers have noted, the influence of *Hindutva* was to some extent apparent in foreign policy under BJP rule. This is because under BJP rule, India's foreign policy reflected both ideological and ideational empathy between the government and proponents of *Hindutva*. The relationship developed from the 1980s, when the ideas of *Hindutva* increased in significance in India, finding its chief political expression in the BJP. The BJP was and is closely linked with a variety of organisations and movements promoting *Hindutva*, collectively known as the Sangh Parivar ('family of associations'). The Rashtriya Swayamsevak (RSS), the Bajrang Dal and the Vishwa Hindu Parishad (VHP) are the leading organisations in the Sangh Parivar; all are proponents of *Hindutva* that provide key sources of religious soft power, focused in recent years on three key issues: Pakistan, Kashmir and the post-9/11 'war on terror'.

The rise to prominence of *Hindutva* in India is manifested in both domestic and foreign policy contexts, although here I shall refer only to external issues. After independence in 1947, India's foreign policy was for three decades dominated by a secular vision of non-alignment and 'third worldism'. During Congress rule, India's government sought:

- dialogue with Pakistan;
- expansion of trade and investment relations with China;
- strengthening of ties with Russia, Japan, Western Europe and the United States;
- attempts to help construct a regional organisation, the South Asian Association for Regional Cooperation.
  (Katalya 2004; Kamdar 2004)

Over time, these emphases gradually changed, reflecting four developments. Domestically, there was the political rise of *Hindutva* and the BJP. Internationally, the Cold War ended, globalisation became more prominent and, after 9/11, the continuing 'war on terror' began. Reflecting these developments, BJP foreign policy shifted focus. Now, the aim was to

- build closer relations with the USA and Israel on the basis of a shared 'Islamophobia' and anti-Arabism;
- isolate Pakistan internationally;
- develop a more aggressive and dynamic Indian nationalism.
  (Bidwai 2003)

These goals were reflected in, first, a more abrasive stance towards India's Muslim minority as well as towards Pakistan. The Indian government claimed that the

government of Pakistan was the main sponsor of 'anti-Indian', Muslim terror groups fighting to wrest Muslim-majority Kashmir from Indian control. Second, the BJP government openly 'criticized non-alignment and advocated a more vigorous use of India's power to defend national interests from erosion at the hands of Pakistan and China'. Third, the BJP government 'favored the overt acquisition of nuclear weapons' (Federal Research Division of the Library of Congress 1995). Fourth, the new foreign policy focus also included a desire to 'help create an "Axis of Virtue" against "global terrorism"', linking India's government with those of the USA and Israel (Bidwai 2003). To pursue this goal, India's then National Security Adviser Brajesh Mishra advanced the 'Axis of Virtue' proposal on 8 May 2003, in Washington, DC. Addressing the American Jewish Committee (AJC) and a number of US Congressmen and women, Mishra emphasised his desire to help fashion an 'alliance of free societies involved in combating' the scourge of terrorism. Apart from the fact that the US, Israel and India were all 'advanced democracies', each had also 'been a significant target of terrorism. They have to jointly face the same ugly face of modern-day terrorism'. The aim of the 'Axis of Virtue' would be to seek to 'take on international terrorism in a holistic and focused manner ... to ensure that the global campaign ... is pursued to its logical conclusion, and does not run out of steam because of other preoccupations. We owe this commitment to our future generations' (Mishra, quoted in Embassy of India 2003). A month later, also in Washington, Lal Krishna Advani,[3] then India's deputy prime minister, also spoke in glowing terms about the 'Axis of Virtue' proposal. Stressing democratic 'similarities' between India and the US, he praised the relationship developing between India and the USA. Obliquely referring to Pakistan, he stated that this relationship was not 'an alliance of convenience. It is a principled relationship (Advani, quoted in Bidwai 2003).

The closer relationship with Israel was reflective of 'the BJP's ideology [which] admires people like [the then Israeli prime minister, Ariel] Sharon for their machismo and ferocious jingoism. It sees Hindus and Jews (plus Christians) as "strategic allies" against Islam and Confucianism. … [T]his "clash-of-civilisations" idea has many takers on India's Hindu Right' (Bidwai 2003). But before the BJP government could cement its new triangular relationship with the USA and Israel, it lost power in a general election, held in May 2004.[4] The new Congress Party prime minister, Dr Manmohan Singh, was urged by *Hindutva* supporters 'to follow a foreign policy as pragmatic as his past economic policies, that would better align India with the US policy in the war on terror. We wish him good sense and good luck in his new role' (http://hindutva.org/).

During an earlier period in power in the 1980s, Congress had embraced what Gatade calls 'the path of soft Hinduism', a policy that is said to have facilitated the subsequent rise of 'hard Hindutva' forces. In various ways, including the 'Meenakshipuram conversions in the early 1980s or the genocide of Sikhs in 1984 or the opening of the gates of Babri Mosque supposedly to "free" Ramlalla one could see the growing commonalities of views between the "secular" Congress and the Hindutva brigade' (Gatade 2006).

In conclusion, India's foreign policy under BJP reflected the growing influence of *Hindutva*, primarily emanating from the Sangh Paravar. It also facilitated a process that had actually begun earlier under Congress rule, a move away from core, traditional Indian principles – moderation, pragmatism, non-alignment and defence of the poor – to increased acceptance of Hindu nationalist ideology and principles. It appears that such concerns, including

the focus on 'Islamic terrorism' and 'clash of civilisations' concerns, were not expunged from India's foreign policy after the fall from power of the BJP in May 2004. It is appropriate to conclude that over time there was a shift in Indian perceptions about what foreign policy goals were desirable, which to some extent transcended traditional ideological divisions between Hindu nationalists and the secular Congress Party. Certainly, the post-2004 Congress-led government continued with the broad thrust of the BJP's foreign policy that it inherited, reflecting not only the prominence of *Hindutva* but also the changed international circumstances after 9/11.

Iran

Iran's post-revolutionary foreign policy is best seen in the context of a changed global environment, one characterised by continuous volatility, largely the result of the end of the Cold War and the singular position of the USA. Iran's rulers believe that the country is a pioneering state struggling to find a place in a developing international system, currently dominated by the USA (Ansari 2006). Both countries wish to contain or undermine the other. In this context, we can note competing 'soft power' agendas of the Khatami (1997–2005) and Clinton (1993–2001) presidencies, followed by 'hard power' clashes between George W. Bush (2001–2009) and Mahmoud Ahmadinejad (2005–2009).

Since the revolution in 1979, Iran's foreign policy has been 'shaped, not mainly by international forces, but by a series of intense post-revolutionary debates inside Iran regarding religion, ideology, and the necessity of engagement with the West and specifically the United States' (Sarioghalam 2001: 1; also see Ansari 2006 and Sohrabi 2006). When Iran's material interests conflicted with proclaimed commitments to 'Islamic solidarity' and Islamic revolution, under Presidents Rafsanjani and Khatami, security and economic considerations came first. When appropriate, Iran employed religion as part of a strategy to contend with neighbouring regimes or to seek to force changes in their policies (Tisdall 2006).

Religious figures within the government lost ground following the death of Ayatollah Khomeini in June 1989, a position that appeared to be consolidated after the landslide election of a self-proclaimed reformer, President Mohammad Khatami, in 1997. Khatami was, however, caught between two forces. On the one hand, there were those in government who wanted increased social and political liberalisation. On the other hand, there were religious figures in the regime who did not. The result was a stalemate between reformers and conservatives. Mahmoud Ahmadinejad replaced Khatami as president, following a further election in July 2005. Since then, Iran's foreign policy has focused on three main issues: (1) regional interests, especially in Iraq, (2) relations with the wider Muslim world, and (3) relations with the United States and Europe, notably regarding Iran's civil nuclear power programme (Barnes and Bigham 2006; Melman and Javedanfar 2007).

What was the role of religious soft power? The first point is that even though Iran is not a 'standard' democracy, it is by no means a closed society. Foreign policy debates fill the Iranian press and there are frequent deliberations in the Majlis (parliament) (Sarioghalam 2001). The Ministry of Foreign Affairs is traditionally the main promoter of secular state interests, while religious 'hardliners' – that is, those who are uncompromising in support of the line that religion is the key factor linking people both domestically and internationally – champion various Islamic causes and expressions of Muslim solidarity with co-religionists beyond Iran's borders.

Articles frequently appear attacking Foreign Ministry policies, especially in the pages of a daily newspaper *Jomhuri-ye Islami* (Afrasiabi and Maleki 2003).

Following Ahmadinejad's election, Khatami publicly criticised religious hardliners, including three prominent sets of Ahmadinejad supporters: (1) the Hojjatieh, a radically anti-Bahai[5] and anti-Sunni semi-clandestine society; (2) the Revolutionary Guards, centred on a two-million strong Islamic militia, the Basijis;[6] and (3) followers of a radical Shi'ite cleric, Ayatollah Mohammad Taqi, a key Ahmadinejad supporter and the Hojjatieh's chief ideologue (Freeman 2005; Barnes and Bigham 2006; McFaul and Milani 2006). Khatami's attack also included a reference to Ayatollah Mesbah-Yazdi, another religious hardliner with close ties to the Haqqani theological school in Qom. He had issued a *fatwa* urging all members of the Basijis to vote for Ahmadinejad in the presidential elections (Freeman 2005). Prominent supporters of Khatami included Ali Akbar Hashemi Rafsanjani, head of the Expediency Council and former president of Iran (McFaul and Milani 2006).[7]

Overall, Ahmadinejad's accession to power led to a significant change in the power balance in Iran. Religious hardliners were an important focus and source of influence, including in relation to Iraq and Iran's nuclear programme. Iran is 90% Shi'ite and Iraq is between 60% and 65% Shi'ite, while about one-third of Iraqis are Sunnis, including both Kurds and Arabs. Religious ties between Shi'ites in Iraq and Iran have been encouraged by, among others, Ayatollah Mesbah-Yazdi (Kemp 2005; Freeman 2005). Iran actively supported the position of the United States in advocating elections in Iraq, as the former hoped to see a Shi'ite dominated government in power which Iran would hope to influence, in part because of shared religious affiliation. As Kemp notes, 'current circumstances encourage

Iran to use soft power to help create some sort of Islamic government in Iraq' (2005: 6).

Iran seeks to win hearts and minds in Iraq, a tactic encouraged by the fact that many Iraqis are Shi'ites. Iran continues to promote democratic structures and processes in Iraq – as a strategy to help consolidate a strong Iranian and Shi'ite voice in Iraq's government and thus help build Iran's influence. Note that this is not Western-style liberal democracy – but Islamic democracy. Hamidreza Taraghi, head of Iran's conservative Islamic Coalition Society, has stated that 'what Ahmadinejad believes is that we have to create a model state based on ... Islamic democracy – to be given to the world. ... The ... government accepts this role for themselves' (Taraghi, quoted in Peterson 2005). As Kemp notes, 'Iran's capacity, capability, and will to influence events in Iraq are high in terms of both hard power and soft power' (Kemp 2005: 7). Note, however, that Iran's foreign policy in relation to Iraq is not unusual: it is what any state, secular or religious, would likely do when a near neighbour and rival undergoes considerable political instability. There may be nothing particularly 'religious' in Iran seeking to encourage closer ties with Shi'ites in Iraq, as it also makes sense from a secular, strategic point of view. There is, however, a second key foreign policy issue – that of Iran's nuclear programme – which has a clear religious component.

The United States has tried hard to isolate Iran, branding it a rogue state. US officials have described the Iranian president as a threat to world peace and claim that he faces a popular insurrection at home (MacAskill and Tisdall 2006; Melman and Javedanfar 2007). Despite this, in 2006 Ahmadinejad enjoyed a 70% approval rating at home, as well as growing support abroad, both among Muslim countries (including Indonesia, Azerbaijan, Kazakhstan, Tajikistan and Syria) and

non-Muslim countries, such as China (Tisdall 2006).[8]

In addition to strategic reasons, there is also a religious factor to be noted in relation to Iran's nuclear programme. Fuelled by an apocalyptic vision, Ahmadinejad and religious hardliners believe that Shi'ite Islam's long-hidden 12th Imam, or *Mahdi*, will soon emerge – perhaps at the mosque of Jamkaran[9] – to end the world (Melman and Javedanfar 2007). In September 2005, Ahmadinejad spoke of an aura that wreathed him: 'O mighty Lord, I pray to you to hasten the emergence of your last repository, the promised one, that perfect and pure human being, the one that will fill this world with justice and peace' (Peterson 2005). To prepare the shrine, Ahmadinejad provided $US20 million of state funds. He is said to have told his cabinet that he expects the Mahdi to arrive by mid-2008. In addition, according to Diehl (2006), a cleric, Mehdi Karrubi claimed 'that Ahmadinejad ordered that his government's platform be deposited in a well at Jamkaran where the faithful leave messages for the hidden imam'. The overall point is that religious soft power is influential in encouraging President Ahmadinejad to pursue a determined line on Iran's nuclear programme. 'From redressing the gulf between rich and poor in Iran, to challenging the United States and Israel and enhancing Iran's power with nuclear programme, every issue is designed to lay the foundation for the Mahdi's return' (Peterson 2005).

Overall conclusion

This chapter does not claim to be a systematic survey of the influence of selected religious actors in the USA, India and Iran and the associated projection of religious soft power; that would require far more research than has so far been undertaken. Instead, the main aim was to establish a research agenda to examine the concept of 'religious soft power' and provisionally ascertain how it is wielded in the USA, India and Iran in relation to foreign policy.

Working from the premise that religious soft power is an important factor in the recent foreign policies of the USA, India and Iran, this chapter sought to develop a conceptual innovation. The aim was to extend the use of the term soft power from its original usage – that is, government A exercises influence over government B in order to achieve the former's secular objectives – to help explain how religious actors may influence foreign policy by encouraging policy-makers to incorporate religious beliefs, norms and values into specific foreign policies, with the result that a country's foreign policy takes on religious characteristics. To achieve influence religious actors must 'get the ear of government', establishing and developing close relationships with key individuals who share their religious convictions: in the USA, President George W. Bush; in Iran, President Mahmoud Ahmadinejad; and in India, former prime minister, Lal Krishna Advani. Religious actors do not simply project themselves as traditional pressure groups – but try to influence foreign policy by exploiting key policy-makers' shared religious norms, values and beliefs; in short, by the wielding of religious soft power.

Finally, the chapter also noted a significant problem associated with the concept of religious soft power. That is, how consistently to operationalise religious soft power's foreign policy influence? How can we tell where the dividing line is between 'soft' and 'hard' power? On the one hand, it appears in some cases reasonable to identify congruence of interests between foreign policy-makers and religious actors, but, on the other hand, how can we be sure that this is any more than an opportunistic coming together of two sets of actors who identify common ground that happens to

be informed by religious norms, values and precepts? In other words, how can we *know* when religious beliefs are the key factor in explaining the influence of religious actors in relation to foreign policy? While this chapter has sought to articulate relevant research questions, to answer them thoroughly requires much more research.

Notes

1 The term 'theodemocracy' was coined by the founder of the Mormon church, Joseph Smith. For him, a theodemocracy implied a fusion of traditional republican democracy combined with theocratic elements, a system under which God and the people held the power to rule in righteousness.

2 A religious actor is an individual, group or organisation that seeks to influence domestic or international outcomes through application of religiously derived ideas or ideology.

3 Advani was President of the BJP until the end of 2005. He is now (mid-2008) leader of the opposition in the Indian parliament, the Lok Sabha.

4 The Congress Party and allies gained the largest number of seats in parliament (216, compared to the BJP's 186) although it did not gain enough seats to rule with an overall majority (273 seats would be needed). As a result, a coalition government, led by Congress, was formed.

5 Bahia was founded in 1863 in Persia and emphasises the spiritual unity of all humankind.

6 The Basijis is a paramilitary force founded by Ayatollah Khomeini in 1979. It supplied volunteers for shock troop units during the Iran–Iraq war (1980–8). The Basijis are now a branch of the Revolutionary Guards, loyal to the Supreme Leader, Ayatollah Ali Khamenei.

7 The Expediency Council has the authority to mediate disputes between Parliament and the Council of Guardians. The latter comprises 12 jurists, including six appointed by the Supreme Leader. The Council of Guardians serves as an advisory body to the latter, making it one of the most powerful governing bodies in the country.

8 Later, however, Ahmadinejad's popularity declined, due to rising inflation, high unemployment and increasing petrol costs (Tait 2007).

9 Shi'te tradition holds that the Jamkaran mosque was ordered built by the Mahdi himself.

Bibliography

Afrasiabi, K. and Maleki, A. (2003) 'Iran's foreign policy after September 11', *Brown Journal of World Affairs*, 9, 2, pp. 255–65.

Ansari, A. (2006) *Confronting Iran: The Failure of American Foreign Policy and the Roots of Mistrust*, London: C. Hurst & Co.

Banchoff, T. (2005) 'Thematic paper, August 5, 2005', prepared as background material for Conference on The New Religious Pluralism in World Politics, 16–17 March 2006, Berkeley Center for Religion, Peace & World Affairs, Georgetown University, http://siteresources.worldbank.org/DEVDIALOGUE/Resources/GeorgeTown.doc, accessed 7 April 2006.

Barnes, H. and Bigham, A. (2006) *Understanding Iran: People, Politics and Power*, London: Foreign Policy Centre.

Berger, P. (ed.) (1999) *The Desecularization of the World: Resurgent Religion in World Politics*, Grand Rapids/Washington, DC: William B. Eerdmans/Ethics & Public Policy Center.

Bidwai P. (2003) 'Critical moment for India', *Frontline*, 20, 13, 21 June, http://www.tni.org/archives/bidwai/critical.htm, accessed 6 September 2005.

Bruce, S. (2002) *God is Dead: Secularization in the West*, Oxford: Wiley.

Chiriyankandath, J. (2004) 'Realigning India: Indian foreign policy after the Cold War', *Round Table*, 93, 374, pp. 199–211.

Diehl, J. (2006) 'In Iran, apocalypse vs. reform', *The Washington Post*, 11 May, p. A27.

Dorrien, G. (1993) *The Neoconservative Mind: Politics, Culture and the War of Ideology*, Philadelphia: Temple University Press.

Embassy of India (2003) 'Address by Shri Brajesh Mishra, National Security Advisor of India at the American Jewish Committee Annual Dinner', 8 May 2003, http://www.indianembassy.org/indusrel/2003/nsa_ajc_may_8_03.htm, accessed 6 September 2005.

Federal Research Division of the Library of Congress (1995) 'India: The role of political and interest groups'. Country Studies Series, http://www.country-data.com/cgi-bin/query/r-6130.html, accessed 9 January 2005.

Fox, J. and Sandler, S. (2004) *Bringing Religion into International Relations*, Basingstoke: Palgrave Macmillan.

Frankel, J. (1963) *The Making of Foreign Policy*, London: Oxford University Press.

Freeman, C. (2005) 'The rise of Prof "Crocodile": a hardliner to terrify hardliners', *The Daily Telegraph*, 19 November.

Gatade, S. (2006) 'Encore soft Hindutva?', *Chowk*, 12 January, http://www.chowk.com/show_article.cgi?aid=00006185&channel=civic%20center, accessed 21 June 2006.

Green, J., Rozell, M. and Wilcox, C. (eds) (2003) *The Christian Right in American Politics: Marching to the Millennium*, Washington, DC: Georgetown University Press.

Haynes, J. (2007) *An Introduction to International Relations and Religion*, Harlow: Pearson Education.

Haynes, J. (2008) 'Evangelicals and a human rights culture in America', *Review of Faith & International Affairs*, 6, 2, pp. 73–82.

Hehir, B., Walzer, M., Richardson, L., Telhami, S., Krauthammer, C. and Lindsay, J. (2004) *Liberty and Power: A Dialogue on Religion and US Foreign Policy in an Unjust World*, Washington, DC: Brookings Institution Press.

Hertzke, A. (2004) *Freeing God's Children: The Unlikely Alliance for Global Human Rights*, Lanham, MD: Rowman & Littlefield.

Hudson, M. (2005) 'The United States in the Middle East', in L. Fawcett (ed.), *International Relations of the Middle East*, Oxford: Oxford University Press, pp. 283–305.

Judis, J. (2005) 'The chosen nation: The influence of religion on US foreign policy', *Policy Brief*, 37.

Kamdar, M. (2004) 'India and the new American hegemony', *Connecticut Journal of International Law*, 19, 3, http://www.mirakamdar.com/hegemony.html, accessed 21 June 2006.

Katyala, K. (2004) 'Issues and trends in Indian elections', *South Asian Journal*, 5 (July–September), http://www.southasianmedia.net/Magazine/Journal/previousissues5.htm, accessed 9 January 2006.

Katzenstein, P. J. (ed.) (1996) *The Culture of National Security: Norms and Identity in World Politics*, New York: Columbia University Press.

Kemp, G. (2005) *Iran and Iraq: The Shia Connection, Soft Power, and the Nuclear Connection*, Washington, DC: United States Institute of Peace.

LaFranchi, H. (2006) 'Evangelized foreign policy?', *Christian Science Monitor*, 2 March, http://csmonitor.com/2006/0302/p01s01-usfp.htm, accessed 2 June 2006.

MacAskill, E. and Tisdall, S. (2006) 'A year on Ahmadinejad's popularity is soaring', *The Guardian*, 21 June.

Marty, M. and R. Scott Appleby (1993) 'Introduction', in M. Marty and R. Scott Appleby (eds), *Fundamentalism and the State: Remaking Polities, Economies, and Militance*, Chicago: University of Chicago Press, pp. 1–9.

McFaul, M. and Milani, A. (2006) 'To tame Iran', *The Washington Post*, 28 January, p. A21.

Melissen, J. (ed.) (2005) *The New Public Diplomacy: Soft Power in International Relations*, Basingstoke: Palgrave Macmillan.

Melman, Y. and Javedanfar, M. (2007) *The Nuclear Sphinx of Tehran: Mahmoud Ahmadinejad and the State of Iran*, New York: Carroll & Graf.

Norris, P. and Inglehart, R. (2004) *Sacred and Secular. Religion and Politics Worldwide*, Cambridge: Cambridge University Press.

Nye, J. (1990) *Bound to Lead: The Changing Nature of American Power*, New York: Basic Books.

Nye, J. (2004) *Soft Power: The Means to Success in World Politics*, Washington, DC: Public Affairs.

Page, S. (2005) 'Christian right's alliances bend political spectrum', *USA Today*, 14 June http://www.usatoday.com/news/washington/2005-06-14-christian-right-cover_x.htm, accessed 2 June 2006.

Peterson, S. (2005) 'Waiting for the rapture in Iran', *Christian Science Monitor*, 21 December, http://www.csmonitor.com/2005/1221/p01s04-wome.html, accessed 22 June 2006.

Philpott, D. (2002) 'The challenge of September 11 to secularism in international relations', *World Politics* 55 (October), 66–95.

Reichley, J. (1986) 'Religion and the future of American politics', *Political Science Quarterly*, 101, 1, pp. 23–47.

Sahliyeh, E. (1990) 'Religious resurgence and political modernization', in E. Sahliyeh (ed.), *Religious Resurgence and Politics in the Contemporary World*, Albany, NY: State University of New York Press, pp. 1–16.

Sarioghalam, M. (2001) 'Iran's foreign policy and US–Iranian relations: A summary of remarks by Dr. Mahmood Sarioghalam, National University of Iran, at the Middle East Institute, February 5, 2001', http://209.196.144.55/html/b-sarioghalam.html, accessed 6 January 2006.

Sohrabi, N. (2006) 'Conservatives, neoconservatives and reformists: Iran after the election of Mahmud Ahmadinejad', *Middle East Brief*, Crown Center for Middle East Studies, Brandeis University, April, No. 4.

Stark, R. and Fink, R. (2000) *Acts of Faith: Explaining the Human Side of Religion*, Berkeley: University of California Press.

Tait, R. (2007) 'Iranian president sacks ministers to deflect blame for policy failure', *The Guardian*, 14 August.

Telhami, S. (2004) 'Between faith and ethics', in B. Hehir, M. Walzer, L. Richardson, S. Telhami, C. Krauthammer and J. Lindsay, *Liberty and Power: A Dialogue on Religion and US Foreign Policy in an Unjust World*, Washington, DC: Brookings Institution Press, pp. 71–84.

Thomas, S. (2005) *The Global Transformation of Religion and the Transformation of International Relations. The Struggle for the Soul of the Twenty-first Century*, New York: Palgrave Macmillan.

Tisdall, S. (2006) 'Bush wrongfooted as Iran steps up international charm offensive', *The Guardian,* 20 June.

Wald, K. (2003) *Religion and Politics in the United States*, 4th edn, Lanham, MD: Rowman & Littlefield.

Walt, S. and Mearsheimer, J. (2006) 'The Israeli lobby and US foreign policy', *London Review of Books*, 28, 6, 23 March. Available at www.lrb.co.uk, accessed 6 April 2006.

Wessner, D. (2003) 'Addressing fundamentalism by legal and spiritual means', *Human Rights and Human Welfare*, 3, pp. 65–76.

19

Transnational religious actors and international relations

Giorgio Shani[1]

This chapter focuses on the role which transnational religious actors play in international politics. Conventionally, international politics has been organized around the principle of state sovereignty since the Peace of Westphalia in 1648. The Peace of Westphalia 'secularized international relations by undermining religion as a mode of legitimacy' (Teschke 2003) and enshrined the territorially bounded sovereign state as the basic unit of international relations. Recently, however, globalization has called into question the claims of the state to unconditional sovereignty thereby creating space for the (re)emergence of transnational religious actors in global politics.

A transnational religious actor may be defined as any non-governmental actor which claims to represent a specific religious tradition which has relations with an actor in another state or with an international organization. In this chapter, the activities of transnational actors working from within two different religious traditions will be examined: Roman Catholicism and Sikhism. Using the case studies of the Roman Catholic Church, the Shiromani Gurdwara Prabandhak Committee (SGPC) and UNITED SIKHS, it will be argued that, despite differences in size, scale and

objectives, actors operating from within these two religious traditions have attempted to take advantage of the opportunities afforded by globalization to articulate a transnational identity which, potentially, challenges the international order of territorialized nation-states which dates back to the Peace of Westphalia. It is hoped that the choice of these actors will serve to refocus the debate from an excessive attention to Islam to the relationship between transnational religious actors and international relations in general. For, while it is undeniable that some transnational Islamic organizations, such as Al-Qaeda, pose a direct and often violent challenge to the international order, others, such as the Organization of Islamic Conference (OIC), work to further 'Islamic' interests or goals *within* it (Haynes 2001, 2007). In contrast to the post-11 September (hereafter 9/11) conventional wisdom in Western policy circles, it is argued that there is nothing particularly subversive about Islam *per se* but that there is a fundamental contradiction between the cosmopolitan, universal ideals espoused by some monotheistic transnational religious actors and the *realpolitik* of the Westphalian order.

The foundational principles of the Westphalian order which, it is argued, have been legitimized by the development of the hegemonic realist paradigm of International Relations (IR), will first be outlined before accounting for what Thomas (2000, 2005) identifies as a 'global religious resurgence'. Contemporary processes of globalization, it is argued, are central to the 'return of religion' to IR theory (Petito and Hatzopoulos 2003). Their impact on transnational religious communities in general will be analysed before examining how they have transformed the role of the Roman Catholic Church and the Papacy in particular. The subsequent section will look at how globalization – and its forerunner, colonial modernity – have transformed Sikh identity by facilitating its institutionalization both in India and the 'diaspora'. This has led transnational religious actors representing Sikhism into conflict with territorialized nation-states committed to secularizing civil society. Finally, it will be argued in the conclusion that transnational religious actors have the potential collectively to constitute an embryonic *globalized* transnational civil society – an alternative both to the Westphalian international order and the secularized liberal model of global civil society (Kaldor 2003). According to Lipschultz, a transnational civil society is a result of the 'self-conscious constructions of networks of knowledge and action, by decentred, local actors, that cross the reified boundaries of space as though they were not there' (Lipshultz 1992: 390). Transnational civil society comprises groups and organizations in different states that work together to create cross-border communities that pursue common goals. Following Haynes, it is argued that transnational religious communities, such as Christendom or the *Umma* may be seen as transnational civil societies (Haynes 2007: 45–6, 150). Consequently, a *globalized* transnational civil society refers to a network or coalition of non-state actors representing different transnational religious

communities, sharing a common interest in working together to overcome the forces of militant secularism.

Beyond Westphalia? Globalization, transnational religious communities and international relations

The Peace of Westphalia has been described as a 'constitutive foundational myth' of modern international relations (Teschke 2003: 3). Conventionally, the contemporary international order is understood to have its origins in the 1648 agreements which brought the Thirty Years War (1618–48) to an end and gave rise to a European system or society of sovereign states, which subsequently 'expanded', through imperialism and decolonization, to encompass the non-Western world and therefore form an embryonic 'international society' (Bull 1984). The Westphalian settlement '*secularized* international relations by undermining religion as a mode of legitimacy' (Teschke 2003: 3; italics mine). It achieved this through institutionalizing the principles of firstly, *rex est imperator in regno suo* (that 'the king rules in his own realm'), and *cujus regio, ejus religio* ('the ruler determines the religion of his realm'). This had the effect of dividing the political from the religious community, temporal from spiritual authority.

According to Haynes, there are 'four pillars' of the Westphalian system of international relations. First, states are considered the sole legitimate actors in the international system. Second, governments do not seek to change relations between religion and politics in foreign countries. Third, religious authorities legitimately exercise few, if any, domestic temporal functions, and even fewer transnationally. Finally, religious and political power, or church and state, are separated (Haynes 2007: 32). The Westphalian world order has been 'legitimized' or 'naturalized' within the discipline of IR by the emergence of first 'realism' and later 'neo-realism' as the dominant perspective in international political theory after World War II. Although the hegemony of realism has recently been eroded by the perceived triumph of liberal values following the collapse of the Soviet Union (Fukuyama 1992), most conventional theories of international relations are anchored in the same 'realist' assumptions. First, conventional theories view the state as both the key actor in international relations and as the legitimate representative of the collective will of a community/nation. Second, state leaders' primary responsibility is to ensure the survival of their state in an international system characterized by *anarchy*: defined by Wendt as 'the absence of authority' (Wendt 1996: 52). Third, conventional theories of international relations share the neo-realist assumption that a strict separation of domestic (intrastate) and international (inter-state) relations is possible.

Recent events show that the Westphalian international order, predicated on the territorialization of political communities and the privatization of religion, has come 'under siege' from deterritorialized faithbased communities. In much of the Islamic world, political Islam or 'Islamism', has replaced the discredited forces of secular nationalism as the main oppositional ideology to Western cultural, political and economic hegemony (Sayyid 1997; Esposito and Voll 2001; Mandaville 2001). Although some – primarily French scholars – consider political Islam to be a declining force in global and regional politics since the onset of contemporary processes of globalization (Kepel 2004; Roy 2004), the influence of Islamism on political movements in Islamic cultural zones (Pasha 2005) from the time of the Iranian revolution to the present day is undeniable and can be seen in recent regional conflicts

in, among others: Afghanistan, Algeria, Bosnia, Chechnya, Indonesia, Iraq, Kashmir, Kosovo, Lebanon, Nigeria, Pakistan, Palestine, Philippines, Somalia, Sudan and Thailand. Indeed, the violent manifestation of Islamic radicalism as exemplified by the events of 9/11 in the US have been seen by many as a vindication of Samuel Huntington's 'clash of civilizations' thesis which depicts Islam as a largely homogenous, violence-prone 'civilization' with 'bloody borders' (Huntington 1993: 34). In India, the emergence of the 'Hindu right' under the leadership of the Bharatiya Janata Party (BJP), largely accomplished through strategic regional alliances, has challenged the previously hegemonic ideology of Nehruvian secular nationalism as espoused by the Indian National Congress (INC). India's democratic structures, rather than resulting in the demise of religious identities as predicted by India's post-colonial leaders, led instead to the emergence of a pan-Indian Hindu cultural nationalism, albeit with local variations (Hansen and Jaffrelot 1998; Jaffrelot 1996; Bhatt 2001). Despite its loss in the 2004 elections, it has been argued elsewhere that the BJP has successfully 're-branded' India as a Hindu polity (Shani 2004).

The global religious revival is not, however, confined to the global South. In the wake of the events of 11 September 2001, Christianity has once again become an important component of Western identity. In the US, Samuel P. Huntington famously argued that American identity was founded upon a common 'Anglo-Protestant' cultural heritage which (non-Protestant) immigrants were expected to adopt as their own and defend against an increasingly radicalized Islam (Huntington 2004). Social issues featured prominently in the 2004 elections which saw the incumbent, George W. Bush, re-elected for a second term with a conservative agenda including opposition to stem-cell research, same-sex marriages and the further extension of abortion rights. These proved popular not only with the religious right or 'moral majority' which since the 1980s has enthusiastically supported conservative candidates in the Republican party but also with many Catholics who favoured Bush's stance on social issues over that of the 'Catholic' but more liberal Kerry. In Europe, an increasingly culturally diverse region, religion has become a faultline along which contemporary conflicts over national security and multiculturalism have been fought (Modood 2005). The presence of an increasingly assertive Muslim 'diaspora' (Modood 2005) in Europe has provided opportunities for a re-politicization of Christianity, in opposition to both the secularization and perceived 'Islamization' of Europe. The result has been a rediscovery of the continent's Christian roots, even among those who have long disregarded it, and a renewed sense of European *cultural* Christianity (Jenkins 2007).

The 'global religious resurgence' (Thomas 2000, 2005) has been sustained by the processes associated with the contemporary phase of globalization. As a result of globalization, faith has 'obtained greater significance as a non-territorial touchstone of identity in today's more global world' (Scholte 2005: 245). Three developments in particular have provided a context for a religious resurgence on a global scale. In the first place, globalization has impacted upon the relative power of the secular state – especially via economic restructuring programmes which uniformly necessitated reduced public expenditure in numerous developing countries. It has also reduced state capacity to impose its secular vision of the nation ('nationalism') to the exclusion of other – more fragmented – identities. Increasingly, national identities coexist and compete with other forms of collective identities on an individual level. As a result, assertion

of a national identity no longer necessitates a rejection of pre-national, *communal* identities, particularly those based on ethnicity and religion. Thus it is now possible to articulate a 'hybrid' identity (Pieterse 2004).

Second, globalization has decreased the salience of *territory* in the construction of individual and collective identities. Identity is no longer exclusively defined in terms of place: where one is from no longer allows us to define who one is. As Scholte points out, 'territorialism as the previously prevailing structure of social space was closely interlinked with nationalism as the previously prevailing structure of collective identity' (Scholte 2005: 225). However, one of the significant consequences of contemporary globalization has been to sever the connections between the state – a coercive apparatus of governance defined in terms of its monopoly of organized violence – and the nation – an 'imagined political community' (Anderson 1991), to the point where 'many national projects today no longer involve an aspiration to acquire their own sovereign state' (Scholte 2005: 228). The *deterritorialization* of nationalism has created space for the reassertion of transnational religious identities. Indeed, religious identities seems particularly suited to the needs of a rapidly globalizing world since, despite the attachment to a territorially defined 'holy land' which is often the site of pilgrimage, the core tenets of most religions are in principle universal and can be embraced and practised anywhere on earth.

Finally, globalization has, through the ICT revolution in particular, facilitated the dissemination of these universal core beliefs and tenets on a global scale. Most religious organizations maintain websites to introduce non-believers to the faith and to provide spiritual guidance to the faithful. Information technology has provided followers of transnational religious communities with the opportunity to communicate across the boundaries and transcend the limitations of the territorially defined national community.

Whilst for Benedict Anderson (1991), it was the development of what he termed 'print capitalism' that made the imagination of the nation possible, it can be argued that now ICTs facilitate the (re)imagination of transnational religious communities. Print capitalism, for Anderson, refers to the creation of mechanically reproduced secular, 'print languages' capable of dissemination through the market. These 'print languages' laid the basis for national consciousness first in Europe then elsewhere by creating fixed, unified fields of communication below sacred language and above the spoken regional vernaculars. Books and newspapers, written in these 'print languages' were the first mass market commodities in capitalism, designed for consumption in the new 'domestic' market. Speakers of regional dialects within a particular territory became capable of understanding one another through articles in newspapers, journals and books, even though they might find it difficult or even impossible to comprehend each other in conversation. In the process, they became aware of the hundreds or thousands or even millions of people, who could read their language. These fellow readers formed, for Anderson, 'the embryo of the nationally imagined community' (Anderson 1991: 44). Thus, for Anderson, 'the convergence of capitalism and print technology on the fatal diversity of the human language created the possibility of a new form of imagined community': the nation (Anderson 1991: 46).

As print capitalism helped produce the 'imagined community' of the nation, digital or 'informational' capitalism (Castells 1996: 13–21) has encouraged the formation of *transnational* networks involving individuals and groups sharing background and/or interests. ICTs 'offer new resources and new disciplines for the construction of imagined selves and imagined worlds'

(Appadurai 1996: 3). Information technology has provided the ability to communicate across the boundaries and transcend the limitations of the territorially defined national community, blurring the distinctions between inside and outside, the virtual (or 'imaginary') and the real. ICTs also provide transnational religious actors with an opportunity to articulate narratives which both simultaneously reinforce *and* challenge hegemonic power structures within their traditions.

In this section, it has been argued, following Scott Thomas, that we have experienced a 'global religious resurgence' in recent years. Globalization has facilitated the re-emergence of transnational religious actors in international relations by, first, eroding the capacity of the state to impose its secular vision on society; second, by decreasing the salience of territory in the construction of identities; and, finally, by facilitating the dissemination of these central beliefs and tenets of religions on a global scale. In the next section, we will examine how contemporary globalization has *empowered* both hegemonic and counter-hegemonic transnational religious actors representing two transnational religious civil societies: Catholicism and Sikhism.

The Roman Catholic Church

According to Jose Casanova, 'ongoing processes of globalization offer a transnational religious regime like Catholicism, which never felt fully at home in a system of sovereign territorial nation-states, unique opportunities to expand, to adapt rapidly to the newly emerging global system, and perhaps even assume a proactive role in shaping some aspects of the new system' (Casanova 1997: 121). Indeed, as its very name suggests, *Catholicism* posits an alternative, more universal or even *global* vision of international society, than that represented by the Westphalian system.

The Roman Catholic Church traces its origins to Peter, the 'rock' upon which – according to Matthew – Jesus first built his Church, and to Paul, without whom Küng asserts there would have been 'no Catholic Church' (Küng 2001: 27). However, its historical roots lie in the 'Imperial Catholic Church' of the fourth century AD. The recognition of Christianity by the Emperor Constantine in 313 AD, paved the way for the eventual conversion of the transnational Roman Empire to the message of Christ and, significantly, the hierarchicalization of the early Church of Peter and Paul along the lines of the Roman Empire. The *ecclesia catholica* incorporated many of the features of the old Roman Empire, notably its central command structure with the Bishop of Rome at the apex, its mystification of authority, its legalism, its bureaucracy and intolerance of dissent. Biblical injunctions – most notably expressed in the Ten Commandments and the New Testament – prohibiting the use of force were quickly forgotten as in 'less than a century the persecuted Church had become a persecuting Church' (Küng 2001: 45). The 'Roman' Catholic Church, however, outlived the Empire and was able to survive the various 'barbarian' invasions, the changing constellations of power in European politics, and the transition to 'modernity'. In so doing, it asserted, through its rigid, monotheistic universalism, the superiority of the spiritual over the temporal, Church over state and was able to provide the religious, political, social and cultural framework through which Europe and, subsequently, the 'West' could be imagined.

The ideology of papal absolutism, however, was only completed with the doctrine of papal infallibility at the First Vatican Council (hereafter Vatican I) in 1870. Described as the 'Council of the Counter-Enlightenment' (Küng 2001: 168), the Council confirmed the Church's opposition to 'rationalism, liberalism and materialism' and asserted that when the Roman pontiff speaks *ex cathedra*, he possesses, 'by the divine assistance promised to him in blessed Peter, that infallibility which the divine Redeemer willed His Church to enjoy in defining doctrine concerning faith or morals'. Therefore, Vatican I declared the 'definitions' of the pontiff to be 'irreformable' (The Holy See 1870).

The Second Vatican Council (Vatican II) convened almost a century after Vatican I between 1961 and 1965 did much to reconcile the Catholic Church with modernity. In *Nostra Aetate*, the declaration on the relation of the Church to non-Christian religions passed by an overwhelming majority of Bishops at the Council and proclaimed by Pope Paul VI on 28 October 1965, the Church condemned 'as foreign to the mind of Christ, any discrimination against men or harassment of them because of their race, colour, condition of life, or religion' (The Holy See 1965a). This seemed to (belatedly) affirm a commitment to universal human rights which the Papacy had steadfastly opposed since the French Revolution. Furthermore, in *Dignitatis Humanae* (7 December 1965), the right of individuals and communities to religious freedom was affirmed (The Holy See 1965b). It was recognized that, although the Vatican Council believed that Roman Catholicism remained the 'one true religion', there were, in principle at least, other paths to salvation.

After Vatican II, the Church could claim to be global in at least two different ways. In the first place, it was no longer an exclusively Roman or European institution. Whereas only one-tenth of the assembled Bishops who attended Vatican I were from outside Europe, Europeans no longer formed a majority at Vatican II. This may explain their unwillingness to rubber-stamp the recommendation of the *curia* and redefine the Church as the 'light of nations'. Furthermore, the use of the vernacular in the liturgy facilitated the 'indigenization' of the Church and allowed it to reach a younger and wider audience outside of its traditional European heartland. This has been reflected in the sharp increase in the number of Catholics globally – from 600 million to one billion by the mid-1990s – with a clear shift from North to South (Casanova 1997: 120; Haynes 2001: 150). Although we still wait the election of a non-European Pope, the fact that the last two Popes have not been Italian clearly illustrates the extent to which the Church is internationalizing (albeit without obviously accepting the shift of focus to the South!).

Furthermore, the Church's centralized hierarchy, centred on the pontiff in Rome, allows it to articulate a coherent and consistent 'ideology' or vision of God, man and the world, affirmed in its constitution, *transnationally*. Since Vatican II, there has been, as both Jose Casanova and Jeff Haynes have pointed out, a 'homogenization and globalization of Catholic culture at elite level throughout the Catholic world' (Casanova 1997: 120; Haynes 2001: 150). This process of globalization and homogenization finds expression in three directions. Firstly, it finds expression in the ever widening publication of papal encyclicals dealing not only with doctrinal matters but also with secular issues affecting all of humanity. According to Jose Casanova, these pronouncements have:

> consistently presented the protection of the human rights of every person as the moral foundation of a just social and political order, the substitution of dialogue and peaceful negotiation for violent confrontation as the means of resolving conflicts and just grievances between people and states, and universal human solidarity as the foundation for the construction of a just and fair national as well as international division of labour and a just and legitimate world order.
> (Casanova 1997: 112)

The second direction in which it finds expression is in the increasingly active role of the papacy in issues dealing with international relations, as can be seen in the opposition of Pope John Paul II to communism and the Iraq War and his championing of democracy in Poland and elsewhere in Eastern Europe in the 1980s. The Pope's encyclical of January 1991 (*Redemptoris Missio*) which stressed the Church's duty to 'relieve poverty, counter political oppression and defend human rights' may in particular be seen as a statement of the transnational *political* aspirations of the Church, and its effects were felt throughout the developing world, particularly in Africa where senior Roman Catholic figures became centrally involved in the transition to democracy (Haynes 2007: 139). Finally, globalization has generally increased the public visibility of the person of the Pope 'as the high priest of a new universal civil religion of humanity as the first citizen of a global civil society' (Casanova 1997: 116).

However, this global civil society cannot be understood as a 'liberal' global civil society. Global civil society, in a liberal sense, refers to the 'space of uncoerced human association' (Walzer 1995: 7), existing in opposition to the state and a states-system representing the interests of *particular* national communities. The liberal conception of global civil society is secular in nature and assumes the existence of the 'unencumbered individual', that is, individuals unfettered by religious or cultural social norms and values. However, this vision of global civil society is at odds with the 'post-secular' vision espoused by the present pontiff.

Although Pope Benedict XVI sparked a furore in the Islamic world when, during a lecture at Regensburg, he quoted a Byzantine emperor who described some of the Prophet Muhammad's teachings as 'evil and inhuman' (The Holy See 2006), he shares an opposition to secularism with many Islamists. Benedict opposes secularism because it is both absolute and arbitrary: in the name of 'neutrality' with regard to values, secularism eliminates all rival worldviews from the public sphere and denies the existence of objective moral truths. Far from being anti-Muslim, the Pope views Islam as a potential ally against the enlightenment secular liberalism that for him corrodes the moral core of society. Indeed, it has been suggested that his visit to Turkey in November 2006 was not only motivated by a desire to repair the damage made by his remarks at Regensburg but also to unite with Islam, and other monotheistic faiths, in order to 'inaugurate a new religious renaissance in Europe' (Blond and Pabst 2006). The pontiff, therefore, sees the Church as a participant in an alternative global civil society composed of transnational religious actors opposed to a militant and self-consciously destructive secular culture centred on the individual.

The hegemony of the papal orthodoxy within Roman Catholicism has, however, not gone uncontested and other counter-hegemonic transnational theologies have evolved within the Church since Vatican II. Perhaps the most influential has been liberation theology which the present pontiff had earlier claimed to constitute a 'fundamental threat to the faith of the Church' (Ratzinger 1984). Liberation theology developed in Latin America in the 1970s and aimed to use a politicized reading of Christianity to further the emancipation of the Third World peoples from authoritarian governments and neo-imperialism. It was profoundly influenced by certain forms of neo-Marxism and by dependency theory in particular (Frank 1969). Although liberation theology is not as influential as it once was, it played a key

role in facilitating the transition to democracy in many developing societies and it lives on through the Ecumenical Association of Third World Theologians (EATWOT): a non-denominational organization independent of the Roman Catholic Church which is committed to the reinterpretation of the gospels 'in a more meaningful way' and the promotion of 'the struggle for the liberation of Third World peoples' (http://eatwot.org/).

In conclusion, the Roman Catholic Church is a global transnational religious actor which potentially challenges the Westphalian order through its assertion of the transnational nature of the Church, of the right of the pontiff to make pronouncements on spiritual issues which are considered binding on all Catholics, and, in particular, in its affirmation of the universal dignity and rights of man. Since Vatican II, the Church has been active in the promotion of human rights, democracy and the elimination of poverty throughout the world, most notably in Communist and developing societies. This has brought it into conflict with repressive state structures which derive their legitimacy from the division of the world into territorialized, sovereign states by the Peace of Westphalia.

Sikh transnational religious actors: the Shiromani Gurdwara Prabandhak Committee and UNITED SIKHS

Whereas the Roman Catholic Church can be termed a *global* religious actor commanding the allegiances of more people than *any* nation-state other than arguably India and China, with a budget to match, the same cannot be said of the Shiromani Gurdwara Prabandhak Committee (SGPC). The SGPC controls all Sikh temples, called *gurdwaras*, in the India state of Punjab where the overwhelming majority of the world's twenty-three million Sikhs live. However, since its inception in October 1920, the SGPC has been central to the articulation of a *transnational* religious identity. It has done so by institutionalizing the orthodox *Khalsa* definition of Sikh identity through the *The Sikh Rehat Maryada* and providing Sikhdom with a central institutional structure within which to make pronouncements on issues concerning Sikhs globally.

The term 'Sikh' refers to the learners or disciples of the first Guru of the Sikh *Panth*, Nanak (1469–1539). Nanak developed during the course of his life, a religious and social philosophy which, although deeply influenced by both Hinduism and Islam, was distinct from both. The Sikh religious tradition is centred around a reading of a holy book, the *Guru Granth Sahib*, written in a sacred script particular to the Sikhs (*gurumukhi*), in a Sikh place of worship, *gurdwara*. Anybody can become a Sikh, as long as one is baptized and conforms to the established practice of the *Khalsa Rahit* (code of conduct). Baptized (*amritdhari*) Sikhs following the edicts of the tenth Guru Gobind Singh (1666–1708), are enjoined to keep their hair, including facial hair, long (*kes*); to carry a comb (*kanga*); wear knee-length breeches (*kachh*); a steel bracelet on the right hand (*kara*); and to carry a sword or dagger (*kirpan*). Those who embody these five symbols of Sikh identity, known as *Kes-dhari* Sikhs, constitute the *Khalsa*, or 'community of the pure', whilst *Sahajdhari* Sikhs, 'slow-adopters', may eventually progress towards full participation in the *Khalsa*.

These five symbols of Sikh religious identity, developed in opposition to prevalent 'Hindu' cultural practices, have been institutionalized by the SGPC and serve to construct boundaries between Sikhs and other communities, making *Kes-dhari* Sikhs an easily identifiable group in both an Indian and diaspora context. According to

the *Rehat Maryada*, a Sikh is defined as any human being who faithfully believes in:

i. One Immortal Being,
ii. Ten Gurus, from Guru Nanak Sahib to Guru Gobind Singh Sahib,
iii. The Guru Granth Sahib,
iv. The utterances and teachings of the ten Gurus and
v. the *baptism* bequeathed by the tenth Guru, and *who does not owe allegiance to any other religion*, is a Sikh.
(SGPC 1994: 1; emphasis mine)

Although this definition is wide enough to include different Sikh sects, it firmly draws the boundaries between Sikhism and other religions. Religious boundaries between Sikhs and other religions are reinforced by Article II of the *Rehat* which states that a Sikh's life has two aspects: 'individual or personal and corporate or Panthic' (SGPC 1994: 1). Whilst the personal life of a Sikh is devoted to meditation on *Nam* (the 'Divine Substance') and to following the Guru's teachings, the corporate life of a Sikh entails a commitment to the *panth*. A single, corporate entity which includes all Sikhs, the *panth* is envisaged as an essentially democratic and egalitarian polity, with the SGPC acting as its Parliament, its Constituent Assembly. The SGPC affords the Sikhs a forum to legislate on all issues concerning the community and its headquarters in the *Akal Takht* inside the Golden Temple complex in Amritsar, is the site of all temporal power within Sikhdom. A comparison, therefore, between the SGPC and the Vatican can be made, although the SGPC is, unlike the Vatican, an elected, representative organization open to all Sikhs. Like Roman Catholicism – and unlike Islam – Sikhism has its own spiritual leader, the *jathedar* or leader of the *Akal Takht*. Although answerable to the SGPC and neither possessing the gift of infallibility nor temporal authority of the Roman pontiff, the *jathedar* can, however, make pronouncements on behalf of the *panth* which, although not binding, have a normative status within Sikhism.

Globalization has influenced Sikhism in two main ways: first, it has brought opportunities for migration from the Punjab; and, second, improved communications, and the development of the Punjabi-language print media and, subsequently, ICTs, in particular, have enabled the construction of a 'diaspora' consciousness (Axel 2001; Tatla 1999; Shani 2005, 2007a, 2007b). Although migration from the Punjab to South-East Asia, East Africa and North America first took place during the colonial period, it was only after the partition of the subcontinent – and the Punjab – into two independent nation-states of India and Pakistan, that large-scale migration took place. The first destination for Sikhs from West Punjab (now Pakistan) displaced by partition was India itself as they replaced Muslims from East Punjab and the capital, New Delhi, going in the opposite direction. Subsequently, labour shortages in the West caused by the adoption of a Keynesian 'full employment' economic model, combined with the underdevelopment of Indian society after two centuries of colonial rule, convinced many Sikhs from mainly agricultural backgrounds to leave their 'homeland' and settle overseas. Initially, the vast majority settled in the UK which was more willing to accept them given the shared Anglo-Sikh colonial heritage (Singh and Tatla 2006). However, particularly after the storming of the Golden Temple complex in 1984 which led to a 'national war of self-determination' in the Punjab (Singh 2000; Pettigrew 1995), Sikhs began to move elsewhere, with North America their preferred destination.

The growth of a sizeable Sikh 'diaspora' settled mainly in the West and, numbering over a million, has posed new challenges for nation-states and the maintenance of Sikh identity. Unlike most other religious identities, Sikh identity is *embodied* and Sikhs have, therefore, found it more difficult to negotiate membership of the 'national' community while retaining the external symbols of the faith. In Britain, the 336,000-strong Sikh community has 'played a crucial role as a bridgehead community which has "pioneered" British multiculturalism' and in so doing has also 'expanded its remit to include greater public recognition of the culture and traditions of other ethnic minority communities' (Singh and Tatla 2006: 210). Although Sikhs have also consistently – and increasingly after 9/11 – faced legal challenges to the maintenance of the five symbols of Sikh identity – as well as employment, educational and legal discrimination – in North America, it is in continental Europe, and particularly France with its Jacobin traditions, that Sikhs have encountered the most difficulties.

In March 2004, the French state passed a law which bans conspicuous religious symbols and attire in public schools in order to uphold the principle of *laïcité*, which promotes the active promotion of secularism in the public sphere. Although the law does not explicitly target the Sikh community, Sikh school children are most affected by the ban since the wearing of the Five Ks is an integral part of *Kes-dhari* Sikh identity and is arguably more important to the maintenance of the Sikh faith than the cross is to Christianity, the skull-cap is to Judaism or the head scarf to Islam. Consequently, many of the 5,000-strong Sikh community in France have been faced with a stark dilemma: either to cease wearing the religious symbols which are the very *embodiment* of their faith; or to face exclusion from state schools. French (and other European) Sikhs have thus been forced to choose between 'faith' and 'nation'. Despite the French government's assurance that a 'satisfactory' solution for the Sikh community in France would be sought, the ban on religious symbols in the classroom has led to the expulsion of six Sikh schoolboys.[2] Furthermore, two adult French Sikh citizens – Shingara Singh Mann and Ranjit Singh[3] – were unable to renew important documents as they declined to remove their turban for the ID photo.

These cases have been taken up by UNITED SIKHS, a transnational, apolitical organization operating outside the Sikh 'political system' and centred on the *Akal Takht* and the SGPC. Often referred to as the Sikh 'Red Cross', UNITED SIKHS aims to 'transform underprivileged and minority communities and individuals into informed and vibrant members of society through civic, educational and personal development programmes, by fostering active participation in social and economic activity' (UNITED SIKHS 2007). Founded in 1999 by a group of Sikhs from the New York metropolitan area who banded together to assist in the 'socio-economic development of immigrant communities in Queens, New York', it now has 'chapters in America, Asia and Europe that pursue projects for the spiritual, social and economic empowerment of underprivileged and minority communities' (UNITED SIKHS 2007). Chapters are in the process of being registered in Africa and Australasia (Mejindarpal Kaur, interview, 25 March 2007).

Specifically, the role of UNITED SIKHS has been to coordinate the litigation by 'instructing counsel and providing input on Sikh issues and definitions' (Mejindarpal Kaur, personal correspondence, 25 March 2007). At the time of writing, the case of the three French boys expelled from school in 2004 is awaiting an appeal in the Conseil D'Etat, the highest French Court, while the appeal of the fourth against his expulsion is pending in the administrative appeal court. Although Shingara Singh Mann lost his appeal in the Conseil D'Etat to renew his driving licence

without having to take off his turban for the ID photo, appeals have been filed at the European Court of Human Rights and the UN Human Rights Committee in New York for all the photo ID cases.

The *globalization* of the French turban cases testifies to the *transnational* aspirations of UNITED SIKHS both to protect the rights of Sikhs throughout the globe and to further the cause of 'religious freedom'. According to European Director and Legal Team Leader, Mejindarpal Kaur, it 'is necessary to appeal these cases to the international courts as if left unchecked the French law, which undermines religious freedom, will have a domino effect on religious rights globally' (UNITED SIKHS 2006). The campaign, she claims, is not only for the French Sikhs, but 'for 25 million Sikhs around the globe as the French Turban problem is one that concerns the whole Sikh community' (Mejindarpal Kaur, personal correspondence, 25 March 2007). Several German states have passed similar legislation that bans the wearing of religious signs and clothing by public servants, and two Belgian Sikh schoolchildren have not been admitted to school because of their turban. It is important to point out that although Sikhs are not the only – or even the main – religious group affected by the ban, they are, as far as I know, the only ones fighting the law *transnationally* and their success may have important consequences for religious freedom globally.

Conclusion

In conclusion, the global activities of religious actors have exposed the 'secular conceit' (Connolly 1999: 19–47) of the Westphalian order which made transnational religious and cultural traditions subject to the disciplinary power of the sovereign state. Now that modern international society, based upon the separation of the 'political' from the 'religious' community and the subsequent subordination of spiritual to temporal authority, is faced with unprecedented global economic, political and social change, it has been argued that the modern secular settlement, which excludes the religious from the public sphere of politics, is unsustainable and that transnational religious actors will become increasingly more important in our 'global age'. However, as Richard Falk has pointed out, all religious traditions have two broad tendencies: the first is to be universalistic and tolerant towards others who hold different convictions and identities; the second is to be exclusivist and to insist that there exists 'only one true path to salvation, which if not taken results in failure and futility, if not evil' (Falk 2003: 184).

It has been argued in this chapter that the Roman Catholic Church after Vatican II has indeed become more tolerant towards other religious traditions and, under the present pontiff, has signalled a willingness to enlist other faiths in its battle against militant secularism. However, a lot more needs to be done if the Church wants to emerge as a truly *global* political actor. According to the Catholic Theologian Hans Küng, the Church needs to satisfy four conditions if it is to have a future in the third millennium: it must not turn back but 'be rooted in its Christian origin and concentrated on its present tasks'; it must not be patriarchal and exclude women from Church ministries; it must not be narrowly confessional but be an 'ecumenically open' church; and, finally, it must not be 'Eurocentric and put forward any exclusivist Christian claims' (Küng 2001: 213). One way in which it could become less Eurocentric and more global in its outlook would be to provide support for the campaign, led by UNITED SIKHS, to overturn the ban on the manifestation of religious symbols in France. In so doing, the Catholic Church would not only advance the cause of religious freedom globally but could also emerge as

a potentially hegemonic actor in a newly emerging globalized 'post-secular' transnational civil society.

Notes

1 The author is Associate Professor, College of International Relations, Ritsumeikan University, Kyoto, Japan. He wishes to thank the editor for the invitation to contribute to the volume.
2 Jasvir Singh, Bikramjit Singh and Ranjit Singh were expelled in 2004. They were joined in 2005 by Gurinder Singh and Jasmeet Singh in 2006. Maha Singh has, furthermore, not been admitted in any school since 2006 on account of his turban (Mejindarpal Kaur, personal correspondence, 25 March 2007).
3 Shingara Singh Mann was unable to renew his driver's licence and passport as he would not take off his turban for a photo ID, and Ranjit Singh, a 69-year-old political refugee, was refused a resident card in 2002 for a similar reason (Mejindarpal Kaur, personal correspondence, 25 March 2007).

Bibliography

Agnew, J. (1998) *Geopolitics: Re-visioning World Politics*, London: Routledge.

Almond, G. A., Sivan, E. and Appleby R. S. (1995) 'Fundamentalism: Genus and species', in M. E. Marty and R. Scott Appleby (eds), *Fundamentalism Comprehended*, Chicago: University of Chicago Press.

Anderson, B. (1991) *Imagined Communities: Reflections on the Origin and Spread of Nationalism*, revised edition (1st edn 1983), London: Verso.

Appadurai, A. (1996) *Modernity at Large: The Cultural Dimensions of Globalization*, Minnesota: University of Minnesota Press.

Axel, B. K. (2001) *The Nation's Tortured Body: Violence, Representation, and the Formation of a Sikh 'Diaspora'*, Durham and London: Duke University Press.

Bhatt, C. (2001) *Hindu Nationalism: Origins, Ideologies and Modern Myths*, Oxford: Berg.

Blond, P. and Pabst, A. (2006) 'Benedict's post-secular vision', *International Herald Tribune*, Wednesday, 29 November, http://www.iht.com/

319

articles/2006/11/29/opinion/edblond.php,
accessed 29 November 2006.

Bull, H. (1984) 'The revolt against the West', in
H. Bull and A. Watson (eds), *The Expansion of
International Society*, Oxford: Clarendon Press.

Carr, E. H. [1939] (1962) *The Twenty Years' Crisis*,
2nd edn, Basingstoke: Macmillan.

Casanova, J. (1997) 'Globalizing Catholicism and
the return to a "universal" church', in
S. H. Rudolph and J. Piscatori (eds), *Transnational
Religion and Fading States*, Boulder, CO:
Westview; reprinted in R. Robertson and
K. E. White (eds) (2003) *Globalization: Critical
Concepts in Sociology*, Vol. V, London: Routledge.

Castells, M. (1996) *The Information Age*, Vol. 1: *The
Network Society*, Oxford: Blackwell.

Connolly, W. E. (1999) *Why I Am Not a Secularist*,
Minneapolis: University of Minnesota Press.

Esposito, J. L. and Voll, J. O. (2001) *Makers of
Contemporary Islam*, New York: Oxford
University Press.

Falk, R. A. (2003) 'A worldwide religious resur-
gence in an era of globalization', in F. Petito and
P. Hatzopoulos (eds) *Religion and International
Relations: The Return from Exile*, New York and
Houndmills, Basingstoke: Palgrave.

Fox, R. G. (1985) *Lions of the Punjab: Culture in the
Making*, Berkeley: University of California Press.

Frank, A. G. (1969) *The Development of Underdevelopment*, Chicago: University of Chicago
Press.

Fukuyama, F. (1992) *The End of History and the
Last Man*, London: Penguin.

Hansen, T. B. and Jaffrelot, C. (eds) (1998) *The
BJP and the Compulsions of Politics in India*,
New Delhi: Oxford University Press.

Haynes, J. (2001) 'Transnational religious actors and
international politics', *Third World Quarterly*, 22,
1, pp. 143–158.

Haynes, J. (2007) *An Introduction to International
Relations and Religion*, Harlow, Essex: Pearson
Longman.

Held, D. and McGrew, A. (2000) 'The great globalization debate', in D. Held and A. McGrew
(eds), *The Global Transformations Reader*,
Cambridge: Polity.

Held, D. and McGrew, A. (2006) 'Introduction:
Globalization at risk?', in D. Held and A. McGrew
(eds), *Globalization Theory*, Cambridge: Polity.

Holy See, The (1870) 'The Decrees of the First
Vatican Council', http://www.dailycatholic.

org/history/20ecume3.htm#Chapter%204.%
20On%20the%20infallible%20teaching%20aut
hority%20of%20the%20Roman%20pontiff,
accessed 20 March 2007.

Holy See, The (1965a) '*Nostra Aetate*', http://
www.vatican.va/archive/hist_councils/ii_vati
can_council/documents/vat-ii_decl_
19651028_nostra-aetate_en.html, accessed
20 March 2007.

Holy See, The (1965b) '*Dignitatis Humanae*',
http://www.vatican.va/archive/hist_coun
cils/ii_vatican_council/documents/vatii_decl_
19651207_dignitatis-humanae_en.html,
accessed 20 March 2007.

Holy See, The (2006) 'Lecture of the Holy Father
to the *Aula Magna* of the University of
Regensburg, 12 September', http://www.vatican.
va/holy_father/benedict_xvi/speeches/2006/
september/documents/hf_ben-xvi_spe_
20060912_university-regensburg_en.html,
accessed 22 March 2007.

Huntington, S. P. (1993) 'The clash of civilization', *Foreign Affairs*, 72, Summer, pp. 22–49.

Huntington, S. P. (2004) *Who Are We? The
Challenges to America's National Identity*,
New York: Simon and Shuster.

Jaffrelot, C. (1996) *The Hindu Nationalist
Movement and Indian Politics, from 1925 to the
1990s*, London: Hurst and Company.

Jenkins, P. (2007) *God's Continent: Christianity,
Islam, and Europe's Religious Crisis*, New York:
Oxford University Press.

Juergensmeyer, M. (1993) *The New Cold War?
Religious Nationalism Confronts the Secular State*,
Berkeley: University of California Press.

Kaldor, M. (2003) *Global Civil Society: An Answer
to War*, Cambridge: Polity.

Kepel, G. (2004) *Jihad: The Trail of Political Islam*,
London: I. B. Tauris.

Küng, H. (2001) *The Catholic Church*, trans.
J. Bowden, London: Weidenfeld & Nicolson.

Lipschultz, R. (1992) 'Reconstructing world politics: The emergence of global civil society',
Millennium, 21, pp. 389–420.

Luke, T. W. (1998) 'Running flat out on the road
ahead: Nationality, sovereignty, and territoriality in the world of the information super-
highway', in G. ó Tuathail and S. Dalby (eds),
Rethinking Geopolitics, London: Routledge.

Mandaville, P. (2001) *Transnational Muslim Politics*,
London: Routledge.

Modood, T. (2005) *Multicultural Politics: Racism, Ethnicity and Muslims in Britain*, Minneapolis: University of Minnesota Press.

Morgenthau, H. (1967) *Politics Among Nations: The Struggle for Power and Peace*, New York: Alfred A. Knopf.

Negroponte, N. (1995) 'Being digital in a wired world', in A. Leer (ed.), *Masters of the Wired World: Cyberspace Speaks Out*, London: Financial Times.

Oberoi, H. S. (1994) *The Construction of Religious Boundaries: Culture, Identity and Diversity in the Sikh Tradition*, New Delhi: Oxford University Press.

Pasha, M. K. (2005) 'Islam, "soft" orientalism and hegemony: A Gramscian rereading', *Critical Review of International Social and Political Philosophy*, 8, 4, pp. 543–558.

Petito, F. and Hatzopoulos, P. (eds) (2003) *Religion in International Relations: The Return from Exile*, New York: Palgrave.

Pettigrew, J. (1995) *The Sikhs of the Punjab: Unheard Voices of the State and Guerrilla Violence*, London: Zed Books.

Pieterse, J. N. (2004) *Globalization and Culture*, Lanham, MD: Rowman and Littlefield.

Ratzinger, Cardinal J. (1984) 'Preliminary notes on liberation theology', http://www.christendom-awake.org/pages/ratzinger/liberationtheol.htm, accessed 25 June 2007.

Roy, O. (2004) *Globalized Islam: The Search for a New Ummah*, New York: Columbia University Press.

Sayyid, B. (1997) *A Fundamental Fear: Eurocentrism and the Emergence of Islamism*, London: Zed Books.

Sayyid, S. (2000) 'Beyond Westphalia: Nations and diasporas: The case of the Muslim umma', in B. Hesse (ed.), *Un/settled Multiculturalisms: Diasporas, Entanglements, Transruptions*, London: Zed Press.

Scholte, J. A. (2005) *Globalization: A Critical Introduction*, 2nd edn, Basingstoke: Palgrave Macmillan.

Shani, G. (2000) 'The construction of a Sikh national identity', *South Asia Research* 20, 1, pp. 3–18.

Shani, G. (2004) 'Rebranding India? Globalization, Hindutva and the 2004 elections', *Ritsumeikan Review of International Studies*, 3, pp. 35–58.

Shani, G. (2005) 'Beyond Khalistan: Sikh diasporic identity and critical international theory', *Sikh Formations: Religion, Culture, Theory*, 1, 1, pp. 57–74.

Shani, G. (2007a) *Sikh Nationalism and Identity in a Global Age*, London: Routledge.

Shani, G. (2007b) 'Provincialising critical theory: Islam, Sikhism and international relations', *Cambridge Review of International Affairs*, 20, 3, pp. 417–434.

Shiromani Gurdwara Prabandhak Committee (SGPC) (1994) *The Sikh Rehat Maryada*, Amritsar: SGPC Publications.

Singh, G. (2000) *Ethnic Conflict in India: A Case Study of the Punjab*, London: Palgrave Macmillan.

Singh, G. and Tatla, D. S. (2006) *Sikhs in Britain: The Making of a Community*, London: Zed Books.

Tatla, D. S. (1999) *The Sikh Diaspora: The Search for Statehood*, London: UCL Press.

Teschke, B. (2003) *The Myth of 1648: Class, Geopolitics and the Making of Modern International Relations*, London: Verso.

Thomas, S. M. (2000) 'Taking religious and cultural pluralism seriously: The global resurgence of religion and the transformation of international society', *Millennium: Journal of International Studies*, 29, 3, pp. 815–884.

Thomas, S. M. (2005) *The Global Resurgence of Religion and the Transformation of International Relations*, New York and Basingstoke: Palgrave Macmillan.

UNITED SIKHS (2006) 'French turban campaign continues in earnest as more Sikh students face expulsion', press release, 18 November, http://unitedsikhs.org/PressReleases/PRSRLS-18-11-2006-00.htm, accessed 25 February 2007.

UNITED SIKHS (2007) 'About', http://www.unitedsikhs.org/about.htm, accessed 21 February 2007.

Waltz, K. (1979) *Theory of International Politics*, Reading, MA.: Addison-Wesley.

Waltz, K. (1986) 'Systemic and reductionist theories', in R. O. Keohane (ed.), *Neorealism and its Critics*, New York: Columbia University Press.

Waltz, K. (1990) 'Realist thought and Neo-Realist theory', *Journal of International Affairs*, 44, 1, pp. 20–40.

321

Walzer, M. (1995) 'The concept of civil society', in M. Walzer (ed.), *Toward a Global Civil Society*, Providence, RI: Berghahn Books.

Wendt, A. (1996) 'Identity and structural change in international politics', in Y. Lapid and F. Kratochwil (eds), *The Return of Culture and Identity in International Relations Theory*, Boulder, CO: Lynne Rienner.

Young, T. (1995) 'A project to be realised: Global liberalism and contemporary Africa', *Millennium: Journal of International Studies*, 24, 3, pp. 527–546.

20

Religion and globalization

David Wessels

Introduction and overview

Globalization has many dimensions in the twenty-first century.[1] The challenges of global politics include the practice of governance and democracy in a world of diverse economic and social realities. As cultures meet, religions act and interact within core areas, along adjoining borders, and in far-flung diasporas. The encounter between religion and globalization is a crucial feature of our world. In the study of politics, a new awareness of religion is evident. In the global transformation that is occurring, religion is basic for the understanding of particular issues such as democracy and fundamentalisms, conflict and reconciliation, tolerance and public religion, standard and track-two diplomacy. Overarching aspects of international relations such as sovereignty and the structure of the international system are intertwined with religion throughout history up to the present. Likewise, religions are moulded by their political surroundings, locally and globally.

The intersection of religion and politics is at the core of the real world of human activity, and especially of what we call globalization today. The tendency of theories on the subject has been to reduce religion to politics or vice versa. Looking at global politics today, practitioners and analysts alike sense that religions and politics and globalization need to be reconsidered, and to be reconsidered together. But how do we do so without just adding one or another variable to an already over-crowded political theory?

There is a pressing need for a new theoretical stance on the theme of *religion and globalization*. Often, analysts have simply treated one or the other of these realities as a selective variable to fill in a few more facts about the dynamics of the other: the question simply becomes one of the direction of influence (of religion on politics or vice versa) in an explanatory model. But an integrated theory of global politics and particular religions must regard religion and globalization in tandem, as fundamental features of the lives of individual persons and whole communities that converge and diverge in many ways. Religion is not some kind of ideological view of politics; global politics is not some kind of rival for the hearts of the religious faithful. Media images of international conflict and violence, juxtaposed with religious claims by the perpetrators of those actions, are merely a conflation of human dramas rather than a considered perception of how politics and religion mingle.

A shorthand for the understanding of global politics may be found in the way political leaders describe that world or prescribe for it. For example, in November 1990 in Paris, leaders of the Conference on Security and Cooperation in Europe (CSCE) formulated what they called the Charter of Paris for a New Europe (Lawson and Bertucci 1996: 202–207), a document which sought to give direction to the changing political and economic realities of Europe at that time of monumental transition when tensions between the military blocs had eased and prospects for a more peaceful future based on common values looked good. Among the Charter's principal points were the emphases on democracy, human rights and economic liberty (market economics) as European, if not global, standards for the conduct of public life in the aftermath of the changes symbolized by the year 1989. After decades of mutual threats, implacable opposition in ideological convictions, and rivalries and conflicts that extended to all corners of the globe, the participants in the CSCE began to envision and discourse about something new. With particular emphases, it was variously called by such names as a new international order, a new global order, globalization; and it resonated beyond the CSCE itself to encompass a variety of political, economic, social and cultural realities throughout the world. 'Global politics' is the term that I will use to address this universal theme.

Global politics thus refers empirically to the practices and discourses that have affected the course of international relations since the 1980s, although it is clearly not limited to such a brief timespan. Many ideas and patterns that fit the term global politics have elements that can be traced back over centuries, even millennia. Institutions that are based on such ideas and that demonstrate such patterns range from ancient Greek city-states to international organizations of the twenty-first century. The term global politics as used here also carries normative meaning.

For example, in the context of today's world, democracy can be contrasted with various forms of authoritarianism and totalitarianism; human rights can be identified with evolving norms based on the key understanding of the dignity of the human person; and free markets demonstrably differ from command-style political-economic systems.

The struggles for democratic freedoms and human rights that continue in our world and the movements against aspects of globalization that arise in many places show that global politics as outlined above remains a contested sphere of thought and action. I will not try to examine all of these cases and issues in this chapter. Instead I will focus on particular religions as a correlative concept that can shed new light on the dynamics of global politics. I will offer a basic stance on religion and politics together that can provide a more integrated understanding of global politics and particular religions than examining either concept alone could yield.

Use of the term 'particular religions' also calls for some efforts at providing a working definition. Some might consider the term pleonasm: of course, all religions are particular. Especially in the context of long-term trends in global politics, the overlap between the spheres of politics and religion in customs, symbols, and even social or hierarchical groups, has been seen throughout the world. Insofar as 'religion' is regarded as a Westphalian invention (Thomas 2003) that differentiates the religious from other spheres of human activity – usually assigning it to a merely private role in making that differentiation – some consider religion excluded from or irrelevant to the public sphere of politics. Also religions that are spread widely across the globe – some with aspirations toward or self-understandings as universal faiths for all people and peoples – manifest particular features of language, rituals and other expressions in diverse lands.

To counterpose particular religions to global politics need not mean that religions have a limited geographical scope while today's politics is worldwide. On the one hand, religions are specific in terms of teachings, rituals, even communities. On the other hand, as the well-known American politician Tip O'Neill was wont to say, 'all politics is local', too. In the study of international relations, scholars have struggled to identify new concepts and have offered neologisms in phrases like 'glocalization' and 'think globally, act locally'. The study of world civilizations and contemporary global dynamics provides abundant evidence that particular religions demonstrate a capacity to spread over the face of the globe, forming inclusive groups of believers that overcome barriers of language, ethnicity and lifestyles.

What these preliminary remarks suggest is that global politics and particular religions have some points of convergence as well as divergence. Furthermore, in the study of international relations, many of the concepts that are used today to characterize global politics are incomplete without additional and complementary notions of particular religions. This poses the question of how we might approach these realities or even achieve an integrated theory that includes or bridges two spheres that some observers consider irreconcilably separate. In an effort to address the theme of 'religion and globalization', we will have to look at their specific and particular empirical conjunctions as well as these abstract concepts.

Given the long history during which religion has been ignored or actively rejected as a factor in the practice and analysis of international relations, it is understandable that some commentators have felt the need to address the question of why religion should be included in the study of international relations (Petito and Hatzopoulos 2003; Fox 2001). I note that apologetic effort here, but will not examine it in detail. Firstly, since the arguments of these earlier writers have already made a good case for bringing religious considerations into international relations, I need not repeat them here. Secondly, building upon the implications of those previous apologies, I will try in these few pages to advance a more substantive argument as to the way to connect these two spheres (global politics and particular religions). In fact, addressing these two realities from a common stance overcomes the difficulty of bringing one of them 'into' the other; their mutuality or connectedness is highlighted.

A less sophisticated but urgent point is the tendency of many to regard religion as a relevant subject merely because of its association with violent events in the world. After the Cold War, ethnic conflicts in many parts of the world had a religious tinge. Each conflict has had unique elements, but attention has been drawn to common aspects of a religious character (Juergensmeyer 1993; 'Religion: politics, power and symbolism' 1996). Even more dramatic was the way in which the terrorist hijackings of 11 September 2001 became associated with religious images. The terrorists themselves imagined their motives and behaviour as religiously inspired; and a typical reaction to those events among governments, scholars and the general public has been to perceive a need to understand religions better to deal with the issues raised by terrorism (Philpott 2002). Questions of conflict and violence certainly need to be addressed, but it would be myopic to reduce a study of religion, politics and globalization to a distorted view of religion only in those terms.

Among the more positive approaches to a re-evaluation of the relationship between religion and international relations are the attempts of scholars to survey the religion and politics landscape. The work of Scott M. Thomas offers a normative perspective particularly influenced by the rich philosophical insights of Alasdair MacIntyre and René Girard. He also identifies the diverse settings throughout the world in which religious roots offer a useful foundation for empirical analysis (Thomas 2005). Eric O. Hanson offers a new paradigm that sees international relations as the set of overlapping political, economic, military and communication systems. Within that paradigm, political and religious perspectives take on powerful independent significance, and lead to a rich appreciation of the various settings of interaction between religion and politics worldwide (Hanson 2006). Jeff Haynes takes a more comparative perspective as he shows the vigour of the religion–politics dialectic in regions, countries and religions all over the globe (Haynes 1998).

Already at this basic level, a number of conundrums present themselves. In the familiar language of social science, the question becomes one of the direction of influence or causation. Does politics coerce religion, or does religion manipulate politics in diverse settings? In subtler ways, do politicians (cynically or otherwise) use the language and symbols of religion to achieve their political agenda? Do people of religion (benevolently or malevolently) cross a border between their legitimate concerns and the arena of politics? Of course, to state these issues is to differentiate the spheres of politics and religion in an analytical way that would be unfamiliar to many people and peoples, past and present. It is also to seek explanations for the behaviour of people in their motives, intentions and goals.

Especially when this kind of analysis draws attention to murky realms of exploitation or violence, to conflict rather than cooperation, it exposes an uncomfortable reality that both politics and religion may fail in achieving the high values that they propose. Politics may be said to have concern for the common good or

public goods, but may in fact be perverted to negative purposes like racial prejudice, exclusionary practices, even genocide. Religions, too, may assert lofty ideals of human dignity but end up pursuing their own advantages against others.

This crucible of imperfection has been well expressed in Scott Appleby's apt phrase concerning religion: 'the ambivalence of the sacred' (Appleby 2000). It could also be applied to the political world as a kind of 'ambivalence of the commonwealth'. While both religion and politics often proclaim goodwill and peace, people acting in the name of one or the other frequently achieve only strife and suffering. As we examine global politics and particular religions, we must be aware of these seeming contradictions and unresolved questions of how the two spheres of human activity do or should relate to each other.

Both religion and politics have had to grapple with problems for which there is no clear dividing line between the two. Moral issues have obviously been such problems. The issues vary from one place to another, but commonly include such contested questions as war, use of force, death penalty, abortion, biotechnology, freedom of religion, social justice. In contemporary polities and global politics, these matters all have ethical and legal dimensions that cannot be separated and to which political institutions address themselves. Likewise, religions stake claims to both their competence and their responsibility in treating these cases. It is not surprising when persons purporting to speak for political or religious communities deal with these issues or disagree about them.

In the long history of global politics, concepts of 'just war' have been used for centuries to address the many moral and legal problems surrounding the use of military force and combat. The formulation and use of just war concepts offer strong evidence that the realms of religion and politics should and can be treated together. The lives of individual persons and whole communities are at stake in the conduct of war, and so it is to be expected that such 'ultimate' questions blur any analytical boundaries that might be suggested for separating religion and politics. The way in which these moral criteria have established the basis for the international law of war demonstrates the intimate link between (religiously based) ethical thought and (politically based) positive law (van der Vyver and Witte 1996; Witte and van der Vyver 1996; Drinan 2004; Freeman 2004). Likewise, the difficult moral and legal questions surrounding the freedom of religion illustrate how religions and politics are intertwined; tolerance as a 'global standard' is a specific way in which this has taken concrete form (Declaration on the Elimination of All Forms of Intolerance and of Discrimination Based on Religion or Belief 1981; Elimination of All Forms of Religious Intolerance 1994).

For decades, if not centuries, sociologists have been examining a 'traditional–modern' distinction in the structures of societies. Without going into that discussion in any detail, it is noteworthy that a widespread assumption in this approach has been that modern societies were experiencing 'secularization'. That is to say, as the patterns of traditional societies gave way to the modern, religions or religious patterns that had been crucial to the character of those societies would change, in many cases to be replaced by secular or non-religious patterns. For some, it meant particularly the privatization of religion, with individual piety replacing group or external expressions of religious identity. Much has been written about the evidence to falsify such assumptions or hypotheses that has been found throughout the world in recent decades. Peter Berger is a prominent advocate of a reversal in the academic forum to a new concept of 'desecularization'

(Berger 1999). This empirical hypothesis is of great significance for this present study of global politics and particular religions because it draws attention to societal aspects of religion prominent today. They are not some kind of second cousin to a hegemonic political or social theory, much less an epiphenomenon to underlying economic trends. Religions with a public expression are central to an understanding of politics, locally and globally.

Another sociological approach with a historical element is associated with the theme of globalization. If classical studies of modern societies discovered secularizing trends in nation-states, recent evaluations of trends perceive globalization or globalizing tendencies that are rooted in religion. As observer-participants people today experience and reflect upon what amounts to elements of a global culture. This reflexive consciousness both enables and restricts people at a global level (Robertson 1992). The inclusive or holistic character of this global identity has a religious quality with a variety of expressions. Public religion (Casanova 1994; Tsushiro 2005), a theme to which I will return later in this chapter, is a vigorous expression of this globalization.

On the one hand, these social trends have led to speculation about the possibility of some sort of religious convergence, meta-religion (for example, based on environmentalism), or supra-religious ethic that would provide a basis for people to coexist in a global world. On the other hand, identifying the *modus operandi* of various religions by the vocabulary of contemporary international relations, these religions can be seen to have a 'global' or 'transnational' character, as Juergensmeyer states:

> In these traditions [Islam, Christianity, Buddhism], the very core of their faith includes the notion that their religion is greater than any local

group and cannot be confined to the cultural boundaries of any particular region. These are religious traditions with universal pretensions and global ambitions. ... These are transnational religions, religions of expansion. But they also have geographic and cultural roots.

(Juergensmeyer 2003)

In any case, the religions that encounter globalization engage this phenomenon with the resources that they have and with the challenges that are implied by the global scope of today's social boundaries. Robertson even suggests that some 'anti-globalism' grows out of opposition to 'secular humanism' (Robertson 1992: 80).

Another approach to the modern encounter between religion and the human and social sciences is exemplified in the vocabulary of 'spirituality'. This reflects several trends in contemporary religiosity. For example, on balance this language emphasizes spiritual experience over institutional forms. To some extent, Hanson's category of 'meditative experience' captures this point (Hanson 2006). A more thorough attempt to integrate the perspective of spirituality with the findings of modern psychology and epistemology is that of Daniel Helminiak (1998), who offers a critique of any spirituality that rests on logical contradictions or on propositions that are not based on true understanding. While noting this dimension of interiority in religious experience, I will focus in this chapter on the social and public aspects of global politics and particular religions.

Cases: problems and issues

At this point I will steer away from the various approaches that have been introduced above and begin a discussion of some of the more substantive problems and issues that link global politics and particular religions. At the risk of conflating different things into a single package or of dissatisfying analysts who are looking for unidirectional influences, I will try to demonstrate the interconnectedness of the political and the religious realms. I have no pretensions of offering a complete survey of the field, but I will try to cover some of the prominent empirical and normative questions that have arisen in recent decades.

Building on the Peace of Augsburg's 1555 formula of *cujus regio ejus religio*, the Westphalian settlement of 1648, taken at face value, seems to enshrine an ideal-type of international political system of independent sovereign states. This formula seems to suggest that states will form along confessional religious lines, or at least that adherence to or deviations from religious confessions are not a matter for co-religionists in other states or for those who follow other religions elsewhere. Of course, the ideal-type was not realized in practice (Krasner 1999). Furthermore, the system actually fostered some elements of secularism (Hurd 2004). It also saw the emergence of moral, political and legal arguments that highlighted the value of toleration of religious beliefs (Zagorin 2003) within states as a primary basis for the legitimacy of those polities in fact, a standard of religious tolerance has taken root in many states as the system spread throughout the world.

Religions constantly developed over the intervening centuries, as well (Juergensmeyer 2004). However incomplete or imperfect these movements may be, ecumenism within Christianity since the twentieth century and religious dialogues – at least among representatives of major world religions – since the Chicago Parliament of World Religions in 1893 have suggested a softer encounter among religionists than a hard shell reinforced by state boundaries. Of course, the religious bodies in question never conformed entirely to the straitjackets of political exclusivity suggested by the Augsburg norm. And migrations in the modern and contemporary world make patently absurd any notion that religions could be or would be confined territorially.

All religions grow and spread by forms of witness, acceptance and conversion. Formal and informal missionary thrusts are a characteristic of the major globe-spanning religious movements. Religious thought and practice have disseminated through many media of communication, for example the printed pamphlets and books of the Reformation and the radio, television and digital media of recent decades. Perennial adaptations and indigenization of universally oriented religions are not new in themselves; but today they constitute the stuff of modern globalization as much as the working of a market system, the structures of nation-states, or the use of technology.

Specifically for this study of global politics and particular religions, it is noteworthy that state sovereignty as a basis for the structure of the international system is under strain today from the forces of globalization. The growth of a global community that encompasses many inter-governmental and non-governmental institutions is a prominent fact of recent history (Iriye 2002). New kinds of networks are spanning the globe, directly and indirectly transforming the way international politics is conducted (Keck and Sikkink 1998). Norms of human rights raise direct challenges to the most cherished norms of state sovereignty (Philpott 2001; Risse *et al.* 1999). Specifically, in the words of Daniel Philpott, 'Religious freedom embodies the moral challenge of an international system that is beginning to move past Westphalia' (Philpott 2003–2004: 997). Religion has never been comfortable with sovereign borders, and particular religions follow dynamic paths

that disregard those borders even as they are affected by many specific political conditions that they encounter locally and globally.

Diplomacy is a traditional institution of international politics that shows evidence of being affected by religions. Of course the unique position of the Holy See (the Vatican) in contemporary diplomatic practice is evident from both the large number of states with which it maintains day-to-day diplomatic relations and from the symbolism surrounding Papal visits (not least being Pope John Paul II's visits to Poland) to various regions, the visits of heads of state to the Pope, and rites such as the funeral of John Paul II. Faith-based diplomacy (Johnston and Sampson 1994; Johnston 2003) has attracted attention as both a necessary ingredient of state-to-state practice (Albright 2006) and a privileged form of track-two diplomatic efforts.[2]

More broadly, religionists have taken prominent roles in social and political reconciliation efforts throughout the globe, within national societies and across national divides. Prominent examples include the peace and reconciliation encounters between Israelis and Palestinians, between Catholics and Protestants in Northern Ireland, among racial groups in South Africa, and in Central America. In the face of military conflicts in such regions, particular religious groups have stepped in to create a basis for security that governments alone have not been able to accomplish.

A vexing problem for this analysis is the working of democracy in societies with exclusionary religious extremists. The word fundamentalism (Almond *et al.* 2003; Marty and Appleby 1990s) has been associated with such extremist movements (not always with beneficial results for intellectual clarity or social harmony). The core of the problem is how freely a political–religious ideology that takes power through democratic processes of majority politics may impose its will on the wider society and polity. The normative question here can be resolved by attention to human rights, particularly those related to religious freedom and toleration. But empirically the procedural democratic principle of majority rule has been in tension with such principles of rights, as in countries like Algeria, Turkey, Iran and India. In a country like Afghanistan that has known much foreign intervention, the question of imposed political norms is even more complex.

As I indicated at the beginning of this chapter, the global politics that we are discussing here includes a prominent norm of democracy. In a comprehensive document like the Charter of Paris, this was balanced with the affirmation of substantive human rights norms that blend with liberal democracy. But the workings of democratic politics, and especially electoral politics, in countries as diverse as Indonesia, Egypt, India, Nigeria and the Netherlands, show the fragility of societal and religious security where religious tolerance fails. The fact that the Universal Declaration of Human Rights of the United Nations affirms religious freedom and that most national constitutions and laws acknowledge the same would seem to be the basis for consensual global politics on this matter. But religious freedom is actually violated by political authorities in many places, often with severe persecutions (Philpott 2003–2004). The tension of the principle of religious freedom with democracy and with the actual practices of various religions, whether at the level of doctrine or of popular belief, creates additional problems.

This brings the discussion back to the issue of public religion that I introduced above. Explicitly religious symbols and values have become more prominent in international and domestic politics even as global politics has emerged as a reality. For example, France's *laïcité* and India's secular constitution coexist uneasily with contemporary desecularization and identity politics on a broad scale. Whether or when men should wear a *fez* cap, women a *chador* veil, or children a crucifix in school have become public issues that are not merely social in a narrow sense of that word but political in a wide sense. Issues such as the imposition of *sharia* law or the representation and expression of religion by various forms of public display have stirred deep emotions globally. While the expressions of religious sentiment are specific to various religions, these issues are no less problems for particular religions than they are for global politics. The particular religions are faced with the question of what they need to do to express themselves and to relate to others in a globalizing world. That is, the religions themselves face questions of self-identity as well as questions of their relationship to politics.

This raises the question of the self-definition of various religions and the degree of uniformity or unity found in them. I would suggest four elements for a working definition of religion: creed (the profession of faith, including doctrine), morality (the ethical dimension of faith in lived behaviour), worship (expressing the believer's notice of the divine or transcendent), community (the human solidarity involved in a common faith).[3] Clearly, all religions show a range of practices on all four of these dimensions, both diachronically and synchronically, and from esoteric to popular forms. Cultures of diverse regions influence the public expressions of all of the more universal religions, an issue that today is often referred to as indigenization. But even religions that are relatively localized in their spread necessarily face similar boundary questions.

What political analysts call public policy also overlaps with religions, with each influencing the other. Everything from public holidays to legal codes, from family life to public associations, bears the imprint of this overlap. If 'modern' societies show a greater differentiation of religion and politics than 'traditional' ones, neither fits an ideal-type of division suggested by a term like 'separation of church and state'. One could speak of religion and politics as integral parts of a brocade fabric, or of the degree of autonomy experienced by religious or political institutions relative to each other. The ascendancy of theories of functionalism (and the differentiation that is said to accompany them) has obscured dimensions of organic unity between politics and religion.

Historically, there has been constant adjustment in various parts of the world in the processes that connect how religion and politics interact and in what results from that interaction. As Don Baker suggests: 'In traditional East Asia, there was no word for religion as a separate and distinct sphere of life' (Baker 1997: 146). When this region was faced with new realities in the late nineteenth century, the Chinese character translation for religion (宗教) that was coined in Japan became the standard for the East Asian region. The Japanese government then claimed that a legitimate religion 'had to have a doctrinal and scriptural base, had to be limited (i.e., sectarian) rather than all-encompassing in its membership, and had to extend beyond the boundaries of one nation' (Baker 1997: 157). The very effort to differentiate and define in public policy illustrates the complexities and dangers involved in separating the religious and political spheres.

Public policy today faces the challenge of allowing mobilized believers to express themselves freely while respecting others' freedoms. This tension is different from the conflicts in societies or in global encounters that are essentially about land, wealth, knowledge, and so on. These tensions or conflicts are accompanied by behaviours ranging from cooperation to force, violence or military confrontation. Due to customs, prejudices or patterns of exploitation, such conflicts are sometimes regarded as religious, and may actually be reinforced by religious communities, while they may be essentially different. For example, intra-religion problems associated with the Hindu caste system or inter-religion problems about sovereignty over Jerusalem cannot be said to be purely or even primarily religious problems. The policies adopted to deal with them must acknowledge religious values and safeguard the values of the common humanity of all persons and communities involved.

This brings our discussion to questions like what those common values might be or how they might be expressed in a common language of religion and politics. These are questions of discourse and of practice. Is there a set of specific circumstances in the contemporary encounter of global politics and particular religions that can help address these questions? Globalization seems to have a universalizing or homogenizing effect on cultures, with impact on everything from language and aesthetics to foods and building materials. Many religions have engaged globalization with renewed awareness of their public character. Rather than seeing particular religions and global politics as somehow veering toward a clash or going off on unrelated tangents, I will try to examine them together in a unified stance of convergence and divergence.

From cases to theory: convergence and divergence

A coherent, unified stance on religion and politics has several aspects. The verbal and other physical behaviours of those engaged in religion and/or politics are the first aspect. These people – I can use the inclusive 'we' here – discourse about moral norms for societies, engage in religious observances, participate in elections, choose public policies, and so on. While some analysts speak of several 'identities' of people, I think that it is more accurate to speak of persons with their potentialities, limitations and capacities. They are enabled by those personal and cultural capacities – and their religious and political commitments – to say and do whatever their concrete actions are. Categories like 'Buddhist' or 'liberal democrat' or 'capitalist' or whatever ultimately capture only part of what these persons are.

The specific aspect of discourse is central to this study. This refers to both the discourse(s) of the people whom we regard as 'speaking' politics and religion and the discourse that we select to talk about them. We all use words to bundle our actions; and, of course, our words are themselves significant and meaningful human actions. We may not like it when Osama bin Laden uses the language of *jihad* to characterize suicide and terrorism, but we do not ignore it. Justifications for armed intervention may not convince us, but we evaluate them by our religious and political standards. Especially in a 'scientific' discourse, we try to specify, for example, what 'just war' or 'legitimate defence' might mean, and use such categories for empirical or normative analysis.

Our theories, then, aim to be relevant to what people are actually doing and saying, and to have a meaning that clarifies rather than distorts those actions and words. A theory that is supposed to elucidate political science or international relations or contemporary religions takes on the task of synthesizing religion and politics as never before. This is no small task, and I can only offer some preliminary suggestions here as to what the contents of that theory might be. The questions that I am posing include this fundamental aspect of theory. Can religion and politics be viewed together after we make all the distinctions that articulate their special characteristics? Does the reality of public religion require a new theoretical discourse about politics? Has global politics changed the way religions are lived or self-consciously perceived? What is the framework of an integrated theory of politics and religion in today's world?

I will begin with a discussion of some of the convergent aspects of religion and politics: common humanity; particular and universal; symbols and rituals; authority. Obviously, my explanation requires a certain level of abstraction and analogous thinking. However, I will not try to make an argument for a specific theory of knowledge or philosophy of science, which would distract from the immediate task.

To note that we share a common humanity that is a basis for convergent thinking about politics and religion may not seem such a remarkable statement, but it has important implications for the current inquiry. This is not a biologist's claim about the common characteristics of the human genome or Aristotle's recognition that politics and ethics are foundational human actions. In fact, there have been quite different understandings of what it means to be human among the various religions and political ideologies. Observing how people actually conduct politics or carry out religious practices gives us pause, as well. There is a great deal of exclusion that takes place in the name of politics and religion: drawing territorial boundaries; designating legal entitlements for certain groups; imagining political or religious communities; legitimizing religious participation. The claim of common humanity affirms that all humans share the basis for religious and political commitment and inclusion.

The claim of the Universal Declaration of Human Rights (adopted by the United Nations General Assembly on 10 December 1948) is that there is an 'inherent dignity' in all humans, and that 'All human beings are born free and equal in dignity and rights'. Philosophers have discussed this claim and similar assertions of what our common humanity implies. It is an invitation to the reader to recognize in himself or herself, and in others, that human dignity is our common heritage. This simple statement is a useful starting point for our search for convergence between global politics and particular religions.

In political thought this affirmation of human dignity is most often associated with the foundations of human rights. A similar line of development is found from the historical arguments of Bartolomé de Las Casas regarding the native populations of the New World in the sixteenth century, through the claims for civil and political rights in Europe in succeeding centuries, and the assertions of freedom of religion and conscience that became ever more specific. More recently the concept of human dignity penetrates political discourse on toleration, basic human needs and human security. Religion and politics mix in both the theoretical foundation and the real-world applications of these principles.

A second convergence between global politics and particular religions is their relationship to the particular and the universal. These are relative terms that both point out a tension within the political and religious spheres and make a bridge between these different spheres of human activity. For example, in the study of international relations, the neologism 'glocalization' (see above) attempts to specify empirical politics today as an interpenetration of the global (universal) and local (particular) spheres. Empirical religions, too, contain a living tension between their universal aspirations and the particular expressions in cultures and communities that have become more prominent today. For example, Joseph Ratzinger (later Pope Benedict XVI) points to the 'European' (particular) cultural features of Christianity within a dynamism of transcendence via cultural encounters (universal) that continues today (Ratzinger 2004: 85ff., 183ff.).

Co-religionists historically maintained contacts and shared traditions, but the transformation of technologies of transport and communication in recent decades have made ideas like 'world-church' or 'networked diaspora' far more concrete to them today. Cultural and political forces impact religious bodies in such a way that they allow or even require religions to both express themselves in local forms and forge global identities.

In the practical world of politics, the universality of political claims is regularly limited by boundaries of cities, states or other group units; and so politics becomes particular. But whenever the political group asserts its legitimacy vis-à-vis individuals, it is staking a claim to a certain universality (this becomes mixed up with the modern European system's concepts of internal and external sovereignty). The political imagination can conjure up Stoic notions of cosmopolis, Kantian ideas of a world federation of states, Wallerstein's world-economy, a world state or a global community as it stretches toward inclusiveness. Religious terminology has favoured words like body, mother, home or temple as analogues or metaphors of religious connectedness.

For both religions and political units there is a constant dialectic between their universal ideals and the particular ways that they are put into practice. I see this as a convergent axis for a theory that integrates these two spheres. For example, when we consider contemporary religion and politics, features of what has been called 'religious nationalism' (Juergensmeyer 1993) become clearer by a critical application of this theoretical insight. Nationalism is a universal abstraction that is epitomized in numerous specific nation-based ideologies. When a nationalism is synergized with a religion, the combination is both powerful and potentially disruptive of the tension between the particular and the universal.

Symbols and rituals are a third kind of convergence between religion and politics. Some theologies lay great stress on the symbolic character of religion in general, and the external symbols and rituals of specific religions are among the prominent ways that observers differentiate them (Dillistone 1986). Less attention is given to analysis of political symbols and rituals, even though they are significant characteristics of political life (Kertzer 1988). The history of Confucian rites in East Asia is a powerful case of how important and how ambiguous these rituals have been (deBary 1998) in a region that did not even have an overarching term for 'religion' until its nineteenth-century encounter with the West (Baker 1997). Flags, anthems, parades, political rallies, and so on are general examples from the political world, while social and political titles, military uniforms, medals, ribbons, and so on are usually restricted to special persons or groups within the polity.

The mixture of the two kinds of symbols and rituals is found in religious ceremonies surrounding the inauguration of persons in political offices throughout the world, as well as the crowning of monarchs, even the *daijōsai* at the accession of the Japanese *Tennō* (emperor). Perhaps the most extreme cases of this mixture have been in 'religions of public life' (Hanson's term), or what might otherwise be called quasi-religions or religious ideologies. Imperial Rome or Confucian China stand as historical examples, while Nazism, Soviet Communism, Chinese Maoism, and the *juche* ideology of North Korea's Kim Il Sung are more recent cases. These illustrate how polities are held together and mobilized by careful manipulation of (quasi-)religious public symbols and rituals.

My point here notes how political leaders or institutions will use existing religious symbols for their own purposes in many instances (from crusade and *jihad* to aggregating political parties and using

soft-sell propaganda of all sorts to promote social, political and economic policies). I also want to emphasize how crucial symbols and rituals are at a broad level of politics. Grand public buildings and monuments, displays of civic unity, observance of political traditions are all the stuff of politics as much as voting or legislating policies. It is useful, therefore, to analyse both global politics and particular religions from this perspective of symbols and rituals.

Of course, religions are commonly associated with the liturgies that they perform. These external signs of worship express the personally held beliefs of the religious adherents and contribute to the identity of the religious community. This public, social character of the religions not infrequently overlaps with political roles. For example, the use of places of worship as locations of sanctuary and refuge for individuals and groups is found in many parts of the world. Churches, mosques and other houses of liturgical worship have been used to reinforce and to resist political ideas.

This leads to a final point of convergence that I will consider: authority in its dimensions of persuasion and teaching. Both politics and religion are characterized by authority; without it the former degenerates into coercive force and the latter into autarchic or autonomous spiritual behaviour. In fact, the two spheres have similar modes in their primary way of exercising authority, which I will call persuasion and teaching.

Legal and political theorists note that sanctions are an ultimate tool of positive political–legal systems, and that the coercive implementation of sanctions is claimed as legitimate. As the issues and norms become broader and more fundamental, however, these systems operate largely as processes of persuasion. By enhancing public understanding of conditions for effective and beneficial action, political leaders and legal norms establish the basis for long-term, widespread conformity with authoritative decisions.

Authority in religion has a similar manner of proceeding by persuasive teaching. Many kinds of religious authority are invoked – sacred texts, community traditions, pronouncements of individuals in hierarchical or charismatic roles, divine revelation, and so on – and taught to the faithful. This teaching needs to persuade if it is to be observed. And when it does persuade it establishes effective identities and patterns of behaviour even for broad civilizations.

While noting the way that global politics and particular religions converge on these dimensions of common humanity, the particular and universal, symbols and rituals, and authority, I will also discuss some aspects in which they tend to diverge. Two aspects that seem particularly noteworthy are the standards that they follow and the matter of rule enforcement. By standard I do not mean some technical measure of uniformity (as is sometimes called 'global standards') but an existential criterion of personal and interpersonal meaning. The standard for global politics is legitimacy, while the standard for particular religions is their orthodoxy and orthopraxy.

Governments, states, international organisations and agencies, and so on require legitimacy to sustain themselves with a meaningful and acceptable identity. Legitimacy is a difficult political concept to define, but it is a kind of litmus test for any political actor. It is perhaps best understood by its absence: without legitimacy, politics does not function smoothly and the mark of authority (analysed above) is lost.

Religions have a somewhat different existential criterion for their unity and continuity, which I will call orthodoxy and orthopraxy. Religions ordinarily have a great range of symbols, teachings, traditions, and

so on from which they draw. But the phenomenon of fundamentalisms demonstrates that this range is tested by changing circumstances inside and outside the religion in question. Orthodoxy and orthopraxy establish boundaries for words and actions in these religions. If political illegitimacy implies a certain failure of the political unit in question, the unorthodox word or unacceptable practice of a given religious unit is rather a sign of a different identity and meaning and may eventuate in a new religion.

Another point of divergence concerns the matter of rule enforcement. A substantial degree of rule enforcement is characteristic of the polity. Actual polities have ranged from totalitarian governments to failed states, and they operate in contexts from political correctness to libertarian attitudes. Institutions and instruments of enforcement include police, administrative agencies, courts, and so on. Ultimately, this may involve physical coercion, but the main point here is that the enforcement is carried out to achieve the polity's own purposes or to maintain its very existence.

In the case of religions, the particular religious community may be a multi-ethnic or global body, or it may be characterized by particular language, territory, or other externals. In any case, rules enforce the behaviour and boundaries of the community. Challenges may arise within the community traditions, as from fundamentalisms, schisms and heresies; developments occur that transform some important features of the religion. The community is the locus of the particular religion, and it ultimately resolves issues of otherwise ambiguous boundaries and identities by a form of rule enforcement.

Conclusions and prospects

At the risk of antagonizing scholars of both politics and religion who may prefer

335

analysing one or the other separately, I have tried to consider both phenomena together in the context of contemporary globalization. And I have deliberately focused on the correspondences or mutual characteristics of global politics and particular religions, rather than examining one as a variable in a theory about the other. But I must admit the limits of my own effort to integrate these two dimensions of human consciousness, life and activity in a unified stance. While the framework of a theory about global politics and particular religions that I have explained above offers the foundation for a unified stance toward these two spheres, establishing a comprehensive theory will require continuing efforts. The problems and issues identified above are critical to our humanity and to our world, and they need to be addressed in a more integrated way than theoretical discourses have hitherto allowed.

I offer a summary of my argument above in the form of Table 20.1. It presents a schematic diagram for an integrated theory of global politics and particular religions. It suggests a basic stance for empirical and normative research in an era of public religion and global governance. The left side of the table under 'Convergence' suggests the overlapping, convergent aspects between politics and religion. While the vocabulary used to specify these realms ordinarily differs, many commonalties abound. The right side of the table under 'Divergence' suggests that the two spheres do constitute different spheres of being and action even as they share common features.

Returning to the post-Cold War frame of reference that I used as exemplary at the beginning of this chapter, I recall the attention that some students of international relations gave a few years ago to the concept of a 'new medievalism'. With the structures of the Cold War crumbling and the emergence of new actors and movements in a range of international issues, they used this concept to illuminate the diversity of power centres and issue areas today by means of an historical analogy. A parallel idea relating more to the sociological literature could be used to suggest the links between religion and politics today. Perhaps phrases like 'new traditionalism' or 'new cohesion' could be used. The failures of classical modernization theory to understand religion might be compared to the inability of international relations scholars to anticipate the end of the Cold War. Religion has a public character that these concepts illuminate. The *traditions* of religion constitute their enduring character (in juxtaposition to the modern) even as they encounter a new globalization. Politics and religion exhibit areas of overlap and convergence that remind us of conditions in historical cases in which *cohesion* was the norm prior to an analytical differentiation of the two spheres.

Indeed, among the concepts put forward recently to examine the kind of overlapping spheres that I have described, the term *public religion* has been particularly

Table 20.1 Global politics and particular religions: convergence and divergence

	Convergence				Divergence	
	Common humanity	*Particular and universal*	*Symbols and rituals*	*Authority*	*Standard*	*Rule enforcement*
Global politics	Human rights	Globalization	Rites	Persuasion	Legitimacy	Polity
Particular religions	Inherent dignity	World church	Liturgy	Teaching	Orthodoxy and orthopraxy	Community

useful. While this phrase by itself may not give full weight to the dynamics of global politics, it has been elaborated within the context of globalization that I have discussed. But the concept of public religion can be expanded beyond the field of the sociology of religion or even beyond sociology. I have tried to inform the term with a broader meaning by my discussion of areas of convergence and divergence between global politics and particular religions. Their converging aspects are common humanity, the particular and the universal, symbols and rituals, and authority. The divergent aspects discussed here are standard and rule enforcement.

The concepts and framework offered here address some of these limitations of comparative and international theories of modernization. But I would not describe them as another 'postmodernism', either. They do not reduce politics and religion to thought-games or functions, but they attend to the stories or discourses in religion and politics as congruent aspects of human activity and identity. Both are essentially human rather than artificial constructs. Cultural particularities and communitarian features abound. And yet this view of human beings is not restricted by the particularistic features of jingoistic nationalisms in recent centuries or of fanatic sectarianisms in many lands.

It is inevitable that there will be extensive discussion of institutions that embody the values and ideas of people and their times. I have tried to present my ideas about an integrated theory of global politics and particular religions in such a way as to include institutions, but also to note the significance of personal human consciousness and identity. The concepts and values that help to open religious and political venues alike are those of tolerance and religious freedom. It goes without saying that our world has not entered a paradise or nirvana of perfect tolerance and freedom.

Among historians and scholars of religion, there is discussion of the concept of an axial age or axial period (Jaspers 1953; Eisenstadt 1982). We are certainly too close to our own age to render a historical judgement about its total significance. But I would suggest that we have a sufficient historical understanding of the last century and of the last few decades in particular to identify an important feature of our own era in the public features of global poli-tics *and* particular religions. I present this study as an effort to understand what that means.

Notes

1 This chapter is a revised version of a paper presented at the International Political Science Association 20th World Congress, Fukuoka, Japan, 11 July 2006.
2 Appleby's book examines several cases of religiously-based efforts by third parties in mediating conflicts (Appleby 2000); the Community of Sant' Egidio's achievements are introduced in Leymarie (2000).
3 This is my own brief formulation of what is involved in religion, inspired in part by ideas of Clifford Howell (Howell 1952: 4, 13, *passim*).

Bibliography

Albright, M. and Woodward, W. (2006) *The Mighty and the Almighty: Reflections on America, God, and World Affairs*, New York: HarperCollins.

Almond, G., Appleby, R. Scott and Sivan E. (2003) *Strong Religion: the Rise of Fundamentalisms around the World*, Chicago, IL: University of Chicago Press.

Appleby, R. Scott (2000) *The Ambivalence of the Sacred: Religion, Violence, and Reconciliation*, Lanham, MD: Rowman & Littlefield Publishers.

Baker, D. (1997) 'World religions and national states: Competing claims in East Asia', in S. H. Rudolph and J. Piscatori (eds), *Transnational Religion and Fading States*, Boulder, CO: Westview Press.

Berger, P. (1999) *The Desecularization of the World: Resurgent Religion and World Politics*, Washington,

337

DC; Grand Rapids, MI: Ethics and Public Policy Center/W. B. Eerdmans Pub. Co.

Casanova, J. (1994) *Public Religions in the Modern World*, Chicago, IL: University of Chicago Press.

De Bary, W. (1998) *Asian Values and Human Rights: A Confucian Communitarian Perspective*, Cambridge, MA: Harvard University Press.

'Declaration on the Elimination of All Forms of Intolerance and of Discrimination Based on Religion or Belief' (1981) United Nations General Assembly Resolution 36/55 of 25 November.

Dillistone, F. W. (1986) *The Power of Symbols in Religion and Culture*, New York: Crossroad.

Drinan, R. (2004) *Can God & Caesar Coexist? Balancing Religious Freedom and International Law*, New Haven, CT: Yale University Press.

Eisenstadt, S. (1982) 'The axial age: The emergence of transcendental visions and the rise of clerics', *Archives Européenes de Sociologie*, 23, pp. 294–314.

'Elimination of All Forms of Religious Intolerance' (1994) United Nations General Assembly Resolution 48/128 of 14 February.

Fox, J. (2001) 'Religion as an overlooked element of international relations', *International Studies Review*, 3, 3, pp. 53–73.

Freeman, M. (2004) 'The problem of secularism in human rights theory', *Human Rights Quarterly*, 26, 2, pp. 375–400.

Hanson, E. (2006) *Religion and Politics in the International System Today*, Cambridge, UK; New York: Cambridge University Press.

Haynes, J. (1998) *Religion in Global Politics*, London; New York: Longman.

Helminiak, D. (1998) *Religion and the Human Sciences: An Approach via Spirituality*, Albany, NY: State University of New York Press.

Howell, C. (1952) *Of Sacraments and Sacrifice*, Collegeville, MN: Liturgical Press.

Hurd, E. (2004) 'The political authority of secularism in international relations', *European Journal of International Relations*, 10, 2, pp. 235–262.

Iriye, A. (2002) *Global Community: The Role of International Organizations in the Making of the Contemporary World*, Berkeley, CA: University of California Press.

Jaspers, K. (1953) *The Origin and Goal of History*, New Haven, CT: Yale University Press.

Johnston, D. (2003) *Faith-based Diplomacy: Trumping Realpolitik*, Oxford; New York: Oxford University Press.

Johnston, D. and Sampson, C. (1994) *Religion: The Missing Dimension of Statecraft*, New York: Oxford University Press.

Juergensmeyer, M. (1993) *The New Cold War? Religious Nationalism Confronts the Secular State*, Berkeley, CA: University of California Press.

Juergensmeyer, M. (2003) *Global Religions: An Introduction*, Oxford; New York: Oxford University Press.

Keck, M. and Sikkink, K. (1998) *Activists beyond Borders: Advocacy Networks in International Politics*, Ithaca, NY: Cornell University Press.

Kertzer, D. (1988) *Ritual, Politics, and Power*, New Haven, CT: Yale University Press.

Krasner, S. (1999) *Sovereignty: Organized Hypocrisy*, Princeton, NJ: Princeton University Press.

Lawson, E. and Bertucci, M. (1996) *Encyclopedia of Human Rights*, 2nd, edn Washington, DC: Taylor & Francis.

Leymarie, P. (2000) 'Heiwa wo yooritsu suru sei-Ejidio no hitobito,' *Sekai*, December, pp. 59-67; in Japanese, translation of 'Les batisseurs de paix de Sant'Egidio,' *Le Monde diplomatique*, September 2000.

Marty, M. and Appleby, R. Scott (eds) (1990s) *The Fundamentalism Project* (six volumes), Chicago, IL: University of Chicago Press.

Petito, F. and Hatzopoulos, P. (eds) (2003) *Religion in International Relations: The Return from Exile*, New York: Palgrave Macmillan.

Philpott, D. (2001) *Revolutions in Sovereignty: How Ideas Shaped Modern International Relations*, Princeton, NJ: Princeton University Press.

Philpott, D. (2002) 'The challenge of September 11 to secularism in international relations', *World Politics* 55, pp. 66–95.

Philpott, D. (2003–2004) 'Religious freedom and the undoing of the Westphalian state', *Michigan Journal of International Law*, 25, pp. 981–998.

Ratzinger, J. (Pope Benedict XVI) (2004) *Truth and Tolerance: Christian Belief and World Religions*, translated by Henry Taylor, San Francisco, CA: Ignatius Press.

'Religion: Politics, power, and symbolism' (1996) Special edition of the *Journal of International Affairs*, 50, 1.

Risse, T., Ropp, S. and Sikkink, K. (eds) (1999) *The Power of Human Rights: International Norms and Domestic Change*, Cambridge: Cambridge University Press.

Robertson, R. (1992) *Globalization: Social Theory and Global Culture*, London: Sage.

Thomas, S. (2003) 'Taking religious and cultural pluralism seriously: The global resurgence of religion and the transformation of international society', in F. Petito and P. Hatzopoulos (eds), *Religion in International Relations: The Return from Exile*, New York: Palgrave Macmillan.

Thomas, S. (2005) *The Global Resurgence of Religion and the Transformation of International Relations: The Struggle for the Soul of the Twenty-first Century*, New York: Palgrave Macmillan.

Tsushiro, H. (2005) *'Kookyoo Shuukyoo' no Hikari to Kage* (in Japanese, *The Light and Shade of 'Public Religion'*), Tokyo: Shunjusha.

Van der Vyver, J. D. and Witte, J. (1996) *Religious Human Rights in Global Perspective: Legal Perspectives*, The Hague; Boston, MA: Martinus Nijhoff Publishers.

Witte, J. and Van der Vyver, J. D. (1996) *Religious Human Rights in Global Perspective: Religious Perspectives*, The Hague; Boston, MA: Martinus Nijhoff Publishers.

Zagorin, P. (2003) *How the Idea of Religious Toleration Came to the West*, Princeton, NJ: Princeton University Press.

Part IV

Religion, security and development

21

On the nature of religious terrorism[1]

Adam Dolnik and Rohan Gunaratna

Introduction

Terrorist violence differs from ordinary crime principally by the presence of an altruistic motive and an ideological justification. In terrorism, ideology is all-important, as an organization's ideological foundation frames the worldview of its members and thus provides a sense of collective identity. Moreover, ideology is instrumental in identifying the enemy, while also providing the necessary explanation and justification for its targeting. In addition, it is again the ideology of a group which determines its core objectives and the strategy for how and by what means these objectives are to be achieved. And finally, ideology is also a critical component in determining a group's ambitions, as well as the overall perception of urgency for armed action in order to fulfil these aspirations. At the operational level, then, the group's core strategy translates into the frequency and intensity of its military operations, in that different ideologies provide different levels of acceptability of mass-casualty and indiscriminate targeting. Consequently, the tactics and targeting preferences of a group are also very much influenced by the given group's belief system. Overall, the understanding of a group's ideology is one of the most important aspects of predictive threat-assessment of terrorist violence.

Since the 1980s, there have been alarming developments in the trends in international terrorism: a continual decrease in terrorist incidents, which has, however, been accompanied by an increasing number of overall casualties in those fewer incidents. In other words, terrorist attacks are becoming increasingly lethal. Besides the rising average casualty rate, qualitative analysis of all terrorist attacks seems to provide additional support for this claim: while the deadliest incidents prior to the 1980s involved 'only' dozens of fatalities, in the 1980s and 1990s, in the most lethal attacks, they numbered hundreds, and in the new millennium the plateau has reached into the thousands for the first time in history. Similarly, until 11 September 2001 ('9/11') and the terrorist attacks on the Twin Towers and the Pentagon, there had been only 76 terrorist bombings in which more than 25 people had been killed. Over the course of the ensuing four years, this number more than tripled.

One of the most common explanations for this trend of increasing lethality has been the proliferation of terrorist campaigns inspired by religion. According to Bruce Hoffman, who was one of one of the first scholars to identify this causal link:

The fact that for the religious terrorist violence inevitably assumes a transcendent purpose and therefore

343

becomes a sacramental and divine duty arguably results in a significant loosening of the constraints on the commission of mass murder. Religion, moreover, functions as a legitimizing force, sanctioning if not encouraging wide scale violence against an almost open-ended category of opponents. Thus religious terrorist violence becomes almost an end in itself – a morally justified, divinely instigated expedient toward the attainment of the terrorists' ultimate ends. This is a direct reflection of the fact that the terrorists motivated by a religious imperative do not seek to appeal to any constituency but themselves and the changes they seek are not for any utilitarian purpose, but are only to benefit themselves. The religious terrorist, moreover, sees himself as an outsider from the society that he both abhors and rejects and this sense of alienation enables him to contemplate – and undertake – far more destructive and bloodier types of terrorist operations than his secular counterpart.

(Hoffman 1993: 12)

As can be seen from the previous quote, an integral part of the argument concerns the core characteristics of religious terrorists, which allegedly set them aside from their secular counterparts. This important hypothesis has contributed to the wide perception that religious terrorists are by default more lethal and more dangerous than secular terrorists, a finding that has a profound impact on the methods of predictive threat-assessment. However, in practice there has been considerable disagreement about the uniformity of categorization of groups as 'religious', as opposed to 'ethnic' or 'nationalist'. This chapter will attempt to shed more light on this issue by providing an alternative perspective on the characteristics of mass-casualty terrorism.

Genesis and scope of religious terrorism

The turn to religion as the main ideological support basis for terrorism since the 1980s did not take place in a vacuum. It has been motivated by a number of factors, among them lack of progress with regard to the widening gap between the West and the rest of the world and the inability of secular organizations to resolve core communal problems, as well as larger issues such as the Israeli–Palestinian conflict, and the overall breakdown of secular ideologies such as Marxism and purely secular nationalism (Laqueur 1999: 128). One of the most important events in this regard has been the Iranian Revolution in 1979, in the sense that it provided evidence of the feasibility of establishing an Islamic state, and also served as a strong support base for violent Shi'a groups such as Amal and Hezbollah in Lebanon or ad-Dawa in Iraq. Another pivotal event in the same year was the Soviet invasion of Afghanistan, the resistance to which quickly became the unifying issue for *mujahidin* from all over the world. This was important in providing personal contacts and battleground experience for many radicals, and, even more important, the addictive taste of victory. These elements would later form the foundation for the phenomenon we now know as al-Qa'ida. But radical Islam was certainly not the only religion that became used as a terrorist ideology during the early 1980s. Christianity was represented by the rise of the Christian Identity and anti-abortion movements in the USA, represented by groups such as the Order, the Covenant, the Sword and Arm of the Lord, Aryan Nations and the Army of God; just as radical Judaism became the main ideological foundation for the Gush Emunim terrorist campaign in Israel. Similarly, the Sikh campaign represented by groups such as Babbar Khalsa International (BKI), Dal Khalsa or the Khalistan Commando Force in India became increasingly religious, following 'Operation Blue Star' in which Indian troops violently raided the holiest Sikh temple in Amritsar. The Palestinian and Kashmiri conflicts have also continually transformed from primarily nationalist to dominantly religious ones from about the end of the 1980s, and the same trajectory could be observed during the 1990s in other conflicts, in, for example, the Balkans or the Caucasus. In the 1990s new-age cults, based on eclectic religious ideologies, also arose, such as the Japanese Aum Shinrikyo, whose apocalyptic mix of prophetic cultic practices derived from a wide array of writings, such as those of Nostradamus, the Book of Revelation in the Bible and imagery from Hindu and Buddhist texts, as well as science fiction elements from the novels written in the 1940s by Isaac Asimov. Other influences were an element of Japanese nationalism, anti-American and anti-Jewish sentiments, the Hindu God Siva, the Old and New Testaments of the Bible, Jesus, nuclear holocaust and the Tibetan Book of the Dead. As we can see from these examples, no major religion has been excluded from being exploited as a divine justification for terrorist violence.

The single most important factor for the observed rise of religion as a dominant characteristic of modern terrorism has been the end of the Cold War, which signified the utter historical failure of communist ideologies, as well as the end of the bipolar world order. These events not only diminished the attractiveness of ideological compliance with one of the two world power centres in order to attract state assistance, but they also triggered immense fear of 'one-worldism', symbolized by the emergence of the unipolar world order, which was perceived by radical members of various cultures as a threat to their identity and survival (Ranstorp 1996). In the absence of alternatives among secular ideologies, many extremists shifted to religion as the main ideological foundation of their activities. This shift in ideological support mechanisms, however, does not necessarily mean that the nature of core terrorist motivations and beliefs has changed, or that religion became the primary *motivating* factor for acts of violence. As previously noted by Walter Laqueur, terrorist belief systems may differ significantly based on history, culture or the influence of charismatic leaders. But the ideological content is only secondary to 'burning passion', which serves as the primary driving force behind terrorist activity (Laqueur 1999: 230).

In other words, while religion has since the 1980s become a more prominent factor as the supporting philosophical basis for many terrorist organizations, the underlying *motives* in the belief systems of the majority of today's terrorists have *not* changed. Even the religious fanatic views his violent activity as an essentially altruistic act of self-defence. It is still the perception of humiliation, victimization and injustice that drives the so-called 'religious terrorist', rather than a perceived universal command from God. The use of holy rhetoric by most groups commonly labelled as 'religious' serves much more as a uniting and morale-boosting tool than as a universal justification for acts of unrestrained violence. That is not to say that for many terrorists religion does not represent a tremendous legitimizing force, and that it does not inspire the perception of enormous gratification and empowerment. But the terrorists are still primarily motivated by a grievance that is very real – even though, just like most ordinary people, they also look for the support of their arguments wherever they can. Religion, then, represents only one of the possible sources of support. The key point to emphasize here is that terrorist *ideology* is fundamentally different from *motivation* for terrorist violence. Motivation in essence refers to an individual's decision to join a violent group, and its sources typically differ even among members of the same terrorist organization. This element is sometimes referred to as the 'root causes' of terrorism, in the sense that it forms the preconditions that make an individual susceptible to joining a terror movement. Ideology then, has the role of an umbrella which enables the unification of frustrated individuals by linking their grievances by an all-encompassing explanation that blames the system, which is so corrupt and unjust that it must be destroyed. In this way a terror group provides its members with a single mindset and objective, together with the firm prescription of violence as the only possible chance for remedy. In addition, ideology provides terrorists with mechanisms for enemy-dehumanization and for the diffusion of responsibility in order to facilitate their ability to kill non-combatants for a higher purpose. The important implication here is that the common perception of religious terrorists as less rational because their motivational drive is a divine call is ultimately incorrect, since religion in the context of terrorism essentially constitutes an ideology and not a motive.

How does one then distinguish between religious and secular groups for the purposes of typology? Most authors confirm that drawing the line between religious and secular terrorists is challenging, as many secular organizations also have a strong religious component, and many religious terrorists in addition possess goals that are of a political nature. This distinction becomes even more blurred in the case of Islamic fundamentalism, as it is often contended that Islam does not differentiate between religion and politics. Further, in trying to make the distinction we should be careful not to fall into the trap of rhetorical nuances. In many cultures the word 'God' figures very strongly in the language and in cultural and political traditions, which can sometimes be misleading. For instance, to an outsider phrases such as

'In God We Trust', printed on American currency, or the use of the popular slogan 'God Bless America' by the American President could easily create the false impression that the USA is essentially a theocratic state. Another factor besides language that has the capacity to mislead us in terms of labelling a terrorist organization as religious is government propaganda. Virtually all states that are victims of a terrorist campaign insist on projecting their opponents as religious fanatics. This is quite understandable, as such labelling can have a delegitimizing effect on the terrorists' cause – someone who views himself as fighting on God's orders is popularly perceived as an irrational zealot, with whom no compromise is deemed possible. Rather, this 'worshipper of evil' is regarded as an exceptionally dangerous creature who uses claims of a just grievance only as a misleading cover, and who can only be stopped by merciless elimination. Israel and to a lesser extent Russia and India are examples of countries that have used such a strategy with some success. But while this strategy of promoting an image of the opponent as an irrational religious fanatic may sometimes be politically successful, it entails the danger of failing to address the actual real-life grievances, which in turn can eventually result in increased support for the terrorists. In sum, while the religious dimension is present in the language of many terrorist organizations, when categorizing terrorist groups for the purposes of threat-assessment we must read between the lines of rhetoric.

Characteristics of religious terrorists

Some terrorism scholars have attempted to define the core characteristics of religious terrorists, pointing mainly to the radically different value systems, mechanisms of legitimization and justification, concepts

346

of morality, mechanisms of victim-dehumanization and an overall worldview. The difficulty, however, is that most of the defined characteristics fail to pinpoint a clear dividing line between religious and secular terrorists.

For instance, Mark Juergensmeyer characterizes religiously motivated struggles primarily as those involving images of divine warfare (Juergensmeyer 2000: 146). Such images represent what Juergensmeyer calls a 'cosmic struggle' which is played out in history as a war between good and evil, order and chaos. Religious terrorists identify with such a struggle and project its images onto the present situation, which they seek to address. Such heavily mythologized conflict between the believers and their enemies then becomes absolute. Juergensmeyer also describes in great detail the creation of martyrs as a distinct characteristic of religious terrorists in their dominant reliance on the concept of martyrdom. In the context of a 'cosmic war', he argues, martyrdom is not only regarded as a testimony of one's commitment, it is also a performance of the most fundamental religious act found in virtually every religious tradition in the world: the act of sacrifice. The images of sacrifice thus transform destruction performed within the religious context into something positive, making killing not only permissible but even mandatory. Juergensmeyer also contends that by giving up their lives, martyrs not only demonstrate their commitment, but they also engage in sacrifice – the most fundamental form of religiosity. But the key to emphasize here is that *all* violent campaigns find it useful to create and glorify martyrs, as documented by the fact that the majority of suicide bombings have been carried out by secular as opposed to religious terrorist groups. An act of self-sacrifice in the name of the organization's cause, whether religious or secular, is a uniting factor. Overt praise of the martyr's accomplishment by prominent members

of the group can also increase the self-sense of group prestige and can inspire future volunteers. The willingness to die for a cause is sometimes also used as evidence of the superiority of the group's members over their adversaries, who are portrayed as pleasure-seekers and who in spite of their military dominance are essentially weak. The resulting perception among the group is that, due to superior determination, their final victory is inevitable.

Another allegedly distinct characteristic of religiously motivated struggles are the aforementioned images of divine warfare, which are equated to the present struggle and are consistently used to create a sense of historical purpose and urgency (Juergensmeyer 2000: 146). This, however, is again a characteristic that is psychologically natural to all ethnic, cultural or national communities, and is consistently used by all violent movements. Juergensmeyer's 'cosmic struggles' are in essence what psychiatrist Vamik Volkan calls 'chosen traumas': 'heavily mythologized historical sufferings that bring with them powerful experiences of loss and feelings of humiliation, vengeance and hatred that trigger a variety of unconscious defense mechanisms that attempt to reverse these experiences and feelings' (Volkan 1997: 82). Such defence mechanisms serve as a powerful dehumanization tool for killing, regardless of ideological context – the new enemies of current conflicts are psychologically transformed into extensions of the old enemy from a historical event. Whether they are the Crusades for the Muslims, the Holocaust for the Jews, Black September for the Palestinians, the Battle of Karbala for the Shi'as, Bloody Sunday for Irish Catholics, the battles of Mahabharata and Ramayana for the Hindus, Operation Blue Star for the Sikhs, the Viet Nam War or 9/11 for the Americans, the Wounded Knee Massacre for the Lakota Native Americans, deportation from Turkey for the Armenians, or the Battle of Stalingrad for the Russians, all of these events can become mythological 'chosen traumas' or 'images of cosmic warfare', which will help to dehumanize the enemy in future conflicts. Religious groups are in this respect no different from secular entities.

As these examples show, religious terrorists are essentially very similar to their secular counterparts: they are narrow-minded individuals who fail to see alternative perspectives on the issues on behalf of which they fight. This is not only a natural, but also an absolutely necessary characteristic for any terrorist – who has to believe in the absolute nature of the cause in order to kill in its name. And while it is true that some organizations are more discriminate and restrained in their violent actions then others, *any* ideology used to support a terrorist campaign becomes in essence a religion – a comprehensive worldview which constitutes an unquestionable higher truth of an absolute nature. Any terrorist is motivated by feelings of frustration and humiliation, any terrorist regards his or her use of violence as a defensive war, any terrorist fights in the name of the absolute good. In addition, any perpetrator of a terrorist act empathizes with his or her own victimization and protests against cruelty towards his or her own people, but at the same time demonstrates minimum empathy for those whom he or she kills. Any perpetrator of such an act feels empowered by the execution of 'just' violence in the name of a great cause. For all of the reasons stated above, Juergensmeyer's characterizations are excellent descriptions of the characteristics of terrorists in general, but fail to provide a useful tool for identifying religious terrorists.

In contrast, Hoffman's analysis of the distinct features of religious terrorists is much more specific, but in the end suffers from a different weakness – virtually none of the terrorist organizations that exist today fit Hoffman's description. For instance, the number of groups that execute their terrorist acts for 'no audience but themselves or God' is rather limited. In fact, most of the existing religious terrorist organizations complement their violence with realistic alternatives to secular rule, by backing their 'military' activities with social, medical and other communal services. As a result, many religious terrorist organizations have over time developed impressive constituencies. Thus, Hoffman's argument that 'the restraints on violence that are imposed on secular terrorists by the desire to appeal to a tacitly supportive or uncommitted constituency are not relevant to the religious terrorists' is hardly valid. Furthermore, religious organizations that 'unlike secular terrorists who see violence as a means to an end, tend to view violence as an end in its self' are also quite scarce. Even though many terrorist groups today carry out acts of violence that are motivated by revenge, the altruistic component of such violence even when accompanied by religious rhetoric cannot be over-emphasized. And while it is true that the goals of some religious terrorists tend to be less clearly defined and seem much less tangible, most organizations commonly labelled as religious, nevertheless, have a clear strategic calculation behind them and seek to benefit a specific group of people. Even Hoffmann more or less confirms this claim by stating that the aims of 'religious political' terrorists are defined as 'the attainment of the greatest possible benefits for themselves and for their co-religionists only, as opposed to the indiscriminately utilitarian goals of secular terrorists'. This observation again shows the complexity of defining the distinct features of religious terrorists. Are not all ethnically or nationalistically based secular organizations also restricted in their violent actions to the attainment of the greatest possible benefits to members of their own ethnic or national community only? And did not, on the other hand, the religiously motivated Algerian Groupe islamique armé (GIA – Armed Islamic Group) indiscriminately kill its co-religionists in some of the most brutal ways imaginable during that country's decade-long civil war?

Conclusion

As this chapter has hopefully demonstrated, the commonly defined characteristics of the 'religious terrorists' as irrational fanatics who do not seek to benefit a constituency and whose violent actions are not a means to an end but rather a self-serving end in themselves, and who are therefore unrestrained in their violence and thus more likely to perpetrate acts of mass destruction, do not apply to the absolute majority of today's terrorists. At the same time, it is true that the religiously ideologized terrorist groups have demonstrated a different worldview and strategy, which is more immune to indiscriminate mass-casualty violence than in the case of nationalist separatist groups. But given the difficulties in making a clear distinction between religious and non-religious terrorists, it may be a more productive approach to focus on more specific elements of a group's belief system than the general dichotomy of 'religious' versus 'non-religious'. This is especially true in view of the absence of any religious element whatsoever in genocides such as those that occurred in Nazi Germany, Stalinist Russia, Rwanda and Cambodia. Clearly, the presence of religion in a group's ideology by itself does not provide a reliable indicator of a group's willingness to progress to causing indiscriminate mass casualties.

A possibly more useful method of threat-assessment may be to focus on the specific ideological characteristics that are responsible for the shifting of the threshold of violence, such as the presence of an apocalyptic justification that could be described by the objective of 'destroying the world to save it'. Religious and other cult-like organizations that share the worldview that the planet requires a radical makeover are not in short supply. Fortunately, most such organizations have yet to resort to outward violence. If that were to occur, however, the potential ability of apocalyptic organizations to justify killing people as actually benefiting them by sending them to a better place than this world makes such groups particularly dangerous. As in most terrorist attacks, the use of violence in this scenario would again be perceived by the terrorists as altruistic, with the critical difference that the constituency in this case would be the victims themselves. In such cases, the victims would not necessarily be regarded as an enemy whom one kills in hate or for symbolic value, but rather as poor human beings who will be saved by being killed. Under such circumstances, killing thousands of people indiscriminately would be psychologically much easier than to do so as part of a political strategy or in revenge.

The most lethal terrorist groups in history have incorporated such an apocalyptic element into their ideology. For instance, Kozo Okamoto, the leader of the secular Japanese Red Army squad which carried out one of the most lethal and indiscriminate terror acts of its era by killing 26 people at Lod Airport, Israel, in 1972, believed that his victims would 'become stars in the sky'. This element was also present in the ideology of Aum Shinrikyo, which adopted a twisted version of the Tibetan Buddhist Tantric concept of 'poa' – the act of merciful killing which would provide the victims with the opportunity for a more favourable rebirth on a higher spiritual plane in their next life. Under such circumstances, the cult's attempt indiscriminately to kill thousands of people was psychologically much easier, especially given the presence of a self-sacrificial element in the sense that the one who killed took the victim's bad karma onto himself. In this way, for Aum members killing people became an act of self-sacrifice for the sake of the victim. The 'benefiting the victim' facet can also be found among the most lethal Islamist terrorist groups, such as the GIA, whose leader had argued that it is justifiable to kill innocent civilians since they would be considered 'martyrs' for the cause. Similarly, Osama bin Laden was also not troubled by the issue of collateral damage or the fact that Muslims also died in the 9/11 attack, arguing that if those killed were good Muslims, they would benefit by becoming martyrs and by being granted special treatment in paradise. A final important point to emphasize is that a terrorist group does not necessarily have to be religious in nature in order to reach an apocalyptic stage. Fundamentalist environmental or animal rights groups, as well as ethnic-based violent movements might under certain circumstances also reach this phase. Consider for instance the RISE, a secular environmentalist group which attempted to culture large quantities of *salmonella typhi* as part of a ludicrous plan to contaminate the water supply of several large cities and indiscriminately kill thousands of people. The logic behind the plot was to kill every human except the group's members, who would later reproduce among themselves in order to repopulate the earth with a more environmentally friendly population. Similarly, Sendero Luminoso (Shining Path), a Peruvian Marxist group, has killed more than six thousand people in the absence of a religious ideology, but in the presence of apocalyptic elements in its interpretation

of Maoist doctrine. Under the slogan 'In the end, we all must mix our warm blood with the cold blood of our death brothers', Sendero Luminoso not only carried out numerous massacres of civilians, but also implemented a quota for casualties *for its own side* in order to monitor its revolutionary progress.

In conclusion, it will be the presence of this type of apocalyptic element in the ideology of a group rather than the generic typologization of the ideology itself that will provide us with a critical insight into a group's potential to commit mass-casualty acts of violence.

Note

1 First published in J. Haynes (ed.) (2006) *The Politics of Religion. A Survey*, London: Routledge, pp. 83–91.

Bibliography

Hoffman, B. (1993) *Holy Terror: The Implications of Terrorism Motivated by a Religious Imperative*, Washington, DC: Rand.

Juergensmeyer, M. (2000) *Terror in the Mind of God: The Global Rise of Religious Violence*, Berkeley: University of California Press.

Lacquer, W. (1999) *The New Terrorism: Fanaticism and the Arms of Mass Destruction*, Oxford: Oxford University Press.

Ranstorp, M. (1996) 'Terrorism in the name of religion', *Journal of International Affairs*, 50, Summer, pp. 41–62.

Volkan, V. (1997) *Blood Lines: From Ethnic Pride to Ethnic Terrorism*, New York: Farrar, Straus and Giroux.

22

Conflict prevention and peacebuilding

Atsuhiro Katano

Introduction

The end of the Cold War enabled human recognition of violence in the world to change dramatically. Three changes can be pointed out: (1) changes in scale and characteristics of armed conflicts; (2) a newly emerged response to these conflicts; and (3) the need to reorganize international institutions for more effective responses.

Changes in scale and characteristics of armed conflicts

Most violent conflicts in today's world are civil wars between domestic communities, rather than wars between independent states. The Stockholm International Peace Research Institute (SIPRI) reported that between 1990 and 2004, the number of 'major armed conflicts' was 57. A 'major armed conflict' is defined as the use of armed force between military forces and/or organized armed groups, with the battle-related deaths of at least 1,000 people in any given year. Only 4 out of 57 were fought between states. Moreover, no inter-state conflict was recognized among 19 'major armed conflicts' fought during 2004 (SIPRI 2005).

It should be noted, however, that the decline in numbers of inter-state conflicts does not exclude what might be called 'global characteristics' of internalized

civil wars. That is, not a few armed conflicts, often referred to as 'protracted', are often strongly sustained by arms supply from foreign countries. As the so-called African 'blood diamond' trade shows, limited mineral resources, including diamond, gold and other rare metals, have both financially influenced, as well as probably prolonging, serious civil armed conflicts in Angola, Congo, Liberia and Sierra Leone.

In addition, global aspects of the internal civil wars are not only economic – but also often religious and cultural. According to John Paul Lederach, these civil wars lead to deeply divided societies where 'people, when threatened, seek security in narrower, more localized identity groups (this often leads to their conflicts being labelled 'ethnic' or 'religious') (Lederach 1997: 18). Since both ethnicity and religion can be identified transnationally, then those who seek security in ethnic or religious identity can be exclusive (i.e. intolerant to other races or faiths) and global (i.e. sharing the ethnic or religious sameness beyond nationality) at the same time.

A newly emerged response to these conflicts

These civil wars often cause severe humanitarian crises, such as mass murder of innocent non-combatants and ethnic or religious minorities, which can encourage the international community seriously to consider so-called 'humanitarian intervention'. Overwhelming arguments have been made in academic circles, and many of them primarily focus on the question of *who* should intervene, as well as *when* and *how*. And out of them has emerged recognition that longer-term commitment to post-conflict social reconstruction is required as a crucial part of successful intervention.

It seems that the arguments relating to humanitarian intervention have encouraged a reconsideration of the normative principle of state sovereignty and non-intervention in domestic affairs. For example, J. Bryan Hehir argues that we need to re-examine the cost and benefit of the non-intervention principle; and that it can be effectively revised by applying 'the just war ethic' from the Christian tradition. As the just war ethic instructs, he says, the military intervention to humanitarian crisis must be the last resort, conducted by the legitimate authority (such as the United Nations Security Council), with restricted use of coercive force (Hehir 1995).

A more in-depth examination of humanitarian crises also calls for a serious exploration of the role of religion in violent conflicts. For instance, Rajmohan Gandhi points out that Hinduism allows 'the link between religion and nationalism', and that the caste system plays 'the divisive, hierarchical, and conflict-generating' function in Hindu society (Gandhi, quoted in Coward and Smith 2004: 50). Eva K. Neumaier mentions that the spiritual and individual understanding of the 'inner peace' and the dualism of the sacred and the secular keep Buddhist religious leaders from active engagement with the daily problems of the secular society (Neumaier, cited in Coward and Smith 2004: 73–4). In the Abrahamic faiths, too, wars and other use of violence have been justified with the words of scriptures and theological application of them. The obedience to one god has been interpreted as sanction enabling harm to 'heretics' and 'infidels' (Sadataka 2005).

The need to reorganize international institutions

A need to reconsider the role of the United Nations (UN) concerning security and peace has become clear in recent years. The original idea of the UN's involvement with world order was envisaged as responding to inter-state use of armed forces (such as aggression) through the means of collective security, which however has not been implemented completely. Instead, the Peace Keeping Operations (PKO) have played a significant role in some conflicts, in intervening between warring parties and helping to maintain ceasefires. However, the roles linked to PKOs have profoundly grown, especially after the Cold War, including the return of refugees, monitoring elections, promoting human rights and policing to help stabilize social order. In this context, the concept of conflict prevention and peacebuilding has emerged as a re-organizing of the UN's peace operations in two ways: (1) to unload the PKO and redistribute peace programmes to other specialized agencies of the UN; and (2) to reframe a new concept to encompass various missions to achieve sustainable peace. In other words, the UN peace operations have come to be expected not only to stabilize conflicts but also to facilitate successful transition from a cycle of violence to a culture of peace.

The UN has also taken some initiative to involve the world religions. In August 2000, a Millennium World Peace Summit of Religious and Spiritual Leaders was held at the UN. The summit presented a document, 'Commitment to Global Peace', to the then UN Secretary-General Kofi A. Annan. The Commitment acknowledges that, 'The United Nations and the religions of the world have a common concern for human dignity, justice and peace … whereas religions have contributed to the peace of the world but have also been used to create division and fuel hostilities.' The document also admits that the 'world is plagued by violence, war and destruction, which are sometimes perpetrated in the name of religion', and that 'a true culture of peace must be founded upon the cultivation of the inner dimension of peace, which is the heritage of the religious and spiritual traditions'. Based on these acknowledgements, the religious and spiritual leaders commit to a collaboration with the UN in the pursuit of peace, the non-violent resolution of religious and ethnic conflicts with condemnation of all violence in the name of religion, and the promotion of peace values such as tolerance, dignity of life, environmental care, economic justice and religious freedom (Millennium World Peace Summit 2000).

The summit also decided to form the World Council of Religious Leaders, aimed at providing the collective wisdom of the faith traditions as a resource to the UN and other international actors. The Council has undertaken various initiatives including promotion of tolerance and a condemnation of racism (in partnership with the UN High Commission for Human Rights), international interfaith dialogue, a Religious Initiative (with the World Economic Forum), and a Global Commission for the Preservation of Sacred Sites (with UNESCO and the World Monument Fund).

The conceptual origin of conflict prevention and peacebuilding

The concept of conflict prevention and peacebuilding has become popular since 1992, when Boutros Boutros-Ghali, then Secretary-General of the UN, issued a report titled *An Agenda for Peace*. In this report, he pointed out four major areas through which the peace-related functions of the UN were to be strengthened: preventive diplomacy, peacemaking, peacekeeping and peacebuilding. Although the term 'conflict prevention' does not appear in *An Agenda for Peace*, the substantive idea was imbedded in Boutros-Ghali's definition of preventive diplomacy as 'action to prevent disputes from arising between parties, to prevent existing disputes from escalating into conflicts and to limit the spread of the latter when they occur' (Roberts and Kingsbury 1993: 475).

According to Hideaki Shinoda, Boutros-Ghali initially conceptualized the UN peace functions in a chronological manner, from pre-conflict phase (preventive diplomacy) through mid-conflict (peacemaking and peacekeeping) to post-conflict (peacebuilding). However, the distinction between pre-conflict prevention and post-conflict peacebuilding was ambiguous, since the report expected that post-conflict peacebuilding 'can prevent the recurrence of violence among nations and peoples' (Roberts and Kingsbury 1993: 475). These concepts were re-organized in the 2000 *Report of the Panel on United Nations Peace Operations*, the so-called 'Brahimi Report', in which the conceptual and functional integrity of conflict prevention and peacebuilding were recognized (Shinoda 2002).

Out of a number of literatures on peacebuilding, W. Andy Knight (2003) has pointed out three trends in this field. First, many works have been published to clarify the concept of peacebuilding. The studies on conceptualization typically take three contexts of thought: viewing violent conflicts (1) from a *political* perspective, which regards the promotion of democratization as a key objective of peacebuilding; (2) from an *economic* perspective, which regards market development solutions as a primary answer for peacebuilding; and (3) from a *military* perspective, which regards disarmament and demobilization as a major task of peacebuilding.

The second trend is that the literature has broadened the vision, scale and scope of peacebuilding. It is in this trend that conflict prevention is closely intertwined with peacebuilding, as some studies call for a shift 'from a culture of reacting to conflicts to one of preventing conflicts before they occur' (Knight 2003: 250). The scale and scope of peacebuilding have been widened, too. Various actors at different levels have been seen to hold significant stakes in peacebuilding: the UN, the Bretton Woods-related institutions, the regional organizations such as the European Union and the African Union, and various international and local non-governmental organizations (NGOs). Not only civilian institutions but also military and police sectors are involved as 'the most recent research indicates that a mixture of military, police and civilian elements may be needed to address the different phases of post-conflict peacebuilding' (Knight 2003: 253).

The third trend is to link peacebuilding and governance. While so-called 'good governance' can be a profound objective of peacebuilding, the specific process and timing are controversial among scholars. On the one hand, there is a call for power to be transferred to the legitimate government as soon as the peace agreement takes place. On the other hand, there is a cautious argument that ill-timed election could do more harm than good to the process. There are also studies to interpret the prevalence of peacebuilding as 'an enormous experiment in socio-economic, political and constitutional engineering', aiming at 'constructing a more stable domestic and international political order by widening the network of liberal democratic societies' (Knight 2003: 255).

Knight's analysis is valuable as it concisely describes the recent trends of peacebuilding research. But since it discusses the issue entirely in secular terms, some religious arguments need to be included here. First, studies to conceptualize peacebuilding need to include *religious*, as well as political, economic, and military, perspectives. As discussed later in more detail, a religious perspective sees the restoration of broken relationships through constructive conflict transformation as a core objective of peacebuilding.

Second, the broadened vision and scope of peacebuilding do include religious actors as well. The World Council of Religious Leaders and its joint initiatives with other inter-governmental organizations are one example. Other international religious organizations, such as the World Muslim League and the World Council of Churches, are also involved with information, research, education and interfaith dialogue. In terms of denominational and grassroots level, a number of NGOs are religiously based. They not only engage in mission and evangelization, but also provide education, healthcare and development programmes, contributing profoundly to the comprehensive social infrastructure.

Finally, the link between peacebuilding and governance needs to be considered from religious perspectives, since the issue involves the problem of power in relationships. Although Knight's discussion focuses primarily on sharing and transition of political power in terms of democratization, a religious perspective can offer two cautions: the negative legacy of missions and the critical examination of modernity. Wilbert Shenk appropriately traces the history of Christian missions over the past two thousand years. He points out two mission strategies, proselytism and conquest, as contradictory to teachings in the Bible. Both strategies justified forcing people to accept a certain truth claim. Historically, such missions went hand-in-hand with colonialist rule by the West.

The modern mission movement replaced them as the third strategy, but it focused on saving individual souls, reflecting the modern notion of the distinction between body (behaviour and ethics) and mind (belief and doctrine) (Shenk 2006). Since the resurgence of religion today calls for a critical review of liberal modernity, these insights from a religious perspective need to be considered, if the prevalence of peacebuilding connotes the contemporary proselytism to liberal democracy.

Scott Thomas argues the religious aspects of conflict resolution and peacebuilding from a more comprehensive viewpoint. He reaffirms that certain religious traditions, such as Buddhism and Christian pacificism, have been actively involved in resolving international conflicts even before the terms conflict prevention and peacebuilding became popular. Against this backdrop, the changing nature of international conflict, as mentioned earlier, encouraged the emergence of so-called 'multitrack diplomacy', based on 'a recognition that civil or internal wars require civil or internal action by societies or communities as a whole if a conflict is to be ended' (Thomas 2005: 177). This is where the religious actors can and should play a role in international peacebuilding, along with other actors such as governments, NGOs, business community, research/educational institutes, media and individual activists.

Thomas goes further to say that the holistic concept of peace (such as Arabic *salaam* and Hebrew *shalom*) found in many religious traditions has influenced the comprehensive vision of sustainable peace that conflict prevention and peacebuilding try to achieve. Reminding us of the fact that many of the societies suffering from protracted conflicts are faith communities in which religious traditions are lived out through rituals, festivals and social customs, he emphasizes 'the transforming power of their faith' as a key impetus for socio-political transformation in a sustainable way (Thomas 2005: 196).

Case studies of conflict prevention and peacebuilding

Since the 1990s, inspired by the interests in achieving sustainable peace in the post-Cold War world, a number of both practices and theorizing efforts have been made in the area of conflict prevention and peacebuilding. Although these are too broad to cover in this single chapter alone, it has to be mentioned that 'the growing literature on peacebuilding, which embraces elements of both praxis and research, is still very much in an embryonic state' (Knight 2003: 242), and that the theoretical integration of the whole process itself is still in the making. In other words, when it comes to a 'case study' of conflict prevention and peacebuilding, two kinds of studies must be considered: (1) cases of specific conflicts and efforts to transform them into durable peace; and (2) trials of integrating the learned lessons into a certain theoretical framework. In the following sections, I would like to illustrate the attempts to examine elements of peacebuilding by Lisa Schirch and John Paul Lederach, as a case of theorization, with in addition some practical analysis from specific conflict and peacebuilding cases.

Both Schirch and Lederach acknowledge, as many other researchers have pointed out, that peacebuilding seeks not only to reduce or eliminate violence, but also to build a social system that stabilizes peace in a sustainable manner. For this purpose, peacebuilding is a multifaceted activity, including various areas of development in terms of demilitarization, local community, human rights, economy and public policy, to name only a few. Thus the work of strategic coordination of various operations is highlighted as an inevitable element of peacebuilding.

Four components of strategic peacebuilding

For effective coordination of strategies, Schirch points out four major aspects of strategic peacebuilding: values, skills, analysis and processes.

Values that peacebuilding seeks can be summarized as fulfilment of needs and protection of rights. These needs and rights are divided into three areas: (1) physical needs such as food, clothes, shelter and health; (2) social needs such as dignity, security, sense of belonging, self-determination and recognition; and (3) cultural needs such as the meaning of life, religious freedom and identity. These values must be pursued with ethics of interdependence, partnership and limiting violence, lest the pursuit of the values should justify depriving those of others (Schirch 2004: 13–17).

It should be noted here that the devotion to local needs could be the very essence of good governance, if the term 'governance' is understood in clear contrast to the term 'government'. For example, Toshiki Mogami critically examines the prevalent discourse of global governance to be conceptually confusing and failing to contribute meaningfully to a clarification of such global phenomena, including: international laws, norms, institutions and international regimes. He suggests that the primary significance of using the concept of 'governance' in international relations is to emphasize the non-coercive and non-authoritarian nature of governance, as opposed to top-down coercive 'government' (Mogami 2006: 320–1). If his argument is relevant, governance can be understood as a way of building and maintaining order not by law enforcement and policing but by responsible and responsive satisfaction of the local needs.

Commitment to these values then helps reaffirm the original meaning of governance and distinguish peacebuilding from the artful imposition of Western-centric solutions, as mentioned earlier.

Peacebuilding owes many *relational skills* to the recent development of conflict transformation theory and practice. Practical skills for effective communication such as self-reflection, active listening, diplomatic and assertive speaking, appreciative inquiry, creative problem-solving, dialogue, negotiation and mediation are understood as foundations for democratic process, and are 'like a grease to the wheels of peacebuilding' (Schirch 2004: 20).

In this regard, development and training of relational skills make a profound impact not only on the local conflicting parties but also on those who intervene in various areas for purposes of peacebuilding. As repeatedly emphasized among practitioners, the comprehensive nature of peacebuilding requires a high degree of communication, a shared sense of common purpose, and accumulated experiences of transforming tensions into creative cooperation among different agencies, both local and international. Well-facilitated relationships among peacebuilding sectors are necessary for successful coordination, and they themselves can be good role models for the local people to build confidence through active listening and assertive speaking.

In addition to practical skills to develop relationships, peacebuilding needs *tools for analysing* complicated conflicts. Basically, conflicts should be analysed: (1) to understand the local context; (2) to identify the unsatisfied needs and the logics that justify the violence; and (3) to discern the relations between various types of violence (Schirch 2004: 21–4). It should be remembered that when Johan Galtung coined the term 'peacebuilding' in the 1970s, his primary interest was to recognize poverty, human rights violation and exploitation of resources as root causes of violent conflict. This insight enabled him to develop the concept of 'positive peace', which seeks the elimination of the various forms of structural violence (Galtung 1975). Structural violence can cause secondary violence – as various forms of reaction: (1) violence against self, such as abuses of alcohol and drugs, suicide, depression and internalized oppression; (2) violence in community, such as crime, interpersonal violence, domestic violence and rape; and (3) violence on national and international levels, such as rebel movements, terrorism, civil wars, revolutions, coups and war (Schirch 2004: 24).

Specific *approaches* for peacebuilding can be categorized into four areas: waging conflict non-violently, reducing direct violence, transforming relationships, and developing capacities.

Waging conflict non-violently

Waging conflict non-violently, such as nonviolent resistance and advocacy, is taken when the powers of the conflicting parties are not balanced and the awareness of the issue is low. It is aimed at making the issue visible and empowering the vulnerable so that the powerful can no longer ignore them (Schirch 2004: 28–34).

Non-violent involvement in conflict necessitates cognitive change of the perspectives on social conflict and human interaction. First, a distinction between conflict and violence must be made. All conflicts do not involve violence and thus there is a possibility of waging conflict non-violently. In reality, conflict of opinions, attitudes and priorities is a natural part of our daily lives, and most of these are dealt with non-violently.

Second, a distinction between problems and people is necessary. As a conflict escalates, it is perceived differently, from people working together to deal with common problems to people regarding each other as problems. Problems and people must be distinguished to avoid such dehumanization (or even demonization) of the opponents.

Third, an alternative view to adversarial approaches to conflict needs to be developed. The adversarial perspective views conflict as irreconcilable, a 'zero-sum' game in which one party's victory automatically mean the other party's defeat. Such a polarized all-or-nothing confrontation depends more on the perceptions of opponents than the actual nature of particular conflict. Then a cooperative problem-solving approach is effective in focusing on the issues rather than the people, brainstorming collaboratively for broad options as imaginably as possible, and pursuing a so-called 'win-win' solution.

Reducing direct violence

Non-violent direct action itself does not build peace, however. In order to reduce direct violence, three major requirements must be met: preventing civilian victims, deterring offenders, and creating safe spaces. The safe space should be considered in three dimensions: physical, emotional and relational. Specific systems for direct violence reduction often overlap with peacekeeping operations in a broader sense. This is the place, as mentioned earlier, where the scope of peacebuilding is enlarged to become a collaborative mission involving military, police and civilian sectors. Programmes for maintaining ceasefires, establishing the rule of law with policing and judicial systems, humanitarian assistance, and early warning and response need to be coordinated to enhance human security and social justice (Schirch 2004: 35–44).

In recent peacebuilding practices in Afghanistan, the UN-mandated International Security Assistance Force was deployed to maintain social order and help establish and train Afghanistan's own security forces. The Security Sector Reform (SSR) process also took place, focusing on five areas of establishing new national military, police reform, judicial reform, policy on drugs and DDR (disarmament, demobilization and reintegration).

Transforming relationships

Transformation of various kinds of relationships is located at the core of peacebuilding. They include personal relationships, family, community, economy, social structure and governmental functions. Several aspects of transformation have to be sought, such as trauma healing, conflict transformation and doing justice.

Take an example of peacebuilding in East Timor. From the time of the military occupation in December 1975, East Timor had been a province of Indonesia. The end of the Cold War in the late 1980s stimulated the move toward democracy in Asian authoritative regimes, and the violation of human rights in East Timor came to increased international attention. The Indonesian government changed its policy and asked the United Nations to take responsibility of holding a referendum. The vast majority (78.5%) expressed their wish for independence and East Timor became independent in May 2002.

Peacebuilding in East Timor is *de facto* nation building. The United Nations got involved in this complicated task by assisting a referendum through the United Nations Mission in East Timor (UNAMET), deploying the International Force for East Timor (INTERFET) to deter violence after the referendum, and achieving the foundation of the government through the work of the United Nations Transitional Administration in East Timor (UNTAET).

While UNTAET played an important role to help the East Timorese start their own country through the establishment of constitution and president, there are many agendas for making peace sustainable.

According to Motoko Shuto (2004), the remaining issues for peacebuilding can be raised in three areas. First, considerable development of socio-economic infrastructure is needed. The rates of unemployment and illiteracy are still high. The legal system covering property rights and land reform must be developed to encourage agricultural and commercial growth. Finally, competent professionals, including administrators and teachers, are needed in sufficient numbers.

Second, enhanced social reintegration needs to be sought through reconciliation and 'doing' justice. The case of East Timor has its own complexity: issues in seeking truth and justice are two-fold: those among East Timorese and those between East Timorese and Indonesians. The Commission for Reception, Truth and Reconciliation (CAVR is the Portuguese abbreviation) was established in 2002 and a final report published in 2005. In the inter-Timorese dimension, CAVR offered procedures for truth telling, amnesty and social reintegration, while in the Timorese–Indonesian dimension, it only researched past human rights violations between 1974 and 1999. Again, the underdevelopment of judicial arrangement needs emphasizing here. On the one hand, domestic laws needed to be created to deal with past wrongs in East Timor. On the other hand, the possibilities of certain international tribunals or other kinds of resolution must be sought to confront the past wrongs under the Indonesian regime (Shuto 2004).

Developing capacities

Capacity development is a way to nurture the culture of peace and justice as an aspect of peacebuilding. Its key term is sustainability and it takes the forms of education, development, military conversion, and research and evaluation. A case study can be found in the grassroots

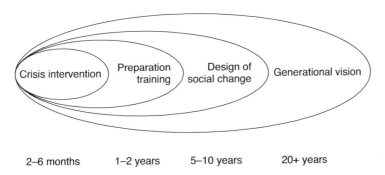

2–6 months   1–2 years   5–10 years   20+ years

Figure 22.1 The time dimension in peacebuilding
Source: Lederach (1997: 77).

peacebuilding initiatives in post-civil war Guatemala. At the end of the 36-year civil war in 1996, the Guatemalan Catholic Church investigated the war violence and started a Trauma Healing Project to respond to the victims. Although the project failed to provide a sufficient number of trained professional facilitators, the use of non-professionals for self-help groups consequently succeeded in empowering the local Mayan people and sustaining the project in terms of both funding and personnel. In addition, there was a consultative project by the UN and Organization of American States (OAS) to gather civil society and governmental leaders to envision a peaceful society. They were divided into six groups and envisioned the future Guatemalan society in the form of small-group consensus conference. The project succeeded in bringing together a variety of people, including former opponents during the war, for the dialogue focused on the common future (Hart 2005).

Strategic 'when': time dimension of peacebuilding

For those living far from armed conflict, violence seems to explode suddenly, when the media starts to cover stories. A need for a 'quick fix' is felt strongly and response to conflict tends to be reactive, short-term and concentrated. Peacebuilding is not that

simple; as the brief description above shows, it must be multi-dimensional, with strategically coordinated operations for almost all aspects of social interaction, from emergent supply of foods and medicine to long-term initiative for trauma healing. Therefore, peace missions need to be coordinated in terms of chronology as well, to ensure the appropriate timing and duration for each activity to be most effective.

Lederach's nested diagram of timeframe is helpful (see Figure 22.1). It starts with the left side, the phase of crisis intervention. It is focused on crisis, a short-term involvement (up to six months) before violence takes place. For example, many conflict transformation practitioners worked at the national election of South Africa in 1994, trying to prevent the public unrest from growing into widespread rioting.

The next step is the preparation and training phase, focused on people, to educate relational skills in one or two years. Relevant training may include both prescriptive and elicitive approaches to conflict transformation. The prescriptive approach is a way to teach a formulated model of communication and mediation by educated professional practitioners, often from abroad. The elicitive approach is more focused on deriving a conflict transformation model from the local context by empowering the local people to through facilitated workshops. Although there is a critical tension between the two approaches, successful training cannot be purely prescriptive or purely elicitive. Prescriptive inputs help the local people to see and reshape the reality with a different view, while elicitive workshops help the trainers respect the local culture as a basis of sustainable practices of conflict transformation (Lederach 1995).

The case of the Majola region in South Africa shows that these two approaches can work hand in hand. When the Mennonite Central Committee (MCC), a North American faith-based relief organization, started the peacebuilding effort in the region, many local people were highly distrustful toward 'outsiders', an attitude that confronted the Mennonite workers. Flexibly enough, however, the MCC 'decided to abandon their original plans for the meeting and put the process where it belonged – in the hands of the people'. By eliciting and satisfying the primary needs of the local people, that was a promise of long-term commitment; and MCC obtained their trust and allowed them to prioritize the issues. The first meeting mainly focused on intensive listening to the stories for trauma healing, and it was the third meeting, the last one, that provided the local Peace Committee members with prescriptive skills of conflict resolution, restorative justice, mediation and trauma healing (Conflict Transformation Working Group 2002: 17).

The right side of the figure shows the longest phase, to envision a peaceful future in generational terms. This phase is focused on *vision*, and not only encourages the conflicted society to become positive about the future, but also seeks to make the collaborative experience easier. As the Guatemalan case showed earlier, it is easier for the divided society to work together when it seeks the common ground for the direction of future life, rather than when it decides whether the past wrongs should be punished or pardoned. The very activity

of searching for common ground is a practice of constructive conflict transformation.

Between the short and long terms comes the middle-term phase of designing social change, within a five- to ten-year timeframe. The purpose of this phase is to focus on developing institutions, a bridge between the short-term experience and long-term vision. The spiral of discernment, experiment, reflection and evaluation overall characterizes this phase. Various capacities, such as funding, dispute system design, violence prediction, cultural resources for peace, and 'flex' funds for peace innovation, need to be developed during this phase (Lederach 1997: 114–15).

Strategic 'who': actors and approaches of peacebuilding

Concerning the actors of peacebuilding, the people in the conflicted society are often categorized into three parts. The top level consists of 'government, big business, and religious leadership in national and international arenas'. The middle range includes 'leaders of national and regional organizations and businesses'. The grass-roots level holds various local community organizations such as youth, women, business and religion (Schirch 2004: 71; Lederach 1997: 39).

Typically, the post-conflict peacebuilding takes the form of a top-down strategy, with concentration on the top-level leaders and their behaviours. No doubt they have a profound impact on the destiny of the conflict, but it is also true that top-led peacebuilding has various problems. One of them is an issue of identity and representation. The status of a top leader is based on the fact that she or he represents a certain group of people in society. The collective identity of the people, typically based on either ethnicity or religion, is attached to the leader. The more the conflict is fuelled by ethnic or religious cleavage, the harder it becomes for the top leader to overcome the collective identity that she or he represents.

The top-down approach poses another dilemma on the grassroots level, too. This approach enables the top level to obtain more information and more comprehensive understanding of the situation. The decisions are made based upon this information, but those who are likely to be most affected by the decision are not the top leaders but the grassroots people who themselves have very limited access to information and bird's-eye understanding. The dilemma takes place here; the powerful decides the future direction even before the powerless start forming their opinions. In terms of the typical process of peacebuilding from ceasefire and peace accord to the forma-tion of transitional government, to general election, the grassroots level cannot parti-cipate in the process until the electoral preparation takes place. By being excluded from the process, citizens at the grassroots level are likely to be uninvolved, without the sense of belonging, responsibility and ownership.

This dilemma is problematic not only for the grassroots level, but also for the top level. Because of exclusion, the local people tend to put too much expectation and pressure on the top leaders. Various requests may be made and some of them can be contradic-tory and irreconcilable. This could put the top leaders in a difficult position, making negotiation and compromise difficult, and they could in addition suffer from help-lessness and an identity crisis.

Lederach comments on these dilemmas by suggesting the organic function of the middle range. He calls this 'the web approach', named after the process that a spider uses in making a web, and affirms that the centre of constructive social change is the web of relationships. In order to bridge and integrate the various peace operations on the top and grassroots levels,

the middle-range leaders need to start, strengthen and solidify the web of relation-ships. In other words, the role of the middle-range leaders is not to make resolu-tions, but, rather, to create the space of relationships where people can keep on making resolutions (Lederach 2005: 75–86).

A case can be found in the Inter-religious Council of Sierra Leone (ICSR), organized by Muslim and Christian leaders in 1997. ICSR succeeded in playing a catalytic role of bridging – between the government, the Revolutionary United Front (RUF) rebels, and the civil society, by maintaining both neutrality and moral authority in 'a country where religion and prayer play an important role in many people's lives' (Conflict Transformation Working Group 2002: 11). In other words, the reassuring presence of the ICSR facilitated creation of a social space where all the groups could function in a shared climate of trust and respect, rather than suspicion and hostility.

Future development: toward institutionalization of reconciliation

Conflict prevention and peacebuilding have become popular terms among researchers and practitioners in international coopera-tion and development. Many universities offer programmes and courses on peace and conflict studies, and a number of books, research reports and conferences have been offered since the early 1990s. In place of a conclusion, I would like to take a brief look at the conciliatory aspect of peace opera-tions in relation to the roles of religion in peacebuilding.

As the experiences and researches of peacebuilding advance, there seems to be a clear tendency to focus more on technical processes to shift the state of civil war to that of orderly social interaction. Various actors in international relations, such as state governments, international organizations and civil society organizations, are involved in funding and evaluation, as well as the actual programmes, of peacebuilding missions. Specific projects are required to make tangible achievement that enables analytical evaluation.

For example, Toshiya Hoshino implies there is a difficulty in promoting conflict prevention, primarily because the successful result of conflict prevention, i.e., the non-existence of conflict, can hardly be proven to be the tangible achievement. He also points out that the Japanese involvement in peacebuilding is mainly based on the idea of development assistance, which is not only familiar with the past Japanese experiences in international cooperation, but also relatively easy to obtain visible outcomes. He suggests that the idea of development assistance should be integrated into a more comprehensive framework of peacebuilding, along with the ideas of peacekeeping, disarmament, rule of law and reconciliation. Not only the tangible achievement in the relatively short term, but also the longer-term programmes concerning the structural change of society must be considered for sustainable peace (Hoshino 2003).

It seems that Lederach's diagram on reconciliation is helpful to respond to Hoshino's concern, as a way to view peacebuilding based on the idea of reconciliation (see Figure 22.2). The nested circles at the centre indicate the dimensions of peacebuilding, while the four squares at the corners show specific aspects of programmes.

The first dimension is to define a specific agenda and tasks. To do that, attention needs to be paid to people, social structure and processes, and many emergent issues, such as disarmament, recovery of social order, and creation of employment, may arise.

The second dimension is to establish the concrete procedure of transition with technical logistics. For example, in order to enable the refugees to return, the roads and railways need to be repaired, process of re-settlement need to be facilitated, and daily lives need to be supported. Without this logistical coordination, hastened return of refugees could become a new concern: creation of another internally displaced people.

The third dimension is to put specific transition into the process of social and structural transformation. For example, the transitional programme for disarmament sometimes takes the form of exchanging firearms with food or money. But this approach may not be successful in a situation where having weapons guarantees certain social status, or the local people, as guards, actually live by their possession and use of weapons. The problem is that the society is structured in such a way that it is meaningful for the people to arm themselves. In such a case, it is important to analyse the social meaning and function of armament, and connect disarmament and social change by giving alternatives, such as a provision of mental care and occupational training in the secured dormitories.

The fourth dimension involves reconciliation, i.e., the restoration of relationships. Reconciliation is dialectic in the sense that it is both an end and a process at the same time. It is not only a result of certain activity but also a beginning of making something new. As the case of MCC's involvement in the Majola region in South Africa (above) shows, transformational and reconciliatory dimensions, such as trauma healing, can be the top priority for the local population.

The four squares of peacebuilding aspects are related to these four dimensions. In many cases, when peacebuilding is viewed mainly in agenda and transition dimensions, the focused areas are mostly socio-political and socio-economic. But once we further highlight the dimensions of transformation and reconciliation, psychological and

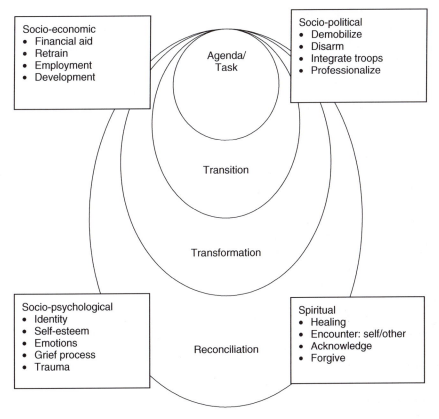

Figure 22.2 The web of reconciliation
Source: Herr and Herr (1998: 187).

spiritual areas come into perspective. For example, DDR is a significant component of peacebuilding, but it cannot cover all the process of reintegration of the former soldiers, especially the psychological aspects. Research on the mental health issues in peacebuilding seems relatively limited, as compared with security and development issues (Kita 2005). In addition, the spiritual aspects cannot be ignored, because it matters when it comes to relating with others (including former enemies), giving and receiving forgiveness, healing past wounds, while the psychological aspect focuses more on the condition and healing of the individual self.

The essence of institutionalization of reconciliation seems to depend on how the social space, which enables restoration

of the web of relationships, can be created. In such a social space, both individuals and groups acknowledge the past, grieve the experience of losses, accept the experiences of pain, confess the past wrongs, and restore broken relationships.

The role of religion in the field of conflict prevention and peacebuilding arises here. As Scott Thomas has suggested, 'in most cultures over the millennia there has been a complementary relationship between healing and religion, and it was their separation that became characteristic of modernity, which is only now being overcome as a part of peacebuilding and conflict resolution' (Thomas 2005: 109). His argument can be expanded to include other aspects such as forgiveness and reconciliation.

It should be noted, however, that the potential contribution of religion in the field of reconciliation and peacebuilding should not be taken as a matter of course. For example, Rodney Petersen reflects on the Christian tradition of forgiveness and points out that forgiveness was privatized in two ways as Christendom took shape in Europe. First, as the church was institutionalized into an active element of statecraft, forgiveness was spiritualized as a matter of inner hearts. Second, as the doctrines of Christian faith were separated from social ethics, forgiveness was individualized as a matter of believer's personal relationship with God. Then another concept, retribution, replaced forgiveness as the tool for maintaining social order. It was in the twentieth century that the public aspect of forgiveness came to be revisited as a response to the massive violation of human dignity such as the Holocaust and apartheid, in which public forgiveness was regarded as the only possible way to constructive future (Helmick and Petersen 2001: 3–25).

According to Thomas, the resurgence of religion in the field of conflict prevention and peacebuilding does not, or should not, stay in the development of multitrack diplomacy, which 'seems to be based on Enlightenment assumptions regarding universal rationality, without any regard for the way rationality may be dependent on different cultural or religious traditions, nor the possibility that different tracks may use different forms of moral reasoning' (Thomas 2005: 178). Instead, he advocates the rise of 'faith-based diplomacy' as a way of bringing religion back to international relations. Faith-based diplomacy 'is rooted in an active integration of faith and life' (Thomas 2005: 183), focused on the transformations of individual and communal lives.

The argument of Luc Reychler seems to support Thomas's bold claim. While acknowledging that religion has played some negative roles in conflict dynamics, either as conflict parties or bystanders,

Reychler recognizes the positive side of religion in both peacemaking and peacebuilding. He especially emphasizes the role of religious organizations in the area of 'field-diplomacy', along with other functions of 'traditional diplomatic efforts' and 'track II' peacemaking (namely, multitrack diplomacy). The 'field-diplomacy' is defined as 'sending non-governmental teams to conflict areas, for an extended period, to stimulate and support local initiatives for conflict prevention' (Reychler 1997). Organizations such as Witness for Peace, Peace Brigade International, International Alert, Search for Common Ground, and Christian Peacemakers Team can be raised.

A possible point of future development emerges here. While the majority of recent studies on conflict prevention and peacebuilding are orientated to the policy side to catch up the peacebuilding praxis, the rise of faith-based diplomacy can provide an alternative by recognizing 'the value of multiple forms of rationality', 'the narrative structure of community formation', 'the distinctive identities of communities grounded in particular cultural and religious traditions', and the corporate response to conflicts through the community of shared convictions (Thomas 2005: 187–9). It can be expected that religious leaders and faith-based organizations engage not only in secular activities of peacebuilding with inner religious motivation, but also in the radical attainment of discipleship (reconnecting of faith and life, theology and ethics), which enables 'the acceptance of the inherent risk of stepping into the mystery of the unknown that lies beyond the far too familiar landscape of violence' (Lederach 2005: 5).

Bibliography

Conflict Transformation Working Group (2002) 'Building peace from the ground up: A call to the UN for stronger collaboration with civil society', http://www.globalpolicy.org/ngos/aid/2002/0802buildingpeace.pdf, accessed 3 November 2006.

Coward, H. and Smith, G. (eds) (2004) *Religion and Peacebuilding*, Albany, NY: State University of New York Press.

Galtung, J. (1975) 'Three approaches to peace: Peacekeeping, peacemaking and peacebuilding', in J. Galtung, *Peace, War and Defense: Essays in Peace Research*, Vol. 2, Copenhagen: Christian Ejlers, pp. 282–304.

Hart, J. (2005) 'Grassroots peacebuilding in post-civil war Guatemala: Three models of hope', *Mennonite Life*, 60, 1, http://raven.bethelks.edu/mennonitelife/2005Mar/hart.php, accessed 7 January 2007.

Hehir, J. Bryan (1995) 'Intervention: From theories to cases', *Ethics and International Affairs*, 9, pp. 1–13.

Helmick, R. and Petersen, R. (eds) (2001) *Forgiveness and Reconciliation: Religion, Public Policy, and Conflict Transformation*, Radnor, PA: Templeton Foundation Press.

Herr, R. and Herr, J. Z. (eds) (1998) *Transforming Violence: Linking Local and Global Peacemaking*, Scottdale, PA: Herald Press.

Hoshino, T. (2003) 'Between conflict prevention and peacebuilding', in the Research Report commissioned by the Ministry of Foreign Affairs, *Conflict Prevention* (in Japanese), Tokyo: Japan Institute of International Affairs, pp. 1–5.

Kita, E. (2005) *The Role of Mental Health during and after Conflict* (in Japanese), Tokyo: Japan International Cooperation Agency.

Knight, W. A. (2003) 'Evaluating recent trends in peacebuilding research', *International Relations of the Asia-Pacific*, 3, 2, pp. 241–64.

Kurimoto, H. (2004) 'Peace mediation of IGAD: Overview and analysis', in the Research Report commissioned by the Ministry of Foreign Affairs, *Possibilities and Trends of Regional Cooperation in Sub-Saharan Africa* (in Japanese), Tokyo: Japan Institute of International Affairs, pp. 45–56.

Lederach, J. Paul (1995) *Preparing for Peace: Conflict Transformation across Cultures*, Syracuse, NY: Syracuse University Press.

Lederach, J. Paul (1997) *Building Peace: Sustainable Reconciliation in Divided Societies*, Washington, DC: United States Institute of Peace Press.

Lederach, J. Paul (2005) *The Moral Imagination: The Art and Soul of Building Peace*, New York: Oxford University Press.

Mogami, T. (2006) *International Organization* (in Japanese), 2nd edn, Tokyo: University of Tokyo Press.

Reychler, L. (1997) 'Religion and conflict', *International Journal of Peace Studies*, 2 (1), http://www.gmu.edu/academic/ijps/vol2_1/Reyschler.htm, accessed 8 December 2006.

Roberts, A. and Kingsbury, B. (eds) (1993) *United Nations, Divided World: The UN's Roles in International Relations*, 2nd edn, Oxford: Oxford University Press.

Sadataka, A. (2005) *Religion of Hatred: The Sacred Hatred in Judaism, Christianity and Islam* (in Japanese), Tokyo: Yosen-sha.

Schirch, L. (2004) *The Little Book of Strategic Peacebuilding Intercourse*, Pennsylvania: Good Books.

Shenk, W. (2006) 'Forming disciples who think and act like Jesus', *Courier*, 4, pp. 4–5.

Shinoda, H. (2002) 'Re-considering the concept of peace-building from strategic perspectives on international peace operations' (in Japanese), *Hiroshima Peace Science*, 24, pp. 21–45.

Shuto, M. (2004) 'Issues in nation-building and conflict prevention in East Timor', in the Research Report commissioned by the Ministry of Foreign Affairs, *Conflict Prevention* (in Japanese), Tokyo: Japan Institute of International Affairs, pp. 37–50.

Stockholm International Peace Research Institute (SIPRI) (2005) *SIPRI Yearbook 2005: Armaments, Disarmament and International Security*, Oxford: Oxford University Press.

The Millennium World Peace Summit of Religious and Spiritual Leaders (2000) 'Commitment to global peace', http://www.millenniumpeacesummit.com/resources/nr/Commitment to Global Peace.pdf, accessed 11 November 2006.

Thomas, S. (2005) *The Global Resurgence of Religion and the Transformation of International Relations: The Struggle for the Soul of the Twenty-first Century*, New York: Palgrave Macmillan.

23

Religion and women

Canadian women's religious volunteering: Compassion, connections and comparisons

Brenda O'Neill[1]

The explosion of interest in the concept of social capital has refocused attention within the political behaviour field of political science on the importance of the private aspects of life, an emphasis long ago adopted and encouraged by feminist researchers in the area (Vickers 1997). One result of this expanded focus is increased interest in religious beliefs and activity and their relevance for political behaviour. As such, this chapter examines the religious volunteering of women as an element of social capital and its relevance for women's political engagement. The importance of religious beliefs and activity in women's lives has been well documented. Women are more likely to report regular religious attendance than men. Sidney Verba *et al.* (1995), for example, found that 55% of American women in the 1990 Citizen Participation Study reported that they attended church services regularly compared to 43% of men. While only 20% of all Canadians aged 15 and over in 1999 reported 'some kind of religious activity on a weekly basis', 23% of women compared with 17% of men did the same (Statistics Canada 2001). Elsewhere I report on the greater relevance of religious values in shaping Canadian women's political opinions (O'Neill 2001). Thus, religious

beliefs play a particularly important role in shaping women's political opinions and behaviour, especially when compared to men, and are deserving of attention. Yet, as noted by Verba *et al.*, 'What is striking … is that arena in which women are clearly more active than men is one that is rarely mentioned in discussions of gender differences in participation: religious institutions' (Verba *et al.* 1995: 257–259).

The importance of religious volunteering as a source of social capital, and through it political participation, has also been documented. High rates of formal volunteering in North America have been partially explained by religious practice (Greeley 1997; Park and Smith 2000; Wuthnow 1991). Very little of this work, however, focuses exclusively on women's religious volunteering and its importance for political participation (Burns *et al.* 2001; Verba *et al.* 1995). American survey evidence makes clear that women's religious volunteering continues to account for a large portion of women's total volunteering (Burns *et al.* 2001). This chapter investigates the relationship between women's participation in religious organizations and the formation of social capital. It is important also to understand whether, if at all, and how that social capital is translated into political participation. That many religious institutions have played an important role in perpetuating gender role stereotypes, in restricting women to a limited and narrow set of responsibilities within their hierarchies, and in advancing policies that tear into the very fabric of the push for women's rights over the past decades is unchallengeable. Yet research has come to identify the various ways in which women's agency allows them to work and develop opportunities, albeit often limited, within religious institutions (Woodhead 2001). That so many women continue to devote their energies and talents to these very organizations demands the attention of social scientists to better understand the public and private consequences of that participation.

Religious volunteering, social capital and political participation

According to Putnam, social capital consists of social networks and associated norms of reciprocity (Putnam 2001: 41). Social capital, then, is made up of both instrumental (group involvement and social networks) and affective (norms of reciprocity and trust) components. Two elements of social capital are important for our understanding of its role in the political system: the mechanisms by which it is created, and its effects on other processes and institutions. While the former provides insight into the particular sources of social capital, the latter provides it on the nature of political participation in modern democracies. Both can be examined for the degree to which they vary across different groups in modern societies. Putnam was clear in identifying that social capital provides both public and private returns, although much emphasis has subsequently been placed on the public side (Putnam 2001: 41). He was also clear in

the distinction between bridging and bonding social capital. Bridging social capital brings people into contact with those who are different from themselves, while bonding leads to stronger ties with members of one's own group. The former has positive benefits for democracy because it is likely to increase levels of trust and strengthen ties across groups. The latter introduces negative externalities in light of the increased tension between members and non-members of the group (i.e., enhances feelings of us versus them). As he made clear, however, 'bonding and bridging are not "either–or" categories into which social networks can be neatly divided, but "more-or-less" dimensions along which we can compare different forms of social capital' (Putnam 2000: 23).

These concepts provide a framework for examining women's religious volunteering. Women's participation in religious organizations can be examined for both its private and public benefits and for the degree to which it develops bridging and bonding capital. Putnam suggests that faith communities are the single most important repository of social capital in the United States (Putnam 2000: 66). These organizations support a wide range of social activities and encourage the development of skills, norms and interests that encourage civic engagement beyond the congregation. According to Putnam, 'religious people are unusually active social capitalists' (Putnam 2000: 67). Religious volunteers have more social connections, are involved in more organizations, and are more civically and politically engaged (Putnam 2000: 66–67). Although religious involvement has decreased over the past few decades, largely as a result of a decline among younger generations, it remains an important source of social capital in many societies.

Research has shown that religious attendance encourages the development of shared community values and, as such, can contribute to the development of social capital and public benefits in turn. Putnam (2000) identifies the connection between religious attendance and volunteering, both secular and religious, and to the donation of time and money to activities beyond those of religious organizations. As identified by Halman and Pettersson, 'religious beliefs are assumed to produce an ethos which is trusting, altruistic and cooperative. ... Religion is also considered a main reason to refrain from pure self-interest' (Halman and Pettersson 2001: 69). Coleman similarly identifies religious beliefs as key factors moving individuals away from self-interest and toward increasing attention devoted to the interests of others (Coleman 1990: 320). Secular resources are important for political participation but the church can encourage participation through direct recruitment for political activity or indirectly by establishing expectations or a 'social contagion' of political activity (Djupe and Grant 2001). Park and Smith suggest that it is less the strength of religious commitment that is a defining factor for volunteering than participation in church activities that leads to church and non-church volunteering (Park and Smith 2000). Additionally André Blais et al. have identified religiosity as a determinant of voter turnout, either by its emphasis on the importance of duty or because of its promotion of community (Blais et al. 2004).

Religiosity increases volunteering in the local community because 'participation in the religious sphere brings with it the development of skills and attitudes reflective of helping others' (Park and Smith 2000: 273). The development of skills among religious volunteers highlights the private benefits that can accrue from such activity.

American research has also shown that many of these generalizations vary across religious groups – namely Protestants and Catholics versus Evangelicals (Wuthnow 1999). Others emphasize differences

between Catholics and Protestants, showing that Catholics are less likely to spend time on church-based activity (Verba et al. 1995: 246). This result stems from the fact that many Protestant churches are smaller than Catholic churches, that they involve greater lay participation in the liturgy, and because greater authority is vested in the membership rather than in the Church hierarchy (Verba et al. 1995: 321). Greeley (1997) finds similar results in a comparison of Canadian Catholics and Protestants. Differences across denominations are also to be found in the degree to which participation in wider community-building efforts are encouraged rather than limited to the religious community itself. In the United States, Putnam identifies evangelical denominations as distinct for the exclusiveness of their volunteering within the congregation (Putnam 2000). The public benefits, or positive externalities, related to religious volunteering should not be assumed to be consistent across all religious communities.

Gender and religious volunteering

The rationale for paying particular attention to women's religious volunteering stems from long-standing evidence of women's greater religiosity. Women are much more likely to belong to a religious organization, to attend services, more likely to volunteer their services to the organization, and to contribute money to it although in smaller amounts than men (Burns et al. 2001: 89; Verba et al. 1995: 259). This pattern holds despite the fact that among those who are religiously active, men are more likely than women to hold lay positions of authority within religious organizational hierarchies (Burns et al. 2001: 89). Much religious doctrine has similarly prescribed a clear gender division of labour: 'breadwinner and provider for males, and moral and religious nurturer for females' (Roof 1993: 221–222). Mothers have traditionally played an important role in their children's religious upbringing. Research suggests that 'When couples of different religions marry or cohabit, the women tend to raise the children in their own tradition, including not having any religion' (Bibby 1997: 26). These differences are also revealed when women and men are asked about their religious volunteering. While women and men are equally likely to provide civic or charitable reasons to explain their volunteering, women are more likely to identify religious reasons for their activity. According to such women, religious volunteering provides unique opportunities: it allows them to affirm their faith and to further the goals of their religion (Burns *et al.* 2001: 106).

Strong critiques of women's involvement in religious organizations have nevertheless been mounted. According to Linda Woodhead, three explanations are often brought forward to explain gendered patterns of religious belief and participation:

- Women's structural locations in society, that is, religious institutions are gendered due to the division of labour.
- Women are differently socialized – the 'ethic of care' leads to their greater religiosity.
- Women's religious involvement is a compensatory response to their material and social deprivation.
    (Woodhead 2001: 73)

Implicit in such arguments is the notion that women's religious involvement does little to challenge the gender status quo; participation in this arena reinforces women's traditional roles of caring for the home and family, and mitigates women's subordinate position in society and the home. She notes, however, that very little

empirical work has tested these hypotheses, and that the sources of the distinctiveness remain unclear. Notwithstanding the dearth of empirical research, religious institutions have been highlighted by much feminist work as the quintessential oppressive patriarchal institutions and as key challenges to the progressive feminist project of freeing women from the binds of the traditional roles they ascribe to women as mothers and homemakers (Manning 1999). Moreover, the role of much organized religion in fighting against reproductive and sexual freedom has necessarily pitched feminists against religious organizations.

There are signs, however, that this rejection of religious organizations is softening. Woodhead identifies an important shift in third-wave feminism thought that challenges a too heavy reliance on patriarchy as a concept for examining complex organizations such as religious organizations and on a too strong willingness to argue that women who remain within religious organizations are suffering from 'false consciousness' (Woodhead 2001: 69). Similarly Manning has discovered that religious conservative women in the United States grapple with feminism in much the same way as non-religious women and work to blend modern and traditional elements in their lives (Manning 1999). The shift has resulted in a fuller appreciation of the various ways in which women can benefit from their religious involvement, and underscores women's individual agency. As an example of such research, Ozarak found that women tend to emphasize the individual benefits derived from their religiosity when queried about their religious involvement. Within Christian churches, she found that women

> emphasized the centrality of caring and community to their religious experience, and remain in the churches because they find such qualities there. … Most of the women

in this study recognized that by hierarchical social standards, organized religion does not treat them as well as it might. ... But in absolute terms, they do not see themselves as disenfranchised. The power of connection and relationship, most essential to their own views of the faith experience, is available to them in abundance.

(Ozorak 1996: 27)

Others highlight that many women in churches are working from within to change those elements of the organization that they find problematic, that is, 'defecting in place' (Winter *et al.* 1994, cited in Woodhead 2001: 73–74).

Research suggests that not all women appear to be equally attracted to religious volunteering. For example, Wuthnow's research identifies a stronger relationship between civic engagement and attendance for married rather than single Catholic women and for women with children. He concludes that this reflects the traditional division of labour in many Catholic families where 'mothers are more likely to attend church than fathers and to take responsibility for the religious upbringing of children' (Wuthnow 1991: 345). Labour force participation also plays a role in shaping women's religious volunteering. According to Roof,

Working women obviously have less time to devote to religious activities – a factor that was sometimes mentioned in our interviews. But more is involved than just time considerations. As the first generation of women to work and pursue careers in great numbers, they also find social and psychological benefits from working that individuals in the past often derived from religious involvement.

(Roof 1993: 221)

Putnam argues that women's entry into the workforce has two opposing effects on community involvement in that 'it *increases opportunity* for making new connections and getting involved, while at the same time it *decreases time* available for exploring these opportunities' (Putnam 2000: 294). The family also appears to play an important role in shaping women's religious volunteering, for as the traditionally family unit declines, so too does participation in churches. Single women, single professional women, and professional women are equally unlikely to be attracted to mainline congregations (Marler 1995 as cited in Woodhead 2001: 75). Hertel argues that for women the combination of marriage and work creates the single biggest challenge to organized religions (Hertel 1995 as cited in Woodhead 2001: 75).

The puzzle, then, is this: how to reconcile the largely positive benefits identified with religious volunteering in the social capital literature with the largely negative view that dominates discussion of women's participation in religious organizations in feminist literature. Putnam's concepts, public versus private benefits and bridging versus bonding social capital, are the tools employed to investigate this puzzle. More specifically, the chapter seeks to better understand the benefits derived from women's religious volunteering and the nature of the social capital that springs from this particular form of volunteering.

It is important to note, however, that the reference point adopted here for comparing women's religious volunteering is women who volunteer in other types of organizations rather than men who volunteer for religious organizations. The comparison between women volunteers allows for an assessment of the benefits derived from, and the nature of the capital derived in, various contexts, a necessary step to evaluating the degree to which women are effectively limited by their choice to volunteer for religious organizations. In this vein, the nature of the private returns to religious volunteering is particularly interesting because it may provide greater understanding of women's participation in organizations that have been historically less than supportive of women's equality generally, and within their own organizations specifically. The public benefits of the social capital developed through women's religious volunteering are also important; specifically, the distinction between bridging and bonding capital, for it allows for a clearer picture of the degree to which women's religious volunteering limits women's connections with others. A final set of questions deals with the transference of the social capital created by religious volunteering to political participation. Does women's religious volunteering correspond with levels of political participation equal to that found among women who volunteer for other organizations? Or put differently, does religious volunteering encourage political engagement to the same degree as other forms of volunteering?

Data and methods

The data come from the 2000 National Survey of Giving, Volunteering and Participating (NSGVP).[2] The survey provides an investigation into the volunteering activities of Canadians and, although more limited, information on their political activities. The survey includes a sample of 8,302 women.[3]

Survey respondents were asked whether they had undertaken a number of volunteer activities in an unpaid capacity for organizations between October 1999 and September 2000 and, if so, the nature of those activities. Among the women included in the survey, 28% reported volunteering in some manner over the past year. Of these, roughly one in four reported that a share of this volunteering occurred within religious organizations. This level of volunteering ties religious

organizations with culture and recreation organizations as the second most common to which women volunteer their time, surpassed only by social services organizations. It also appears that women who volunteer for religious organizations are significantly more likely to volunteer overall; while they report volunteering for 2.0 organizations on average, the remaining women volunteers indicate that they volunteer with 1.6 organizations on average (see Table 23.1). Given the greater number of organizations to which women religious volunteers donate their skills and time, they also report a significantly higher number of hours devoted to all volunteering than other women volunteers: 182 to 147 hours in the last year. On the surface, then, it would appear that women's religious volunteering forms a key component of women's volunteering, and is associated with higher levels of volunteering overall compared to other types of volunteering.

Women who volunteer for religious organizations devote their time to a wide variety of organizations beyond religious organizations, as shown in Table 23.1. Women in the survey were allowed to provide detailed information on the number of events in up to three separate organizations to which they donated their time. The lower half of Table 23.1 provides a comparison of this information between non-religious and religious volunteers net of their religious volunteering. The results suggest that women religious volunteers involve themselves in as wide a set of organizations as non-religious volunteers. If differences are evident, it is in the finding that religious volunteers are more attracted to volunteering in the education and research sectors and less to culture and recreation than non-religious volunteers. This provides some evidence that the social capital generated among women religious volunteers is as much bridging as bonding, at least when compared with other women volunteers, given that they

Table 23.1 Women's volunteering (%)

	Religious volunteers	All other volunteers
Number of organizations★★	2.02	1.64
Number of hours★★	182.43	146.51
N	(549)	(1,787)
Comparison of non-religious volunteering		
Social services	24.5	24.8
Culture and recreation	16.9	20.3
Education and research	24.0	18.0
Health	18.7	17.4
Development and housing	6.3	5.8
Law, advocacy and politics	2.8	3.7
Environment	2.3	3.2
Philanthropic intermediaries and volunteering	1.8	3.2
Business and professional	2.3	2.1
International	0.1	1.4

Notes: ★★ differences significant at $p < 0.01$. Percentages refer to share of volunteers found within each category (allows up to three organizations per volunteer).

do not appear to restrict their volunteering activities to religious organizations.

An examination of the organizations that women volunteers participate in or are members of, apart from their volunteering activities, reinforces this conclusion (results not shown). Respondents were asked about their participation in a dozen organizations ranging from professional associations to cultural organizations. The data suggest that there is little difference in the rates of participation for both groups of volunteers. The few that were apparent were in the lower rate of participation of religious volunteers in sports and recreation groups (21.4% compared to 28.4% for all other volunteers) and their higher rate of participation in religious–affiliated groups (65.5% compared with 16.2% for all volunteers). When comparing the share in each group that belongs to at least one of the groups examined, however, the results reveal that a greater share of religious volunteers are 'civic participants': 85% of religious volunteers participate in at least one of the listed groups compared with 68% of other volunteers. Much of this result is due, however, to the greater share of religious volunteers who participate in

religious–affiliated groups. Once this participation is removed, the two groups become indistinguishable in their civic participation. At the very least, the data suggest that religious volunteers are no less connected to various organizations in the community than other volunteers and that bridging as well as bonding capital has an equal capacity to be created amongst them.

How do women who volunteer for religious organizations differ from women who volunteer in other types of organizations? Table 23.2 provides a comparison of socio-demographic characteristics for the two groups of women. Not surprisingly, women who volunteer for religious organizations are significantly older than other women volunteers, with a majority falling in the 45 and older category. They are also more likely to be married. The difference in age is likely to be a factor in the finding that women religious volunteers are less likely to have children under 18 living in the home. These findings match those found elsewhere and correspond with findings regarding women's religiosity more generally. Income, both personal and family, appears to matter little in differentiating the two groups of volunteers,

Table 23.2 Comparing women volunteers (%)

	Religious volunteers	Other volunteers
Age★★★		
Less than 45	45.9	61.5
45 years and older	54.1	38.5
Household and personal income		
Household income less than $60,000	59.5	54.2
Personal income less than $40,000	81.3	78.4
Education★★		
Less than high school	18.4	18.5
High school	17.9	17.8
Some post-secondary	6.2	11.4
Post-secondary diploma or degree	57.5	52.4
Marital status★★★		
Married/common law	69.8	62.7
Single/never married	17.1	25.0
Widow	6.9	4.5
Separated/divorced	6.2	7.7
Children★		
Children under 18 in the home★	31.5	36.9
Employment status★★		
Employed	59.6	63.5
Unemployed	2.6	4.5
Not in labour force	37.9	31.9
Full- versus part-time employment★		
Part-time	38.1	31.7
Religious affiliation★★★		
No religious affiliation	4.3	26.9
Roman Catholic	27.0	38.8
Protestant	63.0	30.8
Other religious affiliation	5.6	3.4
Immigrant status★★		
Born outside of Canada	17.7	13.2
Length of time in community★★		
New to community (5 years or less)	18.8	25.6
N	(549)	(1,787)

Notes: Entries are percentages. ★★★ indicates $p < 0.001$; ★★ indicates $p < 0.01$; ★ indicates $p < 0.05$ across all categories.

although, perhaps somewhat surprisingly, women religious volunteers are as educated as other volunteers. Although the number of women religious volunteers holding a post-secondary degree or diploma is somewhat higher than the share among other women volunteers, this difference may reflect the age difference between the two groups.

Women who volunteer for religious organizations are less likely to be in the labour force than other volunteers, although those who are employed outside the home are somewhat more likely to be employed part-time rather than full-time. This likely reflects the increased importance placed on family, and women's consequent likelihood of staying home to care for children. Not surprisingly, women who volunteer for religious organizations are more likely to hold a religious affiliation than other women volunteers, and dominant

affiliation among the former group is
Protestant by a ratio of more than two to
one to the next largest group, Roman
Catholic. The 2001 Canadian Census indicates that 43.2% of Canadians identify as
Roman Catholic, 28.5% as Protestant, 12.1%
indicate an affiliation with other religions,
and 12.1 % have no religious affiliation
(Census data available at http://www.
statscan.ca). Thus, the results presented here
reinforce those presented elsewhere of the

greater propensity for volunteering amongst
Protestants compared to Roman Catholics.
Finally, women who volunteer for religious
organizations are more likely to have been
born outside of Canada, although they are
less likely than other women volunteers to
be new to the community.

The next step is to evaluate which of
these characteristics play an independent
role in shaping the likelihood of volunteering for both groups (see Table 23.3). The

Table 23.3 Determinants of women's religious volunteering

Independent variables	Religious volunteers	Other volunteers
Religiosity		
High attendance	**2.399★★★**	0.050
Religion very important	**0.849★★★**	−0.091
Religious identity		
Protestant	**1.149★★★**	**0.151★**
Other	0.259	**−0.339★**
No religion	0.292	**0.205★**
Socio-demographic characteristics		
Education	**0.229★★★**	**0.157★★★**
Household income	0.095	**0.216★★★**
Age	0.043	0.019
Single/not married	−0.253	**0.202★**
Widowed	**−0.476★**	−0.054
Separated/divorced	**−0.415★**	0.073
Children in the home	−0.053	**0.347★★★**
Immigrant	−0.149	**−0.235★★★**
Resident in community 5 years or less	**−0.449★★★**	−0.076
Unemployed	0.041	**0.435★★★**
Not in labour force	−0.091	−0.074
Employed part-time	**0.413★★★**	**0.293★★★**
Student	**0.691★★**	**0.644★★★**
Atlantic	0.174	**0.353★★★**
Quebec	−0.314	**−0.199★**
West	**0.413★★★**	**0.412★★★**
Intercept	−3.606★★★	−1.806★★★
Pseudo-R^2 (Nagelkerke)	0.318	0.084
Log likelihood	2,959.143	8,180.9
N	8,302	8,302

Notes: Entries are coefficients for logit regression analysis; dependent variable is binary with 1 = religious volunteer
and 0, otherwise and 1 = non-religious volunteer and 0 otherwise. Statistically significant effects are in boldface.
★★★ indicates $p < 0.001$; ★★ indicates $p < 0.01$; ★ indicates $p < 0.05$. Comparison groups are Low attendance (less than
once per month), Religion not very important (includes somewhat, not very, and not at all important categories),
Catholic, Married, No children under 18 in the home, Born in Canada, More than 5 years in community, Employed,
Non-student and Ontario. Education is coded as a five-category interval-level variable: less than high school,
graduated high school, some post-secondary, post-secondary diploma and university degree. Age is coded into a
six-category interval-level variable: 15–24, 25–34, 35–44, 45–54, 55–64, over 65. Household income is coded as a five-
category interval-level variable: less than $20,000, $20 to <$40,000, $40 to <$60,000, $60 to <$100,000 and $100,000
and over.

results suggest that different factors contribute to the likelihood of volunteering between the two groups. Religiosity plays a significant role in increasing the likelihood that a woman will volunteer for a religious organization. Respondents who indicated that religion is 'very important in their lives' are significantly more likely to volunteer but the positive effects of a high level of religious attendance on volunteering are striking in comparison. Religious attendance dominates in its relationship with religious volunteering. It would seem, then, that many women who volunteer for religious organizations do so directly as a result of their involvement with the organization. Increased attendance very likely increases the chances that the individual will be asked to volunteer within the organization, by the simple fact that they will be recognized and known within the religious community. And similar to results obtained in the United States, Protestant women are significantly more likely to volunteer than are Catholic women.

The effects of religiosity for non-religious women volunteers are non-existent, although denominational differences in their volunteering activities exist nonetheless. Akin to its effects on religious volunteering, Protestantism has a positive effect on the likelihood of volunteering for non-religious organizations, as does the lack of religious identification. Identifying with other religious organizations significantly decreases the likelihood of volunteering among non-religious volunteers.

Significant differences in the importance of socio-demographic background for shaping the likelihood of volunteering between the two groups are also apparent. One exception is education, which plays a similar role in shaping both types of volunteering; increasing levels of education have a positive effect on volunteering, reflecting the increased personal and financial resources that accompany it, in addition to the likely increased sense of civic responsibility that it engenders. Household income plays no part in shaping the likelihood of religious volunteering; poor women are as likely to volunteer in their religious community as are wealthy women. For other women volunteers, however, increased levels of income enhance the likelihood of volunteering activity, perhaps in light of the increased resources and possibly increased social connections accompanying higher levels of income. Interestingly, age plays no part in shaping the likelihood of any type of volunteering among women.

Single women are much more likely to volunteer in non-religious organizations, which may reflect the greater time available to them for such activities. Religious volunteers, on the other hand, are far more likely to be married or single than widowed or divorced. This finding suggests that marriage may not be as powerful a force in shaping women's decisions to volunteer in their congregation as it is in shaping their decision to become religiously active. The presence of children in the home increases the chances that women will volunteer in non-religious organizations but has no similar effects for religious volunteering.

Although no impact is recorded for religious volunteers, being born in Canada positively influences whether a women will volunteer in some other capacity. This may reflect the time and resource constraints that immigrants face. Religious communities, on the other hand, are immediately identifiable and open to immigrants, which may explain their equal propensity for religious volunteering. Alternatively, being new to the community decreases the propensity for religious volunteering, while having no similar effect for non-religious volunteering.

Labour-force participation affects the two types of volunteering in different ways. Only among the groups of other volunteers does employment status appear to have an effect on the likelihood of volunteering: among this group the unemployed are much more likely to volunteer than those who are employed. No such differences are to be found among religious volunteers. Among both groups, however, part-time employment significantly increases the likelihood of volunteering, no doubt due to time considerations. Putnam was clear in identifying part-time employment for its potential for increasing volunteer activity. And students are far more likely to engage in volunteering activities than others, a result that holds true for both groups. This may well reflect the greater time flexibility available to them, or the self-interested desire to establish a well-balanced résumé.

Finally there are clear regional differences in the nature of women's volunteering in Canada. The West stands out for its increased level of religious and non-religious volunteering. The greatest regional variation appears, however, within non-religious volunteering. When compared with Ontario, living in Atlantic Canada and the West significantly increases the likelihood of volunteering while living in Quebec diminishes its likelihood. There appears to be regional variation in culture that translates into varying patterns of volunteering across the country.

Overall, then, some of the key distinctions to note in the comparison between the factors that increase a woman's likelihood of volunteering between religious and other volunteers, include the strong positive impact of religiosity and religious denomination for religious volunteers. Others to note include areas where an absence of effect among religious volunteers is striking when compared to other volunteers. These include household income, the presence of children in the home, as well as marital and employment status. These factors shape the propensity toward non-religious volunteering in a manner not found for religious volunteer-

ing, possibly reflecting religious organizations' ability to attract members from a mix of backgrounds, the pool from which its volunteers is drawn.

Putnam noted that social capital can have private as well as public benefits and the data provide an avenue for investigating the private benefits that women derive from their volunteering activities. On the one hand, the evidence suggests that women who volunteer for religious organizations undertake a larger set of activities than other volunteers. While women who volunteer in non-religious organizations are more likely to engage in activities aimed at protecting the environment and wildlife, women religious volunteers are far more likely to engage in caring activities such as counselling and visiting, collecting and serving food, driving, maintaining facilities, and to engage in teaching and coaching (see Table 23.4). These activities reflect and to some degree reinforce the traditional gender stereotype embodied in many, but not all, religions of women's role in the division of labour: as nurturer, caregiver, and guide in the religious education of children. Importantly, however, these women are also more likely to report being an unpaid member of a board or committee in their volunteer capacity, diverging somewhat from the gender stereotype and potentially resulting in the development of a set of skills that could be employed in a less stereotypical capacity elsewhere.

And in large measure this bears itself out (Table 23.5). Women who volunteer for religious organizations describe the development of a set of skills through their volunteering that mirrors to some extent that reported by women who volunteer elsewhere. Just over a third of employed women in both groups report that their volunteering provides them with skills that apply directly to their jobs. Over half of women in both groups suggest that their volunteering provides them with

Table 23.4 Women's volunteering activities (%)

	Religious volunteers	Other volunteers
Canvassing/campaigning/fundraising	40.3	44.0
Unpaid member of board/committee*	**44.8**	39.6
Provide information/educate	27.7	29.0
Help to organize/supervisor events	59.7	55.2
Consulting/executive/office/admin. work	29.4	29.6
Teach or coach***	**35.0**	20.7
Care/support/counselling/friendly visiting***	**38.4**	24.5
Healthcare in hospital/senior's home	9.8	8.3
Assist as member of self-help group	8.6	7.3
Collect, serve or deliver food***	**38.8**	22.2
Maintain/build/repair facilities***	**13.3**	8.2
Driving**	**22.0**	16.3
First aid/fire fighting/search and rescue	3.5	3.9
Activities aimed at protecting environment/wildlife**	10.0	**14.6**
N	(549)	(1787)

Notes: Entries are percentage of volunteers indicating they performed the said activities. The higher rate in a statistically significant difference is in boldface. *** indicates $p < 0.001$; ** indicates $p < 0.01$; * indicates $p < 0.05$.

increased organizational and managerial skills, while over two-thirds report the development of communications skills. Women who volunteer for religious organizations are somewhat less likely to report the development of fundraising, technical, and office skills and in increased knowledge, with differences ranging from 5 to 7 percentage points between the two groups. Alternatively, a greater share of religious volunteers report the development of interpersonal skills, 85%, compared with 79% of non-religious volunteers.

When asked why they first became a volunteer, religious volunteers provide responses that are no different from those of other women volunteers: the organization approached them, they were a

Table 23.5 Women's volunteer skills development (self-reported) (%)

	Religious volunteers	All other volunteers
Skills that apply directly to your job/business (applies to employed volunteers only)	35.9	37.7
	(362)	(1,261)
Fundraising skills**	43.4	**48.5**
Technical/office skills** (first aid, coaching, computer)	27.3	**32.1**
Organizational/managerial skills	59.7	56.4
Increased knowledge*[a]	58.6	**65.4**
Communication skills	69.7	66.2
Interpersonal skills*[b]	**85.0**	78.5
N	(535)	(1,739)

Notes: Entries are percentage of volunteers indicating that their volunteering helped develop the said skills. The higher rate in a statistically significant difference is in boldface. *** indicates $p < 0.001$; ** indicates $p < 0.01$; * indicates $p < 0.05$.
[a] Exact wording: Have your volunteering activities provided you with increased knowledge, for example, about health, women's issues, political issues, criminal justice, the environment, etc.?
[b] Exact wording: Have your volunteering activities provided you with increased interpersonal skills, for example, to understand children or other people better, to motivate them, to deal with difficult situations, confidence, compassion, patience, etc.?

Table 23.6 Women's reasons for volunteering (self-reported) (%)

	Religious volunteers	All other volunteers
How first became a volunteer (top 3 responses)		
Organization asked me	32.7	30.4
Was a member in the organization	17.5	17.3
I approached the organization myself	15.7	14.6
Reasons for volunteering		
To help cause in which you personally believe	96.1	95.2
To use your skills and experience★	**83.8**	80.0
To fulfil religious obligations or beliefs★★★	**74.7**	16.0
You (or someone you know) has been personally affected by the cause the organization supports	73.2	69.6
To explore your own strengths★★★	**68.5**	59.5
Because your friends volunteer	27.5	28.1
To improve job opportunities★★★	13.9	**26.9**
N	539	1,741

Notes: Entries are percentage of volunteers identifying the said reason as one behind their decision to volunteer (multiple responses allowed for the reasons for volunteering question). The higher rate in a statistically significant difference is in boldface. ★★★ indicates $p < 0.001$; ★★ indicates $p < 0.01$; ★ indicates $p < 0.05$.

member of the organization, or that they took the first step in approaching the organization (Table 23.6). Almost a third of respondents in both groups indicated that they volunteer because someone in the organization sought them out. When asked to identify the reasons behind their continued decision to volunteer, the largest share in both groups indicate that they devote their time to help a cause in which they personally believe, over 95%. Over two-thirds in both groups indicate that they or someone they know has been personally affected by the cause the organization supports, and just over one in four indicate that they volunteer because their friends do. Where differences are apparent is not surprisingly in the importance of fulfilling religious obligations and beliefs: while three out of four religious volunteers offer this reason, less than one in five of all other volunteers offer the same response. Religious volunteers are also more likely to indicate that they volunteer to use their skills and experience (by 4 percentage points) and to explore their own strengths (by 9 percentage points). Non-religious volunteers are far more likely to indicate

that they volunteer to improve their job opportunities. Religious volunteering would seem, then, to provide an important avenue for women's self-development.

Not all religions are equal when it comes to women's religious volunteering. The rate of volunteering among these groups is highest among women within Protestant denominations: over 15% of respondents in this religious group indicate that they participate in religious volunteering (see Table 23.7). Among Roman Catholic women, the rate is significantly lower: only 4.4% volunteer in their churches, mirroring the results previously recorded in both the United States and Canada. Those affiliated with other denominations record the second highest rate of religious volunteering, almost 7%. Not surprisingly, those with no religious affiliation record a very low rate of religious volunteering, just over 1%. When one turns one's attention to comparing the nature of religious volunteering across denominations, the results suggests that Protestant and Roman Catholic women volunteers are not much different: although Roman Catholic women volun-

Table 23.7 Comparing religious denominations (%)

	Protestant	Roman Catholic	Other denominations	No religious affiliation
Overall volunteering rates				
Religious volunteer	15.2	4.4	6.9	1.3
Non-religious volunteer	24.0	20.4	13.5	26.0
Not a volunteer	60.8	75.2	79.6	72.7
N	2,209	3,268	437	1,778
Comparison of religious volunteers				
Number of hours	181.34	192.46	214.74	87.10
Number of organizations[a,b]	2.01	2.20	1.75	1.35
N	336	144	30	23

Notes: Differences in volunteering rates across the four groups significant at the $p<0.01$ level.
[a] Indicates that the difference between Roman Catholic religious volunteers and those with no religious affiliation is significant at the $p<0.01$ level;
[b] Indicates that the difference between Protestant religious volunteers and those with no religious affiliation is significant at the $p<0.05$ level.

teer for more hours on average and for a slightly larger number of groups, these differences are not statistically significant. Thus while Roman Catholic women are less likely to volunteer overall than Protestant women, women from both groups who do volunteer do so in a similar fashion.

The final question deals with the link between social capital and political participation. The NSGVP provides a limited set of questions relating to political participation but the results suggest that women volunteers, regardless of the type of volunteering, are more politically involved than

other women (Table 23.8). On the surface, then, there appears to be a link between community activity and political engagement. The survey asked women to report whether they had voted in the previous federal, provincial and municipal elections. As shown, women volunteers are much more likely to vote than women who do not volunteer, and in the case of municipal elections the difference between religious volunteers and non-volunteers is 14 percentage points. Where 58% of non-volunteering women report voting at the municipal level, over 67% and 72% of non-religious and religious

Table 23.8 Political participation

	Religious volunteers	All other volunteers	Non-volunteers
Voted in last federal election	83.7	80.8	71.6
Voted in last provincial election	82.6	79.2	70.6
Voted in last municipal election	72.8	67.4	58.0
Follow news or current affairs daily	70.2	66.8	65.7
N (over 18 only)	(509) 537	(1,603) 1,745	(5,346)

Notes: Entries are percentage of respondents who reported engaging in said activity. All differences across the three groups are statistically significant ($p<0.01$). Differences between religious and other volunteers in reported municipal voting statistically significant ($p<0.05$).

volunteers respectively report doing the same. At the level of voting, at least, the evidence is clear that volunteering is associated with increased levels of this political activity.

The only other question in the survey that deals with political engagement is one asking about the frequency of following international, national, regional, or local news and current affairs. The literature makes clear that the politically informed are more likely to participate politically. Here too the results point to a slightly higher level of engagement among volunteers although the differences are smaller than those recorded for voting. While

roughly 70% of religious volunteers report following the news daily, closer to two-thirds of non-religious and non-volunteers report a similar level of attention to the news. A statistically significant correlation ($r \geq 0.22$) between following the news and voting at each of the three levels indicates a connection between the two, although it cannot tell us which of these acts drives the other.

The final task is to assess whether volunteering plays an independent role in spurring women's political participation. Table 23.9 provides an analysis of the independent factors that contribute to women's voting at the federal level.[4] In

Table 23.9 Determinants of women's voting at the federal level

Independent variables	
Volunteer status	
Religious volunteer	**0.500★★★**
Non-religious volunteer	**0.479★★★**
Socio-demographic characteristics	
Education	**0.231★★★**
Household income	**0.147★★★**
Age	**0.441★★★**
Single/not married	**−0.595★★★**
Widowed	0.048
Separated/divorced	**−0.421★★★**
Children in the home	−0.083
Immigrant	**−0.869★★★**
Resident in community 5 years or less	**−0.515★★★**
Unemployed	**−0.432★★★**
Not in labour force	**−0.331★★★**
Employed part-time	0.043
Student	0.090
Atlantic	**0.529★★★**
Quebec	**0.539★★★**
West	0.109
Intercept	**−1.648★★★**
Pseudo-R^2 (Nagelkerke)	0.223
Log likelihood	7,563.4
N	7,788

Notes: Entries are coefficients for logit regression analysis; dependent variable is binary with 1=voted in last federal election and zero otherwise. Statistically significant effects are in boldface. ★★★ indicates $p<0.001$; ★★ indicates $p<0.01$; ★ indicates $p<0.05$. Comparison groups are Non-volunteer, Catholic, Married, No children under 18 in the home, Born in Canada, More than 5 years in community, Employed, Non-student, and Ontario. Education is coded as a five-category interval level variable: less than high school, graduated high school, some post-secondary, post-secondary diploma and university degree. Age is coded into a six-category interval-level variable: 15–24, 25–34, 35–44, 45–54, 55–64, over 65 years of age. Household income is coded as a five category interval-level variable: less than $20,000, $20 to <$40,000, $40 to <$60,000, $60 to <$100,000, and $100,000 and over.

addition to those factors that have been shown in previous research to increase one's likelihood of voting, including increased education, income, age and employment, volunteering exerts a statistically strong and positive independent influence on women's voting turnout. Both religious and non-religious volunteers are more likely than non-volunteers to have voted in the last federal election. Religious volunteering, then, enhances women's political engagement in much the same manner as volunteering in other venues. The increased connection to the community developed through volunteering clearly enhances one's willingness to devote the effort necessary to engage in democracy's most fundamental act. Also intriguing is the finding that married and widowed women are much more likely to vote than are single or separated/divorced women. This might reflect life cycle considerations; the heightened awareness of married and widowed women of the direct impact of government policies and programmes on their day-to-day lives might explain their greater propensity for voting.

Discussion and conclusion

This chapter has sought to resolve a seeming puzzle regarding women's religious volunteering. On the one hand, the social capital literature lauds religious engagement as an important arena for the development of social capital. On the other hand, much feminist literature is critical of women's engagement in patriarchal organizations that are seen as a hindrance to the goal of gender equality. The results suggest that a mix of both accounts defines women's involvement in religious organizations in Canada.

Because it constitutes a significant share of women's volunteering activities, religious volunteering constitutes an important element in the creation of social capital.

A comparison of religious volunteers to other women volunteers suggests a number of similarities. The former group volunteers to the same degree and in as many organizations as the latter group. Similarities are also to be found in the type of activities undertaken by the two groups of volunteers as well as in the skills that they report developing as a result of their engagement. The reasons they offer for having initially volunteered for the organization and for continuing with their volunteering are also comparable. And both groups of women stand apart from other women for the link between their civic engagement and their increased level of political participation.

The comparison nevertheless reveals a number of distinctions between the two groups. Women religious volunteers appear to be slightly more engaged in the community both in terms of the number of organizations for which they volunteer and the number of hours that they devote to them. Women religious volunteers are somewhat older than other women volunteers; somewhat more educated; more likely to be married but less likely to have children in the home; less likely to be employed although if employed are more likely to work part-time; more likely to have been born outside of Canada and to have lived in the community for a longer period of time; and, not surprisingly, are more likely to report a religious affiliation. When comparing the set of factors that helps to account for women's volunteering, religiosity stands apart as a very strong determinant of women's religious volunteering, particularly a high level of religious attendance. To be present and known within any organization increases the chances that one is likely to be asked by it to volunteer in some capacity and this is no different in religious organizations. Although religious volunteers appear to engage in as diverse a set of activities in relation to their volunteering, there is evidence that they more often engage in activities of a caring nature than other women volunteers. The finding that their participation is somewhat dominated by acts that stress the traditional woman's gender role – compassionate and caring – is to be somewhat expected in that many religious organizations are more likely to endorse traditional gender roles than other organizations to which women can volunteer their time. And while many more religious volunteers indicate that they volunteer to fulfil religious obligations, fewer indicate that they do so to improve their job opportunities.

In support of the social capital literature, women's religious volunteering is linked to high levels of volunteering generally, and to greater political participation. As such, the public benefits from the social capital it creates cannot be ignored. Women religious volunteers are well connected to their communities, devote significant time to them, and are more likely to vote and pay attention to current affairs than non-volunteers. In Putnam's terms, significant positive externalities derive from women's religious volunteering.

The results suggest that women who volunteer in religious organizations derive significant private benefits from their participation. Religious volunteering provides women with opportunities for undertaking a wide range of activities that extend beyond those tied to the traditional woman's role of compassion and caring, and for developing a range of skills that benefit them in a number of ways. They volunteer for their religious organizations to use these skills, to pursue causes that are of importance to them, and importantly to explore their own strengths. The private benefits that accrue from their volunteering are multiple.

There is little in the evidence presented here to suggest that women who volunteer for religious organizations are not creating the more beneficial bridging capital referred

to by Putnam. On the contrary, their volunteering spans a number of organizations outside of their religious organizations and, moreover, they are as tied in to their wider community as other women volunteers in that they participate as members in as many other organizations. The breadth of their participation provides reason for concluding that this form of volunteering is to some extent of the type considered most beneficial in social capital terms to the wider community. Devoid of any investigation of religious doctrine, an investigation that might reveal a set of messages more likely to encourage bonding rather than bridging capital, there is at least some reason to suggest that women's religious volunteering assists in the development of bridging capital.

Women's religious volunteering provides a foundation for the development of shared networks, if not norms, that allow for community development. An element to the traditional gender role developed through religious volunteering can be argued to correspond with the affective element of social capital. The development of social norms of trust and reciprocity, although not examined here, would seem easier to develop among communities that develop the values of compassion and caring, so long as they are directed toward the wider community and not restricted to those who are members of one's specific religious community. The compassion and connection found among women religious volunteers might play a beneficial role in communities across the country.

There is also, one might argue, simplicity in the bridging/bonding distinction that falsely dichotomizes organizations and identities. While religious communities are made up of like-minded individuals in terms of their religious beliefs and values, there are a multiplicity of additional identities with which individuals identify and which can be brought to bear on their membership and, additionally, on their volunteering. That income, age and employment status play no part in shaping the likelihood of women's religious volunteering suggests that these women are connecting with women who in other ways are unlike themselves, which in itself can lead to the development of bridging capital, albeit in perhaps a less explicit manner.

Paradoxically, the reinforcement of a traditional woman's role through religious volunteering is precisely what spawns feminist critiques of their involvement in such organizations. Limitations on women's religious leadership roles advance similar critiques. As shown here, however, women derive significant personal benefits from their participation in religious organizations alongside the public benefits that their participation engenders. The development of an extensive set of skills which their participation allows them to exercise, and the reported ability to explore their own strengths, provide important reasons for reassessing women's participation in religious communities. Their religious volunteering additionally corresponds to greater interest and participation in the political arena, which provides the potential for benefiting women in the long run. At the very least, a clearer picture of women's participation in religious organizations emerges from an investigation of their volunteering, one that helps to explain in part their continued involvement. Without dismissing the restrictions that many religious organizations impose on women, within them exist important opportunities for women who choose to volunteer. That the community appears to benefit from their engagement as well provides further reason for encouraging a more balanced assessment of women's religious volunteering.

Notes

1 This chapter was first published in B. O'Neill and E. Gidengil (eds) (2006) *Gender and Social Capital*, London: Routledge.

2 The 2000 survey was conducted by Statistics Canada as a supplement to the Labour Force Survey (LFS). The 2000 NSGVP is based on a representative sample of 14,724 Canadians aged 15 and older who were asked about their giving and volunteering for a one-year period from 1 October 1999 to 30 September 2000. The NSGVP is the result of a partnership of federal government departments and voluntary sector organizations that includes the Canadian Centre for Philanthropy, Canadian Heritage, Health Canada, Human Resources Development Canada, Statistics Canada, and Volunteer Canada.

3 The data for women respondents in the NSGVP were weighted according to the instructions provided in the Microdata User Guide (August 2001, 38). As noted in the document, this procedure is likely to somewhat underestimate variances. Confidentiality concerns prohibit users from correcting for this problem.

4 Analyses conducted for voting at the provincial and municipal levels revealed results that were almost identical to those obtained for voting at the federal level and, as a result, are not shown here.

Bibliography

Bibby, R. (1997) 'The persistence of Christian religious identification in Canada', *Canadian Social Trends*, 44, pp. 24–28.

Blais, A., Gidengil, E., Nevitte, N. and Nadeau, R. (2004) 'Where does turnout decline come from?', *European Journal of Political Research*, 43, 2, pp. 221–36.

Burns, N., Schlozman K.L. and Verba, S. (2001) *The Private Roots of Public Action,* Cambridge, MA: Harvard University Press.

Coleman, J. (1990) *Foundations of Social Theory*, Cambridge, MA: Harvard University Press.

Djupe, P. and Grant, T.J. (2001) 'Religious institutions and political participation in America', *Journal for the Scientific Study of Religion*, 40, pp. 304–14.

Greeley, A. (1997) 'The other civic America: Religion and social capital', *American Prospect*, 32, pp. 68–73.

Halman, L. and Pettersson, T. (2001) 'Religion and social capital in contemporary Europe: Results from the 1999/2000 European Values Study', *Research in the Social Scientific Study of Religion*, 5, 1, pp. 65–90.

Hertel, B. R. (1995) 'Work, Family and Faith. Recent trends', in N. T. Ammerman and W. C. Roof (eds), *Work, Family and Religion in Contemporary Society*, New York and London: Routledge, pp. 81–121.

Manning, C. (1999) *God Gave Us the Right: Conservative Catholic, Evangelical Protestant and Orthodox Jewish Women Grapple with Feminism*, New Brunswick, NJ: Rutgers.

Marler, P. L. (1995) "Lost in the Fifties: The changing family and the nostalgic church", in N. T. Ammerman and W. C. Roof (eds), *Work, Family and Religion in Contemporary Society*, New York and London: Routledge, pp. 23–60.

O'Neill, B. (2001) 'A simple difference of opinion? Religious beliefs and gender gaps in public opinion', *Canadian Journal of Political Science*, 34, 2, pp. 275–98.

Ozorak, Weiss, E. (1996) 'The power, but not the glory: How women empower themselves through religion', *Journal for the Scientific Study of Religion*, 35, 1, pp. 17–29.

Park, J. and Smith, C. (2000) ' "To whom much is given …": Religious capital and community voluntarism among churchgoing Protestants', *Journal for the Scientific Study of Religion*, 39, 3, pp. 272–86.

Putnam, R. (2000) *Bowling Alone: The Collapse and Revival of American Community*, New York: Simon & Schuster.

Putnam, R. (2001) 'Social capital: Measurement and consequences', http://www.oecd.org/dataoecd/25/6/1825848.pdf.

Roof, W.C. (1993) *A Generation of Seekers: The Spiritual Journeys of the Baby Boom Generation*, San Francisco: HarperCollins.

Statistics Canada (2001) 'Religious groups in Canada: Profile series' (Catalogue No. 85F0033MIE), Ottawa: Minister of Industry.

Verba, S., Shlozman, K.L. and Brady, H. (1995) *Voice and Equality: Civic Voluntarism in American Politics*, Cambridge, MA: Harvard University Press.

Vickers, J. (1997) *Reinventing Political Science: A Feminist Approach*, Halifax, NS: Fernwood.

Winter, M.T., Lummis, A. and Stokes, A. (1994) *Defecting in Place: Women Claiming Responsibility for Their Own Spiritual Lives*, New York: Crossroad.

Woodhead, L. (2001) 'Feminism and the sociology of religion: From gender-blindness to gendered difference', in R. Fenn (ed.), *The Blackwell Companion to Sociology of Religion*, Oxford: Blackwell, pp. 67–84.

Wuthnow, R. (1991) *Acts of Compassion: Caring for Others and Helping Ourselves*, Princeton, NJ: Princeton University Press.

Wuthnow, R. (1999) 'Mobilizing civic engagement: The changing impact of religious involvement', in T. Skocpol and M. Fiorina (eds), *Civic Engagement in American Democracy*, New York: Russell Sage Foundation, pp. 331–63.

24

Religion and international development[1]

Gerard Clarke

Introduction

'International development', as a deliberate and planned process of intergovernmental cooperation to promote human well-being, is a relatively new phenomenon. It effectively dates to the end of World War II in 1945, and to a number of initiatives including the establishment of the United Nations in 1945 to encourage peaceful cooperation between nations; the launch of the International Bank for Reconstruction and Development in 1946 to help fund reconstruction in Europe and Japan and to support economic growth in Asia, Africa and Latin America; and the launch of the Marshall Plan in 1947 to provide US economic assistance to European countries in the new Organisation for Economic Cooperation and Recovery. All were instrumental in the launch of multilateral, bilateral and non-governmental organisations which collectively channelled US$2.3 trillion in support of global poverty reduction over the next sixty years (see Easterly 2006: 11).

The first fifty years of 'international development', however, coincided with a distinct secularisation of public policy in Western Europe and North America. Policymakers and academics alike concerned with international development were heavily influenced by 'secularisation theory', the belief (in Wilson's classic formulation) that

'religious institutions, actions and consciousness lose their social significance' over time as societies modernise (Wilson 1992: 49). This influence was evident in two key respects: in 'secular reductionism' – the neglect of religious variables in favour of other sociological attributes such as class, ethnicity and gender – and in 'materialistic determinism' – the neglect of non-material, especially religious, motivations in explaining individual or institutional behaviour (see Luttwak 1994).

In this vein, academics and policymakers perceived poverty as a matter of material deprivation and its elimination a technical undertaking; they systematically ignored the role of faith as an analytical lens through which the poor experienced and rationalised poverty and through which the well-off empathised with their struggles and provided practical support. Heavily influenced by the legal separation of church and state in liberal democracies, they felt that religion was counterdevelopmental, that religious discourses with strong historical resonance were inflexible and unyielding in the face of social and political change.

This antipathy was frequently reciprocated. Faith leaders often saw themselves as the defenders of traditional moral values amid the onslaught of secular modernity and many were wedded to a paternalistic view of poverty and the poor, ready to advocate the charitable obligations of the faithful but less willing to press for political and social change that benefited the faithful as citizens as much as dutiful believers. With notable exceptions, the main faiths emphasised the spiritual and moral dimensions of poverty at the expense of the material, and representative organisations avoided poverty-focused social engagement and policy dialogue with governments and donors.[2]

Since 1997, however, development organisations have become more conscious of the salience of religion in international politics and its import for development policy and practice. In 1997, the then-President of the World Bank, James Wolfensohn, launched a small 'Directorate on Faith' within the Bank,[3] and established a relationship with the then-Archbishop of Canterbury, Dr George Carey, which led to a series of conferences in 1998, 1999 and 2002, bringing together donor representatives and faith leaders. The published proceedings of these, and related conferences point to the 'faith and development' interface as a significant new theme in development policy and discourse (see for instance: Belshaw et al. 2001; Marshall and Marsh 2003; Palmer and Findlay 2003; Marshall and Keough 2004; and Marshall and Van Saanen 2007).

The Millennium Declaration agreed at the United Nations General Assembly in September 2000, and the associated Millennium Development Goals (MDGs), lie at the heart of this new engagement.[4] The Declaration is seen in some quarters as a 'covenant', a solemn contract or agreement with quasi-religious or spiritual significance (see Marshall and Keough 2004: 4). In this sense, the Declaration is an inspirational document which generates a moral commitment among signatories and galvanises the moral energy of the global community. Many years after their approval, however, the MDGs remain poorly understood, much less agreed, on

the ground (2004: 7). Faith communities and organisations to which they give rise are therefore seen as important actors in galvanising the moral commitment on which the MDGs depend and in popularising them in local churches, mosques, temples and synagogues, translating them into the idioms of the faith and mobilising support for organisations and community initiatives that contribute to the Goals.

Donors and faith-based organisations

A key aspect of World Bank work on the 'faith and development' interface has been to challenge faith-based organisations (FBOs) to become more actively involved in the fight against global poverty. This challenge originates in part from the findings of 'Voices of the Poor', a World Bank study (published in three volumes in 2000) which documented the views and experiences of more than 60,000 men and women from sixty countries. FBOs, it noted,

> emerge frequently in poor people's lists of important institutions. They appear more frequently as the most important institutions in rural rather than in urban ones. Spirituality, faith in God and connecting to the sacred in nature are an integral part of poor people's lives in many parts of the world. Religious organisations are also valued for the assistance they provide to poor people.
> (Narayan et al. 2000: 222)

This acknowledgement of faith and associated organisations in the lives of the poor was largely unprecedented in the discourse of major donor agencies such as the World Bank and signalled a significant shift in thinking. The acknowledgement, however, was far from uncritical or insensitive to some of the more negative connotations of faith in the lives of the poor:'[T]he role that religious or faith-based organisations play in poor people's lives', the study concluded:

varies from being a balm for the body and soul to being a divisive force in the community. In ratings of effectiveness in both urban and rural settings, religious organisations feature more prominently than any single type of state institution but they do not disappear when ineffective institutions are mentioned.

(2000: 222)

FBOs, the Bank suggested, can be a potent force in the lives of the poor where they focus on material as well as spiritual poverty, avoid divisive or sectarian agendas, and become more involved in the daily struggles of the faithful.

This bifocal view of faith and FBOs, as both a potent and ineffectual force in the lives of the poor, led to admonitions from the World Bank that FBOs 'must become agents of transformation, using their influence to demand better governance and public accountability' (Narayan 2001: 47). This call was repeated by Clare Short, the cabinet minister responsible for British aid policy between 1997 and 2003 and an active participant in the dialogue begun by Wolfensohn and Carey. At the Canterbury conference in 2002, Short challenged faith leaders to assume a greater role in the fight against global poverty by shifting their focus from charity to justice, and by playing a greater role in making governments politically accountable to their constituencies:

[F]aith groups have to move beyond charity. ... Real charity is justice. We need to mobilize that core of moral teachings that lies at the heart of each of the world's great religions: that life must be just and fair and that all human beings deserve respect and the opportunity to enjoy

their humanity and practice their spirituality. ... The challenge must fall at least partly on faith groups in rich countries to embrace higher ambitions, to convince those countries to back the right policies, to spend money well.

(Short 2003: 8–9)

If faith-based organisations were to adapt in this way, Short suggested, to become more engaged in public policy debates, more embedded in pro-poor alliances and networks at national and international level and more active in representing faith-based constituencies, the potential for positive catalytic change would be enormous (2003). The message from the World Bank and the UK Department for International Development was stern if inviting: donors actively seek dialogue and partnership with FBOs but such organisations must adapt to fulfil their expected roles.

These messages illustrate a realisation on the part of official donors of the growing importance of faith-based or religiously inspired organisations as agents of social change. In the industrialised 'North', FBOs play an important role in providing social services to the poor. In the US, for instance, an estimated 18% of the 37,000 US non-profit organisations involved in social service provision in 1999 had a faith-based ethos (Wuthnow 2004: 141). These FBOs had estimated assets of $25.5bn and annual budgets of $17bn in 1999, equivalent to the annual GNI of medium-sized economies such as Syria, Sri Lanka or Costa Rica.[5]

Faith-based social engagement at home is mirrored in support for the poor in developing countries. Members of Coopération Internationale pour le Développement et la Solidarité (CIDSE, International Cooperation for Development and Solidarity), the largest alliance of Catholic development agencies, had a combined budget of $950m in 2000, members of

APRODEV, the main association of Protestant development agencies, $470m, and World Vision International, the single largest Christian development agency, had a turnover of $600m in 1999 (Clark 2003: 134–136). Including Caritas International, the second main international coalition of Catholic development agencies, the big four faith-based development agencies had a combined annual income of approximately $2.5bn at the beginning of the new millennium, or almost two-thirds of the annual budget of the UK Department for International Development (£2.7bn or $4bn in 2000/2001) (cf. DFID 2001). As such, they have become significant players in the international delivery of aid, the equivalent of large bilateral donors.

Such organisations, however, have been eclipsed in recent decades by the proliferation of missionary organisations, seeking not only to provide services such as health and education to the poor but to win converts to the faith. In the US, for instance, the rise of the Christian right has led to a significant expansion in overseas missionary activity by evangelical and Pentecostal congregations. In 2001, an estimated 350,000 Americans travelled abroad with Protestant missionary agencies, and donations to such agencies totalled $3.75bn, a 44% increase in five years,[6] and significantly greater than the combined annual expenditure of the big four faith-based development NGOs networks (CIDSE, APRODEV, Caritas and World Vision).[7] US evangelical missions in Africa, according to Hearn (2002: 33–34), are critical to the implementation of donor, especially USAID, policy yet effectively function as 'invisible NGOs', invisible because they have been ignored in the separate literatures on development NGOs and on African Christianity.

Similarly, the 1990s and early years of the new millennium have seen an increase in the number and reach of organisations committed to *tabligh wa-da'wa*, preaching

the message of Allah (*da'wa*, or mission, for short) internationally. Throughout Africa, for instance, Arab organisations, including the World Muslim League (Saudi Arabia), the African Muslim Agency (Kuwait) and the World Islamic Call (Libya) fund local *madrasas* (Islamic seminaries or religious schools), promoting conservative Islamic currents such as Wahabism or Salafism which traditionally have had little purchase in African societies. One significant consequence has been the realisation of a distinct cleavage in many regional countries between 'African Islam' and 'Islam in Africa', that is, between traditional local forms of Islamic practice and more conservative currents promoted by organisations from the Arab world (Westerlund and Rosander 1997; Linden 2004).

Missionary activity characterised by active proselytizing, however, is largely confined to Christianity and Islam. In India, some Hindu nationalist FBOs promote the reconversion of *adivasi* ('tribals') who convert from Hinduism to escape the oppressive social hierarchy of caste but otherwise Hinduism lacks the tradition of seeking new converts to the faith, as do other major religions such as Buddhism and Sikhism. Evangelical Christian and Wahabi/Salafi organisations therefore represent a particular case for donors concerned to minimise social conflict in complex cultural settings yet equally concerned to reach constituencies traditionally disenfranchised by secular development discourse.

Government policy: the case of the United States

While the work of faith-based organisations, largely non-governmental in character, has therefore become a significant and controversial theme in development discourse, government policy has been even more central to the growing appreciation of the salience of faith in the international

development community. The most prominent case in this respect is the United States.

US government policy on religion in
the context of international development
has changed enormously since 1980 and the
election of Ronald Reagan as President.
Prior to 1980, the US government channelled small amounts of funding for
international development through organisations associated with the mainstream
Christian churches, respecting established
constitutional conventions on the separation of church and state and generating
relatively little controversy. The election of
Reagan however, provided an enormous
fillip to the US Christian right, to the
evangelical and Pentecostal organisations
and leaders that supported his candidacy.
A born-again (evangelical) Christian,
Reagan mobilised the Christian right
in support of his domestic and foreign
policy, especially his opposition to
communism.

Over the next two and a half decades,
the Christian right grew significantly in
response to White House patronage, transforming US politics. By 2003, for instance,
an estimated 43% of the US electorate was
evangelical (Waldman 2004), a significant
shift away from the mainstream Christian
denominations towards a more fervent,
and ideologically right-wing, form of
faith. In the US, the Christian right has
been influential in the passage of legislation that guides US foreign policy (see
Haynes's chapter (18) on religion and foreign policy in this volume). This influence
is exercised in part by charismatic leaders,
abetted by significant media access, but
organisations that represent the thousands
of evangelical and Pentecostal congregations form a vital bulwark. The National
Association of Evangelicals (NAE), for
instance, had 30 million members in 2005
(up from 2.6m in the 1980s); ('History of
the NAE') and has become an important
participant in debates around US policy
on international development.

This influence become especially evident
in 1996 when the secular-minded Clinton
administration was forced to defer to the
Republican-dominated Senate and to
politicians associated with the Christian
right such as Sen. John Ashcroft in the
passage of the 1996 Welfare Reform Act.
The 1996 Act heralded a revolution in
domestic welfare provision and included
radical 'Charitable Choice' provisions which
eroded obstacles to faith groups securing
government funding and contracts.

With the election of George W. Bush as
President, the Christian right achieved further influence over government legislation.
The Bush administrations of 2001 and
2005 contained more evangelical and
Pentecostal Christians than any previous
US administration (including the President
himself, Secretary of State Condoleezza
Rice and Attorney General John Ashcroft
in the 2005 administration) and legislation
on the separation of church and state was
further diluted. In 2000, faith-based 'compassionate conservatism' was a significant
element in Bush's electoral campaign and
on the hustings Bush lauded the work
of faith-based social service groups. The
message was eagerly received; according
to Kuo (2006: 133), 60% of Bush's votes
'came from evangelical Christians, devout
Catholics and observant mainline
Christians'. In his inaugural speech in
January 2001, Bush spoke again of the religious basis of compassionate conservatism:
'Church and charity, synagogues and
mosques lend our communities their
humanity and they will have an honored
place in our plans and in our laws' (quoted
in Kuo 2006: 140).

The same year, this promise was under-
lined when the 2001 Faith-Based and
Community Initiatives Act was approved by
Congress, consolidating provisions in the
1996 Welfare Reform Act, and Executive
Order 13198 established new Centres for
Faith-Based and Community Initiatives
(CFBCIs) in five federal departments.

In December 2002, Executive Order 13280 created a new CFBCI in the United States Agency for International Development (USAID), designed to ensure that provisions of the 2001 Act are reflected in USAID policy. This was followed by a USAID ruling on 'Participation by Religious Orders in USAID Programs', effective from October 2004 ('Participation by Religious Organizations in USAID Programs').

The 2004 ruling radically transformed USAID policy on engagement with FBOs, reversing the 'pervasively sectarian' doctrine previously upheld by the US Supreme Court. Under the old doctrine, religious organisations which engaged in discriminatory or sectarian practices were barred from government funding or contracts. Under the new ruling, however, USAID cannot discriminate against organisations which combine development or humanitarian activities with 'inherently religious activities' such as worship, religious instruction or proselytisation. USAID-funded activities must be separated 'by time or space' from 'inherently religious activities' but commentators fear that such distinctions will be blurred in practice. (The ruling contains a USAID summary of objections received during a consultation stage and the USAID response.)

The ruling, for instance, prevents discrimination against organisations which provide social services in a religious setting (e.g. a building characterised by religious icons, scriptures or symbols) or which engage in discriminatory practices in the hiring of staff or in their management procedures (i.e. restricting paid employment or election to a board of directors to adherents of a particular faith). This means, in practice, that USAID-funded buildings used for the delivery of social services can also be used (but not at the same time) for 'inherently religious activities'. Similarly, FBOs cannot discriminate against non-believers in the provision of USAID-supported services, but there is no obligation on them to explain that non-believers can avail of such services on an equal basis.

The 2001 Act has been criticised by organisations concerned at the erosion of church–state boundaries and the potential legalisation of discriminatory or sectarian practices by religious organisations (Dedeyan 2004; Bartkowski and Regis 2003: 1–9), but the USAID ruling provokes further concern with its suggestion that less stringent legal standards (than those applicable to domestic programmes) might apply to foreign assistance.[8] Ostensibly designed to equalise the treatment of secular and religious organisations, it effectively tilts the balance in favour of the latter since US or foreign NGOs that provide information on abortion (and which, by definition, are overwhelmingly secular) are ineligible for USAID funding.

The ban on organisations which promote contraception or abortion receiving USAID funding was first enacted under the Reagan administration in 1984 and become popularly known as the 'Mexico City policy' after a speech by Reagan in the city. Rescinded by the Clinton administration in 1993, the policy was restored by President George Bush on his first day in office in January 2001 and later operationalised through the US$15bn President's Emergency Plan for Aid's Relief (PEPFAR) announced in 2003. Donor discourse on the battle against HIV/AIDS emphasises a simple ABC formula, stressing *abstinence* from sex before marriage (A), *being faithful* in marital relationships (B) and *condom* use (C). By 2006, however, reports suggested that over two-thirds of PEPFAR funding was committed to the AB model, with condom promotion and provision limited to particularly high-risk groups (cf. Pearson and Tomalin 2008: 55). In turn, the US has tried to promote this policy in UN and other multilateral fora. At a meeting of the UN Conference on the Status of Women in 2005, for instance, the US representative made it clear that endorsement of the terms 'reproductive health services' and 'reproductive rights' excluded US support for abortion (2008: 54). According to Pearson and Tomalin (2008), '[t]his caveat reflects the insistence of the US administration that the term "reproductive rights" is short hand for abortion [and that] the phrase "consistent condom use", within UN Parlance, as the basis of HIV/AIDS prevention, is taken to indicate tacit approval of under age sex, with the Bush administration backed by the right wing evangelical lobby'.

The case of Saudi Arabia

The political salience of the 'faith and development interface' newly evident in development discourse and policy is also illustrated by the case of Saudi Arabia and by the rise of political and radical Islam as pan-national phenomena affecting international aid as well as international politics or relations. Political Islam is most closely associated with the Muslim Brotherhood, founded by Hassan El Banna in Egypt in 1928 and which has branches today in over seventy countries and a membership of many millions, mostly in the Arab world. In a number of Arab states, it has been associated with armed struggle against colonial rule or against the nationalist but secular regimes which replaced it. It also functions, however, as a pan-Arab and pan-Islamic social movement which feeds on middle-class resentment at often arbitrary state rule and the perceived humiliation of the *ummah* (the global community of Muslims) at the hands of Western powers and plays an important role in the organisation and delivery of social services to the Muslim poor. A controversial force across the Islamic world, the Brotherhood is sometimes attacked for promoting terrorism and exclusive political identities in multi-ethnic and

multi-religious societies yet respected for its social activism and its support (sometimes tactical) for multi-party democracy (for summary details, see Kepel 2002; for country-specific studies, see Wiktorowicz 2001 on Jordan, and Mishal and Sela 2000 on Palestine).

Political Islam is largely concerned with restoring Islam as the organising principle of political power and social order and the political basis of both the nation-state and the pan-national *ummah*. As such, it challenges ruling secular political parties perceived to have marginalised Islam from political life. Moderate political Islam promotes the gradual Islamisation of the nation-state and concedes that the Islamist project must make tactical concessions in pursuit of its strategy. It promotes Islam as the answer to the social, economic and political ills that afflict Muslim societies, effectively that it is the solution (or at least that it frames the solutions), to development dilemmas across the Islamic world. According to Janine Clark, it is partly understood as a reaction against state encroachment on religious authority, including the takeover of mosque-based social services by the state (Clark 2004: 12). In some respects, therefore, moderate political Islam represents the struggle for autonomous civil societies in Muslim countries, where the secular state exists alongside an active community of Islamic FBOs, some of which accept the legitimacy of the state but some of which challenge it.

Radical Islam, on the other hand, is a militant form, predominantly of Saudi Wahabi/Salafi Islam (and of Indian and Pakistani Deobandi Islam), closely associated with loosely organised transnational terrorist networks such as Al-Qaeda or Jemaah Islamiya. At heart, these networks seek the overthrow of the secular state across the Islamic world and the creation of a pan-national caliphate that unifies the world's Muslims under a single political and religious leader, serving as the direct successor of the Prophet Mohammad. This vision is both utopian and apocalyptic and few Muslims subscribe to it, yet, vulture-like, it feeds off a profound concern across the Islamic world at what are regarded as attacks on the *ummah* in Afghanistan, Bosnia, Chechnya, Iraq, Kashmir, Palestine, etc.

The rise of political and radical Islam alike, and the growing importance of faith-based aid in the Islamic world, was triggered by a number of factors, including the Iranian Revolution of 1979, and the Soviet Invasion of Afghanistan the same year, together representing a significant attack on secular nationalism and on communism, and stimulating the proliferation of charitable and development organisations with a conservative Islamic character in Saudi Arabia and in other Gulf states. One result was a dramatic increase in Saudi intervention in the affairs of neighbouring countries, including an expansion in the overseas activities of Saudi-based Islamic organisations.

Following the election of Ronald Reagan as US President, US aid to the Afghan *Mujahidin* increased dramatically, from $30m in 1980 to $250m in 1985 (Burke 2004: 60). In the Arab world, however, the *Mujahidin* struggle was seen as a pan-Islamic one and Arab, especially Saudi, aid increased dramatically – to support the *Mujahidin*, to counteract growing Western influence over the Afghan conflict and to counter militant Iranian Shi'ism which appealed to disaffected Saudi youth. Official Saudi aid to the *Mujahidin* matched, if not exceeded, US aid, but was boosted further by private donations (2004). 'Official' and 'private' funding was channelled through Islamic organisations in Saudi Arabia and other Arab nations, many of which opened offices in Pakistan, paving the way for further activism in other parts of the Islamic world.

Aid to the *Mujahidin* echoed increasing aid from Arab countries to others with a substantial Muslim population. Arab donors are not members of the Development Assistance Committee (DAC) of the Organisation for Economic Cooperation and Development (the main 'club' of official donors) and aid flows from the Arab world go largely unnoticed in the international aid community. Arab countries, however, provided an average of 1.5% of GNP per annum as net official development assistance between 1974 and 1994, significantly more than most DAC members (Neumayer 2003: 135). Such Arab aid is largely provided on a government-to-government basis but significant flows are hidden from public view and channelled through private agencies, including Islamic FBOs at home and in recipient countries. The combination of increased Arab aid flows (in response to the Iranian Revolution and the Afghan war), allied to the adoption of neo-liberal economic policies at home, led to a dramatic growth in the number of FBOs in the Arab world, mostly focusing on domestic issues but with many supporting pan-Islamic causes.

In Saudi Arabia, in particular, a close relationship developed between the Saudi government and various organisations and/or individuals committed to the spread of political or radical Islamic currents abroad. A key feature of Saudi foreign policy in recent decades has been the promotion of Wahabism, or Salafism, the dominant strain of Islam in the Kingdom. Members of the royal family, for instance, are represented on the boards of prominent organisations that combine charitable work abroad with *da'wa*, the propagation of the Muslim faith, and, in the Saudi case, its Wahabi/Salafi doctrines (Burr and Collins 2006: Table 2:1, p. 28). According to one source, Saudi charities, individuals and government agencies have spent almost $90bn in the 30 years to 2005 promoting Wahabism/Salafism overseas (Ehrenfeld 2005).

Saudi charitable organisations have generated significant academic controversy in the West. In *Alms for Jihad: Charity and Terrorism in the Islamic World* (later withdrawn by its publisher, Cambridge University Press, as a result of legal action), Burr and Collins (2006) claim that leading Saudi charities working overseas, such as the International Islamic Relief Organisation, the World Assembly of Muslim Youth and the Al Haramain Islamic Foundation, support terrorist causes in a range of countries.

Kroessin and Mohamed (2008), however, argue that such organisations (and their Wahabi or Salafi ethos) have been unfairly stereotyped in the West, and that their commitment to *da'wa* (the propagation of the faith) is directly comparable with many Western organisations (secular and faith-based) that also propagate distinct value systems.

Private funding channelled by Saudi charitable organisations or individual donors became a key source of conflict between the US and Saudi Arabia in the aftermath of the attacks of 9/11 (2001), and in June 2004, the government announced the closure of some organisations (including the Al Haramain Islamic Foundation) and the establishment of the National Commission for Relief and Charity Work Abroad to funnel and filter private Saudi funding for charitable activities overseas.[9] Three years later, however, the Commission had yet to become operational, provoking further unrest in the United States where Senator Arlen Spector introduced the draft Saudi Arabia Accountability Act in Congress to encourage the Saudi authorities to end support for organisations seen in the US as funding or encouraging terrorism ('Saudi Arabia is the Hub of World Terror' 2007).

The case of the United Kingdom

The US and Saudi cases illustrate the controversial nature of the faith and development interface. The case of the United Kingdom, however, reflects the cautious manner in which many Western donors (bilateral, multilateral and non-governmental) are approaching the issue. In the UK case, the relative caution, in contrast to the US, arises because of the absence of a significant Christian right in Britain.[10] While Evangelical and Pentecostal congregations have grown in recent decades in the UK they have not displaced mainstream Christian denominations, and there is little public demand for legislation that erodes traditional church–state boundaries.

The Department for International Development (DFID; until 1997, the Overseas Development Administration) has traditionally involved FBOs in its operations to a limited extent, normally by co-funding the activities of a small number of specialised development agencies associated with the mainstream Christian churches.[11] DFID regarded such organisations as relatively large and well run, with strong links to Church networks in many developing countries, and a strong support base among adherents in the UK. In addition, to a considerable extent they shared DFID's vision of development and appeared as quasi-secular organisations and therefore compatible with DFID's secular vision of development; they had plural workforces (employing believers and non-believers alike), avoided proselytising activities (i.e. converting non-adherents to the faith), and were non-denominational in their work with local communities (helping believers and non-believers on an equal basis). To the FBOs themselves, however, this quasi-secularism was largely forced on them by DFID's antipathy to faith-based value systems and made for uneasy relationships at times with frequent potential for misunderstanding.

While less significantly than in relation to the World Bank and USAID, DFID policy on engagement with FBOs began to change in 1997. The global 'resurgence' of religion, especially conservative religion, serves as an important backdrop (cf. Berger 1999), but key factors driving the new policy were closer to home. First, DFID began to engage with a wider range of civil society organisations from 1997, including trade unions, faith-based organisations and professional associations. This followed criticism from Clare Short that DFID engagement with civil society organisations focused excessively on non-governmental development organisations. Under Short's leadership, DFID's support to civil society was overhauled and new funding mechanisms introduced.[12] As a consequence, parts of DFID began to think more seriously about relationships with faith communities and with FBOs. Fresh impetus was provided by the launch of the Millennium Development Goals in 2000 and the work of the World Bank in establishing dialogue between donors, governments and faith leaders.

Secondly, DFID was forced to react to the rise of faith-based activism in the form of the Jubilee 2000 anti-debt campaign (and the subsequent Make Poverty History campaign). Founded in 1996, Jubilee 2000 originated in plans in the early 1990s to link demands for debt relief to the old Jewish (and later, Christian) concept of jubilee, a year in every fifty in which creditors forgive their debtors, slaves are set free and forfeited land is returned to its original owners.[13] At its height in the late 1990s, Jubilee 2000 had affiliates in more than 60 countries and by 1999 had collected 24 million signatures and mobilised 50,000 demonstrators at the 1999 G7 meeting in Cologne, creating political pressure that led to the Highly Indebted Poor Countries (HIPC) initiative (Marshall and Keough 2004: 35–48; Wallis 2005: 272–278). In the UK, Jubilee 2000 was significant primarily because it mobilised both mainstream Christian and evangelical/Pentecostal congregations. Chancellor of the Exchequer

(Finance Minister) (and from 2007, Prime Minister) Gordon Brown, for instance, described it as the most important church-led social movement in Britain since John Wesley and William Wilberforce led the campaign to outlaw slavery in the eighteenth century (Wallis 2005: 271–272). In response, Brown began a series of meetings with faith leaders on international debt and trade issues. Clare Short, a Brown ally, was equally impressed with the Jubilee campaign and sought to develop DFID's contacts with faith groups and leaders in response.

Thirdly, the Al-Qaeda attacks of 9/11 and subsequent events brought a greater sense of urgency to these efforts. US-led coalitions, including British forces, overthrew the Taliban regime in Afghanistan in October 2001 and the Saddam Hussain regime in Iraq in March 2003. Many Western governments feared the proliferation of terrorist networks loosely connected or sympathetic to Al-Qaeda as a consequence. In 2003, the British government launched a cross-Whitehall dialogue on faith issues to coordinate inter-departmental engagement with UK faith communities, partly in response to localised inter-faith tensions or the alienation of minority faith communities.[14] DFID was expected to play a significant role in this dialogue on the basis of its links to UK faith-based development organisations and its work in different faith settings overseas but was poorly placed to respond. DFID had no corporate policy on engagement with FBOs and knowledge of current engagement was incomplete at the centre, hindering participation in the dialogue. In addition, DFID was part of a cross-Whitehall dialogue on counter-terrorism while its work in post-Saddam Iraq fell under the auspices of the government's Global Conflict Prevention Pool, linking the Ministry of Defence, the Foreign and Commonwealth Office and DFID. In both cases, DFID's distinct focus on global poverty reduction risked being crowded out by a national security agenda and by the normal rivalries between government departments.

In response to these three factors, DFID has begun to strengthen its understanding of the 'faith and development' interface and its engagement with faith groups and leaders. Members of the ministerial team now speak frequently to faith leaders (mostly drawn from the mainstream Christian churches but also leaders of evangelical/Pentecostal, Islamic and Jewish organisations); a number of country offices have launched projects with significant FBO involvement or are preparing new projects; and the development education arm of DFID has worked with UK Protestant, Catholic, Islamic, Hindu, Sikh and Jewish organisations to publicise the MDGs in the idioms of the faith. Most significantly, perhaps, DFID launched a five-year £3.5m research programme on religions and development in 2005 in conjunction with the University of Birmingham, UK (details of the programme at: http://www.dfid.gov.uk/research/con tractsawardedfaithsindev.asp).

These steps remain tentative, however, and DFID is criticised by representatives of other government departments and of some FBOs for its caution in promoting engagement with faith communities. In practice, however, DFID faces a number of conceptual and programmatic obstacles. Many of these obstacles converge in the absence of a coherent corporate position within DFID on faith and development or on relationships with FBOs. As a result, different parts of the organisation engage with FBOs on an ad hoc basis, confronting a number of significant challenges.

In mid-2004, responsibility for oversight of DFID engagement with FBOs lay with the Information and Civil Society Department (ICSD), and ICSD oversaw DFID's most resource-intensive relationships with FBOs. Among other functions, ICSD supports UK-based development civil society organisations and 70% of its

programme budget in 2004 was committed to Programme Partnership Agreements (PPAs) with such organisations. PPAs provide stable, predictable funding, not tied to specific projects, usually for a period of three years. They support the strategic priorities of PPA agencies where they coincide with those of DFID, for instance, advocacy, networking or capacity-building. DFID supports between 20 and 25 PPAs at any one time, including three with faith-based development NGOs in mid-2004: Christian Aid, the Catholic Fund for Overseas Development (CAFOD) and Progressio (formerly the Catholic Institute for International Relations) (with a total funding commitment of over £25m). All three are associated with the mainstream Christian denominations and other FBOs are critical of the exclusion of organisations from other faith traditions from such a significant funding stream, although DFID has since concluded a PPA with Islamic Relief.[15]

ICSD also supports UK development NGOs and other organisations through the Civil Society Challenge Fund (CSCF), providing matching funds for projects initiated by applicants. Roughly 10% of grants each year are made to FBOs, but FBO representatives suggest that organisations associated with the mainstream Christian Churches benefit disproportionately. FBOs associated with evangelical and Pentecostal churches, for instance, suggest that funding applications are turned down because of DFID fears that funding will be used for proselytising activities, fears which they argue are based on a poor understanding of their mission and activities.

A similar problem arises in the second most resource-intensive form of engagement, between DFID's conflict and humanitarian intervention sections and faith-based NGOs involved in humanitarian or development projects. In 2004, funding was provided almost exclusively to Christian FBOs, even where the local community was not Christian (e.g. CAFOD and Tearfund activities with Muslim refugees in Darfur).[16] Staff are eager to collaborate with FBOs from other faith traditions, including the main Islamic development NGOs, but suggest that such organisations lack expertise in technical areas such as therapeutic feeding. Staff also point to potential contradictions between the principles of humanitarian intervention and the work of FBOs, for instance, sub-contracting to local partners who blur the distinction between the needy and the faithful in disbursing aid. Yet, in this area, as in others, DFID itself suffers from capacity constraints. DFID conflict advisers, for instance, participate in cross-Whitehall dialogue on counter-terrorism strategy yet are constrained by the lack of analytical work on the faith dimensions of conflict and conflict resolution. Research tools employed by DFID such as Strategic Conflict Assessments, often under-analyse issues of faith, undermining DFID's ability to make a distinct contribution based on its poverty reduction focus.

Other challenges arise in DFID's regional and country programmes. Firstly, the changing architecture of British aid hinders engagement with civil society organisations (CSOs), including FBOs. In recent years, DFID has reduced its funding of discrete projects and programmes and increased funding of direct budget support (DBS) and sector-wide approaches (SWAps). DFID has also increased support to multilateral institutions and increasingly funds projects and programmes in alliance with other prominent donors. This new approach aims to strengthen the capacity of central government in developing countries and to make international aid efforts more coherent but it may also serve to distance DFID from CSOs, including FBOs. Since the new millennium, DFID support of UK-based CSOs has increased in absolute terms, amid significant growth in its programme budget, but it has decreased

in relative terms.[17] Pressure on DFID advisory staff to identify opportunities for large funding disbursements may lead to less direct engagement with CSOs; the transaction costs associated with supporting a relatively large number of small organisations often preclude funding support to CSOs, unless it can be funnelled through a single civil society support fund or CSOs can establish consortia and networks with significant absorptive capacity. This creates a distinct challenge for FBOs; to form networks and alliances or to grow in terms of resources and expertise so as to avail of new funding opportunities arising from the changing architecture of aid.

Secondly, DFID engagement with FBOs in practice is at odds with the Department's commitment to the achievement of the MDGs. DFID engages with the Christian churches (Catholic, Protestant and Orthodox) in sub-Saharan Africa and to a lesser extent in Latin American and the Caribbean. It engages to a much lesser extent, however, with FBOs and faith leaders in South Asia. Case studies from the recent literature reveal a similar pattern; the World Bank and other donors have made significant progress in engaging with FBOs and faith leaders in sub-Saharan Africa, Latin America and East Asia but comparatively little progress in South Asia (including India, Pakistan and Bangladesh).[18]

In many countries in sub-Saharan Africa, FBOs account for more than half of health and education provision,[19] and faith groups account for a significant percentage of associational activity. Secular development NGOs and other types of CSOs are weaker than in South Asia, with the result that faith groups and FBOs are attractive partners for donors. The Millennium Development Goals aim primarily to combat extreme poverty by halving the number of people who live on US$1 a day by 2015 yet, in comparison to sub-Saharan Africa, South Asia is home to significantly more people on less than

US$1 a day.[20] This suggests that DFID engagement with FBOs is disproportionately targeted on sub-Saharan Africa and that DFID and other donors need to strengthen engagement with Muslim, Hindu, Sikh and Buddhist FBOs and leaders in the countries of South Asia.

There are significant challenges, however, in engaging with FBOs in South Asia. India, for instance, is defined as a 'secular' republic in the 1949 constitution and both state and federal support of religious organisations is prohibited by law. In these circumstances, it is unclear to what extent foreign donors can fund or otherwise engage with FBOs. Even if the legal position were clearer, moderate Hindu FBOs are significantly less well networked and less committed to political engagement than FBOs associated with *Hindutva* (sectarian Hindu nationalism). Across South Asia, it is difficult to identify obvious interlocutors: Islam, Hinduism and Sikhism are less hierarchically organised than the Christian faiths, so associated FBOs have an ambiguous status as representatives of the faith. In Asian countries, where the state is stronger and exerts greater ownership over policy processes, it can be difficult to secure government agreement to consultation with faith groups. And yet in South Asia, where the institution of caste is central to the social construction of poverty and derives much of its legitimacy from religious discourse, the connections between faith and development are accentuated.

Thirdly, this gap between policy and practice is illustrated by analytical blindspots in DFID such as Islamic education. Conservative *madrasas* (religious schools) and other Islamic schools are often seen in the West as a breeding ground for political extremism,[21] especially where they focus on religious education to the exclusion of the state-approved, and largely secular, curriculum. Pakistani *madrasas,* for instance, have been implicated in providing a military training to young British Muslims

recruited by militant organisations such as Jaish-e-Mohammed and Laskar-i-Toiba, fuelling terrorist attacks in Britain (Lamb 2005). *Madrasa* reform, bringing *madrasas* within the state education system, is seen as a critical component in the war against terrorism in countries such as Pakistan, even though *madrasas* promoting militant ideologies or providing military trainings are in a small minority. (According to Lamb 2005, some reports suggest that roughly 1% of the estimated 13,000 *madrasas* in Pakistan support violence.) DFID and other donors, therefore, face pressures from the security-driven agendas of Western governments. Most *madrasas,* however, play an important role in educating children in countries where the state lacks the resources to fund universal primary education and where parents lack a choice of schools.[22] The better-resourced *madrasas* often provide free food and accommodation to the children of the poor, and employment for a significant minority who go on to work in *madrasas* or mosques.[23] Where they combine secular and religious education, Islamic schools can play a potentially important role in providing poor children with a basic primary school education, and as a significant social safety net.

In contrast to some other donors, DFID does not directly support Islamic schools that combine religious education with the state curriculum.[24] Many countries with a substantial Muslim population, however, are unlikely to attain the MDG with respect to primary school enrolment and completion without innovative and radical measures. Within DFID, five countries in particular give rise to concern vis-à-vis the primary education MDG. In India, Pakistan and Bangladesh, primary school enrolment is high, around 80%, but large population sizes mean that large numbers of children remain outside the primary school system. In Sudan and the Democratic Republic of the Congo, the population is lower, but low enrolment rates, around 40–50%, mean that large numbers of children are still denied a primary school education. In all five countries, state provision is unlikely to deliver the MDG target by 2015 and faith-based schools, including *madrasas*, hold the potential to provide a basic education for the poorest children. By early 2006, however, DFID had yet to fund a significant project or programme in the context of Islamic education.

Conclusion

The country cases reviewed here (the United States, Saudi Arabia and the United Kingdom) illustrate the conceptual and programmatic challenges for donors posed by the emerging faith and development interface. There is now a broad-based agreement that the world's faith communities have an important role to play in the pursuit of the Millennium Development Goals. As Jim Wallis argued in a *New York Times* bestseller, *God's Politics*, 'only a new moral, spiritual and even religious sensibility' can underpin 'the struggle to eliminate the world's worst poverty' (Wallis 2005: 270–271). 'It is social movements', Wallis writes, 'which change history, and the best movements are the ones with spiritual foundations' (2005: xvi). Donor representatives have gone on record in supporting this view and are now faced with a central question: how to harness the latent empathy of the world's major faiths with the plight of the poor and to mobilise faith communities to support the poor and to demand pro-poor change.

Donors have answered this question in significant part by challenging FBOs to become 'agents of transformation', by shedding their traditional focus on charity and by galvanising their moral authority to demand better governance and public accountability. In the UK, former Secretary

of State for International Development Clare Short has gone on record in challenging FBOs to transform in this manner. But this chapter suggests that donors such as the UK Department for International Development (DFID) must also adjust and become equivalent 'agents of transformation' and change in significant respects. Many Western donors, such as DFID, have traditionally promoted a secular and technocratic vision of development, focusing on the material dimensions of poverty at the expense of its cultural, moral and spiritual dimensions. They have traditionally engaged with specialised development agencies associated with the mainstream Christian churches, but largely avoided engagement with organisations from other faith traditions. This secularist bent remains ingrained in donor organisational culture. Some donors are profoundly sceptical of greater engagement with FBOs. DFID staff argue, for instance, that traditional secularism has served DFID well and isolated it from a contentious social milieu, a position supported prominently by Amartya Sen.[25]

This secularist position, however, is under attack on two key fronts. First, 'development' is increasingly seen as a *multidimensional* process, based on a broader conception of *well-being*. This new conception goes beyond the material dimensions of well-being to encompass new variables such as cultural identity. The *Human Development Report 2004*, for instance, identities two distinct forms of cultural exclusion which compound material poverty: *living mode exclusion*, where a state or social custom denigrates or suppresses a group's culture, including its spiritual beliefs, and *participation exclusion*, where cultural identities, including faith-based identities, give rise to discrimination or disadvantage which leads to social, economic or political exclusion.[26] Within this new conception of well-being, faith is a key aspect of cultural identity and FBOs important institutional expressions. Second, development is increasingly acknowledged as an *institutionally complex* undertaking. In contrast to the government-to-government paradigm of old, a new paradigm acknowledges the importance of multi-stakeholder partnerships, of including the private sector and civil society in development policy and of multiple tiers of partnerships and networks from local to global. In this context, faith communities and FBOs are important actors, using the idioms of spiritual belief to provide practical support to the poor and to mobilise the popular moral energy needed to effect political change.[27]

This new conception of development requires significant changes on the part of official donors. USAID's 2004 ruling on participation by religious organisations in its programmes and the Saudi government's difficulties in regulating faith-based charities illustrate many of the dangers that European donors such as DFID perceive in the new interface between faith and development. In particular, it raises the prospect of donor support of organisations committed to active proselytising and/or the denigration of other faiths in some of the poorest and most culturally sensitive countries in the world, generating faith-based tensions which undermine, rather than support, the pursuit of the MDGs. European donors such as DFID, however, must nevertheless change. Conceptually, they must revise their secular and technocratic vision of development, overcome analytical blind-spots such as Islamic education or the work of evangelical and Pentecostal organisations and explore practical overlaps between the previously separate worlds of faith and development. Operationally, they must develop a more coherent corporate position on faith and development, promote faith literacy among staff, adjust their funding modalities to better accommodate FBOs, and diversify their engagement with FBOs beyond the mainstream Christian churches while

working to build their capacity and their inclusion in key development partnerships. With these changes, perhaps, they can become 'agents of transformation', fit for purpose in a new millennium.

Notes

1 This chapter draws on material which first appeared in Clarke (2006, 2007) and in Clarke and Jennings (2008). It is also informed by research in 2004–2005 commissioned by the Department for International Development (DFID) which examined DFID engagement with faith-based organisations and the role of faith groups in poverty reduction.
2 According to the former Archbishop of Canterbury, for instance, faith leaders have 'to admit that sometimes we encourage [material] poverty by focusing on spiritual poverty and maybe confusing the two' (Dr George Carey, Opening Remarks, Leaders Meeting on Faith and Development, Canterbury, England, October 2002 (World Bank transcript)). See also Marshall and Marsh (2003: 29).
3 Wolfensohn, however, was defeated by 24 votes to 0 in the Executive Board when he proposed further Bank expenditure on this new policy thrust (Remarks by James Wolfensohn, Leaders Meeting on Faith and Development). In the acrimonious aftermath, the Directorate was renamed the 'Development Dialogue on Ethics and Values' and its profile reduced.
4 For the full text of the Millennium Declaration, see www.un.org/millennium/summit.htm. For details of the MDGs, see www.un.org/millenniumgoals/index.html.
5 The 37,000 NPOs had assets of approximately $142bn and annual budgets of $93bn in 1999 (Wuthnow 2004: 140 and 325n5). This estimate assumes that FBOs have proportionately similar resources to all NPOs (2004: 142). In 2002, Syria, Sri Lanka and Costa Rica had Gross National Income (GNI) of US$19bn, $16bn and $16bn respectively (http://www.worldbank.org/data/dataquery.html).
6 Peter Waldman, 'Evangelicals give US Foreign Policy an Activist Tinge', *The Wall Street Journal*, 26 May 2004. See Moreau (2000: 45) and Moreau *et al.* (2004: 283 and 285) for equivalent figures for 1996–1999. Moreau (2000), for instance, reports income of $2.93bn in 1999.

7 Although the figures for missionary organisations here include World Vision and other development NGOs associated with the US missionary tradition.

8 See p. 11, footnote 2, of the ruling.

9 See, for instance, 'Saudi Arabia to fold Al-Haramain and other Charities in National Commission', Press Release, Royal Embassy of Saudi Arabia, Washington, DC, 2 June 2004; www.saudiembassy.net. The government announced that a number of prominent organisations, including the Al-Haramain Islamic Foundation, would be closed and their activities absorbed by the new Commission.

10 Indeed, according to Casanova, the US is unique among advanced Western industrial societies in its experience of 'a religious fundamentalist movement of societal importance' in the form of the 'new Christian right' (Casanova 2004: 135).

11 Mainly Christian Aid, the Catholic Fund for Overseas Development (CAFOD) and the Catholic Institute for International Relations (CIIR).

12 Block grants to the main development NGOs and the Joint Funding Scheme (JFS), open to a wider range of development NGOs, were replaced in 2000 with new funding schemes, including Programme Partnerships Agreements (PPAs), the Civil Society Challenge Fund (CSCF) and Strategic Grant Agreements (SGAs).

13 'This fiftieth year you shall make sacred by proclaiming liberty in the land for all its inhabitants. It shall be a jubilee for you' (Book of Leviticus, Chapter 25).

14 The dialogue was accompanied by a government guide, spelling out the steps that government departments were expected to take in developing links to UK faith communities (*Working Together: Cooperation between Government and the Faith Communities*, London: Home Office Faith Communities Unit, 2004).

15 DFID has also concluded PPAs with World Vision, (a prominent development NGO associated with evangelical and Pentecostal Christianity), and with the Aga Khan Foundation, the official development agency of the Ismaili Muslim diaspora and its leader, the Aga Khan.

16 DFID has begun to work more closely with Islamic Relief, especially since Islamic Relief joined the Disasters and Emergencies Committee (DEC), the main network of British NGOs involved in emergency relief and humanitarian intervention.

17 In 1999/2000, for instance, DFID channelled £195m through UK CSOs, equivalent to 7.65% of programme expenditure. In 2003/2004, it channelled £220m, equivalent to 5.54% of programme expenditure, a 28% fall in relative support (DFID 2001: 17 and 87; NS 2005: 168). The relative fall may be less when funding of CSOs through DFID country programmes is included.

18 Of the 15 case-studies in Marshall and Marsh (2003) and the 20 in Marshall and Keough (2004) (with significant overlap between the two case-study sets), none are based on experience in India, Pakistan or Bangladesh.

19 In sub-Saharan Africa as a whole, the World Bank estimates, faith groups account for 50% of education and health service provision (Wolfensohn 2004).

20 Over 450m people survive on less than US$1 a day in four countries in South Asia (India, Pakistan, Bangladesh and Sri Lanka). In comparison, 282m people live on less than a dollar a day in 25 countries in sub-Saharan Africa for which figures are available (UNDP 2003: 199–200).

21 According to Mercer (2006), for instance, an internet search on '*madrasas* and terrorism' in January 2006 revealed 16,347 items.

22 In Bangladesh, for instance, almost 2m children (45% of them girls) attended 7,000 *ebtidai* (primary level and government-recognised) *madrasas* in 2003 while millions of other children attend unrecognised pre-primary or primary level *madrasas*. In Pakistan, the figures are uncertain, but commonly quoted estimates point to between 1m and 1.7m children in up to 10,000 primary and secondary level *madrasas* (Mercer 2006).

23 The employment opportunities for *madrasa* students can be significant. In Bangladesh, for instance, up to 950,000 jobs in *madrasas*, mosques and other institutions (or roughly the total number employed in the public sector) are available to schools leavers or graduates with a religious training (Mercer 2006).

24 This situation is changing slowly. DFID's £26m Girls' Education Project in Nigeria, launched in December 2004, focuses on state provision but also works with non-state providers, especially with *Islamiyya*, an organisation which runs schools combining secular and Islamic education ('Education Project Launched in Nigeria', 9 December 2004, News section, www.dfid.gov.uk).

25 In his own words, a 'strong believer in secularism and democracy' (and what he sees as an intrinsic link between them), Sen rails against

religion-based classifications of people and bemoans 'the confounded view of what a multiethnic society must do', for instance, support faith-based (and state-financed) schools (Sen 2006: 19, 12, 13).

26 The report suggests that faith is the most important element in cultural exclusion, citing evidence that some 359m people are disadvantaged or discriminated against on the basis of their faith, or 70% of the estimated 518m people worldwide who belong to groups that face some form of cultural exclusion (UNDP 2004: 32–33).

27 In 1995, for instance, the UN Commission on Global Governance pointed to distinct attributes of 'religion-based organisations' and other civil society organisations which complement those of official donor agencies in the context of global governance (UNCGG 1995: 32–35).

Bibliography

Bartkowski, J. P. and Regis, H. A. (2003) *Charitable Choices: Religion, Race and Poverty in the Post-Welfare Era*, New York: New York University Press.

Belshaw, D., Calderisi, R. and Sugden, C. (eds) (2001) *Faith in Development: Partnership between the World Bank and the Churches in Africa*, Washington, DC: World Bank and Oxford: Regnum Books.

Berger, P. L. (ed.) (1999) *The Desecularization of the World: Resurgent Religion and World Politics*, Grand Rapids, MI: William B. Eerdmans.

Burke, J. (2004) *Al Qaeda: The True Story of Radical Islam*, Harmondsworth: Penguin Books.

Burr, J. M. and Collins, R. O. (2006) *Alms for Jihad: Charity and Terrorism in the Islamic World*, Cambridge: Cambridge University Press.

Casanova, J. (2004) *Public Religions in the Modern World*, Chicago: Chicago University Press.

Clark, J. (2003) *Worlds Apart: Civil Society and the Battle for Ethical Globalization*. London: Earthscan.

Clark, J. (2004) *Islam, Charity and Activism: Middle-class Networks in Egypt, Jordan and Yemen*, Bloomington: Indiana University Press.

Clarke, G. (2006) 'Faith Matters: Faith-based Organisations, Civil Society and International Development, *Journal of International Development*, 18 (6), pp. 835–848.

Clarke, G. (2007) 'Agents of Transformation? Donors, Faith-based Organisations and International Development', *Third World Quarterly*, 28 (1), pp. 77–96.

Clarke, G. and Jennings, M. (eds) (2008) *Development, Civil Society and Faith-based Organisations: Bridging the Sacred and the Secular*, Basingstoke: Palgrave Macmillan.

Dedayan, D. (2004) 'Faith-based Initiatives: More than Politics', Washington, DC: Institute for Global Engagement, www.globalengagement.org, July 2005.

DFID (2001) *Departmental Report 2001*, London: Department for International Development.

Easterly, W. (2006) *The White Man's Burden: Why the West's Efforts to Aid the Rest Have Done So Much Ill and So Little Good*, London: Penguin Books.

Ehrenfeld, R. (2005) 'Saudi Dollars and Jihad', Frontpagemag.com, 24 October (citing testimony by former Central Intelligence Agency Director James Woolsey before the US House of Representatives' Committee on Government Reform in April 2005).

Hearn, J. (2002) 'The "Invisible" NGOs: US Evangelical Missions in Kenya', *Journal of Religion in Africa*, 32 (1), pp. 32–61.

'History of the NAE', www.nae.net, accessed June 2005.

Kepel, G. (2002) *JIHAD: The Trail of Political Islam*, London: I. B. Tauris.

Kroessin, M. and Mohamed, A. S. (2008) 'Saudi Arabian NGOs in Somalia: "Wahabi" Da'wah or Humanitarian Aid?', in G. Clarke, and M. Jennings, (eds) (2008) *Development, Civil Society and Faith-based Organisations: Bridging the Sacred and the Secular*, Basingstoke: Palgrave Macmillan, pp. 187–213.

Kuo, D. (2006) *Tempting Faith: An Inside Story of a Political Seduction*, New York: Free Press.

Lamb, C. (2005) 'The Pakistan Connection', *The Sunday Times*, 17 July.

Linden, I. (2004) 'Islam, DFID and Poverty Reduction: How to Improve the Partnership', report to the Department for International Development, London, March.

Luttwak, E. (1994) 'The Missing Dimension', in D. Johnston and C. Sampson (eds), *Religion: The Mission Dimension in Statecraft*, Oxford: Oxford University Press, pp. 8–19.

Marshall, K. and Keough, L. (eds) (2004) *Mind, Heart and Soul in the Fight against Poverty*, Washington, DC: World Bank.

Marshall, K. and Marsh, R. (eds) (2003) *Millennium Challenges for Development and Faith Institutions*, Washington, DC: World Bank.

Marshall K. and Van Saanen, M. (2007) *Development and Faith: Where Heart, Mind and Soul Work Together*, Washington, DC: World Bank.

Mercer, M. (2006) 'Madrasas in Bangladesh and Pakistan: Bogeyman or Blessing?', paper presented at the 3rd annual colloquium of the Welsh Network of Development Researchers, Gregynog, 25–27 January.

Mishal, S. and Sela, A. (2000) *The Palestinian Hamas: Vision, Violence and Coexistence*, New York: Columbia University Press.

Moreau, S. (2000) 'Putting the Survey in Context', in J. A. Siewert and D. Welliver (eds), *Mission Handbook: US and Canadian Ministries Overseas 2001–2003*, Wheaton, IL.: Evangelism and Missions Information Service (EMIS), pp. 33–80.

Moreau, A. S., Corwin, G. R. and McGee, G. B. (2004) *Introducing World Missions: A Biblical, Historical and Practical Survey*, Grand Rapids, MI: Baker Academic.

Narayan, D. (2001) 'Voices of the Poor', in D. Belshaw, R. Calderisi, and C. Sugden, (eds), *Faith in Development: Partnership between the World Bank and the Churches in Africa*, Washington, DC: World Bank and Oxford: Regnum Books, pp. 39–50.

Narayan, D., Chambers, R., Shah, M. K. and Petesch, P. (2000) *Voices of the Poor: Crying out for Change*, Washington, DC: World Bank and New York: Oxford University Press.

Neumayer, E. (2003) 'What Factors Determine the Allocation of Aid by Arab Countries and Multilateral Agencies?', *Journal of Development Studies*, 39, 4, pp. 134–147.

NS (2005) *Statistics on International Development 2000/01–2004/05*, London: National Statistics.

Palmer, M. and Findlay, V. (2003) *Faith in Conservation: New Approaches to Religion and Conservation*, Washington, DC: World Bank.

'Participation by Religious Organizations in USAID Programs', http://www.usaid.gov/ur_work/global_partnerships/fbci/fbocomments_101304.doc, accessed March 2006.

Pearson, R. and Tomalin, E. (2008) 'Intelligent Design? A Gender-sensitive Interrogation of Religion and Development', in G. Clarke, and M. Jennings, (eds), *Development, Civil Society and Faith-based Organisations: Bridging the Sacred and the Secular*, Basingstoke: Palgrave Macmillan, pp. 46–71.

'Saudi Arabia is the Hub of World Terror', *The Sunday Times*, 4 November 2007.

Sen, A. (2006) *Identity and Violence: The Illusion of Destiny*, London: Allen Lane.

Short, C., (2003) 'After September 11: What Global Challenges Lie Ahead?', in K. Marshall, and R. Marsh, (eds), *Millennium Challenges for Development and Faith Institutions*, Washington, DC: World Bank, pp. 3–11.

UNCGG (1995) *Our Global Neighbourhood: The Report of the Commission on Global Governance*, New York: Oxford University Press and the UN Commission on Global Governance.

UNDP (2003) *Human Development Report 2003: Millennium Development Goals – A Compact among Nations to End Human Poverty*, New York: United Nations Development Program and Oxford University Press.

UNDP (2004) *Human Development Report 2004: Cultural Liberty in Today's Diverse World*, New York: United Nations Development Programme and Oxford University Press.

Waldman, P. (2004) 'Evangelicals Give US Foreign Policy an Activist Tinge', *The Wall Street Journal*, 26 May.

Wallis, J. (2005) *God's Politics: Why the American Right Gets it Wrong and the Left Doesn't Get It*, San Francisco: Harper.

Westerlund, D. and Rosander, E. E. (1997) *African Islam and Islam in Africa*, London: C. Hurst and Co.

Wiktorowicz, Q. (2001) *The Management of Islamic Activism: Salafis, the Muslim Brotherhood and State Power in Jordan*, New York: State University of New York Press.

Wilson, B. (1992) *Religion in Sociological Perspective*, Oxford: Oxford University Press.

Wolfensohn, J. (2004) 'Millennium Challenges for Faith and Development: New Partnerships to Reduce Poverty and Strengthen Conservation', speech to the Interfaith Conference of Metropolitan Washington, 30 March.

Wuthnow, R. (2004) *Saving America: Faith-based Services and the Future of Civil Society*, Princeton: Princeton University Press.

25

Changing the climate of religious internationalism

Evangelical responses to global warming and human suffering[1]

Noah J. Toly

Introduction

Since the early 2000s, the international affairs community has become significantly more engaged and conversant with religion. This same period has also witnessed religious communities' increasingly intentional engagement with international affairs. However, in response to 9/11 and the subsequent 'War on Terror', most of this mutual interest has been focused upon human suffering associated with potent religious fundamentalisms and the need to secure religious freedom and human rights. While these are important issues, their engagement does not represent a robust commitment by religious internationalists to the breadth of international affairs.

Among religious communities with influential but limited international engagement are Evangelical Christians in the US. Despite the influence of this group, the Evangelical community still marginalizes or ignores many international issues. For example, until very recently, Christian internationalists, in particular, have not explicitly engaged the most pressing global environmental issue of our

time, one that has captured the attention of international relations scholars, foreign affairs specialists, and global activists, alike – anthropogenic climate change.

In a 2004 contribution to *Science*, David King, Chief Scientific Advisor to Her Majesty's Government, went so far as to argue that 'climate change is the most severe problem that we are facing today–more serious even than the threat of terrorism'. Sir John Houghton, former chair of the Intergovernmental Panel on Climate Change Working Group I, has described climate change as a weapon of mass destruction (2003). Notwithstanding such dire warnings, global environmental concerns have garnered little attention among internationally engaged Evangelicals. Until recently, what little attention has been granted to environmental concerns was most often expressed in terms of economics (asking, for example, 'What is the most efficient means of pollution control?'; 'Who will pay for controlling pollutants?') or security ('Is dependence on oil undermining the battle against terrorism?'), with little regard for the human suffering mediated by environmental conditions.

Thus, despite the prominent role of global environmental governance and, specifically, climate governance in the international affairs discourse, Christian internationalists, *qua Christian internationalists*, have not given the issue sufficient attention. This chapter both engages and examines that deficit, presenting climate change as a likely cause of human suffering that merits greater attention from religious communities, briefly analysing religious responses to the problem, and arguing for Christian engagement with this issue in global environmental governance.

The human factors in climate change

Contemporary ecological crises are distinguished from earlier manifestations of environmental change by their human dimensions. Both human origins and consequences set apart phenomena such as biodiversity loss, deforestation, desertification and climate change. This last is especially disturbing, demonstrating an increased scope, scale, and speed of human intervention in ecological systems and processes, and an increased impact upon human populations. In other words, modern – and especially industrial – environmental change is marked by considerable human responsibility and human vulnerability. And this is particularly evident in the case of climate change.

While evidence of contemporary climate change has only recently emerged, the phenomenon is far from novel. Records and reconstructions indicate previous dramatic shifts in global average surface temperature, which were accompanied by associated changes in regional and local climates (Jones *et al.* 2001; Mann *et al.* 1998). Pre-industrial shifts have been attributed to various natural causes and feedback loops related to, among other phenomena, slight shifts in the orbit of the

earth, variability in solar irradiance, changes in the reflectivity of the planet, and volcanic activity (Crowley 2000). The analogous contemporary phenomena of global warming and climate change, however, are set apart by acute onset, increased impact upon human populations, and 'anthropogenesis', the human origins of the crisis itself.

Evidence that the earth is warming is overwhelming. The twentieth century and the beginning of the twenty-first saw an increase of 0.74° Celsius in the global average surface temperature of the earth, a measure of increased energy that will likely contribute to highly differentiated deviations from normal weather patterns across the globe (IPCC 2007a; Karl and Trenberth 2003). That is, deviations from the norm will vary from slight to dramatic over time and space (IPCC 2007a). Differences in temperature are greater at night, at latitudinal extremes, over land, and in winter. Differences in climate are considerably more variable: projections suggest that trapping more energy in the atmosphere will likely lead to some places being colder and some warmer, some wetter and some drier. Many suggest that the beginnings of such patterns – and not just increases in global average surface temperature – are already observable (IPCC 2007a).

However, while the phenomenon itself is generally incontrovertible, the causes of climate change have been hotly debated. A very small and diminishing portion of the scientific community disputes the extent of anthropogenesis, arguing instead that the phenomenon is mostly natural in origin.

Still, the overwhelming balance of scientific opinion and evidence does implicate significant human contributions. Since the emergence of climate change as a field of inquiry in its own right, compelling evidence has been found to support the notion of anthropogenesis.[2] Models including only 'natural forcing' cannot account for observed changes in global average surface temperature; models including only anthropogenic factors approximate observed temperatures, but are not a perfect match; models accounting for natural and anthropogenic forcing match extremely well with observed temperatures and trends (IPCC 2007a; Stott *et al.* 2000).

The Intergovernmental Panel on Climate Change (IPCC),[3] an international scientific community dedicated to understanding the origins and implications of global warming, attributes global warming to two chief causes: land use change and increased greenhouse gas (GHG) emissions from the combustion of fossil fuels, the latter being the most significant cause (IPCC 2007a). Releases of sequestered carbon, alterations in the capacity for carbon sequestration, changes in the reflectivity of the planet, and modifications to the composition of the atmosphere have set the global climate on a path toward serious environmental change (Hasselman *et al.* 2003; IPCC 2007a; Karl and Trenberth 2003). GHG emissions are considered the most pernicious of these causes and current totals – natural and anthropogenic combined – greatly exceed the earth's limited capacity to absorb and recycle such gases (IPCC 2007a).

Another area of some scientific dispute regards the likely consequences of climate change. Some argue that its probable effects are by no means strictly harmful. Increased atmospheric concentrations of CO_2 and other GHGs, along with the poleward spread of temperate weather, are likely to bring such agricultural benefits as longer growing seasons at higher latitudes and decreased exposure-related mortality. However, despite such possibilities, a full reckoning of the effects of climate change strongly suggests that profound global costs will outweigh marginal benefits (IPCC 2007a, 2007b).

With a 1.1°–6.4°C projected warming of global average surface temperatures

over the next century,[4] anticipated adverse effects of climate change are many (IPCC 2007a, 2007b; Karl and Trenberth 2003). For instance, climate change causes biodiversity loss (IPCC 2007b) and is currently among the primary causes – if not the primary cause – of specie extinction (Bakkenes *et al.* 2002; Beaumont and Hughes 2002; Erasmus *et al.* 2002; Midgley *et al.* 2002; Parmesan and Yohe 2003; Pounds and Campbell 1999; Root *et al.* 2003; Thomas *et al.* 2004); it is a chief driver of what Norman Myers has described as a 'biotic holocaust' (1999) as the poleward spread of temperate weather dramatically alters habitat at latitudinal and elevational extremes. Climate change-induced biodiversity loss implies lost social values, as well. Not merely aesthetic, these values carry significant implications for the sustenance of life and livelihood of millions of people across the globe. As the linchpin of ecological integrity, the diversity of ecosystems, species and genetic resources is of central importance to the maintenance of ecological systems and processes upon which many people directly depend. For example, the bleaching of coral reefs due to even minor changes in water temperature can have dramatic ill-effects upon local communities with significant dependence upon marine resources.

And biodiversity loss is not the only potential climate-related threat to society and its values. Others include sea-level rise, increased storm surge, increased intensity and frequency of hurricanes and typhoons, and increased severity of floods and droughts (IPCC 2007a, 2007b). Sea-level rise threatens to flood more than 10% of Bangladesh, a country densely populated with 133,000,000 people, over the next 100 years (IPCC 1996).

Climate change-induced human suffering is not necessarily a far-off, twenty-second-century problem. In many parts of the world, the effects of climate change are already issuing in hard realities. For example, residents of Malasiga, Papua New Guinea and parts of Bangladesh find themselves displaced by rising tides (Goering 2007; Osnos 2006). And sea-level rise has also made environmental refugees of the citizens of Tuvalu, a small island state in the South Pacific, who are retreating from their homeland and seeking safe-haven and new citizenship in New Zealand (Allen 2004, Reuters News Service 2002). Such islands have joined to form the Alliance of Small Island States (AOSIS),[5] which has become a significant contributor to international climate policy negotiations. Potential displacement is among AOSIS's motivating concerns.

The present human suffering generated by climate change goes beyond the hardships of displacement. Recent research attributes more than 160,000 deaths per year – mostly poor children in Africa, Asia and Latin America – to climate change-related causes including, but not limited to, extreme weather and the poleward spread of typically tropical diseases (WHO 2003).[6] A study by Harvard Medical School's Center for Health and the Global Environment notes the likely increased prevalence of malaria, lyme disease, West Nile Virus, and asthma, among other diseases and conditions (2005). These concerns accompany those of increased frequency and intensity of extreme weather, such as floods, droughts and heatwaves, to make climate change one of the most significant, if not the most significant, public health risks facing the world today.

Many believe that climate change will also lead to increased conflict-related human suffering. In 2003, a Pentagon-commissioned study indicated that displacement caused by climate change may be a significant threat to security in the near future (Schwartz and Randall 2003). The United Nations Security Council recently held meetings regarding climate change only days after a panel of retired US military generals and admirals released a report on 'National Security and the Threat of Climate Change'. Such reports suggest significant instability-related security and development linkages for climate change.

Notably, the consequences of climate change threaten poor populations and future generations in disproportionate measure to their GHG emissions, demonstrating the uneven geographic and temporal distribution of climate change's pernicious effects (Agarwal et al. 2002; Agarwal and Narain 1991; IPCC 2007a, 2007b; Qader Mirza 2003; Roberts and Parks 2007). Today's rich populations produce more GHG emissions while the consequent burden of human suffering is borne by today's poor and by future generations.

While the Global North is least vulnerable and most able to adapt, it will not escape this suffering forever. Some consequences may already be evident. Europe's summer of 2003, for example, was the hottest since the sixteenth century, and more than 19,000 deaths on the continent were attributable, at least in part, to the oppressive heat (Luterbacher et al. 2004). Summer temperatures exceeded average summer temperatures of the period 1901–1995 by 6.0° Celsius. While no single weather event may be attributed to global warming, this summer heat wave was consistent with the predicted patterns of global climate change. Meanwhile, average temperatures of European winters since the 1970s have been the warmest since instrumented readings became available in 1750. Harvard's analogue heatwave analysis (Center for Health and the global Environment 2005) suggests that an event in the US similar to Europe's of 2003 would likely result in more than three thousand deaths in New York City, alone.

The largest polluters will not entirely escape the uncertainty and pernicious effects associated with climate change.

But of special concern is (or should be) the fact that global warming victimizes already-vulnerable populations more quickly and more intensely. And the capacity for adaptation to global warming is unevenly distributed around the globe, which exacerbates the global inequalities in human suffering. Capacity for adaptation is generally a function of wealth and geography (Najam *et al.* 2003).[7]

Qader Mirza (2003) has noted that policy mechanisms designed to increase global investment in capacity-building for adaptation currently focus on increasing the capability of developing countries for recovery from climate-related disasters, rather than adaptation to potential environmental hazards. Critics have suggested that these adaptation investment regimes do not address the increasing magnitude of economic and social vulnerability due to the debt incurred in such a recovery effort. Such practices also represent a significant departure from the polluter–pays principle in favour of a victim-pays principle. In this regard, a preoccupation with adaptation may only intensify already significant inequities in the distribution of climate change's effects and the human suffering caused by them.

The international response to climate change

In the face of this crisis, the international community has gathered under the auspices of the United Nations Framework Convention on Climate Change (UNFCCC) in an effort to organize abatement and adaptation. The UNFCCC, along with the Convention on Biological Diversity, was opened for signature at the Earth Summit in 1992 and has enjoyed almost universal participation.

The highlight of the convention has been the emergence of the Kyoto Protocol – opened for signature in 1997 at the third

conference of the parties to the UNFCCC (COP-3) and entered into force in 2005, upon fulfilment of the 55/55 criterion[8] – one of the most ambitious international treaties in history. Kyoto represented a second international effort under the auspices of the norm of universal participation, one operationalized as a 'North-first' principle by the Montreal Protocol (Hoffmann 2005).

Adopting a principle of shared but differentiated responsibilities, the Protocol sets emissions targets for thirty-nine industrialized nations of the treaty's Annex I during its first budget period, 2008–2012. Other parties are exempt from emissions objectives during this initial accounting, but are likely to be assigned targets for a second period and beyond.[9] However, cumulative emissions abatement under the Protocol's targets would constitute a 5.2% reduction in emissions among Annex I nations by 2010, a far cry from the IPCC's indication that 60% reductions from global 1990 levels would be required in order to stabilize sustainable levels of atmospheric GHG concentrations (IPCC 2001).[10]

Faced with the prospect of even minimal emissions reductions, negotiators at the 6th Conference of the Parties (COP-6) began the development of the Protocol's flexibility mechanisms, policy devices designed to limit the necessity of domestic emissions reductions in favour of joint action. Among these flexibility mechanisms is 'emissions trading'. Often described as 'hot air', emissions trading is the mechanism by which countries that have achieved emissions reductions in excess of their targets may sell the difference to countries that would rather not achieve their emissions reductions through domestic action. Notably, the majority of 'hot air' would be provided by countries of Eastern Europe and the Former Soviet Union, the reductions of which have been achieved because of economic recession. Such retrenchments do not represent socially or environmentally sustainable reductions in emissions intensity and stand to be erased by economic recovery, suggesting that, if emissions trading is a viable flexibility mechanism, parties to the Protocol should consider limiting its use to cases in which emissions have decreased because of concerted efforts at efficiency, conservation, or substitution of non-carbon-based fuels.

Also notable are joint implementation (JI) and the clean development mechanism (CDM). JI represents an energy development or GHG sequestration project conducted by one member of Annex I in another Annex I country, in exchange for credits equivalent to the difference between business-as-usual (BAU) and actual emissions. For example, Germany may receive credit for a renewable energy or reforestation project conducted in France.

CDM, on the other hand, represents an exchange between a member of Annex I and a non-Annex I country. In this case, for example, Germany might receive credit for a renewable energy or reforestation project conducted in Mexico.

The Parties have also included carbon sinks, representing already existing sequestration capacity, in accounting for domestic emissions, effectively reducing the emissions reduction requirements of many Annex B nations. As part of the Protocol mechanisms, sinks effectively reduce the assigned targets, as they represent the status quo, rather than any difference from 1990 levels. While applicable sink credits are capped, there are no limits to the use of 'hot air', JI, or CDM.

These policy tools have been designated as means to achieve economically efficient emissions abatement. Unfortunately, the implementation of these mechanisms – apart from caps on their use – will likely lead to emissions increases according to BAU projections, rather than to abatement (Byrne et al. 2004). Indeed, phantom emissions reductions from the application of these flexibility mechanisms, applied to the accounts of Annex B countries, ensure a 'successful' Protocol despite these likely increases in emissions (Toly 2005). Parties may claim to have achieved their target reductions despite significant emissions growth at both national and international levels.

While many of the flexibility mechanisms have been introduced into the protocol under great pressure from the government of the United States (the world's largest polluter), this very same government (along with those of other prominent emitters, such as Australia) has unilaterally opted out of participation in the protocol and has limited participation in international negotiations for the abatement of greenhouse gas emissions (White House 2002a, 2002b; Wirth 2002; van Vuuren et al. 2002). Citing Chinese, Indian and Brazilian lack of targets in the first budget period – and ignoring historical emissions, per capita emissions, differences between 'luxury' and 'livelihood' emissions, and the near certainty of targets for such countries in a second budget period – it has chosen instead to pursue a domestic agenda of voluntary emissions intensity reductions based upon a 'no regret' strategy that invokes the dubious rhetoric of uncertain causes and effects in global climate change.

'No regret' policies for greenhouse gas emissions abatement involve the rectification of market inefficiencies and failures in order to reduce emissions at low or no cost, deriving these benefits from increased market efficiency. Such approaches favour preserving the option values associated with capital that might be invested to mitigate climate change as opposed to the option values associated with a future intact global ecosystem and economy. This approach rejects any relatively costly options for abatement in rhetorical deference to the slight possibility that the effects of climate change may not be as vicious as most scientists are projecting. While the scientific community cannot claim to have achieved the same consensus regarding climate change as exists regarding gravity, for example, the evidence for dramatic changes in climate and some level of human contribution to the problem is more over-whelming now than ever. Yet climate change sceptics are undeterred; they continue to deploy the rhetoric of uncer-tainty as partial justification for 'no regret' strategies.

Religious responses to climate change

In contrast to perspectives that focus only on the economic utility of the natural world or for which economic efficiency is, practically speaking, the only moral guide, adherents of several of the world's major religions have articulated responses to climate change amid increasingly religious engagement with environmental, as well as international, issues. Uniquely Baha'i, Buddhist, Christian, Hindu, Islamic, Jewish and Sikh interpretations have, in some instances, been coupled with action con-sistent with those interpretations. At the same time, many religious groups have issued joint statements or cooperated in projects to reduce emissions.[11]

Intra- and inter-faith ecumenicity is obvious in a December 2005 declaration presented by the World Council of Churches (WCC) at COP-11/MOP-1. The ecumenically Christian WCC drafted 'A Spiritual Declaration on Climate Change', with six statements signed by nearly 2,000 members of various faith-based communities (World Council of Churches (WCC) 2005a):

- We hear the call of the Earth;
- We believe that caring for life on Earth is a spiritual commitment;

- People and other species have the right to life unthreatened by human greed and destructiveness;
- Pollution, particularly from the energy-intensive wealthy indus-trialised countries, is warming the atmosphere. A warmer atmosphere is leading to major climate changes. The poor and vulnerable in the world and future generations will suffer the most;
- We commit ourselves to help reduce the threat of climate change through actions in our own lives, pressure on governments and industries and standing in solidarity with those most affected by climate change;
- We pray for spiritual support in responding to the call of the Earth.

This declaration highlights human vulner-ability and suffering as well as spiritual obligation to care for the environment. In addition, the WCC presented a statement to the high-level segment of the meeting, which also highlighted present and future climate change-induced human suffering (World Council of Churches (WCC) 2005b).

One year after that statement was issued, an Australian-based NGO, the Climate Institute, brought together state-ments from 16 religious groups represent-ing all of the world's major religions (Climate Institute 2006). All of the state-ments – while unique to the religious perspective represented – engaged climate change as a cause of human suffering, a grave threat to human well-being, or an issue of justice, and explicitly or implicitly engaged international dimensions of the issue. Representatives of Christian tradi-tions included Anglicans, members of the Australian Christian Lobby, Baptists, Catholics, Evangelicals, Greek Orthodox, Lutherans and members of the Salvation

Army, all of which called for action to mitigate global warming while drawing attention to its human dimensions. While we might expect such apparent unity to characterize intra-faith dialogue, given the gravity of and evidence for climate change, one notable exception concerns the Evangelical community in the United States, arguably one of the most politically influential religious communities in the world. As others seem to have achieved greater consensus on the issue, US Evangelicals seem to have generated greater controversy.

Evangelicals and climate change

While Evangelical internationalists have exerted considerable foreign policy influence in the US (Mead 2006), they have largely ignored global environmental politics. In the September/October 2006 issue of *Foreign Affairs*, Walter Russell Mead argues that the balance of political and cultural power among religious adherents in the United States has shifted toward conservative evangelicalism and that this shift 'has already changed US foreign policy in profound ways'.[12] The coincidence of this shift with the emergence of concern for the global environment – a largely unpopular cause among conservatives – has left such issues on the margins of Evangelical internationalism.

Though Evangelicals have demonstrated a modest interest in domestically focused engagement with such concerns, they have largely ignored international environmental issues. The United States' public television channel recently aired a lengthy report on Evangelical environmentalists, beginning with a segment on mountain removal/valley fill coal-mining in West Virginia and then focusing a significant portion of the show on climate change and its human impacts without explicitly addressing international dimensions at all (Moyers 2006).

A recent issue of the magazine, *Christianity Today*, in celebration of its 50th anniversary, highlighted the movement of evangelicals 'from cultural curiosities to the "new internationalists"', but its only reference to the Evangelical response to global environmental issues was to be found in its usual 'HeadLines' section, in coverage of the recent intra-evangelical debate on climate change (Blunt 2006).[13] Where climate change, as a global environmental concern, could have been listed independently among the issues highlighted in the magazine's cover stor(ies) on the new internationalists, it was not. Where it might have been coupled with concern for related international issues with which Evangelicals have engaged – justice, poverty, relief or development, for example – it was not. Indicative of the under-examination of religious internationalism, global environmental change and human suffering is the fact that none of the sources above have interacted with all three themes. While such frequent oversights are telling, Mead identifies various foreign policy issues – foremost among them are 'humanitarian and human rights policies' and 'US policy toward Israel' – to which significant portions of the evangelical community have devoted considerable attention, and also mentions the 'heartening development' represented by an emerging evangelical concern for the global environment.[14]

Despite this growing concern, the post-9/11 agenda for Evangelical internationalism has increased attention to terrorism and renewed devotion to security. While evangelicals remain interested in relief, development and human rights (sometimes in the context of undermining terror), they have generally failed to see the connections between environmental issues and these more typical issues of international humanitarianism. That is, they have failed to see that environmental conditions mediate, to a great extent, social conditions and relations. Evangelicals have failed to see that environmental deterioration is a cause of human suffering.

This has, for the most part, inhibited their involvement in the discourse on climate change. Evangelicals have long struggled to engage with environmental issues, whether because of a latent nature/society dualism, a distrust of the regulatory state, or imaginations run wild regarding an idolatrous environmentalist 'mother earth religion'. Yet some have not hastily dismissed climate change as just another *cause célèbre*. Recognizing that climate change and climate politics do indeed rank among the most important challenges we face in our rapidly globalizing world, not only presenting particularly pressing environmental difficulties, but also possessing immense human dimensions, US evangelicals have now begun to interact with the issue.

In the winter of 2006, more than 80 evangelical leaders – theologians, pastors, educators and others – signed 'Climate Change: An Evangelical Call to Action', a document of the Evangelical Climate Initiative (ECI). The 'Call to Action' was more than two years in the making, with retreats and other events serving as precursors to the February 2006 press conference in Washington, DC. The 'Call to Action' made four claims, focusing on the reality of climate change, its consequences for the poor and other vulnerable populations, the consistency of concern with Christian moral convictions, and the urgency of action in public and private sectors.

Not long after the release of the ECI document, a number of responses emerged. Some lacked sophistication and nuance. Others demonstrated considerable sophistication, if not goodwill. 'A Call to Truth, Prudence, and Protection of the Poor: An Evangelical Response to Global Warming', composed by the Interfaith Stewardship Alliance (ISA) and signed by more than 50 natural and social scientists, was presented to the ECI signatories with an open letter,

urging them to remove their signatures from the ECI 'Call to Action' and to sign the ISA 'Call to Truth' (Interfaith Stewardship Alliance 2006; see also Beisner 2006; Spencer *et al.* 2005). The move from 'action' to 'truth' was little more than clever rhetorical one-upmanship: the ISA 'Call' and other responses like it, revealed a lack of sincerity and a want of clarity regarding differences on climate change, and divisions regarding environment and society; economics, poverty and regulation; and appropriate political action.

While some points of disagreement reveal significant differences on considered positions, some appear disingenuous. For example, shoehorning support for nuclear power into an argument that greenhouse gas emissions abatement programmes are too costly compromises the integrity of the argument. Of contemporary modes of electricity generation, nuclear technology is among the most expensive. It is only competitive in the US wholesale electricity market because of a number of cost-externalizing policy measures, including the Price – Anderson Act and the Energy Policy Act of 2005. Apart from limited liability by private generators and cost absorption by taxpayers, nuclear power is completely unviable in the market. Even with the subsidies, nuclear power – from mine to reactor to waste stream – is marked by budget-busting project mismanagement and delays, waste management concerns, considerable risk to public health, and environmental injustice. Shoehorning promotion of nuclear technology into an argument that greenhouse gas reduction is too costly makes such critics appear to be shills for the hard-path energy regime, rather than market fundamentalists, stewards of the environment, advocates for the poor or conscientious internationalists.

Leaving aside apparent insincerities, there is still scope for a discussion of scientific merit. The ECI 'Call to Action' takes for granted the persuasive weight of scientific evidence on climate change and its likely effects. The ISA 'Call to Truth' disputes the existence of consensus on the matter. Too much of the debate regarding climate change is still preoccupied with scientific certainty, or lack thereof, without mention of the nature of scientific disagreement. Parties that frame a call for inaction in the language of scientific uncertainty without discussion of that uncertainty do disservice to the public. Any such discussion should be framed by indicating the scope and scale of controversy – the points on which there is disagreement and the extent of that disagreement. Recognizing that decision and action are informed by science, but are not scientific *per se*, these must be regarded as ethical and political economic issues. Are we disposed toward efficiency or justice (assuming we must sometimes choose)? And what do we know of the global social dimensions of those choices, both now and in the future?

The contention concerns risk management, or the ways in which we act – in this case, collectively – under conditions of uncertainty. It is quite true that the full extent of the phenomenon's ill effects is not yet known. But even under such circumstances, we must decide what option values to preserve: those associated with the capital investment necessary to reduce greenhouse gas emissions or those associated with the integrity of the global environment. Marginal uncertainty regarding a complex adaptive system, such as climate, should spur, rather than stay, our action.

But when the wheat and chaff of argument are separated, there remain at least three genuine points of disagreement among the parties to this debate. The first should be superseded, the second is deserving of continued attention, and the third highlights disagreements regarding how, and with whom, Evangelicals work in society.

Nature vs. society

Some have indicated that they cannot support measures that elevate the non-human created order over the human created order. Without entering into discussion, here, regarding boundaries between nature and society or the extent of a call to stewardship and its relationship to dominion and the cultural mandate, climate change is, in a very real sense, a social problem. To their credit, both the ECI document and the ISA document admit to this aspect of climate change, varying in their presentation of the phenomenon's social causes and consequences. The ISA 'Call' claims that the kind of action advocated by the ECI (though, to be fair, the ECI does not indicate any specific action) would hurt the poor more than the ill effects of climate change would. But both parties agree that climate change is a social issue. And both should continue to clarify this aspect of the problem for those who remain unconvinced, advancing the dialogue by moving toward greater clarity.

Regulation, economics and poverty

Most parties to this debate frame their contribution around concern for the welfare of poor and vulnerable people on the margins of political economy. Some believe that regulating greenhouse gas emissions will serve the planet and the poor, arguing that the most vulnerable populations will suffer most from the ill effects of anthropogenic climate change and that it will serve their interests to mitigate those effects by stunting increases in atmospheric concentrations of greenhouse gases. Others believe that regulating greenhouse gas emissions is inefficient interference with economic activity that would otherwise result in the gently rising tide of economic growth, floating yachts and lifeboats, alike, lifting many out of poverty, and providing the financial means for adaptation to the ill effects of climate change, should it prove to be as burdensome as many predict. It is not true that policies oriented toward emissions abatement or the conservation of sequestration options would require universal reductions in the consumption of final energy. The low-lying fruit of greater efficiency in generation and distribution may be somewhat costly, but is unlikely to destroy the livelihoods of the most vulnerable. And to suggest that the development of distributed renewable and clean energy options fundamentally undermines economic growth is also unhelpful in its plain overstatement. Greater clarity, nuance and sophistication on the actual points of disagreement will benefit all parties to the continued discussion.

Unholy alliances for political action

Some Evangelicals have accused the ECI of making alliance with an unsavoury cast of characters, including foundations that support international causes – abortive means of birth control, among others – typically contrary to the Evangelical current. Evangelicals who disfavour such alliances seem to prefer modes of political action that at least keep such organizations at arm's length. However, Evangelicals have a long history of such alliances, including anti-pornography and anti-abuse campaigns, with pro-choice advocacy organizations. Among global issues, concerned religious internationalists have partnered with such organizations to try to stem the tide of human trafficking related to the sex trade. Why should such partnerships be less acceptable in stemming the ocean tides associated with climate change?

Despite these various deficiencies and significant challenges, this new engagement with climate change represents a significant shift by an evangelical community with demonstrable political clout.

However, it does not yet represent a robust engagement with the global human dimensions of a significant environmental issue.

Conclusion: changing the climate of international affairs

Despite failure to achieve its stated goals of meaningful emissions reductions and to compel the participation of key GHG emitters, the Kyoto Protocol has been hailed by some as a success for the international policy community (Grubb *et al.* 1999; Hovi *et al.* 2003). In some quarters, the formation of an international climate change regime – especially with its recent entrance into force – seems to have become an end in and of itself. Even as the agenda has regressed from abatement to adaptation, many nonetheless defend the Protocol on the ground that it is a building block for future diplomacy and cooperation.

Climate change and climate change policy, however, should not simply be seen as contexts for new experiments in post-Cold War diplomacy and negotiation, but should be recognized as contexts for human suffering and its alleviation. International cooperation is not an unqualified good (as if cooperation to end the world might be good), but rather should be used toward the goal of abatement of GHG emissions for the sake of reducing human suffering.

As clumsy as it may sometimes seem, Kyoto reflects a certain political and technical genius – and, yet, a genius unworthy of our wholehearted commendation (Toly 2005). Absolute, verifiable reductions in the anthropogenic environmental causes of human suffering should be the measure of any international climate change regime, not conformity to ideological presumptions about either governmental or market-based approaches. Indeed, successful engagement of the issue on these terms may require a significant departure from both state-centric diplomacy and market-oriented means in favour of per capita emissions standards in the atmospheric commons.

Fresh approaches to global environmental governance in this policy area will require nothing less than a change in the 'climate' of international affairs, an ambitious project to which the religious international affairs community can and should contribute. Religious internationalists may not only direct the international community away from the means-centric preoccupation of the current debate, but may also be an important voice in reshaping objectives and serving as norm entrepreneurs in the negotiation of climate regimes for a climate-stable and environmentally just future.

In a way, a faith-based international affairs community may even 'subvert' the current climate regime – not in the colloquial sense of subversion, but rather in the sense aptly noted by Cardinal Arns, of São Paulo. In a 1983 address to the annual meeting of the Society for International Development, he described the kind of positive subversion that all disciples of Christ should be bold enough to pursue: ' "Subvert" means to turn a situation round and look at it from the other side ... the side of people who have to die so that the system can go on' (Arns, cited in Rahnema 1997). In so doing, religious internationalists might come to grips with a more holistic view of the multiple contexts for human suffering, including the global environment, while at the same time providing direction and candid truth-telling to the broader international community.

Like other people of faith, Christians recognize a responsibility to empathize with suffering and to use all their God-given talents to help alleviate it. On this score, the global environment merits – indeed, commands – attention; some 160,000 climate change-related deaths per year should be more than enough impetus to rebalance how we are using our resources

(intellectual, financial, political and theological) – resources that are currently lavished upon questions of suffering in other contexts. Christian inquiry into international affairs has been far too slow to adopt questions of environmental justice. The matter of the global environment should be seen as an opportunity to do so. The prospect of climate change demands that we do so.

To be sure, there are difficulties and challenges in turning attention toward the global environment. The inherent ambiguity and structural nature of the global warming problem can make it seem abstract and remote; it is a humanitarian cause that does not 'sell' well amongst donors. For instance, it is easy to externalize the evil of terrorism, both from national and religious perspectives. This is not so easily accomplished with environmental problems; Osama Bin Laden has no analogue in the environmental crisis.

In order to fully appreciate the global environment as a context for human suffering, we must be willing to face the implications of a global political economy (in which we all participate) that militates against environmental integrity and security. Christian inquiry into international affairs should reflect a deep concern for the multiple contexts of human suffering, in spite of ambiguity and structural evil. Climate change and the emerging climate change policy regime should be seen as occasions to articulate a Christian response to environmental crises that threaten the lives and livelihoods of whole populations, and in this way to speak a transformative word into the discourse of the discipline.

Notes

1 The argument advanced in this chapter represents a revised, updated and expanded version of 'Changing the climate of Christian internationalism: Global warming and human suffering' (Toly 2004). The author thanks Jeffrey Haynes, editor of the current

volume, for the opportunity to continue this line of reasoning, and the editors of the *Review of Faith and International Affairs* (www.cfia.org) for permission to re-present the argument.

2 For an interesting and accessible history of climate change science, see Weart (2003).

3 The IPCC was founded in 1988 as a joint effort of the United Nations Environment Programme and the World Meteorological Organization.

4 If emissions were stabilized at year 2000 levels over this period, the IPCC estimates an increase in global average surface temperature of 0.3–0.9°C. Of course, emissions already exceed 2000 levels. Various other IPCC scenarios account for a range of emissions. Even a 2°C warming would be equivalent to the difference between the coldest point of an ice age and the preceding and succeeding warm periods.

5 AOSIS is a network representing the interests of more than 43 states and observers, many of which share basic climate-related vulnerabilities, even if not significant responsibilities. While AOSIS membership is strongest among small island developing states, it includes members that are not states, not islands, not small and not developing.

6 For a contrary position, see Davis *et al.* (2004). This article has received much publicity for its very low estimates of projected marginal mortality increases in US cities due to increased heat. The authors note that marginal increases in mortality during summer heatwaves may be offset by marginal decreases in exposure-related mortality during the winter months. However, the authors examined only the effects of increased heat in US cities, where air conditioning is ubiquitous, even if not universal. The authors do not attend to the relationship between energy use and climate change. Nor do they address the effects of extreme heat in less affluent communities, other examples of extreme weather, or other warming-related phenomena, such as sea-level rise.

7 Some cite this relationship in support of the political economic status quo, suggesting we should give less attention to mitigating climate change and more attention to increasing wealth, or that GHG emissions abatement will destroy wealth- (and, by extension, adaptation capacity-)building opportunities for the most vulnerable. And here the climate change discourse intersects with political economy, begging the question of the production of vulnerability. If one understands our current political economic system and

energy regime as complicit in the production of vulnerability and marginalization – not to mention climate change, itself – one cannot expect business-as-usual to do anything but to perpetuate, if not to deepen, the production of vulnerability.

8 55/55 refers to the ratification of the Protocol by at least 55% of signatories to the UNFCCC and the representation of at least 55% of global emissions by those signatories.

9 The Protocol's *Ad Hoc* Working Group (AWG) is currently negotiating the foundations for future budget periods, discussing both timing and emissions target determination.

10 These IPCC estimates targeted atmospheric concentrations of CO_2 at 450ppm, a level now widely considered out of reach. More recent studies by the IPCC and others have analysed the effects of concentrations of 550ppm, 650ppm, 750ppm, and higher, and the emissions reductions necessary to stabilize at even these extreme concentrations.

11 To put climate-specific religious declarations and actions in a broader context of religious interest in environmental issues, see Haynes (2007: ch. 6).

12 Mead's account of the second shift – the shift in foreign policy concern and influence – is insightful, even if his understanding of the Protestant population in the United States is somewhat confused. See the winter 2006 issue of the *Review of Faith and International Affairs* for a forum discussion on Mead's commentary, as well as Mead's reply.

13 For an analysis of this debate, see Toly (2007).

14 I would agree with Noel Castree, who suggests that ' "environmental" entities are ontologically promiscuous ... inextricably *a part of* those things we conventionally call "economic," "cultural," "social," or "political" entities' (Castree 2002, emphasis in original). Nevertheless, we continue, for the most part, to conceptualize nature as if it were entirely other than society. While I believe that this is problematic, I will use 'environment' and 'environmental' in their colloquial senses for the purposes of this chapter.

Bibliography

Agarwal, A. and Narain, S. (1991) *Global Warming in an Unequal World: A Case of Environmental Colonialism*, New Delhi: Centre of Science and Environment.

Agarwal, A., Narain, S. and Sharma, A. (2002) 'The global commons and environmental justice: Climate change', in J. Byrne, L. Glover and C. Martinez (eds), *Environmental Justice: Discourses in International Political Economy*, New Brunswick, NJ: Transaction Books, pp. 171–199.

Allen, L. (2004) 'Will Tuvalu disappear beneath the sea? Global warming threatens to swamp a small island nation', *Smithsonian Magazine*, August, http://www.smithsonianmag.com/travel/tuvalu.html.

Bakkenes, M., Alkemade, J. R. M., Ihle, F., Leemans, R. and Latour, J. B. (2002) 'Assessing effects of forecasted climate change on the diversity and distribution of European higher plants for 2050', *Global Change Biology*, 8, pp. 390–407.

Beaumont, L. J. and Hughes, L. (2002) 'Potential changes in the distributions of latitudinally restricted Australian butterfly species in response to climate change', *Global Change Biology*, 8, pp. 954–971.

Beisner, E. C. (2006) 'Scientific orthodoxies, politicized science, and catastrophic global warming: Challenges to Evangelicals navigating rough waters in science and policy'. Paper delivered at the 58th Annual Meeting of the Evangelical Theological Society, Washington, DC, 16 November.

Beisner, E. C., Driessen, P. K., McKitrick, R. and Spencer, R. W. (2006) *A Call to Truth, Prudence, and Protection of the Poor: An Evangelical Response to Global Warming*, Burke, VA: Interfaith Stewardship Alliance.

Blunt, S. H. (2006) 'Cool on climate change: New Christian coalition says fighting global warming will hurt the poor', *Christianity Today*, 26 September, http://www.christianitytoday.com/ct/2006/october/8.26.html.

Byrne, J., Glover, L., Inniss, V., Kulkarni, J., Mun, Y., Toly, N. J. and Wang, Y. (2004) 'Beyond Kyoto: Reclaiming the atmospheric commons', in V. Grover (ed.) *Climate Change: Policy and Politics*, Enfield, NH: Science Publishers, pp. 429–452.

Castree, N. (2002) 'Environmental issues: From policy to political economy', *Progress in Human Geography*, 26, 3, pp. 357–365.

Center for Health and the Global Environment (2005) *Climate Change Futures: Health, Ecological, and Economic Dimensions*, Boston, MA: Center for Health and the Global Environment, Harvard Medical School.

Crowley, T. J. (2000) 'Causes of climate change over the past 1000 years', *Science*, 289, pp. 270–277.

Davis, R. E., Knappenberger, P. C., Michaels, P. J. and Novicoff, W. M. (2004) 'Seasonality of climate – human mortality relationships in US cities and impacts of climate change', *Climate Research*, 26, pp. 61–76.

Erasmus, Barend F. N., van Jaarsveld, Albert S., Chown, S. L., Kshatriya, M. and Wessels, K. (2002) 'Vulnerability of South African animal taxa to climate change', *Global Change Biology*, 8, pp. 679–693.

Evangelical Climate Initiative (2006) *Climate Change: An Evangelical Call to Action*, Washington, DC: Evangelical Climate Initiative.

Goering, L. (2007) 'The first refugees of global warming', *Chicago Tribune*, 2 May, http://globalpolicy.igc.org/nations/micro/2007/0502risingwater.htm.

Grubb, M., Vrolijk, C. and Brack, D. (1999) *The Kyoto Protocol: A Guide and Assessment*, London: Earthscan Publications.

Hasselman, K., Latif, M., Hooss, G., Azar, C., Edenhofer, O., Jaeger, C. C., Johannessen, O. M., Kemfert, C., Welp, M. and Wokaun, A. (2003) 'The challenge of long-term climate change', *Science*, 302, pp. 1923–1925.

Haynes, J. (2007) 'Environmental sustainability', in *An Introduction to International Relations and Religion*, New York: Longman, pp. 94–113.

Hoffmann, M. J. (2005) *Ozone Depletion and Climate Change: Constructing a Global Response*, New York: State University of New York Press.

Houghton, J. T. (2003) 'Global warming is now a weapon of mass destruction: It kills more people than terrorism, yet Blair and Bush do nothing', *The Guardian* (London), 28 July http://politics.guardian.co.uk/green/comment/0,9236,1007302,00.html.

Hovi, J., Skodvin, T. and Andresen, S. (2003) 'The persistence of the Kyoto Protocol: Why other Annex I countries move on without the United States', *Global Environmental Politics*, 3, 4, pp. 1–23.

Interfaith Stewardship Alliance (2006) 'An open letter to the signers of "Climate Change: An evangelical call to action" and others concerned about global warming', http://www.interfaithstewardship.org/content/printarticle.php?id=160.

IPCC (Intergovernmental Panel on Climate Change) (1996) *Climate Change 1995: The Science of Climate Change*, Cambridge: Cambridge University Press.

IPCC (Intergovernmental Panel on Climate Change) (2001) *Climate Change 2001: The Scientific Basis*, New York: Cambridge University Press.

IPCC (Intergovernmental Panel on Climate Change) (2007a) 'Summary for policy-makers', in S. Solomon, D. Qin, M. Manning *et al.* (eds), *Climate Change 2007: The Physical Science Basis. Contribution of Working Group I to the Fourth Assessment Report of the Intergovernmental Panel on Climate Change*, Cambridge: Cambridge University Press, pp. 1–18.

IPCC (Intergovernmental Panel on Climate Change) (2007b) 'Summary for policy-makers', in *Climate Change 2007: Impacts, Adaptation and Vulnerability. Contribution of Working Group II to the Fourth Assessment Report of the Intergovernmental Panel on Climate Change*, Cambridge: Cambridge University Press, pp. 1–16.

Jones, P. D., Osborn, T. J. and Briffa, K. R. (2001) 'The evolution of climate over the last millennium', *Science*, 292, pp. 662–667.

Karl, T. R. and Trenberth, K. E. (2003) 'Modern global climate change', *Science*, 302, pp. 1719–1723.

King, D. A. (2004) 'Climate change science: Adapt, mitigate, or ignore?', *Science*, 303, pp. 176–177.

Kyoto Protocol to the United Nations Framework Convention on Climate Change (1997).

Luterbacher, J., Dietrich, D., Xoplaki, E., Grosjean, M. and Warner, H. (2004) 'European seasonal and annual temperature variability, trends, and extremes since 1500', *Science*, 303, 5663, pp. 1499–1503.

Mann, M. E., Bradley, R. S. and Hughes, M. K. (1998) 'Global-scale temperature patterns and climate forcing over the past six centuries', *Nature*, 392, pp. 779–787.

Mead, W. R. (2006) 'God's country?', *Foreign Affairs*, 85, 5, pp. 24–43.

Midgley, G. F., Hannah, L., Rutherford, M. C. and Powrie, L. W. (2002) 'Assessing the vulnerability of species to anthropogenic climate change in a biodiversity hotspot', *Global Ecology and Biogeography*, 11, pp. 445–451.

Moyers, B. (2006) 'Is God green?', http://www.pbs.org/moyers/moyersonamerica/green/watch.html.

Myers, N. (1999) *Biotic Holocaust*, Reston, VA: National Wildlife Federation, pp. 31–39.

Najam, A., Saleemul, H. and Sokona, Y. (2003) 'Climate negotiations beyond Kyoto: Developing countries concerns and interests', *Climate Policy*, 3, pp. 221–231.

Osnos, E. (2006) 'The ocean is slowly claiming Malaysia: They say it's global warming', *Chicago Tribune*, 21 August, http://www.truthout.org/cgi-bin/artman/exec/view.cgi/63/21976.

Parmesan, C. and Yohe, G. (2003) 'A globally coherent fingerprint of climate change impacts across natural systems', *Nature*, vol. 421, pp. 37–42.

Pounds, J. A., Fogden, M. L. P. and Campbell, J. H. (1999) 'Biological response to climate change on a tropical mountain', *Nature*, 398, pp. 611–615.

Qader Mirza, M. M. (2003) 'Climate change and extreme weather events: Can developing countries adapt?', *Climate Policy*, 3, pp. 233–248.

Rahnema, M. (1997) 'Introduction', in M. Rahnema and V. Bawtree (eds), *The Post-development Reader*, London: Zed Books, pp. ix–xix.

Reuters News Service (2002) 'Tuvalu seeks help in US global warming suit', 30 August.

Roberts, J. T. and Parks, B. C. (2007) *A Climate of Injustice: Global Inequality, North–South Politics, and Climate Policy*, Cambridge, MA: MIT Press.

Root, T. L., Price, J. T., Hall, K. R., Schneider, S. H., Rosenzeig, C. and Pounds, J. A. (2003) 'Fingerprints of global warming on wild animals and plants', *Nature*, 421, pp. 57–60.

Schaeffer, F. A. (1982) 'Pollution and the death of man', in F. A. Schaeffer (ed.), *The Complete Works of Francis A. Schaeffer: A Christian Worldview*, Cumbria: Paternoster Press, pp. 2–76.

Schwartz, P. and Randall, D. (2003) 'An abrupt climate change scenario and its implications for United States national security'. Global Business Network, http://www.gbn.com/GBNDocumentDisplayServlet.srv?aid=26231&url=/UploadDocumentDisplayServlet.srv?id=28566.

Spencer, R. W., Driessen, P. K. and Beisner, E. C. (2005) 'An examination of the scientific, ethical, and theological implications of climate change policy', Burke, VA: Interfaith Stewardship Alliance, www.cornwallalliance.org.

417

Stott, P. A., Tett, S. F. B., Jones, G. S., Allen, M. R., Mitchell, J. F. B. and Jenkins, M. R. (2000) 'External control of twentieth century temperature by natural and anthropogenic forcings', *Science*, 290, 5499, pp. 2133–2137.

The Climate Institute (2006) 'The Climate Institute: Australia's faith communities on climate change', Sydney: Climate Institute.

Thomas, C. D., Cameron, A., Green, R., E., Bakkenes, M., Beaumont, L. J., Collingham, Y. C., Erasmus, Barend F. N., de Siquiera, Marinez Ferreira, Grainger, A., Hannah, L., Hughes, L., Huntley, B., van Jaarsveld, Albert S., Midgley, G. F., Miles, L., Ortega-Huerta, M. A., Peterson, A. T., Phillips, O. L. and Williams, S. E. (2004) 'Extinction risk from climate change', *Nature*, 427, pp. 145–148.

Toly, N. J. (2004) 'Changing the climate of Christian internationalism: Global warming and human suffering', *Brandywine Review of Faith and International Affairs*, 2, 2, pp. 31–37.

Toly, N. J. (2005) 'Climate change and climate change policy as human sacrifice: Artifice, idolatry, and environment in a technological society', *Christian Scholar's Review*, 35, 1, pp. 63–78.

Toly, N. J. (2007) 'Are Evangelicals warming to global environmentalism?', *Review of Faith and International Affairs*, 4, 4, pp. 53–55.

van Vuuren, D., den Elzen, M., Berk, M. and de Moor, A. (2002) 'An evaluation of the level of ambition and implications of the Bush climate change initiative', *Climate Policy*, 2, pp. 293–301.

Weart, S. R. (2003) *The Discovery of Global Warming*, Cambridge, MA: Harvard University Press.

White House, The (2002a) 'Executive summary of the Bush climate change initiative, Washington, DC.

White House, The (2002b) 'Transcript of the speech of President Bush delivered at NOAA in Silver Spring, MD', Washington, DC.

Wirth, D. (2002) 'The Sixth Session (Part Two) and Seventh Session of the Conference of the Parties to the Framework Convention on Climate Change', *American Journal of International Law*, 96, 3, pp. 648–660.

WCC (World Council of Churches) (2005a) *A Spiritual Declaration on Climate Change*, Montreal: WCC.

WCC (World Council of Churches) (2005b) *WCC Statement to the High-level Segment of the UN Climate Change Conference*, Montreal: WCC.

WHO (World Health Organization) (2003) *Climate Change and Human Health: Risks and Responses*, Geneva: World Health Organization.

Index